The Psychology of Work and Organizations

Stephen A. Woods
Michael A. West

Second Edition

FURTHER PRAISE FOR WOODS AND WEST'S

The Psychology of Work and Organizations

This highly readable global text presents the results of both historical and leading edge research on work and organizational psychology in a memorable way for students in Australia, Asia, Europe and North America.

Gary Latham, Secretary of State Professor of Organizational Effectiveness, Rotman School of Management, University of Toronto.

This book is the best blend of a textbook in work and organizational psychology that I know of. Woods and West cover all relevant topics of work and organizational psychology as well as its major professional applications. An evidence-based approach is taken to review key theory and research. Difficult content is made accessible, and the reader is encouraged to reflect critically on and to apply pragmatically the lessons learnt. In this brilliant new edition every chapter has been updated incorporating the latest developments in the field. I particularly like the chapter on leadership, which covers not only traditional topics on what makes a leader effective, but also how we can develop leaders that make a positive difference in a globalized world. Without question, it is one book every student and practitioner in work and organizational psychology should own.

Yves R. F. Guillaume, PhD, Chartered Psychologist, Senior Lecturer in Work and Organizational Psychology, Aston Business School, Aston University.

An up-to-date textbook containing all the relevant academic research and applied practices we see in organizations today. Written in an engaging style and with excellent coverage of important contemporary themes such as social responsibility and mobility, this will likely become a definitive introduction for years to come.

Pamela Yeow, Senior Lecturer in Management, Kent Business School.

Woods and West provide a well-balanced and clear introduction to work psychology with lively examples that my students will find highly relevant and informative. The coverage of teams, careers and recruitment and selection is particularly strong, with up-to-date references and innovative learning features used throughout.

Sheena Johnson, Senior Lecturer in Organizational Psychology, Manchester Business School.

There is a need for a genuinely European textbook on Work Psychology and this impressive new work makes some major strides towards filling that gap. The chapters are often state-of-the-art in their coverage yet written in a way that today's students will understand. The coverage of teams, for example, is fun to read and so much better than anything I have seen in other textbooks.

Abigail Marks, Reader in Work and Employment, Heriot-Watt University.

The Psychology of Work and Organizations

Stephen A. Woods

Michael A. West

Second Edition

CENGAGE
Learning

Australia • Brazil • Canada • Mexico • Singapore • Spain • United Kingdom • United States

The Psychology of Work and Organizations, 2nd Edition
Stephen A. Woods and Michael A. West

Publisher: Andrew Ashwin

Commissioning Editor: Annabel Ainscow

Production Editor: Melissa Beavis

Manufacturing Buyer: Elaine Willis

Marketing Manager: Sally Gallery

Typesetter: Integra Software
    Services PVT LTD.

Cover design: Adam Renvoize

For product information and technology assistance,
contact **emea.info@cengage.com.**
For permission to use material from this text or product,
and for permission queries,
email **emea.permissions@cengage.com.**

British Library Cataloguing-in-Publication Data
A catalogue record for this book is available from the British Library.

ISBN: 978-1-4080-7245-5

Cengage Learning EMEA
Cheriton House, North Way, Andover, Hampshire, SP10 5BE
United Kingdom

Cengage Learning products are represented in Canada by Nelson Education Ltd.

For your lifelong learning solutions, visit **www.cengage.co.uk**

Purchase your next print book, e-book or e-chapter at
www.cengagebrain.com

Printed in China by RR Donnelley
Print number 01 Print Year 2014

BRIEF CONTENTS

CONTENTS

PART ONE
FOUNDATIONS OF WORK AND ORGANIZATIONAL PSYCHOLOGY   16

PART TWO
PROFESSIONAL PRACTICE OF WORK
AND ORGANIZATIONAL PSYCHOLOGY 157

PART THREE
ORGANIZATIONS 345

DEDICATIONS

For V.

For Gillian.

ACKNOWLEDGMENTS

Steve Woods:

My sincere thanks go to the production team at Cengage Learning for their support and patience, to Helen Worrall, and to reviewers who were generous with their time and advice. My heartfelt and special thanks as always to my wife Virinder, and to my mother and father, for encouragement and support (and pride) during the writing of this book, and throughout my studies of Work and Organizational Psychology.

Mike West:

Thanks for help and laughter from Ellie Hardy, Tom West, Nik Vlissides and Rosa Hardy. And to Gillian for giving us all support and unswerving direction. Thanks also to the infinitely patient Cengage team and to our wise reviewers.

In addition to the dozens of academics who answered electronic surveys at the start of this project, the publisher would particularly like to thank the following for providing detailed feedback at various stages of the book's development:

David Biggs, University of Gloucestershire
Catherine Collins, University of New South Wales
Sheena Johnson, Manchester Business School
Penny Johnson, University of Sunderland
Annika Lantz, Uppsala University
Abigail Marks, Heriot-Watt University
Peter Morgan, University of Bradford
Johan Naslund, Linköping University
Paula O'Kane, University of Ulster
Birgit Schyns, Portsmouth Business School
Eleni Tzouramani, Norwich Business School, London
Kosheleva Vladimirovna, Saint Petersburg State University
Thomas Waldmann, University of Ulster
Pamela Yeow, University of Kent

The publisher also thanks the various copyright holders for granting permission to reproduce material throughout the text. Every effort has been made to trace all copyright holders but if anything has been inadvertently overlooked the publisher will be pleased to make the necessary arrangements at the first opportunity. Please contact the publisher directly.

ABOUT THE AUTHORS

STEVE WOODS   Dr. Steve Woods is Professor of Work and Organizational Psychology at Surrey Business School, and a Chartered Occupational Psychologist. He received his PhD in 2004. Steve is known for his research on personality and vocational development, psychometric and personality trait assessment, and recruitment and selection. He publishes his research in scientific and professional journals, scholarly books and at national and international conferences. Steve speaks regularly at organizations and universities about personality and work, and contemporary issues in assessment and Work and Organizational Psychology more widely. He is a Director of Aston Business Assessments Ltd, an Aston University spin-out company, and has extensive professional, corporate and practitioner experience working with businesses in the UK and internationally on HRM strategy, policy and practice.

MICHAEL WEST   Michael West is Senior Fellow at The King's Fund, Professor of Organizational Psychology at Lancaster University Management School and Emeritus Professor at Aston University. He graduated from the University of Wales in 1973 and received his PhD on the psychology of meditation in 1977. He has authored, edited or co-edited 20 books and has published over 200 articles for scientific and practitioner publications, as well as chapters in scholarly books. He is a Fellow of the British Psychological Society, the American Psychological Association (APA), the APA Society for Industrial/Organizational Psychology, the International Association of Applied Psychologists, the British Academy of Management, a Chartered Fellow of the Chartered Institute of Personnel and Development and Academician of the Academy of Social Sciences. His specialist areas are team working, organizational culture, leadership and effectiveness, particularly in relation to the organization of health services. He advises governments and organizations on developing health service cultures of high quality and compassionate care and is a sought after public speaker nationally and internationally.

WALK THROUGH TOUR

LEARNING OBJECTIVES each chapter starts with a list of objectives to help you monitor your understanding and progress through the chapter.

KEY THEMES boxed features discuss the issues raised in each chapter and how they relate to the key themes in Work and Organizational Psychology.

AUTHOR EXPERIENCE mini case study examples demonstrate how psychology concepts are applied to real-world experiences.

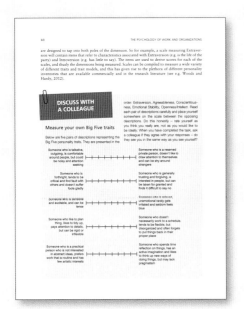

DISCUSS WITH A COLLEAGUE activities appear regularly throughout each chapter to stimulate critical thinking and highlight key questions for discussion.

KEY FIGURE each chapter features a discussion of a prominent figure and their specific area of psychology research.

END-OF-PART CASE STUDIES offer opportunities for student analyses and class discussion.

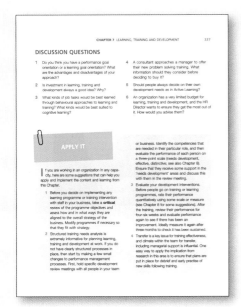

DISCUSSION QUESTIONS are provided at the end of each chapter to help reinforce and test your knowledge and understanding, and provide a basis for group discussions and activities.

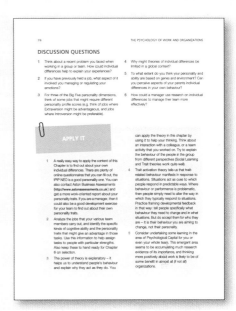

APPLY IT feature helps students apply what they have learned from the chapter to real life.

WEB ACTIVITY a selection of useful web links and resources to complement and boost learning and revision.

DIGITAL SUPPORT RESOURCES

Dedicated Instructor Resources

To discover the dedicated instructor online
support resources accompanying this textbook,
instructors should register here for access:
http://login.cengage.com

Resources include:

* Instructor's Manual containing a range of additional
  material for every chapter of the text
* PowerPoint slides for use in teaching, complementing
  the content and coverage of each chapter
* Testbank

Instructor access

Instructors can access CourseMate by registering at
http://login.cengage.com or by speaking to their local
Cengage Learning EMEA representative.

Instructor resources

Instructors can use the integrated Engagement Tracker in CourseMate to track students'
preparation and engagement. The tracking tool can be used to monitor progress of the class as
a whole, or for individual students.

Student access

Log In & Learn In 4 Easy Steps
1. To register a product using the access code printed on the inside front-cover of the book
   please go to: **http://login.cengagebrain.com**
2. Register as a new user or log in as an existing user if you already have an account with
   Cengage Learning or CengageBrain.com
3. Follow the online prompts
4. If your instructor has provided you with a course key, you will be prompted to enter this after
   opening your digital purchase from your CengageBrain account homepage.

Student resources

CourseMate offers a range of interactive learning tools tailored to the second edition of
The Psychology of Work and Organizations

* Multiple Choice Questions and Quizzes
* Practice Questions
* Onscreen Activities
* Glossary, Flashcards, and more

CHAPTER 1

INTRODUCTION

LEARNING OBJECTIVES

- Define Work and Organizational Psychology.

- List the main areas of Work and Organizational Psychology.

- Describe core values in Work and Organizational Psychology.

- Describe the history of Work and Organizational Psychology.

- Understand the role of historical context in giving rise to Work and Organizational Psychology.

- Identify and know about professional organizations in the field.

- Understand three contemporary challenges facing organizations, and their relevance to Work and Organizational Psychology:

  - Ethics and Corporate Social Responsibility.

  - Globalization and Cross-cultural Issues.

  - Sustainability and the Environment.

We start our book with a scenario and task. Imagine that you are a senior manager in an organization (if you are actually one, then this task requires very little imagination). Perhaps a Human Resource Director. Or a Chief Executive of a medium-sized business or multinational corporation. Or perhaps a group or middle manager with responsibility for 100 members of staff. Think about the tasks and responsibilities you might have if you really were that person. Now think about the day-to-day challenges you would likely face. Finally narrow down your thoughts to focus on people and their behaviour in your organization.

Here is the task. If you really were that person, what do you think would be the seven most important questions you would have about how to understand the people you managed or employed? What would be the most helpful information that someone could give you in respect of people and their behaviour at work? Think hard about these questions. At the risk of suggesting a short break too early in your reading, now would be a good time to get a tea or coffee, while you mull it over. Write down the seven questions on a scrap of paper, and tuck them into the back cover of this book.

Now we are going to make our first assertion of the book. It is our belief that Work and Organizational Psychologists will have, in some way, addressed most, if not all of the questions you have just written down. We also think that by the end of this book, you will have some answers for most, if not all of your questions. Not all of the answers will be as straightforward as you might like, but they will definitely help you to understand the issues raised by your questions with more clarity.

Work and Organizational Psychology is a fascinating area of psychology that deals with all aspects of work, business and organizations. We are enthusiastic about Work Psychology, and believe that it can make highly important contributions to organizations, business and management. Work Psychology has the potential to help people be more productive and prosperous in their jobs, and to feel good about work, and its place in their lives. In this chapter, we will start our exploration of Work and Organizational Psychology by taking a broad overview of the field, looking at the present, the past and some of the major contemporary and future challenges.

THE PSYCHOLOGY OF WORK AND ORGANIZATIONS: FIRST ENCOUNTERS

Work and Organizational Psychology is a field of psychology that applies psychological principles and science to help solve problems of work, business and organizations. To understand the basics of the field, you first have to understand something about psychology. For those of you new to psychology, we can broadly define the subject as 'the study of mind and behaviour'. Psychologists are interested in people's behaviour, in processes of the mind and in understanding how a multitude of factors influence both. Such factors include physiological, developmental, social and cultural influences.

The academic, theory-driven aspect of psychology is sometimes called pure psychology. However, your day-to-day encounters with psychology are more likely to be with the areas of applied psychology. Applied psychology is problem-driven. This means that the purpose of applied psychology is to understand and solve problems that people face in their everyday lives. A great advantage of psychology is that it is adaptive, and it can be applied in many different ways. During its relatively short history, it has permeated many different areas of life, developing and evolving alongside societies and cultures. The major areas of applied psychology are:

- Clinical Psychology: The area of applied psychology concerned with psychological disorders and illnesses.
- Counselling Psychology: Often confused with clinical psychology, but is rather concerned with working with clients with a variety of problems through talking, and relationship-based therapies.
- Health Psychology: Psychology applied to the issues of health and healthy lifestyles, living with and recovering from physical illness and disease.
- Forensic Psychology: Concerned with crime and criminality.
- Educational Psychology: Psychology applied to understand learning, development and education over the whole lifespan.
- Sport Psychology: Psychology applied to performance in sports.
- Work and Organizational Psychology: Psychology applied to work, business and organizations.

The importance and relevance of Work Psychology is evident when you compare it with other areas of applied psychology. Each of us will be educated formally for up to 20 years. We will all get ill from time to time, or spend time improving our general health. Around one quarter of us in Europe will experience some form of psychological disorder (Alonso *et al.*, 2004), and a few of us will experience the pain of being a victim of crime or the excitement of being a top athlete. Most of these areas of applied psychology are relevant to us, but tend to be so infrequently or episodically. The majority of us, however, will work for most of our lives, some of us for 60 years or more, and moreover, we will spend a significant part of our waking hours working. Work and Organizational Psychology is therefore directly relevant to the vast majority of us for most of our lives, and most of the time.

There are a variety of terms associated with Work and Organizational Psychology, and they are not all simply interchangeable. In the UK, the field is known as Occupational Psychology, and in the US, Industrial and Organizational (I/O) Psychology. In Europe, the title Work and Organizational Psychology is most common, and we feel this captures the content of the field most clearly. There are a few other variants that capture specific aspects of the field:

- Business Psychology: Focusing on business development.
- Personnel Psychology: Focusing on core Human Resource tasks and functions.
- Vocational Psychology: Focusing on careers and vocational behaviour.

Work and Organizational Psychology: A Contemporary Definition and Summary

Taking a contemporary perspective on the field, we would define Work and Organizational Psychology as follows:

> *Work and Organizational Psychology is the study of people and their behaviour at work, and of the organizations in which people work; Work Psychologists develop psychological theory and apply the rigour and methods of psychology to issues that are important to businesses and organizations, in order to promote and advance understanding of individual, group and organizational effectiveness at work, and the well-being and satisfaction of people working in or served by organizations.*

The main areas of Work and Organizational Psychology are listed differently depending on the source you read, but broadly comprise:

- Organizational Behaviour, Individual Differences and Attitudes at Work.
- Work Motivation.
- Personnel Selection and Assessment.
- Performance Measurement and Management.
- Learning, Training and Development at Work.
- Careers and Vocational Behaviour.
- Health, Well-being and Safety at Work.
- Teams and Groups at Work.
- Organizational Development and Change.
- Leadership and Management in Organizations.

- Organizational Culture, Strategy and Design.
- Employment Law and Industrial Relations.

The ways in which Work Psychologists approach these areas of interest, is influenced by some core values of Work and Organizational Psychology:

- Science: Commitment to methodological and scientific rigour as ways of understanding people and their behaviour at work, and organizations.
- Pragmatism: Commitment to solving practical problems, and on application of psychology to issues that matter to people at work, and organizations.
- Ethics: Commitment to ethical best practice in the application of psychology to work and organizations (see later section).
- For People and Organizations: Commitment to seeking solutions to organizational problems that enhance organizational effectiveness, and the well-being of people working in organizations. Work and Organizational Psychologists avoid compromising on either of these outcomes, and rather strive to balance and promote both.

Collectively these values give a flavour of the ways in which Work Psychologists conduct applied work in organizations. They are our summary of those values that have emerged from the relatively short history of Work and Organizational Psychology, and to appreciate the present field, it is of course important, and interesting, to understand the past.

A BRIEF HISTORY OF WORK AND ORGANIZATIONAL PSYCHOLOGY

There are a number of accounts of the development of Work Psychology (e.g., Katzell and Austin, 1992; Koppes, 2003), and its rise is an amazing insight into how societal forces necessitate the rise of new ideas and concepts. The emergence of Work Psychology can be credited to the combination of a number of initially unrelated developments around the turn of the 20th century.

1 The applications and successes of science were growing, and entering public consciousness.
2 Modern psychology emerged as a fledgling but quickly developing area of study. In the UK, the work of Francis Galton and Karl Pearson on individual differences heralded the start of the assessment tradition, in which measurement techniques for capturing varied and detailed information about human beings were being designed and tested. At around the same time in the US, psychologists were working on the assessment of intelligence.
3 More widely, the nature of work was changing rapidly, brought about by industrialization. Fuelled by new feats of technology and engineering, the ideas of the early industrialists, people like James Watt, Matthew Boulton and William Murdoch in the English Midlands, a century earlier, had transformed the working and commercial landscape of Europe and the US. Katzell and Austin (1992) quote Sullivan (1927), observing the transformation:

> *Little shops closing down, big factories growing bigger; little one-man businesses giving up, great corporations growing and expanding; ... fewer craftsmen, more factory operatives ... an adjustment of man to [technology].*

Collectively, the context was set for Work Psychology, and the people usually credited with initiating the field in the US are Frank and Lillian Gilbreth, and Frederick Taylor. The only psychologist among them was Lillian Gilbreth, whose work with husband Frank, an engineer, aimed to quantify and measure human behaviour in basic, elementary chunks. The purpose was to measure and manage; to quantify what people did in factory settings, and to make it more efficient. This is the fundamental basis of Scientific Management or 'Taylorism', named after the entrepreneur and management theorist Frederick Taylor.

The emergence of Work Psychology in Europe is usually associated with Hugo Munsterberg, a German psychologist who split his academic career between Germany and the US. He published a book in 1913 called *Industrial Efficiency*, which set down some of the core ideas of the role of psychology in scientific management. In the UK, C.S. Myers was perhaps the first consultant Work Psychologist, working with the British Expeditionary Force during the First World War on the treatment of shell shock. Myers personally saw more than 2000 cases in the first two years of the war.

Work by these early pioneers spawned applications of psychology to work in many industrialized nations, but the major influences were from the US and UK. Notably, it is possible to separate the development of Work Psychology in the US from the UK and rest of Europe.

The First World War was a major catalyst for progress and, after the war, psychologists in both the US and UK exported their new techniques from the military and into industry. In the US, the emphasis was firstly on productivity through personnel selection and training, but Katzell and Austin (1992) also highlight the significance of the Hawthorne Studies in the US as marking a departure from the assessment emphasis. The studies found that changes to working conditions (e.g. environmental changes such as illumination and heat, and work changes such as payment and supervision), irrespective of the actual nature of the change, resulted in improvements in productivity. The Hawthorne Effect refers to outcome changes that are attributed to a specific intervention, when in fact, any intervention would do. The reporting of the Hawthorne studies has been questioned recently (Chiesa and Hobbs, 2008), and their almost mythological status in Work Psychology is surely now in doubt. The criticism is around the science of the studies. They were never subjected to peer review, and the evidence of any effect is weakened because of obvious methodological flaws (Chiesa and Hobbs, 2008). Either way, the Hawthorne studies reflected a growing trend to consider worker rights more clearly during the Great Depression of the 1930s.

In the UK, Myers, with industrialist Henry Welch, founded the National Institute of Industrial Psychology (NIIP) in 1921. Much of the work that the NIIP carried out was concerned with worker well-being. Myers published on worker fatigue, and the group was politically influential, campaigning for the kinds of workers' rights that we still care about now (e.g. limiting work hours, protecting worker dignity and work-life balance, consideration of organizational atmosphere or culture; Kwiatkowski and Duncan, 2006). The NIIP also conducted work on the importance of skills and temperaments in helping people to find suitable employment.

In the rest of Europe, the development of Work Psychology was severely hampered by the Great Depression and the rise of fascism. For example, many gifted German psychologists fell out of favour with the Nazi government, and left to continue their work elsewhere. Perhaps the most well-known of these people is Kurt Lewin, who moved to the US to continue his seminal works on Field Theory and Action Research in Work Psychology.

Like the First World War, the Second World War saw major growth and development of Work Psychology in the US, with hundreds of psychologists employed by the US army in a variety of roles. Some of the main assessment techniques used in organizations today for selection and appraisal of staff originated in the US military during the Second World War, including assessment centres, multi-instrument test batteries and rating forms for measuring performance. Shimmin and Wallis (1994) note similar successes of psychologists in the UK military, but after the war, the initiative was taken primarily by US psychologists, who applied the newly developed techniques extensively in public and private organizations.

In the UK, psychologists likewise transferred methods from the Armed Services, notably to the Civil Service. However, the NIIP changed its emphasis, concerning itself more with the science of Work Psychology rather than practice. Combined with its persistent funding difficulties, it is a choice that probably assisted in its demise in 1977, and the failure to capitalize on past input into Government policy and organizations must be seen as an opportunity missed in the UK. The British

Psychological Society Division of Occupational Psychology (DOP), formed to represent the interests of Work Psychologists in the UK, has never matched the political influence and impact that the NIIP achieved between 1920 and 1940.

Modern Work and Organizational Psychology

Since the 1970s, progress and expansion in Work Psychology has accelerated considerably. In the US, emphasis has consistently been strongly in respect of assessment, personnel selection, performance management and training. Although Work and Organizational Psychology in Europe has followed the US lead in many ways, researchers and practitioners in Europe have carved out some important niches. The work of psychologists such as Cary Cooper and Tom Cox in the 1980s, put the study and management of work stress firmly on the Work Psychology agenda. The work of Peter Warr and others on unemployment and well-being are major contributions to the understanding of the positive and negative psychological consequences of work. Qualitative traditions are much more vibrant in the UK than anywhere else in the world, and the UK assessment industry features some of the major global assessment companies.

Researchers in Scandinavia, and notably in Finland and Sweden, have developed a reputation for producing some of the most influential and powerful findings on work and health. European researchers are at the forefront of research on work teams, and members of the Organization Studies group at Aston University in Birmingham during the 1960s and 1970s carried out some of the most important early studies of whole organizations from a psychological perspective, starting a tradition for such research in Europe. There are therefore aspects of Work Psychology that, over the past 15–20 years, might genuinely be considered European-led.

The difference in emphasis between US and European approaches is a feature in commentaries on research and practice of Work Psychology (e.g. Kwiatkowski, Duncan and Shimmin, 2006), and is evident in comparisons of contents of journals published in Europe and the US. Looking back at the roots of the differences, Highhouse (2006) highlights the importance of the relative power of management and labour in the US and Europe. In the US, management is dominant, and so the preference has been for the application of psychology to improve productivity and organizational functioning, focusing on getting the most out of individuals at work, and measuring their abilities, skills and behaviour. In Europe, labour movements, social welfare and the humanist tradition are stronger, and more widely appreciated, reflected in a closer focus on worker well-being and satisfaction, and on organizational influences on behaviour.

The practice and business of Work Psychology is now established to greater or lesser extents in almost all industrialized countries. Most Work Psychology is delivered to organizations on a consultancy model, with Work Psychologists taking roles as either external or internal consultants with organizations. Work Psychology firms are profitable and, for the most part, disconnected from academic institutions. Educational programmes are popular with trainee psychologists looking to specialize, and Masters programmes in Work Psychology are hosted by Universities in Europe and the US, in Australia and New Zealand and more recently in parts of Asia and Africa. In just one century, Work Psychology has developed from a new idea initiated by an obscure, select group of interested academics to a truly global concern. Work and Organizational Psychologists have joined together in large professional organizations (see Box 1.1).

In 2009, three major professional organizations (the Society for Industrial and Organizational Psychology, the European Association of Work and Organizational Psychology and the International Association of Applied Psychology) signed an agreement to form a new Alliance of Organizational Psychology, aiming to increase visibility and promote the practice of Work and Organizational Psychology globally. Moreover, in 2013, concrete steps were taken towards a Europe-wide specialist certification in Work and Organizational Psychology to provide a common recognized framework for preparation and training of Work Psychologists in Europe

BOX 1.1
Professional Associations of Work and Organizational Psychology

Work Psychologists are supported by a number of different professional associations and organizations. The aims of professional organizations vary, from representation through to educational accreditation and regulation. Broadly though, all attempt to promote good practice in the field, to increase the influence of Work and Organizational Psychology in organizations and government, and to ensure that Work Psychologists stay in touch with developments in the field.

The Society of Industrial and Organizational Psychology (SIOP)

SIOP is a division of the American Psychological Association (APA), has more than 6000 members, and was formally established in 1982.

The European Association of Work and Organizational Psychology (EAWOP)

EAWOP is a relatively young organization, founded in 1991, set up to represent Work Psychology in Europe, and to promote cooperation among professionals in the field across the nations of Europe.

The British Psychological Society and Division of Occupational Psychology

The main UK professional association for Work and Organizational Psychology is the Division of Occupational Psychology (DOP) of the British Psychological Society (BPS). The DOP represents the interests of Occupational Psychologists, the training of whom is accredited by the BPS and regulated by a government regulator (the Health and Care Professions Council; HCPC).

For more on Professional Associations in Work and Organizational Psychology, see the online support materials.

CONTEMPORARY THEMES IN WORK AND ORGANIZATIONAL PSYCHOLOGY

So far in this chapter, we have reviewed some fundamental concepts of Work and Organizational Psychology and the history of the field. In this section, we consider contemporary challenges facing businesses and organizations and discuss the role of Work Psychology in addressing those challenges. We identified these challenges in the first edition of this book. Now, five years on, far from diminishing, their importance has grown significantly, so much so that we have added further coverage of each in this second edition:

- Ethics and Social Responsibility.
- Globalization and Cross-cultural Issues.
- Environment and Sustainability.

Ethical and Socially Responsible Work Psychology

Ethical standards of conduct and practice have always featured strongly in the practice of Work and Organizational Psychologists, but the focus of ethical codes of conduct is very much specific to psychology (for more on this, go to the online support site for this book). Issues of ethics and social responsibility have, however, hit the broader business agenda in a big way in recent years. Lefkowitz (2007) identifies two critical relationships in the moral considerations of business:

1 The relationship between government and business.
2 The relationship between business and the rest of society.

It is the latter that is addressed by the concept of Corporate Social Responsibility (CSR). Moral and ethical perspectives on business suggest that the potential for organizations and corporations to do substantial harm or good, gives rise to a moral obligation to consider all of their direct and indirect effects on society and shareholders. Carroll (1999) identifies three pertinent areas that frame the societal responsibilities of business:

- Economic: To operate profitably and efficiently, returning value to shareholders, and fulfilling economic responsibilities (e.g. taxation) to society.
- Legal: To conform to all aspects of the law, avoiding harmful litigation.
- Ethical: To act in accordance with societal and business moral norms, to promote the overall welfare of society and to avoid doing harm.

Wider issues of ethics and social responsibility in business and organizations are highly relevant for Work Psychology from a number of perspectives (Lefkowitz, 2008), and part of conducting the field in a socially responsible way involves remaining vigilant to areas where Work and Organizational Psychology could indirectly contribute to irresponsible management. Lefkowitz highlights two such areas.

- *Pro-management bias* Work Psychologists are contracted to organizations by management, and the competitive nature of the field means that management can be quite precise in what they require from Work Psychologists. This can lead to a bias for management needs and goals, rather than for employees, that may lead to questionable actions, such as assisting management in organizational changes, for example downsizing without questioning the economic justifications.
- *Focus on means and not ends* Ironically, businesses are often criticized for focusing on ends and not means. Work Psychologists rightly tend to take seriously the methods and practices of their work with organizations. However, the consequence is that they may lower their gaze from the long-term ends and outcomes for individuals, organizations and society.

Lefkowitz (2008) calls for a change in the values of Work Psychology to encompass the ideas about how organizations 'ought' to be, according to ideas of CSR. Lefkowitz believes that this would give Work Psychology the broader values of societal responsibility that a true profession needs. This could influence the methods used, and decisions taken by Work and Organizational Psychologists, in turn, enabling them to act and contribute positively in supporting organizations to function and develop responsibly. In the book, we illustrate how this might work by high-lighting some relevant interfaces of business and Work and Organizational Psychology.

Global, Cross-cultural Work and Organizational Psychology

Over the past quarter of a century, commentators and writers have been talking about globalization or internationalization and its importance for business and organizations. We are now certainly beyond thinking about what is likely to happen – globalization has happened and is happening right now. There is now a near certainty that in the course of your career you will work in another country, or with people from another country or culture as part of your job. It is a reality.

BOX 1.2
A definition of culture

A well-cited definition of culture is that of Kluckhohn (1951)

Culture consists in patterned ways of thinking, feeling and reacting, acquired and transmitted mainly by symbols, constituting the distinctive achievements of human groups, including their embodiments in artifacts; the essential core of culture consists of traditional (i.e. historically derived and selected) ideas and especially their attached values.

Culture is defined in Box 1.2, and an important issue for organizations is the impact of culture on work practices. For example, is it reasonable to expect that theories and practices in HR and management established in Western Europe or the US will apply in other cultures? You would think that the answer to this question was so obviously 'no', that it was not worth asking. However, if you look at trends in the dissemination of knowledge and practice to newly industrialized countries, that is very much what happens. In some areas, the knowledge base that has been established in Work Psychology, for example, is largely exported unmodified from the West to other cultures (Gelfand, Leslie and Fehr, 2008).

There is something of an explicit assumption in this practice that organizations develop in the same way through the process of industrialization. In other words, it is sometimes assumed that organizational progress and development occurs similarly around the globe. This idea was demolished many years ago through contingency theory and studies of organizations. As part of the Aston studies, Childs and colleagues showed that culture should be built into contingency theory of organizations (e.g. Child, 1981). The ways that organizations develop in different countries are similar to an extent, but culture determines the specifics of that development. Child concluded:

> *Culturally derived preferences infuse the exercise of choice between alternative [organizational] structures.*
> *The contingency argument was also seen to be moderated by culturally related influences in the areas of decision-making, managerial roles and behavioural expectations.* Child, 1981 p. 316–318; cited in Aycan, 2000, p. 113.

Research in Work Psychology has made some important contributions to understanding cultural influences, notably in the areas of motivation, values, leadership, expatriation, management, teamwork and diversity. However, a contemporary challenge for Work and Organizational Psychology is to expand and communicate this work more effectively, in order to help people in organizations better understand the influence of culture at work. To do this, culture needs to feature more routinely in theory and research in the field, and there are several ways that this can be achieved (Gelfland *et al.*, 2008; Aycan, 2000):

- Expansion of Cross-cultural Research: Core topics in Work Psychology such as selection, training and performance management particularly need clearer integration of the role of culture.

- Understanding the Implicit Values of Research Questions: This issue is concerned with the influence of Western cultural values on the ways that questions are asked, and the ways that problems are framed in organizations. Understanding the cultural limitations of theory and research involves Work and Organizational Psychologists acknowledging the limitations of culturally nested individual perspectives.

● Theory and Cultural Influence: To adopt a globalized perspective, practitioners and researchers need to firstly consider and understand more clearly the nature of cultural influences at individual, group and organizational levels. How does culture affect individual behaviour? Is this different from the effects it has on team behaviour? What are the cultural contingencies that affect organizational and human resource management strategy? Work Psychology theory should also strive to understand and identify *when* culture matters (Gelfand *et al.*, 2008), and to incorporate that information into models and theories.

All of the chapters in the book comment on cross-cultural perspectives in some form, but in some chapters, we address issues of globalization and cross-cultural Work Psychology directly by highlighting specific areas of importance.

Sustainable Work Psychology

Sustainability is the third global issue that we consider in the book. In some ways the issue of sustainability may be considered an offshoot of CSR in organizations, but we have chosen to consider it as a separate issue given its broader global importance. The most well-cited definition of sustainable development is credited to the Bruntland Report:

> *development that meets the needs of the present without compromising the ability of future generations to meet their own needs.* (Bruntland Commission, 1987.)

Sustainable development is also often represented as a Venn diagram with three interlocking circles. Sustainable development includes attention to sustainable growth in three areas (see Figure 1.1):

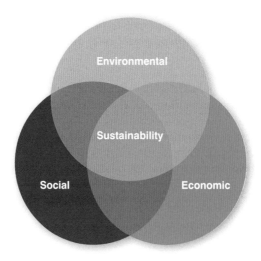

Figure 1.1   Three spheres of sustainability

- Economic: Developing economies in ways that do not threaten long-term economic health.
- Social: Focusing on development that addresses global social issues such as poverty, hunger or inequality.
- Environmental: Developing in ways that allow less environmental resources to be consumed than those that can naturally be replenished.

The current reality of world development is that economic sustainability is the primary focus of growth, followed by social sustainability, and environmental sustainability last. Much international politicking is currently, on the surface, devoted to redressing the balance. Businesses and organizations have a critical role to play in sustainable development, as they represent an important means by which humankind creates social systems, develops economies, distributes wealth and develops new technologies.

Work Psychology has a role to play in promoting sustainable development, but only recently has consideration been given to how applications of Work Psychology might contribute to sustainability (albeit despite some recent emergent thinking, e.g. Carr *et al.*, 2008). Like most of the rest of the world, the preoccupation of Work Psychologists has been with economic outcomes (productivity in organizations) and social outcomes (well-being and satisfaction). Ones and Dilchert (2012) set out some of the challenges for Work and Organizational Psychology in the area of environmental sustainability, and there are several commentaries available on their article (see *Industrial and Organizational Psychology* volume 5, issue 4). The sum of these contributions indicate the potential for Work and Organizational Psychology to contribute to individual behavioural change and management (micro interventions) and development of pro-sustainability cultures, climates and strategies (macro interventions). On the micro side, Work Psychologists understand how attitudes and behaviour might be changed among leaders and employees, thereby helping to ensure individuals contribute to sustainability. Measurement and modelling of individual performance is also a strength of Work Psychologists, and these could be further developed through research and theory to conceptualize the role and place of sustainability in performance metrics for staff. Work Psychologists are also involved in organizational strategy, development and change processes, and this affords an opportunity to counsel for the inclusion and utilization of environmental and social sustainability outcomes in those processes. A central aspect of change at an organizational level is the creation of cultures and climates that support sustainability, (e.g. Norton, Zacher and Ashkanasy, 2012; Alcaraz *et al.*, 2012), and as we will later see in this book, that creation needs to comprise more than simple awareness raising of environmental issues.

More broadly, more consideration is needed about the environmental consequences, direct or indirect, of the work that psychologists do in organizations. We could view such consequences in a number of ways. A direct impact might be observed if psychologists assist in organizational development strategies that in the long term are likely to cause environmental damage. An indirect impact might be ignoring sustainability issues in the selection of powerful leaders, failing to raise such issues with organizations in consulting activities or neglecting to integrate them into models of organizational performance.

Work and Organizational Psychology has a challenge to face in this area and will need to look beyond alliances with HRM to make an impact. A UK survey of sustainable work practices found that 10 per cent of companies enacted environmental sustainability initiatives through their HR department, with facilities and estates, specialist CSR teams or senior management much more likely to be responsible for sustainability policy and activity (Zibarras, Judson and Barnes, 2012). The survey also showed that the vast majority of interventions undertaken were marketing- or awareness-type activities, with much less direct intervention such as training or performance management around sustainable behaviour. As with the other contemporary themes, we consider issues of sustainability in several of the chapters in this book.

THE PSYCHOLOGY OF WORK AND ORGANIZATIONS: THIS BOOK

The final task in this first chapter is to formally set the scene for the rest of this book. As we did in the first edition, we have structured it by dividing the major domains of Work and Organizational Psychology into three sections, moving from foundations, through areas of professional practice and finally onto perspectives about whole organizations.

Foundations of Work and Organizational Psychology

The first section of the book involves some scene setting for Work and Organizational Psychology. We consider some of the core topics in social psychology and organizational behaviour. The section starts with an exploration of research methods and their role in guiding research and practice in Work Psychology. We then consider three further key foundation topics. These are:

- Individual Differences.
- Organizational Behaviour and Attitudes.
- Motivation.

The aim in the first section of the book is to help you develop a broad understanding on psychology and its role in helping us understand people's behaviour at work. Many of the topics in the foundations of Work and Organizational Psychology are fascinating, particularly when encountered for the first time, and so take your time in absorbing new ideas and knowledge.

Professional Practice of Work and Organizational Psychology

In Part Two of the book we cover the major professional applications of Work and Organizational Psychology. Work Psychologists consult and work with businesses and organizations in a number of key areas, and in Part Two we review and discuss these areas. Many reflect the tradition of Work Psychology that focuses on individuals at work, and the chapters represent core tasks for managers in organizations. In each case, the chapters are designed to explore how Work Psychology can help managers and practitioners to better understand and carry out those tasks. The five areas covered are:

- Recruitment, Selection and Assessment.
- Learning, Training and Development.
- Performance Measurement and Management.
- Careers and Career Management.
- Safety, Stress and Health at Work.

Collectively, the content of these chapters considers the major contributions of Work and Organizational Psychology to the effective recruitment and selection of people into organizations, and the management of people's development, and performance once they join an organization. Moreover, the chapter considers people's development across their whole working lives and careers, and how people's welfare, health and safety can be protected at work.

Organizations

The final section of this book takes an organizational perspective by locating our understanding of behaviour at work in the organizational context within which it occurs. This is a perspective which is perhaps less popular or obvious for psychologists whose tendency is to focus on the individual or the small group. However, from Kurt Lewin onwards, we have come to realize just how vital an understanding of context is if we are to understand human behaviour and help to create better communities. Accordingly we consider the following areas:

- Organizations: Structure, Strategy and Environment.
- Leadership.
- Teamworking in Organizations.
- Organizational Culture and Climate.
- Organizational Development and Change.

We propose that an understanding of Work and Organizational Psychology is enhanced by knowledge of organizational strategy, structure and environment since these have a considerable influence on attitudes, behaviour and experience at work. This is an unusual aspect of our text but one we believe will be extremely valuable and, we hope, fascinating for the reader. Second, we focus on what is arguably the most researched area of Work and Organizational Psychology – leadership. But we place leadership in its organizational context rather than simply analyzing it atomistically as traits, behaviours and tactics. The third chapter in this section looks at teamworking in organizations and, in addition to reviewing the research, considers how teamworking can be supported and how it can be developed most effectively in organizations. Finally, there is a chapter on organizational culture, climate and change which takes a whole organization perspective and seeks to give the reader helpful theoretical models with which to understand work organizations and also practical tools for working in them.

In this second edition of *The Psychology of Work and Organizations*, we have updated every chapter to incorporate some of the developments in the field since the first edition. There are some fascinating developments, for example in the area of individual differences and working life (see Chapters 3 and 9), the strategic context of recruitment and selection (see Chapter 6), the development of approaches to competency modeling (see Chapter 8), the role of cognition and emotion in strategy development (see Chapter 11) and new research on team working (see Chapter 13).

As highlighted earlier, we have added more reflection on the key contemporary themes of business in the context of Work and Organizational Psychology. Plus there is a new feature in which we give pointers about how to immediately apply the content of each chapter, called Apply It.

Evidence, Critique, Practice

We have taken a particular approach to writing this book. We both find Work and Organizational Psychology to be a very rewarding field to study and in which to work. We are enthusiastic about the value of Work Psychology, and about the potential for it to make contributions in organizations and to businesses and to the wider society of which they are a part, and we intend this to come across in our writing.

Both of us are academics and practitioners; we conduct research in Business and Management School environments, and also work with organizations, applying Work and Organizational Psychology. Our perspective is therefore critical, but also pragmatic. We have aimed throughout this book to review evidence, research and theory, and to do so in a critical, yet accessible way, and we encourage you to think critically about issues that are raised in the chapters. However, we also adopt a practical focus in each chapter too, and particularly value and report those aspects of Work and Organizational Psychology that have practical utility and relevance to organizations, and make suggestions for how to apply them. We encourage you throughout to think about and understand how the contents of the chapters could, and should be applied in organizations. On that note, it is time that we started doing these things by beginning the journey through the book.

SUMMARY

Work and Organizational Psychology is the study of people and their behaviour at work, and of the organizations in which people work; Work Psychologists develop psychological theory and apply the rigour and methods of psychology to issues that are important to businesses and organizations, in order to promote and advance understanding of individual, group and organizational effectiveness at work, and the well-being and satisfaction of people working in or served by organizations.

The field is known by a number of different titles, such as Occupational Psychology, and Industrial and Organizational Psychology. However, the nature of the field is indicated by the work that psychologists do in organizations, reflected in the contents of this book.

The field has a relatively short history, dating back to the start of the 20th century. Work Psychologists in the US and in Europe developed the field of Work and Organizational Psychology quickly, and along somewhat divergent lines, with the US focusing on productivity, performance, training and assessment, and Europe adopting a stronger focus on well-being and welfare at work.

Global challenges for businesses and organizations are relevant concerns for Work Psychology. Three key challenges facing organizations globally are to strive for Corporate Social Responsibility, to understand the role of culture in globalized business and management and to develop sustainably. These are challenges that Work and Organizational Psychology can help businesses meet.

We are totally serious about our assertion at the start of this book, and if you haven't already done so, write down seven questions now that you might ask about people and their behaviour in organizations if you were a manager. Keep them with this book, and tick them off as you find out something that helps you answer the questions. If you have any that aren't answered, or at least addressed in some way by the time you finish reading the book, then send them to us (we haven't been challenged yet, so please do). They'll be in the next edition.

FURTHER READING

Warr, P.B. (2006) *Psychology at Work* 5th Edition. Penguin.

REFERENCES

Alcaraz, J.M., Kausel, E.E., Colon, C., Escotto, M.I., Gutiérrez-Martínez, I.S.I.S., Morales, D., Prado, A.M., Suárez-Ruz, E., Susaeta, L. and Vicencio, F.E. (2012). Putting organizational culture at the heart of industrial–organizational psychology's research agenda on sustainability: Insights from Iberoamerica. *Industrial and Organizational Psychology, 5(4)*, 494–497.

Alonso, J., Angermeyer, M.C., Bernert, S., Bruffaerts, R., Brugha, T.S., Bryson, H., De Girolamo, G., De Graaf, R., Demyttenaere, K., Gasquet, I., Haro, J.M., Katz, S.J., Kessler, R.C., Kovess, V., Le Pine, J.P., Ormel, J., Polidori, G., Russo, J.L. and Vilagut, G. (2004). Prevalence of mental disorders in Europe: results from the European study of the Epidemiology of Mental Disorders (ESEMeD) project. *Acta Psychiatrica Scandinavica, 109*, 21–27.

Aycan, Z. (2000). Cross-cultural industrial and organizational psychology: Contributions, past developments and future directions. *Journal of Cross-cultural Psychology, 31(1)*, 110–128.

Bruntland Commission (1987). *Our Common Future*, Oxford University Press.

Carr, S.C., Maclachlan, M., Reichman, W., Klobas, J., O'Neill Berry, M. and Furnham, A. (2008). Organizational psychology and poverty reduction: where supply meets demand. *Journal of Organizational Behaviour, 29*, 843–851.

Carroll, A.B. (1999). Corporate social responsibility. *Business and Society, 38(3)*, 268–295.

Chiesa, M. and Hobbs, S. (2008). Making sense of social research: How useful is the Hawthorne effect? *European Journal of Social Psychology, 38(1)*, 67–74.

Child, J. (1981). Culture, contingency and capitalism in the cross-national study of organizations. In L.L. Cummings and B.M. Staw (eds.), *Research in organizational behaviour* (Vol. 3, pp. 303–356). Greenwich, CT: JAI.

Gelfand, M.J., Leslie, L.M. and Fehr, R. (2008). To prosper, organizational psychology should adopt a global perspective. *Journal of Organizational Behaviour, 29*, 493–517.

Highhouse, S. (2006). The continental divide. *Journal of Occupational and Organizational Psychology, 79*, 203–206.

Katzell, R.A. and Austin, J.T. (1992). From then to now: The development of industrial-organizational psychology in the United States. *Journal of Applied Psychology, 77(6)*, 803–835.

Kluckhohn, C. (1951). The study of culture. In D. Lerner and H.D. Lasswell (eds.), *The policy sciences*. Stanford, CA: Stanford University Press.

Koppes, L.L. (2003). Industrial-organizational psychology. In I.B. Weiner (General ed.), D.K. Freedheim (Vol. ed.), *Comprehensive handbook of psychology: Vol. 1. History of psychology* (pp. 367–389). New York: John Wiley and Sons.

Kwiatkowski, R. and Duncan, D.C. (2006). UK occupational/organizational psychology, applied science and applied humanism: Some further thoughts on what we have forgotten. *Journal of Occupational and Organizational Psychology, 79*, 217–224.

Kwiatkowski, R., Duncan, D.C. and Shimmin, S. (2006). What have we forgotten – and why? *Journal of Occupational and Organizational Psychology, 79*, 183–201.

Lefkowitz, J. (2007). 'Corporate social responsibility.' In S. Rogelberg (ed.), *The Encyclopedia of Industrial and Organizational Psychology* (Vol. 1, pp. 114–118). Thousand Oaks, CA: Sage.

Lefkowitz, J. (2008). To prosper, organizational psychology should … expand the values of organizational psychology to match the quality of its ethics. *Journal of Organizational Behavior, 29*, 439–453.

Norton, T.A., Zacher, H. and Ashkanasy, N.M. (2012). On the Importance of Pro-Environmental Organizational Climate for Employee Green Behavior. *Industrial and Organizational Psychology, 5(4)*, 497.

Ones, D.S. and Dilchert, S. (2012). Environmental sustainability at work: A call to action. *Industrial and Organizational Psychology, 5(4)*, 444–466.

Shimmin, S. and Wallis, D. (1994). *Fifty years of occupational psychology in Britain*. Leicester: British Psychological Society.

Sullivan, M. (1927). *Our times: The United States 1900–1925*. London: Scribner's Sons.

Zibarras, L., Judson, H. and Barnes, C. (2012). Promoting environmental behaviour in the workplace: A survey of UK organisations. *Going green: The psychology of sustainability in the workplace*, 84–90.

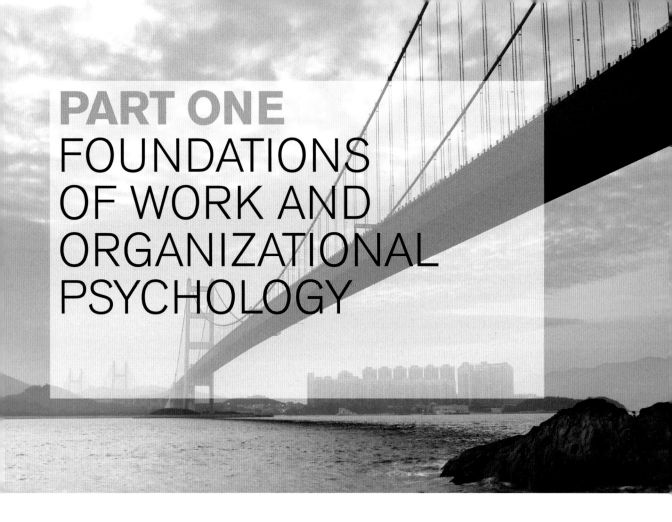

PART ONE
FOUNDATIONS OF WORK AND ORGANIZATIONAL PSYCHOLOGY

The foundations of Work and Organizational Psychology are a heady mix of ideas and concepts from psychology, organizational behaviour, management and science. Collectively they offer fascinating insights into individual behaviour at work, and the ways in which it can be investigated and understood.

The journey through the foundations of Work and Organizational Psychology starts with the scientific principles and techniques that give rise to them. Sound research and science enable the field to establish evidence-based theories about work and organizations. Our path then turns towards the theories and research that help us to understand individuals, and their behaviour at work. Individual differences in personality and ability contribute to understanding people's typical patterns of behaviour, thought and emotion at work, and their potential to perform effectively in increasingly complex work environments. Behaviour at work is also shaped by attitudes, emotions and perception. The ways that people think and feel about their work are important determinants of their behaviour and performance. All of these influences operate in the social contexts of work groups and organizations, and these contexts exert surprising influences on perceptions, decisions and behaviour. And finally, one must ask why people are motivated to work at all? Work satisfies needs, provides purpose, direction and rewards for people's behaviour and effort, all of which are important aspects in understanding motivation. These are the topics of the next four chapters, which will very likely change the ways that you think about people and their behaviour at work.

CHAPTER 2

RESEARCH METHODS IN WORK AND ORGANIZATIONAL PSYCHOLOGY

LEARNING OBJECTIVES

◍ Understand the importance of research methods in Work Psychology.

◍ Describe the elements of the scientific method.

◍ Understand how scientific methods are integrated with the problem-solving cycle in organizational problem solving.

◍ Describe research designs in Work Psychology.

◍ Conduct literature searches and understand the merits and weaknesses of evidence sources.

◍ Describe the need to balance demands of science and practice in organizational research.

◍ Understand critical perspectives on Work Psychology and research methods.

◍ Understand how to critically evaluate theory and research in Work Psychology.

The practical problems that people face every day in relation to work, business and organizations are complex, varied and challenging. Consider the manager who is trying to think about how to improve performance or satisfaction in their team; the new graduate trying to decide which technical specialism to go for in their fast track training scheme; the chief executive trying to understand why their new growth strategy is not producing the expected results. There are a myriad potential answers to these challenges and, usually, no shortage of helpful advice dispensed by colleagues, supervisors, friends, family or costly consultants. Listening to the advice or coming up with solutions might be straightforward. One can use intuition, judgement, perceptions of the credibility of others and so on. Deciding which among the possibilities is best, or most likely to solve the problem is another matter entirely.

Work Psychology research methods and techniques could be used to help understand all of the scenarios highlighted above. The problems could be investigated through conducting new research studies to provide information and evidence to guide decision-making (primary research). There is also an accessible and ever-accumulating body of published research in the field that could be consulted (desk research). Both options require an understanding of methodology in Work Psychology. The purpose of this chapter is therefore to introduce you to research and research methods as used in Work Psychology, with two broad aims:

1 To help you understand scientific research and specific research methods so that you can understand published research.

2 To help you understand how research can be conducted to assist in the solution of problems and challenges that people encounter at work, in business and in organizations.

A REMARKABLE FINDING ABOUT THE VALUE OF HRM

A research article published in 2006 in the *Journal of Organizational Behaviour* reported a remarkable finding about Human Resource Management (HRM). The study (West, Guthrie, Dawson, Borrill and Carter, 2006) examined the relationship between the use of particular HR practices in hospitals in the UK, and patient mortality. The study reported that even after controlling for common predictors of mortality in hospitals (e.g. doctors per number of beds, GPs per 100 000 population in the local area), the use of high performance HR systems was associated with lower mortality in hospitals. In hospitals where effective HR systems were implemented, fewer patients died.

This is a good example of a valuable piece of information about organizations and their management that has real consequences for people's lives, and that could only be established through sound scientific research. How did the researchers arrive at this finding? To understand the answer to that question, you need to understand scientific research methods. All will be revealed at the end of this chapter, by which time you should understand the methods and techniques that were used in the study. There is no better place to start this learning than the scientific method itself.

THE SCIENTIFIC METHOD

Techniques for research and problem solving in Work Psychology are scientific, and draw on the systematic process laid down in the scientific method. Science is a methodological and systematic approach to the acquisition of new knowledge or information (Marczyk, DeMatteo and Festinger, 2005), and scientists try to understand the world around them by taking careful measurements in controlled, systematic and methodical ways. The elements, usually credited to Roger Bacon over 700 years ago, still have relevance to the work that Work Psychologists do in organizations today, and are designed to represent a stagewise process of investigation:

- *Foundations: Empiricism and Rationalism.* Empiricism is a systematic and evidence-based approach to understanding things. Empiricists believe that all knowledge should be based on what can be sensed, observed or measured, rejecting intuition and conjecture. What makes science powerful is the combination of empiricism with rationalism (Hergenhahn, 1997). Rationalists believe that reason and logic can be used to evaluate ideas without always requiring observations or data. Combined with empiricism, a rationalist approach allows scientists to think through and work out the links between various pieces of evidence.

- *Step1: Research Ideas.* For people at work and in organizations, research ideas represent the problems they face at work, problems that need solutions or at least to be better understood. The foci of research in Work Psychology then, come from applied, practical and significant problems.

- *Step 2: Research Questions.* A key step in the scientific method is the translation of problems to research questions. The research question is more than a mere restatement of the research problem. It reduces down the problem to one or more fundamental, answerable questions. The question guides the research completely – the methods and techniques employed are selected because they help the researcher to answer the question.

- *Step 3: Theory.* Good science draws on theory. Theory is a key concept in applied research, and is dealt with in more depth in Box 2.1. Theory is important because it represents preliminary explorations and suppositions about the problem under scrutiny, ultimately leading to a reasoned, rational guess as to the answer to the research question. One way to arrive at this reasoned guess is to look at past research and previously tested theory, and to apply the findings to the research problem. Careful literature searching is required, and is an important skill if you are studying or applying Work Psychology (see Box 2.2).

- *Step 4: Hypotheses.* Effective theories will lead to predictions about what will and will not happen if the theory is correct. These predictions are called hypotheses, and they represent what should be observed if the theory is correct. Methods of investigation are chosen to test the hypotheses.

- *Step 5: Collect Observations or Data.* There are a number of ways to collect research data, and these are covered in more depth later in this chapter. An important first distinction to make is between the collection of quantitative and qualitative data. Quantitative data (numerical data) are often more readily associated with the scientific method compared with qualitative data (text-based data collected through interviews or other methods), but good qualitative research can also follow the principles of the scientific method in the same way as quantitative research. Research design is also a key issue in collecting data and observations because it determines the process by which data are collected. There are two main types of quantitative research study conducted in organizational research, correlational and experimental. They have different purposes and are used to test different kinds of hypotheses and to answer different kinds of research questions (see Box 2.3).

- *Step 6: Analyses.* Once collected, data must be analyzed. Conducted well, analyses are elegant in the sense that they help to simply and clearly make sense of data. They allow conclusions to be drawn about whether hypotheses are supported or rejected by the data the researcher has collected. Basic types of analyses are related to the two major quantitative research designs (correlational and experimental). The first uses correlational analysis to establish the strength and nature of relationships between variables. The second, associated with experimental research, is used to test differences between variables. Qualitative analyses are also used frequently in organizational research, and these techniques use methodical and systematic approaches to understanding the meaning and content of text-based data. Specific techniques are explored in depth later in the chapter.

- *Step 7: Conclusions.* Once analyses of data have been conducted, conclusions can be drawn, stating whether hypotheses have been supported or rejected, and consequently whether the theory is supported or not. Importantly, conclusions can be drawn about the answer to the research question. Where questions have applied value, so the conclusions from research should help to address the original research problem. A critical issue in research is the extent to which the conclusion is based on the data that were collected and analyzed. A fundamental and inexcusable practice in research is to draw conclusions that go 'beyond the data'. This is essentially bad science and unfortunately more common than you might think (see Ben Goldacre's weekly column in the British *Guardian* – Bad Science – for example).

BOX 2.1
Theory in Work Psychology and Organizations

Theory serves a unifying and structural purpose in science, as elegantly expressed by Poincare, 1983:

Science is facts, just as houses are made of stone ... But a pile of stones is not a house, and a collection of facts is not necessarily science.

Theory helps to establish the linkages and patterns between observations and facts, and thereby serves to describe, and explain phenomena. Theory in Work Psychology describes and explains what we know or suppose about people and their behaviour in organizations. Drawing on Whetten (1989), the points below elaborate the basic elements of sound theory in Work Psychology:

- Focus: The theory should clearly focus on a specific individual, organizational or social phenomenon, and in Work Psychology, the phenomenon should have applied value, or in other words be important to organizations and the people that work in them.

- What: The theory should describe factors that might be important in understanding the phenomenon.

- How: The relationships or effects between factors should be described to build a picture of how they affect each other.

- Why: The central crux of the theory and the key to its value is an explanation of relationships between different factors. Why do they occur? Logic or previous research evidence are likely to be drawn on in constructing the 'why' of the theory.

- When, Where, Who: The social and cultural context of theory is critical to understand (i.e. particular theories apply to particular people

in specific kinds of organization, or in particular cultural contexts, or even in specific historical contexts).

- Prediction: Theories should lead to testable predictions about the phenomenon of interest that can be subjected to research. A theory should tell us something about what is and is not likely to happen in organizations. In Work Psychology, such predictions are often about how people will behave in organizations.

A theory about happy and productive workers

Here is an example theory about happy and productive workers (it is a simple one, which we examine in more depth in Chapter 4):

Many organizations make efforts to improve people's working conditions in order to promote satisfaction and happiness at work, in the belief that happier workers will perform better. One theory is that people with higher satisfaction are likely to perform better because they feel more positive about the organization, and are therefore likely to try harder to perform at their best. Satisfaction at work is therefore likely to be related to job performance. The relationship is likely to apply particularly to people who have control over their own performance at work, and in organizations where there are no major mitigating contextual factors, such as redundancies or other negative events. If the theory is correct, and higher job satisfaction *causes* improved performance, then improvements in job satisfaction should be accompanied by improvements in performance.

BOX 2.2
Literature searching

Research in Work Psychology starts at the desk, in what we know rather uncreatively as 'Desk Research'. Desk Research involves searching through, selecting, reading and writing about previously published research that is relevant to your research area or research question. If you are an undergraduate student learning about Work Psychology, or a practitioner in an organization, then the idea of scientific literature searching might be somewhat new to you. 'The literature' in the context of academic study refers to the body of knowledge accumulated about a particular field, reported in books, but most importantly research journals. It is a good idea to start browsing and reading through the research journals in the field. How do you decide what to read though?

Search engines are familiar to us all and there are some easy ways to look for and find relevant research articles. First, if you do not have access to University Library resources, then Google searching can be surprisingly productive, particularly if you use the formal academic search functions in Google Scholar. The latter usually pulls up some relevant material. The main non-public search engines and databases for Work Psychology are PsychInfo and EBSCO. PsychInfo is administered by the American Psychological Association and is a search engine that allows you to search through the major psychology focused journals and these include an excellent group of Work Psychology journals. EBSCO is a dedicated business journal resource, acting as a database for all mainstream business journals. There is some overlap between these two major databases, but generally there is merit in searching through both.

One disadvantage of searching literature in the information age is the sheer volume of the stuff. Sifting through the material and differentiating the unreliable from the robust can seem daunting, but there are a few guidelines to bear in mind:

- Not all published sources are equal. Peer-reviewed journal studies are always the most authoritative source to look at.

Peer-reviewed means that the journal paper has undergone a rigorous review process carried out by at least two other academics in the field. It acts as a quality check on the research to determine whether the methods employed and the ideas communicated are justified and sound. Beware of conference papers or dissertation abstracts in your literature searching, as these are often not reviewed with the same depth as journal papers.

- Never rely on general Internet sources for your information. Online, public-access encyclopaedias are seriously problematic for literature searching because none of the information they contain is verifiable or checked for quality. The same applies to most other Internet resources. However, if you choose carefully and follow advice from people you can trust in the field, some Internet resources can be extremely helpful and informative. We recommend such sources from time to time in this book.

The following literature search strategies are generally the safest to get you started:

- Start by browsing the top journals in the field. Browse editions dating back five years or so to look for relevant articles. The major journals in the field are:
  - *Journal of Applied Psychology*.
  - *Academy of Management Journal*.
  - *Personnel Psychology*.
  - *Journal of Occupational and Organizational Psychology*.
  - *European Journal of Work and Organizational Psychology*.
  - *Academy of Management Review*.
  - *Journal of Personality and Social Psychology*.

- Find a focal article. Once you have found an article that is centrally important to your interest or needs, then use it. Look through the reference list included in the article and use search engines and databases to do a 'search forward'. The latter enables you identify articles citing

your focal article. Such articles will likely be relevant to your interests.

- Identify the major contributors in the area you are researching and access their back-catalogue. Most academics have publication lists available on the Web and many also upload pdf versions of their articles. These can be a very useful resource.

BOX 2.3

Research designs in Work Psychology

Correlational research

Correlational research aims to determine whether different things are related to one another, the 'things' being measurable phenomena like height, weight, age, intelligence, job satisfaction, job performance (referred to as variables; see below). Correlational research is descriptive because it seeks to describe the relationships between different variables, and does not examine cause and effect.

Experimental research

In its simplest form, experimental research aims to establish causative relationships by comparing two groups, treated differently, on the same outcome measure. Experiments are tests of cause–effect relationships, which aim to determine whether one variable influences another. The basic experimental design (Figure 2.1) involves treating two groups of participants in exactly the same way, with one exception, which is referred to as the experimental treatment. One group (the experimental group) receives the treatment, the other (the control group) does not. If all other potential variables are held constant across the two groups, then any difference observed in the two groups post treatment, must logically be caused by the experimental treatment.

For example, imagine that a manager was interested to see if telesales performance was improved by giving people an extra break in the morning. The manager could check using an experiment in which the extra break was given to one group of salespeople, but not another. The change in performance of the two groups could be compared.

In Work Psychology, true experiments are hard to conduct, because the applied nature of research in the field means that it is difficult (near impossible in fact) to control conditions exactly, or in some cases to find 'control groups'. Experimental research in Work Psychology is therefore much more likely to be considered 'Quasi-experimental' (i.e. based on the experimental method, but with imperfections or variations).

Variables in research

'Variable' is the term given to things that we measure in research. Two kinds of variable can be distinguished:

- Independent variable / Predictor: An independent variable or predictor is a variable that is in the control of the researcher, or that is hypothesized to predict an outcome of interest in an organization.

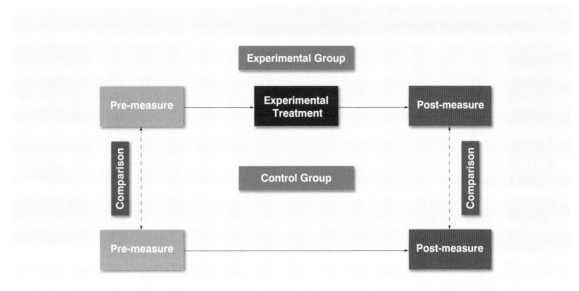

Figure 2.1   Experimental research design

- Dependent variable / Criterion: The dependent variable or criterion is the measureable outcome variable that we are interested in predicting. A good example of a common dependent variable in organizational research is job performance. A great many studies in Work Psychology aim to understand how job performance can be influenced or predicted, and so it is conceptualized as a dependent variable or criterion.

PROBLEM SOLVING USING RESEARCH IN ORGANIZATIONS

The obvious practical value of good research is for evidence-based problem solving. In fact, a whole discipline of evidence-based management is emerging, which attempts to clarify the most effective techniques of management solely based on the sound research and systematic evidence review (see Briner and Rousseau, 2011).

On a more micro-level, research methods may also be applied to solve specific problems at work. The real practical benefits of scientific investigation are realized when they are integrated with a systematic approach to problem solving. The problem-solving cycle is a good way to illustrate how this works. The cycle is a common approach to addressing problems in a variety of fields, adapted for use in organizations. The cycle is presented in Figure 2.2, and follows a series of steps:

- Identification of problem: Specification of the problem.
- Analysis of identified problem: Exploration of the identified problem, capturing information about a wide array of relevant factors and evidence.
- Identification of possible solutions: Evidence and information about the problem are used to guide the generation of several possible solutions.

- Decide on chosen solution: Strengths and weaknesses of possible solutions are evaluated to arrive at a chosen solution.
- Implement chosen solution: The chosen solution is implemented in order to attempt to solve the problem.
- Evaluate solution: The solution is evaluated by using evidence to determine *whether* the problem has been removed or reduced. If not, or if there are unintended consequences, another cycle of problem solving is initiated.

Research has the potential to contribute to all steps of the cycle:

- Desk research could help practitioners to identify and describe the problem, to plan solutions and to work out the best way to implement them.
- Primary research (actual collection and analysis of data from the organization) would be critical to describing and understanding the problem in the organization, analyzing relevant factors to inform generation of possible solutions, planning and implementing solutions and evaluating their impact.

Note that in Figure 2.2, two additional tasks are presented outside the cycle to show it fits with the 'consultancy cycle', a process commonly used for Work Psychology consulting activities in organizations. Contracting and agreeing terms and objectives with client organizations tend to happen at the outset of the consultancy project, with re-contracting happening post-evaluation after reflection on the results of the project. This is a neat way to think about the interface of research processes and practice.

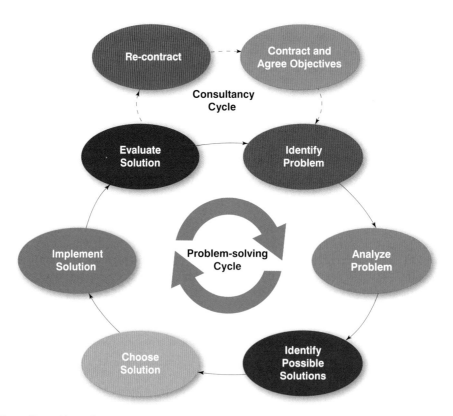

Figure 2.2   The problem-solving cycle

KEY THEME

Corporate Social Responsibility and Research Ethics

How would you judge whether research is ethical? The issue of ethics in research is important in applied psychology. Academic research is regulated closely in terms of ethical treatment of participants. Universities have standing ethics committees who review proposals for research to be conducted by members of staff and also by students for projects and dissertations. In contrast, practitioners who use research techniques in organizations are under no obligation to seek ethical approval for that research. Professional guidelines help in these situations. Members of the BPS, for example, conduct research according to the BPS Ethical Code of Conduct in Research. These and other ethical guidelines for research are designed to highlight and define best practice in research in organizations. The main areas of consideration are:

Privacy and Confidentiality: Participants (i.e. the people participating and 'being researched' in the organization) must be aware of the confidentiality of their data, and confidential data should not be disclosed without prior consent of the participant. An exception is when there is a serious concern about the safety of the participant, the safety of others who may be endangered by the behaviour of the participant, or the health, welfare or safety of children or vulnerable adults.

Informed Consent: Research participants should be given ample opportunity to understand the nature, purpose and anticipated consequences of participating in research, so that they can give their informed consent to participate.

Protection of Participants: Researchers should take account of the potential harm that research might cause to participants and take reasonable steps to manage it. These risks include potential damage to psychological well-being, physical health, personal values or dignity. Participants have the right to withdraw from the research at any time, and may decline to answer questions put to them.

Act within Limits of Competence: Occasionally when researching in organizations, people get the wrong idea about the kind of psychology practiced by Work Psychologists, and may seek advice on personal or wider psychological problems. Under such circumstances, it is important that researchers offer sound advice about where people can seek help.

Debriefing: Following the research, participants should be informed about the outcome of their participation. This might be through reporting general or personal results.

A final point should be made about theory in Work and Organizational Psychology. The value of theory for practice cannot be overstated. This goes beyond the cliché of 'nothing is so practical as a good theory'. Understanding the power of theory is an important development step for anybody working in business. Theories tell us about why we observe relationships between variables, or why certain empirical effects are observed. Theory also helps us to understand how published research may or may not apply in specific businesses or contexts – when we understand *why* a particular idea works, we can adapt it, work with it and see how it fits with the problem we are facing.

DISCUSS WITH A COLLEAGUE

Ethical guidelines help people to make decisions in ethically ambiguous situations, but there are still judgments that have to be made on occasions. For example, should a person inform management if in the course of their research they uncover unethical behaviour of employees (e.g. sabotage, fraud)? Would this violate the privacy and confidentiality of participants? What do you think? Discuss this issue with a colleague.

Is there a Gap Between Science and Practice in Organizational Research?

The role of desk research in the problem-solving cycle highlights the role of published research in informing practice in organizations. For this to work properly, published research needs to have practical implications, but some commentators have noted the emergence of a gap between the concerns of organizational researchers and practitioners in recent times. Representing the practitioner side, Gelade (2006) suggested that too much research in Work Psychology lacks immediate practical relevance for businesses and organizations. He believed that many HR practitioners saw research in Work Psychology as inconsequential or lacking in clear guidance about how to apply findings in practice. In a similar vein, Starkey and Madan (2001) recommended changes for management and organizational research generally, commenting that research in universities needed to move away from the creation of knowledge for academic purposes, and to focus on the creation of knowledge that is relevant for some purpose or practical need. There are plenty of views to the contrary, and representing the academic side, Weick (2001) highlights that the academic–practitioner gap is in part due to the unwillingness of some practitioners to understand the conceptual and research foundations of some management fads and practitioner quick-fixes. Hodgkinson (2006) responded to Gelade commenting that some of his proposals represented a misunderstanding of the roles of researchers and academics in creating robust, defensible new knowledge.

An eloquent representation way to classify and understand research in organizations is presented by Hodgkinson, Herriott and Anderson (2001), reproduced in Figure 2.3. The figure shows four quadrants organized by two features of research, theoretical and methodological rigour (high and low), and practical relevance (high and low). The quadrants show four kinds of research:

- Puerile Science: Low rigour, low relevance. Poorly conducted research with no real relevance to anyone.

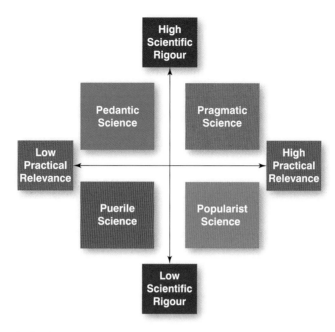

Figure 2.3   Four kinds of organizational research

- Popularist Science: Low rigour, high relevance. Research that meets an immediate practical need, but which lacks theoretical foundations or methodological rigour.
- Pedantic Science: High rigour, low relevance. Research that is highly theoretical and technically competent, but lacks applied relevance.
- Pragmatic Science: High rigour, high relevance. Theoretically meaningful, competent research that meets the needs of users and practitioners.

Of course, Hodgkinson *et al.* (2001) recommend that researchers strive for pragmatic science. They comment that research should meet the needs of users and organizations, but that this should not be at the expense of careful and rigorous research. They also identify the shortcomings of academic research, which, they say, often fails to demonstrate relevance and to communicate research findings in ways that can be understood by practitioners. The counter-argument is presented by Huff and Huff (2001), who warn against jeopardizing future knowledge production by pursuing only those projects that sponsors and organizations find important.

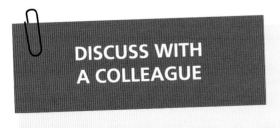

DISCUSS WITH A COLLEAGUE

Problem-driven research focuses on practical, applied problems. Theory-driven research is designed to advance knowledge, without necessarily impacting practice. What do you think should be the focus in research in business and organizations?

Epistemology

There is one final issue to discuss in this initial exploration of research in Work Psychology, and this is related to epistemology. Epistemology is the study of the nature of knowledge. In Work Psychology it essentially refers to how we understand the applied problems that we research in work and organizations. Catherine Cassell has written extensively on this subject in Work Psychology, and her work is thought provoking and critical. Along with colleagues, Cassell challenges the dominant paradigm in Work Psychology, logical positivism, which is represented by scientific research as we have discussed it so far in this chapter. Cassell and colleagues argue that this dominant paradigm prohibits truly critical research in the field (Symon and Cassell, 2006).

This kind of thinking is consistent with social constructionism (sometimes called social constructivism), which holds that we create and maintain our understanding of the world around us through discourse. On the surface, discourses are conversations, discussions or writings. More deeply, discourses represent knowledge structures. So, for example, a Work Psychologist might use science to answer a research question because discourses of science and the scientific method are well embedded in Work Psychology. The Work Psychologist may not question the approach they adopt, because their preference for science represents the accepted way of understanding things.

Ultimately, this issue is about true critical evaluation; scrutinizing not only the evidence upon which research findings are based, but the very foundations upon which they rest. Critical thinking in this sense is about questioning accepted truths about things we encounter.

RESEARCH METHODS IN WORK AND ORGANIZATIONAL PSYCHOLOGY

This chapter has so far covered some of the foundations of research in Work Psychology. Even though some of the perspectives, particularly around epistemology and the academic – practitioner divide, are critical of Work Psychology research, we maintain in this book that Work Psychology is a scientific discipline, and that the most effective approach to solving applied problems in organizations is a scientific one.

In the online support materials, there is a detailed supplement to this chapter that describes and discusses specific methods and techniques in Work and Organizational Psychology. In the next section of this chapter, however, we provide a primer covering some key concepts and terms that will ensure that when we describe research in the rest of our book, it will make sense to you. We organize these in the following headings:

- Collecting Data
- Analyzing Data
- Advanced Techniques in Research.

Collecting Data

Methods of data collection are guided by research aims, but there are a few common techniques that are used in organizational research.

Qualitative Data Collection

Survey methods Survey methods permit researchers to collect a wealth of data quickly, and those data are usually quantitative and easy to analyze. Pre-defined sets of survey items are called scales, and they need to be evaluated in particular ways following the conventions of psychometrics (see Chapter 3). An example of a well-evaluated scale for measuring job satisfaction is shown in Box 2.4.

Survey research can be conducted using several different strategies, and depending on the purpose, data can be collected in different ways:

- **Cross-sectional design** is the simplest and most commonly used in research, and involves collecting survey data at a single point in time.
- **Longitudinal design** in Work Psychology is generally considered to be more robust, and is used for research that investigates change or prediction of future outcomes. In this design, data are collected on several occasions for the same participants, allowing development or change to be tracked over time.
- **Longitudinal cohort design** involves recruiting a group of individuals to participate in research, who then complete multiple surveys over long periods of time. Participants might be asked to complete surveys over 20 years or more.

Observational methods An alternative quantitative data collection method is direct observation. Observation techniques are generally used to capture data on individual behaviour. Casual observation might be used at the start of a research project to help firm up ideas about the phenomenon of interest. Formal observation is a more structured approach, in which systematic methods are employed to guide the observation (Wilkinson, 2000).

Targets of quantitative data collection Quantitative techniques can be applied to measure a myriad of interesting and important phenomena in organizations. Effective measurement is the key, and a lot of research undertaken by Work Psychologists is concerned with how best to measure things in organizations. The main quantitative variables of interest in Work Psychology are:

- Attitudes: Individual attitudes are probably the most commonly measured variables in survey research. Attitudes about specific aspects of work or organizations can be collected easily with surveys. Two very important attitudes in Work Psychology are job satisfaction and organizational commitment (see Chapter 4).
- Individual Differences: Chapter 3 is devoted to the topic of individual differences. The most commonly measured individual differences studied in Work Psychology are personality traits and cognitive ability (intelligence). Cognitive ability is measured using tests that have right and wrong answers. Personality traits are typically measured through self-report surveys.
- Organizational Behaviour: Behaviour in organizations is a key area of interest and research for Work Psychologists. Actual behaviour could be observed directly by psychologists and there are well-defined techniques for observing and evaluating behaviour in work contexts. Survey methods could also be used to measure self-reports of constructs such as motivation or leadership behaviour.
- Job Performance: This is arguably the most important criterion to measure in organizations (Woods, 2008), and as with individual differences, there is a whole chapter devoted to it in this book. Performance can be measured using surveys filled out by supervisors or others. Other measurement techniques include observation, and examination of objective hard data such as sales figures.
- Emotions and States: Self-report surveys can be used to measure emotional reactions to aspects of work, and related phenomena such as mood states. Moods and emotions are transient and therefore changeable, and as a result measures are taken at regular intervals in some studies, following a time-series design.

BOX 2.4
A job satisfaction scale

Introduction

This set of items deals with various aspects of your job. Indicate how satisfied or dissatisfied you feel with each of these features of your present job.

Indicate how satisfied or dissatisfied you are by using this scale:

1 = Highly Dissatisfied.

2 = Somewhat Dissatisfied.

3 = Neutral.

4 = Somewhat Satisfied.

5 = Highly Satisfied.

Items	*Satisfaction level*
1. The physical work conditions.	...
2. The freedom to choose your own method of working.	...
3. Your fellow workers.	...
4. The recognition you get for good work.	...
5. Your immediate boss.	...
6. The amount of responsibility you are given.	...
7. Your rate of pay.	...
8. Your opportunity to use your abilities.	...
9. Industrial relations between management and workers in your firm.	...
10. Your chance of promotion.	...

To score this scale, simply add up the responses to each item, and divide by ten (i.e. the number of items).

Qualitative data collection

Survey and other quantitative methods are arguably the easiest approach to collecting data in organizational research. A limitation of quantitative data however, is the comparative lack of depth and detail. In-depth experiences at work are rarely captured in quantitative data, and are rather the domain of qualitative methods (e.g. interviews and focus groups). Some qualitative research rejects altogether the notion that we can understand psychological and social phenomena through quantitative methods. For qualitative researchers, such phenomena are contextualized against individual experience and consciousness, and to neglect this is to ignore the real essence of psychological research.

Interviews Interviewing is a versatile and widely used methodology in Work Psychology research. It is used in a variety of research contexts. Interviewing is used as the sole method of enquiry in some research, or alternatively it is a useful pre-cursor to quantitative methods, providing rich exploratory data to inform further research design. Interviews can take a variety of different forms, although the common format of the interview is a verbal interaction or exchange between researchers and participants (Breakwell, 2006). The exchange is usually face-to-face, but could also be conducted over the phone. The construction and sequencing of questions is a major design issue for interviews, and it is critical that questions are structured appropriately (e.g. avoiding being leading, ambiguous or assuming), and that they follow a logical progression.

The qualitative data that results from interviews might take several possible forms (brief notes of answers, or full transcriptions of the interview or focus group session).

Focus groups A form of group interview is the focus group, so called because the method involves a group of participants discussing a focal topic in depth. Focus groups can be used as an approach to gather information and to investigate topics of interest in a straightforward manner. From a different perspective, focus groups are interesting because they involve social exchange and interaction between participants, and the analyses of exchanges are illuminating in terms of how people and groups construct social phenomena through dialogue and discourse.

Diary studies Diary studies are not necessarily restricted to qualitative data collection. The diary technique refers to any data collection that takes place over a period of time and at regular intervals (Breakwell and Wood, 2000). Surveys could be used, but diaries can also be open-ended, involving people writing about experiences at work, following a pre-defined schedule and focusing on particular topics.

Research participants

The people who take part in research studies are referred to as participants. Research articles always report the demographics of the research participants, and this information is crucial to understanding how the research findings might apply in organizations. Research studies in Work Psychology are conducted with particular groups of people, usually nested within specific geographical locations or organizational cultures. However, the purpose of research is usually to generalize the findings beyond these contexts (i. e. to be able to say with confidence where and when findings might apply to different groups or organizations). The extent to which research findings can be generalized from one context to another is dependent on how participants are sampled from organizations, and specifically in two aspects:

- Sample size (the extent to which a sample is appropriately large).
- Sample representativeness (the extent to which a sample is adequately representative of the population of interest).

Analyzing Data

As mentioned earlier in this chapter, when conducted well, analytical techniques elegantly explain and elaborate research data. Two other equally true observations about data analyses in Work Psychology and organizational research are:

1 When done badly, data analysis can be confusing, or worse, misleading.
2 Getting it right is easier than people think, and the pseudo-phobia that some people have, particularly about statistics, is probably unwarranted.

From the perspective of research generally, the essence of data analysis is that they should proceed in a logical, systematic way, guided by the research aims, questions and hypotheses.

Quantitative analysis

Quantitative data analyses in Work Psychology vary hugely in their sophistication and complexity. However, when you peel away that complexity, you are left with two pretty straightforward forms of analysis:

- Analysis of differences between variables. These analyses typically compare the means (averages) of different groups on quantitative variables and compute statistics to indicate the extent of those differences.
- Analysis of relationships between variables. These analyses examine whether there are relationships between variables. In simple analyses, the association between two variables may be examined in a correlation analysis. In more complex cases, where there are two or more predictor variables each with associations with an outcome variable, multiple regression techniques are used.

KEY FIGURE

Karl Pearson

In these early chapters of this book, the key people that we introduce are some of the founding figures to whom we owe the field of Work Psychology. Some of the major analytic techniques that form the foundations of our research are without question owed to Karl Pearson (1857–1936), a British, London-born mathematician and philosopher. Pearson read

Mathematics at Cambridge, and developed his expertise in a number of areas after graduating. He was a free thinker and applied his thoughts to the nature of science and to the techniques that could be applied to scientific investigation. Around the turn of the 20th century, Pearson worked with others including Francis Galton (see Chapter 3) on applying mathematical and statistical techniques to biological science. He developed an entire system of statistics, including most significantly, the product moment correlation coefficient (named forever after in honour of Pearson), and the allied techniques of linear regression. These founding techniques have spawned a multitude of variants and more sophisticated analytic techniques, including most recently Structural Equation Modelling. Without these techniques, huge swathes of Work Psychology research would be impossible to conduct, and data would be very difficult to understand or make sense of. In my view, Pearson justifiably retains his place as the key person in the history of Work Psychology research.

Qualitative analysis

Analyses in qualitative research involve making sense of text-based data, which have usually been transcribed from interviews or focus groups, or produced by participants in diary studies. There are several options that could be selected to guide the analysis. As with quantitative analyses, these methods vary in terms of their complexity.

The most basic forms of qualitative analysis are variants of content or thematic analysis. Simple content analysis involves a semi-quantitative treatment of text material, in which categories of text, or specific words are identified and counted. A development of this simple content analysis approach is a more in-depth qualitative analysis of material, in which themes or meanings are the foci of analysis (e g. Krippendorf, 1980). This form of qualitative analysis is sometimes referred to as thematic analysis.

DISCUSS WITH A COLLEAGUE

A retail manager wants to improve customer service in his department store. Think of four ways that research could help the manager understand how best to do this. (Hint: think about the problem-solving cycle.)

Advanced Techniques in Research

There are a number of more advanced research techniques that are worth highlighting briefly, mainly because you are likely to come across them in research articles.

Moderators and mediators

As research in Work Psychology has advanced over recent years, an increasing number of articles are examining the effects of moderating or mediating factors on simple relationships between variables.

- Moderators. Moderators are factors that affect the relationship between variables, representing conditions under which associations are either stronger or weaker. A moderated relationship is typically represented diagrammatically as shown in Figure 2.4.
- Mediators. A mediator is a factor that explains or accounts for the relationship between variables (i.e. x is related to y *because of* mediating factor z). A mediated relationship is also represented diagrammatically in Figure 2.4.

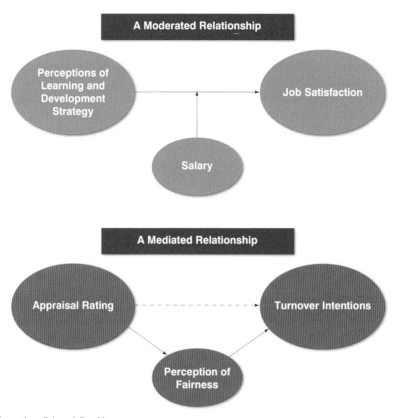

Figure 2.4   Moderator and mediator relationships

Examining very complex relationships

One of the most recent technical developments in the field, which has been made possible by improved statistical capabilities of computers, is Structural Equation Modelling or SEM. SEM is a technique that is used to test the relationships between many different variables altogether. It allows researchers to realize their theory diagrammatically and to see if data they have collected 'fit' their theory.

Beyond individuals as units of study: multi-level modelling

A recent trend in Work Psychology research is multi-level modelling, which refers to research that goes beyond individuals as units of study. For some applied problems or research questions, it is necessary to consider outcomes or phenomena in groups, in teams, or even for whole organizations. The take-home on the idea of multi-level modelling is that Work Psychologists are able to apply research methods beyond the study of individuals in organizations. Groups, teams and organizations are all viable objects of study in research.

Systematic reviews: meta-analysis

Accumulated research evidence allows firmer findings to be established in Work Psychology, and this has been made easier as a result of systematic review methods in the research literature, referred to in Work Psychology as meta-analysis. Meta-analysis (Hunter and Schmidt, 1990) is a technique that allows the results of previous studies to be combined to give an overall result or conclusion.

A good illustrative example is in respect of selection in organizations, and the use of psychometric tests of cognitive ability to aid decision-making. To be viable for use in selection, cognitive ability tests need to be demonstrably related to job performance. They have to tell us something about how people are likely to perform at work if selected. Over a 40–50 year period, a multitude of studies of the issue were published, each reporting their own context- and sample-specific findings. It was hard to say with certainty whether cognitive ability would be useful in a novel context. The application of meta-analysis to the question (e.g. Hunter and Hunter, 1984) resolved that problem by combining the results of all previous studies, correcting them for the idiosyncratic biases arising from sampling and measurement issues, to give an overall result that suggested that cognitive ability was likely to be associated with performance in all kinds of jobs. The findings have fuelled the widespread application of psychometric tests in organizations across the globe since that time. Similar meta-analytic studies have been published in respect of an array of Work Psychology research areas and represent solid, robust evidence of specific research findings for the most part.

The approach has its critics though. Some argue that meta-analysis is sometimes responsible for taking poorly designed and conducted studies and legitimizing them by combining them in an overall result. The quality of that result is in fact closely tied to the quality of the constituent studies, leading to the phrase 'rubbish in – rubbish out'. In my view, a more subtle criticism is more important and to appreciate it, it is helpful to consider another area in which meta-analysis is applied: medicine.

The use of systematic review in medicine has lengthened your life expectancy, and reduced the likelihood that you will die from a curable illness. Simple, but true. In medicine, systematic review combines the results of studies that examine the same research question, perhaps in relation to the effects of a new treatment or drug. They allow medical scientists to quickly establish whether a treatment works, more quickly than if they had to rely on single studies. However, medical research is unlike organizational research in an important way. The physiological reactions of the human body are reasonably predictable, provided that relevant biological parameters are accounted for. The ways in which you would respond to a drug given to you today are the same as the responses would be for a person identical or similar to you living 100 years ago. In Work Psychology, we cannot say the same, because people's behaviour, thoughts, reactions and emotions are all affected by culture and social factors, and those are constantly changing. In meta-analysis, results of studies conducted in the 1960s are combined with those of studies conducted in the 21st century, and there is no accounting for changes in psychological attributes resulting from progress in social and cultural environments.

Notwithstanding these criticisms, the results of meta-analysis are compelling and are considered to contribute in highly important ways to the evidence base of Work Psychology theory and research. We refer to them frequently in this book, and are confident to do so, even though we are mindful of their potential problems.

KEY THEME

Globalization and Cross Cultural Issues

The Cultural Specificity of Research

Cultural specificity in the context of research means the extent to which research findings are specific to particular cultural contexts or settings. In the pure sciences, this is typically not an issue: biological functioning, laws of nature are not typically influenced by the country or culture in which the study was conducted, unless for example, there is some genotype peculiar to a particular culture that would influence biological function.

However, in psychology, cultural context is a critical variable, and immediately invites the question about the cultural specificity of research. The vast majority of research in Work and Organizational Psychology to date is conducted in Europe and the United States, but research from other countries and cultures is now accelerating significantly.

The question for users of research is whether we can take the findings of research conducted in one culture and import them into another, expecting them to apply in the same way. The layperson assumption would I guess be 'no', yet cultural influences on theory and research findings are often poorly elaborated and understood.

The potential for cultural factors to invalidate a theory is easily illustrated. Imagine that we develop theories about decision-making in safety-critical contexts, examining how people decide on behaviour and actions in such situations. We might apply a cognitive model of how people evaluate options and decide logically how to respond. We might also reason that individual differences influence the level or risk that a person is willing to accept.

This all sounds reasonable, but it is developed very much on a 'Western' perspective. In particular, the issue of outcome attribution would be a key cultural factor upon which the theory is built, and which would invalidate it in other cultures. An assumption that one makes in such decision-making theory is that people believe that outcomes are attributable to their actions, and therefore make deliberate decisions. Yet in highly religious cultures, it is common for people to believe that outcomes or destiny are attributable to some higher power – what you personally do will have little effect on the outcome if it has been decided by some higher power that you are going to lose your arm in an accident at work today.

Cultural specificity. It is unfortunately not a requirement for researchers to consider in research articles, so it is up to research users to be proactive, rational and critical in deciding on the relevant cultural parameters that may mean that a theory or finding is valid or invalid in a different culture.

AUTHOR EXPERIENCE

The Potentially Misleading Nature of Research

I was recently asked to work with a major health care company on a project conducted by the management and talent assessment team. The group were responsible for leading the revamp of assessment processes for potential high-flyers in the company. The purpose of these assessments in the organization was to identify people with the potential to rise high and fast in the company early on in their careers. Special development provision would be offered to those individuals. The team I worked with had an incredibly refreshing perspective on the problem at hand. They had invited a number of external consultancies to bid for the work, and had evaluated the proposals against a set of robust, sensible criteria. My role was as an independent reviewer, ultimately with the task of digging down into the evidence base supporting the contractor proposals.

One proposal took more of my time on the project than any of the others. Compared to the elaborate assessment systems presented by the others, this one comprised a single semi-structured interview conducted by an 'expert assessor', lasting for around three hours. The company presented an accompanying portfolio of research findings claiming success rates of their assessment far above what would normally be expected in this kind of process. The review of the underpinning research revealed a confusing, dubiously conducted portfolio of studies carried out, for the most part, thirty years previously. None of the studies had passed rigorous peer review, and the data collection techniques, criterion specification and analytic techniques were all, in my view, questionable. In short, the evidence base was virtually worthless, and did not 'prove' the utility of the technique, as was confidently asserted by the company.

The lesson: beware the uncritical acceptance of research findings. A good appreciation of research is necessarily a critical one. The results of research can lend considerable persuasive weight to arguments or proposals in organizations. Research findings also have the power to be misleading, and bad research is often presented as good evidence by the unscrupulous. Always question, always understand research that is presented to you, and if you can't understand it, know that it is the researcher's fault for not communicating it clearly enough. Ask for it to be clarified and presented adequately, or ask an independent expert. It will save you time and money in the long run. My client rejected all of the proposals in the end – they were unconvinced about the evidence of effectiveness in all of them.

SO HOW DID THEY DO IT?

At the start of the chapter, a remarkable finding about HRM was presented. How did the researchers arrive at the finding?

1 First, they conducted a thorough literature review on the topic, and developed a theory about which HR practices were likely to influence mortality outcomes in hospitals, and why those influences might exist.

2 Second, they identified a population for the research (relevant leaders of 134 UK hospitals). Of this population, a sample of 52 participated, each of whom was in a position that allowed them to comment on the HR practices of their hospital. One person participated per hospital.

3 Third, a survey was designed to collect information on the implementation of various HR practices in the hospital, and people responded either by mail, or by phone (the survey was presented as a structured interview to some participants).

4 Fourth, archived and recorded data were collected from the 52 represented hospitals on mortality rate, and control variables that were theorized to be predictive of mortality rates. These data were matched to the respective survey responses of participants from the 52 hospitals.

5 Fifth, an analytic test (regression analysis) was conducted with the data. Patient mortality was the criterion. Control variables were entered into the regression as predictor variables, followed by survey scores indicating the extent to which HR performance practices were implemented and valued. The analysis showed that the implementation of the identified HR practices predicted mortality rates above and beyond the control variables.

6 Sixth, conclusions were drawn. The researchers concluded that HR practices were associated with mortality rates, but that more research was needed to test the reasons why. Future research, they suggested, should examine the pathways and mediators between HR practice on the one hand, and patient outcomes on the other.

Hopefully, your reading of this chapter should allow you to understand that brief synopsis. If you feel you do, then you are ready to move on. If not, then it might be worth re-reading some relevant sections in the chapter, or looking at the more in-depth material in the Online Support Materials. If you are interested in looking at the study in more detail, the reference is at the end of the chapter.

SUMMARY

This chapter has introduced research methods in Work Psychology. The scientific method forms the basis of the approach that psychologists take to help solve real world problems of work, business and organizations. Understanding research methods and techniques is important for making sense of published research and conducting new research.

Depending on the nature of the research problem, a variety of methods and techniques can be used to collect and analyze research data in organizations. In quantitative research, data are collected and analyzed in numerical forms. Common research designs in Work Psychology are correlational and experimental designs. Survey methods and other forms of measurement are used in quantitative studies, and important statistical tests for dealing with data relate to two broad analytical questions:

- Are variables related to one another?
- Are variables different from one another?

Qualitative research allows deeper understanding of people's experiences at work. Qualitative data can be collected through interviews or focus groups, with resultant text analyzed through techniques based on content and thematic analyses. Some qualitative research is highly critical of the positivist approach to science in Work Psychology.

There is a huge volume of research knowledge reported in books and journals in Work Psychology. Accumulated research findings have helped to establish detailed theories and models that explain the relationships between ever more complex sets of variables and factors in organizations. As more and more research is conducted, some findings are formalized through systematic reviews or meta-analyses, making it possible to report them with increased confidence. Research then, forms the foundations, and facilitates the development of knowledge in the field.

Practically speaking, research helps us to better understand organizations and the way that people behave within them. They also help people to work in more effective and rewarding ways, to make informed decisions and to create and manage healthier and more productive organizations. We (the authors) have an enthusiasm and fascination for theory and research in Work Psychology. We hope to communicate that to you over the next thirteen chapters.

DISCUSSION QUESTIONS

1   A colleague of yours has a theory that absence in their company is caused by stress. What advice would you offer about how to test the theory?

2   Does the potential for science and research to be misleading mean that organizations should ignore scientific research? Why?

3   Can qualitative methods ever be considered scientific in organizations?

4   Can quantitative methods ever capture experiences and intricacies of organizational behaviour?

5   A HR manager would like to understand women's experiences of gender barriers in their organization. How could they do this?

APPLY IT

Unlike the applied recommendations of the rest of this book, which focus on the application of specific research findings, this chapter sets out some specific actions for you to apply research methods and skills in your work:

1   Identify a problem that you are facing at work, or in your team or group if you are at university. Conduct some desk research on this problem. Use search engines such as Google Scholar and EBSCO to identify some relevant research papers. Prioritize those that are highly cited – that means that the articles are influential and substantive. Write a short summary of what you find and what it tells you about a solution to your problem.

2   This action may seem academic, but believe me, may save you or your company money in the future. Look at one HR investment your company makes in an external provider. Next, ask the question 'what is the evidence that this works, and improves our business?'. Review critically the evidence: what are the strengths, and the weaknesses? Consider what your recommendation would be about this investment in the future.

3   If you currently survey staff for any reason in your company, conduct a review of the ethics of the procedures you use. Examine the extent to which they comply with ethical best practice outlined in this chapter. By the way, in doing so, you may find that you don't do something right at present; the major issue is if you do nothing to remedy it.

4   Identify one project that you are working on, for which you might use the problem solving cycle to help develop the project. Try to follow it, work to how you can apply the steps to work through the project scientifically and methodically.

WEB ACTIVITY

Management Gurus: Evidence?

Read the article 'The three habits of highly irritating management gurus', published by *The Economist* Oct 2009, available at the link below or in the digital resources online and discuss the questions below.

http://www.economist.com/node/14698784

1   What are the dangers of presenting ideas to businesses that are not backed up by clear evidence?

2   How would you challenge management gurus to justify their ideas?

3   Write down five strategies or points of enquiry that you could use if you were evaluating the ideas of a management guru.

FURTHER READING

Breakwell, G.M., Hammond, S., Fife-Schaw, C. and Smith, J.A. (2006). *Research Methods in Psychology*. London: Sage.

Dancey, C.P. and Reidy, J. (2011). *Statistics without Maths for Psychology: Using SPSS for Windows*. London: Pearson.

Field, D.L. (2009). *Taking the Measure of Work: A Guide to Validated Scales for Organizational Research and Diagnosis*. California: Sage.

Miles, J. and Shevlin, M. (2001). *Applying Regression and Correlation: A Guide for Students and Researchers*. London: Sage.

REFERENCES

Breakwell, G.M. and Wood, P. (2000). Diary techniques. In G.M. Breakwell, S. Hammond and C. Fife-Schaw (eds.), *Research Methods in Psychology* (pp. 294–325). London: Sage.

Breakwell, G.M. (2006). Interviewing methods. In G. M. Breakwell, S. Hammond, C. Fife-Schaw and J.A.Smith (eds.), *Research Methods in Psychology* (pp. 232–253). London: Sage.

Briner, R.B. and Rousseau, D.M. (2011). Evidence-Based I-O Psychology: Not There Yet. *Industrial and Organizational Psychology, 4(1)*, 3–22.

Gelade, G.A. (2006). But what does it mean in practice? The Journal of Occupational and Organizational Psychology from a practitioner perspective. *Journal of Occupational and Organizational Psychology, 79*, 153–160.

Hergenhahn, B.R. (1997). *An Introduction to the History of Psychology*. Belmont: Wadsworth, Cengage Learning.

Hodgkinson, G.P., Herriot, P. and Anderson, N. (2001). Re-aligning the Stakeholders in Management Research: Lessons from Industrial, Work and Organizational Psychology. *British Journal of Management, 12 (S1)*, S41–S48.

Hodgkinson, G.P. (2006). The role of JOOP (and other scientific journals) in bridging the practitioner–researcher divide in industrial, work and organizational (IWO) psychology. *Journal of Occupational and Organizational Psychology, 79*, 173–178.

Huff, A.S. and Huff, J.O. (2001). Re-focusing the business school agenda. *British Journal of Management, 12 (S1)*, S49–S54.

Hunter, J.E. and Hunter, R.F. (1984). Validity and utility of alternative predictors of job performance. *Psychological Bulletin, 96*, 72–98.

Hunter, J.E. and Schmidt, F.L. (1990). *Methods of meta-analysis: Correcting error and bias in research findings*. Newbury Park, CA: Sage.

Krippendorf, K. (1980). *Content Analysis: An introduction to its methodology*. Newbury Park, CA: Sage.

Marczyk, G., DeMatteo, D. and Festinger, D. (2005). *Essentials of research design and methodology*. Hoboken, New Jersey: John Wiley and Sons.

Poincare, H. (1983). Analytical summary. *Proceedings of Symposia in Pure Mathematics, 39*, 257.

Starkey, K. and Madan, P. (2001). Bridging the Relevance Gap: Aligning the Stakeholders in the Future of Management Research. *British Journal of Management, 12*, S3–S26.

Symon, G. and Cassell, C. (2006). Neglected perspectives in Work and Organizational Psychology. *Journal of Occupational and Organizational Psychology, 79*, 307–314.

Weick, K.E. (2001). Gapping the relevance bridge: Fashions meet fundamentals in management research. *British Journal of Management, 12*, S71–S75.

West, M.A., Guthrie, J.P., Dawson, J.F., Borril, C.S. and Carter, M. (2006). Reducing patient mortality in hospitals: the role of human resource management. *Journal of Organizational Behaviour, 27 (7)*, 983–1002.

Whetten, D.A. (1989). What constitutes a theoretical contribution? *Academy of Management Review, 14(4)*, 490–495.

Wilkinson, J. (2000). Direct observation. In G.M. Breakwell, S. Hammond and C. Fife-Schaw (eds.), *Research Methods in Psychology*. London: Sage.

Woods, S.A. (2008). Performance Measures: The Elusive Relationship Between Job Performance and Job Satisfaction. In S. Cartwright and C.L. Cooper (eds.) *The Oxford Handbook of Personnel Psychology*. Oxford: OUP.

CHAPTER 3

INDIVIDUAL DIFFERENCES AT WORK

LEARNING OBJECTIVES

- Describe the basic principles of differential psychology.

- Understand theories and models of cognitive ability and intelligence.

- Understand different theories of personality.

- Understand trait theories of personality and the Big Five model of personality.

- Describe the ways that individual differences influence behaviour at work.

- Understand the dynamic associations of personality and work, and the developmental influences of work on personality.

- Describe the importance of emotions at work.

- Describe core self-evaluations and psychological capital, and their influences on work outcomes.

- Understand how individual differences are measured.

- Describe principles of reliability and validity, and associated methods.

Like most people, my job involves working with others. I like to think that I know my colleagues quite well, and although they all differ in some respects, the way that we interact is predictable – I have grown accustomed to their styles and characteristics, as they have to mine. There can be no doubt that individual differences influence what people do at work, to suggest otherwise flies in the face of our everyday experience, and a huge volume of research evidence. However, what is even more remarkable in my experience of working with others is the extent to which individual differences exert their effects at different times. In my work with organizations, for example, I often hear about flexible, open and creative people, whose working styles are extremely advantageous at times. However at other times the disorganization, unreliability and carelessness with details that often goes with flexibility and creativity, prove to be equally salient, and usually counterproductive. I am positive that you have your own examples.

Illustrated in this kind of experience are three observations that make the content of this chapter on individual differences so simultaneously interesting and critical for understanding people and their behaviour at work:

1 People do differ in various ways, and those differences do have an impact on their effectiveness and behaviour.

2 The extent to which individual differences are important depends on the context within which they are expressed: the jobs that people do determine whether individual differences are helpful or a hindrance.

3 The extent to which individual differences are helpful or a hindrance is not static, and in fact, characteristics that may be helpful at one point of time may be unimportant at others, or even detrimental to performance.

And, to cap it all, far from this area being a 'classical' discipline in Work and Organizational Psychology, some of the theory and findings to support these points represent very recent contributions to the literature; it is an area that is constantly evolving to reveal new insights. This chapter introduces this fascinating area, covering theory and research on individual differences and their consequences and implications for work and organizations.

INTRODUCTION TO INDIVIDUAL DIFFERENCES

Everyday or layperson intuitions about individual differences are called implicit theories. We all hold implicit theories about the individual differences of those around us. We observe our own behaviour, compare it to the behaviour of others and use the information to decide what kind of person we are and what we think and feel about others. We also use our implicit theories to predict what people will do in certain situations or how they will react to people and events. Implicit theories help us to make sense of the world around us, and also affect our attitudes towards people. We tend to have our own ideas about the relative desirability of certain personality characteristics (e.g. social confidence, friendliness, assertiveness, calmness, openness). The word 'intelligence', for example, has entered everyday language, and has developed a desirability of its own. Rightly or wrongly, high intelligence is a socially valued individual difference, often for no other reason than that it is 'high intelligence'.

For our own purposes of perceiving and understanding the world, and the people we work with, implicit theories are useful. They are no basis for a science of individual differences however, and in this respect psychologists have developed a range of explicit theories designed to represent and explain observations about the differences in individual characteristics and abilities. Only by first understanding these theories can we go on to understand the effects of individual differences on behaviour at work.

The study of individual differences is sometimes referred to as differential psychology. The field aims to explain the differences we observe between individuals in terms of psychological determinants (Chamorro-Premuzic, 2007). Differential psychologists are particularly interested in understanding and measuring consistencies in people's behaviour. They also examine how different patterns of behaviour predict work and other outcomes.

The two major aspects of individual differences that have been studied by psychologists are:

- personality
- intelligence/cognitive ability.

These two components of individual differences have been the subject of research for around 100 years and have given rise to many theories. The history of individual differences is also intertwined with the application of psychology to work and organizations. From early on, psychologists have been interested in how individual differences influence organizational behaviour and performance.

DISCUSS WITH A COLLEAGUE

List the names of six of your colleagues on a piece of paper. Choose three at random and identify what attribute makes two of the three similar, but different from the third (e.g. person one is organized, but persons two and three are disorganized). Write down the attribute, and repeat the process five times. The attributes on your list are the ones that are most important in your implicit theory of individual differences. These are the attributes that you use to differentiate people at work.

INTELLIGENCE

Definitions of intelligence are frequent in the psychology literature and as a result of popular theories of intelligence, across dictionaries as well. Basic verbal definitions often lack consensus, but a group of 52 leading academics in the field of intelligence have provided an agreed working definition of general intelligence:

> *A very general mental capability that, among other things, involves the ability to reason, plan, solve problems, think abstractly, comprehend complex ideas, learn quickly and learn from experience. It is not merely book learning, a narrow academic skill, or test-taking smarts. Rather it reflects a broader and deeper capability for comprehending our surroundings – 'catching-on', 'making sense' of things or 'figuring out' what to do.* (Gottfredson, 1997, p. 13.)

This description sums up the essence of intelligence. It is a general mental capability that can be applied in the understanding of the world around us, for problem solving in a variety of different contexts. One can quickly see why intelligence has the potential to affect such a diverse range of areas of our lives, and in particular why it is important at work.

In the research literature and in most texts, the term intelligence is used interchangeably with cognitive ability, and general mental ability (GMA). Theories of intelligence aim to examine its nature, most often by establishing and testing models of intelligence that tell us more about the way it is expressed in different contexts. The development of such theories and models has tracked the history of intelligence testing, such that the two are impossible to separate.

Francis Galton and Alfred Binet

The first and arguably most eminent figure in the field of individual differences was Francis Galton (see Key Figure Box). Galton's contribution was a theory of hereditary genius, postulating that individual differences in cognitive ability are inherited and normally distributed in the population. Both of his hypotheses have turned out to be largely confirmed in the research literature. In the early

1880s, Galton initiated a programme to test individual cognitive abilities in his Anthropometric Laboratory using fairly crude techniques. With the help of one of his students, Karl Pearson, he also established some groundbreaking and influential statistical techniques – correlation and regression.

These techniques were developed further in the first intelligence test designed by Alfred Binet, working for the French Ministry of Public Instruction. With Theodore Simon, he published the Binet–Simon scale in 1905. The test comprised a series of tasks such as number recall, and sentence completion, along with other practical tasks. Tasks on the test were progressively more difficult in order to differentiate levels of intelligence. The key contribution of Binet and Simon was the establishment of norms of intelligence for different ages. A child's intelligence was worked out by comparing them with children of the same age. Cognitive ability therefore was and always has been a 'relative' construct. Someone is defined as bright or high in cognitive ability because a measure of their ability shows it to be higher than their peers.

KEY FIGURE

Francis Galton

Much has been written about Sir Francis Galton, who is widely accepted as the forefather of differential psychology and psychometrics. He was undoubtedly an exceptional individual, highly intelligent and groundbreaking in the way he thought about people and their attributes. Galton was born and raised in Birmingham in the UK. He was born into a distinguished family, whose ancestors included the founders of the Quaker religion and Barclays Bank. Most notably, Galton's half cousin was Charles Darwin, and Darwin's

'Origin of Species' and other writings on evolution influenced Galton.

As a child, Galton excelled in his schooling, being consistently ahead of his peers. He embarked on medical training before transferring to study mathematics at Cambridge. Galton did not similarly excel as expected at Cambridge and it has been speculated that realizing his own limitations in this field led him to consider why, despite extensive preparation and training, his capabilities were less than those around him. Combining these observations with those of Darwin, Galton theorized on the hereditary nature of genius – that differences in intellectual capability were passed on from parent to child, and that there were innate differences in the intellectual potential of different individuals.

Galton's achievements were multifaceted throughout his life. Having abandoned education after finishing at Cambridge, he became a noted explorer, and developed the first weather map used in meteorology. During his studies of human physical characteristics, Galton also noted the uniqueness of fingerprints, a discovery that led to the use of fingerprinting in criminal investigations and in identification. In his later life, Galton was a figurehead in the Eugenics movement, a phase of his life that is surrounded by controversy, attracting wide criticism. Nevertheless, one cannot deny the huge contribution that Galton made to our understanding of individual differences, and in his life more widely.

Spearman's G

Around the same time, Charles Spearman in the UK examined the intercorrelations or overlaps between scores on different kinds of ability test. Spearman observed that people who scored highly on one kind of ability task, also tended to score highly on others. He proposed that the strong overlap of performance on different kinds of ability task was due to a general underlying factor or construct. He labelled this factor g, to represent general intelligence, and was able to show through a technique called factor analysis, that one could observe the effects of this general factor on a wide range of different ability tests. Factor analysis is a method of examining the relationships between many different variables to identify underlying factors that explain the relationships (more about that later).

Spearman's g is a significant milestone in the history of individual differences and remains one of the most influential findings in the field. Today, researchers still concur with the idea of a general factor of ability, with which all facets of ability are correlated (see Lubinski, 2004), and the definition outlined earlier represents our understanding of g.

The Structure of Cognitive Ability

A challenge for researchers since Spearman originally postulated the existence of g has been how to organize and conceptualize abilities in specific areas (e.g. verbal, numerical, spatial abilities). The earliest effort was that of Thurstone, who rejected the notion of g altogether, instead favouring a model of intelligence that comprised seven primary abilities. Chamorro-Premuzic (2007), describes these primary abilities:

- **Verbal comprehension** – vocabulary (knowledge of words), reading and comprehension skills, verbal analogies (capacity for conceptual association).
- **Word fluency** – ability to express ideas, generating large numbers of words, and use concepts (e.g. anagrams, rhymes, metaphors).
- **Number facility** – ability to carry out mental calculations with speed and accuracy.
- **Spatial visualization** – ability to mentally rotate figures and orientate oneself in space.
- **Associative memory** – rote memory.
- **Perceptual speed** – ability to rapidly spot visual stimuli (similarities, differences, patterns).
- **Reasoning** – inductive, deductive, inferential, logical process of thought.

The definitions of some of these primary abilities are reasonably consistent with some of the more common occupational tests used in organizations. The existence of these specific abilities is largely supported in research, but the idea that these are an alternative to g has by contrast been rejected by most in favour of a hierarchical model, best exemplified by the work of Vernon and Cattel.

Vernon's model included two facets of general ability:

- Verbal/educational intelligence, consisting of verbal, numerical and educational abilities.
- Spatial/mechanical intelligence, which consisted of spatial, mechanical and other practical abilities.

Each was broken down into its constituent levels at lower levels of the hierarchy, culminating in very specific task areas. Models that identify specific forms of ability are highly useful in organizations. Most jobs require people to apply abilities in some areas but not others, and often one area of ability is particularly important. An accountant needs high levels of numerical ability, but spatial ability is less important. For an Air Traffic Controller, spatial ability is highly important. Models of ability allow us to understand how different profiles of ability might be more or less suited to particular jobs.

Cattell also proposed two factors of intelligence, although he did so using a somewhat different rationale. Cattell was a PhD student of Spearman and was influenced by Spearman's work on factor g. His theory and analyses led him to derive two facets of general ability:

- Fluid ability (gf): the ability to solve novel problems with no prior knowledge or education relating to the problem.
- Crystallized ability (gc): learned strategies for solving problems such as those related to education, and cumulative work experience.

Reasoning ability and information processing is captured by gf, whereas acquired knowledge and skills is represented by gc. There is some evidence that gf declines during adult life, whereas gc increases as more culture-relevant information is acquired. It is worth reflecting on the value of both fluid and crystallized ability in organizations. Fluid ability would seem to be related to innovative problem solving, whereas crystallized ability perhaps reflects the collective knowledge and experience of how work has been and should be performed.

The hierarchical model of cognitive ability

The ideas of Vernon and Cattell, and other proponents of the hierarchical model have been consolidated by empirical investigations of the structure of cognitive ability. The best example of such research was carried out by Carroll (1993). In his analyses, Carroll examined the structural relationships between a variety of ability types and tasks. His final model comprised three layers, two of which are shown in Figure 3.1. The figure, adapted from Carroll (1993), and Ackerman and Heggestad (1997), shows g at the top of the hierarchy with ability facets underneath. These include Cattell's crystallized and fluid abilities. All represent mental processes that are influenced in some way by g, or overall cognitive ability. In the third layer of the hierarchy, Carroll included the constituent ability tasks and measures that made up the facets of the second layer. Specific abilities such as verbal and numerical reasoning therefore lie within this third layer, along with the kinds of work tasks that draw on these abilities.

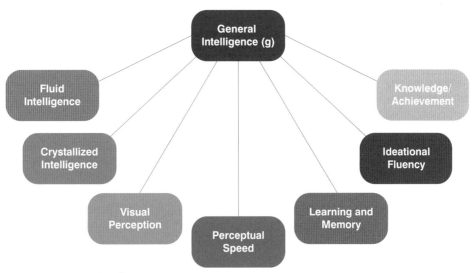

Figure 3.1   Hierarchical structure of intelligence

Ability Testing

The hierarchical model of cognitive ability is consistent with models underpinning a number of ability and intelligence measures. Tests of ability used in organizations are generally designed to address part of the hierarchical model, almost always by testing people's capability to answer intellectual reasoning questions. Tests of cognitive ability have right and wrong answers and are usually timed, so that test-takers complete the test under standardized conditions.

Perhaps the most well-known test was designed by Wechsler. The Wechsler Adult Intelligence Scale (WAIS) was designed with a hierarchical model of cognitive ability in mind and consists of a variety of sub-tests. Other forms of test focus solely on facets of ability. Practitioners have a wide range of tests to choose from, tapping into verbal reasoning, numerical reasoning, abstract reasoning and spatial reasoning. Sometimes the abilities are assessed in job-relevant tasks. An example would be a test that requires people to add up columns of figures quickly, thereby simulating accounts checking or mental calculation of product prices. The task itself would actually be an assessment of numerical reasoning ability, albeit a highly practical one.

Multiple Intelligences

Some people seem to be uncomfortable with the concept of cognitive ability and its measurement. Whatever the reason, such people would often rather identify the virtues of so-called practical (Sternberg) and social (Thorndike) intelligences, which represent skills in interpersonal decision-making and general skills in addressing problems of everyday life. These kinds of constructs hark back to the ideas of Thurstone about multiple intelligences and ideas about the independence of multiple forms of ability.

None of these multiple intelligences has received more attention than Emotional Intelligence, referred to as EI or EQ. Many argue that no other single construct has caused quite the impact that EI caused following its coverage by Daniel Goleman in his bestselling book in 1995 (Chamurro-Premuzic, 2007). EI has been proposed by Goleman, and others (notably Salovey, Mayer and Caruso) as an alternative, more powerful construct than g for predicting success in life and at work. It has found application in organizations, particularly for assessment of managers and leaders, for whom high EI is assumed to be advantageous. There are various definitions of EI, but broadly speaking most would agree with Sternberg and Kaufman (1998) that EI is:

> *the ability to perceive accurately, appraise, and express emotion; the ability to access and/or generate feelings when they facilitate thought; the ability to understand emotion and emotional knowledge; and the ability to regulate emotions to promote emotional and intellectual growth.* (Sternberg and Kaufman, 1998, p. 479.)

Some believe EI to be an ability, similar to other cognitive abilities, and measure EI with tests that have right and wrong answers (e.g. Salovey, Mayer, Caruso and Lopes, 2003). Others believe EI to be a composite personality trait. A good example and operationalization of trait EI comes from the work of Petrides and Furnham (e.g. Petrides and Furnham, 2001). The relative merits of the trait and ability perspectives are hard to evaluate at present because there is not clear evidence to determine whether supporting one or other. There are reported associations between EI and g, which are important if the construct is to be considered as a form of ability (recall that all forms of ability are in some way related to g). There are also established relationships between personality and EI (Petrides and Furnham, 2001), with the debate in that area being whether trait EI adds significantly to what we already know about personality (e.g. Van der Zee and Wakebe, 2004). Whatever form EI takes, there is not consistent evidence that it explains success in life or at work any better than a combination of g and well-defined broad personality dimensions (Antonakis, 2004).

Criticisms of EI can be attributed to a number of sources. In addition to the lack of consensus about exactly how to conceptualize EI, there is also fairly consistent criticism of the measures that are used to estimate it (e.g. Conte, 2005; Fiori and Antonakis, 2011). The demand for measures of EI in organizations has given rise to a supply of poorly designed EI questionnaires sold and used by consultants including, sadly, some Work Psychologists. The call for caution in the application of EI measures (Mayer *et al.*, 1999; Fiori and Antonakis, 2011) appears to be unheeded by some. There remain concerns about the use of EI assessment in organizations, although two recent meta-analyses report evidence that EI is related to job performance (O'Boyle, Humphrey, Pollack, Hawver, and Story, 2011; Joseph and Newman, 2010). More research in this area is needed. There is potential for EI to contribute to our understanding of individual differences in time, but the extent to which it adds anything new beyond personality and cognitive ability remains to be firmly established.

DISCUSS WITH A COLLEAGUE

Think for a moment about the different forms of ability that have been covered in this chapter. Which ones do you think are most important for your job or role? If you are a student, think about which abilities are most important for your course.

PERSONALITY

We are in love with the concept of personality. We are preoccupied with the personalities of others, sometimes obsessed with discussing and understanding them. When you get together with friends, family or colleagues and gossip about the events of the day or the past, or about things at work, the conversation usually comes around to the personalities or characteristics of others whom you know, why you perhaps like them, or why you don't. People like to talk about people, and in that sense we are all personality theorists.

Managers in organizations are also interested in personality. How do we know? Well, firstly we know from anecdotal evidence, which you may agree with. Asking managers about the characteristics or attributes that they value in their employees invariably leads them to comment upon the importance of having employees who are reliable, dependable, able to work under pressure, creative or enthusiastic. All of these reflect personality characteristics. The importance of personality traits to managers was also confirmed in a study by Dunn, Mount, Barrick and Ones (1995), who found that managers cited aspects of personality as often as facets of cognitive ability.

Theories of Personality

Compared to cognitive ability, the theoretical history of personality is more diverse, with a variety of theories proposed. If you are new to psychology, then the existence of multiple theories of the same concept, each with merits in their own right, can seem counter-productive. Surely psychologists could agree on one of them? It is best to view such competing theories as representations of the same phenomenon. Theories of personality all focus on the same phenomenon, namely individual differences in behaviour, thought and emotion. The theories represent the domain in different ways, however. Good theories of personality share a number of features (Maltby, Day and Macaskill, 2006), and these are described in Box 3.1. Keep these features in mind as you review the following major theories of personality.

BOX 3.1

Features of good theories of personality

Description: A theory should be able to describe and simplify the complexities of behaviour.

Explanation: A theory should help in understanding why behaviour occurs in particular situations.

Empirical Validity: A theory should be able to generate hypotheses or predictions that can be tested.

Testable Concepts: Concepts in the theory should be able to be operationalized (defined precisely and measured) so that they can be tested.

Comprehensiveness: A theory should be able to explain normal and abnormal behaviour.

Parsimony: A theory should be economical in the concepts of features it employs, avoiding complexity in favour of acceptable simplicity.

Heuristic Value: A theory should stimulate research and sound scientific development and examination.

Applied Value: A theory should be practically useful, in the sense that it can be applied in different contexts to solve problems or answer important applied questions (in Work Psychology, a theory should help to predict important work outcomes).

Psychoanalysis

Summarizing the theoretical concepts of psychoanalysis concisely is a tricky task. The components of psychoanalytic theory are broad and without compare in our everyday understanding of personality. The theory is based on the hugely influential Sigmund Freud, the renowned Austrian psychologist, working in the early part of the 20th century. Freud was a household name during his life and his work on personality, and in particular on psychopathology and neuroses, stimulated debate and a fashion for the richer classes to be psychoanalyzed by a therapist.

Psychoanalytic theory can be grouped into three parts, covering the structure, development and processes of personality. Freud proposed that personality comprised three basic structures:

- The id represents basic childish drives for instant gratification of our needs. However, these needs cannot always be gratified because of social norms or wider environmental constraints.

- The ego mediates our basic desires, operating on the so-called reality principle. Even though the idea might be appealing in the heat of the moment, one cannot fire a colleague who has annoyed us because one may not have the authority, and more importantly one might contravene employment law.

- The super-ego represents social conscience, that is the knowledge of right and wrong, and what is permissible socially. Firing someone for annoying us is, for most people, against their moral principles of right and wrong.

An important process in Freudian theory is the conflict between these structures, of which people are unaware. Freud proposed that the majority of drives and wants, along with the inner conflicts that occur from regulating them, occur unconsciously. The conflict manifests itself as anxiety.

BOX 3.2
Freud's psychosexual stages of development

Oral Stage: Birth to one year.

Anal Stage: From 18 months to three years.

Phallic Stage: From around three to five years.

Latency Stage: Around age five to 12 years.

Genital Stage: Around 12 to 18 years or older.

Freud also proposed that adult personality is influenced by childhood development. He suggested that there were five distinct stages of psychosexual development. These stages and associated ages of childhood are shown in Box 3.2. The essence of the theory of psychosexual development is that in each stage, the child derives pleasure from the associated part of the body, and that if development fails to progress smoothly, the person will become fixated on pleasure from that same part of the body in later life. An example can be drawn from the anal stage of development, which Freud suggested was affected by the child's toilet training. When this is handled badly by parents, the child can become anally fixated, and this translates through to adult characteristics that might be described as anally retentive (stubbornness, a tendency to hoard things, overly fussy and organized).

During the latency stage, Freud suggested that the child develops some of the crucial processes of personality called defence mechanisms. These mechanisms are designed to combat feelings that are upsetting or harmful to us psychologically. Many of these have entered everyday language, such as repression (moving upsetting feelings into our unconscious), denial (refuting the realities of unpleasant situations) and rationalization (giving reasons for a particular course of action or situation that conceal its true meaning). In his work with clients, Freud believed that these defence mechanisms became unhealthy or problematic if used persistently or randomly.

Freudian theory was highly influential during its own time, but is rejected by most psychologists for its lack of scientific or empirical evidence. Indeed many of Freud's concepts are not testable in nature and so the theory must be considered unscientific. Nevertheless, the ideas endure in the practice of psychotherapy, and in other fields of psychology. There is evidence in research of the existence of unconscious processes, although not quite in the form that Freud hypothesized.

Behaviourism and social learning

Behaviourism is a field of psychology that explores how observable behaviour is shaped by the environment. McAdams (2001) describes the three key elements in behaviourism, the dominant paradigm in US psychology from the 1920s to the 1950s, as observation, environmentalism and learning.

Early behaviourists such as Watson and Skinner rejected the importance of internal cognitions or personality processes in favour of a focus on observable behaviour and its dependence on stimuli in the environment. Their perspective was that thoughts and feelings could not be observed or verified by psychologists and hence could not be considered scientific. This stands in stark contrast to the psychoanalytic approach, which relied almost exclusively on internal processes. Although behaviourists did not necessarily deny the existence of internal thoughts and feelings, they felt that they did not need to be studied, because behaviour could be accounted for adequately by aspects of the environment. This idea is referred to as environmentalism. Behaviourists suggest that in order to predict and explain behaviour, psychologists should look to the environment and the interactions between behavioural responses and environmental stimuli.

The relationship between environmental stimulus and behavioural response is the basis of the behaviourist perspective on learning. In this respect, behaviourism draws on the ideas of learned association and conditioning. The most well-known example of classical conditioning is the case of Pavlov's dog. In his experiments, Pavlov showed that he could condition a hungry dog to salivate in response to a neural stimulus (a ringing bell), if he had previously accompanied the bell with meat that provoked a natural salivation reaction. Watson and Rayner (1920) showed that similar conditioned responses could be provoked in a human baby. Their experiments with 'Little Albert', an 11-month old boy showed that he could be conditioned to fear white rats, by previously exposing him to white rats, and a loud, frightening noise.

Skinner adopted the ideas of classical conditioning in his own theories of human behaviour, which centred on what he referred to as operant conditioning. Operant conditioning examines how behaviour is shaped by both reinforcement and punishment. The concept is straightforward, and suggests that animals and people learn to associate particular behaviours with either punishment or reinforcement (reward). If a particular behaviour leads to a desired outcome, that behaviour is reinforced and repeated, if it punished, then the behaviour is avoided. Skinner was able to show that these processes could shape the behaviour of animals, and they can be applied to aspects of human behaviour as well. In the workplace, the ideas of behaviourism influenced the bestselling book by Kenneth Blanchard and Spencer Johnson (*The One Minute Manager*). In the book, Blanchard and Johnson (1983) describe how employee performance can be managed by carefully praising and rewarding (reinforcing) positive behaviour, and reprimanding (punishing) negative behaviour. The effect is to shape employee behaviour to fit the needs of the manager or organization.

The founding principles of behaviourism fell by the wayside somewhat as psychology developed, and the tradition morphed during the 1960s to become what is today known as social learning or social cognition. Ironically, in the social cognitive perspective on personality, internal processes and the person are highly important. The social cognitive approach is most often associated with the work of Albert Bandura. Bandura emphasized the importance of reciprocal determinism between environment, person and behaviour (Figure 3.2). This means that these three factors are constantly affecting

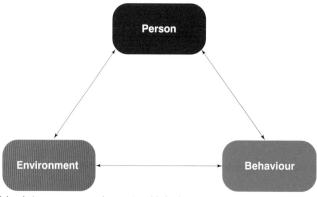

Figure 3.2   Reciprocal determinism between person, environment and behaviour

one another. When a person encounters a particular situation, they perceive that situation in a way unique to them, decide how to respond, and behave accordingly. The results of their behaviour are appraised, and in turn, this appraisal effects how future situations are perceived and dealt with. If whilst at work, I respond aggressively to a colleague during a meeting, and receive a negative reaction from others, I am less likely to behave in the same way again.

Two particularly important concepts in social cognition are observational learning and self-efficacy. Bandura proposed that children learn to behave in particular ways by observing so-called role-model behaviour. The child observes the situation, the behavioural response and the outcome, using all three to decide whether they should behave in the same way. One can hypothesize how this observational learning process might apply in organizations, underlining the importance of leader behaviour in changing and influencing employee behaviour. Self-efficacy refers to the extent of our belief that we can achieve something or successfully behave or perform in a particular way. Self-efficacy is important for people at work, especially in relation to goal setting or objective setting. People feel more committed to their goals if they believe that they can achieve them (see Chapter 4).

Social cognitive theory stands up well against most of the evaluation criteria identified in Box 3.1, with the exception of parsimony and to a lesser extent applied value. Social cognitive approaches are complex and represent behaviour and cognitive processes in complicated ways. This has proved a barrier to their widespread application in applied psychology. Nevertheless, the broad ideas are influential in our thinking about organizational behaviour.

Personality Traits

In personality psychology, the idea of 'traits' is inevitable (Hofstee, 1984). Personality trait theory taps into our intuitions about personality characteristics, that people are orderly and predictable. If a group of people with no knowledge of psychology worked together for a few hours on developing a theory of personality, they would most likely arrive at a position that was similar to trait theory. When we observe the behaviour of others, we try to find order and regularity in it. You probably have your own understanding about the behaviour of people you know and the people you work with, and feel that you can predict how they will respond to you, and how they will respond to particular situations. These stable patterns of behaviour can be described as dispositional or trait-like. Martin is organized, so he will work through this task methodically. John is somewhat disorganized, so he may not develop a plan or schedule for completing the task.

Personality traits are typically conceived as internal dispositions that remain generally stable over time (Chamorro-Premuzic, 2007). Example traits are friendly, talkative, organized, calm. Trait theory suggests that individual differences in behaviour, thought and emotions can be described and explained by personality traits (McCrae and Costa, 1995).

Although the concept of personality traits is fairly simple, psychologists have grappled with the definition over the past fifty years. The original consensus about personality traits is summarized nicely by Hampson (1988), who described assumptions that personality traits are internal, stable (unchanged over time), consistent (apply across different situations) and different. Among these assumptions, consistency has provoked the most challenging responses. Trait theory implies that behaviour should be consistent in different situations. However, this is transparently untrue. People's behaviour varies according to context or situation. The 'you' that you know at home is likely to be different in important ways from the 'you' that you know at work. Situational inconsistency was the observation of Walter Mischel (1968), who published a powerful critique of trait theory suggesting that situations should be the object of focus in understanding personality, rather than internal traits. His critique led to the situationist perspective, that threatened to wipe out the study of personality traits altogether.

Trait theory survived this critique, but the conceptualization of personality traits has subtly changed as a result. Personality psychologists now generally accept that individual differences in behaviour, thought and emotion occur in specific contexts, and that it is hard to separate dispositions from the situation or context in which they occur. Traits can therefore be seen as coherent responses to particular situational cues. The extent to which a person will behave in a consistent manner across two different situations depends on the similarity of the features of those situations. A good illustration of this is team meetings. People behave predictably in team meetings provided that the members of the team and the context of the meeting remain similar. People's behaviour might change subtly though if others are added or removed from the team, or if the context or task is changed. The value of away-days and team-building activities is that the features of working situations are changed, promoting changes in the behaviour of individual team members.

More recently, the stability of traits has been challenged from a development point of view, an area we return to later.

The lexical approach to personality traits

An early pioneer of personality trait theory was Allport, who started the lexical tradition in personality psychology. This line of work is based on the lexical hypothesis, which states that the most important personality characteristics will have been encoded in natural language as society has evolved (John and Srivastava, 1999). Allport and Odbert (1936) therefore studied the English dictionary, extracting all personality-relevant words. They presented a list of almost 18 000 words, which they proposed as the comprehensive account of human personality from the English language. Although this work was doubtless crucial to the development of the trait approach, the resultant set of personality terms was virtually impossible to use or comprehend.

The challenge of simplifying the picture was taken up by Cattell, who applied methods from the study of intelligence to personality traits. He used factor analysis. Recall that factor analysis is a statistical technique that aims to reduce complexity in datasets and models by identifying underlying factors or dimensions that explain the relationships between the variables. This is a useful way to study personality traits because there are obvious relationships between certain personality traits. Relaxed and calm intuitively go together, as do talkative, gregarious and outgoing, likewise warm and friendly. Cattell factor analyzed a small set of traits drawn from the list created by Allport and Odbert, arriving at the conclusion that there were 12 dimensions of personality that could be used to group the list of terms he included in his study (Cattell, 1947). At around the same time, the British psychologist Eysenck (1947) was applying similar methods in his own theory of personality, concluding that fewer, bigger dimensions were a better solution. He proposed two such dimensions, later adding a third to his model, giving extraversion, neuroticism and psychotism.

The Big Five Personality Dimensions   The winning number in the debate about the optimal number of factors or dimensions of personality is undoubtedly five (Hampson, 1999). In the early 1960s, three separate sources reported five factor solutions from factor analyses of personality traits (Tupes and Cristal, 1961; Norman, 1967; Borgatta, 1964). There followed a period of dormancy in the study of traits as a result of the challenge of Mischel and situationism. The gauntlet was taken up again by Goldberg and Digman in the early 1980s, who began work on analyzing a set of 1710 personality traits compiled by Norman many years earlier (Norman, 1967). The result of their work was the identification and description of five broad dimensions of personality, collectively termed the Big Five or Five Factor Model.

The Big Five model suggests that the most adequate representation of personality traits is to group them into five broad bipolar dimensions. These are:

- Extraversion: The extent to which a person is outgoing and sociable versus quiet and reserved.
- Agreeableness: The extent to which a person is warm and trusting, versus cold and unfriendly.
- Conscientiousness: The extent to which a person is organized and dependable, versus impulsive and disorganized.
- Emotional Stability: The extent to which a person is calm and stable, versus neurotic and anxious.
- Openness/Intellect: The extent to which a person is imaginative and open to new experiences, versus narrow-minded and unimaginative.

The Big Five model has heralded a revolution in personality trait psychology and over the past twenty years has become the largely agreed classification of personality traits, permitting the accumulation of a huge literature on their effects at work and in life more broadly. The implication of the model is that individual differences in personality traits can be described and understood effectively by determining how people differ on these five personality dimensions. Importantly, the dimensions are theoretically independent or unrelated to one another. A person's level of Extraversion is theoretically unrelated to their level of Conscientiousness.

It is important that trait models are not confused with type models of personality. The differences, and the problems with type models are discussed in Box 3.3.

BOX 3.3
Types and traits

Theories of personality traits usually strike a chord with our intuitive ideas about personality, but ironically, the first encounter that most people have with personality theory in organizations is personality type theory, usually peddled ably by consultants and practitioners using the Myers Briggs Type Inventory (MBTI). The MBTI is one of the most widely used (indeed, probably *the* most widely used) personality questionnaire in organizations, and draws on the psychological theories of Carl Jung. The important aspect of Jung's theory that is applied in the MBTI is that personality should be represented as a typology rather than as dimensional traits like those of the Big Five model.

To illustrate, in the Big Five model, Extraversion is a dimension, so people can be described as having varying degrees of Extraversion (i.e. very introverted, slightly introverted, neither introverted nor extraverted, slightly extraverted, very extraverted). On the MBTI typological model, Extraversion-Introversion is represented as a dichotomy, so that a person is either introverted (labelled I) or extraverted (labeled E). The MBTI contains four such dichotomies, and the combinations of the various letter codes for each gives a total of sixteen personality types.

Criticisms or type theory

- There is a technical shortcoming of type theory, which is that if Extraversion and Introversion were a true dichotomy, there should be clear divide between the two when extraversion is examined in the population (for the statisticians: a bimodal distribution should exist; Mendelsohn, Weiss and Feimer, 1982). Although this has been disputed (Hicks, 1984), others remain convinced that it is a salient issue (Pittenger, 2005). No such breaks are observed in any of the MBTI dichotomies. Personality dimensions are invariably continuous in populations so that most people cluster around the middle of the dimension (e.g. they are somewhat introverted or somewhat extraverted) with fewer people represented at the extremities or poles of the dimension.

- Conceptually, a type theory of personality is weak. Most accept that a person's personality traits are influenced by a huge variety of different factors. Genes certainly play a part, evidenced in the heritability of personality traits (Bouchard, 1994). However, there is not likely to be one gene for extraversion, or any other personality trait for that matter. Rather, traits are based on the small additive and interactive effects of multiple genes (e.g. Comings, Gade-Andavolu, Gonzalez, Wu, Muhleman, Blake, Mann, Dietz, Saucier and MacMurray, 2000), and similarly small additive effects of life experiences and environmental factors. This conceptualization supports a trait model rather than a type model, whereby small factors combined together lead to many different degrees of extraversion and other traits.

Criticisms of the MBTI

In addition to problems with type theory, there are also important criticisms of the MBTI measure:

- The model underpinning the MBTI is an incomplete representation of personality, omitting emotional stability, one of the key factors of personality (Furnham, 1996).

- The construct validity of the MBTI is questionable, because the four-dichotomy structure often fails to replicate in research studies (Pittenger, 2005).

- The four-letter codes that are assigned to people are unstable, and over periods as short as four or five weeks, around 35 per cent to 50 per cent of people receive a different four-letter classification (Pittenger, 2005).

- By reducing personality dimensions to dichotomies, the MBTI discards important information about personality which limits findings in research, and which can lead to poor personnel decisions when used in organizations.

Some practitioners bat away such criticisms with much talk of practical utility, of the exploratory, non-definitive nature of the MBTI, and the in-depth discussion process that typically follows an assessment. However, these are weak arguments. All of these advantages could equally apply to the use of trait assessments, with the added confidence that comes from using an approach endorsed by the weight of scientific evidence in the field.

Trait models

Although the Big Five is a parsimonious model, it should not be seen as the only way to represent personality traits. One way to elaborate the Big Five is to view them as one level of a hierarchical model of traits, in much the same way that cognitive ability can be modelled as a hierarchy. Researchers have explored the levels immediately above and below the Big Five. Digman (1997) showed that the Big Five could be grouped into two broader dimensions:

- Factor alpha, comprising Agreeableness, Conscientiousness and Emotional Stability.
- Factor beta, comprising Extraversion and Openness/Intellect.

KEY THEME

Globalization and Cross-Cultural Work Psychology

The Big Five: A Human Universal?

Are personality traits the same the world over? Two approaches to the study of personality traits have diverged since the emergence of the Big Five model. The first continues in the vein of the lexical tradition and has explored the structures of personality traits in languages drawn from around the world. This bottom-up or emic approach has shown that the Big Five are most often found in Northern European languages (English, German and Dutch). Culture specific factors are often found in other languages, and although the Big Five are often found in some form, the model is far from universal. The emic approach adopts a philosophy that personality traits are descriptive representations of patterns or regularities in behaviour. Through the development of tradition, custom and language, different cultures have developed different ways of understanding and representing personality traits. By contrast, work by Costa and McCrae has explored the structure of traits using an ethnic approach. They have shown that analyses of translations of their Five Factor Model questionnaire (the NEO-PIR) produce five factor structures in all the cultures that they have studied. They believe the Big Five to be universal for humans (McCrae and Costa, 1997), suggesting that the five dimensions reflect some underlying biological system. So there is evidence for and against the idea that the Big Five personality traits represent the structure of personality in all cultures. This debate obviously has implications for cross-cultural working. If we are used to understanding people's traits in our own culture, then we are inevitably likely to misperceive or completely ignore aspects of personality that are salient in other cultures. These ideas are important to bear in mind when interacting with people from different cultures.

Evidence if also emerging in the personality research literature of a single general factor of personality (the GFP) (e.g. Musek, 2007; Van der Linden, te Nijenhuis, and Bakker, 2010; Woods and Hardy, 2012). This general factor may represent general desirability of behaviour.

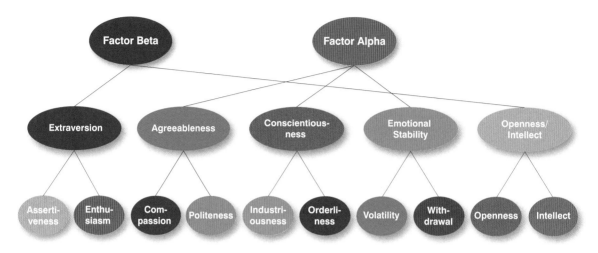

Figure 3.3   The hierarchical structure of personality

Recent work by De Young *et al.* (2007) has explored the narrower personality dimensions that sit underneath the Big Five. Their ten-dimension taxonomy is shown in Figure 3.3, along with the Big Five, factor alpha and factor beta. De Young *et al.* showed in their analyses that each of the Big Five dimensions could be conceptualized as comprising two narrower components or facets.

The model shown in Figure 3.3 is an inductive model of personality (meaning that it is derived from research). There are, however, alternative 'construct-driven' or deductive models of personality traits (Burisch, 1984). These models are derived from theories about how traits could or should be represented. Most are associated with specific personality assessment tools, some of which are popular in organizational assessment. A good example is the Occupational Personality Questionnaire (OPQ). The model underlying the OPQ comprises thirty-two narrow personality dimensions that are designed to be relevant in organizations (see Box 3.4).

BOX 3.4
Scales of the occupational personality questionnaire

Outgoing	Relaxed	Trusting	Behavioural
Emotionally controlled	Worrying	Independent minded	Modest
Affiliative	Socially confident	Detail conscious	Outspoken
Persuasive	Optimistic	Conscientious	Decisive
Controlling	Conventional	Vigorous	Evaluative
Caring	Variety seeking	Forward thinking	Data rational
Democratic	Conceptual	Achieving	Rule following
Competitive	Innovative	Tough minded	Adaptable

Trait measures

So far, this section has explored trait theories and models of personality. How exactly are trait models applied in the measurement of individuals though? Personality traits are most commonly measured by self-report questionnaires or personality inventories. These inventories usually comprise lists of items or statements, and require people to indicate the extent to which they agree or disagree with the statements. Example personality inventory items are shown in Box 3.5, drawn from the IPIP measure of the Big Five dimensions.

Each trait or dimension measured by a particular inventory has a number of items associated with it, collectively referred to as scales. The bipolar nature of personality traits means that items are designed to tap into both poles of the dimension. So for example, a scale measuring Extraversion will contain items that refer to characteristics associated with Extraversion (e.g. is the life of the party) and Introversion (e.g. has little to say). The items are used to derive scores for each of the scales, and thus the dimensions being measured. Scales can be compiled to measure a wide variety of different traits and trait models, and this has given rise to the plethora of different personality inventories that are available commercially and in the research literature (see e.g. Woods and Hardy, 2012).

One of the implications of measuring personality traits in this way is that we essentially rely on people's judgements about traits and behaviour. How effective are people at perceiving and judging consistencies in their own behaviour and the behaviour of others? Funder has examined this question in a number of studies and articles (e.g. Funder, 1989, 1995; Funder and West, 1993). Funder is critical of research that focuses solely on the shortcomings of human observers (the so-called error paradigm), and instead provides evidence that shows that people are actually surprisingly good judges of personality traits. Evidence for the accuracy paradigm is found in studies that show that people agree to an extent in their judgements of others (Funder, 1995) and that self-ratings of personality

BOX 3.5
Example personality inventory items

Indicate the extent to you which you agree or disagree with the following statements.

1 = Strongly disagree.
2 = Disagree a little.
3 = Neither agree nor disagree.

4 = Agree a little.
5 = Strongly agree.

I see myself as someone who...

Doesn't mind being the centre of attention *(Extraversion)*.	....
Has a soft heart *(Agreeableness)*.	....
Follows a schedule *(Conscientiousness)*.	....
Is relaxed most of the time *(Emotional Stability)*.	....
Has a vivid imagination *(Openness)*.	....

tend to correlate with ratings of others (so people's self-perceptions are a good indicator of how they are seen by others; Johnson, 2000). Agreement between self- and other-perceptions is higher for visible traits such as those related to Extraversion than for less visible traits like Openness/Intellect. The evidence is encouraging for the self-report method of trait assessment as it shows that people are pretty accurate judges of their own personality traits.

DISCUSS WITH A COLLEAGUE

Measure your own Big Five traits

Below are five pairs of descriptions representing the Big Five personality traits (taken from Woods & Hampson, 2005). They are presented in the order: Extraversion, Agreeableness, Conscientiousness, Emotional Stability, Openness/Intellect. Read each pair of descriptions carefully and place yourself somewhere on the scale between the opposing descriptions. Do this honestly – rate yourself as you think you really are, not as you would like to be ideally. When you have completed the task, ask a colleague if they agree with your responses – do they see you in the same way as you see yourself?

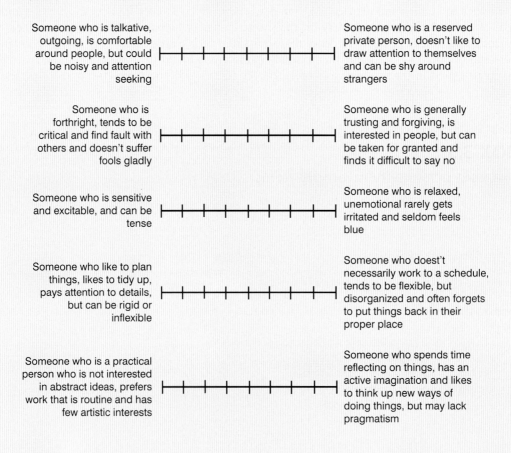

Someone who is talkative, outgoing, is comfortable around people, but could be noisy and attention seeking ⟷ Someone who is a reserved private person, doesn't like to draw attention to themselves and can be shy around strangers

Someone who is forthright, tends to be critical and find fault with others and doesn't suffer fools gladly ⟷ Someone who is generally trusting and forgiving, is interested in people, but can be taken for granted and finds it difficult to say no

Someone who is sensitive and excitable, and can be tense ⟷ Someone who is relaxed, unemotional rarely gets irritated and seldom feels blue

Someone who like to plan things, likes to tidy up, pays attention to details, but can be rigid or inflexible ⟷ Someone who doest't necessarily work to a schedule, tends to be flexible, but disorganized and often forgets to put things back in their proper place

Someone who is a practical person who is not interested in abstract ideas, prefers work that is routine and has few artistic interests ⟷ Someone who spends time reflecting on things, has an active imagination and likes to think up new ways of doing things, but may lack pragmatism

INDIVIDUAL DIFFERENCES AT WORK

How do individual differences influence behaviour at work? This is a key question of interest for Work Psychologists, who have accumulated a broad knowledge of how individual differences are associated with organizational behaviour. The evidence of the effects of cognitive ability and personality are considered in this section.

Cognitive Ability at Work

Interest in cognitive ability in Work and Organizational Psychology has undergone something of a renaissance over the past twenty years. Past dismissal of the importance of individual differences in cognitive ability has been challenged and overcome by advances in the field in respect of the structure of cognitive ability (Carroll, 1993), the study of its longitudinal stability (cognitive ability has been shown to be stable up to 65 years; Deary, Whalley, Lemmon, Crawford and Starr, 2000), and the considerable heritability of cognitive ability, prompting studies to identify relevant marker genes.

The major breakthrough for the study of cognitive ability at work was the development of methods of meta-analysis (Hunter and Schmidt, 1990). Until that point, the accepted wisdom in Work Psychology was that cognitive ability predicted performance at work in some contexts but not others. Ability might be associated with performance in a particular job in a particular organization, but unrelated to performance of that same job in a different organization (Schmidt and Hunter, 2004). Inconsistent associations between cognitive ability and performance in different studies seemed to confirm this. Through meta-analysis, psychologists were able to determine that the inconsistencies in results were actually attributable to unreliable measurement, errors in sampling and restriction of score ranges in datasets. Contrary to popular belief, cognitive ability predicts job performance to varying degrees in all jobs. Moreover, the correlations between cognitive ability and performance are large compared to other effects in psychology:

- Hunter and Hunter (1984) reported a meta-analysis, in which general cognitive ability correlated strongly with job performance (in excess of 0.50 for medium and high complexity jobs, with smaller values for less complex jobs, 0.23 for the least complex).
- When performance during training is examined, the associations are higher still (up to 0.65).
- Meta-analysis of the validity of cognitive ability in European samples are similarly high (Salgado *et al.*, 2003).

These meta-analyses clearly indicate the importance of cognitive ability for performance at work. People with higher levels of ability tend to perform better at work. The finding lacks a theoretical foundation however. Why does cognitive ability lead to better job performance? Schmidt and Hunter (2004) considered this question and reported that the key process is acquisition of job knowledge. People with higher levels of cognitive ability are able to acquire more knowledge about their job and to acquire it quickly. They point out that even relatively simple jobs depend on the incumbent drawing on surprisingly detailed job knowledge, and so the ability to acquire, maintain and develop that knowledge is always an advantage. In more complex jobs, there is more knowledge to acquire, and it is more likely that knowledge acquisition will continue to be important for performance. In less complex jobs, some tasks can be learned thoroughly to the point of automation. This in part explains the differences in the validities for jobs of varying complexity. The importance of job knowledge acquisition for explaining the relationship between cognitive ability and job performance has been highlighted in numerous studies (e.g. Borman, Hanson, Oppler, Pulakos and White, 1993; Schmidt, 2002; Schmidt and Hunter, 1992).

In their review, Schmidt and Hunter (2004) also describe evidence of the prediction of occupational attainment from cognitive ability. Occupational attainment refers to the level that one rises to in an organization along with salary achieved. The most powerful evidence about the association of cognitive ability with attainment comes from longitudinal studies. Murray (1998) examined the earnings of siblings reared together and found that those with higher cognitive abilities consistently earned more than their siblings when aged in their late 20s. Perhaps more astonishingly, a study of the associations between childhood cognitive ability and occupational level show a clear and strong correlation even over periods up to 30–40 years (Judge, Higgins, Thoresen and Barrick, 1999). Cognitive ability seems to influence not only job performance, but also career success.

Personality at Work

Personality traits have been found to be associated with an array of organizational and other behaviours (Ozer and Benet-Martinez, 2006). The resurgence of interest in personality traits at work has been influenced by the emergence of the Big Five model of personality. As highlighted earlier, the Big Five can be viewed as an organizing framework for personality traits and scales. This means that the dimensions can be used to organize the results of previous studies of personality and work criteria that may have used different trait measures. The results from these studies can then be meta-analyzed. Meta-analysis of the criterion effects of the Big Five have examined the prediction of a wide variety of work outcomes from personality traits, showing convincingly that personality traits do relate to organizational behaviour.

Personality traits have been found to predict various forms of job performance. Barrick and Mount (1991) examined the prediction of job performance from the Big Five, reporting that Conscientiousness was particularly important for a variety of performance outcomes (e.g. general job performance, training outcomes). Subsequent meta-analyses were reviewed by Barrick *et al.* (2001), who concluded that Conscientiousness predicted job performance to some extent in all occupations. Emotional Stability and Extraversion also emerge as important predictors of performance in some, but not all occupations (Ozer and Benet-Martinez, 2005).

Although the associations of personality and job performance are typically lower than those between cognitive ability and performance, higher correlations are observed if job contexts are taken into account. Hogan and Holland (2003) examined the associations of job performance with personality traits in studies that had carefully considered which traits might be relevant for performance in particular jobs. In these studies, the correlations appear to be higher, suggesting that specific personality traits are more or less important in different jobs. The extent to which traits predict performance depends on the kind of work that a person is required to do.

What are the pathways from personality to job performance and why do some personality traits seem to predict performance in a wide variety of jobs? One particular research line has considered this question by focusing on job performance more closely, and in particular how cognitive ability and personality relate to different aspects of performance (e.g. Motowildo, Borman and Schmitt, 1997). The findings from these studies suggest that personality traits relate most strongly to 'organizational citizenship behaviours (OCB)', sometimes called contextual performance. These are general pro-social behaviours that support the core aspects of task performance of individuals, teams and organizations. The importance of OCB across most jobs is the likely reason that traits such as Conscientiousness predict job performance so consistently.

In addition to job performance, there is plenty of evidence of associations between the Big Five personality traits and other organizational behaviour criteria.

- Traits related to affective styles (extraversion and neuroticism) along with conscientiousness are associated with job satisfaction (Judge, Heller and Mount, 2002). Personality traits seem to affect how a person appraises aspects of their job and organization.

- Personality also relates to a person's commitment to their organization (Erdheim, Wang and Zickar, 2006) with higher levels of Extraversion being most consistently associated with higher levels of organizational commitment.

- Occupational interests (see Chapter 9) are also associated with personality traits, with good evidence that traits from the Big Five Model overlap with interests and preferences for particular kinds of work and working environments. Of particular note is openness/intellect, which is related to preferences for artistic or investigative occupations (Barrick *et al.*, 2003; Larson *et al.*, 2002).

- Team processes and teamworking are related to the traits of the team members (Van Vianen and De Dreu, 2001; Barrick, Stewart, Neubert and Mount, 1998). Having generally higher extraversion, agreeableness, conscientiousness and emotional stability is generally beneficial, although there is evidence that having a range of profile scores on extraversion and emotional stability is beneficial. In the case of extraversion, having members high and low on the dimension may allow leaders and followers to emerge, and in the case of emotional stability, people low on the dimension may bring a sense of urgency to the team in respect of goal attainment.

- Personality is related to leadership behaviour (see Chapter 12). In meta-analyses (Judge, Bono, Ilies and Gerhardt, 2002; Bono and Judge, 2004), the Big Five have been found to be associated with leader emergence (extraversion and conscientiousness positively associated) and leadership effectiveness (extraversion, conscientiousness, emotional stability and openness all positively associated).

As with cognitive ability, some of the most interesting findings in this area have come from longitudinal studies. Judge *et al.* (1999) examined data from a number of longitudinal studies on the relationships between traits in adolescence and later life career success. They looked at both extrinsic success (e.g. salary and status) and intrinsic success (e.g. job and career satisfaction). conscientiousness, openness and emotional stability at an early age all predicted later life intrinsic success, and perhaps even more interestingly, agreeableness negatively predicted extrinsic success. Woods and Hampson (2010) examined the longitudinal associations between childhood personality and the kinds of job environments where people worked in middle age. They found that children high on openness/intellect were more likely to work in investigative or artistic jobs in later life.

Consider for a moment the implications of these findings combined with those on cognitive ability. Collectively, they show that individual differences in psychological attributes, measured through psychometric methods, are crucial factors in determining people's work experiences, successes, performances and choices. Moreover, individual differences at a very early age can give important insights about how a person's working life will develop over long periods of time.

A DYNAMIC AND DEVELOPMENTAL MODEL OF PERSONALITY AND WORK

Recognizing the need to expand understanding of how personality traits relate to organizational behaviour across people's working lives, Woods, Lievens, De Fruyt and Wille (2013) reviewed the literature on the dynamic influences of personality traits on work outcomes, and also the reciprocal influences of work on personality. They noted that in the research literature on personality and work outcomes, the preoccupation of researchers on validities of the Big Five, whilst having established a huge volume of literature in the field, had two undesirable consequences. First, the relations of personality traits with work outcomes are implicitly treated as static, even though the demands of work change dynamically over time. Second, personality is almost exclusively conceptualized only as a predictor variable. For theory building, personality traits, as highlighted earlier, are considered to be stable over time. However, recent evidence has suggested that personality may not only affect work behaviour, but may also be affected by work (e.g., Wille, Beyers and De Fruyt, 2012).

The changing influences of personality on work outcomes over the course of people's career can be examined through Trait Activation Theory (TAT; Tett and Burnett, 2003). TAT proposes that behaviour results from an interaction between person and situation, in which situations act as cues to activate specific traits. For example, when a person is placed in a social situation, and has freedom to decide how to behave in that situation, their Extraversion is activated and is expressed in their behaviour. Woods *et al.* (2013) applied this theory and considered how demands of work changed in the short- and long-term.

With regards to performance, there is accumulating evidence that the influences of personality on job performance change over even relatively short periods of time. This is linked to the idea that performance demands change (Murphy, 1989). For example, when a person begins a new job (transitional stage), job requirements, problems and tasks are all novel. However after a period of time, the job has been learned (the maintenance stage) and the requirement is rather to maintain performance. Thoresen, Bradley, Bliese and Thoreson (2004) demonstrated how personality was related to performance in sales at these different stages. Openness and agreeableness were associated with performance for sales people in the transitional stage, probably reflecting adaptability and network building respectively. Conscientiousness was associated with performance at the maintenance stage, most likely reflecting the long-term motivational aspects of that dimension. Lievens *et al.* (2009) showed similarly changing associations of the Big Five with performance of students at medical school over time.

Woods *et al.* (2013) also examined three ways in which work has a developmental influence on personality. Although personality traits may still be considered to be generally stable, there is also emerging consensus that traits continue to develop across people's lives (e.g. Roberts, Robins, Caspi and Trzesniewski, 2003). There are three ways that work might affect our personality development through the course of our working lives:

1 Through normative change. Normative development affects people generally in the same way and is related to how our lives typically develop as human beings. People tend to engage in age-related social norms (e.g. education, finding a job, settling down and having a family) at roughly the same times of their lives, and these drive changes such as increased conscientiousness as they get older.

2 Through deepening and strengthening of traits. Personality traits lead people to seek out particular job environments that are consistent with those traits. As a consequence traits are persistently activated, with people's characteristics becoming deepened and strengthened. This process is referred to as the correspondence principle (Roberts, Caspi and Moffitt, 2003).

3 Through unique experiences. There is recent evidence that personality traits change and develop in response to unique working experience. For example Ludtke, Roberts, Trautwein and Nagy (2011) found that traits developed differently for young adults during education depending on whether they took vocational or non-vocational pathways. Wille, Beyers and De Fruyt (2012) also reported evidence that engagement in certain job roles resulted in personality traits development that ran counter to normative developmental trends.

The combined evidence of dynamic influences of personality on work, and developmental influences of work on personality led Woods *et al.* (2013) to propose a dynamic developmental model of personality and work. They proposed that personality traits are in constant interaction with work-related activities and environments and are activated in response to changing work demands and career challenges. As we will see in Chapter 9, traits influence career choices, setting people on pathways to certain kinds of work activities. As demands change over time, different traits influence how people perform, behave and succeed at different stages within these careers, and these experiences in turn influence the development of personality traits throughout working life. By these mechanisms, work really does become a core part of who we are.

A FINAL NOTE ON COGNITIVE ABILITY

You might rightly be curious about how cognitive ability fits with the ideas around dynamic influences of personality and work. The answer is 'quite neatly'. Recent research on performance trajectories suggests that people's performance at work increases linearly in early stages of the job, but then plateaus (see Figure 3.4) following a so-called learning curve (Zyphur, Chaturvedi and Arvey, 2008). Murphy (1989) proposes that cognitive ability is critical in the learning phase of performance, when the job is being learned, and job knowledge is acquired. However, over time, motivational aspects become more important in maintaining performance and may influence whether performance continues to increase, plateau or decline. Gottfredson (2002) refers to the 'can-do' and 'will-do' of performance, which are correspondingly related to cognitive ability and personality. What we can deduce from the idea of performance trajectories is that cognitive ability is most important when people need to learn quickly and solve novel problems. As jobs become more familiar and practiced, the influence of cognitive ability is likely to decrease, and the influence of personality to increase.

EMOTIONS

Although there are questions around the concept of emotional intelligence in the research literature, there is plenty of evidence that emotions themselves are important influences on work outcomes. The study of emotions at work has grown substantially in recent years (Brief and Weiss, 2002). Studies have helped to clarify the nature of emotions, differentiating a variety of terms, described in Box 3.6. Key distinctions are between moods, emotions and trait affect. Moods represent general positive or negative feelings. Emotions are discrete constructs (e.g. anger, joy, hate, jealousy, love) usually

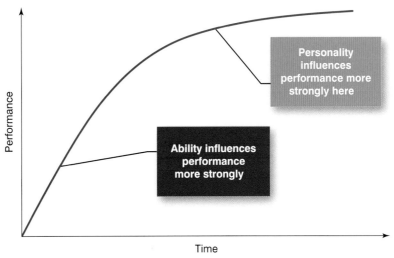

Figure 3.4   A performance trajectory curve (learning curve), and influence of individual differences at different times.

directed towards a specific target or cause. Trait affectivity represents the intersection between personality dispositions and emotions. Positive and negative affect are respectively tendencies to experience positive and negative feelings, moods and emotions. Positive affect is related to Extraversion, and negative affect to Neuroticism (Rusting and Larsen, 1998).

Trait affectivity has been shown to relate to job performance, with positive affect predicting higher levels of performance (Cropanzano and Wright, 2001). This finding has been interpreted alongside

AUTHOR EXPERIENCE

The Orthogonal (Independent) Nature of Personality and Ability: Implications For Potential

Orthogonal means independent. It's a statistical term, and is often used to describe the domains of cognitive ability and personality, because broadly speaking, and with the exception of one or two areas of overlap, cognitive ability (intelligence) is unrelated to personality. And this is evident in my interactions with people in organizations, leaders and managers and with students. What I mean by this is that it is obvious to me that the two are independent in the differences between people. I have worked with many managers who have high levels of intellectual ability, evidenced in their obvious technical skills (in engineering for example), and in their problem solving. Some of these man-

agers are unlikely to make it to board level, however, because they lack key interpersonal competencies, drive or ambition or confidence to communicate persuasively and charismatically. Having the right level of ability doesn't go hand-in-hand with having the right personality traits.

Likewise I meet plenty of students who come across well when you talk to them, but who evidently struggle with some aspects of their work. These students tend to find jobs less quickly than those with high ability coupled with confident, collected interpersonal styles. Perhaps a final permutation is one MD I recall meeting who appeared to have a high level of ability (he was able to grasp ideas quickly), and was also clearly driven (it may well have been what had got him to the level of MD). However, he was also incredibly defensive – his social confidence perhaps stood alongside personal insecurity. He corrected and put-down his subordinate colleagues during the meeting, and had an awkward interpersonal style, that would not suit some organizations or job roles.

It's the orthogonal nature of individual differences that gives us such a rich diversity of people in the world, and in our organizations. Occasionally, people do emerge with exceptional abilities, combined with desirable or charismatic traits, and the motivation to succeed, and they normally rise quickly in organizations. Consider top CEOs in light of your new knowledge about individual differences. But these people are rare. Most people generally have strengths in their attributes alongside weaknesses, and having the right ability is no guarantee that one's personality will be well suited to one's job, or desirable to others and vice versa. And a good thing too. Life would be far too orderly otherwise.

BOX 3.6
Terms associated with affect and emotion

Affect: Umbrella term encompassing a broad range of feelings that individuals experience, including feelings, discrete emotions and traits.

Discrete Emotions: Emotions are focused on a specific target or cause – generally realized by the perceiver of the emotion; relatively intense and short lived (e.g. love, anger, hate, fear, jealousy, happiness, sadness, grief, rage, aggravation, ecstasy, affection, joy, envy, fright). Can sometimes transform into a mood.

Moods: Generally take the form of a global positive (pleasant) or negative (unpleasant) feeling – tend to be diffuse, not focused on a specific cause. May last for a few moments to a few weeks or more.

Dispositional Affect: Overall personality tendency to respond to situations in predictable ways. Positive affectivity relates to the tendency to experience positive moods, whereas negative affectivity relates to the tendency to experience negative moods.

Emotion Regulation: Individual's attempts to influence the emotions they have, when they have them, and how they experience and express these emotions.

Emotional Labour: The suppression or induction of feelings in order to fulfil a particular job requirement (e.g. appearing outwardly enthusiastic and cheerful in customer-facing roles).

the so-called happy-productive worker hypothesis. This hypothesis suggests that happy, satisfied workers are also likely to be productive workers. Although there are several potential theoretical relationships between satisfaction and performance, meta-analysis in the area shows that there is a moderate relationship between the two (Judge, Heller and Mount, 2002). A related line of research has examined the effects of affect and mood on decision-making. Positive affect seems to be associated with more effective decisions, possibly because it allows people to focus more clearly on the requirements of the situation at hand (Barsade and Gibson, 2007).

Affect is also linked with counterproductive and prosocial behaviours. Negative affectivity is associated with increased absence, intention to turnover and actual turnover from the organization (Thoresen, Kaplan and Barsky, 2003). Prosocial behaviours seem to be more dependent on an individual's current mood and the situation (Barsade and Gibson, 2007). One other important organizational consequence of affect is creativity and creative problem solving. Both have been shown to be associated with positive mood (Brief and Weiss, 2002), with clear implications for fostering positive working environments as an intervention for enhancing creativity and innovation at work.

A common question is whether we are in control of our emotions, and to what extent we can regulate them. Rafaeli and Sutton (1989) distinguish between felt and displayed emotions. The emotions that people display in their facial expressions and tone of voice can be different from the emotions they experience internally, and so people are able to regulate the emotions they display to others. At work, such regulation is referred to as emotional labour (Hochschild, 1983), which comprises the demonstration of emotions that are consistent with job requirements or normative rules for emotional display (e.g. positive, enthusiastic behaviour demonstrated by salespeople). Although there is potential for the masking of emotions to cause strain on the individual, the balance of evidence suggests that there are not consistent effects of emotional labour on well-being, particularly if the employee perceives the presentation of particular emotions as a part of their job role (Barsade and Gibson, 2007).

Core Self-Evaluations

The association of Neuroticism with negative affective style is central to a model of general affective style called core self-evaluations (CSE). Judge, Locke, Durham and Kluger (1998) proposed the concept of CSE as a single unifying trait or disposition linking four key affective tendencies:

- Self-esteem: The extent to which people feel good about themselves.
- Self-efficacy: How confident people feel about their capabilities.
- Locus of Control: The extent to which people feel in control of events.
- Neuroticism: As described earlier from the Big Five model.

People high in CSE tend to be more confident, positive and feel in control. People low on CSE have a relatively lower opinion of themselves, feel less capable and fearful or threatened by the world around them. High CSE have been found to be predictive of higher job performance and higher job satisfaction (Judge and Bono, 2001).

To establish the mechanisms explaining the associations of CSE with job satisfaction, Judge, Bono and Locke (2000) tested two hypotheses, both of which were confirmed. First, CSE influences how people perceive their job characteristics and the extent to which they see them positively versus negatively. This has a direct impact on subjective job satisfaction. Secondly, people with high CSE actually attain intrinsically more rewarding jobs. Their higher levels of confidence and self-belief mean that they take on more complex tasks, tend to perform better in them and therefore attain more positive job characteristics.

This tendency to take on more challenging jobs and tasks may be related to the ways in which people approach things at work more generally. High Neuroticism is associated with an avoidant approach (Ferris, Rosen, Johnson, Brown, Risavy and Heller 2011), whereby people select tasks, activities and behavioural strategies that minimize the level of threat or the chances of failure that a person experiences. People low on Neuroticism, and correspondingly high on CSE, tend to accept more individual responsibility and more challenging goals (Erez and Judge, 2001). CSE may therefore have a long-term impact on work and the attainment of success and happiness at work over time.

Psychological Capital

The final aspect of individual difference comes from the literature on positive psychology (e.g. Peterson, 2006), which focuses on the importance of positivity for behaviour and well-being. Adopting a positive psychological stance, Luthans and colleagues have developed a line of research on a concept that they refer to as Psychological Capital (PsyCap; Luthans and Youssef, 2004; Luthans, Youssef and Avolio, 2007). Luthans, Avolio, Avey and Norman (2007) describe PsyCap as a positive psychological state of development, which comprises:

- Hope: persevering towards goals and redirecting effort in order to attain them
- Optimism: having a positive outlook and feeling personally responsible for success
- Resilience: bouncing back and maintaining effort in the face of setbacks
- Self-efficacy: As with CSE, having confidence in one's own capability.

PsyCap is proposed to give an advantage in work activity, promoting people having confidence to work towards and attain their goals. Like CSE, PsyCap has been found to be associated with job performance and job satisfaction (Luthans *et al.*, 2007). The relationship with job performance appears to generalize across cultures. Associations of PsyCap with supervisory rating of performance were reported by Luthans, Avolio, Walumbwa and Li (2005).

Interestingly, in modelling PsyCap, Luthans and colleagues make the distinction between traits and states (e.g. Luthans *et al.*, 2007). They propose that PsyCap is 'state-like', meaning that it is relatively changeable and open to development. This contrasts with 'states' which are transient feelings (rather like the discrete emotions or moods in Box 3.6. They apply this reasoning to theorize that PsyCap can be developed and improved (Luthans, Avey, Avolio, Norman and Combs, 2006). In an intervention study, they showed that application of simple web-based training interventions improved PsyCap in a sample of managers (Luthans, Avey and Patera, 2008). Organizational strategies to develop and promote the positive psychological dispositions captured in PsyCap may also have performance benefits. Luthans, Norman, Avolio and Avey (2008) showed the PsyCap mediated the link between supportive organizational climate and employee performance and commitment. This finding places individual differences firmly in the line between organization management and individual effectiveness at work.

KEY THEME

Sustainability

The content of this key theme box is somewhat speculative, but is an illustration of how theory in Work and Organizational Psychology can be reasoned with logically to offer hope in addressing applied problems.

The issue is pro-environmental behaviour, that is the kind of behaviour that is voluntary and beneficial to the environment. The kinds of things that we don't have to do, which probably cause us mild inconvenience, but which we do anyway because there is a benefit for the environment.

Most of the literature in this area examines attitudinal predictors (which we consider in Chapter 4), but there are no direct studies to date of whether personality traits influence such behaviour. Why might traits be relevant? Well a very similar concept is pro-social helping, likewise voluntary behaviour, but this time designed to benefit another person

(Eisenberg, Fabes and Spinrad, 1998). Pro-social helping has been studied from a dispositional perspective, with traits such as Agreeableness and its facets of Cooperation and Altruism being associated with such tendencies (Graziano and Eisenberg, 1997). Maybe similar traits might predict pro-environmental behaviour.

Applied social psychologists would say 'so what?', and assume that any associations with personality permit little room for behavioural change because of the stability of personality traits. However, this may not be the case. First, we know that amongst the Big Five, Agreeableness is one with lower heritability, with developmental influences having more influences (Johnson and Krueger, 2004). Second, in this chapter, the review of the developmental influences of work on personality suggests that experiences through education and work can shape and influence personality development. So there may be a case for identifying the traits that predict pro-environmental behaviour, and ensuring that they are activated and developed early on in people's lives, and then continuously through their working lives, through among other things, organizational actions and sustainability policy.

MEASURING INDIVIDUAL DIFFERENCES: PSYCHOMETRICS

The last part of this chapter in concerned with the principles of measuring individual differences, which are relevant to a variety of techniques and methods in Work Psychology. Unlike the measurement of physical characteristics, individual differences involves the measurement of unseen or intangible attributes. Measuring height or weight is easy. All one needs is an agreed metric (metres or kilograms) and a tool to do the measurement (tape measure or weigh-scale), and the physical attribute can be objectively perceived and assessed. Psychological attributes are different and are sometimes referred to as latent constructs. This means that we infer that they exist because we can see their effects. A psychologist could not examine your brain and point to your cognitive ability or your Extraversion. However, we know that some people are able to complete reasoning problems more effectively than others and that some people are more talkative than others.

The measurement of individual differences is referred to as psychometric or psychological testing. This chapter has introduced the common forms of test that are used to measure individual differences. These are tests of cognitive ability and self-report personality inventories. Once designed, the measurements derived from these tests need to be evaluated to determine whether they are accurate. In addition, because psychological attributes are unseen, it is not always obvious that a test is tapping into the attribute of interest. How do we know for example, that a test of extraversion, is actually measuring Extraversion and not something else? These are the important questions that psychometrics aims to address. Two key concepts in psychometrics are:

- Reliability (the accuracy of psychological tests).
- Validity (the extent to which a test measures what it claims to measure).

Reliability

Tests measuring individual differences are always imperfect. This means that the score we obtain on a test will reflect two components. The first is the actual or true score of the individual (i.e. the score that someone would obtain if our measure was perfect) and the second is test error (i.e. the degree of inaccuracy in the test). This is the basic tenet of classical test theory, summarized as:

Test Score = True Score + Error

Evaluating the accuracy of the test scores we obtain from a test therefore involves estimating or quantifying the amount of error in the measurement and this is the purpose of assessing test reliability. The reliability of a test is evident in two properties:

1 The extent to which the test produces scores that are stable over time.
2 The extent to which the items on a test are consistent.

Stability over time

The first and most straightforward way to measure test reliability is to examine whether the scores we obtain for people are stable over time. An assumption of theories of cognitive ability and trait theories of personality is that the attributes themselves are stable over long periods of time. The test score that a person receives on one occasion should therefore be similar to the score that he or she receives on another, provided that the test conditions are similar on both occasions. This can be evaluated by administering the test to groups of individuals at two time points. Test scores are then correlated to see the degree of concordance between them. High positive correlations (above 0.7, and ideally above 0.8) indicate that the scores are generally stable. This form of reliability is called test-retest reliability.

Internal consistency

A theoretical assumption in the design of psychometric tests is that the items on the test all tap into the attribute of interest. In order to measure Conscientiousness from the Big Five model, test items are designed to represent the dimension. The IPIP Conscientiousness scale is shown in Box 3.7 (Goldberg, 1999), and you should be able to see that the items are consistent in the sense that they all refer in some way to dimension of interest. However, this assumption needs to be tested and that is the purpose of evaluating internal consistency reliability. There are two ways that internal consistency can be calculated, both of which are designed to examine the agreement or consistency in the items of psychological tests or scales.

Split Half Reliability The most basic way to assess internal consistency is to split the items on a test in half so that there are two half-size tests. Scores on the two half-tests are then correlated to see whether they are consistent. The resultant computed correlation is always an underestimate of reliability because it only reflects half of the test. The value can be corrected using a formula called the Spearman-Brown formula.

Cronbach's Alpha More commonly used than the split-half method is the computation of Cronbach's alpha or coefficient alpha. Coefficient alpha overcomes the problem inherent in the split-half technique (that the reliability coefficient you end up with depends on how you split the items) by considering the correlations of each individual item with the overall score obtained from the test. These item-total correlations are used to calculate an overall reliability coefficient for the test. You'll often see these reliabilities reported in journal articles as indicants of the adequacy of the measurements used in research studies. Values above 0.7 are desirable for internal consistency reliability.

Using reliability information

Information on the reliability of psychometric tests is useful for a number of reasons. First, the information enables practitioners to decide whether or not a test provides adequate, accurate measurement. Second, it allows practitioners to decide how cautious they should be in making decisions from psychometric test results, because the amount of error in the test is precisely specified.

BOX 3.7

Items from the IPIP conscientiousness scale

Am always prepared   Likes order

Follows a schedule   Get chores done right away

Pays attention to details   Am exacting in my work

Validity

The validity of a psychological test indicates the extent to which the test measures the attribute that it claims to measure. This can be termed measurement validity. Equally important in applied psychology is criterion validity, which examines the extent to which the test predicts important criteria. There is not one method of establishing test validity, and test developers will usually address validation from a number of perspectives. The result is the development of an overall case that supports the test validity. The major forms of test validity are reviewed below.

Face validity

Face validity is concerned with the way that the test looks to the people who are completing it. It is a qualitative judgement about whether the test items appear relevant for their purpose. In applied psychology, relevant items help to show people that completing the measure is worthwhile, thereby increasing their motivation.

Content validity

Content validity is a similarly qualitative appraisal of the test validity, but made by subject matter experts rather than the test-takers. Personality scales serve as a good illustration. Imagine that a scale was compiled to measure Emotional Stability from the Big Five model. The domain of Emotional stability is broad, and as discussed earlier encompasses a range of narrower personality facets. The test developer may wish to seek advice on whether the item set they had generated covered the full domain. To do this, they could consult with a personality psychologist or researcher and ask them to review the scale.

Construct validity

Overall, construct validity is the closest form of validity to the general conceptualization of measurement validity (that the test measures what it claims to measure). Unlike other forms of validity, showing that a test has construct validity does not involve single method or technique. Rather a range of statistical analyses are performed in order to establish an evidence base for the validity of the test. Such analyses will usually include evaluation of convergent and divergent validity (establishing that a test correlates with variables that it should correlate with, and is uncorrelated with variables that it is not; Campbell and Fiske, 1959), analysis of the factor or dimensional structure of the test and correlations of test scores with other relevant indicators. For example, a test designed to measure Extraversion could be correlated with observational data recorded during social interaction. People scoring highly on the test of Extraversion, should also demonstrate more extraverted behaviours in their interactions with others.

Criterion validity

Criterion validity is concerned with showing that the test predicts important criteria. In Work Psychology, this is a prerequisite for the use of testing for contributing to personnel decisions. In order to use tests with employees in organizations, practitioners need to be confident that the test predicts the outcome of interest. In order to establish criterion validity, test scores must be correlated with scores from criterion measures. In Work Psychology, this is most commonly job performance, but other work-related behaviours and attitudes such as counterproductive work behaviour, satisfaction, commitment and engagement are also important.

The timing of the administration of the test and the measurement of criteria gives rise to two forms of criterion validity:

- Concurrent validity is demonstrated by correlating test scores with criterion scores measured at the same time (concurrently).
- Predictive validity is demonstrated by collecting test scores first, followed by criterion scores at some future time (with a time lag that is usually in the range of three months to one year).

Predictive validity is arguably more robust in most cases, because it shows that the individual difference being measured predicts a future outcome. It is remarkable to think about the implication of what is on the face of it, a dry statistical test. Fundamentally, predictive validity data show that by measuring individual differences, psychologists can predict with varying degrees of accuracy, likely future behavioural, attitudinal and performance outcomes.

Using validity

Like reliability, validity data help practitioners to be confident in the tests that they use, and in the decisions that they make based on test scores. If a test is to be used in a selection context, then the test should be able to demonstrate criterion validity with job performance. If a test is used to help advise a person about their career choices, then the test should be related to performance potential, or well-being, satisfaction, or 'fit' with particular job environments or organizational cultures. Validity is also important for defending personnel decisions. If tests or assessments of any form are used to make decisions about people's work and jobs, then those assessments should be proven to be valid, both in terms of measurement and criterion prediction.

Item Response Theory

An alternative approach to testing altogether uses Item Response Theory (IRT) as an alternative to the classical model of testing. IRT is gaining popularity, particularly for cognitive ability testing, for which it is well suited, aided by advances in computer development that enable the complex analyses to be easily run. The major difference in IRT is the focus of the analyses, which focuses on the properties of items rather than whole tests. Rather than determine whether a particular test is reliable or not, IRT examines the properties of individual test items. It adds to the mix a continuous representation of the construct being measured (e.g. cognitive ability), labelled theta. IRT analyses aim to establish how test-items perform at different levels of theta. In plain terms this enables researchers to establish the effectiveness of each item for measuring or differentiating people with particular levels of cognitive ability. This means that tests can be designed, for example, for people in the high ability range, with their responses used to accurately estimate their specific level of ability. The advantage is that the test could be used with confident knowledge that the items were ideally suited to the people being assessed, thereby giving a better measurement of cognitive ability than might be achieved with a test designed for the general population. There are other design benefits practically of using IRT such as easier creation of parallel tests, adaptive testing (that presents questions based on previous item responses) and flexible use of so called 'item banks' to create multiple tests.

Psychological Testing: Beyond Cognitive Ability and Personality

The methods of psychological testing are presented in this chapter in the context of measuring cognitive ability and personality traits. However, the principles of psychometric theory and methodology apply to any form of quantitative measurement in psychology. Measures of work-related attitudes, behaviours, job performance, job interests, well-being and emotions can all be evaluated to establish their reliability and validity using the methods outlined. The research literature contains a multitude of examples of scales designed to measure particular aspects of individual differences, attitudes, work behaviours and outcomes. Articles evaluating the psychometric properties of such scales are commonplace, and yet there are as many scales and measures used in organizations with little or no evidence of reliability and validity. One clear principle from this chapter is that measurement of individual differences should be robust and accurate, and there are well-established procedures for determining that a measure or test is psychometrically sound. Applying the findings and theories from studies of individual differences at work relies on sound measurement techniques. Now you know, ensure that the survey measures you use in your work are reliable and valid.

SUMMARY

T he study of individual differences involves the examination of key psychological attributes. Two of the most important individual difference attributes are cognitive ability and personality. Cognitive ability (or intelligence) represents a range of reasoning and mental capabilities that can be represented as a hierarchy, with Spearman's factor g at the top. Higher levels of cognitive ability predict higher levels of job performance in a range of jobs, most likely because people with higher abilities are able to acquire more job knowledge more quickly.

Personality has been studied from a number of different perspectives, but the most important of these in Work Psychology is the trait approach. Personality traits are coherent or characteristic patterns of behaviour, demonstrated in response to particular situational and contextual cues. Research into personality traits led to the emergence of the Big Five model of personality, which most psychologists would agree to be the most adequate and widely accepted classification of personality traits. The Big Five have allowed the accumulation of a huge literature on personality traits and work outcomes, including clear evidence that personality traits do predict job performance, and in particular organizational citizenship behaviour. Recent theoretical developments in the field have examined the dynamic associations of personality traits with criteria, and begun to explore and explain the developmental influences of work on personality.

Individual differences in emotional style also have effects on people's behaviour and well-being at work. Affective tendencies such as core self-evaluations, and Psychological Capital have accumulating evidence of their associations with important work outcomes.

The measurement of individual differences is referred to as psychometric or psychological testing. Psychological tests measure unseen or latent constructs and should be evaluated in terms of their reliability and validity. There are a number of techniques that can be used to assess reliability and validity, which in turn tell practitioners about the accuracy and adequacy of specific tests.

DISCUSSION QUESTIONS

1 Think about a recent problem you faced when working in a group or team. How could individual differences help to explain your experiences?

2 If you have previously held a job, what aspect of it involved you managing or regulating your emotions?

3 For three of the Big Five personality dimensions, think of some jobs that might require different personality profile scores (e.g. think of jobs where Extraversion might be advantageous, and jobs where Introversion might be preferable).

4 Why might theories of individual differences be limited in a global context?

5 To what extent do you think your personality and ability are based on genes and environment? Can you perceive aspects of your parents individual differences in your own behaviour?

6 How could a manager use research on individual differences to manage their team more effectively?

APPLY IT

1 A really easy way to apply the content of this chapter is to find out about your own individual differences. There are plenty of online questionnaires that you can fill out, the IPIP NEO is a good personality one. You can also contact Aston Business Assessments (**http://www.astonassessments.co.uk**) and get a more work-oriented report about your personality traits. If you are a manager, then it could also be a good development exercise for your team to find out about their own personality traits.

2 Analyze the jobs that your various team members carry out, and identify the specific kinds of cognitive ability and the personality traits that might give an advantage in those tasks. Use this information to help assign tasks to people with particular strengths. Also keep these to hand ready for Chapter 6 on selection.

3 The power of theory is explanatory – it helps us to understand people's behaviour and explain why they act as they do. You can apply the theory in this chapter by using it to help your thinking. Think about an interaction with a colleague, or a team activity that you worked on. Try to explain the behaviour of the people in the group from different perspectives (social learning and trait theories work quite well).

4 Trait activation theory tells us that trait-related behaviour manifests in response to situations. Situations act as cues to which people respond in predictable ways. Where behaviour or performance is problematic, then people simply need to alter the way in which they typically respond to situations. Practice framing developmental feedback in that way: tell people specifically what behaviour they need to change and in what situations. But do accept them for who they are – it is their behaviour you are aiming to change, not their personality.

5 Consider undertaking some learning in the area of Psychological Capital for you or even your whole team. This emergent area seems to be accumulating much research evidence of its importance, and thinking more positively about work is likely to be of some benefit in almost all (if not all) organizations.

WEB ACTIVITIES
Personality Clashes

Read the article 'When personalities clash: dire traits that can lead to workplace dismissal' by Philip Landau and published by *The Guardian* March 2012, by navigating to it online (see below) or by following the link in the digital resources online and discuss the questions below.

www.theguardian.com – search for 'When personalities clash: dire traits that can lead to workplace dismissal'

1 What personality traits might be relevant to the issue in this story?

2 How might emotion impact this kind of work situation?

3 How could we try to resolve conflict through so-called 'personality clash' before resorting to disciplinary action?

FURTHER READING

Chamorro-Premuzic, T. (2007). *Personality and Individual Differences*. Oxford: BPS Blackwell Ltd.

Anastasi, A. (1996). *Psychological Testing* (7th ed.). New York: Macmillian.

Furnham, A. (2008). *Personality and Intelligence at Work*. Sussex: Routledge.

Barrick, M.R., Mount, M.K. and Judge, T.A. (2001). Personality and performance at the beginning of the new millennium: What do we know and where do we go next? *International Journal of Selection and Assessment, 9*, 9–30.

Hogan, R., Hogan, J. and Roberts, B.W. (1996). Personality measurement and employment decisions. *American Psychologist, 51*, 469–477.

Schmidt, F.L. and Hunter, J.E. (2004). General Mental Ability in the world of work: Occupational attainment and job performance. *Journal of Personality and Social Psychology, 86*, 162–173.

REFERENCES

Ackerman, P.L. and Heggestad, E.D. (1997). Intelligence, personality and interests: Evidence for overlapping traits. *Psychological Bulletin, 121(2)*, 219–245.

Allport, G.W. and Odbert, H.S. (1936). Trait names: A psycho-lexical study. *Psychological Monographs, 47*, Whole No. 211.

Antonakis, J. (2004). On why "emotional intelligence" will not predict leadership effectiveness beyond IQ or the "big five": An extension and rejoinder. *International Journal of Organizational Analysis, 12(2)*, 171–182.

Barrick, M.R. and Mount, M.K. (1991). The Big Five personality dimensions and job performance: A meta-analysis. *Personnel Psychology, 44*, 1–26.

Barrick, M.R., Mount, M.K. and Gupta, R. (2003). Meta-analysis of the relationship between the Five Factor Model of personality and Hollan's occupational types. *Personnel Psychology, 56*, 45–74.

Barrick, M.R., Mount, M.K. and Judge, T.A. (2001). Personality and performance at the beginning of the new millennium: What do we know and where do we go next? *International Journal of Selection and Assessment, 9*, 9–30.

Barrick, M.R., Stewart, G.L., Neubert, M.J. and Mount, M.K. (1998). Relating member ability and personality to work-team processes and team effectiveness. *Journal of Applied Psychology, 83(3)*, 377.

Barsade, S.G. and Gibson, D.E. (2007). Why does affect matter in organizations? *Academy of Management Perspectives, 21(1)*, 36–59.

Blanchard, K.H. and Johnson, S. (1983). *The one minute manager*. New York: Blanchard Family Partnership and Candle Communications Corporation.

Bono, J.E. and Judge, T.A. (2004). Personality and transformational and transactional leadership: a meta-analysis. *Journal of Applied Psychology, 89(5)*, 901.

Borgatta, E.F. (1964). The structure of personality characteristics. *Behavioral Science, 9*, 8–17.

Borman, W.C., Hanson, M.A., Oppler, S.H., Pulakos, E.D. and White, L.A. (1993). The role of early supervisory experience in supervisor performance. *Journal of Applied Psychology, 78*, 443–449.

Bouchard, T.J. Jr. (1994). Gene, environment and personality. *Science, 264,* 1700–1701.

Brief, A.P. and Weiss, H.M. (2002). Organizational behaviour: Affect in the workplace. *Annual Review of Psychology, 53,* 279–307.

Burisch, M. (1984). Approaches to personality inventory construction. A comparison of merits. *American Psychologist, 3,* 214–227.

Campbell, D.T. and Fiske, D.W. (1959). Convergent and discriminant validation by the multitrait-multimethod matrix. *Psychological Bulletin, 56(2),* 81–105.

Carroll, J.B. (1993). *Human cognitive abilities: A survey of factor analytic studies.* New York: Cambridge University Press.

Cattell, P.B. (1947). Confirmation and clarification of primary personality factors. *Psychometrika, 12,* 197–220.

Chamorro-Premuzic, T. (2007). *Personality and Individual Differences.* Oxford: BPS Blackwell Ltd.

Comings, D.E., Gade-Andavolu, R., Gonzalez, N., Wu, S., Muhleman, D., Blake, H., Mann, M.B., Dietz, G., Saucier, G. and MacMurray, J.P. (2000). A multivariate analysis of 59 candidate genes in personality traits: the temperament and character inventory. *Clinical Genetics, 58,* 375–385.

Conte, J.M. (2005). A review and critique of emotional intelligence measures. *Journal of Organizational Behavior, 26,* 433–440.

Cropanzano, R. and Wright, T.A. (2001). When a 'Happy' Worker Is Really a 'Productive' Worker: A Review and Further Refinement of the Happy–Productive Worker Thesis. *Consulting Psychology Journal: Practice and Research, 53(3),* 182–199.

Deary, I.J., Whalley, L.J., Lemmon, H., Crawford, J.R. and Starr, J.M. (2000). The Stability of Individual Differences in Mental Ability from Childhood to Old Age: Follow-up of the 1932 Scottish Mental Survey. *Intelligence, 28(1),* 49–55.

De Young, C.G., Quilty, L.C. and Peterson, J.B. (2007). Between facets and domains: 10 Aspects of the Big Five. *Journal of Personality and Social Psychology, 93,* 880–896.

Digman, J.M. (1997). Higher-order factors of the Big Five. *Journal of Personality and Social Psychology, 73,* 1246–1256.

Dunn, W.S., Mount, M.K., Barrick, M.R. and Ones, D.S. (1995). Relative importance of personality and general mental ability in managers' judgements of applicant qualifications. *Journal of Applied Psychology, 80(4),* 500–509.

Eisenberg, N., Fabes, R.A. and Spinrad, T.L. (1998). Prosocial development. *Handbook of Child Psychology* 5th ed.: Vol 3. Social, emotional, and personality development., (pp. 701–778). Hoboken, NJ, US: John Wiley & Sons Inc.

Erdheim, J., Wang, M. and Zickar, M.J. (2006). Linking the big five personality constructs to organizational commitment. *Personality and Individual Differences, 41,* 959–970.

Erez, A. and Judge, T.A. (2001). Relationship of core self-evaluations to goal setting, motivation, and performance. *Journal of Applied Psychology, 86(6),* 1270.

Eysenck, H.J. (1947). *Dimensions of Personality.* London, U.K.: Routledge.

Ferris, D. L., Rosen, C. R., Johnson, R. E., Brown, D. J., Risavy, S.D. and Heller, D. (2011). Approach or avoidance (or both?): Integrating core self-evaluations within an approach/avoidance framework. *Personnel Psychology, 64(1),* 137–161.

Fiori, M. and Antonakis, J. (2011). The ability model of emotional intelligence: Searching for valid measures. *Personality and Individual Differences, 50(3),* 329–334.

Funder, D.C. (1989). Accuracy in personality judgment and the dancing bear. In D.M. Buss and N. Cantor (eds.), *Personality psychology: Recent trends and emerging directions* (pp. 210–223). New York: Springer-Verlag.

Funder, D.C. and West, S.G. (1993). Consensus, self-other agreement, and accuracy in personality judgment: An introduction. *Journal of Personality, 64,* 457–476.

Funder, D. (1995). On the accuracy of personality judgement: A realistic approach. *Psychological Review, 102,* 652–670.

Furnham, A. (1996). The Big Five versus the big four: The relationship between the Myers-Briggs Type Indicator (MBTI) and the NEO-PI face factor model of personality. *Personality and Individual Differences, 21,* 303–307.

Goldberg, L. R. (1999). A broad-bandwidth, public domain, personality inventory measuring the lower-level facets of several five-factor models. In I. Mervielde, I. Deary, F. De Fruyt and F. Ostendorf (Eds.), *Personality Psychology in Europe,* Vol. 7 (pp. 7–28). Tilburg, The Netherlands: Tilburg University Press.

Gottfredson, L.S. (1997). Mainstream science on intelligence: An editorial with 52 signatories, history and bibliography. *Intelligence, 24,* 13–23.

Gottfredson, L.S. (2002). Where and why g matters: Not a mystery. *Human Performance, 15(1-2),* 25–46.

Graziano, W. G. and Eisenberg, N.H. (1997). Agreeableness: A dimension of personality. In. Hogan, R., Johnson, J. and Briggs, S. (Eds.). (1997). *Handbook of Personality Psychology.* Academic Press.

Hampson, S.E. (1988). *The construction of personality: An introduction.* London: Routledge.

Hampson, S.E. (1999). State of the art: Personality. *The Psychologist, 12,* 284–288.

Hicks, L.E. (1984). Conceptual and empirical analysis of some assumptions of an explicit typological theory. *Journal of Personality and Social Psychology, 46,* 1118–1131.

Hochschild, A.R. (1983). *The managed heart: Commercialization of human feeling.* Berkeley: University of California Press.

Hofstee, W.K.B. (1984). What's in a trait: reflections about the inevitability of traits, their measurement, and taxonomy. In H. Bonarius, G. Van Heck and N. Smid (eds), *Personality Psychology in Europe: Theoretical and Empirical Developments,* pp. 75–81, Swets and Zeitlinger, Lisse.

Hogan, J. and Holland, B. (2003). Using theory to evaluate personality and job-performance relations: A socioanalytic perspective. *Journal of Applied Psychology, 88(1),* 100–112.

Hunter, J.E. and Hunter, R.F. (1984). Validity and utility of alternative predictors of job performance. *Psychological Bulletin, 96,* 72–98.

Hunter, J.E. and Schmidt, F.L. (1990). *Methods of meta-analysis: Correcting error and bias in research findings.* Newbury Park, CA: Sage.

John, O.P. and Srivastava, S. (1999). The Big Five trait taxonomy: History, measurement, and theoretical perspectives. In L.A. Pervin and O.P. John (eds.), *Handbook of personality theory and research* (pp. 139–153). New York: Guilford.

Johnson, J.A. (2000). Predicting observers' ratings of the Big Five from the CPI, HPI and NEO-PI-R: A comparative validity study. *European Journal of Personality, 14,* 1–19.

Johnson, W. and Krueger, R.F. (2004). Genetic and environmental structure of adjectives describing the domains of the Big Five Model of personality: A nationwide US twin study. *Journal of Research in Personality, 38(5),* 448–472.

Joseph, D.L. and Newman, D.A. (2010). Emotional intelligence: an integrative meta-analysis and cascading model. *Journal of Applied Psychology, 95 (1),* 54.

Judge, T.A. and Bono, J.E. (2001). Relationship of core self-evaluations traits – self-esteem, generalized self-efficacy, locus of control, and emotional stability – with job satisfaction and job performance: A meta-analysis. *Journal of Applied Psychology, 86(1),* 80.

Judge, T.A., Bono, J.E. and Locke, E.A. (2000). Personality and job satisfaction: the mediating role of job characteristics. *Journal of Applied Psychology, 85(2),* 237.

Judge, T. A., Bono, J. E., Ilies, R. and Gerhardt, M. W. (2002). Personality and leadership: a qualitative and quantitative review. *Journal of Applied Psychology, 87(4),* 765.

Judge, T.A., Locke, E.A., Durham, C.C. and Kluger, A.N. (1998). Dispositional effects on job and life satisfaction: the role of core evaluations. *Journal of Applied Psychology, 83(1),* 17.

Judge, T.A., Heller, D. and Mount, M.K. (2002). Five Factor model of personality and job satisfaction: A meta-analysis. *Journal of Applied Psychology, 87,* 530–541.

Judge, T.A., Higgins, C.A., Thoresen, C.J. and Barrick, M.R. (1999). The Big Five personality traits, general mental ability and career success across the life span. *Personnel Psychology, 52,* 621–652.

Larson, L.M., Rottinghaus, P.J. and Borgen, F. (2002). Meta-analysis of Big Six interests and Big Five personality factors. *Journal of Vocational Behaviour, 61,* 217–239.

Lievens, F., Ones, D.S. and Dilchert, S. (2009). Personality scale validities increase throughout medical school. *Journal of Applied Psychology, 94(6),* 1514.

Lubinski, D. (2004). Introduction to the special section on cognitive abilities: 100 years after Spearman's (1904) 'General Intelligence, objectively determined and measured.' Journal of Personality and Social Psychology, 86, *96–111.*

Lüdtke, O., Roberts, B.W., Trautwein, U. and Nagy, G. (2011). A random walk down university avenue: life paths, life events, and personality trait change at the transition to university life. *Journal of Personality and Social Psychology, 101(3),* 620.

Luthans, F., Avey, J.B., Avolio, B.J., Norman, S.M. and Combs, G.M. (2006). Psychological capital development: toward a micro-intervention. *Journal of Organizational Behavior, 27(3),* 387–393.

Luthans, F., Avey, J.B. and Patera, J.L. (2008). Experimental analysis of a web-based training intervention to develop positive psychological capital. *Academy of Management Learning & Education, 7(2),* 209–221.

Luthans, F., Avolio, B.J., Walumbwa, F.O. and Li, W. (2005). The psychological capital of Chinese workers: Exploring the relationship with performance. *Management and Organization Review, 1(2),* 249–271.

Luthans, F., Avolio, B.J., Avey, J.B. and Norman, S.M. (2007). Positive psychological capital: Measurement and relationship with performance and satisfaction. *Personnel Psychology, 60(3),* 541–572.

Luthans, F., Norman, S. M., Avolio, B. J. and Avey, J. B. (2008). The mediating role of psychological capital in the supportive organizational climate – employee performance relationship. *Journal of Organizational Behavior, 29(2)*, 219–238.

Luthans, F. and Youssef, C.M. (2004). Human, Social, and Now Positive Psychological Capital Management: Investing in People for Competitive Advantage. *Organizational Dynamics, 33(2)*, 143–160.

Luthans, F., Youssef, C.M. and Avolio, B.J. (2007). *Psychological capital: Developing the human competitive edge*. Oxford University Press.

Maltby, J., Day, L. and Macaskill, A. (2006). *Personality, Individual Differences and Intelligence*. Harlow: Pearson.

Mayer, J.D., Caruso, D.R. and Salovey, P. (1999). Emotional intelligence meets traditional standards for an intelligence. *Intelligence, 27*, 267–298.

McAdams, D.P. (2001). *The person: An integrated introduction to personality psychology* (3rd ed.). Fort Worth, TX: Harcourt

McCrae, R.R. and Costa, P.T., Jr. (1995). Trait explanations in personality psychology. *European Journal of Personality, 9*, 231–252.

McCrae, R.R. and Costa, P.T. (1997). Personality trait structure as a human universal. *American Psychologist, 52*, 509–516.

Mendelsohn, G.A., Weiss, D.S. and Feimer, N.R. (1982). Conceptual and empirical analysis of the typological implications of patterns of socialization and femininity. *Journal of Personality and Social Psychology, 42*, 1157–70.

Mischel, W. (1968). *Personality and assessment*. New York: John Wiley and Sons.

Motowidlo, S.J., Borman, W.C. and Schmitt, M.J. (1997). A theory of individual differences in task and contextual performance. *Human Performance, 10*, 71–83.

Murphy, K.R. (1989). Is the relationship between cognitive ability and job performance stable over time?. *Human Performance, 2(3)*, 183–200.

Murray, C. (1998). *Income Inequality and IQ*. Washington: AEI Press.

Musek, J. (2007). A general factor of personality: Evidence for the Big One in the five-factor model. *Journal of Research in Personality, 41(6)*, 1213–1233.

Norman, W.T. (1967). *2800 personality trait descriptors: Normative operating characteristics for a university population*. Ann Arbor: University of Michigan, Department of Psychology.

O'Boyle, E.H., Humphrey, R.H., Pollack, J.M., Hawver, T.H. and Story, P.A. (2011). The relation between emotional intelligence and job performance: A meta-analysis. *Journal of Organizational Behavior, 32(5)*, 788–818.

Ozer, D.J. and Benet-Martinez, V. (2006). Personality and the prediction of consequential outcomes. *Annu. Rev. Psychol., 57*, 401–421.

Peterson, C. (2006). *A primer in positive psychology*. Oxford University Press.

Petrides, K.V. and Furnham, A. (2001). Trait emotional intelligence: Psychometric investigation with reference to established trait taxonomies. *European Journal of Personality, 15(6)*, 425–448.

Pittenger, D.J. (2005). Cautionary Comments Regarding the Myers-Briggs Type Indicator. *Consulting Psychology Journal: Practice and Research, 57(3)*, 210–221.

Rafaeli, A. and Sutton, R.I. (1989). The expression of emotion in organizational life. *Research in Organizational Behaviour, 11*, 1–42.

Roberts, B.W., Caspi, A. and Moffitt, T.E. (2003). Work experiences and personality development in young adulthood. *Journal of Personality and Social Psychology, 84(3)*, 582.

Roberts, B.W., Robins, R.W., Caspi, A. and Trzesniewski, K.H. (2003). *Personality trait development in adulthood*. In J. Mortimer and M. Shanahan (Eds.), *Handbook of the life course*. New York: Plenum Press.

Rusting, C.L. and Larsen, R.J. (1998). Extraversion, neuroticism, and susceptibility to positive and negative affect: A test of two theoretical models. *Personality and Individual Differences, 22*, 607–612.

Salgado, J.F., Anderson, N., Moscoso, S., Bertua, C., De Fruyt, F. and Rolland, J.P. (2003). A meta-analytic study of GMA validity for different occupations in the European community. *Journal of Applied Psychology, 88*, 1068–1081.

Salovey, P., Mayer, J.D., Caruso, D. and Lopes, P.N. (2003). Measuring emotional intelligence as a set of abilities with the Mayer–Salovey–Caruso Emotional Intelligence Test. In S.J. Lopez and C.R. Snyder (eds.), *Positive psychological assessment: A handbook of models and measures* (pp. 251–265). Washington, DC: American Psychological Association.

Schmidt, F.L. (2002). The role of general cognitive ability and job performance: Why there cannot be a debate. *Human Performance, 15*, 187–210.

Schmidt, F.L. and Hunter, J.E. (1992). Development of a causal model of processes determining job performance. *Current Directions in Psychological Science, 1*, 89–92.

Schmidt, F.L. and Hunter, J.E. (2004). General Mental Ability in the world of work: Occupational attainment and job performance. *Journal of Personality and Social Psychology, 86*, 162–173.

Sternberg, R.J. and Kaufman, J.C. (1998). Human abilities. *Annual Review of Psychology, 49*, 479–502.

Tett, R.P. and Burnett, D.D. (2003). A personality trait-based interactionist model of job performance. *Journal of Applied Psychology, 88(3)*, 500.

Thoresen, C.J., Bradley, J.C., Bliese, P.D. and Thoresen, J.D. (2004). The big five personality traits and individual job performance growth trajectories in maintenance and transitional job stages. *Journal of Applied Psychology, 89(5)*, 835.

Thoresen, C.J., Kaplan, S.A., Barsky, A.P., de Chermont, K. and Warren, C.R. (2003). The affective underpinnings of job perceptions and attitudes: A meta-analytic review and integration. *Psychological Bulletin, 129*, 914–945.

Tupes, E.C. and Cristal, R.E. (1961). *Recurrent personality factors based on trait ratings (ASD-TR-61–97)*. Lackland Air Force Base, TX: Aeronautical Systems Division, Personnel Laboratory.

Van der Linden, D., te Nijenhuis, J. and Bakker, A.B. (2010). The general factor of personality: A meta-analysis of Big Five intercorrelations and a criterion-related validity study. *Journal of Research in Personality, 44(3)*, 315–327.

Van Vianen, A.E. and De Dreu, C.K. (2001). Personality in teams: Its relationship to social cohesion, task cohesion, and team performance. *European Journal of Work and Organizational Psychology, 10(2)*, 97–120.

Van der Zee, K. and Wabeke, R. (2004). Is Trait-Emotional Intelligence Simply or More Than Just a Trait? *European Journal of Personality, 18(4)*, 243.

Watson, J.B. and Rayner, R. (1920). Conditioned emotional reactions. *Journal of Experimental Psychology, 3*, 1–14.

Wille, B., Beyers, W. and De Fruyt, F. (2012). A transactional approach to person-environment fit: Reciprocal relations between personality development and career role growth across young to middle adulthood. *Journal of Vocational Behavior, 81(3)*, 307–321.

Woods, S.A. and Hardy, C. (2012). The higher-order factor structures of five personality inventories. *Personality and individual differences, 52(4)*, 552–558.

Woods, S.A. and Hampson, S.E. (2005). Measuring the Big Five with single items using a bipolar response scale. *European Journal of Personality, 19(5)*, 373–390.

Woods, S.A. and Hampson, S.E. (2010). Predicting adult occupational environments from gender and childhood personality traits. *Journal of Applied Psychology, 95(6)*, 1045.

Woods, S.A., Lievens, F., De Fruyt, F. and Wille, B. (2013). Personality across working life: The longitudinal and reciprocal influences of personality on work. *Journal of Organizational Behavior, 34*: S7–S25.

Zyphur, M.J., Chaturvedi, S. and Arvey, R.D. (2008). Job performance over time is a function of latent trajectories and previous performance. *Journal of Applied Psychology, 93(1)*, 217.

CHAPTER 4

ATTITUDES AND BEHAVIOUR IN ORGANIZATIONS

T hink for a moment about the things that you did last week either at work or, if you are a student, at college or university. How did you perform do you think? How did you interact with other people? Did you make any important decisions? Do you think that others would have been able to predict your behaviour? Now consider some of the underlying reasons for your behaviour last week. Perhaps you felt good about work and this meant that you were better disposed towards colleagues or more motivated to perform well. Perhaps you felt less committed towards your employer or university course for some reason, and made decisions that reflected these feelings. Whatever your feelings or attitudes towards work last week, could you say with any certainty why you felt the way you did?

Understanding our own behaviour at work is complex, and so to understand behaviour of tens, hundreds or even thousands of people interacting everyday in organizations is a very challenging task indeed. The field of organizational behaviour (conventionally shortened to OB) has taken on this challenge, combining a wide range of approaches to social science to study how and why people behave in organizations. For managers, lessons from OB help to explain the behaviour of subordinates and leaders, enabling them to start to make sense of the complex organizational role they fulfil. We consider some of them in this chapter.

WHAT IS ORGANIZATIONAL BEHAVIOUR?

OB acts as a background context for this chapter, which is focused principally on the behaviour of individuals at work. Robbins and Judge (2009) define OB as:

> *A field of study that investigates the impact that individuals, groups and structure have on behaviour within organizations, for the purpose of applying such knowledge toward improving an organization's effectiveness.* (Robbins and Judge, 2009, p. 45.)

You will see that the broad definition captures some of the aspects of our definition of Work and Organizational Psychology in Chapter 1. The field of OB acts as a meeting point for the application of theory from several areas of social science to business and organizations. Figure 4.1, adapted from Robbins and Judge, shows how psychology, social psychology, sociology and anthropology contribute to the study of the units of analysis in OB: individuals, groups and organizations. The multi-level nature of OB as an approach to understanding behaviour has been a consistent theme in the development of the field (e.g. Schneider, 1985; Mowday and Sutton, 1993).

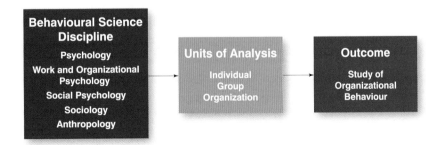

Figure 4.1   The study of organizational behaviour

In this chapter, we distil the field of OB to capture some of the most important topics of theory and research that are not covered in other chapters of this book. Our emphasis in the chapter is primarily on aspects of individual behaviour, the causes and the consequences of that behaviour. We also consider the group context of behaviour in this chapter, but not the organizational context, which is covered in depth in the third part of this book. This chapter sits alongside Chapter 3 on individual differences and Chapter 5 on motivation, and examines some of the other factors that affect behaviour at work. These comprise:

- management influences on behaviour
- attitudinal influences on behaviour
- wider behavioural influences of emotions, perceptions and decision-making
- social influences on behaviour.

MANAGEMENT INFLUENCES: SHAPING AND CONTROLLING BEHAVIOUR AT WORK

A basic approach to examining behaviour at work aims to understand simply how to control, shape and modify behaviour. Stop for a moment and think briefly about how you might propose to modify or influence the behaviour of people at work if you were a business owner or manager. Chances are that you would hit upon a strategy that involved some form of reward or encouragement for the behaviour you desired, and reprimand or punishment for behaviour that was undesirable. You will note that these basic ideas are the hallmarks of behaviourism, and the basic principles of that approach are still evident in behaviour modification theory.

Conditioning and Reinforcement

Be honest. When you thought about shaping behaviour in an organization as you read the previous paragraph, was the role of money one of the first things that popped into your mind? Money has been considered to be a key reinforcer of behaviour since the earliest management theorists such as Frederick Taylor, and it continues to feature in research on behaviour modification (Stajkovic and Luthans, 2003). However, to understand the role of something like pay on behaviour, it needs to be contextualized against theories of behavioural conditioning and reinforcement.

Learning theories offer the clearest way to understand the role of conditioning and reinforcement. The first such theory was presented by Pavlov (see Chapter 3), in which classical conditioning was used to condition the salivation response of a dog. This was developed further by Skinner in theories of operant conditioning. Operant conditioning involves applying four kinds of reinforcement to modify and control behaviour: positive reinforcement, negative reinforcement, punishment and extinction. In behaviour modification, Skinner's theory may be applied in the following ways:

- Positive reinforcement can be applied to encourage desirable behaviour. Monetary reward could be a reinforcer, provided that it is designed to reinforce specific behaviour (Luthans and Stajkovic, 1999). Praise or social recognition are other examples of positive reinforcers used by managers with employees.

- Negative reinforcement involves the withdrawal of something unpleasant in response to desirable behaviour. Imagine that a manager checks up on the performance of an employee on a daily basis, until such time as the employee begins to improve. The discomfort of daily checks is avoided by improved performance, an example of negative reinforcement.

- Punishment involves giving or administering something unpleasant in response to undesirable behaviour. This could include verbal reprimand, or withholding bonus payments for example.

- Extinction is the discontinuation of reinforcement interventions in order to encourage discontinuation of the reinforced behaviour. This could involve the removal of reinforcement from particular behaviours or aspects of performance at work. They could be reallocated to new desirable behaviours so as to result in behavioural change.

Learning theories were developed further by Bandura (e.g. Bandura, 1977) who added the social aspect of learning. There are two additions that are particularly salient in the context of behavioural shaping and control:

1 The role of social modelling. The simple behaviourist paradigm suggests that people approach problem solving as stimulus responders. The social learning perspective adds the notion that people have already accumulated knowledge of the likely efficacy of responses by observing the behaviour of others, along with the consequences.

2 The role of cognition. Social learning theory conceptualizes people as decision-makers, with decisions and behaviour resulting from perception of environmental stimuli, and the cognitions and emotional reactions that result from perceptions. Social cognitive personality theory (e.g. Cervone and Shoda, 1999) indicates how habitual or dispositional behaviour results from repeatedly responding to particular situations in the same way, almost rehearsing responses that become increasingly automatic, and eventually habitual. Such processes could apply to behaviours at work.

In the context of organizational behaviour control, reinforcement is still centrally important in the social learning approach. According to this perspective, in order to encourage desirable behaviour, however it is learned, reinforcement should be applied. For example, a person might learn behaviour through observation of another employee at work. If they observe a colleague stealing from work, then the learning is counterproductive, and punishment might be used to prevent it. If they observe the colleague providing excellent customer support, and model that behaviour accordingly, positive reinforcement would increase the likelihood that the behaviour was repeated, and over time, performed more automatically.

Contemporary research on reinforcement

Behavioural management continues to attract attention in the contemporary research literature, and reinforcement remains a major area of focus. Stajkovic and Luthans (2003) summarize the concept of behavioural management:

> The main premise of behaviour management is that employee behaviour is a function of contingent consequences. Simply, behaviours that positively affect performance must be contingently reinforced. Contingently administered money, feedback and social recognition are the most recognized reinforcers in behavioural management at work. (Stajkovic and Luthans, 2003, p. 156.)

Contingent reinforcement means that reinforcers (i.e. money, feedback and social recognition) must be applied only if the desired performance behaviour is exhibited (Komaki, Coombs and Schepman, 1996). Does it work? Evidence in the research literature appears to suggest that it does. Stajkovic and Luthans (2003) conducted a meta-analysis of studies examining the effect of behaviour management through reinforcement on job performance. They considered the individual and joint effects of the three main reinforcement strategies:

- Money. Money is probably the most basic reinforcer, and is one that is generally attractive to employees, but which is limited because it has no informational value. In other words, giving money to people does not provide information about behaviour or performance.

- Feedback. The role of feedback in performance management is covered in more depth in Chapter 8. The purpose of feedback is to provide information on performance and behaviour to clarify performance expectations. Feedback could focus on either discrepancies between actual and required outcomes, processes by which performance is executed or a combination of both.

- Social Recognition. Recognition of effective behaviour or performance through public praising, awards or through highlighting achievements in media such as newsletters, are forms of recognitional reinforcement. Information about performance can be communicated through recognition, although not as clearly as in specific feedback. The risk of recognition as a sole reinforcer is that if it is not linked with a tangible outcome, it may be perceived as an empty reward (Bandura, 1986).

In their analyses, Stajkovic and Luthans (2003) found that performance was improved by all three reinforcement strategies, with money improving performance on average by 23 per cent, feedback by 17 per cent, and social recognition by 10 per cent. The most powerful effects on performance were exhibited when a combination of all three was used, with performance improving by 45 per cent.

Wider factors in reinforcement

Reinforcement schedules One of the factors in operant conditioning that interested Skinner was the timing and scheduling of reinforcement. Does regular or random reinforcement improve behaviour most effectively? The same issue has been raised in behaviour management in organizations. There are several strategies for scheduling reinforcement, and most in organizations would be considered intermittent (i.e. reinforcement is applied at particular points in time). Consensus seems to suggest that variable schedules of reinforcement produce the most stable and consistent performance (Robbins and Judge, 2009). In such schedules, reinforcement is offered at times when it is most justified. Fixed schedules of bonus pay for example provide no incentive for behaviour change, because employees expect it and know it will be provided. In a variable schedule, a bonus might be paid based on changing outputs, or at various different times. The theory is that such schedules keep people alert and sharp to the reinforcement and the behaviours that give rise to it.

AUTHOR EXPERIENCE

Changing Behaviour Through Reinforcement in a UK Police Force

A project I worked on in one of the UK's regional police forces was grounded very clearly in behavioural modification theory. The project was designed to improve adherence to procedures and systems in police work that governed things like the completion of arrest paperwork, filing of intelligence reports, preparation of documentation for court hearings and so forth. The system of intervention was very simple. Constables, detective-constables, sergeants and detective-sergeants were all awarded points for getting these basic procedures correct. They were deducted points when things were done incorrectly, or if, for example, negligence for procedure or paperwork led to an arrest or court case falling through. Each week, the scores of individuals,

and teams of constables were published. The points were unrelated to any bonus or incentive. They fed into performance assessment, but they did not equate directly to tangible reward or punishment. It did seem to work though, and the quality of work produced by those in the scheme improved markedly, probably because the system provided two things: 1) feedback on performance quality; 2) reinforcement of quality through award of points, and punishment of carelessness or sloppiness through the removal of points.

However, this example also illustrates the dangers of viewing behaviour in the limited ways afforded by behaviour modification theory. As a researcher on a project to examine some of the wider effects of the intervention, one of my contributions was to interview those who were assessed under the system. Although they could perceive the benefits, many reported unintended consequences, such as removal of discretion and decision-making latitude in dealing with petty offenders (points were allocated for arrests for all offences, including minor ones, if they were seen through to conviction). Some felt an erosion of public trust might result in the long term, and many reported dissatisfaction with the publication of scores.

The lesson: simple interventions to change behaviour probably work best in simple jobs. For those jobs with complex demands, impacts and interpersonal contexts, reinforcement and punishment strategies will almost always have unintended consequences of some variety. One could quite easily scale up this example to bonuses in the financial industry. Working for short-term gain in order to maximize personal bonuses encouraged bankers to take decisions that led to the recent financial crisis. Simple financial reinforcement of behaviour at work, with unintended global consequences.

Valence of reinforcement Imagine a person at work who is financially comfortable. Perhaps their earnings provide sufficient means to live a contented life. It is unlikely that the availability of monetary reinforcers would be as effective at managing the behaviour of such a person compared with someone who urgently needed additional money to fund their kids' schooling. The key factor that differentiates the effectiveness of the reinforcement is valence, that is the importance of the reinforcer to the individual. We will pick up on this idea again in Chapter 5 when we consider Expectancy Theory

(Vroom, 1964). In cognitive approaches to organizational behaviour (e.g. Ilgen and Klein, 1988), behaviour results from reinforcement via stages of cognitive processing. Employees perceive a reward or reinforcer as being associated with a particular behaviour, decide whether that reward is important or valuable to them, and then use that information to decide whether to change behaviour or act in such a way as to receive the reward. This theory provides a critical step towards integrating behaviour management with individual differences. Accounting for individual differences in management could, for example, involve considering the kinds of reinforcement that work best for specific individuals, and then making sure that they are abundant in their work environment.

ATTITUDES AND BEHAVIOUR

Are you satisfied at work? What do you think about the managerial capability of your line super-visor? How do you feel about your organization and its mission? All of these represent attitudes at work, and they are important because they potentially have an impact on people's behaviour and performance at work. In this section, we will consider the antecedents, processes and consequences of attitudes at work. We will also consider arguably the most important question in the history of people management (more on that shortly).

What is an Attitude?

Attitudes represent evaluative statements or beliefs about something or someone. They are always directed towards a target (person, object or event) and represent the degree to which that target is perceived favourably or unfavourably. The clearest way to understand attitudes in more detail is to consider three different components (Breckler, 1984). These are cognitive, affective and behavioural:

- Cognitive component. The cognitive part of the attitude represents the thought or belief about the target. For example, in the attitude, 'my office space is too small', the statement itself represents the cognitive part of the attitude.
- Affective component. The affective part of the attitude represents the emotions associated with the attitude. Perhaps the person is frustrated, angry or disappointed that their workspace is too small.
- Behavioural component. The behavioural component represents the behavioural intentions or consequences that result from the attitude. In this case, maybe the individual would request a different workspace, or create more space if possible, or complain to their line manager.

What makes attitudes particularly important in organizations is the behavioural part, and the extent to which positive attitudes result in positive behaviours, and negative attitudes in unhelpful behaviour.

Linking Attitudes and Behaviour

Attitudes do not always lead to behaviour at work, and the circumstances that facilitate the transla-tion of attitude to behaviour are obviously of interest to people working in organizations. Some research has attempted to outline the factors that enhance the prediction of behaviour from attitudes (e.g. Glasman and Albarracín, 2006, reported that stable attitudes that were easy to recall tended to predict behaviour most effectively), but such studies are quite abstract. Two well-established, relevant theories provide more clarity about the links between attitudes and behaviour:

1 Cognitive dissonance theory
2 The theory of planned behaviour.

Cognitive dissonance theory

Have you ever been asked to do something that went against your attitudes or values? Perhaps your job required you to say something that you inwardly disagreed with? How did that, or how would that make you feel? Quite likely uncomfortable, and it is that inner psychological discomfort that is important in Festinger's (1957) cognitive dissonance theory. A key aspect of the theory is the consistency between attitudes and behaviour. When attitude and behaviour are dissonant or inconsistent, the discomfort associated with that dissonance motivates people to act to reduce it (Harmon-Jones and Mills, 1999; Elliot and Devine, 1994).

Harmon-Jones and Elliot review the major perspectives on dissonance research and comment that although there are alternative perspectives on understanding dissonance (e.g. Bem, 1967), many of the assertions of dissonance theory stand up reasonably well in experimental settings. There are two main implications for understanding the attitudes-behaviour link:

1 Under situations where people are free to behave as they wish, behaviour is likely to be consistent with attitudes in order that dissonance be avoided. The greater the importance that a person places on the attitude, the more likely they are to behave in accordance with it (Robbins and Judge, 2009). In organizations though, choices and behaviour are rarely 'free' from constraints, and so social pressures, obligation or incentive might lead people to behave in ways not reflected in their attitudes.

2 The relationship between attitudes and behaviour may be more complex than anticipated. Typically the assumption is that behaviour follows from attitudes. However, the opposite can also be true. Assume that a manager has to tell their team that because of cuts this year, there will be no pay rise for them, and that this is fair and justifiable. The manager may feel inwardly that this is unfair, but has no choice in the matter (i.e. I believe that it is unfair not to give a pay rise, but I told my team that it was fair and justifiable). Once they have communicated this to their team, the behaviour cannot be undone. So whatever the strategy for reducing the dissonance, changing behaviour is not viable. Experimental evidence suggests that the manager in this case would either modify their attitude slightly so that they felt that withholding pay rises was somewhat justifiable, or would attempt to find a reason, excuse or justification for their action. The more important the justification, the less likely they would be to change their view. So, if the manager had accepted the promise of a promotion themselves in return for breaking the news to their team, they might reason 'I know that I don't believe what I told the team, but I did it for the money, or reward'. If there was no incentive, they might reason 'I know that I thought it was unfair to withhold the pay rise, but it is for the good of the company in the long run'. Both represent the alteration of attitudes as a consequence of behaviour.

The theories of reasoned action and planned behaviour

A more clearly defined theory of the pathway from attitudes to behaviour is the theory of planned behaviour (Ajzen, 1988; 1991), which builds on the earlier theory of reasoned action (Ajzen and Fishbein, 1980; 2005). The theory describes some of the antecedents of attitude formation, and the factors that determine whether behavioural intentions are formed, and expressed in actual behaviour. The theory is represented diagrammatically in Figure 4.2. There are a number of key implications of the model:

● Attitudes and beliefs are formed based on a variety of individual, external and contextual variables. Personality, education, life experience and other factors contribute to the formation of beliefs, and even if those beliefs are irrational or unreasonable, they nevertheless act as foundations for action or behaviour.

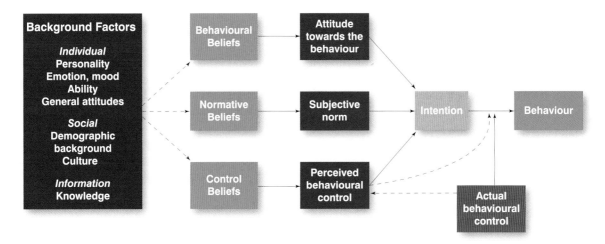

Figure 4.2   The theory of planned behaviour

- The key aspect of the model relating to attitudes is around behavioural beliefs, which lead to attitudes about behaviour. This is a subtle point and relates to the observation that attitudes predict behaviour only when they are considered in similar ways and levels of specificity (Ajzen and Fishbein, 1977). For example, the general attitude 'I like my job' is unlikely to predict whether someone will stay late at work to finish an assignment. The attitude is general, and the behaviour specific. However, the attitude 'I think it is reasonable to stay late to finish work if required' is likely to be a good predictor of the same behaviour. The attitude is specific, and directed toward the behavioural act.

- Alongside behavioural beliefs, the model also includes beliefs about social norms and perceptions of control. Perceptions of social norms comprise judgements about what is socially acceptable in respect of behaviour. So for example, a person may feel that staying late is an unreasonable request, but this could be mitigated if all of their colleagues stay late regularly. Perceptions of behavioural control concern the extent to which people feel able to perform actions or behaviours. An individual may feel it both reasonable and usual to stay late at work, yet be unable to do so because they need to leave early to meet another commitment. The behaviour is out of their hands in this case.

- The key step in the model is the formation of behavioural intention. According to the model all demonstrated behaviour flows from behavioural intention. Attitudes, subjective perceptions of social norms and perceptions of behavioural control all contribute to the formation of behavioural intentions. The pathway from intention to actual behaviour is then moderated by actual behavioural control.

The theory is elegant and provides a very flexible framework for considering the pathways from attitudes to behaviours. The value of the theory is, however, of course dependent upon the extent of empirical support. The theory of planned behaviour has given rise to a multitude of empirical studies, and some of these were included in a meta-analysis conducted by Armitage and Conner (2001). Their study showed that the theory was a good predictor of the formation of behavioural intentions and a reasonably good predictor of actual behaviour.

In applied psychology, the theory has been used to examine topics such as health-related behaviour, as well as purchasing behaviour in marketing research. Surprisingly, the theory has been applied less often in organizational research, although it is clearly relevant, and can help managers and practitioners to understand why attitudes do and do not manifest themselves in behaviour. In the case of organizational change, for example, the theory could be a useful way to understand how behavioural change might be promoted. According to the model in Figure 4.2, managers would need to consider individual attitudes to the new behaviour, social normative pressure from groups and teams in the organization, and the extent to which work was designed so that employees felt a sense of control in performing the new behaviour.

Despite the obvious utility of the theory, and good empirical support, there are some criticisms. For example, a much-disputed aspect of the model concerns perceptions of behavioural control. Ajzen (2002) attempted to clarify what 'control' actually means. He included perceptions of self-efficacy (the extent to which a person feels capable of performing an action), and locus of control (the extent to which a person believes behaviour to be attributable to internal or external constraints). However, even the most recent research remains pessimistic about the clarity of the role of control (e.g. Kaiser F.G., Schultze, P.W. and Guericke, O. (2009)). Another criticism is around the amount of variance in actual behaviour that is left unexplained by the theory. Despite its complexity, the meta-analysis of Armitage and Conner (2001) reported that 80 per cent of the variance in people's behaviour was unexplained by factors in the theory.

KEY THEME

Corporate Social Responsibility

The theory of planned behaviour and socially responsible management

The theory of planned behaviour presents a hugely practical framework for understanding people's attitudes and how they might influence their behaviour. The model has much potential in the area of corporate social responsibility (CSR) and in particular for understanding behaviour that may be problematic for organizations meeting their CSR responsibilities.

A good example of this is in the area of safety and health at work. There is a clear alignment on safety and health at work with CSR: safety at work might be argued to be an ethical and moral obligation of organizations to prevent harm to employees (see Zwetsloot and Starren, 2004). Traditionally, behavioural safety and health has been seen as an issue of putting in place sufficient controls, and a general culture and climate for safety. However, this neglects to address differences

in individual behaviour: why do some people continue to behave unsafely despite the best efforts of organizations?

The theory of planned behaviour has an obvious role to play in framing possible answers to this question. In particular, the theory is comprehensive in this respect because it enables the integration of individual factors with organizational cultural and control factors. Modelling unsafe behaviour using the theory would incorporate the formation of intentions to behave unsafely, derived from attitudes about how positive the behaviour is, how socially acceptable it is considered to be, and perceptions about how easy the behaviour is to perform. Individual differences such as personality traits around risk taking might be particularly important in regard to the formation of positive attitudes about unsafe behaviour. There are examples of applying the theory of planned behaviour to safety behaviour in the literature (e.g. Fugas, Silva and Meliá, 2012).

Using the theory to develop strategies to promote safety provides a systematic approach to addressing problems of behavioural safety. Organizations need to intervene not only to apply controls, and change social normative expectations about safety, but also to acknowledge that there may be those with particularly risky attitudes around unsafe behaviour, who may need more individualized development to change individual attitudes.

Work-Related Attitudes

The theories reviewed in this section could be applied to attitudes in any domain of life. Two important *work-related* attitudes are job satisfaction and organizational commitment, and they have been the subject of extensive research in Work and Organizational Psychology, particularly in relation to a critical management question: Are happy and satisfied workers also productive workers? There is an implicit assumption amongst many people that happy employees are also productive employees. You hear this assertion bandied about in organizations, yet most people would probably concede that they had no robust evidence for the link, only anecdotes and clichés. We will find out what the research says shortly. First though, let's think about what job satisfaction and organizational commitment actually represent.

Job satisfaction

Job satisfaction refers to a person's general feelings about their job, and more specifically the extent to which they feel positive or negative about it. Satisfaction can be considered in different ways. It may be thought of as a general attitude, reflecting overall feelings about work. It may also be considered as a composite of more specific attitudes. In Chapter 2, you saw a measure of job satisfaction (see Box 2.4), which illustrates the concept nicely. In the survey, the items all refer to satisfaction with a specific aspect of work (for example, pay, supervision, workload). Each item asks the individual to respond indicating how satisfied they feel with those aspects of their job. Job satisfaction is taken as the aggregate of those judgements.

You can see right away that the judgement is subjective. In relation to pay for example, people are not asked to comment on their satisfaction with pay relative to others doing similar jobs, only to say whether or not they are satisfied. Of course, most people's satisfaction with pay is influenced to some degree by social comparison or perceptions of fairness (e.g. McFarlin and Sweeney, 1992). These judgements fall under the heading of 'distributive justice', or the extent to which people feel that they are treated fairly in comparison with others in their organizations. However, there are also individual differences that contribute. Some people are more inclined than others to appraise aspects of their jobs positively or negatively, and this is reflected in the associations of job satisfaction with personality traits (Judge, Heller and Mount, 2002). The important factor is 'affect' or the general disposition for feeling positive or negative about things (Judge and Hulin, 1993).

Furthermore, people's satisfaction with pay might also reflect satisfaction with other aspects of work. A person might reason that their pay is low, but that there are other benefits associated with their job that mitigate the lower salary (perhaps the organization has a brilliant childcare support system for example). Satisfaction with pay in this case reflects judgements about the acceptability of pay, accounting for wider job aspects or characteristics. Taken together, this suggests a model of job satisfaction as shown in Figure 4.3, in which job satisfaction is formed from three sources: 1) personality and dispositions, 2) job characteristics, and 3) perceptions of distributive justice. Some have also added culture as an antecedent of satisfaction based on the idea that people in different cultures may be more or less inclined toward satisfaction, although this is not as clearly evidenced in the literature (e.g. Saari and Judge, 2004).

Organizational commitment

Organizational commitment is concerned with the extent to which an individual feels they have a positive relationship with their organization, or conversely, are locked into a relationship with their organization (Mowday, Porter and Steers, 1982). The concept has evolved over time, and the most effective model is that of Meyer and Allen (1991), who differentiate three forms of organizational commitment:

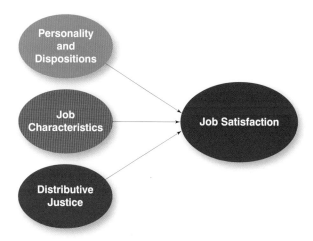

Figure 4.3   The three factors that contribute to job satisfaction

● Affective Commitment. The emotional attachment that a person feels towards their organization is referred to as affective commitment. People feel attached to their organization when the goals and values of the organization are largely consistent with their own, and when they 'buy-in' to the mission and philosophy of the organization.

● Continuance Commitment. When an individual remains in an organization simply because the costs of leaving are too great, they would be described as having high continuance commitment. This form of commitment is obviously less desirable to foster amongst employees.

● Normative Commitment. Sometimes an individual may feel dissatisfied with their job, or may think that their organization is moving in the wrong direction, yet still feel obliged to be loyal and committed, and to stay with the organization. Meyer and Allen (1991) describe this sense of moral obligation as normative commitment.

One implication of the three-component model of commitment is that each form of commitment has different antecedents. So for example, affective commitment is likely to result from a combination of work experiences and perceptions of the organization, alongside personal characteristics such as personality traits. The link between personality and commitment has been established empirically (Erdheim, Wang and Zickar, 2006), and so it seems that in a similar way to job satisfaction, some people are more predisposed than others to develop a commitment to their organization.

Continuance commitment is more likely to reflect perceptions of the viability of alternatives to employment with the organization. It could be argued that personal characteristics may also play a part in this form of commitment, because people who are more driven and ambitious are more likely to examine alternative forms of employment. Normative commitment is fostered by socialization or social experiences. These might be cultural, familial and organizational (Meyer and Allen, 1991). The sense of moral obligation developed as a result of socialization interacts with perceptions of investments made by the organization. If an individual perceives that an organization has made significant investment in them, and feels obliged to reciprocate, then normative commitment is likely to be high. These relationships are shown diagrammatically in Figure 4.4.

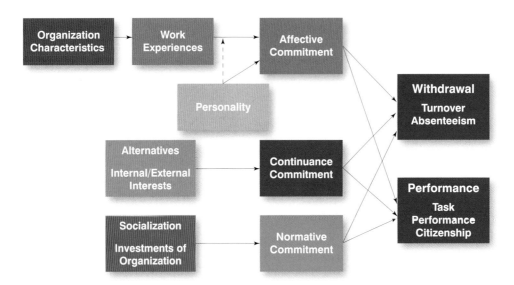

Figure 4.4   Antecedents and the effects of organizational commitment

Consequences of satisfaction and commitment

The extent to which attitudes at work are important rests heavily on their implications for behaviour in organizations. Do job satisfaction and organizational commitment have consequences for behaviour at work? The outcomes of these work-related attitudes have been considered in terms of job performance and withdrawal or counterproductive behaviours such as absence or turnover.

Job performance The relationship between job performance and job satisfaction has preoccupied managers and Work Psychologists for more than 70 years, since the publication of the Hawthorne Studies in the 1930s. Ruch, Hershauer and Wright (1976) describe the issue as the productivity puzzle, describing the 'paradoxical notion that although some happy workers are productive, there are also many happy workers who are unproductive' (p. 5). However, when one thinks in more depth about the simple idea that happy employees are productive employees, the lack of a consistent relationship is less surprising. We have already seen that the pathway from attitude to behaviour is a complex one.

However, practitioner interest in the question means that there are plenty of research studies addressing it, and subsequently, several meta-analyses since 2001 have begun to build our understanding. The first step is to understand the various forms that the relationship between job satisfaction and job performance may take. The assumption that people will perform better *because* they are happier at work is not necessarily true, and Judge, Thoresen, Bono and Patton (2001) review seven potential models:

1 Job satisfaction causes job performance. This model represents the typical implicit perspective on satisfaction and performance.

2 Job performance causes job satisfaction. Attaining high levels of performance at work is likely to result in extrinsic and intrinsic rewards, thereby fostering positive job attitudes.

3 Satisfaction and performance cause each other. A combination of effects from the first and second models give rise to a reciprocal relationship.

4 It is possible that there is no direct link between satisfaction and performance, with any observed correlation reflecting overlap with an unmeasured variable.

5 There may be no relationship between satisfaction and performance at all.

6 The relationship between performance and satisfaction may be moderated by another variable. If an individual is satisfied in their job, but lacks some of the skills required to perform it, he or she is unlikely to be productive. Job knowledge, skills, abilities and characteristics may moderate the relationship between satisfaction and performance.

7 Both satisfaction and performance could be reconceptualized to provide a better understanding of the relationship. For example, job attitudes such as satisfaction and commitment might actually reflect affectivity (the predisposition for either positive or negative emotional states), which in turn, may be related to some, but not all aspects of job performance.

Judge *et al.* (2001) tested the relationship between job satisfaction and job performance and tested a number of moderator variables. Based on 312 studies, assessing more than 54 000 participants, they found a moderate overall relationship between job satisfaction and job performance (meta-analytic correlation = 0.30). It seems that satisfied workers do tend to be higher performing workers. Longitudinal studies (where satisfaction was measured at time one and performance at time two) reported weaker associations than cross-sectional studies (r = 0.23 and 0.31 respectively). There is some support for the notion that satisfaction leads to higher job -performance. However, Harrison, Newman and Roth (2006) reported similar associations between satisfaction and performance regardless of which was assessed first, providing support for the idea that performance leads to satisfaction.

Job commitment was similarly examined by Riketta (2002). The meta-analyses of 111 studies (N = 26 344) revealed a weaker relationship with performance than was observed for satisfaction (meta-analytic correlation = 0.20). Meyer, Stanley, Herscovitch and Topolnytsky (2002) also examined commitment and performance and reported strongest associations of commitment with so-called Organizational Citizenship Behaviour (OCB; see Chapter 8). OCB represents aspects of performance that facilitate performance of core job tasks (such as cooperation with others, representing the organization positively and self-development).

Job satisfaction and organizational commitment tend to be associated with one another and this has led some investigators to combine the constructs to give an -overall job attitudes variable. Harrison *et al.* (2006) examined the association of these combined job attitudes with a very broad measure of job performance. Remarkably, the association between job performance and job attitudes in their study was 0.59, almost double the size of the correlation reported by Judge *et al.* (2001). Collectively there is enough evidence to say that employees with more positive attitudes do tend to perform better at work.

Withdrawal or counterproductive behaviour In addition to job performance, some researchers have examined the associations of commitment and satisfaction with withdrawal or counterproductive behaviour, including absence, lateness and turnover (leaving or intending to leave the organization). As would be expected, lower levels of job satisfaction and organizational commitment tend to be associated with higher levels of absence, higher frequency of lateness and stronger intentions to leave the organization (Harrison *et al.*, 2006; Tett and Meyer, 1993; Eby, Freeman, Rush and Lance, 1999; Woods, Poole and Zibarras, 2012).

Organizational consequences The studies reviewed so far relate to individual aspects of performance or behaviour, but what about outcomes for organizations? Do organizations with greater numbers of satisfied staff tend to perform better? This was the question that interested Harter, Schmidt and Hayes (2002). They examined associations between satisfaction and business unit performance, and found that units in which the members were more satisfied tended to attract higher levels of customer satisfaction, generate high profit, be more productive and experience lower turnover rates and fewer accidents. There seem to be tangible business benefits of positive attitudes at work.

Other work attitudes

Although job satisfaction and organizational commitment are the most widely researched work-related attitudes, there are three others that are worth noting:

Employee engagement Employee engagement represents the extent to which people are not only satisfied, but also enthusiastic about and actively involved with their job and organizations. People who are highly engaged tend to be passionate about their work, whereas those who are disengaged are likely to put time, but not effort or attention into their work (Robbins and Judge, 2009). Engagement is a hot topic for organizations and it seems justifiably so. Harter *et al.* (2002) reported that engagement predicted customer satisfaction, profit, productivity, turnover and accidents in the same way as job satisfaction.

Job involvement Job involvement is concerned with how invested a person feels in their job in an organization. People with higher levels of involvement tend to care more about, and believe in the value of their work.

Justice and fairness Folger and Konovsky (1989) differentiated two aspects of attitudes about fair treatment and pay in organizations. Distributive justice refers to the perceived fairness of the amounts of compensation received, and procedural justice refers to the perceived fairness of the systems and processes that are used to determine that compensation. The concept can be broadened out beyond pay, so that justice perceptions represent both perceptions of fairness of treatment, and fairness of processes and systems in organizations. We will pick up on perceptions of justice and fairness again in Chapter 5 on Motivation.

DISCUSS WITH A COLLEAGUE

Research evidence suggests that people who are more satisfied, committed and engaged at work tend to perform better at work. Discuss your own attitudes towards work and organizations and then, based on your discussions, come up with ten ways that organizations could try to improve satisfaction and commitment of employees.

Attitude Change: Persuasion and Influence

Much communication in organizations aims to be persuasive, and that often means changing people's attitudes. There is a huge literature on persuasion and attitude change in social psychology, and if these issues really interest you, then it would be worth taking a browse through some social psychology texts. The main questions of interest to people in organizations, however, are to do with the factors that contribute to attitudinal change, and some of these are discussed below:

● Major contributions to understanding the process of attitude change are captured in process models. Crano and Prislin (2006) highlight two important models; the Elaboration Likelihood Model (ELM) and Heuristic/Systematic Model (HSM), both of which have similar implications for understanding the process of attitude change. The models are based around the idea that there are two general mechanisms by which attitudes are changed. The first involves individuals evaluating arguments carefully, weighing up the content of arguments, the logic, reasoning and evidence behind the arguments and then deciding whether they are persuasive. The systematic elaboration of new information and the reasoned use of that information has been called the central route to persuasion (Petty and Cacioppo, 1986a; 1986b). Such approaches work best when the target audience is motivated to listen and understand, and when they have the ability to comprehend the evidence. When people are unmotivated or unable to think rationally about the arguments, then they revert to heuristic based processing, perhaps attending to the source of the information, their perceived credibility, or even their attractiveness (i.e. a person might reason that 'I like my manager and they are always right, so their argument must be correct'). This has been referred to as the peripheral route to persuasion (Petty and Cacioppo, 1986a; 1986b). Attitudes that are changed through the central route are typically longer lasting and stronger than those changed through the peripheral route.

● Attitude strength is an important factor in attitude change and it seems reasonable to assume that stronger attitudes are likely to be more resistant to persuasion. However, the influence of attitude strength on persuasion is more complex than this, and in part it reflects internal cognitions (thought processes) about the impact of the persuasion. When people feel that the persuasive attempt has failed outright, then the outcome is to strengthen still further the original attitude (Tormala and Petty, 2004). People are likely to reason that their attitude must surely be right to have resisted the attack of a strong message from a credible source. If the resistance to the persuasion is perceived as difficult or effortful (perhaps a person can only develop weak arguments to counter the persuasion), then the original attitude is likely to remain intact, but be weakened (Petty, Tormala and Rucker, 2004).

● Fear has always been a strategy for attitude change in the arsenal of politicians, but its effectiveness does depend on the extent to which people feel vulnerable to threat being communicated. Fear is likely to operate through the peripheral route to persuasion, although some sources report that appeals to fear might actually stimulate people to evaluate arguments more carefully, thereby promoting central processing (Das, De Wit and Stroebe, 2003). In organizations, fear can be used subtly in organizational change, by communicating the potential adverse consequences for the organization of failure to adapt to new situations. However, the use of threat to personal security (e.g. job security) could be disastrous as an attitude change strategy, and is certainly ethically questionable and likely to generate high levels of employee stress over time.

WIDER INFLUENCES ON BEHAVIOUR AT WORK

Emotion and Behaviour

In Chapter 3, we briefly introduced some concepts about emotions and their effects at work. One distinction that was made in respect of emotional reactions at work was between positive and negative trait affect, which represent broad styles of emotional reaction, or predispositions to experience either positive or negative mood states more frequently and more strongly. Trait affect is an important driver of people's experiences of positive and negative attitudes at work, but the links

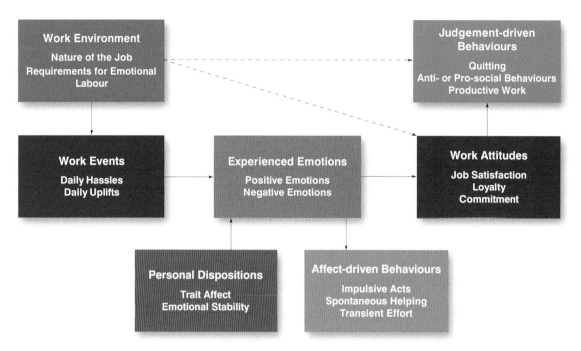

Figure 4.5   Affective Events Theory

between emotions and behaviour at work are more complex. A recent development in theory in this area has elaborated the ways in which emotional reactions to work events translate through to behaviour and attitudes. The theory is called Affective Events Theory (AET; Ashkanasy and Daus, 2002) and it is shown as a model in Figure 4.5.

The pathways highlighted in the model describe the following relationships between events and behaviour:

● The work environment acts as a context for all work-related events and characteristics of jobs and organizations determine the extent to which a person is likely to encounter events that are emotionally demanding. Job demands and the requirement for emotional labour are included in the model. Recall that emotional labour is any form of work that requires an individual to outwardly project emotions that may not really be experienced (e.g. a customer service worker who is asked to consistently project a happy exterior).

● Within the work environment, moods and emotions are affected by daily hassles and daily uplifts. You probably have a wealth of experiences that you can identify with that make you feel good or bad at work. Daily hassles serve to annoy or upset people, and their moods and emotions are influenced accordingly. Daily uplifts such as success, praise or other rewarding events improve mood and promote positive emotions.

● The crux of the model is the link between events and emotions. The theory suggests that daily work events elicit emotional reactions, either positive or negative. The intensity of those emotional reactions is regulated by personal characteristics. These include trait affect, and personality traits such as emotional stability and extraversion.

- The first set of outcome behaviours lead straight from emotional reactions and are therefore described as affect-driven behaviours. These include impulsive or spontaneous acts, and the nature of the behaviour will depend on the experienced emotion. An example of a negative affect-driven behaviour might be losing your temper or saying something that you later regret.

- The second outcome of emotional reactions is related to attitudes. Emotion and mood can positively or negatively influence attitudes like job satisfaction, organizational commitment and loyalty, and we have already considered some of the outcomes that might follow as a consequence.

- In the AET model, attitudes lead to judgement-driven behaviours, which are behaviours that result from changes in work attitudes. These will include performance related behaviours, and withdrawal behaviour such as absence and turnover.

- Dashed arrows in the model serve to recognize that not all of the effects of work environments on attitudes and behaviour act through emotional experiences, and rather job demand and characteristics have direct influences on attitudes and performance.

The AET model is a very neat framework for understanding how emotional reactions regulate the effects of events on attitudes and behaviour. How does it stand up to empirical tests though? One recent meta-analytic study used the model to examine how breaches in the 'psychological contract' were related to outcomes such as trust, job satisfaction and effectiveness (Zhao, Wayne, Glibkowski and Bravo, 2007). We consider the psychological contract in depth in Chapters 6 and 9, but briefly, it represents the unwritten set of expectations that a person has about their relationship with their employer (i.e. what they expect to give and receive at work). The findings of the study were consistent with AET. Affective or emotional reactions were an important mediator of the relationship between psychological contract breach and work outcomes. When people perceive that their employer has reneged on the deal implicit in their psychological contract, their response in terms of behavioural or attitudinal change depends on how they respond emotionally.

Perception and Behaviour

Perception represents the judgements that people make about their environments and people they encounter. They are important processes because they affect the way that people respond to others and to situations they encounter in organizations (Huczynski and Buchanan, 2007). By this reasoning, objective reality is relegated as an influence on outcomes, rather it is the perception of that reality that counts. In Work Psychology, interpersonal perception has been the focus of attention, largely because person perception is a key process in activities that involve judging or assessing other people. Activities such as selection assessment and performance appraisal require that managers and others make judgements about people at work.

People form perceptions based on a variety of cues. These include information gauged about the target, and the situation that frames the target. Information is processed by the perceiver, and is therefore filtered through their values, personality traits and emotions. People also develop shortcuts in perceptions that enable them to quickly make sense of the world around them. This idea features in Personal Construct Theory (Kelly, 1955), which proposes that people have a unique, but limited set of features that they instantly attend to when they make judgements about people. Some of the commonest perceptual shortcuts are shown in Box 4.1.

BOX 4.1

Interpersonal perceptual shortcuts

- Selective Attention. This happens when people pay attention primarily to information that they understand or are familiar with. People tend to have a bias for perceiving and remembering aspects of situations or characteristics of people that are in some way important personally. Imagine a manager listening to a presentation from their CEO, who judges the effectiveness of the speech afterwards. The process of selective attention suggests that he or she would base their judgement primarily on the points that were relevant for their area of the business, neglecting wider aspects of the presentation.

- Stereotyping. Stereotypes are mental models that people hold about others, usually based on physical features or membership of demographic groups (based on factors like gender, ethnicity, sexual orientation or lifestyle preferences).

- Halo Effect. The halo effect occurs when you perceive something positive about a person and then tend to evaluate everything about that person overly positively. This usually involves neglecting any negative information.

- Contrast Effects. This occurs when a person is judged in comparison to a recently perceived other. This is a key issue in selection, where interviewers, for example, might see groups of people one after another, each being judged in relation to the performance of the previous interviewee.

- Similar-to-me Effects. This happens when an individual perceives positively those characteristics that appear to be consistent with their own.

Attribution theories

One of the most informative aspects of research and theory in perception are attribution theories, a set of theories that aim to understand how people perceive the behaviour of others and, importantly, how they attribute cause to that behaviour. Gilbert and Malone (1995) comment on the themes in attribution theories, which are all concerned with how behaviour is attributed to internal or external forces:

> *Although [attribution] theories differ in both focus and detail, each is grounded in a common metaphor that construes the human skin as a special boundary that separates one set of causal forces from another. On the sunny side of the epidermis are the external or situational forces that press inward on the person, and on the meaty side are the internal or personal forces that exert pressure outwards.*

The fundamental attribution error (Ross, 1977) describes how people overemphasize the role of internal forces (dispositions, characteristics, personality traits) when attributing cause to the behaviour of others, when in fact, situational factors also have important influences. Moreover, Watson (1982) suggested that in comparison to causal attribution in perceptions of the behaviour of others, people tend to more strongly attribute their own behaviour to situational factors. So my perception is likely to be that I submitted a recent article manuscript late because my workload was high that month making it impossible to complete it. On the other hand, when my colleague down the hall is late in delivering manuscripts and reports, it is because they are disorganized and generally tardy about getting things done. This error in perception represents a major weakness in the way that people perceive the behaviour of others at work.

Decision-Making

A closely allied field of study to perception and judgement is decision-making or choice. People in organizations have to make decisions on a daily basis, ranging from small decisions like how to organize their working day, right through to huge decisions that might affect large groups of people inside or outside the organization. The major contributions of psychology to understanding decision-making have focused on how people choose or decide between competing options or problem solutions. You might assume that a rational approach to problem solving or decision-making is most desirable or effective in organizations. The problem-solving cycle introduced in Chapter 2 follows a logical, evidence-based process of solving problems. The choice of solution depends on the analysis of evidence relevant to the problem. However, is it reasonable to say that any human decision is ever really completely rational?

DISCUSS WITH A COLLEAGUE

Think about the last time you were disappointed or irritated by the behaviour of another person at work. At the time, why did you suppose the person behaved in the way they did? Was it down to their disposition or personality? Could there have been situational factors that drove their behaviour? What might those situational factors have been?

What might be the risks of attribution error at work? How could you avoid making biased judgements about people and their behaviour?

Many argue not, and an influential idea in decision-making research is the concept of bounded rationality, proposed by Simon (1972). In the theory of bounded rationality, human decision-makers are conceived as limited in their capacity to understand problems objectively. People appraise situations and problems based on their own limited perspectives, and Simon (1972) identifies three main limitations of people's capacity to understand problems:

- Introduction of Risk and Uncertainty: People are not good at evaluating probability and risk when making decisions and choices. Decision-making under uncertainty was the theme of Nobel Prize winning research by Kahneman and Tversky (e.g. Kahneman and Tversky, 1973; Kahneman, 2003). Their experiments suggest that a major determinant of how people weigh up risk in decisions depends on the likelihood of experiencing losses as a result of the decision. People are essentially loss averse, and are essentially much more likely to appraise risk positively if the alternative is a loss. One of the fascinating findings of Kahneman's and Tversky's research, however, is that this aversion is so powerful, that the way in which decisions are framed can influence choices, even when the net results of those choices are exactly the same. Box 4.2 illustrates this.

- Incomplete Information about Alternatives: People may be required to make decisions based on incomplete information, or assume that they have all of the information when actually they do not. This would happen in cases where people's searches for information are limited in scope meaning that they may feel they have evaluated alternatives accurately, when really they have failed to test alternatives thoroughly.

- Complexity: In many cases, a complete set of problem parameters would be so complex for people to appraise that they would simply be unable to rationally evaluate them. Rationality in this case is bounded by the limitations of people's capability to weigh up the parameters of decisions.

BOX 4.2
Loss aversion in decision-making

Here is a decision problem. There has been an outbreak of a serious virus in a small town. There is no risk of the virus spreading further afield, but after conducting investigations within the town, doctors expect that 600 residents will die from the illness. You are in charge of making a decision about what to do next, and you have to decide between two vaccination programmes to combat the virus:

Programme 1: If adopted, 400 people will definitely die.

Programme 2: If adopted, there is a one-third chance that nobody will die, but a two-thirds chance that 600 people will die.

Which would you choose?

In this situation, most people choose the risky option (Programme 2). Now consider the following two choices:

Programme 1: If adopted, 200 people will definitely be saved.

Programme 2: If adopted, there is a one-third chance that everyone will be saved, but a two-thirds chance that nobody will be saved.

When the problem is presented this way, most people opt for Programme 1, avoiding the risky choice. You will of course have noted that the two sets of options are identical, except that in the first example, the options are presented in terms of losses, and in the second, the options are presented in terms of gains.

Kahneman and Tversky (1979) used a similar scenario in their research that showed that framing of problems alters people's decisions. The key factor is that people tend to be loss averse – they take a gamble to avoid certain loss, but avoid a gamble in order to ensure certain gain.

Intuition

Are people really always striving for rationality in their decision-making, or is there a role for intuition in decisions? In organizations, people often go with their gut feeling or use intuition to make decisions. Typically, such decision-making strategies have been derided as weak or flawed, but there is some emergent literature that examines the concept of intuition and which may, in time, help to establish when intuition results in good decisions.

Intuitions have been captured in a variety of theories and research studies on decision-making, and are generally considered to represent decisions that are emotionally or affectively charged, arising through fast, non-conscious processes, in which problems are viewed holistically rather than as constituting components for analysis (Dane and Pratt, 2007; Burke and Miller, 1999).

Dane and Pratt (2007) propose a theory of intuitive decision-making, which includes some implications about when intuitive decision-making is likely to be most effective. They propose that intuition is likely to be most beneficial when:

1 Decision-makers have developed deep knowledge of the context of problems and the domain areas that frame problems. Such deep knowledge includes so-called 'mental schema' for dealing with situations. These are not merely comprised of facts, but rather of routines, ways of thinking and ways of behaving in response to particular problems.

2 Problems and the tasks associated with them are judgemental rather than intellectual. Judgemental problems are those in which outcomes are context dependent (i.e. right and wrong outcomes are subjective). For example, assume a situation in which a person is repeatedly absent from work. A manager's intuition might lead them to adopt a supportive stance, trying to help the employee and to understand the reasons for the absence. In one organization, this might be deemed effective and responsible, in another it may be viewed as weak and capitulating. The theory implies that because intuition takes account of thing like organizational values, the intuitive decision is likely to reflect, and be right for the context. Intellectual problems have objective markers of outcome success (i.e. right and wrong solutions are objective, and the same regardless of context), and in those cases, rational rather than intuitive decisions are more likely to be effective.

KEY FIGURE

Timothy A. Judge

One of the major contributors to the organizational behaviour literature is Timothy Judge. Dr Judge is interested primarily in personality, moods and emotions at work, job attitudes, leadership and careers. His work in the field is impressive because it is consistently high impact and relevant. In this chapter, we have explored his work on job satisfaction and job performance, but you will see his name peppered around this book in many key areas of Work and Organizational Psychology. He has had a prolific career, receiving

awards for distinguished contributions as an early career scientist in 1995 (from the Society for Industrial and Organizational Psychology) and as a mid-career scientist in 2001 (from the OB division of the Academy of Management).

Major features of his work include numerous meta-analytic studies on key questions in OB, and longitudinal studies examining career success. A recent study is worth highlighting, as it illustrates how longitudinal studies can reveal important things about the ways in which people develop over time in societies. The study, published in 2008, examined how core self-evaluations (see Chapter 3) relate to career success. The fascinating finding of the research suggested that people who were more self confident and self-assured were much more likely to achieve early life success, and moreover, that these early successes led to steeper success trajectories – early advantages were extended over time, explaining in part the ways that people attain extraordinary life success.

Timothy Judge has an excellent repository of his research articles available online, which is well worth browsing, as there are many similarly interesting articles in his back catalogue.

Judge, T. A. and Hurst, C. (2008). How the rich (and happy) get richer (and happier): Relationship of core self-evaluations to trajectories in attaining work success. *Journal of Applied Psychology, 93*, 849–863.

Self-regulation

Self-regulation is a process that has attracted increasing attention in the Work and Organizational Psychology research literature (Wood, 2005). In general social psychology, self-regulation is a process of self-control of behaviour. Bandura (1991) highlights three key functions underlying self-regulation:

- Self-monitoring: monitoring one's own behaviour and being able to perceive one's own actions.
- Self-judgement: forming judgements of one's own behaviour against personal standards and expectations.
- Affective self-reaction: forming affective responses about one's own behaviour, such that it is evaluated positively or negatively.

Self-regulation is therefore about actively monitoring and managing our behaviour against certain internalized standards. It does not involve external influences on behaviour, and rather represents self-imposed interventions and controls. Interestingly, Muraven and Baumeister (2000) propose that such self-control is like a muscle, and argue that self-regulation is a limited resource, use of which depletes energy or resource available for subsequent use. They also argue that like a muscle, self-control can be rested or strengthened through exercising it. Bandura (1991) also highlights the role of self-efficacy, relating to self-belief about ability to control behaviour.

In the organizational field, self-regulation is associated most frequently with the combination of the core social cognitive perspective already described, and goal setting theory (see Chapters 5 and 8). In these perspectives, self-regulation is applied to the processes of goal establishment, planning, striving to achieve goals and revision of engagement to goals (Vancouver and Day, 2005). Goals that are subject to self-regulation are necessarily internalized, and become desired states to be attained through behaviour. The self-regulatory processes here serve to monitor progress and influence behaviour and effort as a consequence.

Kanfer (2005) highlights potential applications around promoting commitment to difficult goals at work, and to providing people with competencies for perceiving and overcoming obstacles encountered in goal-directed behaviour, therefore promoting goal attainment. Recent studies have found that helping team leaders develop self-regulatory competencies improves team performance. Yeow and Martin (2013) reported this effect in a longitudinal field experiment in a business simulation context. Similarly in learning and development, Sitzmann and Johnson (2012) found that interventions designed to promote people planning their learning and development were only effective when combined with interventions to promote self-regulatory processes.

Self-regulation is a contemporary area of research, and a potentially important influence on behaviour at work. However, more work is needed to establish more clarity of the concept theoretically, and to accumulate more empirical evidence about the effects of self-regulatory processes (Wood, 2005).

SOCIAL INFLUENCES ON BEHAVIOUR

What are the effects of social context on behaviour in organizations? Research into social context and influence are rooted in social psychology, producing some of the most fascinating findings about people and their behaviour. The ideas tell us much about how factors such as group membership determine people's reactions, interactions and behaviour at work. In the final section of this chapter, we consider the social context of behaviour in organizations. The intention is not to pre-empt Part Three of this book on organizations, but rather to highlight some of the major social influences on the way that people behave in organizations.

People in Groups

In Chapter 13, we consider the differences between *groups* and *teams,* but there are some important processes that happen in groups that affect individual behaviour. Hogg and Vaughan (2008) define a group as:

> *Two or more people who share a common definition and evaluation of themselves, and behave in accordance with that definition.* (Hogg and Vaughan, 2008, p. 268.)

You can see from this definition that 'group' can be used to refer to a very wide range of different collections of individuals, including teams, bigger departments or groups in organizations, clubs or interest groups, ethnic groups, religious groups, families, friendship groups and so on.

DISCUSS WITH A COLLEAGUE   List all the groups that you consider yourself to be a member of inside and outside of work or university.

Behaviour in groups is affected by the mere fact that people are acting in groups rather than acting alone, and there are social processes that drive these changes in behaviour. One intriguing process is called social facilitation, which refers to changes in individual behaviour when others are present or observing. You will have experienced this yourself. In the presence of others, people typically raise their game slightly and perform better than they would ordinarily. There is an element of competitiveness or 'being seen to be performing well' in this effect. Allport (1920) speculated that this social facilitation of performance was down to the simple presence of others.

The performance-enhancing effects of social facilitation were elaborated further by Zajonc (1965) in drive theory. The theory predicts that the presence of others results in arousal, which in turn affects behaviour. The major difference between Drive Theory and earlier models of social facilitation is that the presence of others can serve to inhibit as well as to promote behaviour. This can be illustrated in an example. Imagine that you were required to make a short presentation on Work Psychology to a group of 100 or so peers. You are putting together the presentation and deciding what to include. You are very familiar with theories of individual differences and understand the material completely. Drive Theory suggests that because this material is well learned and understood, you will likely include it in presentation. However, you are not so confident about the history of Work Psychology, you cannot remember all of the stages and dates that are involved. Drive Theory suggests that because you perceive that you are likely to make mistakes or errors in presenting this material, you will be socially inhibited about including it in the presentation. Drive Theory provides a way of understanding when performance or behaviour is likely to be inhibited or improved by the presence of others. Two possible explanations of this effect are:

1 Evaluation Apprehension (Cottrell, 1972). In this perspective, performance is altered because people are apprehensive about how they will be evaluated by others. This means that because people desire to be evaluated positively, they fall back on well-learned or 'dominant' behavioural responses, avoiding novel responses.

2 Distraction-conflict Theory (Baron, 1986). In distraction-conflict theory, the emphasis is on attention and cognition as drivers of performance. The theory suggests that when an audience is present, people get distracted, focusing attention on both the task at hand, and the audience. As a result of diverting attention and cognition away from the task, people respond by behaving in ways that do not require much thought – in other words, well-learned dominant behaviours and responses.

Social loafing

The examples so far have examined social effects on individual behaviour. One of the special features assumed in social facilitation theories is that individuals are accountable, that is to say that others can observe their behaviour and hold them responsible for the outcome. In other words, the outcome of behaviour may be attributed to one person. You may be thinking to yourself that you have plenty of anecdotal evidence of how individuals perform less well or poorly in the presence of others. These examples (assuming you have some) are probably drawn from group-working activities, in which a group is working together on a task or activity. The effect is a real one, which has been considered by social psychologists, and termed social loafing (Latane, Williams and Harkins (1979). Social loafing occurs when people make less effort on tasks because they perceive that others are also working on them. Importantly, social loafing applies when results or outcomes of group tasks are attributable to whole groups and not individuals. People sometimes feel that they are more anonymous in a group and therefore they are less concerned with being held responsible for performance. It is a robust social effect, demonstrated across multiple studies in a meta-analysis by Karau and Williams (1993). Their study showed that in research on social loafing, 80 per cent of comparisons between individual performance and group performance showed reductions in performance in groups. It has obvious implications for organizations, where tasks and performance are almost always mobilized in groups. It highlights why it is so important for managers to understand things like performance management and effective teamworking.

Social Identity

How do social groups shape our sense of personal identity? This is the question that has motivated the development of social identity theory over the past forty years (Tajfel, 1969; Tajfel and Turner, 1979; Hogg, 2006). Social identity theory is concerned with examining group membership and intergroup relations and behaviour, from the perspective of understanding how group members see themselves in relation to their own group and other groups.

Your personal identity represents the idiosyncratic traits and individual differences that give you a sense of who you are. Your social identity on the other hand represents the way in which you perceive yourself as a result of being a member of a particular social group. You might attribute part of your identity as being defined by your nationality for example. For example 'I am resilient as is typical of the English'. Alternatively, people can derive aspects of their identity from much smaller social groups, which can include membership of organizations or teams or groups within organizations.

The very essence of social identity is the idea of the prototype that represents the typical member of a group. The prototype is a mental representation held by people about the main or dominant characteristics or features of a group member. Importantly, these perceptions are held about the groups of people by members (in-groups) and those that they are not (out-groups). The effect of thinking in prototypical ways is depersonalization (Hogg and Vaughan, 2008). This occurs when people are no longer seen as individuals in their own right, but rather simply as members of a group. Social identity becomes the only way in which others are perceived. It causes people to reinforce social identity by behaving more like their own group prototype, in order to differentiate themselves further from out-groups. Such behaviour serves to bolster or enhance our own view of ourselves.

Some of the consequences of social identity have clear relevance for organizations. One consequence is concerned with how positive people feel about their social group. If people perceive that others see their group positively, then social identity is likely to be enhanced. People like to be seen positively by others. This perception might of course depend on the values of the individual and the extent to which the social group reflects those values. These issues become particularly important when either individuals change, or social or societal contexts change. When others perceive a group negatively, the individual members, as a consequence of their social identity, are also perceived negatively. This can have a number of outcomes. The first is that individual members attempt to leave the group and find a more positive social identity elsewhere. However, this can be difficult in many cases. Take, for example, prejudiced negative evaluations of people based on their nationality or ethnicity. The alternative outcomes include bolstering in-group identities by comparison with lower status groups (i.e. finding an enemy to galvanize social cohesion) or conflict with those that perceive the in-group as negative. This is one of the major processes behind inter-group conflict.

In organizations people hold social identities based on memberships of teams or professional groups. Important aspects of individual identities are grounded in those group memberships and when people feel that those social identities are threatened in some way, they react. For managers and others in organizations, an awareness of the salience of group memberships and social identities is important, as it helps them to understand intergroup behaviour, cooperation and conflict. This can extend to informal groups as well as formal teams. You probably have your own examples of informal groups among your work or University colleagues. These can be as important, and in some cases more important, to people's sense of self than formal groups. Interventions or systems in organizations that threaten such groups can meet resistance and difficulties, and social identity theory helps us to understand why.

Work Group Diversity

One particular area of interest for organizations around social identity and its influence on people's interactions and performance at work is the issue of diversity and how to make it work in business. The word 'diversity' is most commonly taken to mean variation in ethnic or cultural background within a work group. However, diverse groups might equally be made up of people with wide differences in other characteristics such as age, disability, or individual differences such as personality traits.

Research literature offers two main perspectives on the issue of diversity and work performance (van Knippenberg, De Dreu and Homan, 2004; Williams and O'Reilly, 1998). The social categorization perspective draws on the social identity literature and proposes that people adopt different orientations to group members based on perceived similarity or dissimilarity to the self. This social categorization may lead to problematic sub-group relations, leading to conflict and lower cohesion. The information/decision-making perspective, by contrast, adopts a positive view of diversity, and proposes that diverse workgroups benefit from having a wider array of skills and backgrounds that may be drawn upon for problem solving. In challenging tasks, such groups are likely to be more innovative and creative in the way that they approach tasks. So by one perspective, diversity seems positive, yet by another, more negative.

The challenge of reconciling these two perspectives was taken on by van Knippenberg and colleagues (van Knippenberg, De Dreu and Homan, 2004), who proposed the Categorization-Elaboration Model (CEM). In the model, the two perspectives are combined with moderators of the effects of diversity based on work-group and task characteristics. The model explains that social categorization may lead to intergroup biases under certain conditions of identity threat (when people feel threatened by diversity in their group). This opens the possibility of cohesion resulting from diversity, if members of the workgroup are positively oriented towards diversity (e.g. van Dick *et al.*, 2008). Likewise, the benefits of information elaboration and generation of diverse solutions to problems are also dependent on certain conditions, specifically that the task being undertaken is sufficiently complex to require sophisticated problem solving. When tasks are simple, too many perspectives and opinions on how to carry out the task may be detrimental. Combining the two, van Knippenberg, De Dreu and Homan (2004) also theorized that conflict that may arise from intergroup bias and interaction would interfere with task-related performance and information elaboration. Therefore, the extent to which the positives of diversity in task performance are realized depends upon the nature of the task being undertaken, and the social processes occurring within the group.

The foundations of the CEM are certainly from Work and Organizational Psychology theory. Recognizing the need to integrate this more closely with the HRM research literatures in order to facilitate application of theories of diversity, Guillaume, Dawson, Priola, Sacramento, Woods, Higson, Budhwar and West (2013) reviewed both literatures and presented an integrative model of managing diversity in organizations. The model is shown in Figure 4.6. Like the CEM model, social categorization and innovation perspectives feature. However, the key additions are the management practices that influence, for example, whether diversity is perceived positively by workgroups, and therefore less likely to result in negative biases and conflict. Guillaume *et al.* (2013) examine these influences on different levels. Societal factors such as legislation and culture set the context for diversity management, and there are obvious international differences about how diversity is perceived. Societal perspectives are also changeable of course, and may evolve slowly, or change rapidly in response to significant local or world events.

The societal context influences how organizations respond, and top management are responsible for developing organizational policy and procedures around diversity management. Top management beliefs about diversity are influential at this stage. Moving to more operational levels, diversity management then requires the implementation of policy and procedure, and Guillaume *et al.* (2013) highlight the importance of managers and leaders creating a climate in which individual differences are integrated, equitable employment practices are applied, and decisions are taken inclusively. These practices in combination facilitate the individual psychological factors that enable diversity to lead to positive innovation, effectiveness, and well-being.

The modelling of multiple influences on the outcomes of diversity at work challenges the simple assumption that diversity is always positive. Rather, these models show that obtaining the benefits of diversity requires careful awareness and management of the factors that contribute to those positive outcomes.

Conformity

Conformity is a classical concept in social psychology, and the most famous experiments on conformity were conducted by Solomon Asch (1952; 1956). There is some excellent video footage of the experiments on the web (search Asch conformity on YouTube or similar) and this really gives a feel for the experiments. They were designed to test whether group pressure would lead individuals to conform in a very straightforward task, which involved judging the length of lines.

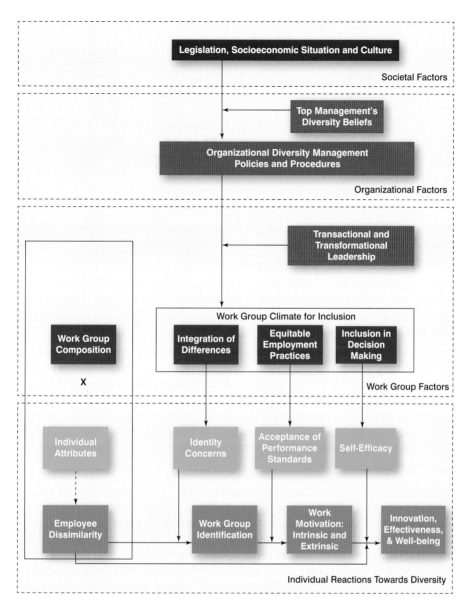

Figure 4.6 A model of managing diversity in organizations.

Participants were presented with four lines as shown in Figure 4.7. All they had to do was say which of the comparison lines was the same as the standard line. In a control experiment, Asch recorded that out of 37 participants, 35 made no errors at all on the task, one person made one error and one person made two. In sum this equates to 0.7 per cent errors.

In the experiment, the participant was placed in a line of confederates. The confederates had been instructed to give consistent, but incorrect answers on 12 out of 18 trials. The participant heard six people give the incorrect response, and then had to call out their answer. Asch found that compared with 95 per cent in the control, only 25 per cent of participants made no errors at all in the task, and that overall errors rose to 37 per cent.

Figure 4.7   Example trial in Asch's experiment
Participants were asked which of the comparison lines was identical in length to the standard lines.

The findings showed that the majority of participants gave incorrect answers in the task, even though those answers were obviously incorrect. The distortion of their judgement can be viewed on two levels, and both are relevant in organizations:

1 Distortion of perception. In this distortion, people genuinely believe that the group are correct. This might be seen in organizations where a person listens to the views of a group or team, and although incongruent with their views, they believe that the weight of consensus must mean that the group view is true.

2 Distortion of response. This represents the alteration of response due to normative pressure (e.g. Van Avermaet, 2001), but not belief. An example at work might be if a person listened to views of colleagues during a team meeting, all of whom agreed with one another. They might go along with the group to avoid the discomfort of disagreeing, even though deep down, their view had not changed. Such conformity could be damaging in organizations, as people may be inclined to agree in public, but privately continue to behave in ways that are inconsistent with the needs or objectives of the organization. Alternatively, they may simply avoid voicing dissent with group decisions.

Additional conditions were added in Asch's experiments to explore potential moderators. For example, conformity was reduced when one of the confederates gave the correct answer, acting as an ally for the participant. Likewise, conformity was reduced when participants were asked to privately write their answers rather than publicly announce them. The conformity experiments have been replicated on several occasions, with similar results evident in the 1980s (e.g. Vine, 1981) and 1990s (e.g. Abrams, Wetherell, Cochrane, Hogg and Turner, 1990: Neto, 1995) challenging the assumption that levels of conformity reflect the particular historical context of the Asch experiments. Critical perspectives on the findings are apparent however (e.g. Hodges and Geyer, 2006), with a significant criticism being that the experimental situation was very peculiar and the findings may not therefore generalize to everyday situations. Nevertheless, the paradigm is an enduring one, and is certainly informative in respect of why people conform to group pressure in organizations. The role of culture in conformity is explored in the Key Themes Box for this chapter.

Obedience to Authority

A similarly fascinating set of studies of social influence on behaviour were those of Stanley Milgram in the 1960s and 1970s (Milgram, 1963; 1965; 1974). As with the experiments of Asch, you can watch these on video, and replications and the originals can be accessed online if you search for them. Milgram was interested in why regular people could bring themselves to commit atrocities during war. His questions related particularly to the Holocaust, but could similarly be applied to the behaviour of American soldiers at Abu Ghraib prison in Iraq, and at Guantanamo Bay. His question was whether people who commit terrible atrocities are evil, or just obedient. In other words, would regular people in the general population obey authority if instructed to cause harm to others?

The experiment involved two confederates and a participant. One confederate played the role of the experimenter, who was dressed in a white coat with clipboard, and who coordinated the experiment. The participant was informed that the experiment was about punishment on learning. In a faked random allocation, they were assigned the role of teacher, and a second confederate (playing the role of a second participant) was assigned the role of learner. The participant watched the learner being strapped into a chair with electrodes placed on their arms. They were then taken away to another room, where they sat down in front of a machine that administered electric shocks from 15V up to 450V in a series of stages. The highest levels were even labelled as 'Severe Shock' or 'XXX'. The participants themselves were given a shock of 45V to gauge the feeling of the shock. They were asked to read out a series of memory questions, and to administer electric shocks to the learner if they answered incorrectly, increasing the voltage each time an incorrect answer was given. Of course, no electric shocks were administered, but the participants were played recordings of the learner crying out in pain, asking for the experiment to stop, and even complaining of a heart condition. If the participant objected, the experimenter simply said that the experiment required that they continue, or that they must continue with the experiment.

The startling finding was that contrary to expectation, 62.5 per cent of the participants continued right up to the highest shock level, even after hearing the learner in obvious pain. Subsequent manipulations demonstrated that the influential factor was the authority figure insisting that the experiment continue. Without threatening sanctions or punishment to the participant, the simple insistence of the experimenter caused the majority of participants to administer lethal electric shocks to another person, who was obviously in discomfort. Ah, you may say, but that was then, surely now people are far too independent minded to obey such authority. Burger (2009) reported a replication of Milgram conducted in 2006, and the findings were near identical. The majority of people in the replication obeyed and continued to administer harmful electric shocks. The findings of these studies tell us much about why people carry out appalling behaviour when instructed to do so by an authority figure.

What are the implications of these findings for organizations though? Quite simply, they tell us about the role of leaders and managers in organizations, who hold positions of authority. At a basic level, they show how the obedience to authority keeps organizational hierarchies intact and leads people to obey instructions from managers and leaders. When you think about it harder though, there are implications for understanding unethical behaviour in organizations. Are people who work for phamaceutical companies all evil, cure-withholding mercenaries? Unlikely, but they might obediently make decisions that cause problems for people who need access to drugs in the poorest nations. Are oil and gas engineers all careless, callous polluters, exploiting the world's resources and the people who live amongst them? No, but the vast majority will obey authority when asked to make decisions about, or contribute to activities that cause damage or harm.

The bottom line is that organizational behaviour results from more than just individual factors. Social influences such as social facilitation, social identity, conformity and obedience have important effects on how people behave at work.

KEY THEME

Globalization and Cross-cultural Perspectives

Social psychological phenomena like conformity and obedience must be viewed as nested within particular cultures. Culturally influenced values are important determinants of the ways in which people react to others in social situations. These influences have been examined by Bond and Smith (1996) in relation to conformity. Their meta-analysis aimed to test the popular stereotypical assumption that some cultures are more submissive or conforming than others. They drew on the cultural values research of Hofstede (1980), Schwartz (1994) and Trompenaars (1993), focus-ing on the well-defined differences in cultures on the collectivistic individualistic continuum. In individu-alistic cultures, people are assumed to form a sense of identity that is independent of social groups, rather reflecting their own concerns and achievements. In collectivist cultures by contrast, self and identity are closely related to group or cultural identity. In the study, countries such as US and UK represented individualistic cultures, and countries such as Brazil and Hong Kong repre-sented collectivist cultures.

In the meta-analysis, Bond and Smith (1996) examined how culture-influenced conformity rates in replications of the Asch experiment conducted in the different countries. The findings showed that culture was influential, with collectivist cultures gen-erally demonstrating higher conformity than indivi-dualistic cultures.

There is an implication of this finding for global working, particularly around the working styles of expatriate workers travelling to new cultures. Non-conformity might be viewed differently by people in organizations in collectivist cultures compared to those in individualistic cultures. Moreover, those in collectivist cultures may be less likely to object or disagree with others' views. This could mean that new ideas or innovation could be stifled in such organizations, highlighting the importance of systems and social supports to help people improve their own areas of work with-out feeling that they going against their peers or managers.

SUMMARY

The complexities of behaviour at work have been examined from numerous perspectives by Work and Organizational Psychologists, and researchers in management and organizational behaviour, their interest sustained and promoted because individual behaviour and performance affect organizational effectiveness and productivity, and well-being and satisfaction at work.

Basic management influences on behaviour are explored in the behaviour modification literature, which draws heavily on behaviourism. Key processes in this perspective are social learning (through observation of behaviour of others), and reinforcement of behaviour. Reinforcement involves applying strategies such as reward and punishment to manipulate and control employee behaviour.

The link between attitudes and behaviour is a key area of research in social psychology, with obvious implications for organizations. The theory of planned behaviour explains how attitudes lead to behaviour, and the mechanisms that promote or inhibit the translation of attitude to intention, and intention to behaviour. Key attitudes at work include job satisfaction and organizational commitment. Research evidence reviewed in this chapter suggests that people who are satisfied and committed at work do tend to perform better, although the relationship between positive attitudes and performance is probably more complex than is usually supposed. There is evidence that higher satisfaction is also related to better outcomes at the level of groups, and to fewer withdrawal behaviours (e.g. lower frequency of absence from work).

Wider individual influences on behaviour include emotion and perception. Emotional reactions to the daily hassles and uplifts at work influence the way that people react and respond. The Affective Events Theory suggests that emotions can lead to behaviour in two ways. Spontaneous or impulsive behaviour results directly from emotions, judgement-driven behaviour results from formation or alteration of attitudes. Perceptions of the work environment, and particularly of people at work, are influential in behaviour and decision-making. Attribution theories tell us how people tend to incorrectly judge the causes of the behaviour of others, and research on decision–making shows how people appraise risk, and use intuition to make decisions and solve problems at work. Into this mixture of influences we can add self-management of behaviour (referred to as self-regulation), in which people monitor and manage their own behaviour.

Alongside individual influences on behaviour are social influences that come from the group and social context of work in organizations. Important social contextual processes such as social facilitation and social loafing influence individual behaviour. Decisions and behaviour are also affected by social pressure, as demonstrated by classic experiments in social psychology on conformity and obedience. Social context also gives rise to the formation of social identity, and theory in this area helps to explain how people perceive different groups at work, and how prejudice, conflict and cooperation arise between different groups. These issues have clear implications for managing diversity at work, and recent research and theory has expanded understanding beyond social factors, to more complex interactions of task performance, problem solving and HRM factors.

DISCUSSION QUESTIONS

1 Looking back at your experiences of work and education, what are the ways in which your behaviour was modified or influenced by reinforcement interventions?

2 This question involves some reflective thought. Can you think of an attitude that you held at work or university that you either did or did not act on? Use the theory of planned behaviour to explain why your attitude did or did not lead to behaviour.

3 Which form of organizational commitment do you think is commonest among people at work in your country currently? Why?

4 Are affect-driven behaviours always to be discouraged at work? Should people always suppress behaviour resulting from emotion rather than judgement?

5 How have your perceptual biases led you to make assumptions about people this week?

6 Think of a recent difficult decision you had to make. Use theories of decision-making to help explain the decision you made.

7 How could a manager use research on social influences on behaviour to more effectively manage a team?

APPLY IT

1 Practise using non-monetary reinforcement with your team. The recent research literature highlights social recognition and feedback as key contemporary reinforcers, so use these more regularly with your staff.

2 Identify an issue you are facing at work that may have some attitudinal factors involved. Analyze the problem using the theory of planned behaviour – what does it tell you about how behaviour might be linked to attitudes? Use your analysis to develop a solution to the problem.

3 Consider conducting an audit of job satisfaction, commitment and engagement among staff in your organization. You may want to find a work and organizational psychologist to help you with this. Use the information to try to identify management and HR areas that you could improve to promote more positive attitudes, and then follow-up to check the impact.

4 Reflect on an incident at work where you did something in haste or in the 'heat of the moment'. Such behaviour is generally 'affect-driven' in Affective Events Theory. Use the theory to try to understand what led you to behave in that way, the consequences, and importantly, how you could be mindful of such situations in the future, so that you act differently.

5 Practise enhancing your self-regulation around achieving goals and objectives at work. The literature on self regulation suggests that key self-regulatory behaviour involves establishing an objective for yourself, planning its achievement, monitoring your progress towards it, and adapting your approach to meet it. Set yourself one objective to achieve in the next three weeks, and set about working on it.

6 Critically review the way that you manage diversity in your team based on the models and literature reviewed in this chapter. Come up with four ways in which you could improve what you do so that you develop greater social cohesion, and incorporate a more diverse set of perspectives and greater information in problem solving.

WEB ACTIVITY

The Best Place to Work

Watch the video clip 'CNN – SAS Named #1 in Best Companies to Work For' on **www.youtube.com** or by following the link in the digital resources online and discuss the questions below.

1 What specific elements of the video do you think have contributed to SAS being voted as the best place to work?

2 How might these elements impact on the work-related attitudes of SAS employees?

3 How might more positive work-related attitudes impact on job performance at SAS?

Leadership and Diversity

Read the article 'Does a lack of diversity among business leaders hinder innovation?' by Sylvia Ann Hewlett, Melinda Marshall and Laura Sherbin and published by *The Guardian* October 2013, by navigating to it online (see below) or by following the link in the digital resources online and discuss the questions below.

www.theguardian.com – search for 'Does a lack of diversity among business leaders hinder innovation?'

1 How could research and theory help to elaborate further on the ideas in this article?

2 What are some of the challenges of managing diverse teams at work?

3 What recommendations could you give to an organization that was aiming to increase diversity?

FURTHER READING

Hogg, M.A. and Vaughan, G.M. (2008). *Social Psychology*. Essex: Pearson Education Limited.

Ashkanasy, N.M. and Daus, C.S. (2002). Emotion in the workplace: The new challenge for managers. *Academy of Management Executive, 16,* 76–86.

Robbins, S.P. and Judge, T.A. (2009). *Organizational Behavior (Pearson International Edition)*. London: Pearson/Prentice-Hall.

Judge, T.A., Thoresen, C.J., Bono, J.E. and Patton, G.K. (2001). The job satisfaction–job performance relationship: A qualitative and quantitative review. *Psychological Bulletin, 127,* 376–407.

Ajzen, I. (2005). *Attitudes, Personality and Behaviour*. Berkshire: Open University Press.

REFERENCES

Abrams, D., Wetherell, M., Cochrane, S., Hogg, M.A. and Turner, J.C. (1990). Knowing what to think by knowing who you are: Self categorization and the nature of norm formation, conformity and group polarization. *British Journal of Social Psychology, 29,* 97–119.

Ajzen, I. (1988). *Attitudes, personality and behaviour*. Chicago: Dorsey.

Ajzen, I. (1991). The theory of planned behaviour. *Organizational Behaviour and Human Decision Processes, 50,* 179–211.

Ajzen, I. (2002). Perceived behavioural control, self-efficacy, locus of control and the theory of planned behaviour. *Journal of Applied Social Psychology, 32,* 665–683.

Ajzen, I. and Fishbein, M. (1977). Attitude–behaviour relations: A theoretical analysis and review of empirical research. *Psychological Bulletin, 84,* 888–918.

Ajzen, I. and Fishbein, M. (1980). *Understanding attitudes and predicting social behaviour*. Englewood-Cliffs, NJ: Prentice-Hall.

Ajzen, I. and Fishbein, M. (2005). The influence of attitudes on behaviour. See Albarracín *et al.* (2005), pp. 173–221.

Allport, F.H. (1920). The influence of the group upon association and thought. *Journal of Experimental Psychology, 3(3),* 159.

Armitage, C.J. and Conner, M. (2001). Efficacy of the theory of planned behaviour: A meta-analytic review. *British Journal of Social Psychology, 40,* 471–499.

Asch, S.E. (1952). *Social psychology*. Englewood Cliffs, NJ: Prentice-Hall.

Asch, S.E. (1956). Studies of independence and conformity. A minority of one against a unanimous majority. *Psychological Monographs, 70(9)*, 416.

Ashkanasy, N.M. and Daus, C.S. (2002). Emotion in the workplace: The new challenge for managers. *Academy of Management Executive, 16*, 76–86.

Bandura, A. (1977). *Social learning theory*. Englewood Cliffs, NJ: Prentice Hall.

Bandura, A. (1986). *Social foundations of thought and action*. Englewood Cliffs, NJ: Prentice Hall.

Bandura, A. (1991). Social cognitive theory of self-regulation. *Organizational behavior and human decision processes, 50(2)*, 248–287.

Baron, R.S. (1986). Distraction-conflict theory: Progress and problems. In L. Berkowitz (ed.) *Advances in Experimental Social Psychology* (Vol. 20, pp. 1–40). New York: Academic Press.

Bem, D.J. (1967). Self perception: An alternative interpretation of cognitive dissonance phenomena. *Psychological Review, 74(3)*, 183–200.

Bond, R. and Smith, P.B. (1996). Culture and Conformity: A Meta-Analysis of Studies Using Asch's (1952b, 1956) Line Judgement Task. *Psychological Bulletin, 119(1)*, 111–137.

Breckler, S.J. (1984). Empirical validation of affect, behaviour and cognition as distinct components of attitude. *Journal of Personality and Social Psychology, 47*, 1191–1205.

Burger, J.M. (2009). Replicating Milgram: Would People Still Obey Today? *American Psychologist, 64(1)*, 1–11.

Burke, L.A. and Miller, M.K. (1999). Taking the mystery out of intuitive decision-making. *Academy of Management Executive, 13(4)*, 91–99.

Cervone, D. and Shoda, Y. (eds.) (1999). *The Coherence of Personality: Social-cognitive Bases of Consistency, Variability and Organization*. New York: Guilford Press.

Cottrell, N.B. (1972). Social facilitation. In C. McClintock (ed.), *Experimental social psychology*. New York: Holt, Rinehart and Winston.

Crano, W.D. and Prislin, R. (2006). Attitudes and persuasion. *Annual Review of Psychology, 57*, 345–374.

Dane, E. and Pratt, M.G. (2007). Exploring intuition and its role in managerial decision-making. *Academy of Management Review, 32(1)*, 33–54.

Das, E.H.H., De Wit, J.B.F. and Stroebe, W. (2003). Fear appeals motivate acceptance of action recommendations: evidence for a positive bias in the processing of persuasive messages. *Personality and Social Psychology Bulletin, 29*, 650–664.

Eby, L.T., Freeman, D.M., Rush, M.C. and Lance, C.E. (1999). Motivational bases of affective organizational commitment: A partial test of an integrative theoretical model. *Journal of Occupational and Organisational Psychology, 72*, 463–448.

Elliot, A.J. and Devine, P.G. (1994). On the motivational nature of cognitive dissonance: Dissonance as psychological discomfort. *Journal* of *Personality and Social Psychology, 67*, 382–394.

Erdheim, J., Wang, M. and Zickar, M.J. (2006). Linking the big five personality constructs to organizational commitment. *Personality and Individual Differences, 41*, 959–970.

Festinger, L. (1957). *A theory of cognitive dissonance*. Stanford: Stanford University Press.

Folger, R. and Konovsky, M.A. (1989). Effects of procedural and distributive justice on reactions to pay raise decisions. *Academy of Management Journal, 32*, 115–130.

Fugas, C.S., Silva, S.A. and Meliá, J.L. (2012). Another look at safety climate and safety behavior: Deepening the cognitive and social mediator mechanisms. *Accident Analysis & Prevention, 45*, 468–477.

Gilbert, D.T. and Malone, P.S. (1995). The Correspondence Bias. *Psychological Bulletin, 117(1)*, 21–38.

Glasman, L.R. and Albarracín, D. (2005). Forming Attitudes That Predict Future Behavior: A Meta-Analysis of the Attitude–Behavior Relation. *Psychological Bulletin, 132(5)*, 778–822.

Guillaume, Y.R., Dawson, J.F., Priola, V., Sacramento, C.A., Woods, S.A., Higson, H.E., Budhwar, P.S. and West, M.A. (2014). Managing diversity in organizations: An integrative model and agenda for future research. *European Journal of Work and Organizational Psychology* (ahead-of-print), 1–20.

Harmon-Jones, E. and Mills, J. (1999). An introduction to cognitive dissonance theory and an overview of current perspectives on the theory. In E. Harmon-Jones and J. Mills (eds.), *Cognitive dissonance: Progress on a pivotal theory in social psychology* (pp. 3–21). Washington, D.C: American Psychological Association.

Harrison, D.A., Newman, D.A. and Roth, P.L. (2006). How important are job attitudes? Meta-analytic comparisons of integrative behavioural outcomes and time sequences. *Academy of Management Journal, 49(2)*, 305–325.

Harter, J.K., Schmidt, F.L. and Hayes, T.L. (2002). Business-Unit-Level Relationship Between Employee Satisfaction, Employee Engagement and Business Outcomes: A Meta-Analysis. *Journal of Applied Psychology, 87(2)*, 268–279.

Hodges, B.H. and Geyer, A.L. (2006). A Nonconformist Account of the Asch Experiments: Values,

Pragmatics and Moral Dilemmas. *Personality and Social Psychology Review, 10(1),* 2–19.

Hofstede, G. (1980). *Cultures consequences: International differences in work-related values.* Beverly Hills, CA: Sage.

Hogg, M.A. (2006). Social identity theory. In P.J. Burke (ed.) *Contemporary Social Psychological Theories* pp. 111–136. Paulo Alto, CA: Stanford University Press.

Hogg, M.A. and Vaughan, G.M. (2008). *Social Psychology.* Essex: Pearson Education Limited.

Huczynski, A. and Buchanan, D.A. (2007). *Organisational Behaviour: An introductory text.* Essex: Pearson Education Limited.

Ilgen, D.R. and Klein, H.J. (1988). Organizational Behaviour. *Annual Review of Psychology, 40,* 327–351.

Judge, T.A., Heller, D. and Mount, M.K. (2002). Five-factor model of personality and job satisfaction: A meta-analysis. *Journal of Applied Psychology, 87,* 530–541.

Judge, T.A. and Hulin, C.L. (1993). Job-satisfaction as a reflection of disposition: A multiple-source causal analysis. *Organizational Behaviour and Human Decision Processes, 56,* 388–421.

Judge, T.A., Thoresen, C.J., Bono, J.E. and Patton, G.K. (2001). The job satisfaction–job performance relationship: A qualitative and quantitative review. *Psychological Bulletin, 127,* 376–407.

Kahneman, D. (2003). A perspective on judgement and choice. *American Psychologist, 58,* 697–720.

Kahneman, D. and Tversky, A. (1973). On the psychology of prediction. *Psychological Review, 80,* 237–251.

Kahneman, D. and Tversky, A. (1979). Prospect theory: An analysis of decisions under risk. *Econometrica, 47,* 263–291.

Kaiser, F.G., Schultze, P.W. and Guericke, O. (2009). The Attitude–Behaviour Relationship: A Test of Three Models of the Moderating Role of Behavioural Difficulty. *Journal of Applied Social Psychology, 39(1),* 186–207.

Kanfer, R. (2005). Self-Regulation Research in Work and I/O Psychology. *Applied Psychology, 54(2),* 186–191.

Karau, S.J. and Williams, K.D. (1993). Social loafing: A meta-analytic review and theoretical integration. *Journal of Personality and Social Psychology, 65(4),* 681–706.

Kelly, G.A. (1955). *The Psychology of Personal Constructs.* New York: Norton.

Komaki, J., Coombs, T. and Schepman, S. (1996). Motivational implications of reinforcement theory.

In R.M. Steers, L.W. Porter and G.A. Bigley (eds.), *Motivation and leadership at work* (pp. 34–52). New York: McGraw-Hill.

Latane, B., Williams, K. and Harkins, S. (1979). Many hands make light work: The causes and consequences of Social Loafing. *Journal of Personality and Social Psychology, 37,* 822–832.

Luthans, F. and Stajkovic, A.D. (1999). Reinforce (not necessarily pay) for performance. *Academy of Management Executive, 13,* 49–57.

McFarlin, D.B. and Sweeney, P.D. (1992). Distributive and procedural justice as predictors of satisfaction with personal and organizational outcomes. *Academy of Management Journal, 35(3),* 626–637.

Meyer, J.P. and Allen, N.J. (1991). A three-component conceptualization of organizational commitment. *Human Resource Management Review, 1,* 61–89.

Meyer, J.P., Stanley, D.J., Herscovitch, L. and Topolnytsky, L. (2002). Affective, continuance and normative commitment to the organization: A meta-analysis of antecedents, correlates and consequences. *Journal of Vocational Behavior, 61,* 20–52.

Milgram, S. (1963). Behavioural study of obedience. *Journal of Abnormal and Social Psychology, 67,* 371–378.

Milgram, S. (1965). Some conditions of obedience and disobedience to authority. *Human Relations, 18,* 57–76.

Milgram, S. (1974). *Obedience to authority: An experimental view.* New York: Harper and Row.

Mowday, R.T., Porter, L.W. and Steers, R.M. (1982). *Employee-organization linkages. The psychology of commitment, absenteeism and turnover.* New York: Academic Press.

Mowday, R.T. and Sutton, R.I. (1993). Organizational Behaviour: Linking Individuals and Groups to Organizational Contexts. *Annual Review of Psychology, 44,* 195–229.

Muraven, M. and Baumeister, R.F. (2000). Self-regulation and depletion of limited resources: Does self-control resemble a muscle?. *Psychological bulletin, 126(2),* 247.

Neto, F. (1995). Conformity and independence revisited. *Social Behavior and Personality, 23,* 217–222.

Petty, R.E. and Cacioppo, J.T. (1986). The elaboration likelihood model of persuasion. In L. Berkowitz (ed.), *Advances in experimental social psychology* (Vol. 19, pp. 123–205). New York: Academic Press.

Petty, R.E., Tormala, Z.L. and Rucker, D.D. (2004). Resisting persuasion by counterarguing: an attitude strength perspective. See Jost *et al.* (2004), pp. 37–51.

Riketta, M. (2002). Attitudinal organizational commitment and job performance: A meta-analysis. *Journal of Organizational Behavior, 23,* 257–266.

Robbins, S.P. and Judge, T.A. (2009). *Organizational Behaviour (Pearson International Edition).* London: Pearson/Prentice-Hall.

Ross, L. (1977). The intuitive psychologist and his shortcomings. In L. Berkowitz (ed.), *Advances in experimental social psychology* (Vol. 10, pp. 173–220). San Diego, CA: Academic Press.

Ruch, W.A., Hershauer, J.C. and Wright, R.G. (1976). Toward solving the productivity puzzle: worker correlates to performance. *Human Resource Management, 15,* p. 2–6.

Saari, L.M. and Judge, T.A. (2004). Employee attitudes and job satisfaction. *Human Resource Management, 43(4),* 395–407.

Schneider B. (1985). Organizational behaviour. *Annual Review of Psychology, 36,* 573–611.

Schwartz, S.H. (1994). Cultural dimensions of values: Towards an understanding of national differences. In U. Kim, H.C. Triandis, C. Kagitcibasi, S.C. Choi, and G.Yoon (eds.), *Individualism and collectivism: Theory, method and applications* (pp. 85–119). Thousand Oaks, CA: Sage.

Simon, H.A. (1972). Theories of bounded rationality. In C.B. McGuire and R. Radner (eds.) *Decisions and Organization: A Volume in Honor of Jacob Marschak.* (pp. 161–76). London: North-Holland Publishing Company.

Sitzmann, T. and Johnson, S. K. (2012). The best laid plans: Examining the conditions under which a planning intervention improves learning and reduces attrition. *Journal of Applied Psychology, 97(5),* 967.

Stajkovic, A.D. and Luthans, F. (2003). Behavioural management and task performance in organisations: conceptual background, meta-analysis and test of alternative models. *Personnel Psychology, 56,* 155–194.

Tajfel, H. (1969). Social and cultural factors in perception. In G. Lindzey and E. Aronson (eds.) *Handbook of Social Psychology* (Vol. 3, pp. 315–394). Reading, MA: Addison-Wesley.

Tajfel, H. and Turner, J.C. (1979). An integrative theory is intergroup conflict. In W.G. Austin and S. Worchel (eds.) *The Social Psychology of Intergroup Relations* (pp. 33–47). Monterey, CA: Brooks/Cole.

Tett, R.P. and Meyer, J.P. (1993). Job satisfaction, organizational commitment, turnover intention and turnover: A path analysis based on meta-analytic findings. *Personnel Psychology, 46,* 259–293.

Tormala, Z.L. and Petty, R. (2004). Resistance to persuasion and attitude certainty: the moderating role of elaboration. *Personality and Social Psychology Bulletin, 30,* 1446–1457.

Trompenaars, F. (1993). *Riding the waves of culture.* London: Economist Books.

Van Avermaet, E. (2001). Social influence in small groups. In M. Hewstone and W. Stroebe (eds.), *Introduction to social psychology* (3rd ed., pp. 403–443). Oxford, England: Basil Blackwell.

Van Dick, R., Van Knippenberg, D., Hägele, S., Guillaume, Y.R. and Brodbeck, F.C. (2008). Group diversity and group identification: The moderating role of diversity beliefs. *Human Relations, 61(10),* 1463–1492.

Van Knippenberg, D., De Dreu, C.K. and Homan, A.C. (2004). Work group diversity and group performance: an integrative model and research agenda. *Journal of applied psychology, 89(6),* 1008.

Vancouver, J.B. and Day, D.V. (2005). Industrial and organisation research on self-regulation: from constructs to applications. *Applied Psychology, 54(2),* 155–185.

Vine, I. (1981). [Letter to the editor]. *Bulletin of the British Psychological Society, 34,* 145.

Vroom, V.H. (1964). *Work and motivation.* New York: John Wiley and Sons.

Watson, D. (1982). The actor and the observer: How are the perceptions of causality divergent? *Psychological Bulletin, 92,* 682–700.

Williams, K. and O'Reilly, C.A. (1998). Demography and Diversity in Organizations, in *Research in Organizational Behavior,* pp. 77–140.

Wood, R. (2005). New Frontiers for Self-Regulation Research in IO Psychology. *Applied Psychology, 54(2),* 192–198.

Woods, S.A., Poole, R. and Zibarras, L.D. (2012). Employee Absence and Organizational Commitment. *Journal of Personnel Psychology, 11(4),* 199–203.

Yeow, J. and Martin, R. (2013). The role of self-regulation in developing leaders: A longitudinal field experiment. *The Leadership Quarterly.*

Zajonc, R.B. (1965). Social facilitation. *Science, 149,* 269–274.

Zhao, H., Wayne, S.J., Glibkowski, B. and Bravo, J. (2007). The impact of psychological contract breach on work-related outcomes: A meta-analysis. *Personnel Psychology, 60,* 647–680.

Zwetsloot, G. and Starren, A. (2004). *Corporate social responsibility and safety and health at work.* European Agency for Safety and Health at Work. Luxembourg: Office for Official Publications of the European Communities.

CHAPTER 5

MOTIVATION AT WORK

The classic BBC comedy 'The Office', written by Ricky Gervais and Stephen Merchant, is a wonderful satirical take on modern management and office working culture. I believe that it should be required viewing for all aspiring managers. Although the enduring storyline of 'The Office' centres on two members of staff in the company, it is the cringe-worthy behaviour and actions of Wernham Hogg Regional Manager, David Brent, that stand out as a highlight of the show, providing a mine of observational opportunity to those interested in the psychology of work, organizations and management.

On the surface, Brent is a hapless manager, self-important and self-interested. However, when you actually look at his behaviour towards his staff more closely, you quickly see a theme. The vast majority of what he does is his way of trying to motivate his staff. Somewhere along the line, he has picked up what he thinks are the cornerstones of motivation – flattery, encouragement, inspiration through the media of comedy and charity work – and he applies them in spades, even to the point of presenting a short lecture on motivation techniques, rounded off with Tina Turner's 'Simply the Best'.

All managers know implicitly that part of their job is about motivating staff, but I wonder how many are like David Brent in that they know what is required, but then use only ill-judged guesswork, cliché and intuition to deliver it. It is unnecessary. Motivation theories in the research literature are amongst the most varied and well defined of any area of Work and Organizational Psychology (Latham and Pinder, 2005). This chapter is about motivation work, how to understand it and how to foster it in organizations. The chapter will consider what motivates people, how and why.

A FRAMEWORK FOR MOTIVATION THEORIES

One appealing feature of motivation theories in the Work and Organizational Psychology is their diversity. Work motivation has been considered from a number of different perspectives and rather than being in competition with one another, they can be seen as complementary, each offering a slightly different insight about the concept of motivation at work. In this chapter, we examine five perspectives, grouping similar theories together according to the themes within them. Collectively, these perspectives consider how people are motivated:

- To satisfy needs.
- By personal traits.
- In response to cognition of their work environment (i.e. the way people think about their work).
- When they feel fairly treated at work.
- By characteristics of their jobs.

There are plenty of general definitions of motivation, but the two below capture the essence effectively:

1 'A set of energetic forces that originate both within as well as beyond an individual's being to initiate work-related behaviour and to determine its form, direction, intensity and duration'. (Pinder 1998, p. 11)
2 'The processes that account for an individual's intensity, direction and persistence of effort toward attaining a goal'. (Robbins and Judge, 2009, p. 209)

Taking these two definitions together, you can see that the study of work motivation is concerned with why people initiate behaviour and effort at work, and the processes that determine its intensity, direction towards goals and maintenance over time. In short, how can we account for the reasons why people are motivated to attain goals at work, and how can we understand the processes that promote and sustain that effort? These are among the major questions in motivation theory and research.

DISCUSS WITH A COLLEAGUE

What motivates you at work or in your studies at university? Based on your intuition and discussion with a colleague, write down five ways in which you are motivated. See how many of them correspond to, or are explained by the theories in this chapter.

NEED THEORIES OF MOTIVATION

Early theories of motivation focused on the needs of employees as the main source of motivation. Ask most managers about theories of motivation, and the one they tend to remember is Maslow's Hierarchy of Needs. Maslow's theory is a need theory of motivation, which describes how people are motivated to satisfy inner needs such as the need for affiliation with others. According to the theories, people with unfulfilled needs will be motivated to initiate action to satisfy them (Wright, 1989). Need theories therefore aim to identify what motivates employees at work. The theories are simple to understand and have high face validity with managers and practitioners, which is undoubtedly part of their appeal. They are less popular with Work and Organizational Psychologists traditionally, for reasons that we will see shortly.

Maslow's Hierarchy of Needs

Maslow (1943; 1954) identified a hierarchy of five needs, which he suggested exist within all human beings. The theory proposed that people are motivated to fulfil each of these needs in a series of sequential steps whereby higher needs become dominant as lower ones become satisfied. The needs are presented in a hierarchical fashion in Figure 5.1, which shows the order in which Maslow proposed they operate. The five sets of needs are:

- Physiological. These are the basic needs that people need to fulfil in order to survive. They include hunger, thirst, sex and other needs that relate to basic physiological processes.
- Safety. Safety needs include the need for security, stability, freedom from physical and psychological harm and fear.
- Social. Maslow originally referred to these as 'love' needs, and they relate to the need for affiliation and close relationships with others.
- Esteem. This group of needs may be broken into two subsets. The first refers to the need for mastery of tasks, striving for personal accomplishment and competence. The second refers to the need for reputation and prestige, in other words, the esteem of others.
- Self-actualization. The final set of needs in the hierarchy are characteristic of many theories like Maslow's, which come from the humanistic tradition. They represent the need to self-actualize, which essentially refers to the need for people to fulfil their potential and to become all that they can possibly be.

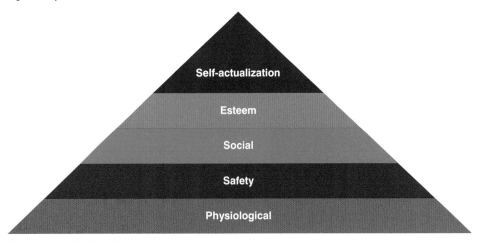

Figure 5.1   Maslow's hierarchy of needs

The hierarchical nature of the theory suggests that people are most strongly motivated to fulfil basic needs before the higher needs such as esteem and self-actualization come into play. However, there is a common misconception of the theory in which once basic needs are fulfilled, they cease to drive behaviour. Maslow rather believed that behaviour was multi-motivated (Pinder, 2008), suggesting that the satisfaction of lower order needs diminishes rather than extinguishes their effects on behaviour.

At work, Maslow's theory gels with managerial intuition about motivation. In a work context, the theory implies that in order to motivate an individual, it is necessary to 1) promote motivation to fulfil higher-order needs by ensuring that the lower-order needs are fulfilled through work design (e.g. through providing pay, job security, a supportive social environment); 2) identify ways in which work tasks can fulfil the higher order needs, thereby helping to motivate individuals to work on those tasks. An employee who is concerned about job security, or who is struggling to provide for their own basic needs and the needs of their family, is unlikely to be concerned to any great degree with mastering new skills or tasks or becoming the very best they can be at work. Their concerns would be more basic and based around fulfilling the lower-order needs.

Is there evidence that the theory works? One would have to say the evidence is marginal at best. Early studies consistently failed to validate the theory, leading to the pessimistic conclusion that unsatisfied needs do not necessarily lead to motivation in the workplace (Lawler and Suttle, 1972; Wahba and Bridwell, 1976; Rauschenberger, Schmitt and Hunter, 1980). One positive aspect of the theory is the way that Maslow grouped the needs, which appears to be reasonably well supported. Ronen (2001) examined data from employees in 15 countries, and demonstrated that Maslow's taxonomy of needs was indeed accurate, with other studies reporting similar supportive results (Kluger and Tikochinsky, 2001; Van-Dijk and Kluger, 2004). Overall, the data appear to suggest some support, albeit not overwhelming, for some of the propositions in Maslow's theory alongside the obvious practical value of the theory (Kamalanabhan, Uma and Vasanthi, 1999; Benson and Dundis, 2003).

Alderfer ERG theory

Alderfer (1969; 1972) presented an alternative model, representing a reclassification and reorganization of human needs. The model contains three basic groups of needs, and is therefore simpler than Maslow's model:

- Existence Needs. Include aspects similar to physiological and safety needs in the Maslow hierarchy.
- Relatedness Needs. Similar to the social needs in Maslow's theory and the needs for prestige and reputation (esteem of others).
- Growth Needs. Refer to needs for self-esteem and self-actualization.

In addition to reorganizing needs, Alderfer's model is also different from Maslow because it removes the hierarchical structural organization. Alderfer suggested that people are consistently motivated by all three sets of needs simultaneously, but to varying degrees at different times. The implications for management is that the aspects of work fulfilling the different needs need to be provided in a steady supply.

Herzberg's Two-Factor Theory

The theories of Maslow and Alderfer describe how people are motivated by the inner fulfilment of needs through situation and life experiences. A different emphasis on motivation at work was adopted in Herzberg's (1959) two-factor theory. The two-factor theory, which has also been termed motivation-hygiene theory (Herzberg, Mausner and Snyderman, 1959) was developed as a result of research into factors at work that promote satisfaction and dissatisfaction at work. Herzberg examined the reasons that led people to feel either very good, or very bad about their work, asking them to describe situations that illustrated these feelings. His analysis of people's responses revealed a distinction between factors that cause dissatisfaction and those that promote satisfaction. He termed these as hygiene factors and motivators respectively, although they have also been termed extrinsic and intrinsic motivators.

- Hygiene Factors. Hygiene or extrinsic factors include things like pay, quality of supervision, work conditions, company policies and administrative procedures. When these do not meet expectations of employees, they tend to result in dissatisfaction and demotivation.
- Motivators. Motivators are factors that tap into internal or intrinsic needs. These include achievement, advancement and promotion, recognition, nature of work and responsibility at work.

The implications of motivation at work are based around the separation of extrinsic and intrinsic motivators. The removal of job characteristics that are dissatisfying only serves to reduce dissatisfaction in Herzberg's theory. Such measures do not promote satisfaction or enhance motivation. To do this, organizations and managers needs to provide opportunities for intrinsically rewarding experience at work by providing things like promotion opportunities, interesting work tasks, and decision-making latitude, autonomy and responsibility.

As with all theories, the utility of the two-factor theory depends on how well it stands up to empirical tests. Early studies offered mixed support for the theory (Ewen, Smith, Hulin and Locke, 1966; House and Wigdor, 1967; Soliman, 1970) with the majority of criticisms directed at the methodology used by Herzberg to derive his theory. These criticisms included questions about the reliability of the procedures used in the research. Another important problem for the theory is the assumed link between satisfaction on the one hand, and effort and productivity on the other. The factors identified by Herzberg are those that lead to either satisfaction or dissatisfaction, and as we saw in Chapter 4, the relationships between satisfaction and performance are far from simple.

Perhaps more fundamentally, the argument behind Herzberg's model faces problems in the wider motivational literature. As highlighted by Tang (1992), the proposal that hygiene factors cannot motivate people in their jobs goes against a body of research demonstrating the motivational effectiveness of one specific hygiene factor: money (Whyte, 1955; Opsahl and Dunnette, 1966; Lawler, 1981). Sachau (2007) points out that Herzberg recognized that money could 'move' people, and that the assertion that pay is a hygiene factor, and thereby not a motivator should not be taken too literally. Either way, this conceptual fuzziness, the lack of empirical support, alongside questions over the methodological groundings of Herzberg's motivation theory raise serious doubts about its validity in organizations. Similar to Maslow's theory of motivation, Herzberg's model provides clear practical recommendations, but lacks a solid evidence base. Interestingly, though, some of the ideas about job factors that promote motivation at work have permeated through to more recent perspectives and ideas about motivation. These are picked up later in the chapter.

BOX 5.1
Money and motivation

To what extent are you motivated by money? Would you work without pay? The debate about the motivating properties of money is an old one, and within your peer group, you will always find people willing to take the two sides of the argument. Those who tend to believe that money is a significant motivator tend to point to people's reliance on money for life satisfaction. They have scientific evidence on their side. Furnham and Argyle (1998) report overall correlations between money and life satisfaction of 0.25, which is weak, but meaningful. At work, there is a significant literature on the motivating properties of financial incentive, used as a form of reinforcement for performance behaviour (see Chapter 4).

Yet the relationship between pay and performance is not as high as you might think. In a meta-analysis, Mitra, Jenkins, Gupta and Shaw (1997) report a relationship of 0.24. Moreover, the way

that individuals perceive money as a motivator also varies, such that money motivates different people in different ways (Mitchell and Mickell, 1999). For example, materialistic people tend to value and seek high pay, individualists prefer pay schemes that are individually-focused, people who are risk averse value fixed pay schemes (Cable and Judge, 1994; Judge and Bretz, 1992). By focusing on the provision of money alone, it is possible to miss some of the more subtle motivating properties of reward, such as the methods by which it is distributed.

An often-quoted example that would seem to dispute the motivating properties of money is concerned with voluntary work. Why do people do charity work and voluntary work for no personal reward, if money is a fundamental motivator? What do you think? How realistic is it in contemporary society for people to work for intrinsic reward alone through volunteering?

MOTIVATION AS A TRAIT

Need theories of motivation adopt a uniform view of human motivation. They suggest that all people are motivated to fulfil similar needs. Theories that we have already covered in this book around individual differences (Chapter 3) might lead you to the conclusion that this is unlikely, given that individual differences have such wide-ranging influences on behaviour and performance at work. Is it reasonable to suppose that people are all motivated in the same ways?

These are the issues addressed by McClelland's (1961) theory of motivation, which conceptualizes motivation as stemming from trait-like inner needs for achievement, affiliation and power:

- Need for Achievement (nAch): This represents the need for, or drive to excel and achieve success.
- Need for Affiliation (nAff): The need to develop close and meaningful interpersonal relationships.
- Need for Power (nPow): The need to control or influence the behaviour of others.

McClelland supposed that these inner needs were trait-like, so that people differed in the extent to which they were motivated by achievement or power needs for example. He also suggested that these traits stemmed from experience and therefore that they could be developed. He believed that achievement motivation, for example, could be developed during childhood, through provision of experiences that lead to success and positive outcomes (Pinder, 2008). Ideas such as these are consistent with our understanding of factors such as self-efficacy (people's beliefs about their own capability and probability of success in activities).

Measurement of nAch, nAff and nPow

One of the limitations of McClelland's theory is concerned with its application in organizations. In the theory, the needs are proposed to be unconscious processes, meaning that people are not directly aware of their influences on behaviour and performance at work. This has a knock-on implication for the measurement of the three needs, which must be done in a way that accesses unconscious processing. One measure which has been widely applied in research is the Thematic Apperception Test (TAT) which requires participants to tell a story based on a series of pictures. Once coded, the stories are intended to reveal the person's aspirations and fantasies and thereby provide a measure of their need for achievement, power and affiliation. The test is a projective measure, which means that responses need to be judged by expert raters, and this makes research and application dependent on the expertise of specific individuals. The technique also lacks psychometric accountability.

Current research is beginning to consider alternative measures for assessing the three motives. A study by Langan-Fox and Grant (2007) examined the use of sentence cues in eliciting motive imagery in a sample of students and entrepreneurs. Their results showed that sentence cues were effective in eliciting imagery related to achievement and affiliation motives, but not power motives.

Outcomes of nAch, nAff and nPow

How do the different needs in McClelland's theory relate to outcomes at work and in organizations? Research has examined this question, particularly in relation to job performance. The most widely studied is need for achievement. Early research documented an association between nAch and success in entrepreneurial roles that require innovation and planning for the future (Hundal, 1971). This has since been supported by a meta-analysis conducted by Collins, Hanges and Locke (2004) who showed that a high need for achievement predicted both choice of an entrepreneurial career, as well as performance in an entrepreneurial role. High nAch tends to give budding entrepreneurs and business owners an advantage.

A fascinating extension to the theory that helps to elaborate this point comes from Atkinson (1964), who considered perceptions of task difficulty. According to Atkinson, achievement-motivated effort is a product of three factors:

- A person's level of nAch.
- Individual perceptions of the probability of success in the task.
- Intrinsic rewards associated with accomplishment.

Atkinson suggested that achievement-motivated effort is highest for people with high nAch, when they perceive the odds of success as about 50/50. People high on nAch are not really motivated by very long odds, as they may attribute success to luck or chance, rather than to their own efforts. Very short odds are also not motivating because they are not challenging enough. Implications for management are to structure tasks that are challenging, but which do not carry very low probabilities of success. This dependence on the link between success and effort differentiates the need for achievement from a more general form of ambition (Judge and Kammeyer-Mueller, 2012).

Looking beyond nAch, research has also examined the optimal pattern of needs for managerial effectiveness in large organizations. Evidence from McClelland and Boyatzis (1982) found that effective managers are strongly motivated by power, moderately motivated by achievement but unmotivated by affiliation. Here is an example of how a combination of trait-like needs is related to effectiveness in a particular job.

Evidence in the literature has also examined how motivation to fulfil trait-like needs impacts job-related decisions over time. Winter (1988) reported that those with a high need for power tended to attain power-relevant jobs such as business management. Jenkins (1994) developed this area of study further by examining the careers of women specifically. The study looked at two different types of power-relevant roles:

- Relational power jobs that provide the job holder with frequent opportunities to exert influence over others, such as in teaching or psychologist roles.
- Directive power jobs, which do not allow for as many opportunities to exercise power over others but can require a certain amount of administration and paperwork, such as in business management roles.

Results showed that women with high nPow did tend to choose high-power jobs, but that over a period of fourteen years, those in relational power jobs actually experienced increases in need for power. These results suggest that gratifying one's need for power in a power-relevant role providing many opportunities for influence on others, does not necessarily satisfy or alleviate the need, but rather nurtures it and helps it to grow further.

COGNITION AND MOTIVATION

One of the mechanisms by which people are motivated highlighted at the start of this chapter is through the ways that they think about their work and work environment. These factors can be grouped under the heading of cognition or cognitive processes. In this section, we cover two theories about how cognition affects motivation. The first examines how people are motivated by their expectations about outcomes at work. The second is probably the most influential idea in contemporary motivation theory and research, and concerns how people think about and respond to goals at work.

Expectancy Theory

Think about something that you want in your life that could feasibly be provided through working hard. How important is it to you? How likely is it that working hard will result in you achieving your goal? Are you working to achieve this goal right now?

If you are working to gain something important in your life right now, then chances are that you have made the following decisions:

1 I really want this outcome.
2 By performing well, I can get access to this outcome.
3 By working hard, I will be able to perform well, so work hard is what I will do to get access to the outcome.

These are the basic elements of Vroom's (1964) expectancy theory of motivation, which explains motivation in terms of the factors that influence an employee's decision to exert effort at work. Specifically, the theory identifies three factors that determine work effort:

- Valence: The desirability of an outcome to an individual, which can be positive or negative. This represents the extent to which a person values some outcome at work.
- Instrumentality: The perceived probability that effective performance will result in the desired outcome.
- Expectancy: The perceived probability that effort will result in the required level of performance.

Collectively, these are referred to as the VIE variables, and Vroom represented them in an equation:

$F = V \times I \times E$
$F = Effort\ or\ Force;\ V - Valence;\ I = Instrumentality;\ E = Expectancy$

The logic of the equation reveals the implications of the theory. People tend to expend most effort at work when they perceive that their efforts will result in good performance, leading to a valued, desirable outcome. People are likely to work less hard if:

1 They do not perceive a desirable or positive outcome resulting from their efforts.
2 They perceive that no amount of effort will result in the level of performance required to gain the outcome.
3 They do not believe that performance, however effective, will lead to the positive outcome.
4 Combinations of 1, 2 and 3 together.

If you are not working to achieve the outcome you identified at the start of this section, then it is likely for one of these reasons.

DISCUSS WITH A COLLEAGUE

Think a bit harder about something that you want in your life that could feasibly be achieved through success at work. Even if that 'something' is a future aspiration, could you identify a pathway from something you are currently working on, to this outcome?

For example, if you are studying at university, how could working harder in your studies lead to your desired outcome? What other effort could you make to achieve it?

The implication of expectancy for motivating people at work, and encouraging and promoting performance, is that managers need to ensure that people perceive that work will lead to desirable outcomes, and that these can be accessed through effort-related performance. Understanding the things that matter to people is a key component of this approach to motivation. This has led to the emergence of measures of individual preferences for particular outcomes at work (e.g. the Motives, Values and Preferences Inventory; Hogan and Hogan, 1996).

Evaluation of expectancy theory

The appealing logic of expectancy theory is backed up by scientific evidence. Early examinations generally accepted the theory as a valid explanation for motivation at work (Pritchard and Sanders, 1973). A meta-analysis by Van Eerde and Thierry (1996) also provided moderate support for the theory. Their analysis examined the relation of the VIE variables with a range of work-related criteria. One less encouraging finding for managers applying expectancy theory was that it tended to predict attitudinal components of motivation such as intentions and preference much more effectively than behavioural components of motivation such as actual performance and effort. This is perhaps unsurprising given the complex processes that determine whether attitudes and intentions lead to behaviour (see Chapter 4), but the failure to develop a clearer account of the pathway from the VIE equation to performance and action, alongside the absence of advances in the theory generally, must be seen as a weakness (Ambrose and Kulik, 1999).

Nonetheless, researchers have continued to examine the model. A study by Erez and Isen (2002) provided support for the motivational effects of the VIE model as part of their wider analysis on the influence of emotion and affect on motivation. The study found that more positive perceptions of valence, instrumentality and expectancy did increase levels of motivation, and that all three perceptions were associated with having a generally more positive outlook in life (positive affect).

Vansteenkiste, Lens, De Witte and Feather (2005) used expectancy theory in research into unemployment, and their study illustrates how the theory could be misunderstood with potentially damaging consequences. They considered the influence of valence and expectancy on unemployed individual's motivation to seek work. Results predictably revealed a positive relationship between valance and job-search motivation in that those who strongly valued being employed were more motivated to engage in job-search activities. By contrast, a negative relationship was reported between expectancy and job search motivation. How could this be explained? The researchers provided numerous hypothetical explanations for the unhypothesized negative relation, which seemingly contradicts the proposals of expectancy theory, but the most likely one is a misconception of the 'expectancy' variable. In the study, this represented participant's expectation that they would get a job in the near future. In other words it consisted of a judgement of how likely it would be that they would get a job soon, *and not* the extent to which they thought that job-seeking behaviour would lead to employment. People who felt confident that they would get their desired outcome, did not see the need to expend additional effort to achieve it. Viewed in this way, the finding seems to support expectancy theory rather than contradict it.

The danger in applying expectancy theory is that desirable outcomes may be seen as too easy to obtain. If that is the case, then people are likely to be less motivated to work hard to achieve them. The processes by which people judge the difficulty of achieving outcomes is just one aspect of another cognitive perspective on motivation: goal setting theory.

Goal Setting

Goal setting theory is the most influential of all motivation theories in management practice, and with good reason given the extent of research on the theory, and its development over time. The seed of the theory was planted by Locke (1968), who was interested to answer a very simple question in a basic research study (Latham and Locke, 2007): Does goal setting affect a person's performance on a task? The answer was 'yes', and what followed was the evolution and development of goal setting theory by Latham and Locke, integrating their own research with a multitude of studies conducted and published by others. This theory development may be considered as 'live' in that new perspectives on the original ideas continually emerge in the literature. Broadly speaking, the theory examines *what* types of goal are most successful in generating high levels of motivation, *when* these effects occur, and *why* they occur.

Goal setting and job performance

The value of setting goals for employees at work was underlined in the meta-analysis of Locke and Latham (1990). This study showed that performance was markedly higher when employees were set goals, as compared with no goal setting. Recent meta-analytic research has also underlined the importance of goal setting in teams (Kleingeld, van Mierlo and Arends, 2011). Moreover, Locke and Latham (1990) also identified a number of features of goals that made them more or less effective:

1 Goals must be specific and challenging. Goals that urge people to 'do their best' result in lower performance than specific, challenging goals, a robust finding about the influence of goal setting on performance supported in numerous studies (e.g. Zetik and Stuhlmacher, 2002). 'Do your best' goals are subjective and do not identify a standard of performance. Consequently people are unable to evaluate the value or acceptability of their work.

2 Motivating goals must be measurable. There should be an objectively measurable outcome that indicates accomplishment of the goal, providing further scope for evaluation of performance.

3 Goals must be attainable and time-bound. Together, these two properties of goals motivate a person to perform highly at work. Goals that are unattainable are demotivating, because people perceive that regardless of the effort they put in, the goal will not be accomplished. Goals should stretch people, but still be achievable. Time-boundedness is encouraged through applying deadlines and timescales for goals, and enables people to decide how much effort is required to achieve a goal within the specified time.

Goals and motivation

Given that there is strong evidence of the link between goal setting and performance, it is important to understand the mechanisms by which goal setting promote performance. There are four, and they are at the heart of the role of goal setting in motivation:

1 Goals direct attention and effort towards activities that are relevant for achieving the goal. Goals therefore affect cognition and behaviour. This mechanism has been reported in several early studies of goal setting (Rothkopf and Billington, 1979; Locke and Bryan, 1969).

2 Goal setting energizes behaviour. Goals lead people to expend effort to facilitate their achievement.

3 Goals induce persistence and prolonged effort. Evidence from LaPorte and Nath (1976) showed that when subjects were allowed to control the amount of time they spent on a task, difficult goals led to sustained effort.

4 Goals influence the acquisition and use of task-relevant knowledge and strategies that increase the chances of task success (Wood and Locke, 1990). Indeed, a study by Knight, Durham and Locke (2001) found that difficult goals affected job performance by influencing how people used particular job-relevant strategies.

The motivational properties of goals are tied to these four mechanisms. Imagine a salesperson is set a target of doubling their monthly sales income in six months. We will assume that the goal is attainable, it is certainly measurable, and the deadline means that it is time-bound. The theory suggests the motivational effects of the goal will first serve to focus the salesperson's attention on the challenge of doubling monthly sales. Behaviour to achieve the goal will be energized so that the person exerts effort and takes steps to improve, and that effort will be prolonged until such time as the goal is achieved, with further effort applied as needed to maintain the improved performance. In order to do all of these things, the salesperson might examine their performance behaviours and develop new strategies to improve.

When do goals lead to motivation and performance?

More precisely, under what conditions do goals lead to motivation and performance? The mere presence of a goal is not enough to ensure that people will be both motivated and that they will perform as a result. There are a number of factors that help to explain why some people are motivated by goals and others are not:

- Locke and Latham (2002) argue that the relationship between goal setting and job performance is at its strongest when individuals are committed to their goals. Furthermore, when goals are difficult, commitment becomes even more significant because challenging goals demand increased effort and have a lower success rate compared to easy goals (Klein, Wesson, Hollenbeck and Alge, 1999; Erez and Zidon, 1984). Goal commitment in turn is affected by two key factors; the importance of the goal to the individual and their personal belief that they are capable of achieving their goal (self-efficacy; Locke and Latham, 2002). People are likely to be more committed to their goals when they perceive that goal achievement is associated with a valued outcome, and that the outcome is attainable. Echoes of expectancy theory are evident here.

- Feedback on progress and performance enhances goal-related behaviour. Feedback increases the effectiveness of goals because it enables individuals to better understand how they are progressing towards the attainment of their goals. Without this information, the person cannot alter important factors such as strategy and level of effort to match goal requirements (Locke and Latham, 2002). People also use feedback in alternative ways depending on their individual differences. For example, Brown, Ganesan and Challagalla (2001) found that individuals with high self-efficacy use feedback to decrease anxiety and increase their motivation, effort and task focus.

- The goal setting–performance relationship is moderated by task complexity. The link between goals and performance is clearest for low complexity tasks. For highly complex tasks, goal attainment is likely to be much more strongly affected by the extent to which a person has the ability to discover and use appropriate strategies and skills (Locke and Latham, 2002).

- The final constraints on the link between goal setting and performance are situational or contextual (Latham and Locke, 2007). Aspects of work and organizational design might interfere or prevent people achieving or working towards goals, as indeed would non-work factors that affect performance, and that are beyond people's control.

A model of goal setting and performance

A number of models of the processes and mechanisms of goal setting and its effects on performance have been presented (e.g. Latham and Locke, 2002; 2007), and the most recent is termed the High Performance Cycle (HPC). An adapted version of this model is shown in Figure 5.2. It highlights all of the factors relevant in determining the effectiveness of goals in promoting motivation and performance, but also adds reward mechanisms, tying the model more closely to performance management (the role of goal setting in performance management is discussed in Chapter 8). Contingent reward is tied to goal accomplishment, non-contingent reward refers to general rewards and features of employment related to satisfaction and commitment.

Emergent perspective on goal setting

Aspects of goal setting theory highlighted so far are well established in research, and form core parts of the theory. As already mentioned though, this is one theory for which development is live and ongoing. There are a number of emergent areas of focus in goal setting research.

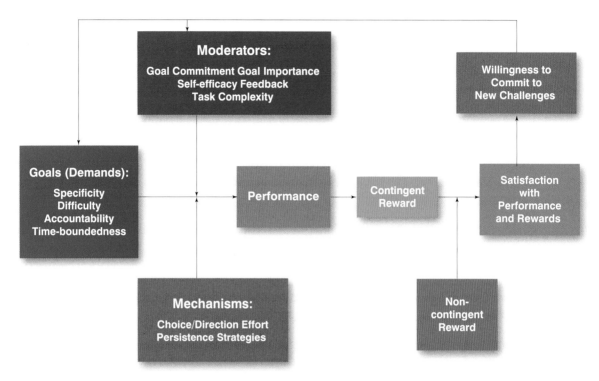

Figure 5.2   Model of goal setting: the high performance cycle

Goal orientation A full introduction to the concept of goal orientation is given in Chapter 7, but it is worth briefly picking up on its role in goal-related motivation and performance here. The goal orientation concept (Dweck, 1986; Dweck and Leggett, 1988) posits that people are generally inclined to adopt one of two orientations in work-related activities:

1 To adopt a learning goal orientation (LGO), in which they strive to master tasks and learn all that they can about a particular task or activity, a style in which errors are central to the learning process.

2 To adopt a performance goal orientation (PGO), in which they strive to meet certain performance benchmarks, avoiding activities or strategies in which they might be seen as unsuccessful.

Goal orientation has been shown to be associated in various ways with the outcomes of goal setting. 'Do your best' goals, used in situations where people have high autonomy and low influence from work and organizational structures tend to be associated with higher performance for people with high LGO. The same goals are associated with low performance for those with high PGO (Seijts, Latham, Tasa and Latham, 2004). By contrast, when people are set specific and challenging goals, which include objectives around learning and acquiring new performance strategies, differences in outcome performance of people with LGO and PGO are extinguished. This indicates that LGO and PGO may be better conceptualized as states that are specific to particular tasks or objectives at work. The implication is that people's typical or preferred goal orientation seems to influence task motivation and performance if people are left to organize their own work. Effective goal setting can help to overcome the effects.

Edwin A. Locke and Gary P. Latham

Goal setting theory has had a major impact on research, practice and, more importantly, thinking in Work and Organizational Psychology, organizational behaviour and human resource management. The establishment and development of the theory can be credited to two individuals, Edwin A. Locke (Dean's Professor Emeritus, University of Maryland) and Gary P. Latham (Secretary of State Professor for Organizational Effectiveness, University of Toronto). Both have exceptional career histories, making contributions in multiple areas of management science, recognized in each being awarded Lifetime Achievement Awards in Organizational Behaviour from the Academy of Management (Locke in 2005, and Latham in 2007).

The first sketches of goal setting theory were set out by Locke in a 1968 paper, worked up further with collaboration with Latham in an early 1975 paper, but firmly established in their joint paper of 1979, entitled 'Goal Setting: A Motivational Technique that Works'. Their collaborative efforts since have formalized, extended and revised the theory, always based on sound science, and always based on the idea that goals, when set in the right way, enhance motivation, performance and ultimately well-being and satisfaction. Recent important works on the theory are the 2007 paper cited in this chapter, and a robust defence of the theory in 2009 in *Academy of Management Perspectives*.

Relevant sources

Latham, G.P. and Locke, E.A. (1975). Increasing productivity with decreasing time limits: A field replication of Parkinson's law. *Journal of Applied Psychology*, 60, 524–526.

Latham, G.P. and Locke, E.A. (2007). New Developments in and Directions for Goal setting Research. *European Psychologist*, 12(4), 290–300.

Locke, E.A. (1968). Toward a theory of task motivation and incentives. *Organizational Behaviour and Human Decision Processes*, 3, 157–189.

Locke, E.A and Latham, G.P. (2009). Has goal setting gone wild, or have its attackers abandoned good scholarship? *Academy of Management Perspectives*, 23, 17–23.

Unconscious goals Goals discussed so far in this chapter are explicit and conscious. They may be verbalized in exchanges between manager and employee, and people are aware of the goals and their implications. Latham and Pinder (2005) suggest a future direction of goal setting theory would be to go beyond these goals to examine unconscious goals and processes that direct behaviour. Early theory in this area suggests that a key process is implementation intention, 'a mental link that is created between a specific future situation and the intended goal-directed response' (Latham and Pinder, 2005, p. 498). These intentions are stored unconsciously and triggered by situations and contexts that people encounter, resulting in behaviour. So, for example, if you possessed an unconscious intention to learn everything you read, then you would automatically read this book very carefully. You would not have to make a conscious decision to read the book carefully, you would just do it.

Two experimental studies suggest that there might be some merit to this unlikely theory. Evidence from Stajkovic, Locke and Blair (2006) showed that unconsciously priming participants by asking them to unscramble sentences containing achievement-related words, improved performance on a brainstorming task in exactly the same way as setting conscious goals. Shantz and Latham (2009) examined this issue further in a sample of employees in a call centre who were taking part in a fund raising day at a university. Results showed that both primed employees and those who were set a specific, difficult, conscious goal, raised more money than those employees who were told 'to do their best'. The effect of the conscious goal remained strongest in this experiment however.

What is really interesting in this research development is that it shows how the essence of ideas and theories can develop over time. Goal setting started as a deliberately cognitive theory, with no place for non-conscious processes or influences on performance, but perspectives change. These emergent findings reflect in some ways the ideas of McClelland, suggesting that we may not even be directly aware of some of the processes that affect motivation on a day-to-day basis.

TREATING PEOPLE FAIRLY: JUSTICE AND EQUITY PERSPECTIVES ON MOTIVATION

Anyone who has been treated poorly, unfairly or uncaringly, been fired, demoted or even just moved to another job or activity without consultation knows the feelings that it brings. It hurts, it feels bad and it is demotivating (Pinder, 2008). The notion that motivation stems from treating people fairly at work, or more specifically, from people's subjective perceptions that treatment at work is just and fair, is the basis of equity and justice theories.

Equity Theory

Equity theory (Adams, 1963) posits that people decide on how fairly they are being treated by examining their inputs and outputs, and then comparing them with others at work. The basic equity equation that guides equity theory is shown in Box 5.2. People feel equitably treated if they perceive

BOX 5.2

The equity equation

$$\frac{Outcomes_{self}}{Inputs_{self}} = \frac{Outcomes_{Others}}{Inputs_{Others}} \qquad \text{Equity}$$

$$\frac{Outcomes_{self}}{Inputs_{self}} < \frac{Outcomes_{Others}}{Inputs_{Others}} \qquad \text{Inequity due to under-reward}$$

$$\frac{Outcomes_{self}}{Inputs_{self}} > \frac{Outcomes_{Others}}{Inputs_{Others}} \qquad \text{Inequity due to over-reward}$$

that their input and outcome ratio is equivalent to others. If people perceive inequity, then the theory suggests that people experience inequity tension: in the case of over-reward, guilt, in the case of under-reward, anger. The comparison 'others' in equity theory are typically thought of as co-workers and colleagues, as these individuals provide the closest and most accessible comparison points. However, people can use other reference points in determining equity:

- Previous Job. A person could compare their current input/outcome ration with that in a previous job role, either within or outside the organization. A person may look back fondly on treatment by a past employer, or conversely may have left past employment because of poor treatment, making them more tolerant of inequity in a new job.
- External Company Employee. People may look outside their current organization to judge how fairly they are being treated. Examining the working conditions of network colleagues in alternative companies allows people to judge the acceptability of their own experience. This kind of comparison might prompt people to leave the organization if they feel that their lot is unlikely to improve.

The predicted outcomes of equity theory are all based on the idea that people behave in ways that will restore equity. If they are under-rewarded, then they will reduce their inputs to restore equity, if they are over-rewarded, then they will work harder to restore equity. Mowday (1991) reviewed the evidence for the accuracy of these predictions, concluding that although there was generally positive support for equity theory in research, methodological problems abound in empirical studies of the theory, and so one could not be totally confident about the validity of the theory.

Organizational Justice

More recently in Work and Organizational Psychology, the basic ideas of equity theory have been developed and extended in the concept of organizational justice. The essence is still around fairness and people's perceptions of how fairly they are treated at work. Three kinds of justice perception are differentiated:

1 Distributive Justice. This captures the essence of equity perceptions, based on the extent to which a person feels fairly rewarded for the work they provide, in relation to others.

2 Procedural Justice. This form of justice perception is targeted towards the organizational systems used to determine how rewards are distributed. The definition could also be broadened to encompass perceptions of the fairness of systems generally in an organization.

3 Interactional Justice. Although the focus of theory and research has typically been on distributive and procedural justice, interactional justice provides a contemporary, and less transactional approach to understanding how people perceive their treatment at work. There are two components. Interpersonal justice concerns the extent to which people feel treated with respect and dignity. Informational justice refers to the ways in which decisions or procedures at work are communicated and explained. At the start of this section, we highlighted the example of being moved or reassigned without consultation. This would be an example where employees would likely perceive low informational justice.

As with equity theory, perceptions of justice at work are hypothesized to affect motivation, and ultimately work behaviour. Hirschman (1970) presented a model of responses to inequity that is still relevant in understanding reactions to perceptions of injustice at work. He presented three typical responses:

- Exit. Leaving the organization.
- Voice. Protesting, or making dissatisfaction known.
- Loyalty. Accepting unfairness, and remaining generally committed.

Pinder and Harlos (2001) add Silence to the list of responses, which represents quietly taking, but not accepting unfairness at work, and harbouring resentment as a result. This is the kind of response that might lead to presenteeism at work, a state of being at work, yet not being productive or engaged.

Research on organizational justice continues to build our understanding of the effects of justice perceptions. Perceptions of distributive justice exert effects on motivation and behaviour in ways similar to inequity tension. More interesting findings have examined the effects of the wider aspects of justice. Brocker and Siegel (1996) examined both procedural and distributive justice, examining their interaction. They reported that if people perceived procedures and systems as unjust, they tended to perceive decisions favourably provided that distributive justice was high. This suggests a self-serving tendency. People might reason that 'the system is bad, but at least I am fairly treated overall'. When procedural justice was high, distributive justice became less important. People effectively had trust in the system and the people that used it to make decisions.

Zapata-Phelan, Colquitt, Scott and Livingston (2009) examined the effects of procedural and interactional justice on intrinsic motivation and task performance. Results showed that procedural justice was positively related to intrinsic motivation and further that intrinsic motivation, in turn, affected task performance. This suggests that perceived fairness of procedures in organizations can have a positive effect on intrinsic motivation, leading to improved job performance.

Zapata-Phelan et al.'s (2009) study failed to report any significant relationships between interactional justice, intrinsic motivation and task performance. The researchers note the body of evidence revealing an inconsistent link between interactional justice and job performance, some studies reporting significant relationships (e.g. Aryee, Budhwar and Chen, 2002) and others disconfirming the link (e.g. Colquitt, Scott, Judge and Shaw, 2006). Part of the reason for inconsistent findings may be that the influences are not direct, and rather mediated. Colquitt, LePine, Piccolo, Zapata and Rich (2012) reported that experienced trust was a mediator between justice perceptions and performance. People trusted their employer more as a consequence of high justice perceptions, which led to better performance. Aryee, Chen, Sun and Debrah (2007) report that perceptions of interactional justice mediate the pathway from perceived abusive supervision to performance outcomes and organizational commitment. When people felt badly treated by their supervisor, this affected their sense of interpersonal treatment at work generally, and this led to reduced citizenship behaviour, and lower organizational commitment. There are other supervisory effects as well. Ambrose, Schminke and Mayer (2013) reported that supervisory perceptions of interactional justice was associated with subordinate perceptions, and that this was most strong in teams that had a flexible, decentralized structure.

Organizational justice is a concept that has influenced research broadly in Work and Organizational Psychology, and we will return to these in other chapters of the book. It appears that justice perceptions influence attitudes and behaviour in relation to a wide variety of HR functions and processes, including selection and recruitment (Bell, Wiechmann and Ryan, 2006), training and learning (Liao and Tai, 2006) and appraisal and performance management (Roberson and Stewart, 2006).

AUTHOR EXPERIENCE

Equity Theory and the Brain Drain

This author experience is a simple observational one, which has wider, more serious implications.

Some management development work I carried out with an oil company illustrated to me how issues of inequity can cause difficulties at a national level. The oil company in question was government owned, and located in a fast-developing economy. Among the managers we worked with were highly skilled engineers, many of whom had received support for development and education abroad to build expertise. Conditional on that support was a mini-

mum period of service with the company, but afterwards they were free to pursue their careers as they saw best.

Here is where the issue of equity comes into play. The salaries offered at this company were good in comparison to local standards, but lower than the going rates paid by multinational companies for top engineers. Many of the managers and engineers knew this, and significant numbers knew colleagues who had moved abroad to take more lucrative jobs, or were planning to do so themselves. Globalization has provided a new referent in judging equity, comprising other people of similar skill and status, in other countries or in companies originating from other countries. In this example, the organization had developed a strong set of cultural values, fostering affective commitment, but skill retention remained a key issue for HR management.

On a bigger scale, this kind of response to global inequity only serves to consolidate it. When highly skilled workers leave their home country to seek better returns elsewhere (and it is a perfectly reasonable decision on their part), they take with them critical knowledge and skills that may speed the progress of developing nations. Knowing how to address the issue is complex, and challenging, but perhaps there are aspects of motivation theory that could help.

What steps do you think that organizations and governments could take to prevent the drain or loss of people with talents, expertise and abilities?

JOB DESIGN AND MOTIVATION

For some people, the content and nature of the work that they do is all they need to motivate them. The nature of work as a source of motivation is the focus of the job characteristics model (Hackman and Oldham, 1980), which examines the features of work that lead to intrinsic work motivation. The theory proposes that a standard set of features should be built into jobs in order to make them rewarding and motivating. The purpose is to foster three work-related psychological states, which are associated with motivation:

- Sense of Personal Responsibility. Jobs should provide opportunities for individuals to feel personally responsible for the outcomes of work.

- Meaningfulness. This concerns people's sense of purpose about work. Meaningfulness is a perception that work *matters* in some way.
- Knowledge of Results. Individuals should be able to determine how they are performing, so that they develop a sense of their own effectiveness at work.

KEY THEME

Environment and Sustainability

Motivation to Act at Work and Beyond

One of the craziest aspects of the impending environmental catastrophe that human beings are presiding over on Earth is the reticence of people to do anything about it. World leaders attend numerous summits and conferences attempting to make progress on agreeing measures for reducing emissions of carbon dioxide and other greenhouse gases that cause climate change (and they do – if you doubt this fact, then you need to re-read Chapter 2; science has shown conclusively that greenhouse gases are heating the Earth).

Yet what are we as citizens doing right now while we wait for one of these meetings to end well? If most of us are honest, nothing, or very nearly nothing. Why? Why are we not motivated to do more?

Equity theory could help to understand why people are not motivated to reduce their consumption. How many of you are thinking right now: 'I could cut back, but then why should I, when people in other parts of the world consume more'. A sense of inequity demotivates us from changing. Is this belief rational, or indeed based on evidence?

Moreover, consider goal setting theory for a moment, and then consider the kind of advice that most of us are given about recycling and other ways to be more energy efficient. Essentially it comes down to 'do your best to do your bit', and we now know that 'do your best' goals are the least effective of any goal that could be set. When people are given targets for improvement, they tend to meet them. In some parts of the UK, people are required to reduce their waste, with government refuse collection being limited to a set amount each week. People whinge about it, but they do it. The specific quantifiable target is met on a weekly basis.

Could goal setting theory not be applied further? First at work, specific measurable targets for energy usage for each person could be set and monitored. Feedback would allow people to see how they compared to others – most people have no idea what constitutes good versus bad energy efficiency for example, so feedback would help them to understand better. If there was a contingent incentive attached, that would likely increase people's commitment to the goal. Could these same principles be scaled up to the population as a whole? Offer people a £500 tax rebate if they reduce their energy usage to a sensible level during the year (the goal must be attainable remember), and I'm pretty sure those meters would stop ticking so fast.

In what other ways could motivation theory be applied to understanding why people fail to change behaviour in respect of climate change?

Hackman and Oldham (1980) identify five job characteristics that promote the three psychological states. The first three create meaningfulness, the fourth fosters responsibility and the fifth facilitates knowledge of results:

1 Skill Variety. The extent to which people are required to draw on a diverse set of job skills and abilities. Meaningful work requires that people use their capabilities.

2 Task Identity. The extent to which a job allows people to complete a whole, identifiable piece of work, the outcome of which they can perceive.

3 Task Significance. The extent to which the output of work has an impact on others, either people at work, or outside such as service/product users.

4 Autonomy. Freedom to decide how to work and to accomplish goals. Autonomy at work is central to developing a sense of personal responsibility.

5 Feedback. Performance feedback (see Chapter 8) is critical for enabling people to gain knowledge of the results of their work.

There are elements of Herzberg's theory in the model, and the basic tenet of the JCM is that intrinsic motivation will be higher if these characteristics are present in people's jobs. In organizations, this means paying attention to job design, structuring jobs and work activities to ensure that the characteristics are present as far as is possible. How likely is it that such intervention would actually improve motivation?

Convincing support for the theory was provided by the meta-analysis by Fried and Ferris (1987), who found that the five job characteristics identified by the JCM were strongly positively related to internal job motivation and job satisfaction, although relationships with job performance and absenteeism were far weaker. Some studies have also tested specific aspects of the model.

Grant (2008) looked specifically at the effect of task significance on job performance. In the first experiment, fund-raising callers were given a task significance intervention in which they read stories about how the work of former callers had benefited others. Those subjects who received the intervention significantly increased the number of pledges made and the amount of money raised one month later. In the second experiment, lifeguards were given a similar task significance intervention in which they read stories about other lifeguards rescuing victims. Those subjects who received the intervention significantly increased the number of voluntary hours worked and the frequency of helping behaviours one month later. These two studies illustrate the positive impact emphasis on task significance can have on performance.

The trend towards greater freedom and autonomy in jobs generally means that the autonomy characteristic has taken on contemporary relevance. Morgeson, Johnson, Campion, Medsker and Mumford (2006) examined the consequences of moving from a traditional work group setup to a semi-autonomous team structure over a twelve month period. Results showed an increase in effort expended, skill usage and problem solving in employees who moved into semi-autonomous teams. Autonomy does appear to relate to increased effort and motivation.

Developments of the JCM

The empirical support for the JCM has maintained research interest in the model, and very recent studies have sought to develop and extend it. Through this development, the JCM might be seen as central to wider perspectives on job design, rather than as a definitive model. Humphrey, Nahrgang and Morgeson (2007) present a comprehensive model of job design features, differentiating motivational,

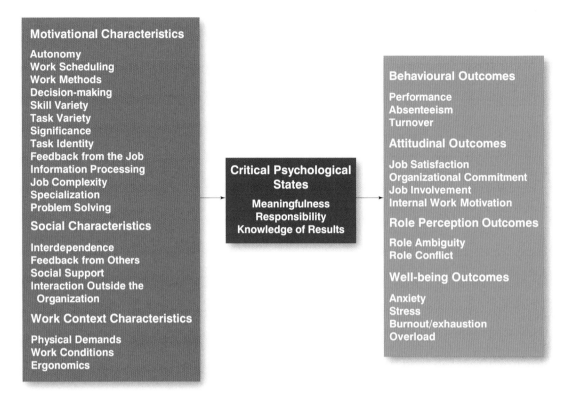

Figure 5.3   Job characteristics, psychological states and work outcomes

social and work context characteristics, all of which they propose affect work outcomes such as performance, satisfaction, commitment and well-being. They maintain that the links between job characteristics and outcomes at work operate through the three psychological states in the JCM. Their model is shown in Figure 5.3, and was tested through meta-analysis.

The results suggested substantial relationships between job characteristics and outcomes, providing further support for the idea that motivation can be improved through job design. Among the most interesting of findings were that:

● Motivational and social characteristics accounted for 64 per cent of variance in organizational commitment, 87 per cent of variance in job involvement, 35 per cent of variance in subjective job performance, 7 per cent of variance in absence levels and 26 per cent of variance in turnover intentions.

● Motivational, social and work context characteristics accounted for 55 per cent of variance in job satisfaction, 38 per cent of variance in people's experience of work stress and 23 per cent of variance in burnout and exhaustion.

For managers and practitioners in organizations, the results of this meta-analysis clearly point to the value of considering carefully, and investing in job design. The returns in terms of performance, well-being and, importantly, motivation appear well established in the research literature.

Humphrey *et al.*'s study also showed strong relationships between job characteristics and the three psychological states, and some support for the role of responsibility and meaningfulness as mediators. However, it appears that not all of the effects of job characteristics can be explained by the three psychological states, and this had led some to call for further refinements of the theory to really understand the mechanisms by which job characteristics lead to outcomes at work including motivation, satisfaction and performance. Other attitudes such as engagement may need to be factored into theorizing (e.g. Woods and Sofat, 2014).

Pierce, Jussila and Cummings (2009) propose a promising line of enquiry based on a single, integrative concept: psychological ownership. They suggest that the five core job characteristics give rise to a state of job-related psychological ownership. This comprises a sense of *mine-ness* about one's job – that it is more than simply a job role, rather it is '*my job, I own it, and control it, and it matters to me*'. (Pierce, Kostova and Dirks, 2003). Job characteristics are theorized to give rise to psychological ownership. For example, Pierce *et al.* (2009) suggest autonomy is likely to provide employees with more opportunities for control over their work, while task identity requires the person to invest themselves personally into the job and establish an intimate relationship with their work. Both could develop a person's sense of job-related psychological ownership. This theory remains to be tested empirically, but does provide a good illustration of how the JCM continues to be relevant in research and practice, and how it might develop in the future.

DISCUSS WITH A COLLEAGUE

Talk to a colleague about a current or past job (full- or part-time). Try to establish the extent to which the five job characteristics in the JCM are present in that job.

MOTIVATING PEOPLE AT WORK: INTEGRATING THEORIES OF MOTIVATION

One of the barriers to applying theories of motivation in practice is a sense of which one to apply and when. With so many implications coming from the theories, how would managers be best advised to motivate their staff, and more broadly, how would an organization use the ideas to motivate all of their employees? To answer these questions, the main theories of motivation need to be integrated and viewed alongside one another so that interventions draw jointly on multiple theories. In this section, we will discuss and explore the main emergent recommendations from theory and research on motivation. These are grouped into five strategies for promoting motivation at work.

Strategy 1. Remove Sources of Demotivation and treat People Fairly

Herzberg's theory, along with equity theory and organizational justice research, all point to the potential for hygiene factors, including pay and rewards, to cause demotivation if people are dissatisfied with them. Research on justice suggests that one strategy to address potential sources of demotivation is to ensure that people feel they are receiving adequate return for the work that they give to an organization. More importantly, perceptions of the fairness of systems used to distribute benefits and rewards are critical, captured the concept of procedural justice. Systems and procedures in organizations, including those used to determine reward have high potential for creating demotivation and dissatisfaction. Avoiding the negative consequences associated with these factors is likely to depend on improving systems and procedures, and ensuring people feel adequately and fairly rewarded for their work compared to others.

Strategy 2. Ensure an Abundance of Valued Outcomes of Work

Expectancy theory tells us that people are motivated to work on tasks and activities that lead to valued outcomes. Part of the challenge for managers is to understand those things that are important to people as individuals, essentially those outcomes from work that are valued by people. The next task in this strategy is to ensure that those things are abundant as far as is possible in the individual's work environment. This strategy is only likely to result in increased motivation if people are able to perceive the link between effort and performance on the one hand, and attaining the desired outcome on the other. Access to valued outcomes should be contingent on performance.

Strategy 3. Set People Goals and Objectives

If managers could only implement one strategy to improve motivation and performance among their staff, then this should be the one. The overwhelming evidence for the effectiveness of goal setting as a performance improvement strategy underlines its importance in management. Goals should be specific and challenging, attainable, measurable and subject to deadlines that indicate the time-frame for achieving them.

Setting goals is only part of ensuring their effectiveness, however. Commitment to goals is important to address, and it is likely that this can be encouraged in two ways: 1) By ensuring that outcome rewards are visible and valued (as in Strategy 2), so that employees feel that achieving the goal will be recognized and rewarded in ways that they appreciate; 2) Through participative goal setting, in which people contribute to the development of their own goals.

Not addressed in this chapter is the issue of capability, competence and skill. Goal accomplishment will obviously be dependent on people having the right knowledge, skills, abilities and competencies to achieve them, and so systems of employee development (see Chapter 7) are important to integrate with goal setting interventions.

Strategy 4. Give People Feedback

Feedback on performance has been included as a key motivational process in goal setting theory, and in the job characteristics model (JCM). Feedback on performance allows people to determine whether they are on track to achieving goals, and to better understand the results of their work. Both are important for directing effort and behaviour, and thereby for influencing motivation. The mechanisms for providing feedback may need careful consideration, and some important issues in feedback are picked up in Chapter 8.

Strategy 5. Design Jobs in ways that make them Rewarding to People

The features or characteristics of work are important sources of motivation. Again, the ideas of motivation factors in Herzberg's theory provide a basic idea about the kinds of work features that are important to people, but the JCM and subsequent developments specify these much more precisely and clearly. Moreover, the elements of the JCM have been clearly demonstrated as linked to positive work outcomes. Managing the features and characteristics of jobs is at the heart of job design. However, simply recommending that managers include rewarding features in job design is probably neglecting the practical realities of management in organizations. For example, most managers have limited control over the ways that they can change the design of work for their staff, which may rather be under the control of HR or other corporate groups. Secondly, the characteristics in Figure 5.3 seem like a long shopping list to attend to, which may dissuade managers from attempting to intervene in issues of work design.

However, such barriers can be overcome, and the application of models of motivation through job design may be more straightforward than it would appear. There is no research to suggest that motivation requires all of the job characteristics to be present. Certainly, it is likely to be highest when they are, but nevertheless the effects of rewarding job characteristics are likely to be additive. This means that implementing subsets of the characteristics is likely to be beneficial, provided that they are thought through clearly.

For example, a manager might introduce more autonomy into people's work, giving greater freedom for people to decide how to organize their work. This could foster the sense of responsibility highlighted in the JCM. However, without goal setting, increased autonomy is unlikely to work. How would people organize their work if they do not know what they are working towards? Unhelpful systems and procedures that interfere with work would also need to be considered, and may need to be revised or redesigned. Otherwise, the combination of autonomy with administrative barriers may provoke frustration.

The key point in this strategy is that work design can be addressed in various ways and to varying degrees to improve motivation, but that regardless of the scale of the intervention, careful attention needs to be given to the interaction of work requirements with organization systems and procedures. On a grand scale, work design is a key part of organization design, a subject that we return to in Chapter 11.

Motivating People at Work: From Science to Practice

These five strategies tie together some of the key practice implications of motivation theory and research. They provide a good illustration of how core theory in Work and Organizational Psychology can translate through to practical application. The most important aspect of the strategies from the perspective of Work and Organizational Psychology is that they are backed up by theory and sound science. This harks back to the lessons of Chapter 2 around science, research and evidence-based practice and problem solving. As we approach the end of this first part of the textbook, having covered a substantive volume of core theory and research in Work and Organizational Psychology, it is useful to reflect on motivation theory as a clear illustration of the links between science and practice. The illustration makes it easy to see the value of sound scientific theory, which gives managers and practitioners confidence in making important decisions in organizations. These kinds of links feature even more strongly in Part Two of the book.

KEY THEME

Ethics and Corporate Social Responsibility

Decent Work and Motivation Theory

The International Labor Organization (ILO) promotes what it calls the 'Decent Work Agenda'. They describe Decent Work as reflecting the aspirations of all people for their working lives, describing it as having:

> opportunities for work that is productive and delivers a fair income, security in the workplace and social protection for families, better prospects for personal development and social integration, freedom for people to express their concerns, organize and participate in the decisions that affect their lives and equality of opportunity and treatment for all women and men.
>
> ILO, 2013

The ILO highlight some key aspects of decent work (creating jobs, guaranteeing rights at work, extending social protection and promoting social dialogue) and provide framework guidelines for assessing it in countries, measuring hard indicators like labour market participation (e.g. employment and unemployment; women and children at work), alongside more psychosocial aspects (e.g. working hours, and consequent opportunities for balancing work, social and personal life).

The recognition in the Decent Work Agenda is the potential for work to contribute in positive and rewarding ways to people's lives provided that is organized fairly, ethically, and in the context of sound economic, societal, and governmental structures, with respect for people and their rights at work.

There are parallels and lessons from Work and Organizational Psychology in the literature on motivation, all relevant for the pursuit of decent work. For example, basic equity theory and extensions of concepts of distributive, procedural, and interactional justice, all form a foundation of some of the key elements of decent work as set out by the ILO.

More interesting overlap perhaps is evident by considering what we know from Herzberg's theory and the Job Characteristics Model (JCM). First, we might see many of the fundamental aspects of decent work as *critical* hygiene factors: basic rights and features of work that make it decent.

However, there is more room for development of course. Morgeson (2011) in a conference speech, talked about *good* work, and talked about this in the context of job design and the JCM. Good work is not only *decent*, but is designed to enhance well-being and meaningfulness. Here there is good research from the motivation literature to apply to consider how and in what ways positive job features can be integrated in job design.

A further implication from the ILO Decent Work Agenda is the need for wholly integrated perspectives on what constitutes decent or good work. From a psychology point of view, there is a need to capture core aspects of equity and job design, literature on careers, women at work, diversity and fairness at work, alongside the real wider context (social, organizational, economic) within which work exists. A truly unifying concept when considered in this way.

ILO (2013) Retrieved from: **http://www.ilo.org**, 13th April, 2013.

Morgeson, F.P. (2011). Who is responsible for good work? *Proceedings of the 15th European Congress of Work and Organizational Psychology,* Maastricht, The Netherlands.

SUMMARY

The study of work motivation is concerned with why people initiate behaviour and effort at work, and the processes that determine its intensity, direction towards goals and maintenance over time. Theories of motivation abound in the Work and Organizational Psychology literature, each addressing the topic in slightly different ways.

Simple early motivation theories examined the role of work in satisfying basic employee needs. Humanistic theories of Maslow, and later Alderfer, suggested that people were motivated to satisfy internal needs, and that work was one way of doing so. An alternative perspective was Herzberg's theory, which looked at work features specifically, differentiating hygiene factor from motivators, or extrinsic from intrinsic motivation.

McClelland considered motivation as trait-like, suggesting that people were more or less driven to satisfy inner needs for achievement, power and affiliation. Although trait-like, McClelland supposed that the needs could be developed. Research on this theory has focused on the performance-enhancing effects of need for achievement.

Two cognitive theories of motivation examine how motivation arises from thought processes. Expectancy theory describes how perceptions of desirable outcomes, and the belief that effort and performance will lead to those outcomes, combine to influence motivation and behaviour. Expectancy theory stands up reasonably well to empirical tests, and is practically very useful. Goal setting theory has received more attention in research than any other motivation theory. Research clearly supports the idea that goal setting increases effort and performance, and more recent elaborations of the theory provide thorough explanations of why they do so, and when they do so. The nature and content of goals is also critical to their effectiveness.

The role of fair treatment at work in motivation and demotivation is considered in equity theory and in research on organizational justice. As organizations become more concerned about corporate social responsibility, models of organizational justice will become increasingly important. The most recent models consider how people feel treated fairly in terms of the rewards they receive, by the systems for delivering those rewards, and by other people at work.

A broader perspective on motivation examines how it is linked to job design. The most well-defined explication of this idea is the job characteristics model, which describes five core job characteristics (skill variety, task identity, task significance, autonomy and feedback), which through three psychological mechanisms affect intrinsic motivation and work outcomes, including job performance. The model, along with developments and extensions stands up well in empirical research studies.

There are a variety of ways in which managers in organizations may apply theories and models of motivation at work in practice. Effective application involves integrating some of the concepts to develop overall strategies for improving motivation. Motivation serves as a good illustration of how sound research and scientific theory can be applied in practice.

The application of science and theory to practice is the central theme of Part Two of this book, which considers the professional applications of Work and Organizational Psychology, building on the foundations established in this, and the preceding three chapters. We hope that the topic of motivation at work has whetted your appetite.

DISCUSSION QUESTIONS

1   A manager of a customer services team has noticed that many staff in the team do not seem to be motivated to give the best possible service to customers. What could the manager do to improve motivation in this area?

2   Does Maslow's hierarchy of needs have any value as a theory of motivation in contemporary organizations?

3   Think about a time that you felt really motivated to accomplish something. Use motivation theories to explain this experience to colleagues.

4   Goal setting is an individual-specific exercise, yet organizational justice tells us that people compare their own experiences with others in determining

whether they are treated fairly. How can these two observations be reconciled?

5   How could you persuade a manager of the importance of fair treatment of employees at work?

6   How could a manager motivate employees in ways consistent with the ideas and values of corporate social responsibility?

7   One of your friends finds out that you have studied motivation theory and quips 'all you really need to know is that people are either motivated or not, and it is all down to their personal choice'. How could you knock down this proposition using scientific evidence?

APPLY IT

In this chapter, we presented five strategies for integrating and applying work motivation theories. These give a clear idea about how to apply the ideas covered in the chapter – however, here are a few specific actions to help kick-start the strategies:

1   Open up conversations with people in your team or organization and find out what are the sources of demotivation or motivation that they experience. This kind of fact-finding can help you to remove sources of demotivation, and also understand how to provide abundant valued outcomes.

2   Ensure you are familiar with the full goal setting model, and try writing some summary goals/objectives to ensure that you understand how to set goals effectively. Ensure that they are specific and challenging, attainable, measurable and subject to deadlines that indicate the time-frame for

achieving them. Use these as a checklist to help summarize your goal setting, and also add further headings 'skill/training requirements' and 'potential barriers' to consider these potential moderating factors.

3   If you manage people, arrange a fortnightly/monthly feedback session, which can double as an objective setting session. Get into good habits for giving feedback by recognizing positive behaviour and identifying negative behaviour. Importantly, for negative feedback, ensure you understand the difference between telling people about negative aspects of their behaviour, and making global negative attributions (i.e. tell people what they did wrong, rather than telling them they are an incompetent person).

4   Conduct a job design audit by looking at the various jobs within your team and identifying how the features in the JCM (and beyond if you work through the section in this chapter) are evident or not in the jobs. Where they are not present, consider how they could be introduced.

WEB ACTIVITY

Change in Goal Setting in Banks after the Financial Crisis

Read the article 'HSBC removes sales targets from staff incentives' by Hilary Osborne and published by *The Guardian* February 2013, by navigating to it online (see below) or by following the link in the digital resources online and discuss the questions below.

> **www.theguardian.com** – search for 'HSBC removes sales targets from staff incentives'

1 How would you expect the new goal-setting structure in the banks to change employee behaviour?

2 What factors could undermine this change?

3 How else could bank motivate their staff to give excellent customer service?

Designing Workspaces

Read the article 'Workplace design: how office space is becoming fun again' by Tim Smedley and published by *The Guardian* February 2012, by navigating to it online (see below) or by following the link in the digital resources online and discuss the questions below.

> **www.theguardian.com** – search for 'Workplace design: how office space is becoming fun again'

1 How could you explain the motivational benefits of improving workspaces in the ways described?

2 In addition to designing the physical environment, companies could also improve people's job design. What recommendations could you make about how to do this?

FURTHER READING

Pinder, C.C. (2008). *Work Motivation in Organizational Behaviour*. New York: Psychology Press.

Latham, G.P. and Pinder, C.C. (2005). Work motivation theory and research at the dawn of the 21st century. *Annual Review of Psychology, 56*, 485–516.

Latham, G.P. (2012). *Work Motivation: History, Theory, Research and Practice*. California: Sage Publications.

REFERENCES

Adams, J.S. (1963). Toward an understanding of inequity. *Journal of Abnormal Psychology, 67*, 422–436.

Alderfer, C.P. (1969). An empirical test of a new theory of human needs. *Organizational Behaviour and Human Performance, 4*, 143–175.

Alderfer, C.P. (1972). *Existence, Relatedness and Growth*. New York: Free Press.

Ambrose, M.L. and Kulik, C.T. (1999). Old friends, new faces: motivation research in the 1990s. *Journal of Management, 25(3)*, 231–292.

Ambrose, M.L., Schminke, M. and Mayer, D.M. (2013). Trickle-Down Effects of Supervisor Perceptions of Interactional Justice: A Moderated Mediation Approach. *Journal of Applied Psychology, 98*, 678–89.

Aryee, S., Chen, Z.X., Sun, L.Y. and Debrah, Y.A. (2007). Antecedents and outcomes of abusive supervision: test of a trickle-down model. *Journal of Applied Psychology, 92(1)*, 191.

Atkinson, J.W. (1964). An introduction to motivation. Oxford, England: Van Nostrand.

Aryee, S., Budhwar, P.S. and Chen, Z.X. (2002). Trust as a mediator of the relationship between organizational justice and work outcomes: Test of a social exchange model. *Journal of Organizational Behavior, 23*, 267–285.

Bell, B.S., Wiechmann, D. and Ryan, A.M. (2006). Consequences of organizational justice expectations in a selection system. *Journal of Applied Psychology, 91*, 455–466.

Benson, S.G. and Dundis, S.P. (2003). Understanding and motivating health care employees: integrating Maslow's hierarchy of needs, training and technology. *Journal of Nursing Management, 11*, 315–320.

Brockner, J. and Siegel, P. (1996). 'Understanding the interaction between procedural and distributive justice: the role of trust', in Kramer, R.M. and

Tyler, T. (eds),*Trust in Organisations*, Sage, Thousand Oaks, CA, pp. 390–413.

Brown, S.P., Ganesan, S. and Challagalla, G. (2001). Self-efficacy as a moderator of information-seeking effectiveness. *Journal of Applied Psychology, 86*, 1043–1051.

Cable, D.M. and Judge, T.A. (1994). Pay preferences and job search decisions: A person-organization fit perspective. *Personnel Psychology, 47*, 317–348.

Collins, C.J., Hanges, P.J. and Locke, E.A. (2004). The relationship of achievement motivation to entrepreneurial behaviour: A meta-analysis. *Human Performance, 17(1)*, 95–117.

Colquitt, J.A., Scott, B.A., Judge, T.A. and Shaw, J.C. (2006). Justice and personality: Using integrative theories to derive moderators of justice effects. *Organizational Behaviour and Human Decision Processes, 100*, 110–127.

Colquitt, J.A., LePine, J.A., Piccolo, R.F., Zapata, C.P. and Rich, B.L. (2012). Explaining the justice–performance relationship: Trust as exchange deepener or trust as uncertainty reducer?. *Journal of Applied Psychology, 97(1)*, 1.

Dweck, C. S. (1986). Motivational processes affecting learning. *American Psychologist, 41*, 1040–48.

Dweck, C.S. and Leggett, E.L. (1988). A social-cognitive approach to motivation and personality. *Psychological Review, 95*, 256–273.

Erez, A. and Isen, A.M. (2002). The influence of positive affect on the components of expectancy motivation. *Journal of Applied Psychology, 87(6)*, 1055–1067.

Erez, M. and Zidon, I. (1984). Effects of goal acceptance on the relationship of goal setting and task performance. *Journal of Applied Psychology, 69*, 69–78.

Ewen, R.B., Smith, P.C., Hulin, C.L. and Locke, E.A. (1966). An empirical test of the Herzberg two-factor theory. *Journal of Applied Psychology, 50(6)*, 544–550.

Fried, Y. and Ferris, G.R. (1987). The validity of the job characteristics model: A review and meta-analysis. *Personnel Psychology, 40(2)*, 287–322.

Furnham, A. and Argyle, M. (1998). *The Psychology of Money*. London: Routledge.

Grant, A.M. (2008). The significance of task significance: job performance effects, relational mechanisms and boundary conditions. *Journal of Applied Psychology, 93(1)*, 108–124.

Hackman, J.R. and Oldham, G.R. (1980). *Work design*. Reading, MA: Addison-Wesley.

Herzberg, F., Mausner, B. and Snyderman, B. (1959). *The motivation to work*. New York: John Wiley and Sons.

Hirschman, A.O. (1970). *Exit, voice, and loyalty: Responses to decline in firms, organizations, and states*. Cambridge, MA: Harvard University Press.

Hogan, J. and Hogan, R. (1996). *Motives, Values, Preferences Manual*. Tulsa, OK: Hogan Assessment Systems.

House, R.J. and Wigdor, L.A. (1967). Herzberg's dual factor theory of job satisfaction and motivations: A review of the evidence and criticism. *Personnel Psychology, 20(4)*, 369–389.

Humphrey, S.E., Nahrgang, J.D. and Morgeson, F.P. (2007). Integrating motivational, social and contextual work design features: A meta-analytic summary and theoretical extension of the work design literature. *Journal of Applied Psychology, 92(5)*, 1332–1356.

Hundal, P.S. (1971). A study of entrepreneurial motivation: comparison of fast and slow progressing small scale industrial entrepreneurs in Punjab, India. *Journal of Applied Psychology, 55*, 317–323.

Jenkins, S.R. (1994). Need for power and women's careers over 14 years: Structural power, job satisfaction and motive change. *Journal of Personality and Social Psychology, 66(1)*, 155–165.

Judge, T A. and Bretz, R.D. (1992). Effects of work values on job choice decisions. *Journal of Applied Psychology, 77*, 261–271.

Judge, T. A. and Kammeyer-Mueller, J. D. (2012). On the value of aiming high: The causes and consequences of ambition. *Journal of Applied Psychology, 97(4)*, 758.

Kamalanabhan, T.J., Uma, J. and Vasanthi, M. (1999). A Delphi study of motivational profile of scientists in research and development organizations. *Psychological Reports, 85*, 743–749.

Klein, H.J., Wesson, M.J., Hollenbeck, J.R. and Alge, B.J. (1999). Goal commitment and the goal setting process: conceptual clarification and empirical synthesis. *Journal of Applied Psychology, 84*, 885–896.

Kleingeld, A., van Mierlo, H. and Arends, L. (2011). The effect of goal setting on group performance: A meta-analysis. *Journal of Applied Psychology, 96(6)*, 1289.

Kluger, A.N. and Tikochinsky J. (2001). The error of accepting the 'theoretical' null hypothesis: the rise, fall and resurrection of commonsense hypotheses in psychology. *Psychological Bulletin, 127*, 408–423.

Knight, D., Durham, C.C. and Locke, E.A. (2001). The relationship of team goals, incentives and efficacy to strategic risk, tactical implementation and performance. *Academy of Management. Journal*, 44, 623–639.

Langan-Fox, J. and Grant, S. (2007). The effectiveness of sentence cues in measuring the big three motives. *Journal of Personality Assessment*, 89(2), 105–115.

LaPorte, R. and Nath, R. (1976). Role of performance goals in prose learning. *Journal of Educational Psychology*, 68, 260–264.

Latham, G.P. and Locke, E.A. (2007). New Developments in and Directions for Goal setting Research. *European Psychologist*, 12(4), 290–300.

Latham, G.P. and Pinder, C.C. (2005). Work motivation theory and research at the dawn of the 21st century. *Annual Review of Psychology*, 56, 485–516.

Lawler, E.E. (1981). *Pay and Organization Development*. Reading, MA: Addison-Wesley Publishing Co.

Lawler, E.E. and Suttle, J.L. (1972). A causal correlation test of the need hierarchy concept. *Organizational Behaviour and Human Performance*, 7, 265–287.

Liao, W. and Tai, W. (2006). Organizational justice, motivation to learn and training outcomes. *Social Behavior and Personality: An International Journal*, 34(5), 545–556.

Locke, E.A. (1968). *Toward a theory of task motivation and incentives*. Organizational Behavior & Human Performance, 3, 157–189.

Locke, E.A. and Bryan, J. (1969). The directing function of goals in task performance. *Organizational Behaviour and Human Performance*, 4, 35–42.

Locke, E.A. and Latham, G.P. (1990). *A Theory of Goal Setting and Task Performance*. Englewood Cliffs, NJ: Prentice Hall.

Locke, E.A. and Latham, G.P. (2002). Building a practically useful theory of goal setting and task motivation: a 35-year odyssey. *American Psychologist*, 57, 705–717.

Maslow, A.H. (1943). A theory of human motivation. *Psychological Review*, 50, 370–396.

Maslow, A.H. (1954). *Motivation and Personality*. New York: Harper & Row.

McClelland, D.C. (1961). *The achieving society*. New York: Van Nostrand Reinhold.

McClelland, D.C. and Boyatzis, R.E. (1982). Leadership motive pattern and long-term success in management. *Journal of Applied Psychology*, 67, 737–743.

Mitchell, T.R. and Mickell, A.E. (1999). The meaning of money: An individual difference perspective. *Academy of Management Review*, 24, 568–578.

Mitra, A., Jenkins, J.D., Gupta, N. and Shaw, J. D. (1997). *Financial incentive and performance: A meta-analytic review*. Paper presented at the annual meeting of the Society for Industrial and Organizational Psychology, St. Louis. Cited in: Mitchell, T.R. and Mickell, A.E. (1999). The meaning of money: An individual difference perspective. *Academy of Management Review*, 24, 568–578.

Morgeson, F.P., Johnson, M.D., Campion, M.A., Medsker, G.J. and Mumford, T.V (2006). Understanding the reactions to job redesign: A quasi-experimental investigation of the moderating effects of organizational context on perceptions of performance behaviour. *Personnel Psychology*, 59(2), 333–363.

Mowday, R.T. (1991). Equity theory predictions of behavior in organizations. In R.M. Steers and L.W. Porter (eds.) *Motivation and Work Behavior* (5th ed. pp. 111–130).

Opsahl, R.L. and Dunnette, M.D. (1966). The role of financial compensation in industrial motivation. *Psychological Bulletin*, 66(2),94–118.

Pierce, J.L., Jussila, I. and Cummings, A. (2009). Psychological ownership within the job design context: revision of the job characteristics model. *Journal of Organizational Behaviour*, 30, 477–496.

Pierce, J.L., Kostova, T. and Dirks, K.T. (2003). The state of psychological ownership: Integrating and extending a century of research. *Review of General Psychology*, 7(1), 84.

Pinder, C.C. (1998). *Work Motivation in Organizational Behaviour*. Upper Saddle River, NJ: Prentice Hall.

Pinder, C.C. (2008). *Work Motivation in Organizational Behaviour*. New York: Psychology Press.

Pinder, C.C. and Harlos, K.P. (2001). Employee silence: quiescence and acquiescence as responses to perceived injustice. *Research in personnel and human resources management*, 20, 331–369.

Pritchard, R.D. and Sanders, M.S. (1973). The influence of valence, instrumentality and expectancy on effort and performance. *Journal of Applied Psychology*, 57, 55–60.

Rauschenberger, J., Schmitt, N. and Hunter, J.E. (1980). A test of the need hierarchy concept by a Markov model of change in need strength. *Administrative Science Quarterly*, 25(4), 654–670.

Robbins, S.P. and Judge, T.A. (2009). *Organizational Behaviour (Pearson International Edition)*. London; Pearson/Prentice-Hall.

Roberson, Q.M. and Stewart, M.M. (2006). Understanding the motivational effects of procedural and informational justice in feedback processes. *British Journal of Psychology*, 97(3), 281–298.

Ronen, S. (2001). Self-actualization versus collectualization: Implications for motivation theories. In M. Erez, U. Klenbeck and H.K. Thierry (eds.), *Work motivation in the context of a globalizing economy* (pp. 341–368). Hillsdale, NJ: Lawrence Erlbaum.

Rothkopf, E. and Billington, M. (l979). Goal-guided learning from text: Inferring a descriptive processing model from inspection times and eye movements. *Journal of Educational Psychology*, 71, 310–327.

Sachau, D.A. (2007). Resurrecting the Motivation-Hygiene Theory: Herzberg and the Positive Psychology Movement. *Human Resource Development Review*, 6(4), 377–393.

Seijts, G.H., Latham, G.P., Tasa, K. and Latham, B.W. (2004). Goal setting and goal orientation: An integration of two different yet related literatures. *Academy of Management Journal*, 47(2), 227–239.

Shantz, A. and Latham, G.P. (2009). An exploratory field experiment of the effect of subconscious and conscious goals on employee performance. *Organizational Behaviour and Human Decision Processes*, 109, 9–17.

Soliman, H.M. (1970). Motivation-hygiene theory of job attitudes: An empirical investigation and an attempt to reconcile both the one- and the two-factor theories of job attitudes. *Journal of Applied Psychology*, 54(5), 452–461.

Stajkovic, A.D., Locke, E.A. and Blair, E.S. (2006). A first examination of the relationship between primed subconscious goals, assigned conscious goals and task performance. *Journal of Applied Psychology*, 91, 1172–1180.

Tang, T.L. (1992). The meaning of money re-visited. *Journal of Organizational Behaviour*, 13(2), 197–202.

Van-Dijk, D. and Kluger, A.N. (2004). Feedback sign effect on motivation: Is it moderated by regulatory focus? *Applied Psychology: An International Review*, 53, 113–135.

Van Eerde, W. and Thierry, H. (1996). Vroom's expectancy models and work-related criteria: A meta-analysis. *Journal of Applied Psychology*, 81(5), 575–586.

Vansteenkiste, M., Lens, W., De Witte, H. and Feather, N.T. (2005). Understanding unemployed people's job search behaviour, unemployment experience and well-being: a comparison of expectancy-value theory and self-determination theory. *British Journal of Social Psychology* 44(2), 268–286.

Vroom, V.H. (1964). *Work motivation*. New York: John Wiley and Sons.

Wahba, M.A. and Bridwell, L.G. (1976). Maslow reconsidered: a review of research on the need hierarchy theory. *Organizational Behaviour and Human Performance*, 15, 212–240.

Whyte, W.F. (1955). *Money and Motivation – An Analysis of Incentives in Industry*. New York: Harper and Row.

Winter, D.G. (1988). The power motive in women and men. *Journal of Personality and Social Psychology*, 54, 510–519.

Wood, R. and Locke, E. (1990). Goal setting and strategy effects on complex tasks. In B. Staw and L. Cummings (eds.), *Research in organizational behaviour* (Vol. 12, pp. 73–109). Greenwich, CT: JAI Press.

Woods, S.A. & Sofat, J. (2014) Personality and work engagement: The mediating role of psychological meaningfulness. *Journal of Applied Social Psychology*. (in press)

Wright, P. (1989). Motivation and job satisfaction. In C. Molander (ed.), *Human Resource Management*. Lund, Sweden: Studentlitteratur.

Zapata-Phelan, C.P., Colquitt, J.A., Scott, B.A. and Livingston, B. (2009). Procedural justice, interactional justice and task performance: The mediating role of intrinsic motivation. *Organizational Behaviour and Human Decision Processes*, 108(1), 93–105.

Zetik, D.C. and Stuhlmacher, A. (2002). Goal setting and negotiation performance: a meta-analysis. *Group Processes and Intergroup Relations*, 5, 35–52.

CASE STUDIES FOR PART ONE: FOUNDATIONS OF WORK AND ORGANIZATIONAL PSYCHOLOGY

CASE STUDY 1.1

Call Centre: Improving Staff Retention

This case study takes place in a fictional telesales call centre for a soft drinks manufacturer. Read the case and answer the questions that follow.

An Introduction to Call Centres

A call centre can be described as a space where the majority of work tasks are performed over the telephone, either in calls to customers (or potential customers) or calls from customers. Call centres are popular in large organizations, especially in the areas of sales and customer services. Call centres generally have a poor reputation in terms of low staff morale and levels of pay, strict working practices, monotonous (and often stressful) tasks with few opportunities for career progression. This is often associated with low retention rates. A CIPD report in 2009 stated that turnover within call centres was 34 per cent (on average), compared with 15.7 per cent across all UK organizations surveyed.

Mercher's Drinks Case Study: Background to the Case

Mercher's Drinks is a large soft drinks manufacturer in the UK. The company have had an on-going issue with high levels of staff turnover in their call centres, which include telesales, customer care and technical support. The highest level of turnover has consistently been in telesales and has been creeping up over the last few years. Six months ago the recorded figure was 37 per cent.

Work and Work Environment

The telesales staff at Mercher's Drinks are split into two teams, one for outbound sales calls to current customers and one for inbound calls from current customers. Each team are line managed independently. The managers have their own offices and are rarely in the call centre space. Staff are strictly monitored and have targets on call times, number of calls answered/made and time spent in 'wrap up' (unavailable whilst completing administration from previous call). Inbound calls and calls to be made by outbound staff are allocated by a computer system; staff may receive calls from any type of outlet or be selected to make calls to any outlet. Staff can earn commission on extra products that they 'sell-in' to outlets. Busy periods are during the run-up to Christmas and summer, when short-term members of staff are taken on to deal with high call volumes.

The Task Force and Procedure

The HR Director was aware that high levels of turnover were driving up the company's hiring and training costs as well as negatively impacting sales and customer retention. She gained buy-in from the rest of the company board to proceed with a 'retention initiative' in an attempt to reduce turnover. A task force was set up to investigate areas for change and to produce recommendations. The task force comprised the HR Director, the HR Business Partner for Telesales and Telesales Line Managers. Exit interviews were studied and focus groups were conducted with members of the front-line telesales staff.

The Findings

The most common areas for change highlighted in exit interviews and focus groups were as follows:

- Staff were reprimanded for not meeting targets but rarely recognized for meeting targets.
- Lack of clear career development opportunities.
- Staff were pleased that managers regularly take complaint calls off them, but staff rarely found out how complaints were handled and resolved.
- Between annual performance reviews, staff unclear on their performance (unless being reprimanded for performing below target).
- Inbound call staff felt it was unfair that outbound call staff were able to read notes about outlets before calling, as they always received calls 'cold' and claimed it was therefore more difficult to sell-in products.
- Little interaction with colleagues allowed, so low morale in the office.
- Short term members of staff had quick inductions to the company so they didn't feel like they understood the organization.
- Strict targets over 'wrap-up' and call times were at odds with benefits of spending longer on one account to sell in products to make commission.
- Leavers often got bored with their role and wanted a change.

Recommendations

The task force discussed the findings and decided some issues they were unable to rectify, such as rivalry between the inbound and the outbound teams and the quick inductions of short-term staff. However, they made several recommendations to improve retention, based on the other areas for change:

1 **Increasing supervision.** Managers should have more regular one-to-ones with staff to discuss performance, complaint handling and career progression.
2 **Break areas.** Staff should be encouraged to socialize during breaks and lunch in specially provided break areas with TV, sofas, books, games console, etc.
3 **Incentives.** Staff should be provided with incentives like shopping vouchers for meeting targets, provided with payslips each month.
4 **Fun Days/Team building.** Fun days and team building activities to be arranged during the working days within the office to boost morale, add interest and encourage team bonding.

Questions

1 Based on your reading of Part One, what theories and models could help us to understand this case better?

2 What suggestions would you make to improve the recommendations of the task force to improve retention rates?

CASE STUDY 1.2

TESCO PLC
Introduction

Tesco was created in 1919 by Jack Cohen and the first store opened in 1929. Since then the company has grown exponentially, expanding into other sectors such as clothing and more recently banking and telecoms, and opening stores outside of the UK. The first customer loyalty card, which allows Tesco to track the shopping habits of customers, was launched in 1995 and soon after Tesco was the UK's most visited supermarket. Sir Terry Leahy became the supermarket's chief executive in 1997 and presided over unprecedented supermarket expansion across the UK. In March 2011 Tesco Plc's CEO Sir Terry Leahy retired and new CEO Philip Clarke arrived. Expansion into the USA was abandoned in 2013 after operating at a loss for several months and Tesco experienced its first fall in profits for over 20 years.

Six-Point Plan

After spending some time overseeing UK operations, as well as continuing with the Group CEO role, in April 2012 Clarke announced a new plan to 'Build a Better Tesco'. This comprised six points:

1 Giving better customer service through hiring more staff and specialist training.

2 Making the stores more inviting; changing layouts, signage and lighting.

3 More straight pricing and promotions that customers want.

4 Updating products and re-launching Tesco brands.

5 Updating branding and marketing with a new advertising agency.

6 Improving online offering and allowing customers to collect an increased variety of items from more locations.

Purpose and Values

As well as the six-point plan, Clarke introduced a new 'core purpose' for Tesco: 'We make what matters better, together'. This phrase highlights Tesco's increasing focus on CSR, being seen to do the right thing and to encourage trust and loyalty from customers, suppliers and employees. To strengthen this, an extra value was added to Tesco's two core values, which have been in place for over a decade. These two core values are: *No one tries harder for customers*, which is about providing excellent customer service and *We treat everyone how we like to be treated*, which is about respect and team work. The newest addition, *We use our scale for good*, is about CSR, with aims specifically around opportunities for young people, tackling obesity and reducing food waste.

The core purpose and values of the brand translate into how people are managed within Tesco. Employees are treated with trust and respect by the organization, in the belief that this will translate

into excellent customer service. This culture also means employees stay with the company for a long time; many members of staff have been working at Tesco for 25 years or more (including the CEO). Another aspect of this is that Tesco believe in developing staff that perform well and around 80 per cent of managers have been appointed from internal positions.

'Be a Great Employer'

To be a great employer is one of the four Essential Elements of Tesco's approach. Tesco aim to ensure staff are happy and proud in their work, develop employee potential and enable equal opportunities. As such, Tesco take the business of motivating, developing and rewarding their employees seriously, although this is a difficult job. The size and scope of Tesco's operations mean the roles occupied by employees are extremely varied, spanning various market sectors and countries. For example, apart from their main business in the UK, Tesco now operate across countries in Europe and Asia and as well as the main food retailing business, the company has arms in clothing, technology and telecoms. This means that the ways employees are motivated, rewards they are offered and development opportunities that are available need to be suited to such varied positions as customer assistants in store to customer analysts in head office; from warehouse pickers to marketing managers.

Reward and Recognition

To ensure reward is managed in a structured way, despite these varying demands, Tesco have an overarching framework in place to motivate and recognize employees. This is called Tesco Reward Principles. This is implemented in ways that focus staff on the goals of the company, whilst promoting a sense of pride and loyalty towards the brand. The principles are:

● Competitive:
  ○ Assessed on a total rewards basis, including financial and non-financial rewards.

- ○ Reflects an individual's role, experience and contribution.
- ○ Set with reference to external market practices and internal relativity.
- Simple:
  - ○ Simple, clear and easy to understand.
  - ○ Avoids unnecessary complexity.
  - ○ Delivered accurately.
- Fair:
  - ○ Transparent and applied consistently and equitably.
  - ○ Trusted and properly governed.
  - ○ Legal and compliant.
- Sustainable:
  - ○ Aligned to the business strategy, reflects performance and is affordable.
  - ○ Flexible to meet the changing needs of the business.
  - ○ Responsible.

There is a large range of benefits on offer to employees, as part of the reward package. A few of the more innovative financial incentives include the 'Shares in Success', 'Save as you Earn' and 'Buy as you Earn' (BAYE) schemes. The shares scheme entitles employees who have been with Tesco at least one year to free shares and a proportion of the company's profits; the saving scheme encourages staff to save out of their salaries for a set time period, with tax-free incentives; and the BAYE scheme is an opportunity to buy shares with tax saving advantages. Other benefits include the Privilege card, which gives staff 10 per cent off shopping, as well as discounts on a range of products and services including gym memberships, private medical insurance and holidays. There is also the opportunity to take a career break after two years' service.

Tesco make their employees feel recognized in other ways too, as demonstrated by the Students At Tesco website. This website is specifically designed for and accessible only to the many students who work in stores for Tesco during A levels and university, and includes articles on a range of subjects as well as Tesco cooking recipes.

Development

As already acknowledged, Tesco are keen to develop internal talent for future roles in senior positions, as well as to more generally provide opportunities for individuals to increase their skill-sets and move around the organization. At any one time Tesco have around 7000 staff members on development courses to enable them to change roles successfully within the company, and there are specific training programmes for each major career stage within Tesco. Where possible these programmes are tailored to the individual's specific requirements. One training and development offering is the Options programme, which trains individuals for the next job level or a different role through on-the-job training and specific training courses to up-skill them in the required areas.

A well-known way of developing potential future leaders quickly within Tesco is the Graduate Scheme, although there are also Apprenticeship and A level leavers schemes. There are three main strands to the scheme: Store Management, Distribution and Offices (which incorporates many different strands from commercial food, to supply chain to the dot.com side of the business). Each of these strands look for different individual qualities in applicants. Store managers have to be good communicators, have the drive to implement change, be self-aware and able to influence others. Individuals are expected to be running their own store within two years. After five years they are expected to be working towards becoming a Store Director, managing a number of Store Managers around a certain location.

In distribution individuals need to be able to make decisions quickly and be able to work with individuals from all backgrounds. In this area of the company graduates run projects to increase efficiency within the distribution networks, specifically focusing on how items are received in warehouses, picked and loaded for delivery. After the scheme

Graduates take on senior management roles, with a more strategic role over distribution operations. The Offices graduate scheme strands are specific to the department involved, but all Graduate Scheme employees are developed quickly, often being promoted within one year and given a wide variety of training and development opportunities to propel them into more senior roles rapidly.

Communication

An additional way that Tesco engage their staff is through communication. Regular blog posts are made by selected members of the group about a range of topics, from activities in-store to partnering with charities. Importantly, the CEO and UK Managing Director, as well as Heads of Group in Asia and Europe, regularly contribute to the blog. The visibility of the senior team and their posts which show them to be 'living to values' of the company keep them in contact with staff and engage employees with what is happening in the wider business. Senior staff also take part in a programme for one week each year called TWIST (Tesco Week In Store Together), where they spend five days on the shop floor. This helps to connect colleagues and promote conversations between employees who ordinarily work in separate areas of the business.

Another important part of this communication strategy is the annual anonymous staff engagement survey, where employees are free to comment about changes they would like to see. The senior team act on these suggestions; for example, a recent survey highlighted that employees wanted more opportunities to voice their suggestions and concerns and subsequent efforts are being made to make this happen, and ensure staff recognition for their suggestions. Tesco also measure how well they are meeting their aims of happy and proud workers, developing potential and providing equal opportunities through metrics collected from the survey. The 2012/2013 figures available show that the target for numbers of individuals on the Options Programme was missed by 0.1 per cent, although other development opportunities have been in

place for more staff as Tesco increased store staff numbers and provided specialist training.

Diversity

A key aim of Tesco's drive to be a great employer is around diversity and equal opportunities: 'To build an environment where all our colleagues contribute, make a difference and can be themselves'. The Group-wide plan also has a key element of 'Everyone is welcome'. Diversity in the leadership team is an important focus for Tesco, as they aim to increase the number of women working at the top level. Between 2007 and 2013 93 per cent more women were appointed as Directors or Business Leaders, and as of April 2013 30 per cent of the Tesco Plc Board were women (three people). In 2010 Tesco launched their Women in Leadership development programme in order to progress and retain women in senior positions. This programme is also working in other countries where Tesco operate, such as South Korea, where it is more unusual for women to take leadership roles.

Tesco UK also have a policy in place to encourage staff to work beyond the traditional retirement age if they wish to, and currently 2500 individuals do so. Additionally, the company has policies and networks in place to encourage further diversity within the workforce. For example, there is a growing LGBT (lesbian, gay, bisexual and transgender) employee network, a new in 2011/2012 ABC (African, Black British and Caribbean) network and longer running Women in Business and Asian networks. Tesco also work with external organizations to encourage applications from individuals with disabilities and long-term unemployed people, as well as ex-service personnel and ex-offenders. All of these policies move Tesco closer to ensuring that their staff members reflect the wider society.

Teamwork

Many of the staff members at Tesco also talk about the camaraderie of the teams within the stores. One way this is fostered is through social events as all stores have their own social committees, who organize events such as five-a-side football tournaments and fancy-dress competitions. The teamwork culture of Tesco is also highlighted by the fact that many senior staff members go to work on the shop floor during the busy Christmas period as part of the 'Helping Hands' programme. In 2013 over 5000 members of staff from the Tesco offices spent time working in store to help keep the shelves stocked.

Sources and further reading:

www.**tescoplc.com** search for careers and graduates

www.**marketingweek.co.uk** – search for article 'Sir Terry Leahy to retire in Tesco board overhaul' by Russell Parsons, 2010

www.**telegraph.co.uk** – search finance/newsbysector/retailandconsumer for 'Tesco the six point turnaround plan' with Philip Clarke

www.**bbc.co.uk/news/magazine** – 'Tesco: How one supermarket came to dominate' by Denise Winterman, 2013

www.**managementtoday.co.uk** – search for 'Tesco boss Philip Clarke: I feel Bloody Great' by Chris Blackhurst 2013

Case Questions

1 a. What Big Five personality traits do you think are important for the Store Manager and Distribution Manger graduate schemes, based on the information in the case?

   b. Why do you think these qualities would be important?

2 How do you think emotions, core self-evaluations and psychological capital would impact the work of Graduate Store Managers?

3 How can we apply information from Chapter 4 about social influences on behaviour in groups, to the Tesco case?

4 How could we use the models of motivation from Chapter 5 to explain the policies and procedures in place at Tesco?

5 What evidence is there in the case that Tesco is attempting to create a satisfied and committed workforce? What else could they do?

PART TWO
PROFESSIONAL PRACTICE OF WORK AND ORGANIZATIONAL PSYCHOLOGY

Areas of professional practice in Work and Organizational Psychology have the potential to make important contributions to improving people management processes and systems in businesses, resulting in better performance and effectiveness, and more positive psychological and physical health. Part Two of this book will show you how businesses and organizations can improve decisions about recruitment and selection, ensuring that those decisions are ethical and fair; make better investments in training, learning and development; manage people's individual contributions more effectively through improved performance measurement, better and more useful feedback, and more systematic performance management and development interventions.

From the perspective of individuals themselves, these and other experiences at work are accumulated over many years and even decades from the stories of careers. We will see how organizations have a role to play in facilitating career development, and understanding the new expectations of people about work and its role in life. And furthermore, we'll also look at the effects of work on health. The demands of work and modern life are very different from those experienced by our ancestors, and humans have not evolved to cope with these new kinds of life pressures. Organizations have a responsibility to ensure demands of work in the 21st century are not damaging to people's health and well-being, and this study of safety, stress and health at work have a pivotal role to play.

The next five chapters encourage you to think in new ways about people management systems in organizations, identifying practical ways in which they can be changed and improved.

CHAPTER 6

RECRUITMENT AND SELECTION

LEARNING OBJECTIVES

- Describe the importance of recruitment and selection in organizations.

- Describe the process of recruitment and selection.

- Understand the contribution of work psychology to selection.

- Describe methods of job and competency analysis.

- Understand the importance of reliability and validity in selection.

- Understand specific assessment techniques (application forms and biodata; psychological testing; selection interviewing; assessment centres).

- Understand the competency approach to selection.

- Describe methods for the evaluation of selection processes.

- Describe diversity and fairness issues in selection.

- Understand the experience of recruitment and selection from the candidate's perspective.

My office is a 25-minute walk from my home in Birmingham, and the walk takes me across the City. Two things strike me as I walk. The first is just how diverse the working world is, even in this one city. My walk takes me past a series of shops, including one serving breakfast to construction workers starting their day. I walk past the council offices, where several thousand people work in a huge variety of public sector jobs. I walk past some of the main finance and investments companies in the city where investments, savings, and pensions are made or broken. My walk takes me past St Philips Cathedral and onto the much bigger retail outlets of the city. The final 300 metres take me past the Crown and Magistrates Courts, where I see solicitors and their clients, and a fairly heavy police presence. The children's hospital is next, shortly followed by the fire service headquarters, and finally I arrive at my own place of work, Aston University.

Just try to build a picture in your mind of the diversity of the jobs that exist in these different organizations. Now try and think about what kinds of knowledge, skills, abilities, and characteristics would be needed for those different roles. The skills required to work with children in a hospital are quite different from those required by your average solicitor or investment banker. Moreover, jobs that appear similar, may actually have quite different requirements based on the specific work styles or organizational cultures of different businesses.

The extent to which people are suited for different kinds of jobs of course depends on their individual attributes. I feel able to judge the attributes of my colleagues at work reasonably well – I have worked with them for a long time. However, when I meet people for the first time, it is almost always difficult to perceive their traits, and even harder to perceive anything about their skills and abilities. Yet this is exactly the same situation as a job interview, which is usually the first time that an employer is able to meet a prospective employee.

The challenge facing recruiters and selectors in organizations is therefore three-fold. First, they need to be able to measure individual differences that are often hard to perceive. Second, they need to be able to make a judgement about whether those individual differences are suited to a particular job role in a particular organization. Finally, they need to understand how the needs of specific organizations, and the business environments that they exist within, should be incorporated into selection decisions. Recruitment and selection is therefore about matching people to jobs and to organizations.

THE ORGANIZATIONAL IMPERATIVE

The challenge to recruit highly skilled or talented people into organizations is increasingly important. Globalization and continual developments in technology mean that product innovations are quickly adopted by competitors (Cooper, Robertson and Tinline, 2003), and so do not offer persistent competitive advantage. Cooper *et al.* also point out the brand advantage can easily be eroded by customer experiences. Competitive advantage in organizations therefore arguably lies in the people that it can attract, recruit and retain. Their performance has a critical impact on the performance of the organization. Utility analysis (the analysis of the financial benefits of increased employee productivity; Schmidt and Hunter, 1983) indicates that the difference in productivity between a below average performer and an above average performer is worth about 80 per cent of their salary. This underlines why selecting those people who are likely to be high performers is so important. This chapter will explore some of the ways that organizations recruit and select their employees, focusing on the contributions of psychologists to recruitment and selection methodology.

EFFECTIVE RECRUITMENT AND SELECTION

It is possible to examine recruitment and selection from both micro and macro perspectives. The micro perspective (not to be confused with *simple*) is concerned with the processes and procedures of recruitment and selection. The macro perspective considers the wider factors and demands that influence how recruitment and selection are applied in organizations. These include strategic demands of the organization that may apply at a specific point of time. In this chapter, we begin from the micro perspective, and look at specific procedures and techniques of recruitment and selection, considering relevant evidence in each case. We then consider these in the context of the macro perspective. Taking what we know from both perspectives though, we may define an effective approach to recruitment and selection as one that is:

- Evidence based – this means that research and empirical evidence is used to inform the processes and procedures of recruitment and selection.

● Systematic – this means that processes follow a logical pathway whereby decisions are made sequentially and on the basis of sound analyses.

● Strategic – this means that recruitment and selection are performed with due attention to the strategic context of the HR function and the strategic needs of the organization.

Recruitment and selection is best conceptualized as a longitudinal process, comprising a series of stages. Figure 6.1 is a good representation of the process. Figure 6.1 shows the practical tasks of recruitment and selection as well as the activities that underpin them. The aim of these activities is to ensure that the process is undertaken systematically and according to methodological best practice. The emphasis in most of this literature is towards the effectiveness of such systematic or structured techniques of selection (Zibarras and Woods, 2010). These might be defined as techniques that have a high degree of procedural methodology, and clear processes of measurement and evaluation. The research literature virtually without exception, points to the merits of such techniques (e.g. Hunter and Schmidt, 1998). If followed, the benefits are that relevant job competencies are assessed reliably and fairly, giving the most adequate indication of later job performance.

Systematic approaches to selection, follow a series of sequential steps and applies problem-solving logic to the recruitment and selection problem (see Figure 6.1). The selection process starts

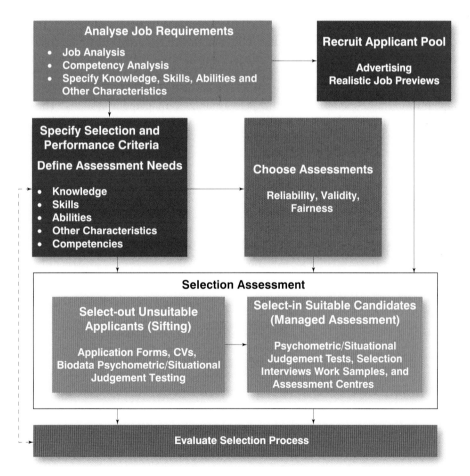

Figure 6.1   A model of the recruitment and selection process

with an analysis of the job to be selected for. Information about the job role and its associated tasks are used to derive a specification of the knowledge, skills, abilities and other characteristics (KSAOs) that are essential or desirable for a person performing the job role. Based on the job analysis, recruitment activities are carried out to advertise and communicate job vacancies and attract job applicants by describing the tasks and person requirements alongside benefits and other information.

Job analysis information is also used to define selection criteria (i.e. the criteria that determine whether someone should be selected or rejected), reflecting the eventual performance requirements of the employee. Practitioners must then decide how best to assess job applicants and candidates against those criteria, and there are a range of different assessment methods that may be used to do this. The major methods used in organizations are shown in the figure, and information about the reliability and validity of selection assessments also guides choices about which techniques to use. Finally, best practice in selection includes an evaluation phase, in which selectors investigate whether the process was successful. The practical job of recruitment and selection is to attract a pool of job applicants, *select out* unsuitable applicants, *select in* potential candidates, and finally make a hiring decision.

Fit with Wider Organizational Systems

Recruitment and selection can be viewed as core HRM activities (Davis and Scully, 2008), and it is useful to conceptualize them alongside other HR functions. Broadly speaking, recruitment and selection aim to identify from a group of individuals, the person or persons with the highest potential for job success as indicated by a profile of KSAOs. The key word there is potential. Realizing the potential for success depends on a variety of other HR processes including job design, management and leadership, training and socialization, and performance management systems. These interact to determine whether the individuals who are selected will go on to perform effectively in the organization (Figure 6.2). It is of course possible to extend this reasoning further to encompass the effects of team climate, organizational cultures, and ultimately market environments on individual performance (see Part Three of this book).

Figure 6.2   Selection in the context of other human resource systems

Systematic Selection: Perspectives in Work and Organizational Psychology

Psychologists have a reputation for designing and implementing effective selection systems, and this is an important area where some psychological techniques have proven potential to contribute to practice. Psychologists have contributed significantly to recruitment and selection through the development, improvement and evaluation of an array of assessment approaches and methodologies, drawing on some of the core principles of psychological testing outlined in Chapter 3.

Much of the work that psychologists have undertaken has aimed to reduce the subjectivity of selection, minimizing the biases that selectors bring to the assessment processes, the most common of which are shown in Box 6.1. Although assessments of people to determine their suitability for particular jobs can be traced back centuries, the first applications of psychological assessment in selection were carried out by the military after the First World War. A basic personality inventory (Woodworth's Personal Data Sheet) was used to differentiate soldiers predisposed to experiencing 'shell shock' (a condition that may now be referred to as Post Traumatic Stress Disorder; Winter and Barenbaum, 1999). This first venture into assessment for selection has developed over the past 90 years into a variety of different assessment methods. The most widely applied psychological assessment techniques include psychological or psychometric testing, biodata, and work-sample techniques such as assessment centres. Psychologists have also improved the understanding and application of more traditional techniques such as interviewing, and application forms. A more recent approach, which is gathering popularity and much evidence in the literature, combines techniques for measuring situational judgements. Psychologists have also contributed substantially to job analysis methods that form the foundations of recruitment and selection, and other HR functions.

JOB ANALYSIS

What exactly are we trying to assess in selection processes? Overall, the purpose of selection assessment is to measure those attributes that enable an effective decision about the suitability of a particular job candidate. How would one identify and prioritize such attributes? Methods of job analysis represent the way that work psychologists answer this question, and are essential foundations of personnel selection processes. Job analysis is the catch-all label given to a range of techniques

BOX 6.1
Subjective biases in people perception

Halo Effect: Perceiving a person as positive and henceforth seeing only their positive features.

Horns Effect: Same as the halo effect, but perceiving only negative information about a person.

Similar-to-me: Holding oneself as the 'gold standard' and comparing all others to one's own attributes.

Stereotyping: Making prejudiced assumptions about a person based on their appearance or demographic background (ethnicity, gender, age, regional dialect/accent)

Self-delusion: Believing oneself to be immune from subjective bias.

that are designed to help us understand what people do at work, and why some people do it better than others. Brannick, Levine and Morgeson (2007) give a clear definition of job analysis:

> *Job analysis is the systematic process of discovery of the nature of a job by dividing it into smaller units, where the process results in one or more written products with the goal of describing what is done on the job or what capabilities are needed to effectively perform the job.* Brannick, Levine and Morgeson (2007; p8)

The purpose of job analysis is to determine the characteristics of the job, to use these to state the KSAOs that should be demonstrated by the employee, and ultimately their performance criteria. Traditional job analysis is described as 'work-oriented' analysis, because the focus of the analyst is on the job and its associated tasks. There are a variety of different methods for conducting job analyses, and most are covered in depth in specialist texts (e.g. Smith and Robertson, 1993; Pearn and Kandola, 1988; Searle, 2003). Box 6.2 provides a summary of the main methods that are used in organizations. These methods supplement basic desk research techniques used by practitioners such as reference to existing sources such as training manuals and past job specifications.

The product of job analysis is a job description, which describes concisely the main tasks and responsibilities of the job. The production of such task lists assumes that the tasks associated with the job remain stable over time (Robertson, Bartram and Callinan, 2002). This may be a false assumption for some jobs, and the incorporation of anticipated changes to the job tasks is not something that is clearly addressed by conventional job analysis methods.

Once the job description has been produced, the next step is to translate the information into measurable performance outcomes and to a specification of the KSAOs and behaviours to be demonstrated by the employee. This step relies heavily on the expertise of the practitioner, who may draw on their experience and knowledge of the job, combined with consultation with managers and other relevant stakeholders to produce a specification of KSAOs. This process is therefore quite intuitive, and often based on the specific knowledge of the analyst. The product of 'worker-oriented' analysis is a specification of competencies to be demonstrated by the employee. There are a number of methods that may be used for worker-oriented analysis, also listed in Box 6.2.

In contemporary HRM practice, a very widely used approach to job analysis is competency modelling or profiling. Competencies can be defined as '*observable workplace behaviours* [that] *form the basis of a differentiated measurement* [of performance]' (Bartram, 2005, pp. 1185–1186). So generally, competencies are seen as behaviour patterns that are performance related (Cooper, Robertson and Tinline, 2003; Woodruffe, 1997), and in that sense they may integrate attributes from K, S, A and O (Roberts, 2005).

Competency modelling involves the construction and design of frameworks of competencies that may be applied to a range of different job roles in an organization. The frameworks are usually quite generic, specifying behaviours that would contribute to job success in a variety of contexts. Practitioners may select relevant competencies from the framework that apply to a particular job role based on their own judgement or by seeking contributions from managers and others. These can then be assessed as part of a selection process. One exception to this practice is where competency frameworks are designed to apply in their entirety to a specific employee group. This applies frequently to leadership and management roles, with many organizations having company-wide corporate competency frameworks that reflect strategic goals and values. The growing interest and popularity of competencies and competency models has led to some advances in our understanding of their structure and nature (e.g. Tett, Guterman, Bleier and Murphy, 2000). Important advances in competency modelling have aimed to standardize the main classifications of job competencies (e.g. planning and organizing, communicating and presenting), most recently by relating them to core aspects of individual differences in personality, motivation and ability (Bartram, 2005).

BOX 6.2
Methods of job and competency analysis

Job analysis methods (work-oriented)

Questionnaires: There are several off-the-shelf questionnaires that can be used for job analysis. They contain lists of job tasks that are endorsed by job holders to indicate the extent to which they characterize their job role. An example is the Position Analysis Questionnaire (PAQ).

Observations: Workers are observed carrying out specific job tasks, and the behaviours demonstrated are recorded.

Self-records/Diary Methods: Workers can be asked to talk through particular job tasks, or asked to keep a diary of activities for a short period of time.

Hierarchical Task Analysis: Broad work tasks are sequentially broken up in increasingly narrow tasks to result in a hierarchy of job responsibilities and activities.

Worker-oriented methods

Critical Incidents Interviewing: Critical incidents interviewing involves conducting interviews with workers about particularly important or critical job occurrences. The aim of the interview is to understand the behaviours that made the outcome of the situation either particularly effective or ineffective.

Repertory Grid: The repertory grid examines the personal attributes that make effective workers different from ineffective workers. Interviewees nominate effective and ineffective workers. Two effective and one ineffective worker are drawn at random from the list and the interviewee must identify what makes the ineffective person different from the two effective workers (e.g. the former is disorganized, whereas the latter are organized). The interviewer then probes

the competency to identify exactly what the interviewer means when they describe the attribute.

Combination job analysis methodology

The combination job analysis method (CJAM) is one of the most useful and complete techniques for job analysis. It comprises a systematic approach to job analysis that can incorporate information from a variety of methodologies, combining them to produce a job description and person specification for use in selection and other HR activities. The CJAM uses a team of subject matter experts, and job analysts (e.g. work psychologists) to guide the process, and proceeds in a series of steps (Pearn and Kandola 1988; Brannick, Levine and Morgeson, 2007):

- The team generate lists of tasks associated with the target job, using a variety of work-oriented methods to supplement their own ideas about tasks of the job.

- Sets of tasks are combined together to generate broad job activities or duties. These are rated by the group, and other key stakeholders, to determine their relative difficulty and importance in the job.

- Job activities and duties are considered by the team, and used to generate lists of KSAOs or competencies that are required for effective performance.

- Generated KSAOs and competencies are combined, defined and elaborated, to give a clear, parsimonious set. These are rated by the group, and other stakeholders, to determine their relative importance in newly appointed employees.

In recruitment and selection, the goal of job analysis is to provide an evidence-based specification of attributes that act as criteria for decision-making during the selection guide the choice of assessment techniques, and to therefore establish their content validity (Schmidt, 2012). Assessments are selected based on correspondence between the attributes they assess, and those identified in the job analysis.

Try to list the KSAOs required for a job that you are familiar with. Write down around 12–15 different person requirements. If you have time, search for your chosen job on the O*NET (**http://www.oneton line.org**) database to compare your person requirements with the listings on the site.

RECRUITMENT: ATTRACTING PEOPLE TO WORK

The success of any recruitment and selection process hinges on attracting a pool of good applicants. Given the importance of this stage of the recruitment and selection process, it is surprising that the findings of research are not more directive or insightful. Indeed some critics point out that many findings from recruitment research are somewhat obvious (e.g. see critical evaluation by Ployhart, 2006). However, there is sufficient evidence to help practitioners in applying systematic approaches. For example, Breaugh (2008) identifies the following key steps in recruitment activities:

- Recruitment Objectives: identifying the specific recruitment need, the kinds of individuals to be recruited (drawing on findings of the job analysis), the time frame, and the required levels of performance and retention needed from the process.

- Strategy Development: working out a strategy for the recruitment activity, in which key questions about who and where to recruit, how to reach targeted people, and what to communicate during the recruitment, are all considered.

- Recruitment Activities: application of specific methods of recruitment to attract the applicant pool, typically involving decisions about who will do the recruitment, whether it will be outsourced, the nature of the information to be conveyed, and the use of various media.

Breaugh (2008) also highlights the moderating effects of applicant characteristics. Applicant perceptions of the company and the attractiveness of the job, alongside their own expectations and relevant job interests, all impact on decisions to apply. This kind of thinking features clearly in Schnieider's Attraction-Selection-Attrition model (ASA; Schneider, 1984). The ASA framework describes how people are attracted to organizations principally on the basis of their judgement about whether they fit with the job and organization. Initial decisions may be based on perceptions of job fit, but during the recruitment and selection phase, according to the ASA model, applicants and organizations undertake a mutual fact-finding exercise, designed to ascertain the degree of fit between them. When person-organization fit is high, people are more likely to be selected. Within the organization, employees who are a poorer fit to the organization are more likely to leave (attrition), resulting in an iterative homogenization of the organizational culture. This model highlights the importance of subjective fit perceptions in decision-making with implications for how jobs are marketed during recruitment. A further implication is that recruiters should be mindful about whether their objective is recruit 'for fit' or 'for diversity' to avoid creating overly homogenous teams and groups.

Other research has examined specific practices, which can be interpreted against contingencies of recruitment and selection. For example, in situations in which there is likely to be a large applicant pool for a particular job, recruiters often use realistic job previews (RJPs) to ensure a good fit between person and job characteristics. Such previews might highlight any negative aspects of the job in order to ensure the seriousness of job applications. The administration of this and other practices is equally important. Chapman, Uggerslev, Carroll, Piasentin and Jones (2005) found that receiving timely responses to enquiries and applications led to higher perceptions of the attractiveness of the recruiting company.

Of course, not all recruitment happens through external marketing. Van Hoye and Lievens (2009) for example, examined word-of-mouth influences on applicant behaviour (i.e. receiving word-of-mouth recommendation from specific others). They found that word-of-mouth effects were dependent upon characteristics of the applicant and the source. Alongside certain personality characteristics, source credibility and independence was important. Interestingly, the influences of word-of-mouth went beyond those of exposure to mass media, and were particularly positive when received early on in the recruitment process. More such psychological research is likely to enrich our understanding of recruitment, particularly if researchers turn attention to more integrated perspectives on recruitment processes (Breaugh, 2008; Rynes and Cable, 2003).

Often neglected in research on recruitment activity is the huge industry of recruitment consultancy services (Ordanini and Silvestri, 2008). This is part of a bigger trend to outsourcing of HR services, but recruitment is particularly of interest given the vast size of the recruitment industry. Ordanini and Silvestri (2008) examined some predictors of the use of outsourced recruitment. They found that bigger companies, which required less specialist workforces, and in which the internal HR provision tended to be perceived as under-resourced or inadequate, were more likely to outsource their recruitment. Studies of the effectiveness of outsourced recruitment are sorely needed.

SELECTION: ASSESSING AND HIRING PEOPLE

Foundations of Selection Assessment: Reliability and Validity

Reliability and validity have been introduced in Chapter 3 as fundamental concepts in psychological assessments. Assessments of individuals for selection in organizations are also very strongly underpinned by these concepts. In a critical approach to selection assessment, questions over reliability and validity must always be addressed. At this point, it is helpful to clarify the meanings of reliability and validity in selection practice.

Reliability

Reliability in selection assessment relates to two particular aspects of the assessment:

- Internal consistency reliability of the selection assessment, which provides an index that tells us whether tests and other assessments are consistently or accurately measuring the attribute of interest. Internal consistency is generally used to evaluate assessments made using self- or other-report scales or tests (such as biodata, personality tests or cognitive ability tests).

- Inter-rater reliability, which provides an indication of the extent to which two different assessors agree in their assessments of a particular job candidate. If a selection process is to be objective, then different individuals should be able to use the assessment process and system and agree on their findings. This would provide evidence that the assessment reflected the competencies or attributes of the candidate, rather than the idiosyncratic judgements of the assessor.

Validity

Validity takes several forms, all discussed in Chapter 3, and summarized in Box 6.3. Robertson, Bartram and Callinan (2002) point out that among these different types of validity, construct and criterion validity are particularly important. Construct validity is concerned primarily with whether the assessment measures the competencies or attributes that it claims to. Whilst these analyses are straight-forward for psychometric tests, construct validity is harder to establish for other selection assessments, and the approach that most practitioners take is to build a case for the validity of a particular assessment. Triangulation of measurement can be a useful way to do this. Selection processes that measure multiple attributes or competencies using several different methods are often referred to as a multi-trait, multi-method approach (MTMM). The essence of these approaches is that each competency or attribute is measured using a number of different methods. One way of checking the construct validity of the process as a whole is to establish that the scores on each construct converge across assessment methods, and diverge from other attribute scores where they are expected to.

BOX 6.3

Main types of validity in selection, and the questions answered by each

Face Validity: Does the assessment look appropriate to job candidates?

Content Validity: Does the assessment look relevant to job experts (managers, job holders) in terms of its relevance to job requirements?

Convergent Validity: Does the assessment correlate with other relevant measurements? Do assessment components correlate strongly with a common 'factor' or construct, extracted through factor analyses?

Divergent Validity: Is the assessment uncorrelated with other non-relevant measurements?

Construct Validity: Can an overall case be made to support the validity of the assessment?

Criterion Validity: Does the assessment correlate with job performance or some other relevant work criterion measured at the same time (concurrent validity) or at a later date (predictive validity)?

These techniques tell us about the quantitatively aspects of validity, but they do not tell the whole story in terms of the comprehensiveness or relevance of the assessment. To address these issues, practitioners can pay attention to the face and content validity of the assessments.

- Face validity in selection relates to how relevant the assessment looks to the job candidates. It is often overlooked by the statistically minded, but in practice it is amongst the best predictors of perceptions of procedural fairness (Hausknecht, Day and Thomas, 2004). This means that job candidates are more likely to feel that they have been treated fairly by the selecting organization if they believe the assessment to be relevant to the job they have applied for.

● Content validity is a similar qualitative judgement, made by subject experts rather than job candidates. In the case of tests, these are usually test designers and researchers, but for other forms of assessment, job holders could review assessments to determine their relevance to tasks and attributes that feature in their design.

The fixation of most selection research conducted over the past fifty or so years has undoubtedly been criterion validity, and with good reason. Criterion validity reflects the ultimate aim of selection assessments in organizations – to predict individual job performance. Asking a job candidate to participate in an assessment is a waste of time unless we know that it predicts how people tend to perform in the job we are selecting for. How can this be established? There are two approaches to criterion validation, and both involve correlating assessment scores with outcome criteria, usually job performance measures:

● The concurrent approach: assessment scores are correlated with job performance measured at the same time (i.e. concurrently). This approach is generally used in the development of assessments with current job holders.

● The predictive approach: assessment scores are correlated with job performance measured at some point in the future. This can be used to evaluate selection processes, enabling practitioners to check that the assessments of candidates made during the selection predicted their future job performance. A challenge with this approach is that only high scoring candidates are selected, and we are unable to measure the performance of low scoring candidates who were rejected from the selection process. This effect is called range restriction, which must be addressed in validity evaluations.

A challenge for practitioners seeking to evaluate criterion validity is the so called 'criterion problem'. The criterion problem refers to the typical unavailability of robust job performance measures in organizations. In many organizations, job performance indices are either absent or unreliable. This is critical for criterion validity evaluations. Selection processes might be incorrectly judged as having high or low validity as a result of poor measurement of criteria.

The picture is not all bad however. Some organizations do collect relevant job performance data, and moreover, it is probably short-sighted to view criterion validation solely from the perspective of job performance. In some jobs, organizations may not require high-flying performers, instead valuing reliable workers who are likely to stay with the organization for some time. One could think of the example of call centres, where turnover of staff has traditionally been problematic. In such cases, a well-defined, objectively measurable criterion such as tenure, absenteeism or turnover could be constructed and used.

Evidence of validity, reliability and fairness (see later in this chapter) are essential in verifying the effectiveness of selection processes. These therefore act as important evaluation criteria for selection processes. I'm always disappointed about how few organizations and practitioners conduct robust evaluations of selection processes, despite sizable investment in assessments upfront. The reluctance to invest in evaluations makes life easier for selectors and comfortable for assessment suppliers, who may rarely need to prove that selection tools or processes work for specific jobs in specific organizations. When done well, examining the reliability and validity of selection processes and assessments is extremely valuable. First, it helps us to determine whether the selection process worked or not. Second, demonstrable validity ensures that selection systems are defensible. Third, it allows the calculation of utility or the financial benefit of selection.

AUTHOR EXPERIENCE

Why Should Managers Care about Validity in Selection?

Many business decisions incur a degree of risk, and organizations typically aim to minimize this risk or at least balance it with the potential for return. It always surprises me that so many practitioners are therefore uninterested in the concept of validity because it actually permits a highly accurate estimate of risk in selection decision-making. Imagine that organization were to select people for a job at random. The probability that they would select an above average performer would be 50 per cent, and if they selected a number of people, then they would certainly choose as many good performers as poor performers. Random selection represents a validity of zero. As validity increases little by little, the probability of selecting a good performer increases and more and more risk is taken out of the decision. The bottom line is that by using valid selection tools, the risk in selection decisions is reduced considerably and as a result, we are more likely to select individuals who will be more productive for the organization. So validity matters.

In fact, in my experience, managers in organizations understand this concept perfectly and when validity is accurately explained and the implications illustrated, they are keen to improve what they are doing with their selection processes. I believe that we as psychologists are equally to blame for the disinterest in validity in practice. I once wrote up Hunter and Schmidt's (1998) findings for a Human Resource newsletter in an organization, communicating the implications. The Training Manager was unfamiliar with the findings, and yet had completed an MBA as well as other courses on assessment. Why had he not come across these key findings in the area? My view is that some of the writing that psychologists use in academic work is simply not practical or clear enough, nor is it publicized sufficiently by researchers to have a widespread applied impact.

UTILITY ANALYSES

Related to the issue of communication of validity research is the technique of utility analysis, first applied to selection processes by Schmidt, Hunter, McKenzie, and Muldrow (1979), and Schmidt and Hunter (1983). They proposed a method that estimated the financial benefits of improvements in selection processes based on the validity of the process, ratios of selected to rejected candidates, and estimates of the monetary value of different levels of job performance. Recent developments to the technique have retained many of these original features (e.g. Sturman, 2001). Schmidt and Hunter (1983) provided the well-cited estimate of the value of improved job performance. A one standard deviation improvement in job performance is estimated to equate to 40 per cent of the employee's salary in productivity gains. We can use this assumption to evaluate the productivity returns of improving validity and consequently selecting people with higher levels of job performance.

Psychologists originally developed utility analysis to help them communicate the benefits of their assessments to managers in clearer business language. They believed that managers would be more convinced by the bottom-line financials than by explanations of validity. However it appears that their belief may have been incorrect. Latham and Whyte (1994) reported that managers were more likely to endorse a new selection method if the validity of the assessment was explained clearly. However, the presentation of utility analyses has no influence on their decision-making. Perhaps psychologists should just try to make a better job of explaining what validity means rather than trying to express the effects financially.

SELECTION ASSESSMENT METHODS

Figure 6.1 showed that different assessments have different purposes. Early stage assessment is designed to select-out unsuitable applicants. Those individuals remaining (job candidates) are assessed using more detailed assessment methods, designed to thoroughly assess their competencies. The purpose of these later stage assessments is to select-in the most suitable candidates. In each case, assessment methodology is critical. The next sections review the major methods of assessment in selection processes.

CVs, Application Forms, and Biodata

The first contact that a job applicant has with an organization is usually through a Curriculum Vitae (CV) or application form, and this means that they have a high potential for affecting the outcomes of the selection process (Robertson and Smith, 2001). CVs provide a summary of relevant biographical information such as education and previous job experience. CVs are unique to the individual and in that sense the applicant leads their development. The unstandardized nature of CVs has led to questions about the effect it has on selection outcomes (Robertson and Smith, 2001; Searle, 2003). Many applicants include personal statements or other descriptive content highlighting relevant KSAOs, and these, along with the inclusion of applicant photographs can affect the evaluation of the CV and the assessment of the applicant at later stages of the selection process (see Bright and Hutton, 2000 for a review).

Application forms often contain similar information to CVs, but are organization-led, allowing some control over the format and contents of the initial submission by the applicant. The evaluation of application forms is open to bias, and in some cases to mistakes or failures of procedure (such as failure to verify information). Whilst one might assume that people screening job applications act consistently with established selection criteria, there does appear to be some evidence of the potential for subjective biases in the decision to select or reject an applicant (McKinney *et al.*, 2003). Moreover, meta-analyses show that typical factors that are examined on application forms (e.g. years of job experience and education) are poor predictors of job performance.

Biodata

Application forms can be enhanced by the addition of using scoreable biographical background information rate or evaluate applications, commonly applied in the biodata (biographical data) method. There is some confusion across different authors about exactly what constitutes biodata, but from a practical point of view, it is possible to draw on the definition by Owens (1976):

> *autobiographical data which are objectively or scoreable items of information provided by the individual about previous experiences (demographic, experiential, or attitudinal) which can be presumed or demonstrated to be related to personality structure, personal adjustment, or success in social, educational, or occupational pursuits.* Owens (1976) p. 53

Biodata may be captured quantitatively through answers to questionnaires, or qualitatively through provision of narrative text. Biodata scales are similar to personality scales, but items focus on the specifics of past behaviour and experience rather than behavioural preferences. Some example biodata items from Oswald, Schmitt, Kim, Ramsay and Gillespie (2004) are shown in Box 6.4. The items tend to ask people about the extent to which they agree or disagree with a particular statement, or about the frequency of a particular experience or event. One of the defining features of biodata is the way that data are dealt with. The empirical keying method follows the principles of prediction outlined earlier. In this approach, the association of each item with the outcome of interest is computed, and the most predictive items are retained and weighted. This method is criticized because little regard is paid to why an item predicts the outcome, and as such it is theoretical.

In the rational keying approach, desirable job relevant attributes or competencies are defined and a set of biodata items constructed to measure each one. The psychometric properties of the items are then evaluated, usually with existing job holders. Related items are compiled into reliable scales, and are then retained on the basis of their associations with the outcome of interest. By introducing theory into the development of the items, this method avoids some of the criticisms of the empirical keying method.

The form of biodata that you will more likely encounter at some stage of your career (and very soon if you are applying for graduate jobs) is qualitative. Qualitative biodata questions are open-response and ask applicants to provide a descriptive account of a job-relevant example from their past experience. Some examples are shown in Box 6.5. These items are scored in different ways from other forms

BOX 6.4
Example biodata items and associated measurement constructs

Knowledge: Think about the last several times you have had to learn new facts or concepts about something. How much did you tend to learn?

    a. Usually not enough.

    b. Sometimes not enough.

    c. Just what is needed.

    d. A little more than what is needed.

    e. Much more than what is needed.

Leadership: How many times in the past year have you tried to get someone to join in an activity in which you were involved or leading?

    a. Never.

    b. Once.

    c. Twice.

    d. Three or four times.

    e. Five times or more.

BOX 6.5

An example open biodata question plus behaviourally anchored rating scale (BARS)

Describe a recent project that you had to plan in advance. What were the important features that you factored into your plan? How did you ensure you achieved your objective? (answer in 200 words).

Competency and BARS

Planning and organization
Identifies priorities, sets deadlines, and plans schedules. Effectively manages own time to achieve goals. Gives considerations to wider implications of plans made.

1 The participant has not exhibited this competency in the exercise and/or has not followed instructions. Attempts to plan are ineffective through inappropriate prioritization or organization.

2 Plans are short-term, reactive and not related to objectives or outcomes.

3 Plans are linked to objectives but tend to be short term.

4 Plans are linked to objectives, are longer term and are based on priorities and deadlines.

5 Identifies priorities, sets deadlines, and plans schedules. Manages own time to achieve goals and gives considerations to wider implications of plans made.

of biodata. They could be scored against a competency framework using behaviourally anchored rating scales (BARS), which define the behaviours that constitute particular scores (see Box 6.5). The assessor might alternatively seek to confirm specific points from the applicant's answers, which could then be scored on a Yes/No or True/False binary basis.

Psychometric Testing

Psychometric testing (sometimes referred to as psychological testing) can be used in two ways in selection. It can be used to sift and reduce applicant pools to manageable sizes. It can also be used as part of a more detailed assessment of job candidates. It therefore covers both select-out and select-in activities, and the way that it is applied depends very much on the context of the selection process.

In Chapter 3, the common forms of psychological test were discussed:

- Tests of Maximum Performance, consisting of tests of ability and aptitude, linked to general intelligence, or specific facets of intelligence, such as verbal, numerical, abstract, spatial or mechanical abilities.

- Tests of Typical Performance, which in selection are almost exclusively trait assessments of personality.

Tests are popular for selection because they are easy to use, and cost effective. Logistically, many people can complete a test at the same time, requiring minimal supervision and input from selectors, and developments in online testing mean that people do not even need to visit the organization in order to complete a psychometric test.

Tests of ability and aptitude

Tests of ability and aptitude can be designed to measure overall reasoning ability or conversely to assess a very narrow aspect of an individual's ability, depending on job requirements. They may be used to establish a candidate's learning potential, or because requirements of the test are aligned to job tasks (Schmidt, 2012):

- Jobs that involve working with numerical data are likely to require a reasonable level of numerical ability for example. Similar cases could be made for verbal abilities, with most jobs drawing to some extent on skills in comprehending, understanding, and communicating verbally either orally or in writing.
- Jobs involving the mental manipulation of three dimensional shapes or spaces (such as for architects, air-traffic controllers, or fire-fighters) draw on spatial ability, and jobs that involve an appreciation of how things move require job holders to apply mechanical abilities.
- Abstract ability (the ability to recognize and use patterns presented in abstract forms) taps into an individual's fluid or novel problem solving ability, and in that sense is often applied to jobs that require flexible problem solving or systems thinking. For these reasons, they are popular for changeable, or complex roles.

Tests also vary in their difficulty, and pitching this correctly determines the utility of the information that is gained from the testing process. Tests that are too easy will produce data that are skewed to the top end of the ability range and those that are too difficult will likely produce very low scores across all candidates. Test suppliers have addressed this issue by providing guidelines on the appropriateness tests for different job types. Developments in test design have also moved towards 'item banking' that allow tests to be constructed flexibly to suit different levels of ability. Increasingly, ability tests are delivered online, adding to their procedural practicality (see Bartram, 2005).

The use of psychometric testing can be viewed as one of the successes of work psychology in the sense that the methodology draws on important psychological theory and research, and is incredibly popular with organizations, not to mention profitable. One of the reasons for its success is the high criterion validity values reported for ability testing, particularly in the research literature. In Hunter and Schmidt's (1998) meta-analysis, general ability tests are right up there with work samples and structured interviews with a validity of 0.51. In combination with an integrity test (which would extend to a personality assessment drawing on integrity-relevant traits), the validity rises to 0.63. In a European context, Salgado and Anderson (2003) reported extraordinarily high validities for the use of general mental ability (GMA) (0.60 – 0.70).

Theoretically speaking, the mediating pathway from ability to performance is learning (Schmidt and Hunter, 2004). People with higher ability tend to acquire job knowledge more quickly and in greater quantity, and proceduralize that knowledge more effectively (Kuncel, Ones and Sackett, 2010). As a consequence they adopt a steeper learning curve or performance trajectory. This theory helps to understand when ability assessment is most relevant; when jobs are complex and require fast learning. Job complexity is an important moderator of the validity of ability tests (Salgado *et al.*, 2003) with tests working best in more complex jobs.

The major criticisms of ability testing are based on their potential to cause adverse impact in recruitment and selection, thereby having the potential to unfairly discriminate against some ethnic groups. This is a significant issue, which we discuss later in the section on fairness.

Personality assessment

Personality traits are assessed in a number of different ways during the selection process. Selectors make informal judgements about personality traits during interviews and observational assessments. However, the assessment of traits is formally operationalized in personality trait inventories or questionnaires. These are self-report inventories that require candidates to respond to questions or statements, rating their agreement with them, or their perceptions of their accuracy as a description of their personality.

There are a multitude of different personality tests available on the market for practitioners to use, and these are of variable quality. Well-designed tests can be highly useful in selection. Poorly designed tests are at best useless, and at worst potentially damaging to businesses and the well-being of job candidates. Without knowledge of testing theory and practice, it can be difficult for users to distinguish good from poor tests. Training in the use of personality testing is therefore essential for the ethical use of assessments in organizations. However, the most common problems with personality tests are shown in Box 6.6.

As we saw in Chapter 3 the key differences in personality measures are how they measure the personality domain. Underlying each personality inventory is a personality structure, representing the dimensions or traits that are measured by the inventory. Inventories might measure broad traits similar to the Big Five personality factors, or at the facet level. The relative merits of each approach really depend on the performance criteria that selectors are trying to predict. If criteria are broad, then broad trait assessment is typically more useful; if the criteria are narrow, then more accurate assessment may be achieved through measuring at facet level (this is known as the bandwidth-fidelity trade-off).

The most prevalent approach to using personality assessment for selection is to undertake a profile-matching exercise. This usually draws on the practitioner's detailed knowledge of a specific personality instrument and the different traits that it assesses. Relevant traits are matched to aspects of the personnel specification, and an overall 'ideal' or 'desirable' personality profile constructed. For example, for jobs requiring social confidence, high Extraversion is ideal, whereas for jobs requiring lone working, low Extraversion may be a better fit. Candidates are then evaluated in terms of how well their profile fits with the ideal profile. This approach may be thought of as theoretically-driven, because there are good conceptual reasons established as to why certain traits are more or less

BOX 6.6

Three common problems with commercially available personality tests

If you are ever in the position of needing to evaluate the strengths and weaknesses of a personality tool for use in business, consider the three following common shortcomings of such test to help you:

- Incompleteness: Many tests claim to be comprehensive, but are not. Completeness of coverage involves covering the major personality domains of the five-factor model, and in selection, it is often helpful to be able to measure at the facet level (i.e. assessing two or more components of each of the Big Five).

- Gimmicks: Companies always try to market their products as different, but presenting

personality profiles on pretty 3D shapes, as colours, or as mountain peaks (I'm not making this up incidentally), is gimmickry at its worst – it adds nothing, and should be avoided to make decision-making as straightforward as possible.

- Lack of Evidence: Many tools have poor research evidence behind them. Always ask to scrutinize the evidence behind a test you might purchase, and always look at the detail of the studies as well as the key findings. If the evidence is poor, use an alternative.

desirable. For example, Shaffer and Postlethwaite (2013) reported that Conscientiousness has strongest validity for predicting performance in jobs that were highly routinized, reflecting the alignment of job requirements with the organized, structured and planned approach taken by those high on Conscientiousness. The way in which personality assessment is used has a clear impact on its validity.

There has been criticism of personality assessment validities (Morgeson, Campion, Dipboye, Hollenbeck, Murphy and Schmitt, 2007), but the overwhelming evidence is that when they are used in the right way, reliable assessments of personality do predict job performance. Traits are associated with performance in two ways. Firstly, Conscientiousness particularly appears to predict performance fairly consistently (e.g. Barrick, Mount and Judge, 2001). This probably reflects the association of Conscientiousness with organizational citizenship behaviour (see Chapter 3), which is important to some extent in almost all jobs. More relevant for selection however, is the improvements in validity that result from adopting the theory-driven approach as described above. Hogan and Holland (2003) showed that when traits were matched to job demands the validities of all of the Big Five were substantially improved. They reported validities of 0.43 for Emotional Stability, 0.35 for Extraversion, 0.34 for Agreeableness, 0.36 for Conscientiousness and 0.34 for Openness.

Finally, there is emergent evidence that personality assessment validities may change and increase for predicting performance after several years. Lievens *et al.* (2009) examined this effect in medical school students, but their theory is relevant for assessment for selection. In their analyses, they observed increases in the validity of Extraversion and Openness for predicting performance at year 7 compared to year 1. The theoretical rationale is that later stage training drew more on these dimensions as trainees interacted with real patients to solve medical problems. Thoresen, Bradley, Bliese and Thoresen (2004) observed that personality validities changed for predicting performance at different job stages, and Minbashian, Earl and Bright (2013) also reported that Openness was associated with better performance maintenance over time. Using personality assessment in selection may therefore have dual benefits of predicting performance in the short term where traits are matched to job requirements, but also in the long term by influencing motivation and emergent skills as people become more experienced in their work.

Criticisms about personality assessment by practitioners tend to focus on the potential for faking one's responses to personality inventories. There is a substantive literature on this issue (see Box 6.7) and a variety of different perspectives. Some researchers believe it to be problematic for selection practice (e.g. Murphy and Dzieweczynski, 2005; Morgeson *et al.*, 2007), and others do not (e.g. Hogan, 2005). One thing that is clear is that the effects of faking in selection are not fully understood, or well communicated, and while this remains the case, the concerns of practitioners are probably justified. Efforts to explore the nature of faking versus honest responding (e.g. König, Merz and Trauffer, 2012) represent the most effective starting point to improve this situation.

Selection Interviewing

Interviews are the most commonly experienced and applied selection assessment method, and involve an interaction between the job candidate and one or more interviewers for the purpose of determining their suitability for the job. Judgements about the candidate's suitability are made based on his or her orally presented responses to orally presented questions. The delivery of the interview by the organization varies considerably (Cook, 2004). For example, interviews can vary in their duration, the number of interviewers present, and in terms of how candidate input is prompted and evaluated. All of these points affect the reliability, validity and candidate reactions to the interview process and so are important to consider in the design of interviews.

BOX 6.7
Social desirability in personality testing

One of the most well cited concerns of managers and practitioners in respect of personality assessment in organizations is the potential for faking or socially desirable responding. The principle is straightforward: personality measures do not have right and wrong answers and so in theory, test takers could a) try to make themselves seem more desirable than they really are, or b) try to spot what the selectors are looking for and respond in a dishonest way to make themselves appear more suitable than they really are. On the face of it, it is a valid concern, but there are those that argue against the importance of the issue.

Amongst the most direct of critics are Robert Hogan and Joyce Hogan. Robert Hogan (2005) makes the point that the issue of faking or socially desirable responding is blurred in assessment in the same way that it is blurred in life. All people make efforts to conform to social norms and expectations, suppressing their true urges, inclinations and desires. All people take steps to create a good impression in particular life situations. Think about the last time you went on a first date, or indeed the last job interview that you attended. You probably managed your behaviour and impression somewhat. The point is that perhaps impression management should not be viewed as faking per se.

J. Hogan, Barrett and Hogan (2007) note three observations on socially desirable responding. First, individuals are able to fake their personality profile when instructed to do so. Second, the base-rate of faking in selection is quite low, a finding supported by Hogan, Barrett and Hogan's (2007) study and by Ellingson, Sackett and Connelly (2007). Third, and perhaps most curiously, there is mixed evidence about the effects of response distortion on validities of personality measures. Hough, Eaton, Dunnette, Kamp and McCloy (1990) argued that they remain stable, even if distortion is present. This may be because socially desirable responding represents an important individual difference in its own right. Others argue that validity is affected (e.g. Birkeland et al., 2006).

Numerous methods are available for detecting and reducing socially desirable responding in selection assessment. These include validity or social desirability scales designed to detect faking and impression management, instructional warnings about faking, and forced choice items. The effectiveness of these interventions is unclear in the research literature, although instructional warnings do appear to mitigate the risk of faking (Dwight and Donovan, 2003), but all continue to be used to address the practical concerns of managers and practitioners.

The broad finding from a wide range of research sources is that the structured interviews comprehensively outperform unstructured interviews in terms of their validity and reliability (Moscoso, 2000; Robertson and Smith, 2001). In Salgado's (1999) review of selection interviewing the validities of highly structured and highly unstructured interviews were 0.56 and 0.20 respectively. Moreover, structured interviews achieve higher levels of inter-rater reliability than unstructured interviews (0.92 and 0.69 respectively between the most and least structured panel interviews; Conway, Jako and Goodman, 1995), a finding replicated in meta-analyses by Huffcutt, Culbertson and Weyhrauch, 2013). So structure in the selection interview is clearly important, but what exactly does this mean?

One of the key aims of adding structure to interviews is to reduce the subjective biases that affect interviewers questioning and evaluation during the interview process. Campion *et al.* (1997) outline a number of ways that structure can be added to the selection interviews:

- Standard questioning could be adopted to ensure that each candidate is asked exactly the same questions. This ensures that comparisons between candidates are made based on consistent information.

- Scoring and evaluation procedures are also key foci for adding structure. The use of competency dimensions or scales for the scoring of candidate performance improves the structure of assessment during the interview. This involves providing interviewers with definitions and notes about how to evaluate particular answers or candidate behaviours, which helps to improve consistency.

- Further structure can be added to the scoring of candidate performance by the use of rating scales.

- Information provided to interviewers about the job under scrutiny can be standardized.

- Multiple rather than single interviewers can be used.

- Procedural guidelines around aspects such as follow-up questions, and overall interview duration can be applied.

Specific approaches to interviewing also help to add structure. More common structured formats are behavioural, competency, and situational interviews. Examples of question formats from all three kinds of interviews are shown in Box 6.8.

BOX 6.8
Example interview questions

Behavioural

Describe a recent project that involved you working as part of a team. How did you keep the group on track? How did you ensure that everyone's opinions were taken on board?

Competency is similar to behavioural, but focused on a specific competency.

An example question for teamwork could ask you to describe a project that involved you working as part of a team. What was your role, and how did you contribute? Give an example of how you contributed to the co-operation within the team.

Situational Judgement

Imagine a situation where you were part of a team working on a product design project. How would you help to ensure co-operation in the team, and facilitate the achievement of the team's objective?

- Behavioural interviews are based on key job requirements and ask interviewees to describe past experiences of performing such tasks. Behavioural interviews reflect the theory that past behaviour predicts future behaviour. The aim is to uncover positive job behaviours through past examples of fulfilling similar job requirements. Interviewers look for actual behavioural evidence (e.g. specific examples of the behaviour in question).

- Competency based interviewing (e.g. Roberts, 1997) has proved popular with practitioners, most likely because it allows interviews to be integrated with other forms of assessment such as assessment centres. Like behavioural interviews, the method uses questioning that requires the candidate to provide specific examples from their past experience to highlight relevant performance of job-relevant behaviours. However, in competency interviewing, questions are designed to tap into particular competency areas, and candidate responses evaluated against competency definitions. Behavioural and competency interviews focus on past behaviour.

- Situational interviews are based on the theory that intentions predict behaviour (Sue-Chan and Latham, 2004). Candidates are presented with a particular situation and forced to describe how they would respond. Their answers are evaluated by comparing them with a pre-defined set of responses that vary in desirability.

In his review of structure in interviews, Salgado (1999) reported that past-oriented questions had higher validities than future-oriented questions. However, as the literature on situational interviews is comparatively more recent, research data are accumulating (e.g. Banki and Latham, 2010), and so the relative merits of each question type is not clear at present.

Despite the relative straightforwardness with which structure can be introduced to interviews, and the consistent evidence of improved reliability and validity, the use of less effective, unstructured interviews is generally more common in organizations (Van der Zee, Bakker and Bakker, 2002). Some argue that the technical or prescriptive design of structured interviews can put off managers and practitioners from using them (e.g. the multi-modal interview; Schuler and Moser, 1995). Managers may even favour unstructured methods in some cases, perhaps because of convenience or habit, or a perception that structured methods are beyond their control or capability (Van der Zee, Bakker and Bakker, 2002). It is clear that more needs to be done to clarify the ways in which research implications in this area are communicated (Roulin and Bangerter, 2012), and indeed there are some readable and practical accounts published recently (e.g. Huffcutt, 2010).

Assessment Centres

Assessment centres are processes that enable the in-depth assessment of job candidates. They are used in a variety of formats, and defined by the International Taskforce on Assessment Centre Operations (2001) as:

> *a standardized evaluation of behavior based on multiple inputs. Multiple trained observers and techniques are used. Judgements about behaviors are made, in major part, from specifically developed assessment simulations. These judgements are pooled in a meeting among the assessors or by a statistical integration process.*

The definition captures the key components of assessment centres; multiple exercises, multiple assessment dimensions, multiple assessors. The strength of assessment centres is undoubtedly the richness of the assessment system and the data they produce.

Assessment centre design

Assessment centres are often described as multi-trait, multi-method approaches to selection. This reflects their design, which is based around the idea of assessing multiple competency dimensions in multiple exercises or activities. Competency dimensions form the basis of the assessment of candidates at the assessment centre. Exercises are designed to elicit specific competency dimensions, and the essence of the assessment centre design is to include a variety of activities that give an adequate representation of the different elements of the job. The exercises themselves are referred to as work samples. This is because they simulate job tasks, enabling candidates to provide a 'sample' of their job behaviour. Work samples may be used in combination in an assessment centre, or on their own as standalone assessments. Some common forms of work sample are listed in Box 6.9. Once the competencies are selected, and exercises designed, a matrix of competencies against exercises is constructed (Figure 6.3). This shows which competencies are assessed in each exercise and is used by assessors to guide their evaluations of candidates.

Assessors and assessment procedures

Assessors at the assessment centres are usually a variety of different stakeholders in the selection process. Lievens (1999) found that whilst psychologists tended to be most effective at differentiating competencies behaviours, managers tended to give ratings that more accurately reflected the values of the organization. Training of assessors has been found to affect the validity and reliability of their ratings (Lievens, 2001), and yet many organizations continue to provide very limited training to assessment centre assessors.

The assessment of candidates at assessment centres is structured and methodical. The most common format is the ORCE method of assessment (Observe, Record, Classify, Evaluate). In this method, the assessor is trained to observe candidate behaviour, recording (in writing) everything that the candidate says or does during the exercise. Once recorded, the behaviours are classified against competency dimensions before being evaluated or rated. This last stage is usually guided by anchored rating scales. A recent development in assessment procedures is the frame-of-reference method of

BOX 6.9
Common forms of work sample tests

Inbox exercises. In these activities, candidates provide responses to a typical set of email inbox items. They are usually assessed based on the content of responses and overall prioritization.

Group tasks. These can include business games and team activities. Candidates are assessed on interpersonal and leadership competencies among others.

Group discussions. These activities involve group discussion of a work related issue or task, generally with the purpose of reaching a decision or conclusion. The discussions can be leader-assigned or leaderless, and can have assigned or unassigned roles (i.e. participants can be given a brief or purpose in the discussion, or be given no guidance on how they should contribute). Asses-

sors consider the interactions of group members to assess communicative, interpersonal and leadership competencies.

Role-play or fact-finding interviews. These often involve examples of one-to-one management of people, or face-to-face interviews for conducting investigations. For example, the activities might require the candidate to deal with a staff performance issue.

Presentations. Presentations tend to be used for jobs that require people to present in public, such as sales or managerial roles. Candidates are asked to present on a particular topic, or given a free choice. They are usually assessed on communicative competencies, as well as on the content of the presentation.

Competency	Exercises		
	Group Activity	**In-tray**	**Presentation**
Communication	X		X
Planning	X	X	
People Management		X	X
Decision-Making	X	X	
Problem Solving		X	X
Assertiveness	X		X

Figure 6.3   An example competency x exercise matrix

assessment (Lievens and Klimoski, 2001). The frame-of-reference method encourages assessors to compare episodes of candidate behaviour against specific models of job performance that incorporate behaviour that is set within an organizational context. Rather than focusing solely on behaviour as in the ORCE method, the assessor would be encouraged to draw on knowledge of effective performance as expressed in a particular work context, using this information to judge the overall performance of the candidate. There are some encouraging findings from studies of this assessment method (e.g. Schleicher, Day, Mayes and Riggio, 1999).

Assessment centres are set up so that each candidate is assessed by several different assessors. At the end of the assessment centre, their judgements are integrated in a 'wash-up' meeting. The purpose of the integration session is to standardize ratings to some extent (providing a check that each assessor is using the assessment procedures in a similar way), but mainly to pool the ratings of the candidates from the various exercises. Given the importance of this issue for deciding on overall evaluations of candidates, it is surprising that there are no published research findings on the impact of this process.

Validity of assessment centres

The validity of assessment centres is somewhat disappointing given the high level of investment that is required to design and implement them. Gaugler, Rosenthal, Thornton and Bentson (1987) reported a meta-analysis that found that overall assessment centre ratings predicted supervisory ratings of job performance, with a validity coefficient of 0.36. More recent meta-analyses reported validity of 0.28 (Hermelin, Lievens and Robertson, 2007) and 0.39 (Arthur, Day, McNelly and Edens, 2006)

KEY FIGURE

Filip Lievens

Filip Lievens is Professor at the department of Personnel Management, Ghent University in Belgium, and is highlighted in this chapter because of his ongoing and influential work in the area of selection. He is a prolific researcher, his achievements recognized by his rising from PhD

Graduate to Full Professor in only seven years at Ghent. What makes his perspective on selection assessment compelling is a commitment to construct-driven selection assessment. A great deal of research in the field of selection is concerned with prediction of job performance, but Lievens emphasizes the need to understand why particular assessments predict performance. This is likely to become a key focus in the next generation selection research.

Lievens also has an interest in non-cognitive predictors of job performance, writing on personality assessment, situational judgement, and assessment centres. His perspective represents a subtle distinction between emphasis in the US and EU on selection assessment. The US has focused on cognitive ability and predictive validity, work spearheaded by Frank Schmidt and John Hunter in the 1990s. The European research emphasis is arguably somewhat more open to non-cognitive assessment, and to a greater extent oriented to understanding why certain assessments predict job performance.

Lievens has one of the best online repositories of writings of any academic in work psychology, which is well worth browsing:
http://users.ugent.be/~flievens/

DISCUSS WITH A COLLEAGUE

Go back to the list of KSAOs that you generated for a familiar job earlier in this chapter. Identify how each one could be assessed at a selection process.

A recurrent concern for assessment centres is their construct validity. Within the assessment centre, the competency dimensions are set up as the constructs to assess. Their construct validity rests on the assumption that they are indeed individual attributes that can be measured in different contexts. For example, if a candidate is given a score of 3 for Problem Solving in one exercise, then they should achieve a similar or identical score for Problem Solving in other exercises. Remember that we are assuming that the rating reflects their level of competency. The problem for assessment centres is that this assumption is not confirmed in empirical investigations, and scores appear to be much more consistent within exercises than they are within competencies. Scores on different competencies within the same exercise are rated similarly. The result is low convergent and discriminant validity. This is referred to as the exercise effect (Sackett and Dreher, 1982), and several sources have tried to explain why it occurs and how to reduce it (e.g. Lievens, Chasteen, Day and Christiansen, 2006; Lievens, De Koster and Schollaert, 2008). Clearly more work is needed in this area to determine exactly what is being measured at assessment centres. For example, it may be unreasonable to expect competency scores to be equal across exercises. Each represents a unique situation, and people generally are more or less effective in different work contexts. More important is to understand the potential effects on criterion validity.

Selection Assessments: What Does Research Tell us Works Best?

Criterion validity research has developed considerably over the years. Early studies tended to report findings from small samples in specific selection contexts, and studies that aggregated data reported disappointing cross-context validities. The result was a strong endorsement of the value of local validation. Research has moved beyond local validation studies however. In 1984, Hunter and Hunter published a highly influential meta-analysis of selection techniques. As discussed in previous chapters, meta-analyses take account of the methodological artefacts that suppress validity coefficients, allowing a more accurate aggregation of results from different studies. Table 6.1. presents the findings from several of the most widely cited, and shows the validity coefficients for a variety of different assessments, and some combinations of assessments. A good updated review of criterion validities is presented by Schmitt and Fandre (2008). Amongst the updates are psychometric test data specifically from Europe (Bertua, Anderson and Salgado, 2005; Salgado, Anderson, Moscoso, and Bertua 2003).

MACRO PERSPECTIVES ON RECRUITMENT AND SELECTION

Whilst the processes and procedures from the micro perspective are certainly robust, many see this methodology as quite traditional (Cascio and Aguinis, 2008). At the heart of such processes are validity and reliability of selection, and the seminal works on validity almost feel somewhat 'last century'; Hunter and Schmidt published their major meta-analyses more than 15 years ago (Hunter and Schmidt, 1998), drawing partly on work published more than 30 years ago (Hunter and Hunter, 1984).

Bringing the literature into the 21st century requires examining the evidence base for structured and systematic recruitment and selection against a more strategic perspective on HRM framework (e.g. Cascio and Aguinis, 2008; Ployhart, 2006). One key theme in the strategic HRM literature is the role of contingencies on the effectiveness of HR and management practices (e.g. Lengnick-Hall, Lengnick-Hall, Andrade and Drake, 2009). Contingency theories emphasize that in certain scenarios, specific practices are likely to be more or less effective than in others. This is a point less frequently acknowledged in the Work and Organizational Psychology selection literature, which by contrast, treats systematic selection as universally effective (Lengnick-Hall *et al.*, 2009).

Table 6.1 Selection Assessments and their Associated Validities

Assessment or Combination of Assessments	Criterion Validity Values
Test of General Cognitive Ability plus Structured Interview	0.63 (Schmidt and Hunter, 1998)
Test of General Cognitive Ability plus Work Sample Test	0.63 (Schmidt and Hunter, 1998)
General Cognitive Ability Test	0.51 (Schmidt and Hunter, 1998) 0.50–0.60 (Bertua et al., 2005)
Structured Interview	0.56 (Salgado, 1999) 0.44 (McDaniel et al., 1994)
Work Sample Test	0.54 (Schmidt and Hunter, 1998) 0.33 (Roth et al., 2005)
Personality Assessment	0.34–0.43 (Hogan and Holland, 2003) 0.31 (Schmidt and Hunter, 1998)
Assessment Centres	0.39 (Arthur et al., 2006) 0.28 (Hermelin et al., 2007)
Biodata	0.35 (Schmidt and Hunter, 1998)
Unstructured Interview	0.20 (Salgado, 1999) 0.33 (McDaniel et al., 1994)
Reference Check	0.26 (Schmidt and Hunter, 1998)
Job Experience	0.18 (Schmidt and Hunter, 1998)
Years of Education	0.10 (Schmidt and Hunter, 1998)

This is reasonable given the evidence from meta-analyses is consistently that structured selection is more effective than unstructured, informal techniques. Nevertheless, the utility of such techniques is predicated on being able to be very selective in decision-making. The fact is that is some economies, there is a dramatic under-supply of people with key skills and knowledge, meaning that selectors often do not have the luxury of selecting one person from a candidate pool of 20. Rather they may be required to select one from three, one from two, or even two from every three candidates. So selection ratio, based on economic context, is a key contingency that influences the effectiveness of structured selection practice.

Contingencies such as these and other strategic demands and objectives of organizations influence how best to deploy effective strategic recruitment and selection. Tsui, Pearce, Porter and Tripoli (1997) identify how organizations typically have multiple HR systems used for different purposes. The challenge is to adapt the approach taken to fit the objectives of selection. For example, Lepak and Snell (1999) proposed that positions in a company should be classified on two dimensions: uniqueness of skills (how specific skills were to the company need) and value of skills (strategic importance). Where jobs are high uniqueness and high value, employee development is key, and correspondingly, selection might focus on capacity to learn. Where jobs are low uniqueness, but high value, a market-based external approach to recruitment and selection is needed, where assessment might follow closely the models we have reviewed, and invest heavily in the late-stage select-in techniques.

EXAMPLES OF DEPLOYING EFFECTIVE RECRUITMENT AND SELECTION

Developing effective selection systems calls for adapting approaches to meet specific or strategic needs in organizations. Two high-impact recruitment and selection tasks are the recruitment and identification of talented and high potential employees, and leadership and managerial selection.

Talent and High Potential Selection

Talent management is an often-quoted activity in HRM that might range in meaning from managing people generally, through to managing top-level managers and directors. However, it broadly refers to (e.g. Collings and Mellahi, 2009):

1 Identification of key positions in a business that contribute to the achievement of strategic business objectives.

2 Identification of high-potential individuals, either externally or internally that can be developed and managed into those positions.

There is obviously a clear need and role for sound and robust assessment and selection in the process of talent management. Identifying high potential, selecting such individuals and keeping them is a critical strategic organizational task.

The challenge for assessment and selection is to first understand the nature of high potential. Also relevant is to understand the career context for high potential employees. When an employee or recruit is added to a high potential pool of people, that person is entered onto a steep career trajectory that will involve experience of multiple areas of a business, and fast progression quickly to leadership roles. The person is not so much selected for a job, rather for a career that involves frequent learning, and adaptation.

Defining the nature of high potential has attracted surprisingly little research attention until recently. Silzer and Church (2009) review the literature on high potential and formulate a model capturing three key elements that define high potential individuals:

- Foundation Aspects: high cognitive ability to facilitate learning, and key personality traits such as achievement orientation.
- Growth Aspects: motivation to learn and master things, and resilience to grow and develop.
- Career Aspects: typically leadership, but also career-specific specialty or competence that might include technical excellence in a field.

For deploying assessments for selection, one implication for assessment and selection is that a combination of assessments is needed. For foundation aspects, *prospective assessment* is needed to inform decisions, looking forwards at predictors of learning and performance maintenance such as personality traits and cognitive ability. For career aspects, *retrospective assessment* is needed to examine capability and competencies developed through the career to date. Interviews or work samples might be used, or potentially peer-assessments for current employees. For growth aspects, a combination of these techniques may be needed to look at prospective and actual past learning and adaptation.

KEY THEME

Globalization and Cross Cultural Issues

Economic growth and recruitment and selection

An environmental contingency of recruitment and selection is the economic environment within which businesses operate. Over the past several years I have worked on recruitment and selection activity in a number of different countries with corporate clients. The effects of contingencies are very easy to observe in practice. For example, in the UK, at the time of writing this, austerity measures by the incumbent government are hitting employment hard. In the UK, there is therefore an oversupply of labour, most notably in the graduate market, where young people struggle to find employment. From a selection practitioner point of view, the challenge is to assess in high volumes, and ensure that processes are maximally selective to ensure that the very best people are hired.

In SE Asia by contrast, two countries are particularly illustrative of the environmental influences on selection practice. The Indonesian economy has been growing at 6–7 per cent annually, yet is immature in terms of applying formalized HRM effectively. Practitioners there have the dual challenge of an emerging undersupply of highly skilled applicants, because supply cannot always meet growing demand, and lack of selection skills in decision-makers. This creates problems for attrition rates, because good people can move organizations easily, and poor decision-making leads to unsuitable people being selected, who quickly leave or do not produce as a consequence.

The second country in the ASEAN region to note is Myanmar, which is opening up to the world and industrializing at a significant rate. There, the selection challenge is a dramatic underdevelopment of skills for effective working in the corporate organizations that are now moving into the economy and introducing high performance management systems. The selection challenge is most definitely about identifying potential to learn and develop, so that through on-job development or internship-type arrangements, people with high potential can be nurtured, developed, and advanced through organizations quickly.

Managerial and Leadership Selection

Managerial and leader selection is a preoccupation of many organizations, understandably so given the impact leaders have on businesses (see Chapter 13). Most people can connect with the obvious issue that the technical expertise and excellence is not enough for effective leadership and management. Promoting people or selecting leaders for technical excellence often means losing an excellent technician and gaining an average leader.

Fiedler (1996) considered the issue of leadership and management selection and pointed to the contradictory findings of the validity of intelligence assessments in this context. Intelligence was, it appeared, an inconsistent predictor of effectiveness as a leader.

In unpicking the literature, Fiedler identified some key issues in these findings. Firstly, intelligence is only important to the extent that the leader has subsequent capacity and autonomy to learn and solve problems. Leaders and managers operating under hierarchical systems of control are likely to have less such autonomy, and in such contexts, cognitive ability is less important. Secondly, leadership effectiveness itself is highly contingent. Leader behaviour, for example varies in terms of two dimensions: person-orientation (the focus of the leader of people and their welfare), and initiation of structure (task-focus of the leader). Neither approach to leadership is universally effective, and so the context of the leadership role is critical.

The case of leadership selection is one that illustrates the issue of context. The context within which the leadership role is performed requires a contextualized assessment approach, in which the demands of the organization and the job environment are built into assessment design. Assessment centres are a good example, which may simulate aspects of the organization. Lessons from literatures on frame-of-reference techniques (Lievens, 2001) are likely to improve selection. Likewise, Cascio and Aguinis (2008) describe 'in-situ' performance, which represents understanding of both performance, and the context within which performance occurs. The incorporation of contextual information to assessment is therefore highly relevant for effective managerial and leadership selection.

The literature on personality and leadership may also inform the selection of leaders and managers. For example, Judge, Bono, Illies and Gerhardt (2002) report a meta-analyses of the associations of personality traits with leader emergence and leader effectiveness. They reported that:

- Traits related to Extraversion and Conscientiousness in the Big Five model were associated with leader emergence.
- Traits related to Conscientiousness, Extraversion, Emotional Stability and Openness were associated with leader effectiveness.

The use of personality assessment as a component of leadership and managerial selection therefore seems sensible from an evidence-based perspective.

APPLICANT PERSPECTIVES: THE EXPERIENCE OF RECRUITMENT AND SELECTION

The methods that have been explored so far in this chapter conform to a single paradigm in selection practice – the positivist or psychometric paradigm. Bilsberry (2007) comments that this paradigm considers selection primarily from the perspective of the organization, focusing on how good selection decisions should be made in order to maximize performance. Neglected by the paradigm is the perspective of the applicant or candidate. As highlighted earlier, the social process or constructionist perspective focuses on the social nature of the selection process. Bilsberry identifies that the social process approach is rarely integrated into the selection literature adequately, and rather serves as a theoretical counterpoint, presented as a critical perspective to the psychometric paradigm. However some of the issues raised by the social process approach have been developed in empirical research.

Herriot (1984) developed ideas of the social exchanges that occur during the selection process in depth and examined some of the implications of a theory of social exchange at the selection process. Perhaps the most widely investigated area amongst those that he covers concerns applicant reactions and perceptions of the selection process and the organization. In a review of forty studies conducted between 1985 and 1999, Ryan and Ployhart (2000) identify two trends in this research. The first is the influence of applicant perceptions on attitudes and behaviours towards the organization. The second is the influence of applicant perceptions on their subsequent performance at the selection process. These two sets of relationships were elaborated by Hausknecht, Day and Thomas (2004) and included in a theoretical model of the antecedents, contents, and outcomes of applicant perceptions of selection processes (see Figure 6.4).

A key element of the model concerns organizational justice, with the most commonly studied aspect being perceptions of procedural justice (perceptions of the overall fairness of the procedures used in the selection). In their meta-analyses of the components of their model, Hausknecht *et al.*, (2004) reported clear associations between applicant perceptions of face and predictive validity, and

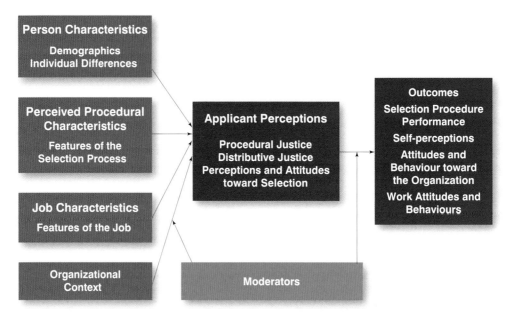

Figure 6.4   A model of applicant perceptions of selection processes, plus antecedents and consequences

positive perceptions of the fairness of the selection process. Moreover, those who perceived the selection positively were more likely to perceive the organization favourably, accept job offers, and to recommend the organization as an employer to others. Note also that perceptions of fairness are not necessarily aligned with actual fairness (Anderson, 2011), and so organizations need to consider both the process and presentation of selection.

As you may expect however, the effects of perceived selection fairness may not be so straightforward. In a study of real job applicants, Schinkel, van Vianen and van Dierendonck (2013) reported that affective well-being was related differently to perceptions of fairness depending on the selection outcome. Those who were selected reported higher well-being if they perceived the selection to be fair. However, for those who were rejected, well-being was higher if they thought the selection was unfair. This makes sense when you think about it: people could compensate for the negative effects of rejection by at least feeling that it was not because of a lack of competence, but rather a problem in the selection. The practical implication is that organizations should be aware of the potential negative impacts of rejection and alongside designing fair processes, should take steps to mitigate the negative impacts of rejection.

So which selection methods are generally preferred by applicants? Hausknecht *et al.* (2004) reported that work samples and interviews were judged most favourably, followed by cognitive ability tests, with personality tests and biodata being rated less favourably.

FAIRNESS IN SELECTION

Fairness in selection processes stands alongside reliability and validity as a third critical ethical consideration. The concept of fairness is difficult to define however. It requires one to consider three interacting factors that collectively determine whether a selection process can be considered to be fair:

1 Models of adverse impact and differential validity.
2 Legal concerns.
3 Best practice procedures and conventions.

Models of Adverse Impact and Differential Validity

Next to validity, adverse impact is perhaps the most consistently studied research area in selection. Adverse impact (sometimes referred to as indirect discrimination) is related to individual assessments, as well as selection processes overall. Adverse impact occurs when one particular demographic group scores lower than others on a particular assessment (i.e. their mean score is lower than that of other groups). The net result is that a smaller proportion of candidates from that group will make it through the selection process compared to others. The group is systematically disadvantaged as a result of the use of the assessment technique. This form of discrimination can be contrasted with direct discrimination, which reflects particular prejudices of the selector. Indirect discrimination does not imply that the assessor or selector is prejudiced, rather it is an unseen form of discrimination – a property of the assessment rather than the assessor.

The four-fifths rule of thumb is a statistical convention for judging the severity of adverse impact. The rule states that the proportions of one group 'passing' a component of the selection should not be less than four-fifths or 80 per cent of another. If the proportion is less than 80 per cent, then adverse impact is effectively confirmed. A variety of procedures for determining adverse impact according to this rule of thumb have been developed (Collins and Morris, 2008). Hough, Oswald, and Ployhart (2001) reviewed adverse impact evidence for a variety of assessment methods, collating data on the differences in assessment scores between different demographic groups (e.g. men, women, black candidates, white candidates, older and younger workers). Their findings are summarized in Table 6.2.

On its own, adverse impact does not necessarily constitute unfairness, and it is actually validity that is the key to deciding whether a method is unfair. Criterion validity tells us the extent to which an assessment predicts job performance. If the assessment is valid, then selecting high scoring candidates will give the highest probability of selecting a high performing employee. Organizations cannot be challenged on these grounds, and even if the assessment causes adverse impact, using it to select job candidates is justifiable. This holds true unless the assessment is found to predict performance differently for different demographic groups. This is referred to as differential validity. The implication of differential validity is that estimates of job performance are different depending on the demographic group of the candidate (e.g. different performance estimates could be derived from two candidates with the same assessment scores). Procedures for determining differential validity were proposed by Cleary (1986), but are very difficult to implement, particularly in small samples of candidates (e.g. Woods, 2006). If differential validity is demonstrated, then the assessment can be considered to be unfair.

Legal Concerns

Globalization of organizations means that they may operate selection processes in a variety of different legal contexts, each treating fairness in selection differently. In Europe and the US, there are some common threads however. Employment law generally covers discrimination based on gender, ethnicity, disability and age. Recruitment material such as advertisements are prohibited from stating preferences for individuals from specific groups, unless it is essential for fulfilling a job requirement (e.g. in the case of disability, if the organization could not make a reasonable adjustment to the job).

Indirect discrimination is covered in most employment laws (e.g. the Equality Act 2010 in the UK), but only in the US is it operationalized in the four-fifths rule of thumb. The essence of most legislation in

Table 6.2 Assessment Methods and Adverse Impact (potential for adverse impact highlighted where appropriate) (summarized from Hough, Oswald and Ployhart, 2001)

Assessment Method	Potential Adverse Impact
Cognitive Ability Tests	**High potential for adverse impact:** **Ethnicity Moderate potential for adverse impact: Gender, Age** ● In US data, white groups score higher than black groups on many forms of ability test, higher than Hispanic groups, and lower than East Asian groups on measures of g. ● Men and women score equally on general ability tests, women score higher on verbal tests, men on spatial and numerical. ● Older workers tend to score lower on measures of g.
Personality Measures	**Moderate potential for adverse impact: Gender** ● Small or negligible differences on the Big Five across ethnicities. ● Women score higher on agreeableness, and traits relating to affiliation and dependability.
Biodata	● Small differences in scores across ethnicities, gender and younger/older workers. If scores captured educational background, potential for adverse impact against some ethic groups increases.
Assessments Centres	**Moderate potential for adverse impact: Ethnicity, Age** ● In US data, black candidates score lower than whites. ● Older candidates surprisingly score lower than younger ones considering that managerial skills supposedly develop with experience. ● No information on gender differences, but higher performance on work sample test may lead to higher AC score.
Interviewers	● White scored slightly higher than blacks and Hispanic groups in US data. ● Evidence less clear for gender, but difference likely to be negligible overall (Moscoso, 2000), but moderated by perceptual factors such as interviewer biases.
Work Sample Tests	**Moderate potential for adverse impact: Ethnicity** ● In US data, black group score lower than white groups, men score lower than women. Ethnic differences are much smaller than those on cognitive ability test difference for the same participants, however, and so are preferable in terms of reducing advance impact.

KEY THEME

Corporate Social Responsibility: Fairness, Ethics, and the Law

One issue that is highlighted in this chapter is adverse impact: indirect discrimination against particular groups based on systematic differences in their assessment scores compared with others. It's a complex issue, because as highlighted in the section on Fairness, the legal position around adverse impact is not clearly defined. An assessment method could cause adverse impact, yet still be lawful on the grounds that it is a legitimate way to identify individuals with the highest potential for performance.

On the issue of adverse impact, organizational culture and values are relevant. This might seem to contradict the majority of this chapter, which has primarily drawn on the technical and evidence based application of selection methods, removing subjectivity in decision making. Yet culture and values are important on this point. In work psychology research, we know about the potential adverse impact associated with some selection methods, most obviously with cognitive ability testing. Research has established that differences exist across ethnicities, and that even when combined with non-cognitive predictors, adverse impact or indirect discrimination may still occur. Plus, international working raises the issue of the effects of non-native speakers completing tests in the same language as native speakers. Evidence shows that our estimates of ability are suppressed when the test-taker completes verbal tests in non-native languages, with the test tapping into language proficiency rather than ability (e.g. te Nijenhuis and van der Flier, 2003).

The fairness of the test depends on whether it predicts performance differently across demographic groups. There is little reported evidence of differential

validity in the research literature (e.g. Hunter, Schmidt and Hunter, 1979) and many organizations are not in a position to carry out their own validity investigations. Organizations are therefore faced with a dilemma about trying to balance the demands of valid selection and a diverse workforce. According to De Corte and Lievens (2003), this dilemma is 'one of the most perplexing problems facing the practice of personnel selection today' (p.87). Using a cognitive ability test will certainly help to identify high performers, but will most likely reduce diversity in the organization – in different ways for different tests. Even the most recent attempts to develop an empirical account of the problem are limited (e.g. De Corte, Lievens and Sackett, 2007) because conceptualizing and modelling the selection quality – adverse impact trade-off is highly complex, and beyond the technical capabilities of most practitioners.

At present then, organizations must therefore make the decision about whether to use cognitive ability tests for selection based on their own values and these are likely to include consideration of values around CSR. If the organization values productivity over diversity, then the use of a fair test with some adverse impact is justifiable. If the organization values diversity first, then the test is best avoided, particularly if it is unaccompanied by other supporting evidence in the selection process.

The question for work psychologists is whether they should present a position on the issue, and if so what it should be?

respect of selection is that adverse impact or indirect discrimination is only unlawful if it cannot be shown to be a reasonable method of assessment. This usually means that assessments are judged fair if they can be shown to be job relevant through a *priori* job and competency analyses, and if there is some evidence of their validity. US law is peculiar in its specification of differential validity as grounds for unlawful practice, although employers can present a case to show that it was not practically possible to conduct a validity study. A major future challenge is to understand how research findings and implications relate to the legal environments in different countries (e.g. Myors *et al.*, 2008). A related question in this area concerns the difference between legal practice, and ethical, responsible practice (see Key Theme Box).

Best Practice Guidelines

A further determinant of fairness concerns the extent to which best practice guidelines have been followed in the selection process. There are some important sources of guidance on best practice in selection that can be drawn upon. Psychometric testing has well defined guidelines for use. The International Testing Commission (2005) has developed a comprehensive set of guidelines, which are similar to those set down by the British Psychological Society in the Occupational Test User qualifications. There are similar guidelines for Assessment Centres (International Taskforce, 2001). In the UK, the Chartered Institute for Personnel and Development (CIPD) publish best-practice guidance, and in the US, the Uniform Guidelines on Employee Selection Procedures (US Employment Opportunities Commission, 1978) are also comprehensive.

SUMMARY

R ecruitment and selection are key activities for work psychologists in organizations. Effective recruitment and selection processes are those that are evidence-based, systematic, and strategic. Such processes draw on sound science, proceed logically and methodically, and serve the specific strategic needs of particular organizations, or job and roles within them.

From a practical perspective, recruitment and selection are best conceptualized as a longitudinal process following a series of sequential steps. The process starts with job analysis (an examination of the work to be carried out) and the knowledge, skills, abilities, other characteristics and competencies to be demonstrated by the worker). The resultant information is recorded in a job description and personnel specification, which are used to define selection criteria and assessment needs. The information also feeds into recruitment (attraction of job applicants).

Once assessment needs are defined, assessments are chosen on the basis of their match with needs, and their associated reliability, validity and fairness. Among the most common assessment methodologies are CVs, application forms and biodata, psychometric, and situational judgement testing, selection interviewing and assessment centres. Advances in research, most notably meta-analyses, have enabled a huge volume of literature on the criterion validities of different assessment methods to be accumulated. Alongside validity, a further critical issue is adverse impact and fairness, decisions about which draw on statistical methods, best practice guidelines, and organizational culture and values.

Macro-perspectives on recruitment and selection explore how organizational contingencies guide how recruitment and selection are deployed in various ways in different organizations and for different purposes within organizations. Recent examples include a focus on assessment and identification of high potential staff employee. Other wider perspectives focus on the experience of job candidates at selection processes and the impact that their experiences have on behavioural, attitudinal and affective outcomes.

At the start of this chapter, I described my walk to work through the city of Birmingham, and the wide diversity of jobs that people do in the organizations and businesses that I walk past. I must also reflect on the impact of Work Psychology in those businesses. I know that some of the ideas explored in this chapter have made their way into practice, but we could do so much more. What might the impact be of applying effective, sound and fair selection practice in all of these organizations? Businesses could benefit because productivity and performance could be improved, and people would potentially be happier in their jobs, if their unique skills and attributes found expression and utility in their work. They might also feel more fairly treated by organizations. Then imagine this potential impact at the level of the whole city – interacting and co-dependent organizations all performing their functions more effectively, led and staffed by happier, more satisfied employees.

DISCUSSION QUESTIONS

1   What advice would you give to a manager who wanted to select a new administrator for their group?

2   Are tests of cognitive ability the best way to assess people in selection? Why?

3   If you were a selection candidate, what would be important in terms of helping you feel fairly treated?

4   Look at some job advertisements in the press. What information do they communicate about the organization's values?

5   Think about your own judgemental biases. How might they influence your decisions if you were interviewing a job candidate?

6   People can manage their behaviour and the impression they create at a selection process (i.e. they could fake a personality test, or turn on the charm for an interview). How would you advise an organization to protect against this possibility?

APPLY IT

Here are some immediate ways to transfer the content of this chapter in your work activity.

1   Practically critique recruitment practices in your own organization. There is not one right way in selection, but effective processes are evidence-based, systematic, and strategic – use this as a framework for seeking ways to improve selection processes.

2   Review the selection criteria that you use for key positions in your team. Look at each competency or KSAO element that you look for in employees in that job and ask the following questions: Is it essential (yes/no)?; Is it reasonable to expect in the applicant pool (yes/no)?; Does it differentiate good from poor performance (1=Not really, 5=Definitely)?; Could it cause you trouble if you ignored it at a selection (1=Highly unlikely; 5=Highly likely). Use your ratings to prioritize those things that really matter in your selection.

3   Improve your interview processes – everyone can to some extent – by incorporating one or more of the recommendations from the chapter.

4   Learn about psychometric assessment if you have not already done so. The British Psychological Society Occupational Test User Programmes are valuable if you use assessment widely, and there are good programmes offered by test suppliers and consultancy companies (we have one spun-out from Aston Business School: **http://www.astonassessments.co.uk**).

5   Ask for feedback from successful and unsuccessful job applicants and candidates about your recruitment and selection processes, to see how they perceive your company as a consequence. Make improvements where you can, based on the feedback.

WEB ACTIVITY

When Selection Practice is simply... unbelievably bad...

Read the article 'Currys interview *humiliation* as graduate *made to dance*' on **www.bbc.co.uk** or by following the link in the digital resources online and discuss the questions below.

1   What KSAOs and competencies do you think could be important for this role?

2   What methods would you suggest could have been used to assess for this role instead of the chosen... activity?

3 Why do you think your selected methods would be appropriate to the role?

4 What impact do you think the recruitment practices reported in the article would have on applicants and on the company's reputation more widely?

How Names affect Screening Decisions

Read the article 'Undercover job hunters reveal huge race bias in Britain's workplaces' by Rajeev Syal and published by *The Guardian* October 2009, by navigating to it online (see below) or by following the link in the digital resources online and discuss the questions below.

www.theguardian.com – search for 'Undercover job hunters reveal huge race bias in Britain's workplaces'

1 What are the issues raised in this article about ethical and fair selection?

2 What recommendations could you make about how to improve screening processes to address those issues?

FURTHER READING

Searle, R. (2003). *Selection and Recruitment: A Critical Text*. London: Palgrave-Macmillan.

Sackett, P.R. and Lievens, F. (2008). Personnel selection. *Annual Review of Psychology, 9*, 419–450.

Evers, A., Anderson, N. and Smit-Vosguijl, O. (2005). *The Blackwell Handbook of Personnel Selection*. Oxford: Blackwell.

Schmitt, N. and Fandre, J. (2008). Validity of Selection Procedures. In S. Cartwright and C.L. Cooper (Eds.). *The Oxford Handbook of Personnel Psychology*. pp. 163–193. Oxford: OUP

REFERENCES

Anderson, N. (2011). Perceived job discrimination: Toward a model of applicant propensity to case initiation in selection. *International Journal of Selection and Assessment, 19(3)*, 229–244.

Arthur, W., Day, E.A., McNelly, T.L. and Edens, P.S. (2006) A meta-analysis of the criterion-related validity of assessment centre dimensions. *Personnel Psychology, 56(1)*: 125–153.

Banki, S. and Latham, G.P. (2010). The Criterion-Related Validities and Perceived Fairness of the Situational Interview and the Situational Judgment Test in an Iranian Organisation. *Applied Psychology, 59(1)*, 124–142.

Barrick, M.R., Mount, M.K. and Judge, T.A. (2001). Personality and performance at the beginning of the new millennium: What do we know and where do we go next? *International Journal of Selection and Assessment, 9*, 9–30.

Bartram, D. (2005) The Great Eight competencies: a criterion-centric approach to validation. *Journal of Applied Psychology, 90(6)*: 1185–1203.

Bertua, C., Anderson, N. and Salgado, J.F. (2005). The predictive validity of cognitive ability tests: A UK meta-analysis. *Journal of Occupational and Organizational Psychology, 78(3)*, 387–409.

Bilsberry, J. (2007). *Experiencing recruitment and selection*. West Sussex: John Wiley and Sons Ltd.

Birkeland, S.A., Manson, T.M., Kisamore, J.L., Brannick, M.T. and Smith, M.A. (2006). A Meta-Analytic Investigation of Job Applicant Faking on Personality Measures. *International Journal of Selection and Assessment, 14(4)*, 317–335.

Brannick, M.T., Levine, E.L. and Morgeson, F.P. (2007). Job and work analysis: Methods, research, and applications for human resource management (2nd ed.). Thousand Oaks, CA: Sage.

Breaugh, J.A. (2008). Employee recruitment: Current knowledge and important areas for future research. *Human Resource Management Review, 18(3)*, 103–118.

Bright, J.E.H. and Hutton, S. (2000). The Impact of Competency Statements on Résumés for Short-listing

Decisions. *International Journal of Selection and Assessment. 8(2)*, 41–53.

Campion, M.A., Palmer, D.K. and Campion, J.E. (1997). A Review of Structure in the Selection Interview. *Personnel Psychology, 50*, 655–702.

Cascio, W.F. and Aguinis, H. (2008). 3 Staffing Twenty-first-century Organizations. *The Academy of Management Annals, 2(1)*, 133–165.

Chapman, D.S., Uggerslev, K.L., Carroll, S.A., Piasentin, K.A. and Jones, D.A. (2005). Applicant attraction to organizations and job choice: a meta-analytic review of the correlates of recruiting outcomes. *Journal of applied psychology, 90(5)*, 928.

Cleary, T.A. (1986). Test bias: Prediction of grades of negro and white students in integrated colleges. *Journal of Educational Measurement, 5*, 115–124.

Collings, D.G. and Mellahi, K. (2009). Strategic talent management: A review and research agenda. *Human Resource Management Review, 19(4)*, 304–313.

Collins, M.W. and Morris, S.B. (2008). Testing for adverse impact when sample size is small. *Journal of Applied Psychology. 93(2)*, 463–471.

Conway, J.M., Jako, R.A. and Goodman, D.F. (1995). A Meta-Analysis of Interrater and Internal Consistency Reliability of Selection Interviews. *Journal of Applied Psychology, 80(5)*, 565.

Cook, M. (2004). *Personnel Selection: Adding Value Through People*. (4th edition) UK: John Wiley and Sons.

Cooper, D., Robertson, I.T. and Tinline, G. (2003). *Recruitment and Selection: A Framework for Success*. London: Thomson.

Davis, A.J. and Scully, J. (2008). Strategic Resourcing. In Aston Centre for Human Resources (Eds.), *Strategic Human Resource Management* (pp. 95–128). London: CIPD.

De Corte, W. and Lievens, F. (2003). A Practical Procedure to Estimate the Quality and the Adverse Impact of Single Stage Selection Decisions. *International Journal of Selection and Assessment, 11*, 87–95.

De Corte, W., Lievens, F. and Sackett, P.R. (2007). Combining predictors to achieve optimal trade-offs between selection quality and adverse impact. *Journal of Applied Psychology 92(5)*, 1380–1393.

Dwight, S.A. and Donovan, J.J. (2003). Do warnings not to fake reduce faking? *Human Performance, 16*, 1–23.

Ellingson, J.E., Sackett, P.R. and Connelly, B.S. (2007). Personality assessment across selection and development contexts: Insights into response distortion. *Journal of Applied Psychology, 92(2)*, 386–395.

Fiedler, F.E. (1996). Research on leadership selection and training: One view of the future. *Administrative Science Quarterly*, 241–250.

Gaugler, B.B., Rosenthal, D.B., Thornton, G.C. and Bentson, C. (1987). Meta-analysis of assessment center validity. *Journal of applied psychology, 72(3)*, 493–511.

Hausknecht, J.P., Day, D.V. and Thomas, S.C. (2004). Applicant reactions to selection procedures: an updated model and meta-analysis. *Personnel Psychology. 57*, 639–683.

Hermelin, E., Lievens, F. and Robertson, I.T. (2007). The validity of assessment centres for the prediction of supervisory performance ratings: A meta-analysis. *International Journal of Selection and Assessment, 15*, 428–433.

Herriot, P. (1984). *Down from the Ivory Tower: Graduates and their Jobs*. Chichester: John Wiley and Sons.

Hogan, R. (2005). In Defense of Personality Measurement: New Wine for Old Whiners. *Human Performance, 18(4)*, 331–341.

Hogan, J., Barrett, P. and Hogan, R. (2007). Personality measurement, faking, and employment selection. *Journal of Applied Psychology, 92*, 1270–1285.

Hogan, J. and Holland, B. (2003). Using theory to evaluate personality and job-performance relations: a socioanalytic perspective. *Journal of Applied Psychology, 88(1)*, 100.

Hough, L., Eaton, N., Dunnette, M., Kamp, J. and McCloy, R. (1990). Criterion related validities of personality constructs and the effect of response distortion on those validities. *Journal of Applied Psychology, 75*, 581–595.

Hough, L.M., Oswald, F.L. and Ployhart, R.E. (2001). Determinants, detection and amelioration of adverse impact in personnel selection procedures: issues, evidence and lessons learned. *International Journal of Selection and Assessment, 9*, 152–194.

Huffcutt, A.I. (2010). From Science to Practice: Seven Principles for Conducting Employment Interviews. *Applied HRM Research, 12(1)*, 121–136.

Huffcutt, A.I., Culbertson, S.S. and Weyhrauch, W.S. (2013). Employment Interview Reliability: New meta-analytic estimates by structure and format. *International Journal of Selection and Assessment, 21(3)*, 264–276.

Hunter, J.E., Schmidt, F.L. and Hunter, R. (1979). Differential validity of employment tests by race: A comprehensive review and analysis. *Psychological Bulletin, 86(4)*, 721–735.

International Task Force on Assessment Center Guidelines. (2000). *Guidelines and Ethical Considerations for Assessment Center Operations*. Pennsylvania: DDI Inc.

International Testing Commission. (2005). *International Guidelines on Computer-based and Internet Delivered Testing*. Accessed from **www.intestcom.org/_guidelines/guidelines/index.html**, October 15th 2008.

Judge, T.A., Bono, J.E., Ilies, R. and Gerhardt, M.W. (2002). Personality and leadership: A qualitative and quantitative review. *Journal of Applied Psychology*, 87, 765–780.

König, C.J., Merz, A.S. and Trauffer, N. (2012). What is in Applicants' Minds When They Fill Out a Personality Test? Insights from a qualitative study. *International Journal of Selection and Assessment*, 20(4), 442–452.

Kuncel, N.R., Ones, D.S. and Sackett, P.R. (2010). Individual differences as predictors of work, educational, and broad life outcomes. *Personality and Individual Differences*, 49(4), 331–336.

Latham, G.P. and Whyte, G. (1994). The futility of utility analysis. *Personnel Psychology*, 47, 31–46.

Lengnick-Hall, M.L., Lengnick-Hall, C.A., Andrade, L.S. and Drake, B. (2009). Strategic human resource management: The evolution of the field. *Human Resource Management Review*, 19(2), 64–85.

Lepak, D.P. and Snell, S.A. (1999). The human resource architechture: Toward a theory of human capital allocation and development. *Academy of Management Review*, 24(1), 31–48.

Lievens, F. (1999). Development of a simulated assessment center. *European Journal of Psychological Assessment*, 15, 117–126.

Lievens, F. (2001). Assessor training strategies and their effects on accuracy, interrater reliability, and discriminant validity. *Journal of applied psychology*, 86(2), 255–64.

Lievens, F., Chasteen, C.S., Day, E.A. and Christiansen, N.D. (2006). Large-scale investigation of the role of trait activation theory for understanding assessment center convergent and discriminant validity. *Journal of applied psychology*, 91(2), 247–58.

Lievens, F., De Koster, L. and Schollaert, E. (2008). Current theory and practice of assessment centers: The importance of trait activation. In S. Cartwright and L. Cooper (Eds.), *The Oxford Handbook of Personnel Psychology*. Oxford: OUP.

Lievens, F. and Klimoski, R.J. (2001). Understanding the assessment center process: Where are we now? In C.L. Cooper and I.T. Robertson (Eds.) *International Review of Industrial and Organizational Psychology*, vol. 16 (pp. 245–286). Chicester: John Wiley and Sons, Ltd.

Lievens, F., Ones, D.S. and Dilchert, S. (2009). Personality scale validities increase throughout medical school. *Journal of Applied Psychology*, 94, 1514–1535. doi: 10.1037/a0016137.

McDaniel, M.A., Whetzel, D.L., Schmidt, F.L. and Maurer, S.D. (1994). The validity of employment interviews: A comprehensive review and meta-analysis. *Journal of applied psychology*, 79(4), 599.

McKinney, A.P., Carlson, K.D., Mecham, R.L., III, D'Angelo, N.C. and Connerley, M.L. (2003). Recruiters' use of GPA in initial screening decisions: Higher GPAs don't always make the cut. *Personnel Psychology*, 56, 823–845.

Minbashian, A., Earl, J. and Bright, J.E.H. (2013). Openness to experience as a predictor of job performance trajectories. *Applied Psychology: An International Review*, 62, 1–12. doi: 10.1111/j.1464-0597.2012.00490.x.

Morgeson, F.P., Campion, M.A., Dipboye, R.L., Hollenbeck, J.R., Murphy, K. and Schmitt, N. (2007). Are we getting fooled again? Coming to terms with limitations in the use of personality tests for personnel selection. *Personnel Psychology*, 60, 1029–1049.

Moscoso, S. (2000). Selection Interview: A Review of Validity Evidence, Adverse Impact and Applicant Reactions. *International Journal of Selection and Assessment*, 8(4), 237–247.

Murphy, K.R. and Dzieweczynski, J.L. (2005). Why don't measures of broad dimensions of personality perform better as predictors of job performance? *Human Performance*, 18(4), 343–357.

Myors, B., Lievens, F., Schollaert, E., Van Hoye, G., Cronshaw, S.F., Mladinic, A., Rodriguez, V., Aguinis, H., Steiner, D.D. and Rolland, F. (2008). International Perspectives on the Legal Environment for Selection. *Industrial and Organizational Psychology*, 1, 206–246.

Ordanini, A. and Silvestri, G. (2008). Recruitment and selection services: Efficiency and competitive reasons in the outsourcing of HR practices. *The international journal of human resource management*, 19(2), 372–391.

Oswald, F.L., Schmitt, N., Kim, H.B., Ramsay, L.J. and Gillespie, M.A. (2004). Developing a bio-data measure and situational judgement inventory as predictors of college student performance. *Journal of Applied Psychology*, 89, 187–207.

Owens, W.A. (1976). Background data. In M.D. Dunnette (Ed.), *Handbook of industrial and organizational psychology*. Chicago: Rand McNally.

Pearn, M. and Kandola, R. (1988). *Job Analysis: A Manager's Guide*. Oxford, IPD.

Ployhart, R.E. (2006). Staffing in the 21st century: New challenges and strategic opportunities. *Journal of Management*, 32(6), 868–897.

Roberts, G. (1997). *Recruitment and Selection: A Competency Approach*. London: CIPD.

Roberts, G. (2005). *Recruitment and Selection*. London: CIPD.

Robertson, I.T., and Smith, M. (2001). Personnel Selection. *Journal of Occupational and Organizational Psychology*, 74, 441–472.

Robertson, I.T., Bartram, D. and Callinan, M. (2002). Personnel selection and assessment. In P.Warr (Ed.), *Psychology at Work*. (pp. 100–152). London: Penguin.

Roth, P.L., Bobko, P. and McFarland, L.Y.N.N. (2005). A meta-analysis of work sample test validity: Updating and integrating some classic literature. *Personnel Psychology*, 58(4), 1009–1037.

Roulin, N., & Bangerter, A. (2012). Understanding the Academic–Practitioner Gap for Structured Interviews: 'Behavioral' interviews diffuse, 'structured' interviews do not. *International Journal of Selection and Assessment*, 20(2), 149–158.

Ryan, A.M. and Ployhart, R.E. (2000). Applicants' perceptions of selection procedures and decisions: A critical review and agenda for the future. *Journal of Management*, 26, 565–606.

Rynes, S.L. and Cable, D.M. (2003). Recruitment Research in the Twenty-First Century. *Handbook of psychology: Industrial and Organizational Psychology*, vol 12, (pp. 55–76). John Wiley and Sons.

Sackett, P.R. and Dreher, F. (1982). Constructs and assessment centre dimensions: some troubling empirical findings. *Journal of Applied Psychology*, 67(4), 401–10.

Salgado, J.F. (1999). Personnel selection methods. In C.L. Cooper and I.T. Robertson (Eds.), *International Review of Industrial and Organizational Psychology*. New York: Wiley.

Salgado, J.F. and Anderson, N. (2003). Validity Generalization of GMA Tests across Countries in the European Community. *European Journal of Work and Organizational Psychology*, 12, 1–17.

Salgado, J.F., Anderson, N., Moscoso, S., Bertua, C., De Fruyt, F. and Rolland, J.P. (2003). A meta-analytic study of general mental ability validity for different occupations in the European community. *Journal of Applied Psychology*, 88(6), 1068–1080.

Schinkel, S., van Vianen, A. and van Dierendonck, D. (2013). Selection Fairness and Outcomes: A field study of interactive effects on applicant reactions. *International Journal of Selection and Assessment*, 21(1), 22–31.

Schleicher, D.J., Day, D.V., Mayes, B.T. and Riggio, R.E. (1999, May). *A new frame for frame-of-reference training: Enhancing the construct validity of assessment centers*. Paper presented at the meeting of the Society for Industrial and Organizational Psychology, Atlanta, GA.

Schmidt, F.L. (2012). Cognitive tests used in selection can have content validity as well as criterion validity: A broader research review and implications for practice. *International Journal of Selection and Assessment*, 20(1), 1–13.

Schmidt, F.L. and Hunter, J.E. (1983). Individual differences in productivity: An empirical test of estimates derived from studies on selection procedure utility. *Journal of Applied Psychology*, 68, 407–414.

Schmidt, F. and Hunter, J.E. (1998). The validity and utility of selection methods in personnel psychology: practical and theoretical implications of 85 years of research findings. *Psychological Bulletin*, 124, 262–274.

Schmidt, F.L. and Hunter, J. (2004). General mental ability in the world of work: Occupational attainment and job performance. *Journal of personality and social psychology*, 86(1), 162–173.

Schmidt, F.L., Hunter, J.E., McKenzie, R.C. and Muldrow, T.W. (1979). Impact of valid selection procedures on work-force productivity. *Journal of Applied Psychology*, 73, 46–57.

Schmitt, N. and Fandre, J. (2008). Validity of Selection Procedures. In S. Cartwright and C.L. Cooper (Eds.) *The Oxford Handbook of Personnel Psychology*. (pp. 163–193). Oxford; OUP.

Schneider, B. (1987). The people make the place. *Personnel psychology*, 40(3), 437–453.

Schuler, H. and Moser, K. (1995). Validity of the Multimodal Interview. *Zeitschrift fur Arveit- und Organisationspsychologie*, 39, 2–12.

Searle, R.H. (2003). *Selection and recruitment: a critical text*. Milton Keynes: Open University Press.

Shaffer, J.A. and Postlethwaite, B.E. (2013). The Validity of Conscientiousness for Predicting Job Performance: A meta-analytic test of two hypotheses. *International Journal of Selection and Assessment*, 21(2), 183–199.

Silzer, R. and Church, A.H. (2009). The pearls and perils of identifying potential. *Industrial and Organizational Psychology*, 2(4), 377–412.

Smith, M. and Robertson, I.T. (1993). *Systematic personnel selection*. London: Macmillan.

Sturman, M.C. (2001). Utility analysis for multiple selection devices and multiple outcomes. *Journal of Human Resource Costing and Accounting*, *6(2)*, 9–28.

Sue-Chan, C. and Latham, G.P. (2004). The Situational Interview as a Predictor of Academic and Team Performance: A Study of the Mediating Effects of Cognitive Ability and Emotional Intelligence. *International Journal of Selection and Assessment*, *12(4)*, 312–320.

Te Nijenhuis, J. and Van der Flier, H. (2003). Immigrant–majority group differences in cognitive performance: Jensen effects, cultural effects, or both? *Intelligence*, *31(5)*, 443–459.

Tett, R.P., Guterman, H.A., Bleier, A. and Murphy, P.J. (2000). Development and Content Validation of a "Hyperdimensional" Taxonomy of Managerial Competence. *Human Performance*, *13(3)*, 205–252.

Tsui, A.S., Pearce, J.L., Porter, L.W. and Tripoli, A.M. (1997) Alternative approaches to the employee–organization relationship: does investment in employees pay off? *Academy of Management Journal,* 40(5): 1089–1121.

US Employment Opportunities Commission. *(1978)*. *Uniform Guidelines on Employee Selection Procedures (1978)*. Accessed from **www.uniformguidelines. com/uniformguidelines.html**. October 20, 2008.

Thoresen, C.J., Bradley, J.C., Bliese, P.D. and Thoresen, J.D. (2004). The big five personality traits and individual job performance growth trajectories in maintenance and transitional job stages. *Journal of Applied Psychology*, 89, 835–853. doi: 10.1037/ 0021-9010.89.5.835.

Van der Zee, K.I., Bakker, A.B. and Bakker, P. (2002). Why are structured interviews so rarely used in personnel selection? *Journal of Applied Psychology*, 87, 176–184.

Van Hoye, G. and Lievens, F. (2009). Tapping the grapevine: A closer look at word-of-mouth as a recruitment source. *Journal of Applied Psychology*, *94(2)*, 341.

Winter, D.G. and Barenbaum, N.B. (1999). History of modern personality theory and research. In L. A. Pervin and O. P. John (Eds.), *Handbook of personality: Theory and research* (2nd ed., pp. 3–27). New York: Guilford.

Woodruffe, C. (1997). *Assessment centres: Identifying and developing competence*. London: Institute of Personnel Management.

Woods, S.A. (2006). Cognitive Ability Tests and Unfairness against Minority Ethnic Groups: Two Practical Ways to Check for Unfairness in Selection. *Selection and Development Review*, *22(3)*, 2–7.

Zibarras, L.D. and Woods, S.A. (2010). A survey of UK selection practices across different organization sizes and industry sectors. *Journal of Occupational and Organizational Psychology*, *83(2)*, 499–511.

CHAPTER 7

LEARNING, TRAINING AND DEVELOPMENT

LEARNING OBJECTIVES

- Understand learning and development against the context of organization and HR strategy.

- Describe and evaluate the learning and development cycle, its components and associated methods; learning needs assessment, design and delivery of training and other development interventions, training evaluation.

- Understand and evaluate learning theories.

- Understand and evaluate models of learning outcomes.

- Understand factors that contribute to the success and failure of learning, development and training.

- Understand the influence of individual differences on learning and development.

- Describe the concept of transfer, and ways that transfer can be promoted in organizations.

- Understand how training affects organizational outcomes.

A friend of mine is self-employed and owns her own business. My friend is both the owner of, and the only person working in her company, and therefore the set of skills that she needs to draw on is very diverse indeed. If you know anyone who works in this way, then stand back and admire their versatility. They need to simultaneously be a salesperson, strategist, marketer, accountant, not to mention technical expert in actually delivering whatever service or product the company provides. My job is very different, and if you work in a medium or large organization, yours will be too. Most people in such organizations work in niches. The learning that each person accumulates through their lives and careers specializes their contribution so that by developing advanced skills and knowledge, each is able to learn to do things that others cannot.

Yet all of those diverse contributions are important in some way to the health and success of the organization. Whatever the organization's goals, people in the organization need to be able to draw on the right knowledge, skills, abilities and competencies to contribute their part of it. Effective recruitment and selection helps with this, but training, learning and development, alongside performance management, makes the difference once employees are selected. This chapter is about learning, training and development in organizations and the contribution of Work Psychology to understanding and improving it.

LEARNING, TRAINING AND DEVELOPMENT IN ORGANIZATIONS

The development of job-relevant knowledge, skills, abilities and competencies in organizations is called many things (Harrison, 2009). Training is the term traditionally used in Work Psychology sources (e.g. Goldstein and Ford, 2002; Salas and Cannon-Bowers, 2001, but this is restrictive, because training is only one way of developing people in organizations. Harrison (2009) points out that the terms employee development and human resource development (HRD) are disliked by some practitioners, because they seem to imply that people are either subservient or 'a resource'. In the UK, the CIPD use the terms learning and development, simply because these two terms represent what is important in practice: the learning (however it is facilitated) needed to support individual, team and organizational development.

However conceptualized, learning, training and development serve a strategic function in organizations. In strategic performance management, individual performance indicators and targets are linked to strategy, which is filtered down from organizational goals, through unit and team goals to individuals. Strategic learning and development is concerned with facilitating the development of people in ways that enable them to perform effectively. Blanchard and Thacker (2007) identify a number of ways that issues of learning and development can be built into wider organizational strategy:

1 Learning and development specialists can provide overviews of current KSAOs in the organization that can help strategists to determine the gap between actual and required capability in the organization.

2 Information could be provided about the interventions needed to achieve the strategic goals. These might include information about the best ways to develop capabilities, and the specific areas of the organization that would benefit most from intervention, and the associated costs.

3 Learning and development are central to the successful implementation of organizational change, helping managers to identify potential barriers to behaviour and performance change.

Figure 7.1 shows the progression from organizational strategy to individual performance goals, and the role of learning and development in helping to determine whether those goals are achieved in organizational, unit/team and individual performance. We revisit these ideas in Chapter 8. The figure also shows how valuation of performance change can inform the development of more learning and development strategy. The strategic importance of learning, training and development mean that it is a key area of practice for Work Psychologists.

This chapter explores the field based in two main sections. The first considers the process and implementation of training and development in organizations. The second looks at factors that influence whether learning, training and development are successful. Finally, at the end of the chapter, you will find out about the bottom-line in learning, training and development: do they actually benefit businesses and organizations?

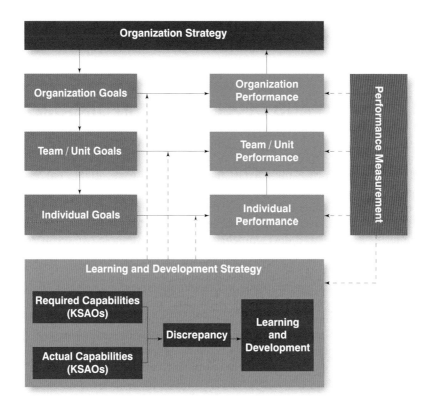

Figure 7.1   A model of the influence of learning and development strategy

THE PROCESS AND IMPLEMENTATION OF LEARNING, TRAINING AND DEVELOPMENT

The learning and development process in organizations is almost always presented as a cyclical process. Depending upon which books or publications you read, the cycle might appear slightly different, but the basic components do not really change that much. The form represented in Figure 7.2 (the training cycle) represents the basic elements of Goldstein's Instructional System Design (ISD) model (Goldstein, 1991; Goldstein and Ford, 2002).

The cycle begins with a needs assessment phase. This phase involves the analysis of learning and development needs at different levels of examination (organizational, team/unit, individual). From this analysis follows the specification of learning and development objectives designed to meet those needs. Once set, objectives guide the design and delivery of learning and development interventions. These may involve formal training, or other kinds of development activity. Careful consideration of individual difference and contextual factors is required in this step. The final step of the cycle is evaluation, which involves systematic examination of whether the objectives have been met and whether the learning and development interventions have had the desired effect. The cyclical nature of the model becomes apparent at this stage as the outcomes of the evaluation will inform the next round of needs assessment. In much of the Work Psychology literature, this model is simply called the training cycle.

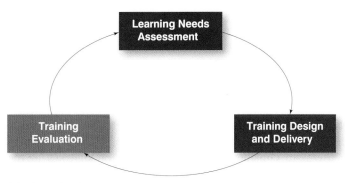

Figure 7.2   The learning and development cycle

Learning and Development Needs Assessment

The needs assessment phase is designed to identify where learning and development interventions are required in the organization. Goldstein and Ford (2002) describe a systematic approach to conducting the needs assessment. Their model is summarized in Figure 7.3. Note that the needs assessment is carried out at different levels within the organization, starting with organizational factors, and moving through to individuals. The general approach advocated in the model is to start with broad needs assessments, and to focus these down to the level of individuals.

Organizational needs and analysis

Examination of the organization comprises a few key steps. The first is to determine the level of support for learning and development in the organization. The thinking behind this step is that interventions and activities in organizations tend to stand a better chance of being implemented and being effective if senior managers and leaders are behind them. Part of establishing such support would require an understanding of the strategic direction of the organization and how learning and development might fit in with that strategy. In addition to liaison with top management, Goldstein and Ford (2002) also highlight the importance of gaining support of other stakeholders in the process. Wider analytical questions are also addressed at this stage such as determining the organizational culture and climate for learning and development (more on that later). Moreover, needs assessment at this stage might also consider external pressures on learning and development, such as legal requirements of particular jobs, or future economic pressures. All of these factors act as a context to jobs being performed in the organization.

Figure 7.3   The needs assessment process

Job and position analysis

Although the terms job and position are often used interchangeably, there is a difference between them. A 'job' is defined by the nature of work that is carried out by people with the same or similar job titles. A 'position' refers to a role in a specific organization, including duties and activities that are specific to the position. The purpose of this step of the needs assessment is to understand both.

Firstly, the relevant positions in the organization need to be identified and examined. The nature and objectives of the position are considered, and in some cases compared with information available about similar jobs elsewhere. Part of this stage would also involve talking to line managers and job incumbents about their experiences of the positions of interest, as well as the team context. The team context can also be useful to consider, especially the division of roles in the team. It would be important to gauge, for example, whether a person is required to carry out all aspects of a particular job, or whether they work collaboratively with others contributing only part of the 'job requirements'. Future requirements of the business are also critical, particularly in contemporary rapidly changing environments (Dachner, Saxton, Noe and Keeton, 2013).

KEY FIGURE

Irwin L. Goldstein

Irwin Goldstein has been a major researcher and thinker in the field of training for over 35 years. The first edition of his book on Training Systems was published in 1974, with the more recent edition, co-authored with Kevin Ford being published in 2002. Goldstein is Professor at the University of Maryland, among other roles, where he has conducted most of his research. His list of honours are inspiring, including serving as President of SIOP 1985–86, and a 1995 award for research excellence from the American Society for Training and Development.

Goldstein's autobiographical article on the SIOP website shows his commitment and passion for using Work Psychology to improve the way organizations train and develop their staff. His systems approach to training was, and continues to be highly influential, but can be seen by some practitioners as overly prescriptive or inflexible. It is unashamedly scientific, emphasizing evidence-based practice and measureable factors in organizing training activities. One nice section in his autobiography also indicates his openness to change and challenge, something that most of us could learn from. It is in relation to the government drive to establish and promote fairness in employment, and working with colleagues from legal professions: 'I have also enjoyed the opportunity to work with the many bright attorneys because they made me think about the public-interest aspects of our field. The problems of discrimination in the workplace became a salient issue for me and I must thank the many attorneys I have worked with, especially those from the US Department of Justice, for expanding my education. I found their questions forced me to expand the systems focus of my own thinking. Some I-O Psychologists felt that court cases negatively affected the advancement of our field. I feel otherwise. To me, this research was right at the intersection of practice and science and it tested our ingenuity in developing new ideas and approaches.'

Task, KSAO and competency analysis

This stage of the needs assessment is focused on defining the tasks required in the target positions, and based on task requirements, defining the KSAOs (knowledge, skills, abilities and other characteristics), and competencies required. This is another process in Work Psychology where methods of job analysis are critical. Methods of job analysis are covered elsewhere in this book (see Chapter 6), and the same kinds of methods are applied in learning and development needs assessment. The basic steps involve using a variety of methods to help specify the tasks and duties associated with the target job or position, analyzing them where possible to identify clusters that are related to one another (e.g. Carlisle, Bhanugopan and Fish, 2013), and then to use further methods to translate these into person requirements, expressed as KSAOs or job competencies. The differences between these aspects of person requirements are as follows:

- Knowledge. Required foundation learning about the context, content, processes or procedures of the job.
- Skills. Capability to carry out tasks relating to the use of tools or equipment, or the application of abilities to specific job tasks or contexts.
- Abilities. Core physical, mental or social capabilities that can be applied in a variety of contexts.
- Other Characteristics. Personality traits, attitudes and motivation.
- Competencies. Performance-related behaviours.

Person analysis

The final step in the needs assessment returns to the focus of learning and development of individual people working in the organization. The purpose is to determine where there are gaps between the KSAO requirements of a position, and the KSAO profile of the job incumbent. Performance measurement and management techniques are used in this step, which aim to establish whether or not someone is performing various aspects of their job satisfactorily. Some work may be required to supplement existing performance assessment systems, however, so that the measurement is clearly focused on understanding where learning or development is required. For example, an overall or objective performance measure (such as sales figures) is unlikely to be helpful in this respect as there is no information about which aspects of behaviour or performance are problematic. Assessment needs to be multi-dimensional so that people's strengths and weaknesses can be distinguished (see Chapter 8).

Some organizations use competency-based or psychometric assessments to help define gaps in KSAOs of current employees. The value of these methods is dependent on the extent to which they focus on KSAOs or competencies that are required in the target position. Participative discussion and input from the incumbent is also valuable, and may help them to self-assess their own training needs.

Learning and Development Interventions

Once gaps in KSAOs are identified through Training Needs Analysis, interventions can be devised to address them. For Work Psychology, interventions are, in part, based on an understanding of how people learn. Two perspectives on learning in Work Psychology are behavioural and cognitive perspectives, and each has implications for training delivery and development interventions (Blanchard and Thacker, 2007).

Behavioural theories of learning

Behaviourism is a basic form of learning theory. The work of Skinner (see Chapter 3) emphasized the role of positive and negative reinforcement in the 'operant conditioning' of behaviour. In this theory, people learn to behave in particular ways to either access more rewards, or to avoid punishment. In organizations, the approach could be adopted in structured environments to modify and control organizational behaviour. More useful is the work of Bandura (e.g. Bandura, 1977), who extended behaviourism to encompass two additional concepts:

- Observational Learning. The idea that people learn by observing role models. Part of the process of observational learning involves perceiving a role-model receiving some kind of outcome that is valued as a result of behaving in a particular way. That behaviour is likely to be mimicked or copied by the observer.

- Affect and Cognition. In the more up-to-date social cognitive theories (e.g. Mischel and Shoda, 1995), behaviour is generated from interacting cognitions and affective responses that result from situational perceptions. The outcome of behaviour is observed and used to update cognition and affect. In an iterative process, ways of thinking, feeling and behaving are learned and increasingly automated (i.e. eventually behaviour, thought and emotion become habitual so that people no longer have to think about their reactions).

A social learning and behavioural approach to learning would facilitate learning in the following ways:

- Learning of new behaviours would be prioritized, and these could be modelled by the trainer to promote observational learning.

- Behavioural procedures might be practised in simulations as part of the training or development activities.

- Affect and cognition would also be targeted, perhaps by explaining the value of new learning. The purpose would be to change the way that trainees perceive and think about aspects of their work.

Cognitive learning

Anderson has proposed a cognitive theory of learning, catchily titled the Adaptive Character of Thought (ACT) Model (Anderson, 1996). The model has developed slowly since the 1980s (e.g. Anderson, 1983), and has a strong logical emphasis on how people learn (see Figure 7.4).

The most basic form of knowledge in Anderson's model is declarative knowledge. Declarative knowledge may be thought of as sets of disconnected facts called 'knowledge chunks'. These chunks are simple components of more complex knowledge, but for Anderson, they underpin everything that human beings do. A major task of learning is to accumulate basic knowledge chunks and to compile them. In this step, the knowledge chunks are compiled and organized into procedures for problem solving. The result is procedural knowledge about how to solve problems or complete tasks.

Figure 7.4   Acquisition of cognitive skills

In its initial form, procedural knowledge is described as 'weak', as it is untested (i.e. when a person decides how to address a problem at work, they have no indication initially about whether it will be successful). Procedural knowledge is strengthened when it is used and found to be successful, eventually becoming automatic. Anderson comments on an interesting implication of his work, which is that human learning develops in parallel with the experience of problems in the environment. People learn because there is some pressing need to do so, and the complexity of human beings is a reaction to the complexity of the environments in which they live. If the world were simpler, there would be no need for people to continually learn and adapt.

A cognitive approach to learning and training would adopt different emphases from a behavioural approach, and would facilitate learning in the following ways:

- Knowledge development would be emphasized, starting with the declarative knowledge and communication of facts of knowledge chunks.

- Activities would be designed to facilitate problem solving using the knowledge, but trainees would probably be allowed to approach problems without seeing examples or modelling. The purpose would be development of procedural knowledge.

- More difficult problem scenarios could be used to strengthen and extend cognitive strategies for problem solving.

In practice, training and development interventions in organizations tend to blend both kinds of approach. The extent to which a particular method is likely to be effective depends on a number of factors. These include the participants or trainees and their individual differences, the learning and development objectives, and the organizational context.

Techniques and methods of training and development

It is true that formal face-to-face training is still among the most common ways that people learn and develop at work, but even within formal training, there are many ways in which learning can be facilitated. Outside of formal training, there are also plenty of other options available for practitioners and organizations to use. There are a number of good texts and reviews that cover training methods in depth (e.g. Goldstein and Ford, 2002; Blanchard and Thacker, 2007).

Lectures The most basic learning and development method is the stand-up lecture. (If you are a student, you are probably reading this after having the content presented to you in a lecture!) Lectures aim to present participants with a wealth of information about a particular topic. Their advantage is that a lot of information can be conveyed in a short amount of time. The disadvantage is that if badly implemented, the lecture can be perceived as dull or dry, and this is likely to inhibit learning and retention.

AUTHOR EXPERIENCE

My Life as a Trainer

One of the roles I perform as a Work Psychologist is to be a trainer for various groups. I work with clients in public and private sector organizations, and it is an interesting part of my job, particularly when I am working with a single client organization and running training on-site for their staff. You quickly get a feel for the organization's culture and climate. Four groups of staff, all of whom were being trained to use psychometrics, stick in my mind because they illustrate some of the different approaches the organizations took to learning and development. The first was a small group of Senior HR managers, who were leading the introduction of psychometrics in their group within a local government organization. They took the learning on the course seriously, perhaps because they had a good idea about how it would be applied. A second group were sent to a training course by their manager. Several were unsure why they were attending, but just in case they were put off, the manager did come to take a register of those that had attended during the lunch break. He clearly saw learning and development as something he did *to* rather than *with* staff. The third group were corporate HR officers and senior officers from a large bank. Many worked together as a team and were attending the course as a team. The positive, upbeat culture of the group was evident as they enthusiastically got involved with the training activities. I worked with the same bank, in other HR groups, away from the policy-making roles in Corporate HR. Here, attitudes were completely different. As with the earlier example, some people had been instructed to attend training without knowing why, and had been packed in to large training groups. Some of the delegates were very anxious about being seen as failing.

What do I take from these experiences? I think the key message is about the importance of people having agency and purpose for learning and development. Where people had no control over their attendance, and were unsure exactly how the training was to be applied, they tended to be both demotivated and worried. People who knew how they were going to use the training, or alternatively, knew that they would be able to help decide how the training was applied, on the whole were more positive, and in my view, learned more as a result.

Lecture and discussion A variant of the basic lecture is lecture and discussion. This is where the lecturer or trainer presents information, but also facilitates exploration and discussion with trainees on specific issues. This kind of approach works best in reasonably small participant groups. Questioning and facilitation skills of the trainer are also critical to making this method work in practice.

Demonstrations Where a procedure or skill is to be learned by trainees, demonstration is highly effective, particularly if there is a standard or ideal way of performing. The demonstration can allow trainees to get a feel for what kinds of behaviour are required in respect of their learning and development. Demonstrations may be less effective for highly complex tasks, and the provision of follow-up information and explanation is likely to be important. One limitation of demonstration is that people are not encouraged to think about how to deviate from the demonstration and address novel situations.

Simulations Simulations are useful for developing skills or cognitive strategies for problem solving. Equipment simulators can be used to allow trainees to get a feel for how to use them prior to starting the job. More complex simulations could also be utilized such as business games.

Role-play Role-play activities are used to simulate activities at work or in interpersonal situations. They can be set up so that participants work alone or in groups and can vary in terms of their structure, so that the scenarios are tightly structured or quite loose.

Development centres Development centres are a variation of assessment centres that are used in selection. The basic format is much the same – performance is observed in multiple exercises or simulations by a team of assessors. However, the purpose is the production of in-depth development reports, which are usually fed back to the participant in a face-to-face interview. Some development centres allow for instant feedback that can be applied right away in a follow-up development exercise.

Case studies These techniques comprise in-depth exercises relating to specific scenarios or situations. They are often used to illustrate similar scenarios to those that might be encountered in the work environment.

On-job training Most of the methods reviewed so far involve people stepping out of their work environment for learning and development. The alternative approach is on-the-job learning, where people learn how to carry out job duties through actually doing them. People probably never stop learning at work, but the focus here is on pro-active on-job training. Structured guidance would be provided, which could be supported by a work programme, shadowing activities and mentoring. A special kind of on-job training is an apprenticeship, which represents a partnership between several parties to sponsor the development of a junior worker (usually the employer, government and trade unions are involved to some degree). Apprenticeships are typically associated with skilled trades such as carpentry, car mechanics or plumbing, but are also used in more technical disciplines such as engineering, and even in office-based environments.

Coaching Coaching is a very popular method of development with senior managers who may feel that formal training is not bespoke enough for them. The one-to-one nature of the relationship between coach and participant allows a more tailored exploration of specific learning and development needs. Coaching can be provided by independent external coaches, who use a variety of techniques including psychometric tests and counseling techniques to work with the participant. Some organizations also set up coaching relationships between people within the organization, and most expect managers to engage in some coaching activities with staff. With internal coaches, the development is usually less structured than if an external coach is used. Whichever approach is adopted, some key issues for the coach are to fully understand the job role of the participant and to spend sufficient time collaboratively agreeing learning and development goals.

KEY THEME

Environment and Sustainability

E-learning and sustainable learning

An often overlooked cost of training in organizations is to the environment. The carbon impact of organizing and delivering training can be considerable. Delegates often need to travel to training venues, sometimes long distance. Trainers can be required to travel internationally to deliver sessions if they have specialist knowledge. Training materials are often paper-based unnecessarily.

One of the benefits of e-learning beyond the increased flexibility of learning and reduced costs, is the potential for reducing carbon costs. E-learning, and particularly activities and courses that are delivered online can reduce the carbon costs of learning and development by presenting courses at distance, so that participants do not need to travel, and by cutting down on the use of paper and other physical resources.

There are lessons for organizations however, even if e-learning is not adopted in full. There are obvious ways that the environmental costs of learning and development could be reduced – electronic distribution of materials, use of video-conferencing or delivery of presentations by video podcast. Cutting down on travel for learning is probably the most important change that organizations could make to learning and development activities. Is this worthwhile? There is a neat 'learning footprint' calculator online (HT[2] http://www.learningfootprint.com) for just this purpose, and we plugged in some modest values whereby a company ran one course per month off-site, with six delegates travelling 90 miles by car, four delegates travelling 450 miles by air and one trainer travelling 200 miles by car. Removing air travel, and cutting down all travel by 20 per cent, reduces the overall carbon impact by over 74 per cent.

Mentoring Mentoring can be thought of as coaching with a lighter touch, conducted over a long period of time. Mentoring comprises the formation of a relationship between a participant and a more senior colleague, who can provide guidance when required, or on specific issues at work. Mentoring is particularly useful for developing awareness about informal norms and cultures, in addition to developing KSAOs.

E-learning The group of learning and development methods that are delivered by computer are referred to as e-learning, and a whole literature on the integration of technology into workplace learning is emerging (e.g. Bell and Kozlowski, 2009). One driver of e-learning is the combination of the demands of providing ever more development to staff, whilst cutting costs of that development. E-learning permits both, and is making a substantial impact on practice. For example, in 2004,

BOX 7.1
Active learning

Active learning is an approach to learning and development in organizations whereby the employee has control over how and when they learn and develop. They are given the freedom to decide how they will develop in particular areas, and to structure that development around their job responsibilities. In some cases, employees may also take the initiative to identify development areas. The use of e-learning is obviously useful to support active learning, as resources and courses are available constantly and employees are in control of the schedule and pace of their learning. A key advantage of active learning is also that it allows flexible adaptation to new job demands. In short, employees can monitor their own performance and elect to undertake some development if their job gets harder for some reason. There are some key issues in active learning, particularly around individual differences and learning outcomes. For example, does active learning assume that people have reasonable metacognitive ability (also see Chapter 4 on self-regulation), allowing them to question and identify their weaknesses? Bell and Kozlowski (2009) highlight the need for more understanding about the pathways from individual differences through active learning interventions to learning outcomes.

around 58 per cent of all training days at IBM were delivered through e-learning, with the company reportedly having an on-demand learning database of 54 000 short courses. The rise in e-learning has also provided the tools to facilitate so-called active learning (see Box 7.1). Different forms of e-learning include:

- Programmed Instruction. Online courses comprising text, graphics and multimedia enhancements.
- Intelligent Development Systems. Intelligent systems are adaptive in the sense that the nature of the course changes depending on the responses or input of the participant.
- Simulations. Computer-based simulations of situations or scenarios encountered at work. An important variable in simulation is its level of fidelity (the extent to which it replicates the reality of performance, and environment in which it occurs; e.g. Beaubien and Baker, 2004).

Organizational and team learning strategies

The learning and development methods described so far tend to veer towards individual learning. However, from a strategic HRM perspective, practitioners are equally or more interested in learning at team or organizational level (Shipton and Zhou, 2008). The difference in implementing team and organizational learning interventions is that the purpose of learning and development is conceptualized as overall capability within the organization, rather than specific KSAO needs of individuals. A few potential interventions are summarized below:

Secondment   Secondments are short-term postings to new areas of the organization or partner companies. Individuals might complete specific projects or work within teams during the secondment, with the aim of bringing learning back to improve their own team. A particular kind of secondment is the expatriate or international assignment, increasingly valued as organizations become more globalized. A whole area of Work Psychology has examined expatriate assignments, and related issues of international HRM (e.g. Schuler, Budhwar and Florkowski, 2002).

Job rotation Within teams, individuals can be asked to work in a variety of different positions with the express purpose of learning about different areas of business, clients, systems and processes.

Competitor and client placements The purpose of these kinds of learning and development techniques is to raise awareness and develop knowledge of services provided by similar businesses or the perspective of service users. The outcomes for the organization could be a clearer external focus in work and ultimately organizational and business activities.

Team training Team training would involve having complete teams attend training or development programmes, and is a useful strategy where team members work interdependently on work tasks (Kozlowski, Gully, Nason and Smith, 1999).

In addition to these proactive interventions, naturally occurring learning at the team and organizational level can be facilitated and promoted in the following ways:

Encouraging networking Internal and external networking is about developing links with people inside and outside the organization that might work in similar or related areas of practice. The purpose is to promote cross-fertilization of ideas within the organization and to allow pathways for sharing innovations and best practice.

Communities of practice Groups of like-minded employees with shared concerns in an organization, working together to learn from each other and develop new approaches and ways of working have recently been referred to as Communities of Practice (Shipton and Zhou, 2008). Such groups tend to be self-managing, without much direction or management intervention on how they should conduct their work. The potential benefits are wide-ranging, and depend upon the initial purpose of the group, but could include specific projects such as development of work procedures or innovations, or analyses of specific areas of business in the organization.

DISCUSS WITH
A COLLEAGUE

List all the kinds of learning activity you have experienced. Rate them out of ten based on how effective they were at helping you learn. Compare and discuss your ratings with a course colleague.

Training Evaluation

The third stage in the learning and development cycle is evaluation. Understanding the outcomes of training and other learning interventions allows organizations to determine the impact and benefits, and ultimately the value of learning (Kearns, 2005). Work Psychologists have focused on two main issues in training evaluation:

- Defining evaluation criteria to judge the effectiveness of training.
- Designing systematic methods and procedures for training evaluation.

Evaluation Criteria

One of the first questions to address in training evaluation is what should be measured to help decide whether learning, training and development interventions have worked. Kirkpatrick's (1976) widely used framework of evaluation criteria proposes that training should be evaluated against four levels of criteria:

1 Reactions: Trainee attitudes about the training they have received. These are generally measured through the distribution of satisfaction surveys that ask people about the delivery and outcomes of the training.

2 Learning: Knowledge, skills and abilities that trainees have learned. These can be assessed through tests or assessments of post-training learning. There is no rule of thumb about when the assessment should be made.

3 Behaviour: Changes in trainee behaviour at work (training transfer). Assessments in this area would be made at work, and could vary in terms of specificity.

4 Results: Organization or team-level performance outcomes. These assessments are likely to be tangential to the aims of the training, and focused rather on improvements in quality, productivity or profitability.

The four levels of criteria are progressively more difficult to measure. Reactions to training are routinely collected by trainers and are highly accessible. Some courses also employ tests of learning to determine whether the learning objectives of the course have been achieved. Behaviour change is less commonly examined, but can often be adequately tapped by standard appraisal or performance management assessments (see Chapter 8), provided they reflect the content or aims of the training. Typically, if well designed, these kinds of criterion measures can achieve reasonable reliability.

The fourth level of Kirkpatrick's model, training results, presents a major practical challenge for organizations. This is because it is difficult to conceptualize and measure performance outcomes at the level of the organization. A basic model of organization-level outcomes is a combination of profitability, survival and growth of the organization or business (Hamblin, 1974). However these criteria do not map clearly to the objectives of many training programs, which are often designed to improve processes rather than outcomes (e.g. through the development of new technical or interpersonal skills). The 'balanced scorecard' (Kaplan and Norton, 1992) approach suggests that the performance of organizations should be judged against a range of relevant criteria. In this vein, organizational outcomes of training can be gauged by evaluating their impact in a variety of organizational performance indicators (e.g. HR outcomes, organizational performance improvements, profitability and financial outcomes; Tharenou, Saks and Moore, 2007). This kind of approach is adaptable and criteria may be modified so as to be relevant in different kinds of organization. For example, in healthcare organizations, patient/client satisfaction, community engagement, research and learning could all be examples of relevant criteria (Schalm, 2008).

Despite its practical utility, Kirkpatrick's model is criticized in the research literature as being overly simplistic or restrictive (e.g. Kraiger *et al.*, 1993), and there are alternative models that elaborate definitions of the outcomes of learning in organizations. The most notable of these focus specifically on individual learning outcomes.

Modelling Individual Learning Outcomes

Gagne and colleagues (e.g. Gagne, Briggs and Wager, 1992) designed a framework for learning outcomes, in which they distinguished between five kinds of learning outcome:

1 *Verbal Information:* Declarative information that can be stated or recalled by the individual.
2 *Intellectual Skills:* Procedural knowledge about concepts, rules and procedures that can be applied to solve problems.
3 *Cognitive Strategies:* Rules for deciding when to bring verbal information and intellectual skills into play in order to solve a specific problem. Such strategies are important for people when they encounter novel problems for which there is no obvious learned solution.
4 *Attitudes:* Changes in the way people think and feel about specific aspects of their work environment.
5 *Motor Skills:* Physical or movement-based skills such as using tools or physical labour.

A second model of learning outcomes is that of Kraiger, Ford and Salas (1993). In response to criticisms about psychologists' weak understanding of training outcomes (e.g. Tannenbaum and Yukl, 1992), Kraiger *et al.* examined a number of learning and educational taxonomies and proposed a classification system based on three important learning outcomes (see Table 7.1):

- Cognitive Outcomes: Declarative and procedural knowledge, and cognitive strategies for problem solving. The concept of metacognition, is also highlighted, referring to the process by which a person examines and evaluates their own ways of thinking, identifying areas for development. In learning and development, this could be important in respect of changing the way that people think about the way they work.
- Skill-based Outcomes: These are behavioural outcomes, such as learned performance behaviours and the extent to which they can be performed easily, quickly and without error.
- Affective Outcomes: Two constructs are defined in the affective outcome category, attitudes and motivation. Attitudes are related to the way that a person feels about a particular object or target. Motivation comprises a number of different aspects, but notably goal setting, and the nature and difficulty of targets that people set for themselves after training. Self-efficacy is the final aspect of this category. Recall that self-efficacy concerns the belief that one can perform. This is obviously important for transfer of training to the work environment, since the application of learning at work will depend to some degree on whether a person believes it will be successful.

Table 7.1   The learning outcome framework of Kraiger *et al.* (1993)

Learning Outcomes	Sub-categories	Learning Constructs
Cognitive Outcomes	Verbal Knowledge	Declarative Knowledge
	Knowledge Organization	Mental Models
	Cognitive Strategies	Self-Insight Metacognitive Skills
Skill-based Outcomes	Compilation	Composition Proceduralization
	Automaticity	Automatic Processing Tuning
Affective Outcomes	Attitudinal	Targeted Object Attitude Strength
	Motivation	

Comparing Models of Learning, Training and Development Outcomes

Models such as the one by Kraiger *et al.*, (1993) are presented to try to describe learning outcomes in a precise, measureable and detailed way. This could be seen as a scientific retort to the Kirkpatrick's framework, which is non-specific about exactly what should be measured at each of the four levels. However, it is the practical utility and flexibility that goes hand-in-hand with this approach that has probably made it endure. The reviewed psychological models of learning outcomes tend to focus on individual outcomes only, whereas organizations are often as interested in the team and organizational level outcomes. Moreover, the emphasis on measurement could preclude examination of less tangible outcomes of learning. A good example of this is tacit knowledge, a core concept of knowledge management theory in organizations, which has made considerable impact on learning processes in organizations (see Box 7.2).

For all its complexity and sophistication, Kraiger *et al.*'s model has not had the dramatic impact on practice that might have been expected, and this may be because some of the components are simply outside the mindset of managers and practitioners. Ford, Kraiger and Merritt (2009) review progress in the field around the three-category classification, and even the major developments in research are in those areas that tap into simple cognitive dimensions (e.g. declarative and procedural knowledge; Bell and Kozlowski, 2002; Kozlowski and Bell, 2006), and motivational dispositions (see the later discussion of goal orientation). Some of the more complex nuances of the model remain to be justified, and part of that involves explaining the practical utility of these complex quantitative models to people working in organizations.

Evaluation Methods and Procedures

The essence of evaluation is an assessment of change following some form of intervention. Whatever the evaluation criterion (knowledge, skill, ability, competency, behaviour, results and so on), the aim of the evaluation should be whether there is any difference in that criterion before and after the learning and development intervention. Thinking back to Chapter 2 on research methods, you will probably spot that experimental methods are the logical choice, and in an ideal world, all training evaluations would be conducted according to the principles of experimental research design.

Experimental designs allow practitioners to determine the benefits of training by comparing the performance of trained and untrained (control) groups of employees. By taking relevant measurements pre- and post-training, practitioners are able to assess changes in the performance of the two groups and the control group is important because it helps rule out the possibility that any observed change could have occurred regardless of the intervention. For example, imagine that we have observed change in a group of trainees after a training course. We might conclude that the training is effective, when in fact changes to work design or job characteristics could be the real reason that performance has changed, with improvements observed regardless of whether people have attended the training.

In the experimental design, control groups are not subject to any treatment at all, other than criterion measurement. Experimental design is therefore desirable for training evaluation because it allows performance change to be attributed to the training intervention rather than to confounding or unmeasured variables.

BOX 7.2
Knowledge management

In the early 1990s there was a hive of activity around the concept of knowledge management. It is often associated with the article by Ikujiro Nonaka (1991) in *Harvard Business Review*, followed up in depth in a book in 1995 (Nonaka and Takeuchi, 1995). The emphasis of these publications was the importance of knowledge creation, capture and dissemination in the knowledge-worker age. The work was based on processes and procedures in high-profile Japanese companies such as Honda. The imperative for knowledge management was that competitive advantage in the 21st century economy would be linked to knowledge held in a company and not simply to physical assets, technologies or patents, which are mostly easily replicable. Knowledge enables people and companies to change and progress faster than their competitors.

The key contribution of Nonaka was to highlight the importance of the distinction between two types of knowledge:

- Explicit Knowledge: knowledge that can be easily written down, communicated and taught to people.

- Tacit Knowledge: knowledge that cannot be easily communicated and that rather reflects accumulated experience and 'ways of knowing'.

Tacit knowledge has real value in organizations, but is difficult to quantify and identify. It is likely to reside with particular individuals, who have accumulated the knowledge through their experience. Does it give competitive advantage? Well, an example that illustrates the concept might be drawn from Formula 1 racing. In 2008, the Honda racing team were a lower-order team, who did not really challenge the top teams for points or the championship. When the outfit had to be sold during the 2008 economic slump, Honda were purchased by a consortium led by Ross Brawn, who had previously led the successful Ferrari team. Keeping the same workers and drivers, Brawn led his Brawn team to win the 2009 constructors championship and, in part, this surely reflects his tacit knowledge of Formula 1 racing. He did not have an explicit blueprint for the winning car, but rather a way of understanding how to develop the winning team.

So knowledge is valuable, and learning and development interventions might involve determining how to capture tacit knowledge, and how to disseminate and develop it in people in the organization. Nonaka and Takeuchi proposed four processes involved in the creation of knowledge in organizations:

- Socialization: Shared experience that helps to create tacit knowledge within individuals.

- Externalization: The conversion or specification of tacit knowledge so that it becomes explicit knowledge.

- Combination: The combination of individual aspects of explicit knowledge into systems or prototypes.

- Internalization: The absorption of combined explicit knowledge to develop tacit knowledge, and to create more tacit knowledge.

The four processes are cyclical, with Internalization leading to Socialization, which involves collaborative development of tacit knowledge and so on. What is the implication for Work Psychology? One possible implication is that Work Psychologists may need to think more widely than traditional Training Needs Analysis (reviewed later) in understanding.

In practice, training evaluations tend to adopt a quasi-experimental design (Goldstein and Ford, 2002). Trainees are selected for training because they have a particular training need, and their development is compared with colleagues who have not received training (i.e. the control group). The most common deviation from experimental design for many training evaluation procedures is to assess performance post-training only. This prevents the measurement of performance change, which is necessary for assessing the return on investment in training. A common alternative to the quasi-experimental design is the time-series design in which performance change is tracked at several points before and after the training program. This approach can determine whether there is a marked change in performance after the learning and development intervention. Figure 7.5 shows different evaluation methods side-by-side.

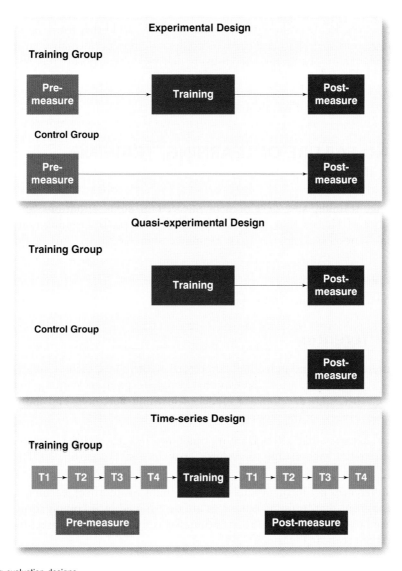

Figure 7.5   Training evaluation designs

A Sales Manager has decided to put her sales team through a sales training programme. How would you advise her to evaluate the training?

A final important issue in evaluation methodology is obviously measurement of outcomes. Practitioners need to think practically about the ways that different learning outcomes can be measured and assessed. At the individual level, aspects of performance measurement need to be considered and would help practitioners decide on how performance at work, and other learning outcomes could be measured in organizations (see Chapter 8 for detailed discussion of performance measurement). Work Psychologists also place a lot of emphasis on ensuring that measurements are reliable and valid. These are key issues to consider in the measurement of learning outcomes because they allow evaluation data to be viewed with more confidence. Even if research designs in training evaluation are very elaborate, poor measurement still equals poor decision-making.

SUCCESS AND FAILURE OF LEARNING, TRAINING AND DEVELOPMENT

Why does learning, training and development succeed in some situations and fail in others? There are a number of factors that influence the likely success of training and development in organizations, and Work Psychologists have examined some of these. This section considers two perspectives:

- individual difference factors
- training transfer and organizational factors.

Individual Differences

People learn in different ways, and individual differences in attributes, such as ability, personality and motivation will all, to an extent, affect the way that people respond to learning and development at work. Gully and Chen (2009) developed a model of learning outcomes and individual differences (Figure 7.6). The key aspects of the model are:

- Trainee characteristics that affect learning outcomes include abilities, personality traits, demographics such as age (Bertolino, Truxillo and Fraccaroli, 2011), interests and values.
- Individual differences act through intervening mechanisms to affect learning outcomes. Gully and Chen comment that 'training outcomes are determined by a combination of mechanisms that influence how people process information, focus their attention, direct their effort and manage their affect during learning'.

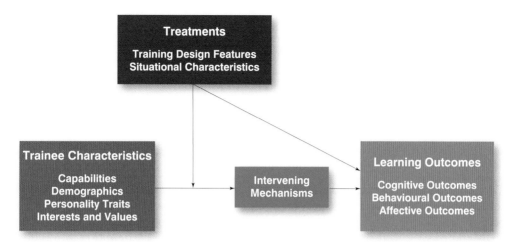

Figure 7.6 The pathway from individual differences to learning outcomes

- The pathway from individual differences to learning outcomes is also moderated by attribute-treatment interactions. This means that learning outcomes for an individual depend on how they respond to a specific training and development intervention, and outcomes are a product of the interaction of learning methods and individual differences.

Three areas of individual differences are particularly worth exploring to understand how individuals react to training and development:

1 Ability and Cognition.
2 Personality Traits.
3 Goal Orientation.

Ability and cognition

General cognitive ability is an important predictor of learning outcomes. Remember that general cognitive ability is consistently predictive of job performance, particularly in complex jobs. One of the major pathways by which general ability predicts performance is through the acquisition of job knowledge. People with higher ability acquire job knowledge faster and in greater volume. Colquitt, LePine and Noe (2000) reported moderate–strong associations between cognitive ability and learning outcomes of declarative knowledge, skill acquisition, training transfer and self-efficacy. If this result is viewed alongside the other models and theories of learning reviewed so far, then it is fairly straightforward to suppose why cognitive ability is so important for learning outcomes. People with higher ability are likely to absorb more information and to be able to organize, recall and adapt that information more effectively than those with lower abilities. One of the implications for learning and development is that people higher in cognitive ability learn and develop more effectively through exploration and problem solving, whereas people with lower cognitive ability tend to respond better to more structured learning (Gully and Chen, 2009).

Another cognitive construct touched upon earlier is metacognition or self-regulation. People with greater metacognitive ability should learn more effectively because they are able to monitor their progress and improve where needed (Gully and Chen, 2009). The practical implications of this finding is that the process of reflection in training is important. People may not automatically reflect on their own progress and learning, or question their established styles of problem solving and working. Guided reflection could encourage those lower in metacognitive abilities to think about their learning, and thereby promote better learning outcomes and transfer to the work environment. Second, learning and development interventions in organizations should include some activities or components that facilitate reflection and metacognition.

Personality traits

As with other areas of Work Psychology, the emergence of the Big Five model of personality traits (Chapter 3) has clarified the associations of personality and learning outcomes. Four of the Big Five have exhibited associations with learning outcomes.

- Conscientiousness. Barrick and Mount (1991) reported a positive association between conscientiousness and training success. Conscientiousness may be related to training success because people high on conscientiousness are more likely to set challenging personal goals and to stick to them (Barrick, Mount and Strauss, 1993). Colquitt et al. (2000) report an association with motivation to learn, but not with skill acquisition and declarative learning. This may be because these latter two outcomes are more clearly linked with cognitive ability. The implication is that learning may be most effective when people have a high motivation to learn, and also have the abilities needed to acquire knowledge and skills quickly.

- Openness to Experience. Openness to experience was related to training success, but not job performance in the meta-analysis of Barrick and Mount (1991). Openness probably affects learning because people high on openness are simply more likely to be open to new ideas.

- Extraversion. Extraversion was found to be positively associated with training success by Barrick and Mount (1991), although it is unclear exactly why. One possibility is that higher levels of extraversion mean that people appraise learning opportunities more positively, and are more open to training in social or group-based scenarios. The majority of learning and development interventions involve some form of social or interpersonal interaction (with the exception of self-directed or e-learning). Esfandagheh, Harris and Oreyzi (2012) reported that extraversion was associated with higher training self-efficacy, which had a subsequent positive effect on learning outcomes.

- Emotional Stability. Emotional stability was found to have a weak association with training success by Barrick and Mount (1991). However, facets of Emotional Stability related to anxiety seem to be most important. Colquitt et al. (2000) reported that anxiety was strongly negatively related to motivation to learn, self-efficacy post training and acquisition of declarative knowledge and skills. Potential explanations for these findings include the negative effects of anxiety on learning experience – anxiety or nervousness may distract people's attention from learning activities, limiting their impact. Additionally, anxiety is related to negative affect, and high negative affect may mean that people feel less confident in the face of setbacks experienced during training or at work afterwards. For some people, the anticipation of setbacks or failure may be enough to lower motivation to learn or to engage with training.

Goal orientation

The concept of goal orientation emerged from the education literature, but has received a great deal of research interest in organizations in recent years. Dweck (1986) proposed that goal orientation was a motivational construct that explained some of the differences in achievement of children during their education. She suggested that goal orientation was linked to a child's belief about ability and intelligence. If they believed it to be fixed, then they were likely to adopt a performance goal orientation (PGO) based around avoiding negative feedback and gaining positive feedback. If they believed ability to be improvable, then they were likely to adopt a learning goal orientation (LGO), being driven to master a task for its own sake. Dweck (1986) suggested that learning goal orientation was associated with more positive outcomes than performance goal orientation.

The concept was quickly adopted by Work Psychologists (Farr, Hofmann and Ringenbach, 1993) and it is easy to see why. On the face of it, these two different goal orientations seem immediately relevant to understanding why and how people learn and develop in an organization, and why the outcomes for some are more favourable than others. Some research in the area has examined the goal orientation construct in more detail. From the definitions, we might assume that the LGO and PGO are polar opposites, so that the presence of a strong learning goal orientation automatically prohibits that presence of a strong performance goal orientation. However, contrary to this belief, it appears that the two kinds of performance goal are independent, so that a person may simultaneously hold strong performance and learning goal orientations (Van de Walle, 1997).

Another important distinction in the literature is the difference between conceptualizing goal orientation as a trait or a state. In the trait conceptualization, goal orientation is taken to be a stable disposition that does not really change over time. In the state conceptualization, goal orientation is a temporary orientation towards a particular task or activity that may change over time. Payne, Youngcourt and Beaubien (2007) comment that it is likely that goal orientation could be conceptualized as both trait and state, with the experience of the state likely to be influenced in part by the trait. This means that is possible that goal orientation can change.

The attention given to goal orientation is justified because it appears to be a predictor of learning outcomes. In their meta-analysis, Payne, Youngcourt and Beaubien (2007) reported that LGO was linked to motivation and positive attitudes as well as learning and job performance. The implication is that if goal orientation is at least partly state-like, it would be sensible to promote the adoption of learning goals during training. However, the picture may not be that simple. There is some evidence that post-training self-efficacy is highest when training goal structure is consistent with goal orientation (Martocchio and Hertenstein, 2003). People feel more able to apply their learning if the learning environment has suited their goal orientation.

Furthermore, organizational climate and leadership are likely to affect goal orientation. Potosky and Ramakrishna (2002) report that people performed better and felt better able to learn and perform when they simultaneously had high LGO, and perceived a supportive organizational climate for updating skills. Dragoni and Kuenzi (2012) reported that goal orientation of team members was associated with leader goal orientation. The benefits of LGO might therefore depend on the organizational context.

Training Transfer

A marker of the success or failure of learning, training and development is whether learning is transferred to the work environment. Just because a person has acquired knowledge and skills, there is no guarantee that when they return to work, they will apply what they have learned. Most of us have our own experiences of this dilemma, particularly in respect of training courses. They are generally very useful, and during the course there is time to learn and reflect, but when we return to work it is too easy to slip back into the established ways of doing things. This is a big problem for organizations (Ford and Weissbein, 1997) because the benefits of learning and development can only be realized if learning is utilized and applied at work. To be justified, the investment in learning and development must result in some return such as improvements in quality or productivity. Yet, a well-cited estimate of the percentage of training that is applied at work is a woefully low 10 per cent (Fitzpatrick, 2001).

Salas and Cannon-Bowers (2001) conceptualize training transfer as the extent to which KSAOs acquired in a training programme are applied, generalized and maintained over some time in the job environment.

There are a few immediate questions that emerge in respect of the issue of transfer. For example, is transfer a product of individual or organizational factors? What are the processes that facilitate application? What could an organization do to promote transfer?

Some researchers have developed models to disentangle the process of training transfer and answer some of these questions (e.g. Baldwin and Ford, 1988; Cheng and Hampson, 2008). Figure 7.7 summarizes these models, showing how different factors could combine to promote training transfer in organizations.

In the model, learning outcomes are affected by individual differences, training design and organizational factors, but these outcomes are not sufficient for transfer. The transfer of learning to the work environment requires 'intention to transfer' (Cheng and Hampson, 2008), with individual differences, training design and work environment factors influencing this intention (Beier and Kanfer, 2009). Perceived usefulness of training is also important (Van Eerde, Tang and Talbot, 2008; Alliger, Tannenbaum, Bennet, Traver and Shotland, 1997). When trainees perceive course content as having high relevance and utility, they are more likely to transfer their learning.

Organizational factors influence transfer intentions and transfer directly in the model, and there is some evidence for this from research. Quinones, Ford and Seko, (1995) highlight the importance of work design and 'opportunity to perform' at work. Their theory is simple and describes how

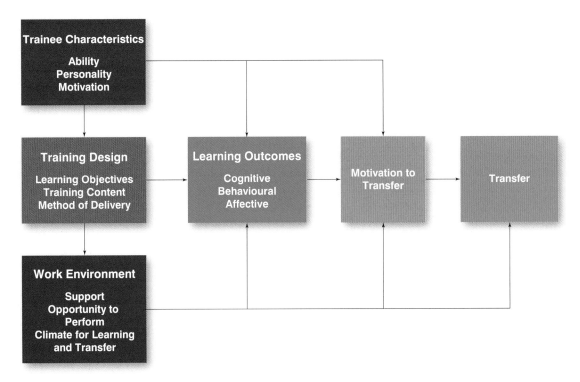

Figure 7.7   A model of training transfer.

transfer is promoted when people are given an opportunity to perform skills learned during learning and development activities. Building in 'opportunity to perform' into learning and development plans is likely to enhance transfer. Arthur, Bennett, Stanush and McNelly (1998) highlight the value of timely application, and reported that long delays between training and application at work result in significant learning decay. Opportunities for quick application of learning could help to facilitate transfer.

Wider organizational factors are also important. Social support from supervisors, peers and subordinates before and after training all helps to promote transfer (Salas and Cannon-Bowers, 2002). Saks and Belcourt (2004) reported that supervisor and trainee involvement in development planning, as well as supervisor and organizational support post-training were all significantly related to training transfer.

Success and Failure of Learning, Training and Development: Summary

The message from research is that individual differences and organizational factors do have clear influences on learning and development outcomes in organizations, including transfer of learning. Learning and development outcomes depend on a combination of a person's abilities, personality traits, cognitive styles and motivational style. One method of development may be more effective for one person compared with another, and to complicate the picture, individual differences and organizational factors interact to determine whether a person applies their learning at work. There are a few key implications for learning and development strategies and interventions:

1 Organizations must aim to use a variety of learning and development techniques because a 'one size fits all' approach will certainly fail to appeal to a significant proportion of people regardless of the approach that is adopted.

2 Participative learning and development goal setting is important, but only so long as it genuinely allows for people's individual differences to be expressed and is taken into account during training and development planning. The purpose of developmental discussion should be to help find the most suitable and appealing learning and development activities to address learning needs.

3 Active intervention to promote successful outcomes from training can be used. For example, Sitzmann and Johnson (2012) reported that learning was more effective when people were instructed to create learning plans and to actively reflect on this plans as they undertook learning activity. Shantz and Latham (2012) reported similar benefits of writing 'self-guidance' for transfer of training, and goal setting also has the potential to increase application of training at work (Brown, McCracken and Hillier, 2013).

4 Learning and development activities should take account of organizational performance management activities and climate so that learning outcomes are consistent with the way that people are expected to work in the organization. Moreover, managers should be aware of the effects that learning and development activities, and subsequent performance expectations, have on climate for learning in their organizations.

5 Work design and team processes should be considered and steps taken to give people timely opportunities to apply their learning, supported by peers and supervisors in the team.

KEY THEME

Globalization and Cross Cultural Issues

Does cross-cultural training help people work internationally?

The globalized working world comes complete with the requirement for people to work internationally. Such working most commonly takes the form of expatriate assignments, which involve people working for extended periods in another country or culture. Working in cross-cultural context brings new challenges and places demands on individuals that are unlike those they experience day-to-day. They include, for example, challenges of language and communication, adjustment to new social and cultural customs, dealing with the unfamiliar, not to mention the loss of home comforts, and routines.

Given these new demands, it is no surprise that organizations invest in preparation training for expatriates, often called cross-cultural training or CCT. The intention is that giving some preparatory training will help people to adjust more quickly making it more likely that they will perform and complete their assignment. Such training could focus on the specific host culture, or cross-cultural working generally, and could adopt a formal or experiential approach (Gudykunst and Hammer, 1983). The question is though, does it really help? Because if not, then businesses might be better off focusing on the alternative research perspective in this area: the selection of effective expatriate workers

The evidence seems mixed, such that it is not clear cut that such training always helps. Morris and Robie (2001) conducted a meta-analysis that examined 41 studies. Overall, the results indicated that cross-cultural training had some positive impact on adjustment and performance outcomes, but the effects were quite small and there was considerable variability in the studies they included. This suggests that there are factors moderating the effectiveness of the training, or potential mediators that explain why some people benefit and others do not.

More recent studies have begun to address these gaps in understanding. Littrel *et al.* (2006) conducted a qualitative review and proposed moderating factors such as the timing of the training relative to the assignment, and wider factors such as the adjustment of the expatriate's partner or spouse (who may have to accompany them on assignment). Puck, Kittler and Wright (2008) examined the effectiveness of training for a sample of German managers and found that whilst general training had no impact on adjustment, language training was predictive of three outcomes (general, interactional, and work adjustment). Focusing on the psychological processes of adjustment, Osman-Gani and Rockstuhl (2009) reported the mediating effect of self-efficacy in translating training to effective adjustment outcomes. When training led to a genuinely improved expectation of success, then adjustment outcomes were more positive.

So in this case, training is not always a guaranteed benefit, and careful attention is needed it seems to the design of programmes. Indeed, if CCT raises anxieties or apprehension about working in another culture, then it may potentially be detrimental. The area of CCT provides a good insight into factors affecting success and failure of training at work.

THE BOTTOM LINE: DOES LEARNING AND DEVELOPMENT MAKE A DIFFERENCE IN ORGANIZATIONS?

The simple answer to this question is that there appears to be plenty of evidence that learning, training and development do contribute to the overall performance of organizations. A recent meta-analysis (Tharenou, Saks and Moore, 2007) examined the effects of training on three categories of organization outcomes (HR outcomes, organization performance outcomes and financial outcomes). Training provision was associated with a range of beneficial HR outcomes. These included more positive employee attitudes such as higher satisfaction, involvement and commitment; lower incidence of grievances and absenteeism; higher employee retention and lower turnover. Training provision also predicted higher levels of overall human capital or employee skill levels, suggesting that training did transfer to some degree in the organizations studied.

With respect to organizational performance, training was found to predict key outcomes, specifically productivity, quality (including higher levels of customer satisfaction), objective organizational performance and managerial perceptions of performance. Training was also found to be associated with perceptions of the financial performance of organizations, but only negligibly related to actual financial outcomes. There was some evidence that the effects of training on organizational and financial performance were stronger when the training was clearly aligned to the organization's strategy.

The strength of the association between training provision and managerial perceptions of organizational effectiveness can be affected by the design and delivery of training. A study of 457 managers (Aragon-Sanchez, Barba-Aragon and Sanz-Valle, 2003) from a variety of small and medium organizations found that most forms of training were associated with perceived improvements in HR outcomes (reduced absenteeism and turnover, reduced accidents, reduced external recruiting of services), whereas only on-job training was associated with improved perceptions of service quality and profitability. Training provision is related to perceptions of the quality of innovation in organizations (Shipton, West, Dawson, Birdi and Patterson, 2006). Organizations that train managers tend to perform more effectively than those that do not (Aragon and Sanz Valle, 2013). Moreover, training and development opportunities are included as one aspect of 'High Performance HR Practices', which are collectively associated with improved work-related attitudes such as commitment and satisfaction (Kooij, Jansen, Dikkers and De Lange, 2010).

A meta-analysis of a wider range of training evaluation criteria (Arthur, Bennet, Edens and Bell, 2003) examined all four of Kirkpatrick's criterion levels (reactions, learning, behaviour, results). Training was found to positively influence criteria in all four levels, importantly providing further evidence that training does lead to positive organizational outcomes.

A really powerful finding about the value of learning and development comes from the British NHS, as part of a study highlighted in Chapter 2. As part of ongoing staff satisfaction and HR research in the Health Service, there have been a number of studies that have examined the organization-level outcomes of training, including benefits for patient care. Within these studies, it has been shown that the sophistication of and satisfaction with training policies within PCTs is directly related to patient mortality, even after controlling for hospital size, number of doctors per 100 beds and prior and region-specific mortality rates (West, Borrill, Dawson, Scully, Carter, Anelay, Patterson and Waring, 2002). Fewer patient deaths occur in hospitals where learning and development is organized effectively.

SUMMARY

This chapter has examined learning and development in organizations and the contribution of Work Psychology to understanding and improving learning and development systems and processes. Learning and development are important HR functions that help to ensure that people learn and apply knowledge, skills, abilities and competencies that are needed to deliver the strategy and goals of the organization.

The practice of learning and development is structured around the 'training cycle', which comprises a needs assessment phase, the design and delivery of training, plus systematic evaluation. Needs assessments are conducted at different levels, focusing on organizations, jobs and positions in team contexts, job tasks, required KSAOs and individual development needs. All are used to specify objectives for training and learning.

Behavioural and cognitive theories of learning are relevant to the design of training and development interventions and there are a variety of techniques that practitioners can use to help people develop in ways that they find rewarding. The concept of active learning describes how people take an active role in their own development by deciding on their own development needs, and when and how they will address them. New technology in the form of e-learning is likely to facilitate the development of this approach in future years.

Evaluations of training should ideally follow experimental research designs, which permit the analysis of change, and ultimately the examination of the value and benefits of learning and development. Such rigorous evaluation is quite rare in practice. Key challenges include defining and measuring outcome criteria, and psychologists have proposed several models of learning outcome criteria.

Success and failure of learning, training and development in organizations depends on many different factors, including individual differences, training design and organizational factors. Models of training transfer help to understand these issues more clearly. Getting learning, training and development right might be tricky, but it is worthwhile. Research examining the outcomes of training at an organizational level overwhelmingly points to the organizational and business benefits of investment in learning and development.

DISCUSSION QUESTIONS

1 Do you think you have a performance goal orientation or a learning goal orientation? What are the advantages and disadvantages of your approach?

2 Is investment in learning, training and development always a good idea? Why?

3 What kinds of job tasks would be best learned through behavioural approaches to learning and training? What kinds would be best suited to cognitive learning?

4 A consultant approaches a manager to offer their new problem solving training. What information should they consider before deciding to buy it?

5 Should people always decide on their own development needs as in Active Learning?

6 An organization has a very limited budget for learning, training and development, and the HR Director wants to ensure they get the most out of it. How would you advise them?

APPLY IT

If you are working in an organization in any capacity, here are some suggestions that can help you apply and implement the content and learning from this chapter.

1. Before you decide on implementing any learning programme or training intervention with staff in your business, take a **critical** review of the programme objectives and assess how and in what ways they are aligned to the overall strategy of the business. Modify programmes if necessary so that they fit with strategy.

2. Structured training needs analysis is extremely informative for planning learning, training and development at work. If you do not have clearly structured processes in place, then start by making a few small changes to performance management processes. First, hold specific development review meetings with all people in your team

or business. Identify the competencies that are needed in their particular role, and then evaluate the performance of each person on a three-point scale (needs development, effective, distinctive; see also Chapter 8). Ensure that they receive some support in the 'needs development' areas and discuss this with them in the review meeting.

3. Evaluate your development interventions. Before people go on training or learning programmes, rate their performance quantitatively using some scale or measure (see Chapter 8 for some suggestions). After the training, review their performance for four-six weeks and evaluate performance again to see if there has been an improvement. Ideally measure it again after three months to check it has been sustained.

4. Transfer is a key issue for training effectiveness, and climate within the team for transfer, including managerial support is influential. One easy way to apply the implication from research in this area is to ensure that plans are put in place for debrief and early practise of new skills following training.

WEB ACTIVITY

Bite-size Learning: the future?

Read the article 'The best and worst of bite-size learning' at **uk.themindgym.com** or by following the link in the digital resources online and discuss the questions below.

1 How might bite-size learning be incorporated into HRM strategy more widely?

2 How could organizations promote transfer of learning from short learning activities?

3 What could organizations do to maximize and measure the return-on-investment for training and learning?

FURTHER READING

Goldstein, I.L. and Ford, J.K. (2002). *Training in organizations: Needs assessment, development and evaluation*. Monterey, CA: Brooks Cole. An excellent introduction to systems of training in organizations. In S.W.J. Kozlowski and E. Salas (eds.), *Learning, training and development in organizations* (pp. 65–98). New York: Routledge.

Harrison, R. (2009). *Learning and Development*. 5th ed. London: CIPD. A more practically oriented book on learning and development, giving an HR perspective.

Blanchard, P.N. and Thacker, J.W. (2007). *Effective training: Systems, strategies and policies*. Upper Saddle River, NJ: Pearson Education.

REFERENCES

Alliger, G.M., Tannenbaum, S.I., Bennett, W., Traver, H. and Shotland, A. (1997). A meta-analysis of the relations among training criteria. *Personnel Psychology, 50(2)*, 341–358.

Anderson, J. (1983). *The Architecture of Cognition*. Cambridge, MA: Harvard University Press.

Anderson, J.R. (1996). ACT: A simple theory of complex cognition. *American Psychologist, 51*, 355–365.

Aragon-Sanchez, A., Barba-Aragon, I. and Sanz-Valle, R. (2003). Effects of training on business results. *International Journal of Human Resource Management, 14(6)*, 956–980.

Aragon, I.B. and Sanz Valle, R. (2013). Does training managers pay off?. *The International Journal of Human Resource Management, 24(8)*, 1671–1684.

Arthur, W., Bennett, W., Stanush, P.L. and McNelly, T.L. (1998). Factors that influence skill decay and retention: a quantitative review and analysis. *Human Performance, 11*, 79–86.

Arthur, W. Jr., Bennett, W. Jr., Edens, P.S. and Bell, S.T. (2003). Effectiveness of training in organizations: a meta-analysis of design and evaluation features. *Journal of Applied Psychology, 88*, 234–245.

Baldwin, T.T. and Ford, J.K. (1988). Transfer of training: A review and directions for future research. *Personnel Psychology, 41(1)*, 63–105.

Bandura, A. (1977). *Social Learning Theory*. Upper Saddle River, NJ: Prentice Hall.

Barrick, M.R. and Mount, M.K. (1991). The Big Five personality dimensions and job performance: A meta-analysis. *Personnel Psychology, 44*, 1–26.

Barrick, M.R., Mount, M.K. and Strauss, J.P. (1993). Conscientiousness and performance of sales representatives: Test of the mediating effects of goal setting. *Journal of Applied Psychology, 78*, 715–722.

Beaubien, J.M., & Baker, D.P. (2004). The use of simulation for training teamwork skills in health care: how low can you go?. Quality and Safety in Health Care, 13(suppl 1), i51–i56. Chicago

Beier, M.E. and Kanfer, R. (2009). Motivation in training and development: A phase perspective. In S.W.J. Kozlowski and E. Salas (eds.), *Learning, training and development in organizations* (pp. 65–98). New York: Routledge.

Bell, B.S. and Kozlowski, S.W.J. (2002). Goal orientation and ability: interactive effects on self-efficacy, performance and knowledge. *Journal of Applied Psychology, 87(3)*, 497–505.

Bell, B.S. and Kozlowski, S.W.J. (2009). Toward a theory of learner centred training design: An integrative framework of active learning. In S.W.J.Kozlowski and E. Salas (eds.), *Learning, training and development in organizations*. New York, NY: Routledge Academic.

Bertolino, M., Truxillo, D.M. and Fraccaroli, F. (2011). Age as moderator of the relationship of proactive personality with training motivation, perceived career development from training, and training behavioral intentions. *Journal of Organizational Behavior, 32(2)*, 248–263.

Blanchard, P.N. and Thacker, J.W. (2007). Effective training: Systems, strategies and policies. Upper Saddle River, NJ: Pearson Education.

Brown, T. C., McCracken, M. and Hillier, T. L. (2013). Using evidence-based practices to enhance transfer of training: assessing the effectiveness of goal setting and behavioural observation scales. *Human Resource Development International, 16(4)*, 374–389.

Carlisle, J., Bhanugopan, R. and Fish, A. (2013). Latent factor structures affecting the occupational profile construct of the training needs analysis scale. *The International Journal of Human Resource Management, 23(20)*, 4319–4341.

Cheng, E. and Hampson, I. (2008). Transfer of training: A review and new insights. *International Journal of Management Reviews, 10(4)*, 327–341.

Colquitt, J.A., LePine, J.A. and Noe, R. (2000). Toward an integrative theory of training motivation: A meta-analytic path analysis of 20 years of research. *Journal of Applied Psychology, 85*, 678–707.

Dachner, A.M., Saxton, B.M., Noe, R.A. and Keeton, K.E. (2013). To Infinity and Beyond: Using a Narrative Approach to Identify Training Needs for Unknown and Dynamic Situations. *Human Resource Development Quarterly, 24(2)*, 239–267.

Dragoni, L. and Kuenzi, M. (2012). Better understanding work unit goal orientation: Its emergence and impact under different types of work unit structure. *Journal of Applied Psychology, 97(5)*, 1032.

Dweck, C.S. (1986). Motivational processes affecting learning. *American Psychologist, 41*, 1040–1048.

Esfandagheh, F.B., Harris, R. and Oreyzi, H.R. (2012). The impact of extraversion and pre-training self-efficacy on levels of training outcomes. *Human Resource Development International, 15(2)*, 175–191.

Farr, J.L., Hofmann, D.A. and Ringenbach, K.L. (1993). Goal orientation and action control theory: Implications for industrial and organizational psychology. In C.L. Cooper and I.T. Robertson (eds.), *International Review of Industrial and Organizational Psychology* (pp. 193–232). NY: New York, Robertson Wiley.

Ford, J.K. and Weissbein, D.A. (1997). Transfer of Training: An Updated Review and Analysis. *Performance Improvement Quarterly, 10(2)*, 22–41.

Ford, J.K., Kraiger, K. and Merritt, S.M. (2009). An updated review of the multidimensionality of training outcomes: New directions for training evaluation research. In S.W.J. Kozlowski and E. Salas

(eds.) *Learning, Training and Development in Organizations*. New York: Routledge.

Fitzpatrick, R. (2001). The Strange Case of the Transfer of Training Estimate. T*he Industrial-Organizational Psychologist*, 18–19.

Gagne, R., Briggs, L. and Wager, W. (1992). *Principles of Instructional Design* (4th ed.). Fort Worth, TX: HBJ College Publishers.

Goldstein, I.L. (1991). Training in work organizations. In M.D. Dunnette and L.M. Hough (eds.), *Handbook of industrial and organizational psychology* (Vol. 2, 2nd ed., pp. 507–620). Palo Alto, CA: Consulting Psychologists Press.

Goldstein, I.L. and Ford, J.K. (2002). *Training in organizations: Needs assessment, development and evaluation*. Monterey, CA: Brooks Cole.

Gudykunst, W.B. and Hammer, M.R. (1983). Basic training design approaches to intercultural training. In D. Landis and R. Brislin (Eds.), *Handbook of intercultural training, 1*. NY: Pergamon.

Gully, S. and Chen, G. (2009). Individual differences, attribute-treatment interactions, and training outcomes. In S.W.J. Kozlowski and E. Salas (eds.) *Learning, Training and Development in Organizations*. New York: Routledge.

Hamblin, A. (1974). *Evaluation and Control of Training*. London: McGraw Hill.

Harrison, R. (2009). *Learning and Development*. 5th ed. London: CIPD.

Kaplan R.S. and Norton D.P. (1992) The balanced scorecard – measures that drive performance. *Harvard Business Review, 70*, 71–79.

Kearns, P. (2005). *Evaluating the ROI from Learning*. London: Chartered Institute of Personnel and Development.

Kirkpatrick, D.L. (1976). Evaluation of training. In R.L. Craig (ed.), *Training and development handbook*. New York: McGraw-Hill.

Kooij, D. T., Jansen, P. G., Dikkers, J. S. and De Lange, A. H. (2010). The influence of age on the associations between HR practices and both affective commitment and job satisfaction: A meta-analysis. *Journal of Organizational Behavior, 31(8)*, 1111–1136.

Kozlowski, S.W.J., Gully, S.M., Nason, E.R. and Smith, E.M. (1999). Developing adaptive teams: A theory of compilation and performance across levels and time. In D.R. Ilgen and E.D. Pulakos, (eds.) *The Changing Nature of Work Performance: Implications for Staffing, Personnel Actions and Development* (pp. 240–292). San Francisco: Jossey-Bass.

Kozlowski, S.W.J. and Bell, B.S. (2006). Disentangling achievement orientation and goal setting: effects on self-regulatory processes. *Journal of Applied Psychology, 91(4)*, 900–16.

Kraiger, K., Ford, J.K. and Salas, E. (1993). Application of Cognitive, Skill-Based and Affective Theories of Learning Outcomes to New Methods of Training Evaluation. *Journal of Applied Psychology*, *78(2)*, 311–328.

Littrell, L.N., Salas, E., Hess, K.P., Paley, M., & Riedel, S. (2006). Expatriate preparation: A critical analysis of 25 years of cross-cultural training research. *Human Resource Development Review*, *5(3)*, 355–388.

Martocchio, J.J. and Hertenstein, E.J. (2003). Learning orientation and goal orientation context: Relationships with cognitive and affective learning outcomes. *Human Resources Development Quarterly*, *14*, 413–434.

Mischel, W. and Shoda, Y. (1995). A cognitive-affective system theory of personality: Reconceptualizing situations, dispositions, dynamics and invariance in personality structure. *Psychological Review*, *102(2)*, 246–268.

Morris, M.A. and Robie, C. (2001). A meta-analysis of the effects of cross-cultural training on expatriate performance and adjustment. *International Journal of Training and Development*, *5(2)*, 112–125.

Nonaka, I. (1991). The knowledge-creating company. *Harvard Business Review*, *69*, 96–104.

Nonaka, I. and Takeuchi, H. (1995). *The knowledge creating company: How Japanese companies create the dynamics of innovation*. New York: Oxford University Press.

Osman-Gani, A.M. and Rockstuhl, T. (2009). Cross-cultural training, expatriate self-efficacy, and adjustments to overseas assignments: An empirical investigation of managers in Asia. *International Journal of Intercultural Relations*, *33(4)*, 277–290.

Payne, S.C., Youngcourt, S.S. and Beaubien, J.M. (2007). A Meta-Analytic Examination of the Goal Orientation Nomological Net. *Journal of Applied Psychology*, *92, (1)*, 128–150.

Potosky, D. and Ramakrishna, H.V. (2002). The moderating role of updating climate perceptions in the relationship between goal orientation, self-efficacy and job performance. *Human Performance*, *15(3)*, 275–297.

Puck, J.F., Kittler, M.G. and Wright, C. (2008). Does it Really Work? Re-Assessing the Impact of Pre-Departure Cross-Cultural Training on Expatriate Adjustment. *International Journal of Human Resource Management*, *19(12)*, 2182–2197.

Quinones, M.A., Ford, J.K., Sego, D.J. and Smith, E.M. (1995). The effects of individual and transfer environment characteristics on the opportunity to perform trained tasks. *Training Research Journal*, *1*, 29–48.

Saks, A.M. and Belcourt, M. (2004). An investigation of training activities and transfer of training in organizations. *Humans Resources Management 45(4)*, 629–648.

Salas, E. and Cannon-Bowers, J. (2001). The science of training: A decade of progress. *Annual Review of Psychology*, *52*, 471–499.

Schalm, C. (2008). Implementing a balanced scorecard as a strategic management tool in a long-term care organization. *Journal of Health Services Research Policy*, *13(1)*, 8–14.

Schuler, R.S., Budhwar, P. and Florkowski, G. (2002). International Human Resource Management: Review and Critique. *International Journal of Management Reviews*, *4(1)*, 41–70.

Shantz, A. and Latham, G.P. (2012). Transfer of training: Written self-guidance to increase self-efficacy and interviewing performance of job seekers. *Human Resource Management*, *51(5)*, 733–746.

Shipton, H., West, M.A., Dawson, J.F., Birdi, K. and Patterson, M. (2006). HRM as a predictor of innovation. *Human Resource Management Journal*, *16(1)*, 3–27.

Shipton, H. and Zhou, Q. (2008). Learning and development in organizations: Intervention or Informality? In Aston Centre for Human Resources (eds.), *Strategic Human Resource Management*. London: CIPD.

Sitzmann, T. and Johnson, S. K. (2012). The best laid plans: Examining the conditions under which a planning intervention improves learning and reduces attrition. *Journal of Applied Psychology*, *97(5)*, 967.

Tannenbaum, S.I. and Yukl, G. (1992). Training and development in work organizations. *Annual Review of Psychology*, *43*, 399–441.

Tharenou, P., Saks, A.M. and Moore, C. (2007). A review and critique of research on training and organizational-level outcomes. *Human Resource Management Review*, *17*, 251–273.

Van de Walle, D. (1997). Development and validation of a work domain goal orientation instrument. *Educational and Psychological Measurement*, *57*, 995–1015.

Van Eerde, W., Tang, K.C.S. and Talbot, G. (2008). The mediating role of training utility on the relationship between training needs assessment and organizational effectiveness. *International Journal of Human Resource Management*, *19*, 63–73.

West, M.A., Borrill, C.S., Dawson, J.F., Scully, J., Carter, M., Anelay, S., Patterson, M. and Waring. J. (2002). The link between the management of employees and patient mortality in acute hospitals. *International Journal of Human Resource Management*, *13*, 1299–1310.

CHAPTER 8

PERFORMANCE MEASUREMENT AND MANAGEMENT

LEARNING OBJECTIVES

- Understand the role of performance management in organization strategy.

- Describe and critique objective measures of performance.

- Understand multi-dimensional models of job performance.

- Understand the difference between task performance and organizational citizenship behaviour.

- Describe competencies and their use in performance management.

- Describe and evaluate methods of performance appraisal.

- Understand the importance of goal setting, feedback and intervention in performance management.

- Understand how goal setting and feedback can be made more effective in performance management.

- Describe coaching as a performance improvement intervention.

- Understand when disciplinary proceedings might be invoked in performance disputes.

How do you know if you are performing at work? Think about your job, and what it involves. What are the key tasks associated with your job? How do you know if you are carrying them out well or poorly? Does your manager give you feedback on your performance, and if so, how does he or she present it to you? Performance management in organizations is the task of measuring and improving the performance of employees. It is an important task for managers because it helps to ensure that the people in an organization are all working towards a common goal, and to the best of their ability. However, performance feedback, and particularly the content or absence of it, is a common source of dissatisfaction in organizations, and it seems that many get performance measurement and management wrong. Perhaps you have your own examples. It is unnecessary, and the fact that some organizations do get it right attests to this fact. Research and theory actually tells us much about how to measure and manage job performance effectively. In fact, one of the most practical, yet robust and well-supported findings in Work Psychology comes from this area of study (more on that later). This chapter is about the measurement and management of people's performance at work, and covers what we know about these processes from Work Psychology theory and research.

THE IMPORTANCE OF PERFORMANCE MEASUREMENT AND MANAGEMENT

Understanding organizations is a complex task, which we will tackle later on in this book. However, a brief consideration of organization theory is important at the outset of this chapter. Systems models of organizations emphasize the importance of conceptualizing organizations as interconnected systems of processes. One such model is the Burke–Litwin Model (Burke and Litwin, 1992), shown in Figure 8.1. The Mission and Strategy, Leadership, and Organizational Culture boxes in the model are called the transformational factors in the organization. When an organization seeks to develop or change significantly, these transformational factors are the enablers, often prompted by change in the external environment. If you follow the logic of the figure, you see that change in these transformational factors is filtered down through smaller-scale processes to individual employee performance. The model illustrates that in order for the organization to achieve its strategic goals, people in the organization need to perform in a way that contributes to them. The key process in translating strategy to individual behaviour is performance management. Strategic performance management is about aligning individual performance goals with those of the organization, determining whether individuals perform satisfactorily against those goals, and intervening when they do not. Performance management therefore involves assessment of performance at work, but also employee development, comprising identification and closure of gaps in knowledge, skills, abilities and behavioural dispositions that hinder or prevent people performing at work. Two tasks of performance management are therefore identified:

- Performance Measurement.
- Performance Improvement.

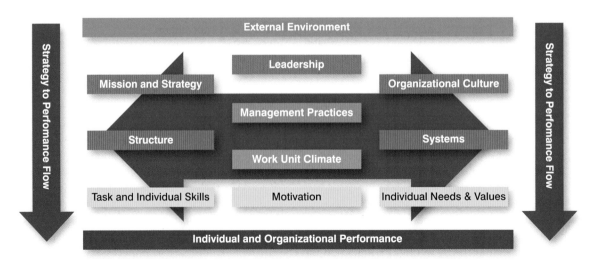

Figure 8.1   Adapted from the Burke–Litwin model

The first part of this chapter is concerned with performance measurement. Later sections examine performance improvement by looking at performance management more broadly.

MEASURING JOB PERFORMANCE

It is a common problem in management and human resource practice that a high proportion of managers tend to know intuitively whether staff are performing well or poorly, but are at a loss about exactly how to quantify performance (Woods, 2008). The problem of quantifying job performance is also prevalent in research in Work Psychology and management. Job performance is so important in Work Psychology that it is often known simply as 'the criterion' (Dalal, 2005), with the 'criterion problem' referring to the unavailability of robust job performance criteria in applied research (Austin and Villanova, 1992; Thayer, 1992). This is of real concern for researchers and practitioners because alongside performance management, many other activities also rely on job performance measurement: validation of selection systems and individual difference measures, training and development evaluation, and promotion planning to name but a few. So performance measurement is an important process, but what exactly does it involve? Tannenbaum (2006) describes job performance measurement as:

> *The collection and use of judgements, ratings, perceptions or more objective sources of information to better understand the performance of a person, team, unit, business, process, program or initiative in order to guide subsequent actions or decisions.*

Highlighted in this definition are a number of potential ways that performance can be measured, but the basic issues that arise from all of them are around what actually constitutes job performance (i.e. what is job performance, and how could it be defined?) and how it should be measured (i.e. what methods should be used to measure performance). The two issues are closely linked such that the definition of job performance that is adopted will usually dictate how it is measured.

Objective Measures of Performance

A basic approach to performance measurement is to use objective outcome data collected by organizations, and this is relevant in specific kinds of jobs where data are easy to capture. Some objective measures reflect the core task or the job:

- Sales figures: Sales volume is easily measured in sales jobs, and can be represented in various ways including absolute monetary value, performance above target, or values adjusted for factors such as 'sales patch'.
- Service duration: Service jobs, such as those carried out in call centres can be measured objectively, usually through examining call or service times.
- Utilization: Some organizations monitor the 'on-job hours' of employees. This is commonly used with consultants who are charged at daily rates. The time spent working on-contract versus off-contract could be measured.
- Results: Objectively measureable results are those that are not based on the perceptions of a rater or manager.
- Production: Any job that involves producing things can be measured by monitoring output.

- Quality: The products associated with some jobs have objective markers of quality (number of defects for example), which can be measured.

Proxy measures are objective data that are not directly associated with the task or function of the job. These are actually a poor substitute for relevant job data:

- Absence: Absence from work is sometimes used as a performance indicator, as it is assumed to detract from productivity. Absence data are difficult to collect accurately.
- Safety record: These data might be collected in industrial jobs, recorded as number of accidents in a given period.
- Tardiness/Timekeeping: Where 'clocking-in' is used in an organization, records of tardiness at the start of the day, or during breaks could be collected.

Objective measures are sometimes considered to be more robust and therefore more accurate indicators of performance compared with subjective measures. However, there are questions about exactly how objective such data are. Campbell (1990) argues that determining the boundaries for acceptable versus unacceptable objective performance is a subjective task (e.g. a supervisor has to decide what constitutes acceptable sales figures), and so many 'objective measures' could easily be conceptualized as subjective.

Perhaps more importantly, objective performance data are limited because they fail to tap into why some people perform better than others. To understand that, the focus of performance measurement needs to be on behaviour. Behaviour represents what people actually do at work, and Motowidlo, Borman and Schmitt (1997) argue that behaviour should be the focus in performance measurement because results and outcomes can be affected by many factors outside the control of individuals. The results achieved by poorly performing employees and managers can be compensated by a buoyant business environment or co-worker support. Conversely, a person who performs all of the desirable behaviours required in their job might achieve poor results because the product or service that he or she is delivering is inadequate, or not in demand, factors that may be outside the employee's control. Does that make them poor performers, or is the shortcoming in the market research department of the organization? For Work Psychologists, the best way to establish fairly whether someone is performing at work is to examine behaviour at work.

Models of Job Performance Behaviour

Think for a moment about your colleagues, or if you supervise people, your subordinates. You probably feel able to form an overall impression about their performance at work. There is likely to be some validity to your judgement (Viswesvaran, Schmidt and Ones, 2005), but there are a number of problems with measuring performance in this way. First, your judgement is affected by bias, and particularly the halo effect (Viswesvaran *et al.*, 2005). The halo effect is perceptual bias that affects how people perceive others. Before someone assesses another person's job performance, they form an impression about that individual's overall merit, and this influences the way that they evaluate the person's performance on a range of different performance dimensions. The halo effect occurs when people form a favourable impression and consequently overly positive judgments about a person's performance. The opposite is the horns effect. The second limitation is similar to that of objective measures; there is no information in the evaluation to determine which aspects of performance are weak or strong.

Jobs are diverse and therefore make diverse demands on people, eliciting a multitude of different behaviours, and this inevitably leads to multi-faceted or multi-dimensional models of job performance. Multi-dimensional models allow us to make sense of complex behavioural phenomena, and to measure performance in ways that are more useful to people at work, and to organizations. Constructing them involves clustering performance behaviours into broad homogenous dimensions.

Each dimension is defined according to the common theme among its constituent behaviours. For example, key management performance behaviours include formulating short- and long-term team objectives, and organizing and prioritizing work. These two activities are conceptually related, and might be grouped under a broader heading of 'planning and organizing' (e.g. Borman and Brush, 1993). This multi-dimensional approach has led to two similar, yet divergent approaches to understanding job performance, explored in the next sections of this chapter:

- The first has examined the job performance in organizations generally, with the aim of understanding how performance can be conceptualized across all jobs.
- The second is the competency approach, which has drawn on the practice of competency modelling in organizations to construct broad models of job performance that can be applied in different ways across different jobs and organizations.

General models of job performance

Whilst most psychologists emphasize the need to conduct thorough job analyses to define job performance in specific jobs, this does not mean that the basic elements of job performance change across different jobs (Viswesvaran and Ones, 2000). Research on models of job performance aims to define these basic elements. There is a huge and complex research literature examining the best way to model job performance, and the methods used in such studies are complicated, making it difficult for managers and HR practitioners to engage with the implications. However, once you cut through the complexity, these studies offer a wealth of information about job performance, and how to measure it. The starting point is to break down overall performance into constituent parts. There are different ways of doing this (e.g. Viswesvaran *et al.*, 1996; Campbell, McCloy, Oppler and Sager, 1993), but by far the most widely supported approach to take is to differentiate task performance from organizational citizenship behaviours (Woods, 2008).

Task performance versus organizational citizenship behaviours

Probably the most influential advance in job performance modelling in the past 20 years is the differentiation of task performance and organizational citizenship behaviour (OCB; e.g. Motowidlo and Van Scotter, 1994; Motowidlo, Borman and Schmitt, 1997). These two categories of job performance sit underneath general job performance in the hierarchical model. The traditional view of job performance restricted the domain of interest to the way that people performed the core tasks of their job. Task performance has a direct impact on organizational performance and is defined by Borman and Motowidlo (1997) as 'the effectiveness with which job incumbents perform activities that relate to the organization's technical core' (p. 99). Motowidlo, Borman and Schmitt (1997) expand this definition to encompass two basic kinds of task performance activities:

- Conversion of raw materials into goods and services that constitute the products of the organization (such as selling merchandise, operating machinery, teaching a class, performing surgical procedures).
- Activities that maintain and service the technical core of the organization (such as the supervision of staff, planning core activities, distributing supplies and products).

Components of task performance   There are a variety of different perspectives in the research literature on how to break down task performance into more specific components, but an influential idea came from the Project A studies conducted by Campbell and colleagues (see Key Figure box on page 242). Their simple model of performance distinguishes two aspects of task performance:

● Job-specific Task Performance: This can be thought of as core task proficiency, or performance of tasks that are central to a person's job role. Put simply, this is how well a person fulfils the tasks listed on their job description.

● Non-job-specific Task Performance: This is a general proficiency dimension, representing performance of tasks that may not be core to a person's role in the organization. This might be thought of as being performance on tasks or assignments outside areas of core responsibility (short-term projects for example).

These two components are still rather abstract in their definition, and their purpose is to provide a framework around which more specific task performance behaviours can be organized. The use of job analysis for example could define the important task performance behaviours for different jobs.

Organizational citizenship behaviour

More recently, theories and models of job performance have acknowledged the importance of work behaviours that fall outside the domain of task performance, often referred to as discretionary or extra-role behaviours. In contemporary business environments characterized by flatter structures, international competition and increased employee autonomy, such behaviours are now considered critical to effective organizational performance (Podsakoff, MacKenzie, Paine and Bachrach, 2000). The most widely used term for these aspects of job performance is organizational citizenship behaviour (OCB).

The concept of OCB was proposed by Organ in the late 1980s (e.g. Organ, 1988), who observed that to a varying extent, people tend to contribute to the continued existence of their organization beyond their core task activities. Such contributions include helping and cooperating with others, and general support for the organization and its mission. OCB was initially defined as extra-role behaviour, not directly recognized through formal reward systems. Such behaviour was therefore considered desirable, but not enforceable (Smith, Organ and Near, 1983). This definition was modified by Borman and Motowidlo (1993), who proposed an alternative construct labelled contextual performance. They defined contextual behaviours as those that 'supported the organizational, social and psychological environment in which the technical core must function' (p. 74), elaborating this with examples such as helping co-workers, volunteering for extra work and describing the organization in a positive way. They noted that whilst task behaviour is job specific, contextual behaviours were desirable across all jobs. An important development of the theory was recognition that such behaviours need not fall outside formal job responsibilities, later recognized in Organ's model (Organ, 1997).

Components of organizational citizenship behaviour   There are several models of OCB in the research literature. The first was proposed by Organ (1988), who identified five dimensions labelled altruism, courtesy, conscientiousness, sportsmanship and civic virtue. A simpler two-dimensional structure was described by Williams and Anderson (1991), who distinguished between citizenship behaviours directed towards individuals (OCB-I) and organizations (OCB-O). These two dimensions are also represented in a model proposed by Coleman and Borman (2000), in the dimensions Personal Support and Organizational Support respectively. Their model incorporated a third dimension labelled Conscientious Initiative. Box 8.1, taken from Hanson and Borman (2006), describes the model. Hanson and Borman provide a fuller discussion of the overlaps and relationships between the various models of OCB.

When you start to think about OCB and its implications for job performance, it is also tempting to think about the opposite of citizenship behaviour. Counterproductive work behaviours are reviewed in Box 8.2, and there is a surprising conclusion from research about how they relate to OCB.

BOX 8.1

Dimensions of organizational citizenship behaviour

- Personal Support — Helping others by offering suggestions, teaching them useful knowledge or skills, directly performing some of their tasks and providing emotional support for their personal problems. Cooperating with others by accepting suggestions, informing them of events they should know about and putting team objectives ahead of personal interests. Showing consideration, courtesy and tact in relations with others, as well as motivating and showing confidence in them.

- Organizational Support — Representing the organization favourably by defending and promoting it, as well as expressing satisfaction and showing loyalty by staying with the organization despite temporary hardships. Supporting the organization's mission and objectives, complying with organizational rules and procedures and suggesting initiatives.

- Conscientious Initiative — Persisting with extra effort despite difficult conditions. Taking the initiative to do all that is necessary to accomplish objectives even if not normally a part of own duties and finding additional productive work to perform when own duties are completed. Developing own knowledge and skills by taking advantage of opportunities within the organization and outside their own organization using own time and resources.

BOX 8.2

The flip-side of performance: counterproductive work behaviours

Theories of OCB tell us numerous ways that employees can engage in behaviours that enhance working practices, environments and relationships. Conversely, employees can engage in behaviours that are damaging to other individuals, to productivity and to the organization as a whole. Such behaviours fall under the overarching concept of counterproductive work behaviours (CWB). Viswesvaran and Ones (2000) include CWB as a third broad performance dimension next to task performance and OCB. They identify several kinds of common CWB:

- Property damage (including theft and misuse of resources).

- Substance abuse at work.

- Violence (which may also include workplace bullying).

- Lateness, absenteeism, social loafing and turnover.

Viswesvaran and Ones (2000) point out that all of these behaviours are considered by supervisors when they rate the performance of their employees.

If one thinks for a moment about the kinds of things that a bad organizational citizen would be guilty of, some, if not all of the behaviours listed above intuitively spring to mind. The implicit perspective on OCB and CWB is therefore that they are at opposite ends of a single continuum. However, this assumption is misguided. In a meta-analysis addressing the question, Dalal (2005) reported an association of −0.32 between the two performance domains. This moderate negative relationship is too small to conclude that they are polar opposites. A better perspective is to view OCB and CWB as separate but related constructs (Kelloway, Loghlin, Barling and Nault, 2002). It appears that employees can be rated as both reasonable organizational citizens and as engaging in counterproductive behaviours.

The Competency Approach to Performance Measurement

Models of job performance in the literature are not immediately accessible for managers and practitioners in organizations. More familiar are competencies and the competency approach to performance measurement. Competency modelling is a popular contemporary approach to analyzing job performance, and the skills, abilities and attributes underlying performance. The approach has grown substantially in the past 20 years (Campion, Fink, Ruggeberg, Carr, Phillips and Odman, 2011) and most large organizations now use some form of competency modelling or competency-based assessment as part of their HR strategy. There has been no general consensus in the academic literature about exactly how to define 'competencies'. However, recent commentaries in the literature (e.g. Campion *et al.*, 2011; Soderquist, Papalexandris, Ioannou and Prastacos, 2010), combined with past contributions (e.g. Bartram, 2005) point to a general definition as referring to the combined knowledge, skills, abilities and other characteristics that underlie effective performance, and are observable, measurable, and distinguish superior from average performance.

Critics of the concept of competencies correctly point out that competency definitions are currently a conceptual muddle. There is no standard format for how competencies might be represented (Voskuijl and Evers, 2008), yet significant advances have been made to describe and review best practice in competency modeling (Campion *et al.*, 2011). Moreover, the major appeal of competency modelling as a tool for HRM lies in their applied benefits. Soderquist *et al.* (2010) highlight that competency modeling allows horizontal integration of HRM processes, such that selection, development and performance management can all be aligned, and vertical integration such that strategy and organization-level objectives can be built in directly to performance (i.e. competency) requirements of individual staff. The vertical integration aspect reflects the discussion earlier in this chapter regarding the importance of strategy in performance management.

A key property of job competencies is that they are behaviourally defined (Aguinis, 2009). Competencies used for assessment in organizations tend to comprise a label, a broad definition and several behavioural indicators or descriptors (see Figure 8.2). Box 8.3 presents an example job competencies. Behavioural descriptors or indicators are used to facilitate assessment of competencies, to elaborate their meaning, and to differentiate standards of proficiency. The behaviours described in the indicators, if observed in a person's performance, are taken as evidence of effective job performance, or presence of the competency. Some competency definitions also contain negative behavioural indicators (i.e. behaviours that constitute ineffective performance) to aid performance measurement. Assessment of competencies generally involves judgement based on observation about how effectively the individual has demonstrated the behaviours associated with the competency.

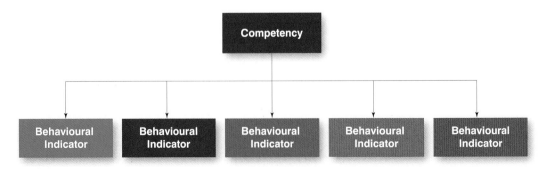

Figure 8.2   Competency and behaviour indicators

BOX 8.3
Example competency

Project Management

Project Management is the art of creating accurate and effective schedules with a well-defined scope while being personally accountable for the execution and invested in the success of the project. People who exhibit this competency effectively and continuously manage risks and dependencies by making timely decisions while ensuring the quality of the project.

Proficiency Level 1

- Identifies risks and dependencies and communicates routinely to stakeholders.
- Appropriately escalates blocking issues when necessary.
- Understands project objectives, expected quality, metrics and the business case.
- Champions project to stakeholders and articulates business value.

Proficiency Level 2

- Develops systems to monitor risks and dependencies and report change.
- Works effectively across disciplines and organizational boundaries to gain timely closure on decisions that impact own project/portfolio/solution.
- Develops methods to track and report metrics, gains agreement on quality and relates it to business value.

- Asks the right questions to resolve issues and applies creative solutions to meet project objectives.

Proficiency Level 3

- Anticipates changing conditions and impact to risks and dependencies and takes preventative action.
- Effects timely, mutually beneficial outcomes on decisions that impact the whole product, multiple projects or portfolios.
- Evaluates quality and metrics based on return on investment and ensures alignment to business need.
- Proactively inspires others to take action on issues and implications that could prohibit projects success.

Proficiency Level 4

- Proactively identifies implications of related internal and external business conditions to risks and dependencies.
- Instills a system and culture that facilitates effective decision-making across organizations, product lines or portfolios.
- Evaluates project results against related examples and incorporates best practices and key learning for future improvements.
- Champions business value across multiple organizations and gains alignment and commitment to prioritization to ensure long-term project deliverables.

Competencies are a development of the behavioural perspective on measuring performance (Aguinis, 2009) and are used by organizations to help structure employee performance assessments. Competencies can be constructed to reflect different kinds of jobs in organizations, and conceptualized as narrow aspects of performance or very broad overarching constructs. Their flexibility is in some ways responsible for the criticisms around lack of structure and coherence associated with the competency approach.

From an applied perspective, it is possible to differentiate two approaches to the task of competency modeling. The first aims to identify universal competencies that apply across all jobs or within a specific kind of job. At a broad level of abstraction, Bartram (2005) identified the 'Great Eight' competencies. These were derived from considering the influence of major individual difference dimensions on work activity (the Big Five, general mental ability, and need for power/achievement). The resultant eight competency dimensions (Box 8.4) were designed to be applied across jobs, with different jobs drawing more or less heavily on each of the eight.

BOX 8.4
The Great Eight competencies (from Bartram, 2005)

Leading and Deciding	Creating and Conceptualizing
Supporting and Cooperating	Organizing and Executing
Interacting and Presenting	Adapting and Coping
Analyzing and Intepreting	Enterprising and Performing

At a slightly less general level of abstraction are approaches that identify universal competencies for specific kinds of jobs (e.g. sales or management). Tett *et al.* (2000) presented a hyperdimensional taxonomy of management competencies. Their model incorporated 53 management competencies, grouped into nine broader areas. The 53 management competencies are shown in Box 8.5. These competencies are designed to specifically tap into important managerial job performance behaviours.

The alternative to the universal approach might be termed a strategic or contextual approach. Rather than removing context and seeking general competencies that might be used across jobs and organizations, this approach begins with the context of performance and the strategy of the organization in mind. This enables competencies to be defined that fit with the strategic needs of the business, and that reflect the current and anticipated future performance needs (Campion *et al.*, 2011). This approach recognizes the unique performance demands and requirements of different sectors and businesses.

Each of the two approaches has something to contribute to the process of using competencies to measure job performance. The more general and universal approach recognizes that at job-level, there are common factors that influence successful performance across businesses. However, neglecting the context within which those competencies are performed may seriously limit their utility, which is the clear implication of a more organization-specific, contextual and strategic approach.

BOX 8.5

The 53 managerial competencies proposed by Tett *et al.* (2000)

Traditional Functions

1 Problem Awareness
2 Decision-Making
3 Directing
4 Decision Delegation
5 Short-term Planning
6 Strategic Planning
7 Coordinating
8 Goal Setting
9 Monitoring
10 Motivating by Authority
11 Motivating by Persuasion
12 Team Building
13 Productivity

Task Orientation

14 Initiative
15 Task Focus
16 Urgency
17 Decisiveness
18 Compassion
19 Cooperation
20 Sociability
21 Politeness
22 Political Astuteness
23 Assertiveness
24 Seeking Input
25 Customer Focus

Dependability

26 Orderliness
27 Rule Orientation
28 Personal Responsibility

29 Trustworthiness
30 Timeliness
31 Professionalism
32 Loyalty

Open Mindedness

33 Tolerance
34 Adaptability
35 Creative Thinking
36 Cultural Appreciation
37 Resilience
38 Stress Management

Communication

39 Listening Skills
40 Oral Communication
41 Public Presentation
42 Written Communication

Developing Self and Others

43 Developmental Goal Setting
44 Performance Assessment
45 Developmental Feedback
46 Job Enrichment
47 Self-Development

Occupational Acumen and Concerns

48 Technical Proficiency
49 Organizational Awareness
50 Quantity Concern
51 Quality Concern
52 Financial Concern
53 Safety Concern.

KEY FIGURE

J.P. Campbell and colleagues The Project A studies

Rather than focus on an individual in this chapter, we highlight instead a team of Work Psychologists. Possibly the most in-depth studies of job performance criteria are those conducted as part of the US army's job performance measurement project by J.P. Campbell, C.H. Campbell and colleagues. The most detailed of these was conducted within the US army in 'Project A'. These projects were designed to produce comprehensive models of performance for service personnel and to inform selection and recruitment activities for the military. The studies have provided Work Psychologists with a wealth of material on the structure and analysis of job performance criteria (Knapp, 2006). C.H. Campbell, Ford, Rumsey, Pulakos, Borman, Felker, Vera and Riegelhaupt (1990) describe the techniques and processes used to develop job performance measures for the broad sample of jobs within the army. Job content was first analyzed using task-analysis and critical-incidents analysis. From these job-analysis data, an array of work sample tasks, pencil-and-paper tests and performance rating instruments were constructed, supplemented by archival performance data. Across all the jobs analyzed, more than 200 individual performance indicators were generated.

J.P. Campbell, McHenry and Wise (1990) subjected the performance indicators to a structural analysis based on the data from over 9000 job-holders. The starting point of their analysis was an assumption that there are two general factors of job performance: 1) performance dimensions that relate to a specific job or role; 2) performance dimensions that are relevant across jobs and roles. In their structural analysis, J.P. Campbell *et al.* identified five factors that best represented the data. The first was core technical proficiency, representing the performance of tasks central to the specific job role. The second was general proficiency dimension that represented the performance of tasks that were important in all roles. The remaining three factors also represented aspects of performance that generalized across roles, assessed through performance ratings. These were Effort/Leadership, Maintaining Personal Discipline and Fitness/Military Bearing.

Although the model was specific to army personnel, the results of these and other US military studies led to the development of the widely cited eight dimensional model of J.P. Campbell, McCloy, Oppler and Sager (1993). This model extended the five-dimension model to encompass job performance criteria applicable across all jobs. The eight dimensions are: 1) job-specific task proficiency; 2) non-job-specific task proficiency; 3) written and oral communication; 4) demonstrating effort; 5) maintaining personal discipline; 6) maintaining peer and team performance; 7) supervision/leadership; 8) management/administration. The model may be thought of as a job performance framework applicable to any occupation, with the eight categories populated with job-relevant information and assigned specific weights depending on the nature of the job.

DISCUSS WITH A COLLEAGUE

What are the key dimensions of performance in your current or past job? If you are a student, think about your performance as a student, or about a familiar job. Discuss and compare with a colleague.

The Process of Performance Measurement: Appraisal

Models of job performance tell practitioners what to measure or assess in respect of a person's performance at work. The various models reviewed so far can be used in conjunction with information about peoples' jobs and the organizational contexts of those jobs (i.e. job or competency analysis information) to decide on the dimensions or competencies to measure. How is the performance assessment actually implemented in organizations? The process of measuring performance at work is usually referred to as performance appraisal. As we will see later in the chapter, the definition of appraisal might be broadened out to encompass performance improvement activities, but pragmatically for most practitioners, the measurement of employee performance is synonymous with performance appraisal. There are a number of different methods for collecting performance data, reviewed below.

Survey items and rating scales

Simple rating scales are perhaps the most common means of collecting performance judgements. Performance dimensions are broken down into their constituent parts, and raters are asked to indicate judgements about performance using specific rating scales. Some examples of different rating scales are shown in Box 8.6. You'll see that the scales are being used to rate 'Teamworking'. However, there is no information provided in the measure to allow the rater to see exactly what is meant by Teamworking. Performance appraisal survey items might take more detailed forms, breaking down performance dimensions into specific behaviours. An example is provided in Box 8.7. This measure is taken from Williams and Anderson (1991) and shows three scales measuring In-role Behaviour, Organizational Citizenship Behaviour (OCB) directed towards Individuals and OCB directed towards the organization. These items have been designed to be behavioural, helping the rater to judge performance more clearly.

BOX 8.6
Different types of rating scales

Verbally anchored Likert scales

The level of this employee's Teamworking is:
1 = Unsatisfactory.
2 = Less than adequate.
3 = Fair.
4 = Good.
5 = Very Good.
6 = Outstanding.

Unanchored Likert scales

Unsatisfactory 1 2 3 4 5 6   Outstanding

Graphic Scale
Unsatisfactory   [− − − − − − −]   Outstanding

Comparative scales

In the area of Teamworking, this employee:
1 = Is one of the very poorest performers.
2 = Performs less well than most.
3 = Performs the same as most.
4 = Performs better than most.
5 = Is one of the top few performers.

Improving rating scales and appraisal measures

Ratings collected using the basic kinds of appraisal measure shown in Box 8.7 are inevitably subjective. As such, the common biases that human judges bring to assessment are likely to affect ratings. As outlined in Chapter 6, such biases include stereotyping, halo versus horns effect,

BOX 8.7

Measuring three dimensions of job performance

Use the following items to rate the performance of a colleague, subordinate or supervisor. Use the rating scale below:

This person:

1 Adequately completes assigned duties.

	Almost Never 1 2 3 4 5 Almost Always

2 Fulfils responsibilities specified in the job description.

	Almost Never 1 2 3 4 5 Almost Always

3 Performs tasks that are expected of him/her.

	Almost Never 1 2 3 4 5 Almost Always

4 Meets formal performance requirements of the job.

	Almost Never 1 2 3 4 5 Almost Always

5 Engages in activities that will directly affect his/her performance evaluation.

	Almost Never 1 2 3 4 5 Almost Always

6 Neglects aspects of the job he/she is obligated to perform.

	Almost Never 1 2 3 4 5 Almost Always

7 Fails to perform essential duties.

	Almost Never 1 2 3 4 5 Almost Always

8 Helps others who have been absent.

	Almost Never 1 2 3 4 5 Almost Always

9 Helps others who have heavy workloads.

	Almost Never 1 2 3 4 5 Almost Always

10 Assists supervisor with his/her work (when not asked).

	Almost Never 1 2 3 4 5 Almost Always

11 Takes time to listen to co-workers' problems and worries.

	Almost Never 1 2 3 4 5 Almost Always

12 Goes out of way to help new employees.

	Almost Never 1 2 3 4 5 Almost Always

13 Takes a personal interest in other employees.

	Almost Never 1 2 3 4 5 Almost Always

14 Passes along information to co-workers.

	Almost Never 1 2 3 4 5 Almost Always

15 Attendance at work is above the norm.

	Almost Never 1 2 3 4 5 Almost Always

16 Gives advance notice when unable to come to work.

	Almost Never 1 2 3 4 5 Almost Always

17 Takes undeserved work breaks.

	Almost Never 1 2 3 4 5 Almost Always

18 Great deal of time spent with personal phone conversations.

	Almost Never 1 2 3 4 5 Almost Always

19 Complains about insignificant things at work.

	Almost Never 1 2 3 4 5 Almost Always

20 Conserves and protects organizational property.

	Almost Never 1 2 3 4 5 Almost Always

21 Adheres to informal rules devised to maintain order.

	Almost Never 1 2 3 4 5 Almost Always

To score your responses:

In-role Behaviour (Task Performance): (1+2+3+4+5+6R+7R) / 7

Organizational Citizenship Behaviour – Individual: (8+9+10+11+12+13+14) / 7

Organizational Citizenship Behaviour – Organization: (15+16+17R+18R+19R+20+21) / 7

The scale calculations produce scores on the original 1–5 scale.

similar-to-me effect and so forth. A challenge for Work Psychologists is therefore how to reduce the influences of subjective biases on ratings. Fletcher (2008) outlines a number of ways that rating scales might be improved to reduce bias:

● Training: Although rating scales are simple, they can still be used poorly by raters. Training of raters can help them to be aware of their own biases and to challenge them.

DISCUSS WITH A COLLEAGUE

Use the scales in Box 8.7 to rate the performance of someone you work with. What did you find out about their performance from doing this?

● Forced Distributions: Using a five-point scale (Poor, Fair, Average, Good, Outstanding) to rate the performance of a group of employees should, by definition, result in most people being rated as average. However, the value that we attach to the word 'average' (people do not like to be labelled as average), combined with a reluctance amongst most people to rate the performance of others negatively, means that the majority of people are likely to be rated as 'good' or 'outstanding'. One way to overcome this problem is to use a forced distribution, whereby appraisers are forced to give 10 per cent the highest rating, 10 per cent the lowest rating and so on. Such approaches may be perceived negatively by people in organizations, and certainly seem to be at odds with the principle that performance should be evaluated on the basis of what people actually do (i.e. their behaviour). Rigid forced distribution systems are uncommon, although GE are famed for their system. Under the GE appraisal system, 10 per cent of managers each year are given the lowest performance rating. If they receive the same low rating the next year, they are asked to leave the company (Aguinis, 2009).

● Multiple Raters: Combining the judgements of multiple raters overcomes the problem of the idiosyncratic judgement of one rater having a disproportionate effect on the appraisal rating. Several supervisors might rate the performance of the individual, or more commonly, supervisor ratings might be combined with ratings provided by peers, subordinates or even customers or clients. Multi-source appraisal (known as multi-source feedback) is a popular contemporary approach to performance assessment, and is discussed later in the chapter.

● Behavioural Scales: In the behavioural approach to measuring performance, the role of the rater changes from 'judge' to 'observer'. In this approach, job performance ratings are based on the rater's perception of whether the target has demonstrated particular job-relevant behaviours, and to what frequency. These are Behaviourally Anchored Rating Scales (BARS; see Box 8.8) and Behavioural Observation Scales (BOS; see Box 8.8). BARS have very specific behavioural anchors that indicate the behaviour that a person should demonstrate to be awarded a specific rating. You can observe the increased effectiveness of these behaviours in respect of the performance dimension under scrutiny as the rating increases. By contrast, BOS are closer to the survey-item and rating scale approach outlined earlier. However, the items here are in the form of specific behaviours, and the rating scale requires that the rater makes an overall judgement about the frequency with which the employee demonstrates the behaviour.

BOX 8.8

Behavioural scales used in appraisal and performance measurement

Behaviourally-Anchored Rating Scale: Planning and organization

Identifies priorities, sets deadlines and plans schedules. Effectively manages own time to achieve goals. Gives considerations to wider implications of plans made.

1 The participant has not exhibited this competency in the exercise and/or has not followed instructions. Attempts to plan are ineffective through inappropriate prioritization or organization.

2 Plans are short-term, reactive and not related to objectives.

3 Plans linked to objectives, but these tend to be short term.

4 Plans are linked to objectives, are longer term and are based on priorities and deadlines.

5 Identifies priorities, sets deadlines and plans schedules. Effectively manages own time to achieve goals. Gives considerations to wider implications of plans made.

Behavioural Observation Scales Teamworking

a. Tolerant with others and shows patience with them.
   Almost always 1 2 3 4 5 Almost never

b. Consistently seeks to offer help and support.
   Almost always 1 2 3 4 5 Almost never

c. Plays a balanced role in team discussions.
   Almost always 1 2 3 4 5 Almost never

d. Keeps colleagues informed where necessary.
   Almost always 1 2 3 4 5 Almost never

e. Volunteers for fair share of less popular duties.
   Almost always 1 2 3 4 5 Almost never

f. Willing to change own plans to cooperate with others.
   Almost always 1 2 3 4 5 Almost never

Results-based appraisal

In the results-based appraisals method, employee performance is judged based on what they achieve rather than what they do. The foundations of results-based appraisal lie in the tradition of Management by Objectives (MBO). This approach to performance management holds that the key to motivating employees to perform at work is to set objectives and goals. Objective setting, when executed effectively, certainly has a central role to play in performance management. However, as an approach to measuring and judging performance, attending solely to outcomes is seriously limited for two reasons:

1 It is extremely difficult to compare different employees using the approach (Fletcher, 2008). This is because numerical ratings are not used to assess performance.

2 The assessment is over-simplistic, for the reasons outlined at the start of this chapter. In order to be perceived fairly by employees, the assessment would need to somehow account for wider contextual issues that might affect performance.

BOX 8.9

How reliable are performance assessments in organizations?

Like any other form of measurement in Work Psychology, a key question concerning ratings of job performance is their reliability. Reliability has been discussed at length in previous chapters, and the three forms of reliability are all relevant in performance assessment:

- Internal Consistency: To what extent are performance rating scales internally consistent?

- Test-retest Reliability: To what extent are performance ratings stable over time?

- Interrater Reliability: To what extent do different people's ideas about and judgements of effective performance converge?

These three methods of assessing reliability present interesting applied interpretations when applied to job performance measures. Scale consistency can sometimes be interpreted as poor discrimination of performance dimensions by supervisors. Striving for stability in performance ratings goes against our intuitions that performance can change over time. Interrater reliability raises questions about the frame of reference that people apply when they rate job performance. To what extent does one rater's idea of effective performance generalize to other raters? These issues are important because job performance measurement is central to a substantive volume of Work Psychology research and HRM practice. For example, reliability estimates are critical in meta-analysis, where they are used to correct validity coefficients. Moreover, reliability is important for the practical use of job performance

ratings, for example to determine pay, promotion and training requirements. None of these activities can be adequately carried out if performance measures are unreliable. Studies of the reliability of performance assessments have yielded the following findings:

- Viswesvaran, Ones and Schmidt (1996) conducted a meta-analysis of the reliability of job performance ratings and reported modest interrater reliabilities for overall job performance assessments for supervisors (0.52) and for peers (0.42). Interestingly, reliabilities across dimensions varied, with the dimensions Quality, Productivity and Administrative Competence demonstrating the highest reliability and Communication and Interpersonal Competence the lowest. Borman (1979) suggests that such variations reflect the availability of evidence to raters. Some competencies or performance dimensions are more observable than others, and moreover, some are likely to be more visible to supervisors than peers and vice-versa. The implication is that supervisor and peer ratings of job performance are most reliable when there is available evidence upon which to make a judgement. From their results, Viswesvaran et al. (1996) argued that interrater reliability was the most adequate reliability index for job performance as this reflects the basic question about whether two equally knowledgeable judges would rate the same individual's job performance similarly. As such, interrater reliability determines the effectiveness of, for example, applying single performance standards across organizations (where different supervisors rate the performance of different employees), or in placing team members in new positions or project teams, where their performance may be judged by someone other than their line supervisor. If you are investigating the reliability of appraisal ratings in your own organization, then interrater reliability is a key area to address.

- Coefficient alpha reliabilities tend to be higher than interrater reliabilities. In Viswesvaran et al.'s (1996) analyses, internal consistency reliabilities were 0.86 for supervisors (range = 0.73 – 0.86) and 0.85 for peers (range = 0.61 – 0.85). The implication of this finding is that job performance scales can be reliable. One confound, however, refers back to the issue of halo effect and the error it introduces into ratings. Recall that part of the reason that ratings of performance tend to be consistent across different dimensions is that all ratings are influenced by the bias associated with the halo effect. Viswesvaran et al. (2005) estimate the inflation effect on coefficient alpha reliabilities to be around 30 per cent for supervisory ratings and 60 per cent for peer ratings. In the analyses, supervisors were less influenced by halo than were peers. It seems then, that supervisors are generally better at differentiating multiple aspects of job performance.

- An in-depth examination of the stability of performance measures over time was presented by Sturman, Cheramie and Cashen (2005), and is highly informative in respect of test-retest reliability. Sturman et al. point out that we have to be very careful when we think about test-retest reliability in performance measures. We could test whether a performance measure gives the same result on two different occasions and conclude that the measure was stable, and thus reliable. However, this judgement is only sound if the performance on the people we are assessing is also unchanged. If performance has actually improved or worsened, then a stable measurement is inaccurate. Test-retest reliability should therefore be thought of as the stability of the measurement over time, assuming that performance has actually remained the same. By using complex statistical techniques (Structural Equation Modelling; See Chapter 2), Sturman et al. (2005) were able to determine that in the short term, performance measurements can demonstrate acceptable reliability. However, when looking at stability in the long term (i.e. one year or more), the reliabilities of the measures decreased substantially. The practical implication of their work is that in order to be considered reliable, assessments of employee performance should be conducted regularly.

Competency-based appraisal

The competency approach to appraisal uses competencies and their definitions to structure the assessment of employee performance. The approach is similar to the behavioural approach to appraisal, except that behaviours are not rated in isolation, but are rather clustered together into the competency dimensions. The breadth and detail encapsulated in these dimensions makes the competency approach useful for development purposes, as well as performance assessment. As described earlier, the definitions of competencies can give key information about the positive and negative behaviours associated with a particular dimension. These behaviours obviously help to structure the assessment and judgements of the rater, but also provide clear guidelines on the desirable levels and forms of performance. These can be discussed with ratees so that they can see how to improve. Moreover, a further advantage of this approach is that if competencies incorporate strategically important aspects, individual performance can be shaped around delivering business strategy.

KEY THEME

Ethics and Corporate Social Responsibility

Throughout this chapter, we have taken the perspective that performance management needs to be based on the strategy of the organization, so that the needs of the business are integrated with front-line performance objectives. This vertical integration helps to promote the impact of performance management on business performance.

However, such issues do not always feature in the development of performance management processes in organizations. In particular, there are two risks. The first is from an over-focus on measurement and process. This involves looking inward at the process and principally at the metrics, methods and audit trails, ignoring as a consequence, the strategic aims of performance management. The result is a disconnect between the HRM system and the wider business objectives. It is not responsible management, and places business at risk of poor economic performance, but also may inadvertently miss social responsibility aspects of organizational strategy, which are less easily defined and quantified.

The second risk is from the use of generic performance measurement systems, again ignoring the context of performance. Such systems are often adopted for convenience and their measurement value. Again, the risks are neglect of the wider business needs, and a lack of focus on the potential outcomes or impact of performance (the focus is on the means of performance measurement rather than the ends of performance management).

Where these problems do occur, one must question the connection of HR with the organization; are the systems set up that enable HRM to help implement business strategy through sound performance management systems? This is an issue we return to later in the book, when we look at organizations.

PERFORMANCE IMPROVEMENT AND MANAGEMENT

At the start of this chapter, the Burke–Litwin model of organizational change and performance was briefly discussed, outlining the importance of performance management for organizations. Work Psychologists have concerned themselves principally with performance measurement and appraisal in respect of performance management. Most of the empirical work published in this area is focused on measurement issues. Work Psychologists have nevertheless made a contribution to understanding performance management. Performance measurement or appraisal is one part of performance management, with the key additions being processes designed to improve or develop employee performance. Performance management therefore emphasizes development alongside assessment.

Aguinis (2009) defines performance management as:

> *A continuous process of identifying, measuring and developing the performance of individuals and teams and aligning performance with the strategic goals of the organization.* (Aguinis, H., 2009 p. 2.)

He goes on to comment on the importance of two aspects of the definition. First, the process is continuous. Performance management is ongoing and should not be viewed as episodic, or as a discrete intervention in organizations. Second, the purpose of strategic performance management is to ensure that employee performance is in line with the requirements of the organization. This can only be achieved by aligning performance management with the strategic goals of organizations.

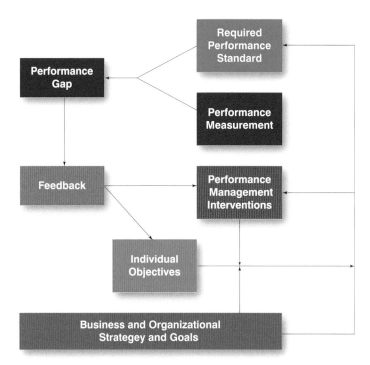

Figure 8.3   A model of performance management

Murphy and DeNisi (2008) present a model of the performance management process (Figure 8.3). The model is relevant in this chapter because it shows how performance appraisal fits into the overall process of performance management. The performance measurement box in the figure represents the assessment of performance. It denotes the observed level of employee performance, however it is measured, at the time of assessment.

In the model, the performance measurement is considered alongside the desired level of performance. If you trace the arrows backwards, you see that the desired level of performance is derived from corporate and individual goals. Performance goals should reflect the strategy of the organization, and the process of setting individual goals involves translating broad organizational strategies to smaller, measureable objectives for units, teams and ultimately individuals. For example, schools might set strategies that include objectives for students to achieve certain percentages of exam passes. These could be translated to individual targets for teachers for their specific classes.

Following the steps of the model leads to developmental processes. Performance assessment information is fed back to people in the organization. Where there is a discrepancy between observed and desired levels of performance (i.e. where performance is below the required standard) performance management interventions would be deployed to prompt improvement in performance. Expectations of performance improvement are then built in to more goals and objectives, forming the basis of the next performance assessment. The cyclical nature of the model again emphasizes the continuous nature of performance management.

Three important processes are identified from this model, each of which is reviewed in the remainder of this chapter:

- *Performance* Goal Setting.
- *Performance* Feedback.
- *Performance* Management Interventions.

Goal Setting

Goal setting is a core part of performance management and is also one area of theory that is particularly well supported in the research literature. This is the practical, yet robust area of research identified at the start of the chapter. Goal theory was covered in Chapter 5 on Motivation, but the relevant points for performance management will be discussed here.

The development of goal-setting theory is usually attributed to Locke and Latham, two American Work Psychologists, and they have written several positional and review articles on the topic (e.g. Locke and Latham, 1990; 2002). From an organizational point of view, goals are important because they ensure that individual performance is in line with the performance standards for the organization. Goals therefore serve a strategic organizational function. However, research in Work Psychology has been more concerned with the extent to which goals are translated through to actual performance or behaviour. Locke and Latham (2002) summarized research in Goal Setting, and presented some of the key findings about the effectiveness of goals:

- First and foremost, goal setting does result in markedly higher performance than no goal setting (Locke and Latham, 1990). More difficult goals also result in higher levels of effort and performance, although this only works insofar as people have the necessary abilities to meet their goals. There is a clear imperative here to balance goal setting in performance management with the development of abilities and competencies.

- Specific goals are better than 'do-your-best' goals. Goal setting results in higher performance if goals are specific and measureable (in other words if the performance standards expected are clearly spelled out, and can be measured). Locke and Latham (2002) neatly surmise that in their research, when people are told to do their best, they do not do so. Goals are not necessarily results-based or outcome-based. Rather goals might blend aspects of results or outcomes with goals that refer to changes in behaviours or specific areas of job performance.

- Goals affect performance through four mechanisms. These are: 1) Direction of behaviour. Goals direct behaviour towards goal-relevant activities and away from irrelevant activities. 2) Energizing of behaviour. Goals lead people to expend greater effort on goal-relevant activities, with harder goals being associated with increased effort. 3) Goals affect persistence. Harder goals tend to promote people prolonging their efforts to achieve those goals. Prolonged high intensity effort cannot be maintained indefinitely however. Tight deadlines tend to result in faster work pace for a short period of time. 4) Goals lead people to develop their approach to work. Goals encourage people to develop achievement and performance strategies, learning job-relevant skills as a consequence.

The relationship between goals and performance is also moderated by a number of factors. This means that the extent to which goals result in performance depends on a number of additional factors:

- Goal Commitment: The relationship between goals and performance is strongest when people are committed to their goals. There are two major predictors of goal commitment. The first is perceived importance of goals. People are more likely to be committed to their goals if they perceive them as important. One way of promoting this is to allow people to participate in goal setting, although the evidence is mixed as to how effective this strategy is. In any case, participative goal setting is likely to be perceived as fairer, even if it does not increase performance. Other ways of promoting perceptions of goal importance are to associate a valued incentive with the goal (such as monetary reward), or to communicate the goals in an inspirational way (bringing in clear interaction with leadership approaches). The second predictor of goal commitment is self efficacy. Self-efficacy concerns the extent to which a person feels able to achieve their goals. It relates to self-perceptions of the extent to which a person has the relevant skills to achieve the goal and also of the achievability of the goal. Social psychologists have written much about the precursors and effects of self-efficacy (e.g. Bandura, 1997).

- Feedback: People perform better when they receive feedback about how they are performing in relation to their goals. Feedback allows people to see how they are doing in respect of their goals and to change their behaviour accordingly to ensure they meet their goals.
- Task Complexity: Goals relate to performance most strongly for tasks which are low complexity. This is because for highly complex tasks, achieving a set goal might draw on a range of strategies and skills, and this in turn is related to people's abilities. Ability therefore becomes a limiter to the achievement of goals related to complex tasks for a great many people.

An emerging area of research related to the Task Complexity moderator is the differences between Performance and Learning Goals (see Chapter 7). Performance Goals refer simply to achieving some level of performance and are typically simpler than Learning Goals, which might refer to the acquisition of new competencies or approaches to work. The picture is enriched further by the theory that people have a preferred style of working, which reflects how they interpret and understand their own goals. According to Goal Orientation theory, two learning approaches are differentiated, Learning Goal Orientation (LGO) and Performance Goal Orientation (PGO). People with LGO are motivated to learn and understand, whereas people with PGO are motivated to achieve their desired standard, but no more. Left to their own devices, people tend to work in their preferred styles, but a study by Seijts and Latham (2001) suggested that goal orientation effects could be overcome by setting goals in the right way. Regardless of preferred style, setting challenging learning goals resulted in similar performances from those with LGO and PGO styles. The implication for performance management is that for complex tasks, goal setting should include learning goals in addition to performance goals.

Locke and Latham (2002) pull together many of these issues in a model of goal setting and performance improvement (Figure 8.4). The model summarizes the processes by which performance is improved or managed through goal setting. Note that a key part of the model is the association of goal achievement with satisfying and important rewards, reflecting parallels with Vroom's Expectancy theory (See Chapter 5). The take home of the model for performance management in organizations is that goal setting is a crucial component of any performance management strategy, provided that it is implemented in the right way. Goal setting is likely to be most effective when managers understand and are attentive to:

- The format and content of goals.
- The mechanisms by which goals are achieved.
- The moderators of the goals-performance relationship.
- The satisfaction of individuals with the rewards they receive for achieving goals.

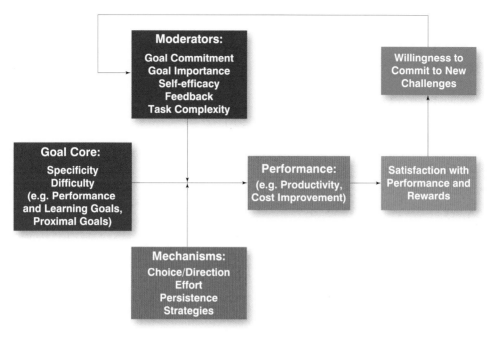

Figure 8.4   A model of goal setting

Performance Feedback

Already highlighted in the discussion of goal setting is the importance of giving people feedback about their performance. Most managers are aware of the need to provide feedback to employees, but when you talk to people in organizations, the quality of the feedback they receive about their performance is a common source of dissatisfaction (see Author Experience box on p. 257). Feedback should clearly communicate progress against objectives, but more importantly serve a developmental purpose. Good feedback allows employees to see what they are doing right, helping to build confidence, identifies areas for improvement, helping to build competence and can also promote engagement and involvement with the organization. Aguinis (2009) lists some of the ways that feedback to employees can be generally improved (Box 8.10).

Feedback provided to employees is likely to be a balance of positive and negative information, although it is the provision of negative feedback that typically concerns many managers. However, negative feedback is clearly crucial to performance management, as without it, employees have no information upon which to make a decision how to improve. A fundamental question in this area is the extent to which constructive or developmental feedback actually results in changes in behaviour. Evidence seems to suggest that giving feedback poorly can be less effective than giving no feedback at all. Indeed, reviews of the effects of feedback on performance indicate that there are robust findings showing that feedback can both enhance and have negative effects on performance (Kluger and DeNisi, 1996).

Research in this area in Work Psychology has examined the cognitive processes underlying people's responses and reactions to feedback on their job performance. The aim of such research is to examine the mechanisms that determine why one person might react positively to feedback, whilst someone else responds negatively. Kluger and DeNisi (1996) present a major review of the topic, and propose a model. Their model lacks something in applied value due to its complexity, but some of the major implications are informative. First, their analyses seem to suggest that perceptions of the nature

BOX 8.10
Characteristics of effective feedback

- Timeliness. Feedback delivered close to the event or performance episode.
- Frequency. Feedback provided regularly and continuously.
- Specificity. Specific behaviours or aspects of performance are reported.
- Verifiability. Focus on accurate, verifiable evidence, not rumour or inference.
- Consistency. The tone of feedback should be consistent, and not subject to huge variation.
- Privacy. Presented at an appropriate time and place to avoid embarrassment.
- Consequences. Consequences and potential outcomes of behaviour are communicated to contextualize feedback.

- Description first, evaluation second. Clear descriptions of performance behaviours precede evaluations of those behaviours.
- Performance as continuous. Focus on how to demonstrate more good behaviour and less ineffective behaviour, communicating that performance is not simply bad/good.
- Pattern identification. Patterns of poor performance behaviours identified rather than isolated mistakes.
- Confidence in the employee. Manager communicates confidence in the employee, emphasizing that negative feedback is targeted at behaviour and not the person.
- Advice and idea generation. Ways of improving performance offered by the manager (advice) and invited from the employee (idea generation).

of feedback are related to behaviour change. Feedback leads to performance improvement when it informs a person of a necessary change in behaviour, or when it challenges assumptions about the best way to do something at work. This is because such feedback leads a person to pay attention to the task at hand and to the way they are completing it. Feedback that is personal (which can include comparing the employee with other team members) promotes a focus on improving or defending oneself, thereby focusing attention away from the task at hand. A second important lesson from Kluger and DeNisi (1996) is that the way these processes work for individual employees is likely to depend on their personality, and the situation.

Kinicki, Prussia, Wu and McKee-Ryan (2004) tested a simpler model of feedback and performance improvement based on a model proposed by Ilgen, Fisher and Taylor (1979). The model is shown in Figure 8.5. The main implications of their model are:

- Feedback is translated to performance through a series of sequential cognitive mechanisms, which represent individual reactions and judgements in respect of feedback.
- A fundamental judgement that employees make about feedback is its accuracy. The perceived accuracy of feedback depends on the credibility of the communicator, and the presence of a so-called 'feedback-rich environment'. A feedback-rich environment is one in which feedback is specific, provided frequently and is positive.
- Perceived accuracy is related to a desire to respond to the feedback, although the credibility of the person providing the feedback also has a direct effect on desire to respond.
- The desire to respond to the feedback leads to the formation of an intended response. There is a modest relationship between the intention to respond, and actual performance change.

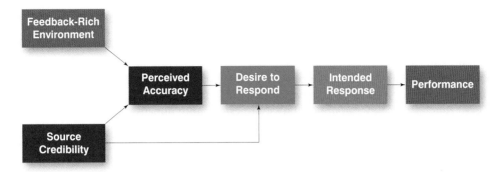

Figure 8.5   A model of performance improvement resulting from feedback

Parallels between this model and the theory of planned behaviour (Ajzen, see Chapter 4) are clear. In particular, the step from intention to behaviour is likely to be affected by a range of attitudinal and cognitive processes. Notably, Kinicki *et al.*'s model does have implications for the provision of negative feedback. It is well documented that people tend to perceive positive feedback as more accurate than negative feedback (e.g. Brett and Atwater, 2001), but perhaps creating a feedback rich environment in which negative feedback is embedded could enhance the extent to which people see it as accurate.

Multi-source feedback

Feedback is traditionally based on supervisor ratings of performance, but a popular contemporary approach to performance assessment and feedback is for ratings to be provided by a variety of people, including peers, subordinates and customers or clients. This form of performance assessment is usually referred to as 360-degree feedback, and has proved very popular with organizations. The profusion of such feedback systems appears to have been more popular initially in the US, migrating to practice in the UK and Europe in the 1990s.

Multi-source performance ratings are valued by organizations because they appear to be more comprehensive than single sources, providing a more thorough assessment of performance across a range of different contexts. Supervisor ratings of performance may be based on limited evidence of employee competence because they may not observe the ratee in interactions with peers or subordinates. Despite practitioner enthusiasm for multi-source systems such as 360-degree appraisal, researchers have remained sceptical. Fletcher has written extensively on this topic in the UK, and points out that this scepticism often arises because 360-degree systems are sometimes poorly operationalized, and because the information collected is not always used effectively (Fletcher, 2001). He identifies some of the key practical components of 360-degree systems in organizations (Fletcher, 2008):

- Rating Instruments. Feedback surveys are typically used to collect ratings of performance. As with other performance measures, raters use rating scales to indicate the effectiveness of particular performance behaviours.
- Raters. Self-ratings of performance are usually used, and the individual being rated is often asked to nominate the people who will assess him or her. The issue of anonymity is important in this respect, as subordinates particularly may feel uncomfortable about rating their boss, knowing that their boss will see their ratings.
- Feedback Process. Data are collected and compiled by a central administrator or by the person giving feedback to the employee. Ratings are typically collated so that an average score is provided for each rating alongside a breakdown of the scores from each rating source. The average is important to report back, but the dispersion of scores across rating sources is often more informative.

A conceptual challenge in multi-source feedback systems is to understand whether different raters conceptualize performance dimensions similarly or differently. Understanding the validity and conceptual basis of multi-source ratings is important because it helps us to understand how best to use them. Studies generally support the measurement equivalence of performance ratings across sources (Maurer, Raju and Collins, 1998; Facteau and Craig, 2001). Overall, it appears that measures of the same construct provided by different sources are conceptually similar. So, for example, a supervisory rating of leadership skill is likely to represent the same kinds of behaviours as a corresponding peer rating. These conclusions may not apply across all performance dimensions however.

Visweswaran, Schmidt and Ones (2002) examined convergence of supervisor and peer ratings on ten performance dimensions. They found that supervisor- and peer-ratings converged for some dimensions but not others. Supervisors and peers may therefore conceptualize some elements of performance differently. In 360-degree assessment systems, individuals may also rate their own job performance. Self-other convergence of performance ratings tend to be lower than other-other convergence (Conway and Huffcutt, 1997). This may be due to personality influences that inflate or suppress self-ratings of performance (e.g. Goffin and Anderson, 2007). People may be overly lenient, or conversely overly harsh on themselves, and this should be noted when implementing 360-degree assessment systems.

Practical concerns in multi-source feedback

If management in an organization decide to introduce 360-degree feedback, practitioners are faced with the choice of using it for either development or formal performance appraisal. There is no clear answer as to the best strategy to adopt, as the issues surrounding 360-degree feedback and its introduction are potentially complex. On the face of it, the approach appears to offer considerable advantages. People often feel that feedback or appraisal assessment based on the views of single individuals is limited, and may not reflect their true performance. Moreover, traditional appraisal assessments are hardly held up as a benchmark of accurate, objective measurement. A further benefit of the multi-source approach is that it empowers people to potentially influence the way they are managed. For subordinates, it offers a way for them to communicate their views about the way they are supervised.

The downside is that if 360-degree assessment was embedded in a company as part of formal performance appraisal, there could be various unintended effects (Fletcher, 2008. The ratings that people provide are likely to be compromised if they know that their assessments will affect the person's pay or status. There is some evidence that subordinate ratings are less useful if used for appraisal compared with development (Greguras et al., 2003). Ratees might be less likely to take on board criticism from the process if it has consequences for them in the organization. There is also a risk that people may use the power that comes with rating performance to exercise influence over those they are rating. Many of these issues would be considered less critical if there was good evidence that 360-degree feedback is effective in terms of improving people's performance.

An important meta-analysis of this issue was conducted by Smither, London and Reilly (2005). They examined only longitudinal studies, and were interested to see whether people improved their performance over time after a 360-degree assessment. Their findings suggest only small performance improvements result from receiving 360-degree feedback. Interestingly it was subordinate ratings that seemed to increase the most. Smither et al. (2005) were unsurprised by their findings and suggest that there are of course, a number of factors that will promote performance improvement following 360-degree. These are summarized in their model (see Figure 8.6). Once again some of the most important factors are around personal dispositions, beliefs about and reactions to the feedback. Beliefs about change in the model echo the issue of self-efficacy in goal-setting theory. As with other performance management mechanisms, the science tells us that simply using 360-degree or multi-source feedback is not enough for performance improvement, rather it is the way the technique is applied in a specific context.

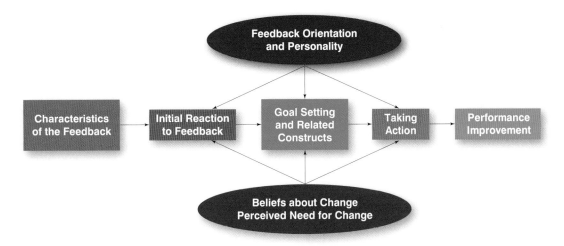

Figure 8.6   Theoretical model of performance improvement following multi-source feedback

Performance Management Interventions

Performance management interventions are applied in organizations when performance assessment identifies areas where performance is below expectations or requirements. Many such interventions are developmental, and designed to address gaps in knowledge, skills, abilities or competencies. Chapter 7 on learning and development covers individual development in organizations in depth, and Chapter 9 also highlights some pro-active development interventions in respect of careers. The ideas in these chapters should be viewed as integral to performance management intervention. Coaching for performance is one intervention that is not covered elsewhere. Another important set of interventions to consider are more challenging for all concerned and they are disciplinary proceedings, invoked in organizations when individual performance problems are serious or chronic. Both of these interventions are reviewed briefly here.

Coaching for performance

A relatively recent development in terms of performance enhancement and management has been the explosive growth of coaching for both managers and non-managers in organizations. Coaching is generally defined as a collaborative relationship between a coach and coachee, which is formed for the purpose of supporting the coachee to attain their professional or personal goals (Grant, Passmore, Cavanagh and Parker, 2010). Coaching involves supporting someone at work to improve their performance by helping them reflect on, explore and clarify problems at work, set objectives and review performance. Grant *et al.* (2010) highlight three forms of coaching at work:

- Skills coaching: designed to help people learn and apply a particular skill set at work.
- Performance coaching: designed to focus on the processes of goal setting and performance delivery over a period of time.
- Developmental coaching: a more widely strategic approach that aims to help people develop competencies and capabilities to deal with current and future demands.

AUTHOR EXPERIENCE

When No News in Considered Good News (But Not for Performance Management)

I recently visited one of my students working on placement (a year-long internship) as an executive search agent for a recruitment company. Such visits always bring home the reality of organizational culture as you can clearly feel immediate differences in the atmospheres of the different companies. We met for around an hour and talked about her progress and experience in the company. One question that it was hard to get an answer to concerned how she felt she was performing, and how her manager felt about her performance so far. The student insisted that her manager had provided her virtually no feedback on how she was performing, and that on the very few occasions she had met her manager, the person had spoken more about herself than the student's performance. The meeting with my student was followed immediately by consultation with the manager, as is procedural.

I confess to being surprised that the caricature painted by the student was entirely confirmed in the first 20 minutes of the meeting with her manager. Her manager openly reported that she told her staff that if she did not tell them anything about their performance, then they should assume they were doing okay (in other words, no positive feedback was provided to her staff). When I asked about the performance of the student, the manager did indeed quickly turn the conversation around to talk about herself and her managerial style. And so this went on for more then half an hour. I found myself in a position of tactfully pointing out the merit and importance of regular feedback for people at work. Gradually the person's initial defensiveness diminished, so that by the end of the discussion, I did manage to get some information on the performance of the student and I encouraged her to communicate her satisfaction to the student.

My impression was that the failure to provide feedback in this case was down to two things: organizational culture, and the personality of the manager. The culture was clear to see – empty offices, people working at home or behind partitions. I did not see a single person talk to anyone else during my visit. The manager in question, in my view, was actually quite an anxious person, and I believe part of the reason she did not give feedback more readily was down to low social confidence, masked by the mild arrogance she demonstrated to others.

The lesson I took: Part of the reason feedback is ineffective in some cases is down to the personality and working style of managers. Understanding the cognitions of the person receiving feedback is only part of the story.

Coaching is usually one-to-one and the coach is often someone from outside the organization. The emphasis is generally developmental, and focused on performance improvement. However, the literature on the benefits of coaching is somewhat limited, which means that there is not clear understanding of how, when, and in what ways coaching is effective. Some research does offer grounds for confidence. Smither, London, Flautt, Vargas and Kucine (2003) showed that coaching led to small improvements in the performance evaluations of managers. In a small sample of teachers, Grant, Green and Rynsaardt (2010) showed improvement in goal attainment, resilience, well-being, and reduction of stress for teachers receiving coaching, compared to no change over the same period for a control group. To address the need for systematic evidence for the effectiveness of coaching Jones, Woods and Guillaume (2014) reported a meta-analysis in which it appears that assuming certain key processes are applied, coaching does result in a positive performance impact.

Coaching may also be used by organizations in a variety of ways to address poor performance issues such as when an individual's performance declines; as a means of reducing exit costs for the organization by 'helping an individual to realize that they don't fit'; for leadership development, providing a 'safe' person to discuss organizational challenges with; to boost an individual's confidence following long-term absence from work; to help with a personal issue which is affecting work. The culture of the organization must be supportive of coaching since it is unlikely to be effective in a highly competitive environment (for example in a sales department where there is a high level of competition between staff).

The relationship between the coach and the coachee is clearly important and, in well developed coaching systems in organizations, there is a commitment to:

- Creating a culture and a set of coaching procedures which are aligned with the philosophy of coaching.
- Building coaching responsibilities into people's jobs and providing appropriate time and recognition for this contribution.
- Assessing the skills of coaches and ensuring they have appropriate training and supervision as well as opportunities for upgrading their skills.
- Selecting staff for coaching roles who have positive attitudes, emotional sensitivity and commitment to the role.
- Monitoring the effectiveness of coaching and its impact within the organization and adapting the system as appropriate (Clutterbuck and Megginson, 2006).

A related developmental intervention is mentoring. Whereas coaching is concerned with improving specific aspects of performance, mentoring involves providing generalized support and guidance to an individual within the organization, usually by a senior colleague but sometimes by a senior and experienced person outside the organization. The growth of coaching and mentoring schemes has been explosive and is now a substantial industry attracting many with psychology training and many more without. The ethical and competency issues raised are often not adequately addressed in many organizations, however. The continued professionalization of the coaching and mentoring field in the coming years will likely begin to address these issues.

DISCUSS WITH A COLLEAGUE

Identify one area of your own performance at work or university that needs to improve. Based on this chapter and Chapter 7, identify five ways that you could improve.

Disciplinary processes

When performance problems become serious, or spill over into behavioural problems, they can result in disciplinary cases, which is usually distressing for all involved and can result in litigation. To avoid disciplinary problems and litigation, HR specialists recommend that individuals at work should know the standards of performance expected of them and the rules to which they are expected to conform (Armstrong, 2009). Where there is a problem, they should be given a clear indication of where they are failing (e.g. not treating customers with consideration or respect) or what rules they are deemed to have broken (e.g. failing to leave the building when a fire alarm sounds, smoking in the building, harassing colleagues). Where disciplinary action is considered, employees should be given the opportunity of improving their performance before disciplinary action is taken. The exception to this is where employees are deemed to have been guilty of gross misconduct (such as striking a colleague, stealing from the organization or endangering the safety of colleagues). In such cases they are subject to summary dismissal.

Under UK law, employees subject to disciplinary processes (other than summary dismissal for gross misconduct) must first be given an informal warning about their performance. The second stage involves a formal warning and often this is supplemented in writing. The nature of the offence must be made clear and the likely consequence of further offences laid out for the employee. The third stage involves the employee being given a final written warning which must include a statement that any recurrence would lead to suspension, dismissal or some other penalty. Such procedures allow individuals to be accompanied to disciplinary meetings by a colleague or a union or other employee representative. There must also be an appeal system.

The nature of these processes and the strong emotions they elicit necessitates that those managing them obtain and carefully record facts and all processes. Managers leading disciplinary meetings would generally have a colleague present (such as a senior HR member) and are usually advised to make a note of what was said in meetings immediately. Further disciplinary action can entail anything from (for example) a number of days' suspension without pay or dismissal.

Many organizations inappropriately use disciplinary procedures to manage staff who have capability difficulties (i.e. when people do not seem able to perform their jobs, as a result of lacking necessary skills or competencies). This is a very destructive approach, having the potential for serious demoralizing negative effects on the staff involved. More enlightened organizations use developmental interventions to help staff develop skills or find more suitable positions for them before resorting to disciplinary action or dismissal.

KEY THEME

Environment and Sustainability

The role of performance management

One of the key ideas introduced in this chapter is that performance management is a critical process for enabling organization to achieve goals and implement strategies. The key step is for organizational goals and objectives to be translated into unit, team and individual goals. Without this, it can be very hard for individuals to comprehend how they might contribute to the strategy.

Issues of environment and sustainable business are increasingly being addressed in organizational statements about mission, company culture and values or strategies. This is not least because customers are more aware of the impact that business has on the environment and of the need for corporate social responsibility in this area more broadly. Companies that show a disregard for these issues may find people dissuaded from buying from them.

The weak link in these statements about sustainable business and management of environmental impact is how they are expressed in individual performance objectives. If there is no clear inclusion of the issues in people's performance appraisal or objective setting, then it is all so much talk or lip service to the zeitgeist of socio-political progress. Organizations could be very pro-active about finding new ways to build specific goals and targets around environmental impact into people's jobs. For example, people could be set the target of finding at least two ways each year for reducing carbon costs associated with their job. It could even be possible to give measureable carbon quotas to employees based on the targets, carbon usage of the organization. More than individual targets, of course, what we know about organizational change also tells us that novel target setting of this kind works best if systems of support are put in place to help people achieve them. The extent to which there is the will to make use of performance management and wider organizational systems to address issues of environment and sustainability probably gives an indication of the company's *real* appetite for change.

SUMMARY

Performance management in organizations is an important process by which organizational goals and strategies are translated down to individuals so that they stand a better chance of being achieved. The process relies on effective measurement of job performance to determine whether people are performing in the required way, with performance management interventions drawn upon when people are not, to help develop capability and address performance problems.

Performance measurement can take a variety of forms. Basic conceptualizations of job performance are based on objective data captured by organizations, but much more information can be examined and incorporated into measurement by focusing on performance behaviour. To help structure assessment of performance, Work Psychologists have developed broad models of job performance dimensions (notably task performance, and organizational citizenship behaviour). They have also worked alongside other practitioners to develop models of job competencies.

The process of measuring job performance is synonymous with the term 'performance appraisal', and there are a number of methods that can be used to measure people's performance at work.

Examining performance management as a system or process helps to frame the core tasks involved. The system starts with objective or goal setting, and there is a huge body of literature on the value of goal setting, and how it can be implemented most effectively. Performance measurement follows, accompanied by the feedback of performance information. The impact of feedback depends on the manner in which it is delivered, the organizational environment, and on the person giving the feedback. Work Psychologists have considered all of these influences on feedback processes.

Performance management interventions include many of the developmental interventions considered in other chapters in this book, but two others reviewed in this chapter are coaching, and disciplinary procedures, the latter being used when performance problems become more serious.

Performance measurement and management are bridging processes in Work Psychology. In fact, they are processes that sit very clearly at the intersection of Work and Organizational Psychology. On the 'work' side, they contribute to understanding about how to select and develop people, and about how to manage organizational behaviour. On the 'organizational' side, they add significantly to a systems view of organizations and the way that people operate with them. For practitioners, these are areas of great need in many organizations, and the theories, models and techniques identified in this chapter give plenty of guidance on how more organizations could improve and enhance the measurement and management of people's performance at work.

DISCUSSION QUESTIONS

1 An employee's appraisal has identified that they would benefit from development in Interpersonal Sensitivity. What should be done next?

2 Is 'no performance management' better than 'bad performance management'?

3 If a CEO wanted their company to be more innovative, how could they use Performance Management to achieve it? What else could they consider?

4 Is Organizational Citizenship Behaviour important in all jobs? Why?

5 What are the issues that a manager should keep in mind before introducing multi-source feedback?

6 Is performance management worthless without effective performance measurement? Why?

APPLY IT

1 Look at the competencies in Box 8.4/8.5, and if you can, look up the original sources to get some more details about them. Select those that are relevant for you own job, and rate your proficiency on each one. Identify 3 or 4 specific areas to develop in.

2 Most objective setting activity could be improved in some way, and the section on goal setting in this chapter offers some key guidance in how to do it. Set objectives for each of your team and review them against the model of goal setting and performance improvement in Figure 8.4. Refine and improve them based on your evaluation.

3 Critically review your performance appraisal tools – how can they be improved based on the content of this chapter? Pay attention to the design of the measurement tools and the content (e.g. strategic foundations) of the tools. If you do not have appraisal tools, consider developing some.

4 Practise giving performance feedback to a colleague. Carefully plan this feedback based on Box 8.10. Ask a colleague who you know well, and let them know that you are practising giving performance feedback. Suggest that you might work with each other as 'critical friends' to help each other learn and improve.

5 Learn about coaching skills and apply them to help a colleague improve. There are many courses available for helping you to develop some coaching skills – some specifically for managers, others for psychologists, including some courses at Aston University (check online).

WEB ACTIVITY

*Performance Management:
the Football Manager*

Read the article 'Middlesborough sack Tony Mowbray as manager after three years in charge' at **www.mirror.co.uk** or by following the link in the digital resources online and discuss the questions below.

1 How was the objective performance of Mowbray measured in this article?

2 What would be the issue with using this objective measure of performance as a 'true' measure of his performance in the role?

3 What methods could have been put in place to improve Mowbray's performance before sacking him?

Performance Management in Global Business

Read the article 'Cloud-based systems enable performance management' by Paul Solman, published November 2013 at **www.ft.com** (print edition) or by following the link in the digital resources, online and discuss the questions below.

1 What are some of the challenges of managing performance globally?

2 In addition to reward, what other mechanisms might be considered by this organization in an effort to improve performance?

FURTHER READING

Fletcher, C. (2008). *Appraisal, Feedback and Development*. London: Routledge.

Aguinis, H. (2009). *Performance Management*. NJ: Pearson/Prentice-Hall.

Woods, S.A. (2008). Job performance measurement: The elusive relationship between job performance and job satisfaction. In S. Cartwright and L. Cooper (eds.), *The Oxford Handbook of Personnel Psychology*. Oxford: OUP.

Budhwar, P.S. and DeNisi, A.S. (2008). *Performance Management Systems: A Global Perspective*. London: Routledge.

REFERENCES

Aguinis, H. (2009). *Performance Management*. NJ: Pearson/Prentice-Hall.

Armstrong, M. (2009). *Armstrong's handbook of human resource management practice* (11th ed.). London: Kogan Page.

Austin, J.T. and Villanova, P. (1992). The criterion problem 1917–1992. *Journal of Applied Psychology*, 77, 836–874.

Bandura, A. (1997). *Self-efficacy: The exercise of control*. New York: Freeman.

Bartram, D. (2005). The Great Eight Competencies: A Criterion-Centric Approach to Validation. *Journal of applied psychology*, 90(6), 1185.

Borman, W.C. (1979). Format and training effects on rating accuracy and rater errors. *Journal of Applied Psychology*, 64, 410–21.

Borman, W.C. and Brush, D.H. (1993). More progress toward a taxonomy of managerial performance requirements. *Human Performance*, 6, 1–21.

Borman, W.C. and Motowidlo, S.J. (1993). Expanding the criterion domain to include elements of contextual performance. In N. Schmitt and W.C. Borman (eds.) *Personnel Selection in Organizations*. San Francisco: Jossey-Bass.

Borman, W.C. and Motowidlo, S.J. (1997). Task performance and contextual performance: the meaning for personnel selection research. *Human Performance*, 10(2), 99–109.

Brett, J.F. and Atwater, L.E. (2001). 360° feedback: Accuracy, reactions and perceptions of usefulness. *Journal of Applied Psychology*, 85(5), 930–942.

Burke, W.W. and Litwin, G.H. (1992). A Causal Model of Organizational Performance and Change. *Journal of Management*, 18(3), 523–545.

Campbell, J.P. (1990). Modelling the performance prediction problem in industrial and organizational psychology. In M.D. Dunnette and L.M. Hough (eds.), *Handbook of Industrial and Organizational Psychology* (pp. 687–731). Palo Alto, CA: Consulting Psychologists Press.

Campbell, J.P., McCloy, R.A., Oppler, S.H. and Sager, C.E. (1993). A theory of performance. In N. Schmitt and W. Borman (eds.) *Personnel Selection in Organizations* (pp. 35–70). San Francisco: Jossey-Bass.

Campbell, J.P., McHenry, J. and Wise, L.L. (1990). Modelling job performance in a population of jobs. *Personnel Psychology*, 43, 313–33.

Campbell, C.H., Ford, P., Rumsey, M.G., Pulakos, E.D., Borman, W.C., Felker, D.B., DeVera, M.V. and Riegelhaupt, B.J. (1990). Development of multiple job performance measures in a representative sample of jobs. *Personnel Psychology*, 43, 277–300.

Campion, M.A., Fink, A.A., Ruggeberg, B.J., Carr, L., Phillips, G.M. and Odman, R.B. (2011). Doing competencies well: Best practices in competency modeling. *Personnel Psychology*, 64(1), 225–262.

Clutterbuck, D. and Megginson, D. (2006). *Making coaching work: Creating a coaching culture*. London: CIPD.

Coleman, V.I. and Borman, W.C. (2000). Investigating the underlying structure of the citizenship performance domain. *Human Resource Management Review*, 10, 25–44.

Conway, J.M. and Huffcutt, A.I. (1997). Psychometric properties of multi-source performance ratings: A meta-analysis of subordinate, supervisor, peer, and self-ratings. *Human Performance*, 10, 331–60.

Dalal, R.S. (2005). A meta-analysis of the relationship between organizational citizenship behaviour and counterproductive work behaviour. *Journal of Applied Psychology*, 90, 1241–1255.

Facteau, J.D. and Craig, B.S. (2001). Are performance appraisal ratings from different rating sources comparable? *Journal of Applied Psychology*, 86(2), 215–27.

Fletcher, C. (2001). Performance appraisal and management: The developing research agenda. *Journal of Occupational and Organizational Psychology*, 74(4), 473–487.

Fletcher, C. (2008). *Appraisal, Feedback, and Development*. London: Routledge.

Goffin, R.D. and Anderson, D.W. (2007). The Self-Rater's Personality and Self-Other Disagreement in Multi-Source Performance Ratings. *Journal of Managerial Psychology*, 22, 271–289.

Grant, A.M., Green, L.S. and Rynsaardt, J. (2010). Developmental coaching for high school teachers: Executive coaching goes to school. *Consulting Psychology Journal: Practice and Research*, 62(3), 151.

Grant, A.M., Passmore, J., Cavanagh, M.J. and Parker, H.M. (2010). 4 The State of Play in Coaching Today: A Comprehensive Review of the Field. *International Review of Industrial and Organizational Psychology*, 25(1), 125–167.

Greguras, G.J., Robie, C., Schleicher, D.J. and Maynard Goff III. (2003). A field study of the effects of rating purpose on the quality of multi-source ratings, *Personnel Psychology*, 56(1), 1–21.

Hanson, M.A. and Borman, W.C. (2006). Citizenship performance: An integrative review and motivational analysis. In W. Bennett, Jr., C.E. Lance and D.J. Woehr (eds.), *Performance Measurement: Current Perspectives and Future Challenges* (pp. 141–74). Mahwah, NJ: LEA.

Ilgen, D.R., Fisher, C.D. and Taylor, S.M. (1979). Consequences of individual feedback on behaviour in organizations. *Journal of Applied Psychology*, 64, 349–371.

Jones, Woods, Guillaume (2014) A Meta-Analysis of the Effectiveness of Executive Coaching at Improving Work-Based Performance and Moderators of Coaching Effectiveness. Paper presented at the BPS DOP Annual Conference, Brighton, England.

Kelloway, K., Loughlin, C., Barling, J. and Nault, A. (2002). Counterproductive and organizational citizenship behaviours: Separate but related constructs. *International Journal of Selection and Assessment*, 10(1–2), 143–51.

Kinicki, A., Prussia, G., Wu, B. and McKee-Ryan, F. (2004). A Covariance Structure Analysis of Employees' Response to Performance Feedback. *Journal of Applied Psychology*, 89, 1057–1069.

Kluger, A.N. and DeNisi, A. (1996). The effects of feedback interventions on performance: A historical review, meta-analysis and a preliminary feedback intervention theory. *Psychological Bulletin*, 119, 254–284.

Knapp, D.J. (2006). The US joint service job performance measurement project. In W. Bennett, Jr., C.E. Lance and D.J. Woehr (eds.), *Performance Measurement: Current Perspectives and Future Challenges* (pp. 113–40). Mahwah, NJ: LEA.

Locke, E.A. and Latham, G.P. (1990). *A theory of goal setting and task performance*. Englewood Cliffs, NJ: Prentice Hall.

Locke, E.A. and Latham, G.P. (2002). Building a practically useful theory of goal setting and task motivation: A 35 year old odyssey. *American Psychologist*, 57(9), 705–717.

Maurer, T.J., Raju, N.S. and Collins, W.C. (1998). Peer and subordinate performance appraisal measurement equivalence. *Journal of Applied Psychology*, 83(5), 693–702.

Motowidlo, S.J., Borman, W.C. and Schmitt, M.J. (1997). A theory of individual differences in task and contextual performance. *Human Performance*, 10(2), 71–83.

Motowidlo, S.J. and Van Scotter, J.R. (1994). Evidence that task performance should be distinguished from the contextual performance. *Journal of Applied Psychology*, 79, 475–80.

Murphy, K.R. and DeNisi, A.S. (2008). A model of the appraisal process. In P.S. Budhwar and A.S. DeNisi (eds.), *Performance Management Systems: A Global Perspective* (pp. 81–96). London: Routledge.

Organ, D.W. (1988). *Organizational Citizenship Behaviour: The Good Soldier Syndrome*. Lexington, MA: Heath.

Organ, D.W. (1997). Organizational citizenship behaviour: it's construct clean-up time. *Human Performance*, 10(2), 85–97.

Podsakoff, P.M., MacKenzie, S.B., Paine, J.B. and Bachrach, D.G. (2000). Organizational citizenship behaviors: A critical review of the theoretical and empirical literature and suggestions for future research. *Journal of Management*, 26, 513–63.

Seijts, G.H. and Latham, G.P. (2001). The effect of distal learning, outcome and proximal goals on a moderately complex task. *Journal of Organizational Behaviour, 22*, 291–302.

Smith, C.A., Organ, D.W. and Near, J.P. (1983). Organizational citizenship behaviour: Its nature and antecedents. *Journal of Applied Psychology, 68*, 653–63.

Smither, J.W., London, M. and Reilly, R. (2005). Does performance improve following multi-source feedback? A theoretical model, meta-analysis and review of empirical findings. *Personnel Psychology, 58*, 33–66.

Smither, J.W., London, M., Flautt, R., Vargas, Y. and Kucine, I. (2003). Can working with an executive coach improve multisource feedback ratings over time? A quasi-experimental field study. *Personnel Psychology, 56(1)*, 23–44.

Soderquist, K.E., Papalexandris, A., Ioannou, G. and Prastacos, G. (2010). From task-based to competency-based: A typology and process supporting a critical HRM transition. *Personnel Review, 39(3)*, 325–346.

Sturman, M.C., Cheramie, R.A. and Cashen, L.H. (2005). The consistency, stability and test-retest reliability of employee job performance: A meta-analytic review of longitudinal findings. *Journal of Applied Psychology, 90*, 269–83.

Tannenbaum, S.I. (2006). Applied measurement: practical issues and challenges. In W. Bennett, Jr., C.E. Lance and D.J. Woehr (eds.), *Performance Measurement: Current Perspectives and Future Challenges* (pp. 297–320). Mahwah, NJ: LEA.

Tett, R.P., Guterman, H.A., Bleier, A. and Murphy, P.J. (2000). Development and Content Validation of a Hyperdimensional Taxonomy of Managerial Competence. *Human Performance, 13*, 205–251.

Thayer, P.W. (1992). Construct validation: do we understand our criteria? *Human Performance, 5*, 97–108.

Viswesvaran, C. and Ones, D.S. (2000). Perspectives on models of job performance. *International Journal of Selection and Assessment, 8*, 216–26.

Viswesvaran, C., Ones, D.S. and Schmidt, F.L. (1996). Comparative analyses of the reliability of job performance ratings. *Journal of Applied Psychology, 81*, 557–60.

Viswesvaran, C., Schmidt, F.L. and Ones, D.S. (2002). The moderating influence of job performance dimensions on convergence of supervisory and peer ratings of job performance: Unconfounding construct-level convergence and rating difficulty. *Journal of Applied Psychology, 87*, 345–54.

Viswesvaran, C., Schmidt, F.L. and Ones, D.S. (2005). Is there a general factor in ratings of job performance? A meta-analytic framework for disentangling substantive and error influences. *Journal of Applied Psychology, 90*, 108–31.

Voskuijl, O.F. and Evers, A. (2008). Job Analysis and Competency Modelling. In S. Cartwright and C.L. Cooper (eds.), *The Oxford Handbook of Personnel Psychology* (pp. 139–163). New York: Oxford University Press.

Williams, L.J. and Anderson, S.E. (1991). Job satisfaction and organizational commitment as predictors of organizational citizenship and in-role behaviours. *Journal of Management, 17*, 418–28.

Woods, S.A. (2008). Job performance measurement: The elusive relationship between job performance and job satisfaction. In S. Cartwright and L. Cooper (eds.), *The Oxford Handbook of Personnel Psychology*. Oxford: OUP.

CHAPTER 9

CAREERS AND CAREER MANAGEMENT

LEARNING OBJECTIVES

- Describe the changing nature of careers in the 21st century.

- Understand the Psychological Contract and how it relates to careers.

- Describe and critique developmental theories of careers and understand contextual and individual difference influences on career development.

- Describe Holland's theory of vocational personality types and environments.

- Understand how personality relates to career interests, and contemporary developmental perspectives on personality and work.

- Understand how gender, cultural and other social factors influence career development.

- Describe the transition cycle and its implications for job changes.

- Understand the concepts of the boundaryless career and employability.

- Understand how theories and models of career interests and development are applied in career management interventions.

Careers might be thought of as the stories of our working lives. They represent a major part of our lives, and to differing degrees for people, are indicators of our successes – not just in terms of monetary or status outcomes, but also in respect of our own perceptions of whether we are achieving what we wanted in life. The story analogy for careers is a good one, and we can retrospectively look back over our decisions, the chances we took and missed, the rewards we gained as well as mistakes we made. Careers are good stories, which have moments of excitement, periods of prolonged happiness and usually some tough times marked by challenge, anxiety and, at times, disappointment. Almost like a novel, only with you as the heroic lead character.

What is your career story? How did you decide what kind of discipline you would like to work in? What kind of issues influenced your decision to work for a particular organization or in a particular career? Why did you decide to study, or learn about Work and Organizational Psychology by reading this book? These are all important questions, and Work Psychologists are concerned with understanding the answers to them. This chapter is about careers and their management. The chapter covers topics of career development, considering how theories of career development apply in the new world of work. The chapter also looks at career decision-making, and in particular at the development and influence of vocational interests, and the interplay of individual differences and careers.

CAREERS IN THE 21ST CENTURY

Much has been written about the changing context of work in the later part of the 20th century and the early 21st century. These important years have indeed witnessed striking changes to the landscape of organizations and to the jobs that people perform within them. Writers have tended to agree on some of the drivers of these changes (Kidd, 2002). Broadly, they comprise:

- Globalization and the internationalization of organizations and markets. Organizations have been required to change in order to meet the challenges of operating in many countries around the world. The pace of globalization has meant that the pace of organizational change has also increased. Employees have found themselves working within new organizational structures, designed to meet these challenges.

- Technological changes and innovations. In order to support rapid change, and to ensure competitiveness, organizations have developed and adopted new technologies. Technology has facilitated global working, so that people working in different countries can communicate and share ideas. Technology has also allowed people to work at home more easily. Looking back a little further, technology has completely changed the face of manufacturing, to the point that human input into manufacturing has become less and less important.

- Changes to employment law and regulations. Important changes to the relationship between employer and employee have occurred in the past 20–30 years. In the UK, the power of the trade unions has diminished, and consequently the enforcement of worker rights is a less pressing issue for many organizations (an issue exacerbated by the extension of the qualifying period for basic worker rights). This means that jobs are seen as more temporary, less secure and subject to fewer benefits. This is juxtaposed against a steadily increasing minimum wage. Employees are essentially asked to accept higher remuneration in lieu of other benefits.

- Changes to organizational structures. The biggest trend in organizations in recent history is restructuring, most notably delayering and downsizing. Organizations have changed to become flatter and leaner. Such changes have important effects on people's careers. Leaving aside the associated increases in workload that accompany reductions in staffing levels, delayering and downsizing inevitably result in fewer opportunities for promotion (because there are fewer levels within the organization), and require people to perform job tasks that are more diverse (because increasingly complex job tasks must be performed by fewer people). Employees should therefore expect fewer promotions and more horizontal moves within an organization, or across organizations, and should expect to be required to utilize a broader range of skills than previously.

Collectively, these issues mean that the traditional 'job for life' is less common in the majority of industries, and this has heralded changes in the mutual expectations of employers and employees. The nature of these expectations has been explored in the concept of the psychological contract.

The Psychological Contract

The idea of a 'psychological contract' has been around for many years, often credited to Argyris (1960). However, a clutch of research and writing on the psychological contract emerged in the mid- to late 1990s led most notably by Rousseau in the United States, and Herriot and Pemberton in the UK. A well-cited definition of the psychological contract is:

> *An individual's belief regarding the terms and conditions of a reciprocal exchange agreement between that focal person and another party.* (Robinson and Rousseau, 1994, p. 246.)

When applied to organizations and careers, the psychological contract refers to an unwritten set of expectations about how the employee will perform at work, and what they can expect from the organization in return. Herriot and Pemberton (1995) commented on the changing nature of the psychological contract generally in organizations, focusing on their experience from a UK context. They differentiate between relational contracts and transactional contracts. The relational contract is a long-term contract based on a relationship between the employee and the organization. Generally speaking, the organization offers loyalty and security, comfortable and fulfilling working conditions and benefits such as generous pension schemes and regular promotion. In return, the employee reciprocates with loyalty to the organization, tolerating lower remuneration in return for the security of knowing that their job is safe, and that management and the organization can generally be trusted. The relationship is an emotional one, with the employee developing an effective or emotional attachment to the organization. The second kind of contract is transactional. This kind of contract represents a short-term economic exchange. The employee expects to receive a specific benefit (financial or otherwise) in return for a specific contribution to the organization.

In his commentary on the psychological contract, Arnold (1997) discusses the trend from relational contracts to transactional ones. These changes reflect some of the changes in the world of work outlined earlier. Fewer layers in organizations, and indeed fewer jobs, mean that people are increasingly willing to accept short-term project or contract work, but will then expect higher levels of tangible benefits such as pay.

The concept of the psychological contract is not without its problems, and its initial influence has waned somewhat in recent years. As early as 1998, Guest presented an influential critique of the concept. Some of the important aspects of this critique are outlined below:

- Guest calls into question the validity of using a legal metaphor to explain the psychological contract. The legal metaphor indicates that both parties are signed up to an explicit documented agreement, and that the terms and conditions are agreed. The psychological contract is quite different, and there is no guarantee that both parties conceptualize the contents of the contract in the same way. Violation of the contract, or changes to its content can be made arbitrarily in the case of the psychological contract, further distinguishing it from a real contract.

- Guest questions the conceptual underpinnings and theoretical foundations of the psychological contract, commenting that there is no agreed definition about what the contract actually represents. Competing definitions emphasize beliefs, obligations, perceptions and promises. The psychological contract is therefore defined inadequately, and there is no agreed method for measuring the contents of the contract, making research in the area difficult.

- Perhaps more importantly, Guest questions the notion that the psychological contract has changed in the way suggested by Rousseau, and Herriot and Pemberton. Rousseau's observations were drawn from her work in the United States, and Herriot and Pemberton worked closely with financial organizations, who experienced some of the biggest restructures and changes during the late 1990s. Their conclusions are therefore based on a particular cultural, and organizational context. Sparrow (1996) highlights differences across cultures in the nature of the psychological contract, and in the extent of changes in its content. He identifies differences between the experiences of employees in the United States and United Kingdom, compared with those of others in Europe. Perhaps ideas about the psychological contract may not apply so readily in other countries. Moreover, Guest questions whether people's perceptions about careers have changed as drastically as is proposed by writers in the area. It is easy to have some sympathy with this view. City bankers are likely to have developed very different expectations in the past ten years compared with their predecessors. Those working in, for example, the public sector may have seen smaller changes, focused principally around the gradual erosion of benefits such as pensions and promotion, coupled with increasing workloads. They may consequently expect more development, autonomy and respect, but are also likely to still value security and a reasonably long-term relationship with one employer, provided that their needs continue to be satisfied.

Practically, the psychological contract is undoubtedly a useful way to think about the unwritten expectation of employees about their careers and their relationship with their organization. More contemporary perspectives on the contract have emphasized the importance of some general aspects of its content and particularly the employee's sense of fairness and trust in the organization and their belief that the organization is honouring and delivering on the deal (Guest and Conway, 2002). The CIPD in the UK summarize typical expectations that characterize the psychological contract for contemporary jobs. Employees: work hard; uphold their company's reputation; have high levels of attendance and are punctual; are loyal; work extra hours when required; develop new skills and update new ones; are courteous, honest and come up with new ideas.

Employers: pay commensurate with performance; provide opportunities for training and development; provide opportunities for promotion; recognize innovation or new ideas; give feedback on performance; provide interesting tasks; provide an attractive benefits package; are respectful; provide reasonable job security; provide a safe and pleasant working environment.

THE DEVELOPMENT OF CAREERS OVER TIME

Careers are metaphorically like stories, autobiographies created by individuals through their career aspirations and decisions. The nature and contents of career stories are inevitably about development, from childhood, to adulthood and eventually to old-age. Psychologists are interested in this development, and developmental career theories aim to identify specific stages of careers. The most influential developmental theories are those proposed by Super, Erikson and Levinson. The context for these theories might be described as a human relations paradigm, by which theories were designed to explain the experiences of most, if not all, people. Parallels can be drawn with Maslow's hierarchy of needs. As theorizing has become more complex and flexible, some of the ideas in the development of theories appear somewhat outdated. Nevertheless, they do provide useful frameworks for understanding career-related development over time.

Career Development Theories

Erik Erikson

Erikson formulated his developmental theory drawing on influences from Freudian theory, most notably the concept of tension between opposing forces (Arnold, 1997). He outlined eight stages of development – four in childhood, and four in adulthood. Erikson suggested that at each stage, there is conflict to resolve, the outcome of which has consequences later on in life. The eight stages are presented in Box 9.1.

BOX 9.1

Eriksson's eight developmental stages

1 Trust vs. Mistrust.

2 Autonomy vs. Shame and Doubt.

3 Initiative vs. Guilt.

4 Industry vs. Inferiority.

5 Identity vs. Role Confusion.

6 Intimacy vs. Isolation.

7 Generativity vs. Stagnation.

8 Ego integrity vs. Despair.

With reference to careers, the final four stages are most important. In the first of these, the young adult seeks to develop an identity. This is perhaps the most well-known of Eriksson's stages, incorporating the so-called adolescent identity crisis. Formation of an integrated identity serves to bolster self-esteem and self-confidence, and is the focus of development at this stage. An important component of identity is the kind of career or work that a person would like to pursue. The potential negative consequence of this stage is role confusion, whereby the adolescent is unable to form a coherent identity for themselves.

The next stage in Eriksson's model is intimacy versus isolation. The principal concern at this stage is to form close relationships with other people without losing a sense of identity. The risk to development is that close relationships are not formed, resulting in isolation. During the later stages of adulthood, Erikson described the conflict between generativity and stagnation. Generativity refers to passing on knowledge to younger generations, and Eriksson saw this as part of the process of coming to terms with mortality.

The final stage of Eriksson's model is ego integrity versus despair. At this stage, the challenge is for a person to be able to be accepting and satisfied with his or her identity, without feeling undue regret (Arnold, 1997). Work contributes significantly to overall life satisfaction and identity, and so careers are an important aspect of this acceptance. The alternative is despair; feeling that life has not worked out as hoped, and feeling helpless to put it right.

Daniel Levinson

It is remarkable that Daniel Levinson's theory has remained so influential, given that the original incarnation was developed on a sample of 40 American males, aged 35–45. He used an in-depth qualitative approach to understanding their career development, and his theory emerged from the analysis of very rich interview data. His theory differentiated three stages of adulthood (early, middle and late adulthood), each comprising a number of stages, and the precision with which Levinson talked about age and development may surprise you. The ten phases he identified in his book *The Seasons of a Man's Life* (Levinson, 1978) are shown in Table 9.1.

Table 9.1 also shows some of the broader concepts from Levinson's theory, including 'Becoming one's own man', a stage characterized by a surge for independence and achievement. Immediately following this is the most enduring idea from Levinson's theory – the so-called 'midlife crisis' accompanying the midlife transition at around age 40. During early adulthood, Levinson proposed that people formulate a 'dream' of how they would like their life to proceed. By around age 40, the individual is able to develop a more realistic picture about whether the dream will be realized. The midlife crisis occurs if the person feels that the dream is unlikely to be fulfilled, and that there is little

Table 9.1 Levinson's ten phrases	
Early Adult Transition (age 17–22)	Leaving the Family
Entering the Adult World (age 22–28)	Getting into the Adult World
Age 30 Transition (age 28–33)	
Settling Down (age 33–40)	Settling Down
Midlife Transition (40–45)	Becoming One's Own Man
Entering Early Adulthood (45–50)	
Age 50 Transition	
Culmination of Middle Adulthood	
Late Adult Transition	
Entering Late Adulthood	

scope to remedy the situation. This idea is very accessible and one could hypothesize that crises of confidence similar to the midlife crisis stimulate career change, or change in lifestyles more generally.

In responding to criticism about the gender specificity of his original study, Levinson repeated his study, interviewing forty women in a variety of careers. 'The *Seasons of a Woman's Life*' (Levinson and Levinson, 1996), co-authored with his wife, was published two years after Levinson's death. The follow-up did not achieve the same impact as the original study, perhaps because Levinson did not make any substantive changes to his theory on the basis of the new evidence.

Donald Super

Super's theory is arguably the most influential amongst the developmental theories, being focused entirely on career development. In its original form, Super's theory proposed a set of five stages set around specific age ranges. They are shown in Table 9.2.

The theory is criticized on several grounds. First, it appears to be too inflexible about assigning ages to the five stages. In truth, however, the ages were deemed to be guidelines, and although Super persisted with organizing his stages across the lifespan, (e.g. Super and Hall, 1978), he also acknowledged that the stages might apply to people at a variety of ages. Consider the person who opts for a career change during their 30s or 40s. Such a person might establish themselves within their new career later in life. Likewise, the decline stage is certainly unlikely to remain applicable to people aged 65 or over. We know that people are already deciding, and in some cases being forced, to work until age 70 or even later. In summary, it is the stages themselves, rather than the associated ages that are the important components.

A second criticism is that as with other developmental theories, Super focused primarily on male careers as the basis for his theory. There appears to be little consideration of career challenges faced by women (e.g. career breaks for having children), and in this sense, the theory begins to show its age.

An interesting interpretation of Super's theory is presented by Savickas (2002; 2005). Adopting a social constructionist perspective, Savickas proposes that career development is triggered by social environmental changes (for example, societal expectations about how people develop during the course of their lives) rather than an internal impetus to develop. The criticism here is that Super's theory seems to neglect social context. In a similar vein, Fouad (2007) highlights that progressing through the various stages of a career depends on the opportunities and resources (skills, abilities,

Table 9.2 The five stages of Super's career development theory	
Growth (0–14)	The key phase for the development of career interests, capabilities and personality traits. At this stage, young people are starting to think about the kind of work that appeals to them.
Exploration (15–24)	This stage involves exploring the world of work and further development of the self-concept and identity, identifying jobs or roles that are consistent with it.
Establishment (25–44)	At this stage, the person finds a job or career that matches his or her identity and interests, and seeks to make a mark in their chosen field.
Maintenance (45–64)	Having established a position in a chosen feel, the person now seeks to retain that position in the face of new challenges, such as changes in technology.
Decline/disengagement (65+)	Here the person begins to disengage from the work environment, focusing more on non-work interests. Retirement follows.

knowledge and external resources such as financial and social support) available to a person, and this varies in terms of associated ages for different people. This explains why some individuals seem to establish themselves more quickly in careers than others. It is a question of adaptability rather than maturity.

These two themes (the influences of social contextual factors, and also individual differences, on career development) are explored further by Woods, Lievens, De Fruyt and Wille (2013). They presented a dynamic developmental model (DDM) of personality and work, in which personality traits dynamically influence, and are reciprocally influenced by work activity and experience. In exploring the influences of individual differences on working life, they adopted Super's framework to consider the changing contexts of work over the course of a career.

Super's framework is appropriate in this regard because it reflects normative developmental challenges. That is to say that embedded within it are challenges that people face in the course of growing up, and despite changes to demography and lifestyle, people are and society are both stubbornly traditional and therefore engage in social institutions at roughly the same times. So, for example, people are educated through to around age 18–25, and become increasingly specialized in that education. This necessitates their exploration of the working world, followed by entering a career and establishing within it. That establishment is often fuelled by settling down, and having children, which places greater financial burden on people, driving them to advance and maximize earnings. These demands eventually plateau, leading to the maintenance phase.

Super's stages may therefore be seen to represent the contexts against which career development plays out. In Woods et al.'s (2013) model, the course of career development is dynamically influenced by individual differences. At different stages, particular traits and characteristics are activated in response to contextual demands, influencing career and work outcomes, which may in turn give advantage or in some cases, hindrance to progression (see also Chapter 3 for more discussion of these mechanisms).

Table 9.3 Integrating developmental theory		
Super	Erikson	Levinson
Growth	Identity vs. Role Confusion	Leaving the Family
Exploration	Intimacy vs. Isolation	Getting into the Adult World
Establishment Maintenance	Generativity vs. Stagnation	Becoming One's Own Man
Decline	Ego Integrity vs. Despair	

DISCUSS WITH A COLLEAGUE

Spend ten minutes individually writing down in note form your career story to-date on a blank sheet of paper. Think about the decisions you made at various stages of your education or career that have brought you to this point. What are your aspirations? Where do you see your career progressing from here? Have your aspirations changed at any point?

Now look at the integration of the developmental theories in Table 9.3. Can you place yourself within any of those stages? Do you think that more than one of the stages applies to you at present? What would the theories suggest to you about the challenges that you will face in the near future? Are the theories reasonable in this respect?

Career Moves: Job Transition

So far we have discussed perspectives on careers development as a whole. These theories tend not to focus on the individual jobs that make up a person's career, however. On this issue, theory and literature on job transition and socialization is relevant. Work–role transitions are broadly conceptualized as being a move in or out of a job or role, moves between jobs or alterations to work duties and responsibilities (Nicholson and West, 1988). Transitions might refer to entering into or retiring from employment, changing organizations, taking a new job, whether that be a promotion, demotion or sideways move, and changes to job tasks that are not necessarily associated with changes of employer or job titles.

Contemplating all of these potential work transitions, Nicholson (1990) put forward a flexible theory that helps to frame and understand the challenges and stages that people progress through during transitions. The transition cycle is shown in Figure 9.1, and comprises four steps.

1 Preparation. This stage refers to the period prior to entering a new job role. You may have your own experiences of starting a new job or role, and anecdotally one hears about organizations that provide very thorough guidance for new starters and those that provide very little. This stage involves the formation of perceptions by the individual about what the new role will be like.

2 Encounter. The second stage in the cycle refers to the first days and weeks in the new role. This involves a sort of reality check, by which the individual quickly learns about the basic characteristics of the job and the group of others that he or she will work with, inevitably comparing reality with previously held perceptions.

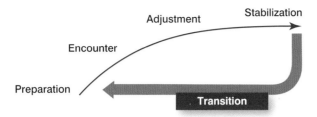

Figure 9.1   The transition cycle

3 Adjustment. At this stage, the individual draws on the knowledge of the work and social environment that they have accumulated and develops their own style of fulfilling the work role. The individual might decide to conform to the requirements of the role as described by the organization, or to innovate and find their own way.

4 Stabilization. In this fourth stage, the work associated with the job role becomes routine, with the person becoming a veteran or 'old-hand' at the job. This stage can prompt further job role change if the stabilization is associated with boredom.

The transition cycle is a very useful framework for understanding a variety of organizational behaviours, bringing our understanding of careers and career management closer to more mainstream management literature. One of the first important influences on the reaction of individuals to their job and organization is socialization. Fisher describes five learning outcomes of socialization:

● preliminary learning
● learning to adapt to the organization
● learning to function in the work-group
● learning to do the job
● personal learning.

During the preparation and encounter stages of the transition cycle particularly, individuals acquire a high volume of information about their new work environment. Formal induction processes help to facilitate socialization, but more powerful is the informal learning that people acquire from their new colleagues and managers (Nicholson, 1990). The initial weeks in a new job role run the risk of being a period of disillusionment (Nicholson and Arnold, 1991), if the initial perceptions of the new employee turn out to be false or unrealistic. Socialization research has more recently examined the influence of individual differences such as pro-active personality traits on the process and outcomes of socialization (e.g. Ashforth, Sluss and Saks, 2007). The strategies that people adopt in respect of their first experiences in a new role do have an effect on socialization outcomes. Such outcomes include effective job performance, and organizational commitment on the positive side, but also stress and negative well-being, turnover, disengagement or other escape strategies on the negative side. Reason enough for organizations to do as much as they can to help new or existing employees to adjust to new work roles.

The transition cycle also tells us something about innovation at work. Schein (1971) identifies three approaches to adjusting to new work:

● Custodian: The person delivers work according to the formal job description.
● Content Innovator: The person develops new ways of delivering the duties and outcomes associated with the role.
● Role Innovator: The person rethinks or reshapes the work role and its position in the organization, including the deliverable responsibilities.

These three potential approaches represent adjustment strategies, and individuals might be influenced by their early encounters with the organization and aspects of its culture. Gabarro (1987) describes how initial innovation in a work role is aimed at 'taking hold' of the role. This is followed by a period of immersion where a person learns and reflects the detail of the job, before further 'reshaping' innovation takes place.

The models we have covered in this chapter lead us to think about how the process of lifelong development leads people to follow particular career paths. Theories about transition and socialization help us to understand how people navigate the various junctions and changes of direction on their journey. One of the biggest transitions that all people have to make at some point in their career is *out* of the work. Retirement brings its own benefits and challenges, and is currently a hot topic for economists and politicians as the population gets older and the proportion of retirees increases. The view of Work Psychologists is discussed in Box 9.2.

BOX 9.2
Retirement

Retirement represents a transition for people out of the working world. Unlike unemployment, retirement is a socially sanctioned move out of work (Warr, 2008), supported by an infrastructure of social and financial benefits, the latter of which are usually tied to success during people's careers, supplemented by Government input that differs across countries.

Retirement is part of the traditional development of careers across the lifespan, and is usually linked to age. In the UK, for example, traditional retirement ages were 65 for men and 60 for women, but these have risen because of the financial strain on pension schemes resulting from people living longer lives. Work Psychologists have been interested in the effects of retiring on health and well-being. There has been a prevalent myth over the years that retirement is bad for health and well-being (Ekerdt, 1987), but as with all such phenomena, the picture is not that simple. Work does provide important sources of life satisfaction (Warr, 2008; see also Chapter 4), but that does not automatically mean that retirement is damaging in the long term.

There are positive changes in lifestyle that can result from retirement including decreased stress and increased physical activity (Midanik, Soghikian, Ransom and Tekawa, 1995). Some sources report increased well-being resulting from retirement (e.g. Kim and Feldman, 2000), but others report no differences between the well-being and physical health of retired and non-retired people of the same age (Ekerdt, Baden, Bosse and Dibbs, 1983; Warr, Butcher, Robertson and Callinan, 2004). One of the reasons for this is that people are likely to experience retirement in different ways. For example, Herzog, House and Morgan, (1991) found that physical and psychological health deteriorated if the decision to retire was constrained by non-controllable external factors. People who were forced to retire for some reason tended to experience retirement negatively. Warr *et al.*, (2004) reported that people who were more committed to work before retirement tended to have lower happiness and well-being in retirement.

Retirement need not be the end of a person's career though, and it is common for retired people to return to work in some form. Such bridge employment is typically part-time, in a different organization to previous employment, and paid less than previous jobs (Warr, 2008). There is evidence that people who take bridge employment in retirement are more satisfied with life and with their retirement (Kim and Feldman, 2000), but this is also likely to be moderated by contextual factors.

VOCATIONAL INTERESTS AND CHOICES

Common to all of the career development models is an exploration phase in which individual differences in self-concept and job interests are formed, followed by choice of a particular career area, and establishment within it. The development of individual differences in work preferences and vocational interests is a crucial step in determining how later career stages progress. This brings us to the next major area of interest for Work Psychologists in respect of careers and career management: the study of vocational interests. Work Psychologists have conducted influential work in this field, seeking to understand why people are attracted to particular kinds of job, and how those interests develop.

Take a moment to think about your ideal job. What kind of work would it involve? What would be some of the key features of that job? It is likely that the ideal job you have identified reflects your particular occupational interests, as does your choice of degree course, and learning activities. Occupational interests begin to develop early on, for most people during childhood and their education (Gottfredson, 1981), and remain relatively constant through their working life.

Recall from Chapter 3 that one of the key contributions of psychology to understanding individual differences is the construction of models and frameworks that help to explain the complexities of differences between people. Similarly, in the study of occupational interests, a key contribution has been a coherent model of occupational interests. This model was proposed by John Holland (see KEY FIGURE box), formalized in the first edition of his book *Making Vocational Choices: Theory of Vocational Personalities and Work Environments* in 1973. His model has become highly influential in career counselling practice, particularly in the United States.

Holland's RIASEC Model

In his work as a career counsellor, John Holland noticed that amongst his clients, preferences and interests for particular kinds of work or job environment tended to co-occur. This led him to believe that he could identify a set of distinct vocational interest types, which in his theory he describes as personality types. He extended this reasoning further to suggest that interests and work environments could be organized on the same typological framework. He explains the basic premises of the theory:

> ❝ *The theory consists of several simple ideas and their more complex collaborations. First, we can characterize people by their resemblance to each of six personality types: Realistic, Investigative, Artistic, Social, Enterprising and Conventional. The more closely a person resembles a particular type, the more likely he or she is to exhibit the personal traits and behaviours associated with that type. Second, the environment in which people live and work can be characterized by their resemblance to six model environments: Realistic, Investigative, Artistic, Social, Enterprising and Conventional. Finally, the pairing of persons and environment leads to outcomes that we can predict and understand, knowledge of the personality types and the environmental models. These outcomes include vocational choice, vocational stability and achievement, educational choice and achievement, personal competence, social behaviour and susceptibility to influence.* ❞

John Holland

In November 2008, Work Psychology lost one of its most influential figures – John Holland, who died in Maryland in the US, aged 89. In the month prior to his death, he was awarded the American Psychological Association Award for Distinguished Scientific Application of Psychology, for his outstanding contributions to vocational psychology and personality. His biography in *American Psychologist* tells a diverse and interesting career story in itself. His parents had intellectual interests and put John through university. After graduating in 1942, he served three years in the army in a variety of roles, including classification interviewer and psychological assistant, roles that triggered his interest in psychology, leading to his completion of a doctorate on personality and art. His work did not sit well with his university department, where evidence and science was strongly valued over other considerations. His preference for the practical over the rigorous appears to have been a

theme in much of his subsequent research and theorizing. Indeed, much of the research he conducted in the late 1950s and 1960s is acknowledged to be only weakly evaluated, and his theory to be poorly evidenced when first presented.

His work as a career counsellor was a huge influence on his thinking. His frustration at having to wait up to ten days for the results of the Strong Interest Inventory (the popular career survey at the time), and at the complexity of the process of matching people's preferences to jobs, stimulated his work in the field. He designed a short, simple questionnaire (the Vocational Preference Inventory) to assess preferences for particular occupations, and by learning more about the Strong inventory, he began to conceptualize people's interests as aspects of personality. By grouping occupations and interests in particular ways, Holland arrived at the first basic formulation of the six RIASEC categories. His eventual theory went through several revisions, and although he was retired at the time, he published the most recent version in 1997.

John Holland's contribution to Work Psychology was an undeniably practical theory. That is its great strength – practitioners are able to grasp and use Holland's model and the associated assessment tools even if they have very little background knowledge about psychology. His work is an example of how theory can be translated into practice, and his legacy is a model that is used every day in the process of advising people about their careers. And moreover, many of Holland's suppositions (e.g the hexagonal circumplex structure, the associations of personality and vocational environments and some of the outcomes of congruence between interests and environment) have been supported in research since the development of the theory. It is an excellent case-study for considering the tensions of science versus practice.

Holland proposed six vocational personality types and six corresponding work environments, suggesting that people can be described in terms of their similarity to the six personality types, and that their most dominant type will give an indication of their preferred working style. Holland described work environments using these same six dimensions, and suggested that people are attracted and find satisfaction in work environments that match their interests (i.e. that match their vocational personality type). The six personality types and corresponding work environments are summarized in Table 9.4.

Table 9.4 Holland's six vocational personality/ environment types

Personality/ Environment type	Personality Traits and Preferences	Typical Work Environments	Occupations
Realistic	A Realistic person prefers activities that involve the manipulation of objects, tools, machines and animals. They are typically conforming, practical, persistent, dogmatic, inflexible, among other traits.	Realistic occupations frequently involve work activities that include practical, hands-on problems and solutions. They often deal with plants, animals and real-world materials like tools and machinery. Many of the occupations require working outside, and do not involve paperwork or working closely with others.	Mechanic Labourer Surveyor Electrician Farmer
Investigative	An Investigative person prefers activities that involve observational, systematic or creative investigation of physical, biological or other scientific phenomena. They prefer abstract problem solving, and often have an aversion to persuasive, social and repetitive activities. They are likely to be analytical, rational, independent and intellectual, among other traits.	Investigative occupations frequently involve working with ideas, and require an extensive amount of thinking. These occupations can involve searching out facts and figuring out problems mentally.	Scientist Anthropologist Engineer Laboratory technician
Artistic	An Artistic person prefers activities that involve the manipulation of physical, verbal or human materials to create art forms or products. They are likely to have an aversion to systematic or ordered activities, and enjoy an environment with few rules. They are likely to be imaginative, intuitive, nonconforming and expressive, among other traits.	Artistic occupations frequently involve working with forms, designs and patterns. They often require self-expression and the work can be done without following a clear set of rules.	Painter Sculptor Interior designer Writer Journalist

Social	A Social person prefers activities that involve working with others, usually teaching, developing or helping others. They are likely to be empathic, friendly, generous, and altruistic, among other traits.	Social occupations frequently involve working or communicating with others or teaching people. These occupations tend to involve helping or providing services to others.	Teacher Counsellor Waiter/waitress Nurse Tour guide
Enterprising	An Enterprising person prefers activities involving managing others to attain organizational goals or economic gain. They are typically ambitious, assertive, extraverted and self-confident.	Enterprising occupations frequently involve starting up and carrying out projects, often dealing with businesses. These occupations can involve leading people, making decisions or risk-taking.	Sales person Manager Lawyer Chief executive Recruitment consultant
Conventional	A Conventional person prefers activities that are rule-regulated, such as working with data, record-keeping and other administrative work. They tend to be averse to ambiguous or unsystematic activities. They are typically careful, conforming, methodical and conscientious.	Conventional occupations frequently involve following set procedures and routines. These occupations can include working with data and details rather than with ideas. Usually there is a clear line of authority to follow.	Accountant Auditor Statistician Cashier Office clerk Secretary Administrator

The structure of vocational interests

Holland's theory proposed that the six types are arranged in a hexagon (see Figure 9.2). This hypothesis has stood up reasonably well in empirical tests (e.g. Armstrong, Hubert and Rounds, 2003; Tracey and Rounds, 1993). The structure represents interests effectively from late adolescence onwards and seems to be largely invariant across gender and ethnicity (Armstrong *et al.*, 2003; Darcy and Tracey, 2007). Each type is conceptually most similar to its adjacent types, and least similar to its opposing type (e.g., the Investigative type is similar to the Artistic type, and least similar to the Enterprising type).

Implications and applications of Holland's theory

If you are reading this book outside the US, then Holland's model is unlikely to have figured highly in your career decision-making or your education. Within the US, Holland's model has been much more influential, and has shaped research and practice in important ways. A few of the implications, perspectives and applications of the model are reviewed below.

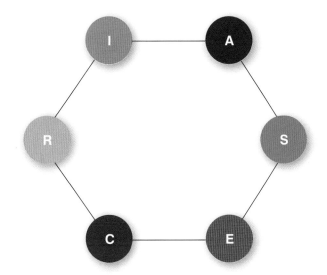

Figure 9.2   Holland's RIASEC hexagon

Application   Although Holland's model has been somewhat neglected in Europe and Asia, its impact is clearly visible in career counselling practice in the US. In the Dictionary of Occupational Titles (US Department of Labor, 1991) and more recently in the O*NET database (O*NET Resource Center, 2003), jobs are categorized according to Holland's six vocational types, and rated on continuous scales representing the degree to which they are characterized by each of the six types. Career counsellors use these resources to help people decide on the kinds of jobs that might best suit their individual interests. Interests are assessed using a number of different self-report questionnaires. Holland's own is the Self-directed Search (Holland, 1994), which continues to be used and can be completed online. Equally as popular is the Strong Interest Inventory (Harmon, Hansen, Borman and Hammer, 1994), and there are now at least two public-domain measures of the RIASEC model available for researchers and practitioners to use (e.g. Armstrong, Allison and Rounds, 2008). All of these questionnaires tend to ask about preferences for jobs and for different work activities. The Self-directed Search also contains questions about people's self-rated competence in particular work activities.

Implications   Like all good psychology theories, Holland's theory makes predictions about behaviour. The key predictive variable is congruence between interests and job environment, and the central tenet of the theory is that people seek out occupations that are consistent with their interests. When occupation and interests are matched, people are supposedly more satisfied, and more likely to perform well. When interests and occupation are not matched, people tend to be less satisfied, and to seek out ways to express their interests, which may include turnover from their current occupation in favour of something new. How well do these assumptions stand up?

The assumption that people gravitate to occupations that match their interests has been examined in a number of studies. A validation study for the Strong Interest Inventory found that RIASEC types predicted occupational group membership 12 years later (Hansen and Dik, 2005), and similar prospective results were reported by Donnay and Borgen (1996) and Betz, Borgen and Harmon (2006), who also found that personality traits added to the prediction of occupational group membership beyond interest assessments. Recent studies such as these, in addition to an earlier review (Fouad, 1999), support the validity of measures of vocational interests as predictors of occupational membership.

AUTHOR EXPERIENCE

Career Choices and Constraints
Author Experience

Over the past five years or so, I have worked with managers at a major national oil company, all of whom are going through assessment and development for promotion to the next level of management. There are two distinct groups of managers that I see during the project – those going for promotion by developing leadership skills and taking on more management responsibility, and those who are seeking to become technical experts, building on their engineering speciality. Notably, virtually all of the managers started their careers by training as engineers.

Career interest theories such as Holland's, as well as Schein's career anchors, are useful models for helping to understand why these individuals who started from the same position diverge in their career aspirations and pathways. Some clearly identify very strongly with a role of technical expert, seeking to understand the fine detail of their particular field, whereas others clearly enjoy management and leading, and perhaps derive more satisfaction from those activities. I also meet some people who seem to be in jobs that do not really inspire them, perhaps because the job duties clash with family life, or because they would rather that the job be different in some way. Here, the theories hit their limit of utility.

A focus on career interests and individual differences in career decision-making overestimates the freedom that people have to choose jobs and careers that they find rewarding. People are limited in their career options because of educational

opportunities, or natural abilities. Social and family commitments also impact on people's options. A mother or father of three may want to go for self-employment and build that new business they had been planning, but the lack of security that such a move would bring makes it possibly irresponsible. The lesson is perhaps that it is wrong to assume that people are in their job because they like it. Building satisfaction at work is in part about understanding whether the job appeals to the interests of the job-holder, and if not, finding possible ways that job duties might be diversified so that at least part of a person's job does allow interests to be expressed.

Spokane, Meir and Catalano (2000) conducted a review of studies testing the congruence hypotheses derived from Holland's model, indicating that satisfaction tends to correlate with congruence at about 0.25 in most studies, an effect strong enough to support the theory. Other investigators are less optimistic about the implications of congruence between interests and occupations. Arnold (2004) reviews a number of potential sources of weakness in the theory, drawing on two meta-analytic studies that strongly question the theory on the grounds that congruence does not predict satisfaction or performance at work convincingly and consistently (Assouline and Meir, 1987; Tranberg, Slane and Ekeberg, 1993). Potential confounds include weak measurement of either the environment or interests, as well as neglect of wider influences on job satisfaction (such as job conditions and characteristics).

Overall, some of Holland's propositions appear to be supported in the literature, but combine these with some strong published critique, and one would have to conclude that the implications of the theory are far from definitive. Nevertheless, for practitioners, understanding the congruence of people's interests and actual occupations offers an enormously heuristic approach for helping people explore preferences, satisfaction and happiness at work. It is a pity that the ideas are not used more often in job design in organizations. If a job does not naturally appeal to an individual's interests, then perhaps it could be redesigned or modified to allow some expression of interests and preferences, especially because different specialty pathways within an occupation can often present markedly different features (a point we return to shortly).

Schein's career anchors Taking a different perspective on individual differences in career development, Schein presented a set of career anchors (Schein, 1993), which he believed guided decisions about jobs and careers. Schein's contribution is an important one because it bridges the gap between theories of career development and vocational interests. He proposes that people develop a preference for a specific career theme, and that this influences their decision-making about how their career should progress. Like vocational interests, the anchors are supposed to lead people to gravitate to particular kinds of work (leading to the anchor analogy). The career anchors are:

- Technical or Functional Competence.
- General Managerial Competence.
- Autonomy/Independence.
- Security/Stability.
- Entrepreneurial Creativity.
- Service/Dedication.
- Pure Challenge.
- Lifestyle.

BOX 9.3
Extensions and alternatives to the Holland RIASEC model

An extension of the RIASEC model was proposed by Prediger (1982), who suggested that there were two dimensions underlying the Holland hexagon:

- Things versus People: A dimension representing the degree to which vocations involve impersonal tasks (Realistic activities) versus interpersonal tasks (Social activities).
- Data versus Ideas: A dimension representing the degree to which vocations involve creative, thinking-related tasks

(Investigative and Artistic activities) versus systematic, data-related tasks (Conventional and Enterprising activities).

These dimensions represent a different way of thinking about vocational preferences and interests, and their simplicity is appealing. Preferences and occupations can be described in terms of their positions on the two dimensions. The relationship between Prediger's two dimensions and Holland's six types is illustrated in Figure 9.3.

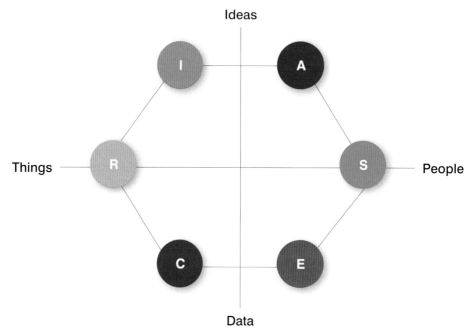

Figure 9.3   Holland's RIASEC hexagon, plus prediger's dimensions

Although the career anchors have had less impact than the theories of Holland and Super, the model and its associated assessment tools are increasingly popular in career counselling practice.

Personality Traits and the RIASEC Model In Holland's theory, the RIASEC types are positioned as personality types. Parsimoniously, in the research literature, the constructs are more commonly described as based on interests rather than personality traits or variables per se. In this vein, six types of vocational interest stand alongside the two other important components of individual differences: cognitive ability/intelligence, and personality traits. How are these three kinds of individual difference integrated to give an overall picture of the person?

There is plenty of research examining the associations of personality traits and the RIASEC types. These studies are summarized in two meta-analyses (Barrick, Mount and Gupta, 2003; Larson, Rottinghaus and Borgen, 2002). There were some differences in the findings of these two meta-analyses, but the most robust associations seem to be observed for Openness with Artistic/Investigative interests, Conscientiousness with Conventional interests, and Extraversion with Social and Enterprising interests. These associations are shown in Figure 9.4.

Ackerman and Heggestad (1997) took a slightly different approach and examined how different forms of cognitive ability, personality traits and interests cluster together. They identified four types or clusters of characteristics:

1   Social: Enterprising and Social interests together with Extraversion from the Big Five model.
2   Clerical/Conventional: Conventional interests, Conscientiousness, and perceptual speed (with the latter representing an ability).
3   Science/Mathematics: Investigative and Realistic interests and numerical reasoning ability.
4   Intellectual/Cultural: Artistic and Investigative interests, Openness, and fluid and crystallized forms of general ability.

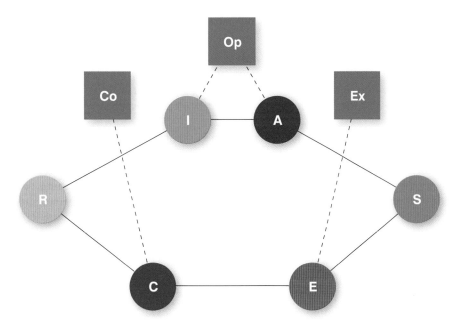

Figure 9.4   Associations between RIASEC types and the Big Five personality dimensions

The associations between personality traits and the RIASEC types are also observed if occupational environments rather than interests are examined. Judge *et al.* (1999) reported that traits measured during adolescence predicted the RIASEC characteristics of participants' occupations many years later. Extending this to even earlier in childhood, Woods and Hampson (2010) reported associations between the Big Five personality dimensions measured at ages 6–12 and the RIASEC characteristics of job environments held by those same participants forty years later, with Openness and Conscientiousness being particularly important (predicting later life occupations characterized as Artistic/Investigative, and Conventional/Social respectively).

Woods and Hampson (2010) present a developmental theoretical model of childhood vocational development, and how this leads to adults working in particular occupational environments. They propose that early childhood personality traits such as Openness/Intellect, Conscientiousness and Extraversion direct children to particular activities and interests, which result in the acquisition of certain competencies. These eventually shape the development of vocational interests that in turn lead people to work in particular occupational environments.

Advancing the developmental perspective of personality and work further, Woods *et al.* (2013) consider the reciprocal influence of work on personality. Following the developmental process proposed by Woods and Hampson (2010), people select themselves into particular occupational environments in which their traits and associated competencies are activated, practised and strengthened. The strengthening and deepening of characteristics resulting from life experiences that draw on those traits is called the correspondence principle (Roberts, Caspi and Moffitt, 2003). According to Woods *et al.* (2013), work influences our personality through these and other developmental processes. Their Dynamic Developmental Model has implications for how we understand the role of career development in people's lives more widely, and they propose that the development and maintenance of stable identities and personality characteristics may rely significantly on working life:

> *Longitudinal stability of personality may owe much to the processes of developing preferences for activities, practising them, applying them in a job, strengthening them, and then remaining in a career in which they are persistently activated from age 25 through to 65.* Woods, Lievens, De Fruyt and Wille, 2013 ppS19

A final addition to the literature on personality and Holland's model extends the scope of focus of the Holland model beyond choice of occupations to choice of specialties within occupations. Different specialties within occupations may represent substantially different work environments. For example, a management pathway might represent a more Enterprising specialty, a teaching pathway more Social. Woods, Koczwara and Patterson (2013) examined the associations of personality traits with the specialty choices of doctors in the UK NHS. These specialties were profiled on the RIASEC model. They found that Neuroticism and Agreeableness were the key associates of specialty choice. Doctors high on Neuroticism were less likely to work in Realistic specialties (e.g. Surgery) and more likely to work in Artistic specialties (e.g. Microbiology). Woods, Koczwara and Patterson (2013) proposed that Realistic specialties in medicine had a greater level of threat (e.g. high consequences of failure in surgical procedures), and were therefore avoided by people high on Neuroticism. Artistic specialties by contrast featured less threatening activities. Agreeableness was positively associated with Social specialties such as public health, most likely because of the opportunities in those specialties for pro-social helping, which might appeal to doctors with high Agreeableness.

In these studies, we can observe the interplay of personality and career development. Holland's RIASEC model provides a robust framework for examining the theoretical concepts and questions that such studies present. It is therefore an excellent example of a model that has both practical and theoretical value.

DISCUSS WITH A COLLEAGUE

Select the two RIASEC dimensions that you think best match your career interests. Use the O*NET database (**http://online.onetcenter.org/**) to search for jobs that match those interests:

Instructions for O*NET: Open O*NET > Find Occupations > Select Browse by Descriptor (Interests) > Click your preferred Interest

What do you think of the results? Discuss the generated career options with a colleague.

SOCIAL, CULTURAL AND ORGANIZATIONAL INFLUENCES ON CAREERS

The theories and perspectives covered so far in this chapter are individual-oriented. Career development and choices is conceptualized as a product of individual differences and developmental processes. However, these are not the only influences, and they neglect the realities of careers in which social, cultural and organization factors also play a part. In this section, we consider some of these influences, and at the same time, examine some more contemporary perspectives on careers.

Careers and Gender

Gender is a major influence on the development of vocational interests and eventual career choices (Lent, Brown and Hackett, 1994). From as young as two–three years, boys and girls aspire to careers that are gender stereotypic (Fouad, 2007). Much of the research on career development and vocational interests has neglected the issue of gender and yet most people are acutely aware of societal pressures and norms around gender and occupations. When we think of some occupations, we tend to automatically assume either a male or female job-holder (e.g. nurse, firefighter, engineer, secretary), with the Think-Manager-Think-Male bias (Schein, 1973) being particularly persistent. For other occupations and careers, gender stereotypes are less strong, but still somewhat evident (e.g. teacher, business owner).

Children absorb these cultural stereotypes in their early preferences for jobs and roles. Girls express preferences for female gender-sterotyped jobs (Miller and Budd, 1999) and girls who express preferences for non-traditional jobs are less likely to persist in their choice than those choosing traditional jobs (Farmer, Wardrop, Anderson and Risinger, 1995; Fouad, 2007). Traditional career choices for men are those that typically confirm aspects of male identity, reflecting selection of masculine attitudes and traits over feminine ones, supporting self-perceptions of toughness and emotional restrictiveness (Jome and Tokar, 1998). Perhaps more interestingly, men and women often give different gender-stereotypic reasons for entering particular careers. For example, men explain entering engineering because of their interests in the field, whereas women tend to cite altruistic reasons such as helping others (Davey, 2001).

One of the most important and well-articulated theories of career and occupational aspirations and development is that of Gottfredson (1981). Her theory fills one of the key gaps in the career development theories outlined earlier because it focuses on children. Gottfredson identifies four stages of development for children in respect of their occupational aspirations:

- Orientation to size and power (ages three–five): At this stage, children grasp the concept of becoming an adult, and growing up.
- Orientation to sex roles (ages six–eight): Gottfredson suggests that gender (sex-role in her model) is the first influence on the development of a vocational self-concept. Children acquire stereotypes about male versus female roles early on in their development.
- Orientation to social valuation (ages 9–13): At this stage, demands of social class and ability become important determinants of behaviour and identity.
- Orientation to the internal, unique self: (age 14 and above): Children develop a greater awareness of their own individual, unique characteristics at this stage, and are able to deal with more complex aspects of their self-concept (this is related to Eriksson's 'identity crisis').

In examining the gender-stereotyped nature of occupations, Gottfredson explores gender preferences for occupation characteristics described on the RIASEC model. The most gender-stereotyped occupations are Realistic (male) and Conventional (female). Artistic and Social jobs are somewhat feminine whereas Investigative and Enterprising jobs are somewhat masculine.

In their study of personality and vocational environments, Woods and Hampson (2010) examined how gender and the Big Five dimensions measured in childhood interact to predict the kind of occupational environments that a person works in later in life. They found that women tended to work in jobs that were more Conventional, Social and Artistic, but also to a lesser extent more Enterprising. Men's jobs tended to be more Realistic, but equally Investigative compared to women. Gender and personality interacted in their study in some interesting ways. For example, men and women high on Openness were more likely to work in Artistic or Investigative jobs. However low Openness predicted job environments differently for men and women. Women who were lower on Openness as children were more likely to work in Conventional jobs, whereas men lower on Openness as children were more likely to work in Realistic jobs. Later-life career environments for boys and girls low on Openness tended to diverge along gender-stereotypic lines. Woods and Hampson proposed the children high on Openness would be more likely to experiment with different activities and potentially buck the trend of gender stereotyping.

These findings have reflected on the differences in the occupational preferences and choices of boys and girls as they develop. One other relevant consideration is opportunity. Career development is in part related to opportunities that a person has to attain the level of status or achievement that they aspire to, and although countries continue to take steps to address inequalities between men and women at work, there remain striking gaps and areas of inequity. These questions are reflected every year in the World Economic Forum's 'Global Gender Gap Report' Hausmann (2012). The report examines a number of areas of inequality (work, health, education and political empowerment), and rank orders countries according to the size of the gap between men and women. According to the 2012 report, no country in any part of the world has achieved equality, and although countries such as the UK, Germany, Sweden, Norway and New Zealand are in the top 20 countries in the list, the rankings of some Western European countries in terms of economic participation and opportunity are much lower (e.g. out of 135 countries, UK 33rd, Germany 31st). Scandinavian, African, Eastern European and Central Asian countries feature heavily in the top 30 countries, with the big emergent economies of China and India ranked 58th and 123rd respectively. Interestingly, the US ranks 22nd overall, but 8th for economic participation and opportunity.

The subject of women in leadership has attracted renewed research and some advances in recent years. A frequently cited metaphor for the barriers preventing women progressing into leadership positions is the glass ceiling; an invisible barrier hindering promotion of women to higher management. However, it appears that the social psychology of women in leadership is much more complex that this simple metaphor. Ryan and Haslam (2005) argue that although women are beginning to break through the glass ceiling, their performance once promoted is placed under close scrutiny. Moreover, there emerge some fascinating findings about the contexts under which women are typically perceived as desirable leaders, and indeed appointed to leadership roles. Examining the performance of the UK FTSE 100 companies, Ryan and Haslam (2005) found archival evidence that women were more likely to be appointed to boards at time of organizational crisis, and especially so when share prices had fallen over successive months. Those organizations that did appoint women in these circumstances tended to perform better in the months that followed. Ryan and Haslam (2005) termed this effect the glass cliff – the appointing of women to precarious positions of leadership at times of crisis.

Developing their work further, Ryan, Haslam, Hersby and Bongiorno (2011) conducted a series of experiments in which they showed that women were perceived as more effective (i.e. ideal) leaders for companies in situations of crisis (confirming the Think-Crisis-Think-Female bias). However, their studies also showed that this applied specifically when the leader was expected to a) stay in the background and endure the crisis, or b) take responsibility for the company failure, or c) manage people and personnel issues through the crisis. There was not female bias if the leader was expected to d) act as a spokesperson, or e) take control and improve performance. This research uncovers some troubling trends for perceptions around women in leadership, strengthening the case for the glass cliff hypothesis. Although more women may be breaking into top leadership, the social psychological forces associated with their appointment may mean that they are essentially set up to lead in situations in which they have a much higher probability of failure than is typically experienced by their male counterparts.

Gender then, influences a child's aspirations for his or her career, including the career choices that he or she perceives as available. Through persistent inequality, gender also acts to limit the career opportunities of women compared to men in a number of important ways, including most notably in terms of leadership, wages, and the proportions of women in professional and technical occupations.

Careers and Culture

The theories of career development and choice that have been reviewed in this chapter are very clearly rooted in Western, and more specifically US experiences of careers. Moreover, the major theories were conceived in the historical context of the US between 1950 and 1980 (Wong and Slater, 2002). In this sense, the theories should be seen as limited in terms of their utility in other cultures. Culture has a strong influence on career appraisal, expectations and decisions. Derr and Laurent (1989) comment that:

> *National cultures have a significant impact on career dynamics in two major ways. First, national cultures shape the individuals self definition of a career ... Second, national cultures also shape the institutional context or design of work, and the individual's perception of it ... through the norms, values and assumptions that the individual has already learned in the culture.* Derr and Laurent, 1991; p. 465–6; cited in Wong and Slater, 2002; p. 354.

Schein (1984) explored how culture affected several aspects of careers. The very notion of a career is based on the aspiration for personal ambition, and this features more strongly in Western cultures. The concept of career in collectivist cultures would be very different. Societies also place values on careers that can determine their desirability. Compare the changing values attached to military careers in the US currently to the negative stereotypes that were held in the late 1960s and early 1970s. The value of a career in life also varies across cultures. Hofstede (1980) found that employees in Singapore, Hong Kong, Columbia, Mexico and Peru did not value family time as an important feature of their careers. Employees in Japan, the Phillipines and Taiwan valued it more, and those in New Zealand, Australia and Canada valued it most. Markers of success in careers are also different across cultures. For example, achieving results is valued strongly in the US, creativity and health in Germany, education in the Netherlands and opinions of others in the UK (Laurent, 1991).

Comparative cross-cultural research is weak in vocational psychology, yet it has the potential to strengthen understanding about cultural differences more widely. Wong and Slater (2002) provide a good example of this. Their study used qualitative methods to explore the careers of managers in China. They comment on four relevant cultural traditions in China that differ from Western cultures:

- Importance of face: giving respect to those of higher social status.
- Respect for hierarchy: respect for seniority and age.
- Importance of collectivism: thinking and behaving within accepted social norms.
- Importance of harmony: keeping good relations by fulfilling reciprocal obligations and duties.

One of the emergent aspects of these values is guanxi, referring to relationships with others. In their interview data, Wong and Slater (2002) found that guanxi remained a significant influence on career progression and development of management careers in China, despite the significant economic and business reforms in the country. Many managers felt that maintaining good guanxi with subordinates and top management was important in career progression, and the implication is that part of maintaining good guanxi is respect for traditions and values.

Against this context of difference, there were also interesting similarities. Family upbringing, social status, individual values, motivation, environmental factors, life stages and organizations all had influences on career decisions and progression. Alongside the limitations of existing theories, there may also be some important strengths. What makes cultural comparison difficult in current times is cultural change. The exportation of Western working cultures and styles, driven in part by the biases that operate in management research, could bring changes to ways that careers are perceived in other cultures. Nevertheless, enduring cultural values are still vital to understanding when and how theories and models of careers are likely to be invalid across cultures.

KEY THEME

Globalization and Cross Cultural Work and Organizational Psycholoy

International career Relocation

The globalization of work means that a substantial number of workers now have the opportunity to relocate their career to a new country. This may take the form of a temporary expatriate assignment, but could also involve a more permanent move. We are seeing the effects of this in many countries around the world already as migrant workers move to meet business demands for a variety of jobs ranging from professional and managerial to semi-skilled or manual work. This presents cultural challenges on the part of people moving to new countries, and the countries and businesses to which they move.

The process of cultural adjustment is referred to as acculturation, and there are a number of strategies that people adopt. For example, some people strive for assimilation (rejecting completely their previous culture and rather completely adopt the new culture), others for integration (adoption of some new cultural values alongside retention of some of original cultural values), still others for different strategies. For organizations, understanding the impacts of this kind of cross cultural working requires knowledge of the processes, antecedents and consequences of different acculturation strategies, and to this end, Samnani, Boekhorst and Harrison (2013) proposed a theoretical model to explore the process. In the model, the salience of cultural identity influences acculturation strategy, a relationship that is moderated by desire for economic reward (e.g. pay) and relational pressure (e.g. pressure from family or friends to adopt a particular approach). Acculturation strategy then influences the kind of organization a newcomer seeks out, and the social networks they interact with, with the degree of similarity of new versus original culture also having an influence. These decisions ultimately impact on long-term career outcomes.

In terms of career management, organizations could apply theorizing such as this to firstly attract applicants from diverse backgrounds, and secondly to help newcomers to settle in and adjust, potentially improving the probability that international career relocation will be successful.

The Boundaryless Career

The latest terminology to be applied to career theory in Work Psychology is the so-called 'boundaryless career'. Arthur and Rousseau (1996) originated the term, and Inkson (2008) identifies six specific meanings:

- Moving across boundaries of separate employers.
- Validating work by seeking information outside the current employer.
- Sustaining work and role with information and networks that reach beyond the current employer.

- Breaking traditional career boundaries.
- Rejecting career opportunities for personal or family reasons.
- Perceiving one's career as without boundaries, regardless of current constraints.

The boundaryless career is one in which the individual is not constrained to career moves or indeed work activities that are restricted within one employer or organization. Although the roots of the idea can be traced back to Gouldner (1957), Inkson (2008) points out that the idea has found particular significance in the past 10–20 years as a result of some of the changes to work and organizations outlined earlier.

Thinking in respect of boundaryless careers has developed beyond the constraints of employer and organization. One focus has been the barriers or boundaries imposed by traditional aspirations and markers of career success. The closely related concept of the Protean Career (Hall, 2002) examines the subjectivity of goal setting, exploring how career goals might be understood as broad life goals, whereby an individual seeks to achieve more that the objective markers of success such as salary and status. These goals might be related to attaining a happiness or contentment through achievement or validation of identity – essentially attaining meaning in life and career.

Other boundaries might also be broken down in the boundaryless career. These include geographical (location), occupational (actual job) and status (promotion, demotion, independence) boundaries. The notion of the boundaryless career incorporates a general rejection of the traditional structural constraints on decisions about their careers, and is therefore timely. The ideas around rejecting structures and societal career traditions find expression because of the rapid development of social and cultural norms over the past 50 years. We now have more flexibility than ever before about how to live our lives and to decide on how we work. Increased access to education, travel and information have broken down some of the traditional boundaries of opportunity, mobility and access. Careers have therefore captured the attention of sociologists, acting as a lens for examining social change. It is naïve, however, to suppose that the boundaries of social class and opportunity have been broken or at least sufficiently eroded to move us closer to a true equality of opportunity. Issues of culture, class and privilege are pervasive in determining why young people of similar abilities aspire and gain access to careers with differing outcomes, including status and salary. Organizations could do more to promote social mobility and this is explored in the key themes box.

The implication of seeking or simply having a 'boundaryless career' is a greater sense of agency and responsibility of the individual for managing and developing his or her career. The organization is seen as doing less to manage career progression, with people taking ownership of factors like development, networking and education for the purpose of initiating and furthering their careers. In this vein, Direnzo and Greenhaus (2011) present a model of job search and voluntary turnover. They argue that in the context of volatile economic conditions, and removal of traditional career progression boundaries, people are more motivated to engage in pro-active job search activity. By maintaining a greater awareness of the job market, employees may be motivated to move jobs (voluntarily turnover) or to engage in self-directed career development strategies such as up-skilling to maintain their marketability with prospective new employers. This marketability is referred to as employability, a concept reviewed in the next section.

Careers and Employability

One impact of changing perspectives on careers and organizations is the concept of employability. The basic idea is that if careers are more fluid, less structured, less hierarchical and more boundaryless, then a person's career progression is enhanced or limited by their employability, or the extent to which they develop or possess a sought-after profile of abilities, skills and competencies. Employability has been defined as 'continuous fulfilling, acquiring or creating of work through the optimal use of one's competences' (Van der Heijde and Van der Heijden, 2006; p. 453) and studied from three perspectives (Nauta, Van Vianen, Van der Heijden, Van Dam and Willemsen 2009):

- Socio-economic perspective: Employability has been considered in relation to socio-economic factors such as culture, gender, ethnicity and disability. The focus in this perspective is often to understand why people from different backgrounds may find it more difficult to progress in their careers. Global boundaries are a current focus in this area, for example, understanding the barriers for international workers with the right skills and abilities finding jobs in Europe and the US (Brown, 2003).

- Individual perspective: Maintaining employability has been the focus of the individual perspectives. Key themes are adaptability to turbulent organizational changes and economies. Employability is a reaction or alternative to job security in this perspective (Forrier and Sels, 2003), and research has looked at some of the ways in which people stay employable, such as pro-active learning across whole careers (Rothwell and Arnold, 2007). That learning seems especially important if it improves self-perceptions of employability. De Vos, De Hauw and Van der Heijden (2011) reported that perceived employability mediated the relationship between competency development and career satisfaction.

- Organizational perspective: Employability has been flagged as beneficial for organizations too (Nauta et al., 2009). This is because employable people in organizations are by definition, multi-skilled and flexible. They are able to move between organizations or between jobs within organizations. Consequently they help organizations to adapt quickly to new demands, and provide versatility because they are able to move between different tasks or jobs within their company.

People differ in the extent to which they are 'employability oriented', so that some are more inclined than others to seek out opportunities to increase employability. An interesting finding is that this orientation can be influenced by fostering a culture of employability in the organization, for example through HR initiatives that promote internal development or mobility, and the promotion of this kind of culture may have important organizational benefits (Nuata et al., 2009). In their study of health and welfare workers in the Netherlands, Nuata et al. reported that development of an employability culture increased employability orientation, but simultaneously reduced turnover intentions. The key factor was a reduction in 'push motives' for turnover (i.e. a desire to leave the company because of dissatisfaction). When people were given more opportunities to develop their employability within the organization, they were more likely to be satisfied with their careers, and less likely to be 'pushed' out.

This finding is also relevant to understanding a practical concern that organizations may have that enhancing employability may increase the likelihood that people will find alternative employment. For example De Cuyper, Van Der Heijden and De Witte (2011) reported a positive association between self-rated employability and turnover intention, so there appears to be some basis for this concern. This association may reflect complex supervisor-subordinate relationships. Supervisors may actually be less likely to promote some workers who they perceive as highly employable, so as to keep them in their own teams (Van Der Heijden, de Lange, Dermerouti and Van der Heijde, 2009), which may lead those individuals to seek alternative employment.

By contrast, Yousaf and Sanders (2012) report a positive association between self-perceived employability and affective commitment, mediated most significantly by job satisfaction. So it appears that enhancing employability of employees can be beneficial for organizations, provided it is against the context of creating an overall positive, satisfying job experience and a climate for competency development and career growth.

Employability is likely to be an increasingly important concept in understanding career development and decision-making, and in particular the differences in people's experiences of careers. Part of the motivation for greater understanding the concept comes from the potential benefits of improving individual employability, which appear wide-ranging. Individuals could progress more easily and swiftly in careers, organizations could become more adaptable, and barriers to global and social mobility could be identified and weakened.

CAREER MANAGEMENT IN ORGANIZATIONS

How do organizations manage the careers of their employees in practice? How might the theories and research outlined in this chapter be applied to the management of careers? There are a number of ways that organizations can help to develop the careers of their employees and likewise, there are things that individuals can do themselves. Not all interventions are equally useful for all people, all of the time. Rather, the theories and models of career development, career interests and work-role transitions lead to the conclusion that different kinds of career management strategies will be more or less relevant for people at different stages of their lives and careers. More than ever, the individual has responsibility for deciding what kind of career management strategy will work best for them, and organizations can help by providing access to suitable activities and interventions. The theories and perspectives in this chapter point to the following broad aims for career management interventions:

- Counselling and advising people so that people better understand their individual differences and the kind of work that would appeal to their traits, skills, abilities and interests.
- Developing new knowledge, skills or abilities through formal learning, practical training or development or on-the-job development.
- Preparing for transition, either into new jobs or positions, or alternatively, out of the organization.
- Facilitating career progression with activities such as networking, or job-seeking skills.

Counselling and Advising

Formal career counselling is the main contributor in this area of career management. Most career counselling is designed to explore a person's current situation, and to allow them to independently work out what might be the most suitable next steps in their career. Like other forms of counselling, career counselling is based on a relationship between the counsellor and the client, which may develop over a number of meetings held regularly over a lengthy period of time. The general stages of career counselling are to first understand the 'now', which is defined by understanding the client's career history to data, and the resources they have available to them (including knowledge, skills, abilities and other characteristics). Preferred career options can be explored using models such as Holland's RIASEC typology, and the individual is then usually tasked with identifying a career goal and working out the action they need to take to achieve that goal.

Traditionally, career counselling has been employed most often at the start of people's careers (i.e. during education), but there is increasingly opportunity for counselling to be applied at various stages of people's careers (Arnold, 1997).

Developing People

If we take on board the implications of the literature on the changing psychological contract, then development would be considered the most useful career management provision from organizations to their employees. Development is empowering to employees in the sense that it allows them to address any self-identified weaknesses or skills gaps. The literature on development is covered in depth in Chapter 7, but a few general strategies are highlighted here:

- Developmental Work Assignments. Work and task assignments designed to allow employees to develop new skills and to experience new areas of responsibility or different parts of the organization.
- Development Centres. A process of assessing employee competencies using the assessment centre method with the purpose of providing detailed feedback about performance and development needs.
- Mentoring. Partnering of an employee with an experienced colleague (usually more senior), who advises and develops them. The aim of mentoring is to provide the employee with an impartial source of support and learning in the organization, who is not his or her line manager.
- Self-directed Development and e-Learning. Many organizations now use online and self-study development materials that allow employees to work at their own pace and at convenient times. The Internet has permitted wider use of self-directed development.

Preparing for Transition

There are a number of interventions that organizations can make to help employees at stages of transition. The transition cycle is useful to remember when considering these interventions. In the preparation stage, the important task for employees is information seeking. A good example of assistance at this stage is the provision of Realistic Job Previews (RJPs; see Chapter 6). The RJP provides an outline or demonstration of the uncensored requirements of the job, and often the organization's values and culture. After selection, the organization can provide an induction process for new employees. This intervention is relevant to the encounter stage in the transition cycle. During this stage, new employees are purported to seek as much information as possible about the job and organization. Induction processes can help them to do this, and provide a formal aspect of socialization that sits alongside the informal learning that new employees acquire from colleagues and other sources.

At some point, employees will leave the organization, either of their own volition, involuntarily in the case of dismissal, or redundancy. In the cases of redundancy and or retirement, organizations can help employees at a potentially difficult stage of their careers by providing outplacement services. Outplacement is designed to support employees consider their options after leaving the organization and with respect to redundancy, to help employees leaving the organization to find new jobs and careers. Outplacement services typically comprise career counselling, and development planning, but might also involve wider counselling for employees suffering stress as a result of job loss, or financial planning and advice. Such services might actually offer little solace to those made redundant, but at least shows the organization to be fulfilling an ethical responsibility.

KEY THEME

Key Theme CSR and Social Mobility

The currency of social mobility as an issue for organizations and society in the UK is illustrated nicely by the publication of the Government's 2009 white paper on the topic (New Opportunities: Fair Chances for the Future). The white paper sets out the central importance of access to jobs as a key indicator and outcome of social mobility. Leaving aside the politics of such initiatives, one must accept the unfairness of social background as a determinant of career success and achievement. The pathway from a privileged background to better jobs and opportunity is easy to trace: a comfortable or wealthy upbringing gives access to more affluent surroundings, better primary or secondary education, leading to better University education, leading to attaining qualifications that are more desirable or appealing for employers, leading to gaining a better job, which fast-tracks the person to a higher status, and probably more money and so the cycle continues. In respect of employment, social mobility is about breaking into jobs or careers that have traditionally been difficult to attain without a particular social background. It is a global issue, with all countries facing the challenge to varying degrees, and with the added complexity that country of birth will also affect access to jobs and careers in globalized companies.

Social mobility is neglected in all of the traditional theories of career development and interests, although research on employability is beginning to address this deficiency. For organizations, there is a role to play in continuing to erode the boundaries of

class and opportunity by actively seeking to encourage people from disadvantaged backgrounds to apply for jobs that initially may appear out of reach. Challenging traditional selection criteria, including educational background, in favour of more objective, competence-based selection could also contribute. However, career management also relies heavily on networking, and so access to influential networks and individuals must also play an important part in an organization's strategy for responsibly encouraging social mobility through employment. These kinds of intervention rely on also broadening the educational aspirations of individuals from disadvantaged backgrounds, and so we come back to politics.

As Work Psychologists, it is important that we understand the social psychology of careers, and contribute to social mobility through career counselling, and ethical recruitment and selection. Career development theory takes on a whole new guise when you start to think about these issues, from a relatively small area of Work Psychology in the research literature, to a force for social change.

What do you think? What practical steps could your organization, or any organization take to help improve social mobility, locally, nationally and globally?

Facilitating progression

A high proportion of new jobs roles never get formally advertised, and instead people are appointed through informal processes or managerial decision-making over task assignment. A key contributing factor in determining whether a person will be considered for new responsibilities is networking. Networking refers to the establishment of social relationships or connections with influential or important people and organizations, within and outside the organization. Effective networking can make the difference for speed of progression within an organization, and a good external network can also act as an information source for a variety of purposes (e.g. new developments in the industry, competitor information, new or forthcoming job roles). Organizations can support networking activities by funding travel and attendance of the employee at visits and meetings at different internal and external sites, as well as at professional events such as conferences.

A further set of skills that are very helpful in career development are job-seeking skills. It can be useful for mentors or managers to help those seeking promotion, or indeed jobs elsewhere, to develop skills in the preparation of CVs, or performing well at interview or other selection assessments. These skills will help facilitate career development, and are particularly welcomed by employees in contemporary careers where job moves are frequent. A concern of some is the extent to which such activities introduce bias into selection processes. My belief is that they do not. Many selection processes are built on the assumption that a person will perform at their best, or give a fair and accurate picture of their skills and capabilities. A surprising number or people find it difficult to do this, and so effectively under-sell their skills and abilities. Development of job-seeking skills may actually helps selectors to make sound decisions by helping candidates communicate their strengths more clearly.

SUMMARY

M odern and contemporary stories of peoples working lives are different in important ways from those told in the past. Although changes to the psychological contracts between people and their employers are sometimes overestimated, there are nevertheless important shifts in people's expectations about their careers.

Careers have been studied in Work Psychology from a number of perspectives. One set of theories has examined how careers develop across the lifespan. Such theories collectively highlight traditional stages of development, and the challenges that people face at different stages of their lives. One of the most important decisions that people make in early adulthood is the kind of occupation in which they would like to work. Understanding why different people choose particular occupations is a central concern of Holland's theory of vocational personality types and environments. His theory suggests that work interests and environments can be described on the same six dimensions, and that people gravitate to environments that appeal to their interests. The process of choosing an occupation, specializing, establishing and maintaining one's career also has developmental implications, with emergent literature suggesting a reciprocal effect of work and careers on personality traits.

Work Psychology has also considered some of the social, cultural and organizational influences on careers. Gender continues to be an important influence, and for women, it seems, a barrier to career development in all parts of the world. Culture also affects careers on many levels, including career development, and judgements about what constitutes career success. By attending to such issues, career stories can be seen as important reflections of social history and change.

Recent perspectives on careers have examined the changing nature of career progression, with some suggesting that careers are now more boundaryless than ever. However, the concept of employability mitigates this view and helps to explain why boundaries and barriers are experienced by some, but not others.

All of these perspectives have the potential to inform career management interventions in organizations, which take the form of counselling and advising, developing people, preparing people for change, and facilitating progression within and beyond the organization.

There is such a thing as a formula for a good story, and when you take the ideas introduced in this chapter together, it seems that there are similarly familiar formulae for the various sections of career stories. Theory helps us to make sense of, among other things, career choices and career development. Does that make the writing and telling of career stories predicable or less interesting? I do not think so – rather it enables Work Psychologists to help people with plot development, or to help organizations be better, more vibrant settings for career stories – in short, applying knowledge and understanding of the career stories of others, to help those who are perturbed or confused about how to write their own.

DISCUSSION QUESTIONS

1   What could an organization do to manage issues of gender and culture in career development strategies?

2   Why don't people always choose a career that matches their interests?

3   Are careers really boundaryless in the 21st century?

4   What are the 'terms' on your psychological contract? What do you expect from an employer?

5   Suggest five ways that an organization could improve employability of staff.

6   Use the transition cycle to describe your experiences of job change, or of starting at your university. Discuss your experiences in a group.

APPLY IT

1   The literature on employability suggests that we have more responsibility than ever for developing our own careers. So undertake a self-reflection exercise on you own. Write down your own career history and try to make sense of it from the perspective of the content of this chapter. Consider where you want your career to take you in the next three years. What skills or competencies might you need to develop to enhance your employability?

2   Undertake career review meetings with your team to better understand their career aspirations. Build the information into their development and work planning.

3   Use the transition cycle to put together an induction process for new colleagues in your team. Think about activities that you can organize to help with Preparation, Encounter, Adjustment and Stabilization.

4   Become a mentor for a less experienced colleague and help them to develop their career. Bring them into networks you have and hold regular meetings to discuss their development. If you have scope in your job, introduce this more formally as a process of development in your team.

WEB ACTIVITIES

Women in Science

Read the article and watch the video '100 Women: Why are there so few female scientists?' on **www.bbc. co.uk** or by following the link in the digital resources online and discuss the questions below.

1   How can Holland's theory of vocational personality types and environments be used to explain the lack of women in science?

2   How can other social factors explain the few women in science roles?

A Life of Work

Obituaries tell you the stories of exceptional working lives – select one or two and explore them in the context of the theories in this chapter. Access them using the link below or by following the link in the digital resources online

http://www.telegraph.co.uk/news/obituaries/

FURTHER READING

Arnold, J. (1997). Managing careers into the 21st century. London, UK: Sage.

Brown, D. (2002). *Career Choice and Development.* San Francisco: Jossey-Bass.

Holland, J.L. (1996). Exploring careers with a typology: What we have learned and some new directions. *American Psychologist, 51,* 397–406.

Conway, N. and Briner, R. (2005). *Understanding psychological contracts at work: A critical evaluation of theory and research.* Oxford: Oxford University Press.

Inkson, K. (2008). The boundaryless career. In S. Cartwright and C.L. Cooper (eds.) *The Oxford Handbook of Personnel Psychology.* (pp. 545–563). Oxford: OUP.

REFERENCES

Ackerman, P.L. and Heggestad, E.D. (1997). Intelligence, personality and interests: Evidence for overlapping traits. *Psychological Bulletin, 121,* 219–245.

Argyris, C. (1960). *Understanding organizational behaviour.* Homewood, IL: Dorsey Press.

Armstrong, P.I., Allison, W. and Rounds, J. (2008). Development and initial validation of brief public domain RIASEC marker scales. *Journal of Vocational Behaviour, 73(2),* 287–299.

Armstrong, P.I., Hubert, L. and Rounds, J. (2003). Circular unidimensional scaling: A new look at group differences in interest structure. *Journal of Counselling Psychology, 50,* 297–308.

Arnold, J. (1997). Managing careers into the 21st century. London, UK: Sage.

Arnold, J. (2004). The congruence problem in John Holland's theory of vocational decisions. *Journal of Occupational and Organizational Psychology, 77(1),* 95–113.

Arthur, M.B. and Rousseau, D.M. (1996). *The boundaryless career: A new employment principle for a new organizational era.* New York: Oxford University Press.

Ashforth, B.E., Sluss, D.M. and Saks, A.M. (2007). Socialization tactics, proactive behaviour and newcomer learning: Integrating socialization models. *Journal of Vocational Behaviour, 70(3),* 447–462.

Assouline, M. and Meir, E.I. (1987). Meta-Analysis of the Relationship between Congruence and Well-Being Measures. *Journal of Vocational Behaviour, 31(3),* 319–332.

Barrick, M.R., Mount, M.K. and Gupta, R. (2003). Meta-analysis of the relationship between the five factor model of personality and Holland's occupational types. *Personnel Psychology, 56,* 45–74.

Betz, N.E., Borgen, F.H. and Harmon, L.W. (2006). Vocational confidence and personality in the prediction of occupational group membership. *Journal of Career Assessment, 14,* 36–55.

Brown, P. (2003). The opportunity trap: Education and employment in a global economy. *European Educational Research Journal, 2,* 142–180.

Darcy, M.U.A. and Tracey, T.J.G. (2007). Circumplex structure of Holland's RIASEC interests across gender and time. *Journal of Counselling Psychology, 54,* 17–31.

Davey, F.H. (2001). The relationship between engineering and your women's occupational priorities. *Canadian Journal of Counselling, 35,* 221–228.

De Cuyper, N., Van der Heijden, B.I. and De Witte, H. (2011). Associations between perceived employability, employee well-being, and its contribution to organizational success: a matter of psychological contracts? *The international journal of human resource management, 22(07),* 1486–1503.

De Vos, A., De Hauw, S. and Van der Heijden, B.I. (2011). Competency development and career success: The mediating role of employability. *Journal of vocational behavior, 79(2),* 438–447.

Direnzo, M.S. and Greenhaus, J.H. (2011). Job search and voluntary turnover in a boundaryless world: A control theory perspective. *Academy of Management Review, 36(3),* 567–589.

Donnay, D.A.C. and Borgen, F.H. (1996). Validity, structure and content of the 1994 Strong Interest Inventory. *Journal of Counselling Psychology, 43,* 275–291.

Ekerdt, D.J. (1987). Why the notion persists that retirement harms health. *The Gerentologist, 27,* 454–457.

Ekerdt, D.J., Baden, L., Bossé, R. and Dibbs, E. (1983). The effect of retirement on physical health. *American Journal of Public Health, 73(7),* 779–783.

Farmer, H.S., Wardrop, J.L, Anderson, M.Z. and Risinger, R. (1995). Women's career choices: focus on science, math and technology careers. *Journal of Counseling Psychology, 42,* 155–170.

Forrier, A. and Sels, L. (2003). The concept employ-ability: A complex mosaic. *International Journal of Human Resources Development and Management*, 3, 102–124.

Fouad, N.A. (1999). Validity evidence for interest inventories. In M.L. Savickas and R.L. Spokane (eds.), *Vocational Interests: Meaning, Measurement and Counselling Use* (pp. 193–209). Palo Alto, CA: Davies-Black.

Fouad, N.A. (2007). Work and vocational psychology: Theory, research and applications. *Annual Review of Psychology*, 58, 543–564.

Gabarro, J.J. (1987). *The dynamics of taking charge*. US: Harvard Business School Press.

Gottfredson, L.S. (1981). Circumscription and compromise: A developmental theory of occupational aspirations. *Journal of Counselling Psychology Monograph*, 28, 545–579.

Gouldner, A. (1957). Cosmopolitans and locals: Toward an analysis of latent social roles, part I. *Administrative Science Quarterly*, 2, 281–305.

Guest, D.E. (1998). Is that psychological contract worth taking seriously? *Journal of Organizational Behaviour*, 19, 649–664.

Guest, D.E., Conway, N. (2002). Communicating the psychological contract: An employer perspective, *Human Resource Management Journal*, 12(2), 22–38.

Hall, D.T. (2002). *Careers in and out of organizations*. Thousand Oaks, CA: Sage Publications.

Hansen, J.C. and Dik, B.J. (2005). Evidence of 12-year predictive and concurrent validity for SII Occupational Scale scores. *Journal of Vocational Behaviour*, 67, 365–378.

Harmon, L.W., Hansen, J.C., Borgen, F.H. and Hammer, A.L. (1994). *Strong Interest Inventory Applications and Technical Guide*. Palo Alto, CA: Consulting Psychologists Press.

Hausmann, R. (2012). The Global Gender Gap Index 2012. *El Fórum Económico Mundial*.

Herriot, P. and Pemberton, C. (1995). *New deals: The revolution in managerial careers*. Chichester, New York: John Wiley and Sons.

Herzog, A.R., House, J.S. and Morgan, J.N. (1991). Relation of work and retirement to health and well-being in older age. *Psychology and Ageing*, 6, 202–211.

Hofstede, G. (1980). *Cultures and Organizations: Softwares of the Mind*. Newbury Park, CA: Sage.

Holland, J.L. (1973). *Making vocational choices: A theory of vocational personalities and work environments*. Odessa, FL: Psychological Assessment Resources.

Holland, J.L. (1994). *Self-Directed Search: Assessment booklet, a guide to educational and career planning*. Odessa, FL: Psychological Assessment Resources.

Inkson, K. (2008). The boundaryless career. In S. Cartwright and L. Cooper (Eds.), *The Oxford Handbook of Personnel Psychology* (pp. 545–585). Oxford: OUP.

Jome, L.M. and Tokar, D.M. (1998). Dimensions of masculinity and major choice traditionality. *Journal of Vocational Behaviour*, 52, 120–134.

Judge, T.A., Higgins, C.A., Thoresen, C.J. and Barrick, M.R. (1999). The Big Five personality traits, general mental ability and career success across the life span. *Personnel Psychology*, 52, 621–652.

Kidd, J.M. (2002). Careers and Career Management. In P. Warr (Ed.), *Psychology at Work* (pp.178–202). London: Penguin.

Kim, S. and Feldman, D.C. (2000). Working in Retirement: The Antecedents of Bridge Employment and Its Consequences for Quality of Life in Retirement. *Academy of Management Journal*, 43(6), 1195–1210.

Larson, L.M., Rottinghaus, P.J. and Borgen, F.H. (2002). Meta-analyses of Big Six interests and Big Five personality factors. *Journal of Vocational Behavior*, 61, 217–239.

Derr, C.B. and Laurent, A. (1989) The internal and external career: a theoretical and cross-cultural perspective. In The Handbook of Career Theory, eds Arthur, M., Laurence, B.S. and Hall, D.T., pp. 454–471. Cambridge University Press, New York.

Lent, R.W., Brown, S.D. and Hackett, G. (1994). Toward a unifying social cognitive theory of career and academic interest, choice and performance. *Journal of Vocational Behaviour*, 45, 79–122.

Levinson, D.J. (1978). *The season's of a man's life*. New York: Knopf.

Levinson, D.J. and Levinson, J.D. (1996). *The season's of a woman's life*. New York: Ballantine.

Midanik, L.T., Soghikian, K., Ransom, L.J. and Tekawa, I.S. (1995). The Effect of Retirement on Mental Health and Health Behaviours: The Kaiser Permanente Retirement Study. *The Journals of Gerontology Series B: Psychological Sciences and Social Sciences*, 50B(1), S59–S61.

Miller, L. and Budd, J. (1999). The development of occupational sex-role stereotypes, occupational preferences and academic subject preferences in children at ages 8, 12 and 16. *Educational Psychology*, 19, 17–35.

Nauta, A., Van Vianen, A., Van der Heijden, B., Van Dam, K. and Willemsen, M. (2009). Understanding the factors that promote employability orientation: The impact of employability culture, career satisfaction and role breadth self-efficacy. *Journal of Occupational and Organizational Psychology, 82,* 233–251.

Nicholson, N. (1990). *On the move: the psychology of change and transition.* Chichester: John Wiley and Sons Ltd.

Nicholson, N. and Arnold, J. (1991). From Expectation to Experience: Graduates Entering a Large Corporation. *Journal of Organizational Behaviour, 12(5),* 413–429.

Nicholson, N. and West, M.A. (1988). *Managerial job change: men and women in transition.* Cambridge: Cambridge University Press.

O*NET Resource Center (2003). *The O*NET analyzt database.* O*NET Consortium. Available: http://www.onetcenter.org/database.html#archive.

Prediger, D.J. (1982). Dimensions underlying Holland's hexagon: Missing link between interests and occupations? *Journal of Vocational Behaviour, 21,* 259–287.

Roberts, B.W., Caspi, A. and Moffitt, T.E. (2003). Work experiences and personality development in young adulthood. *Journal of personality and social psychology, 84(3),* 582.

Robinson, S.L. and Rousseau, D.M. (1994). Breaching the psychological contract: Not the exception but the norm. *Journal of Organizational Behaviour, 15,* 245–259.

Rothwell, A. and Arnold, J. (2007). Self-perceived employability: Development and validation of a scale. *Personnel Review, 36,* 23–41.

Ryan, M.K. and Haslam, S.A. (2005). The glass cliff: Evidence that women are over-represented in precarious leadership positions. *British Journal of Management, 16(2),* 81–90.

Ryan, M.K., Haslam, S.A., Hersby, M.D. and Bongiorno, R. (2011). Think crisis–think female: The glass cliff and contextual variation in the think manager–think male stereotype. *Journal of Applied Psychology, 96(3),* 470.

Samnani, A.K., Boekhorst, J.A. and Harrison, J.A. (2013). The acculturation process: Antecedents, strategies, and outcomes. *Journal of Occupational and Organizational Psychology, 86(2),* 166–183.

Savickas, M.L. (2002). Career construction: A developmental theory of vocational behaviour. In D. Brown and Associates (eds.), *Career choice and development* (4th ed., pp. 149–205). San Francisco, CA: Jossey-Bass.

Savickas, M.L. (2005). The theory and practice of career construction. In S.D. Brown and R.W. Lent. (eds.), *Career Development and Counselling:*

putting theory and research to work (pp. 42–69). New Jersey, USA: John Wiley and Sons.

Schein, E.H. (1971). The Individual, the Organization and the Career: A Conceptual Scheme. *The Journal of Applied Behavioral Science, 7(4),* 401–426.

Schein, E.H. (1984). Culture as an Environmental Context for Careers. *Journal of Occupational Behaviour, 5(1),* 71–81.

Schein, E.H. (1993). *Career anchors: Discovering your real values.* San Diego: Pfeiffer and Company.

Schein, V.E. (1973). The relationship between sex role stereotypes and requisite management characteristics. *Journal of Applied Psychology, 57(2),* 95.

Sparrow, P.R. (1996). The changing nature of psychological contracts in the U.K. banking sector: Does it matter? *Human Resource Management Journal, 6(4),* 75–92.

Spokane, A.R., Meir, E.I. and Catalano, M. (2000). Person–Environment Congruence and Holland's Theory: A Review and Reconsideration. *Journal of Vocational Behaviour, 57(2),* 137–187.

Super, D.E. and Hall, D.T. (1978). Career development: Exploration and planning. *Annual Review of Psychology, 29,* 333–372.

Tracey, T.J. and Rounds, J.B. (1993). Evaluating Holland's and Gati's vocational-interest models: A structural meta-analysis. *Psychological Bulletin, 113(2),* 229–246.

Tranberg, M., Slane, S. and Ekeberg, E. (1993). The relation between interest congruence and satisfaction: A meta-analysis. *Journal of Vocational Behaviour, 42,* 253–264.

US Department of Labor. (1991). *Dictionary of occupational titles* (Rev. 4th ed.). Washington DC: US Government Printing Office.

Van der Heijde, C.M. and Van der Heijden, B.I.J.M. (2006). A competence-based and multidimensional operationalization and measurement of employability. *Human Resource Management, 45,* 449–476.

Van der Heijden, B.I., de Lange, A.H., Demerouti, E. and Van der Heijde, C.M. (2009). Age effects on the employability–career success relationship. *Journal of Vocational Behavior, 74(2),* 156–164.

Warr, P. (2008). *Work, Happiness and Unhappiness.* NJ: LEA.

Warr, P., Butcher, V., Robertson, I. and Callinan, M. (2004). Older people's well-being as a function of employment, retirement, environmental characteristics and role preference. *British Journal of Psychology, 95,* 297–324.

Wong, A.L. and Slater, J.R. (2002). Executive development in China: Is there any in a Western sense? *International Journal of Human Resource Management, 13(2),* 338–360.

Woods, S.A., Lievens, F., De Fruyt, F. and Wille, B. (2013). Personality across working life: The longitudinal and reciprocal influences of personality on work. *Journal of Organizational Behavior*.

Woods, S.A. and Hampson, S.E. (2010). Predicting adult occupational environments from gender and childhood personality traits. *Journal of applied psychology*, *95(6)*, 1045.

Woods, S.A., Koczwara, A. and Patterson, F. (2013). Personality and Occupational Specialty: An Examination of the Big Five and Medical Specialty Choice. *Proceedings of the Division of Occupational Psychology Conference*, 2013, Chester; UK.

Yousaf, A. and Sanders, K. (2012). The Role of Job Satisfaction and Self-Efficacy as Mediating Mechanisms in the Employability and Affective Organizational Commitment Relationship: A Case From a Pakistani University. *Thunderbird International Business Review*, *54(6)*, 907–919.

CHAPTER 10

SAFETY, STRESS AND HEALTH AT WORK

LEARNING OBJECTIVES

⬗ Understand the concepts of occupational health and safety.

⬗ Identify the key causes of accidents at work and how to reduce them.

⬗ Define the concepts of stress and engagement at work.

⬗ Identify the key causes of stress and engagement.

⬗ Understand how to reduce stress and increase engagement at work.

⬗ Understand how health is affected by work factors.

⬗ Identify the ways in which health can be protected and promoted at work.

POSITIVE EMOTION AT WORK

Research evidence now shows convincingly how important positive emotions, such as hope, pleasure, happiness, humour, excitement, joy, pride and involvement are as a source of human strength (Fredrickson, 2009; Lyubomirsky, King and Diener, 2005). When we feel positive emotions we think in a more flexible, open-minded way and consider a much wider range of possibilities than if we feel anxious, depressed or angry. This enables us to accomplish tasks and make the most of the situations we find ourselves in. We are also more likely to see challenges as opportunities rather than threats. When we feel positive, we exercise greater self-control, cope more effectively and are less likely to react defensively in workplace situations. The litany of benefits doesn't stop there. It spills over, too, into what is called 'pro-social behaviour' – cooperation and altruism. When we feel positive emotion we are more likely to be helpful, generous and to exercise a sense of social responsibility.

The idea that we can create effective organizations by focusing simply on performance and ignoring the role of our emotions is based on the false premise that emotions can be ignored at work. Positive relationships and a sense of community are the product and cause of positive emotions. We must work with human needs and capacities and potentials rather than against if we are to create positive organizations that succeed and, at the same time, that foster the health and well-being of those who work within them (Goleman *et al.*, 2002; Layard, 2005). Where there is a generally positive feeling in an organization, it is likely that creativity, cooperation and citizenship are typical, creating a powerful cocktail of factors we know predict organizational performance.

Not surprisingly, the opposite of much of this is depressingly true too. Chronic anxiety and chronic hostility/anger lead to ill health, failure to recover from illness and a generally depressed immune system. Pessimism, anger, anxiety, cynicism and apathy are corrosive in organizations, not just to organizational performance but also to the health and the well-being of the people who work within them. In this chapter we consider some of the dark sides of organizations and how they create tension, anger and fear for some employees and what the consequences of that are for employees. And we examine how the health and safety of people at work can be understood and protected. We begin by examining the topic of health and safety at work.

OCCUPATIONAL HEALTH AND SAFETY

The World Health Organization estimates that there are 270 million occupational health injuries worldwide and 354753 fatalities (Takala, 2002). Canada estimates the cost of such injuries at $6000 per injury and $492000 per fatality. In the UK, there are an estimated 596000 people injured at work each year with a corresponding annual cost in billions of pounds (Health and Safety Executive, 2013). The number of injuries at work has dropped by 40 per cent over the last decade in the UK as a result of legislation and better health and safety policies. Nevertheless, the human costs in pain, misery or bereavement are still enormous. What can Work Psychology offer to help us understand how to prevent injury and illness? First we need to understand the phenomena we are faced with

> Occupational injury *represents a wound or damage to the body resulting from unintentional or intentional acute exposure to energy (kinetic, chemical, thermal, electrical and radiation) or from the acute absence of essential elements (e.g. heat, oxygen) caused by a specific event, incident or series of events within a single workday or shift (Bureau of Labour Statistics, 2013). An occupational injury can be fatal or non-fatal.*
>
> Occupational illness *represents any abnormal condition or disorder, other than one resulting from an occupational injury, caused by exposure to factors associated with employment. It includes acute and chronic illnesses or diseases that may be caused by inhalation, absorption, ingestion or direct contact. There are seven categories: occupational skin diseases, dust diseases of the lungs, respiratory conditions due to toxic agents, poisoning due to the systematic effects of toxic agents, disorders due to physical agents other than toxic materials (welding flash, sunstroke), disorders associated with repeated trauma (carpal tunnel syndrome, noise induced hearing loss) and all other occupational illnesses (adapted from Bureau of Labour Statistics, 2013).*

What protects people from such occupational injuries and illness? 'Safety climate' is considered a key factor (Neal and Griffin, 2004). This refers to employees' perceptions of the policies, practices and procedures relating to safety (Zohar, 2003). It is highly influenced by what managers and leaders say and do in terms of making safety a priority. Zohar (1980) proposed that safety climate had eight dimensions of employee perceptions: importance of safety training; management attitudes towards safety; effects of safe behaviours on promotion; level of risk in the workplace; effects of work pace on safety; status of safety officer; effects of safe behaviour on social status; status of the safety committee. Neal and Griffin have proposed a model for the relationship between safety climate and other factors in understanding how they affect occupational health and safety. It includes organizational factors such as supervision (supervisors with a strong concern about safety will produce safer environments) and work design; individual differences such as conscientiousness; safety knowledge and motivation (likely to be affected by training); and safety performance.

Turner and Parker (2004) have shown, in a review of the literature (particularly research on cockpit crews in aircraft) that teams can have a very positive effect on safety in organizations since they provide a medium within which employees can influence decision-making. This is consistent with work in the UK National Health Service, suggesting that good teamworking is associated with fewer errors and injuries reported by staff (West and Lyubovnikova, 2013). Individual factors also affect occupational health and safety such as anxiety and negative affect. Dunbar (1993) found that depression, anxiety and negative affect were associated with lower use of protective equipment. Probst and Brubaker (2001) proposed that job insecurity was also likely to be associated with workplace accidents and injuries because it affected job satisfaction, which, in turn, influences workplace safety behaviours. These findings extend to casual or contingent work. Quinlan and Bohle (2004) report consistent evidence that temporary work is associated with poor health outcomes. Quinlan, Mayhew and Bohle (2001) reviewed 82 studies across 14 EU countries and Australia, and found that in 76 of them, compared with full-time work, contingent work had worse occupational health and safety outcomes in terms of injury rates and strain. Benavides, Benach, Diez-Roux and Roman (2000) found that, across Europe, fatigue, backache and muscular pain were more prevalent amongst those with precarious employment.

Age is another important factor in considering occupational health and safety. Loughlin and Frone (2004) report that non-fatal injuries at work are highest amongst young workers, especially males, in the 15–24 years age group. This is particularly important since young workers are not typically concentrated in dangerous industries such as mining, construction and petrochemicals. They are more likely to work in restaurants and groceries, yet typical injuries include lacerations, sprains, bruising, burns and fractures. Why? Some researchers suggest this is because those in this age group are more likely to have perceptions of invulnerability, to be sensation seeking, rebellious and to experience negative affect (disappointment at the quality of the work they are required to do). They may also be more likely to abuse alcohol or other substances at work, making it more likely they will be injured (Frone, 1998). Moreover, young workers have less control in the workplace and are less likely to have union representation, so these protection factors are absent.

Occupational health psychology (OHP) aims to improve quality of work life by promoting the health, safety and well-being of workers by applying psychology and by developing evidence-based knowledge. OHP researchers and practitioners focus on psychosocial work characteristics that affect physical and mental health problems. The physical health problems range from accidental injury to cardiovascular disease. The mental health problems include psychological distress, burnout and depression. Two of the leading international OHP organizations are the Society for Occupational Health Psychology (**http://sohp.psy.uconn.edu/**) and the European Academy of Occupational Health Psychology (**http://eaohp.org**). Key journals related to this field are the *Journal of Occupational Health Psychology* and *Work and Stress*.

KEY THEME

Corporate Social Responsibility and Ethics

It is the responsibility of employers to protect the health and ensure the safety of employees at work. This is a key corporate social responsibility but is taken seriously to varying degrees across organizations and across nations. To what extent can HRM and other workplace practices promote health and safety in organizations? Zacharatos and Barling (2004) propose ten HRM practices that will influence workplace safety positively:

1 Employment security – since this encourages a long-term perspective, promoting trust and organizational commitment as well as building experience with safety procedures.

2 Selective hiring – to exclude accident-prone individuals based on drug addiction, alcoholism, emotional maturity and trustworthiness.

3 Extensive training – employees who have workplace safety training have fewer injuries (Colligan and Cohen, 2004).

4 Self-managed teams and decentralized decision-making – a number of studies have

demonstrated higher levels of safety behaviour in teams. One example (Tjosvold, 1990 study) found that flight crews which worked as teams when facing dangerous situations were more effective than those which operated as a hierarchy.

5 Reduce status distinctions – where status distinctions are strong, expressed concerns about workplace safety are likely to be given weight only if the individual is of high status. Milanovich et al., (1998) found that this was indeed the case among airline cockpit crews.

6 Share information – companies where there is more contact and information sharing between managers, and front line employees have fewer accidents.

7 Compensation contingent on safe performance – high pay communicates that the employee is valued. 'If you're getting paid a wage that you're happy with, then you're happy at your work, so you're switched on and alert. You don't mind doing your bit'. (North Sea oil worker, Collinson, 1999, p. 591). And specifically rewarding all workers for group level safety behaviour (lower rates of accidents across the whole organization) is likely to convey a message about the importance that managers and leaders place on safety (Fox, Hopkins and Anger, 1987).

8 Transformational leadership – will be effective in communicating to employees the importance of safety and inspiring them to work safely, a prediction supported among workers in the offshore oil and gas industry (O'Dea and Flin, 2000).

9 High-quality work – high workload can lead to high levels of injury and errors at work (Hofmann and Stetzer, 1996), but so too can work underload among adolescents (Frone, 1998). High job autonomy leads to safety at work (Parker, Axtell and Turner, 2001), along with work role clarity (Houston and Allt, 1997).

10 Measurement of variables critical to organizational success – these include employee attitudes to safety, organizational commitment, job satisfaction, trust in management, initiative taking in respect to safety and participation in safety processes and structures (such as health and safety committees); employment security; safety training experience; job quality; and the extent to which employees work in teams.

Overall, Work Psychologists and occupational health psychologists have made considerable advances in understanding the factors that influence occupational health and safety and it is an area where we have much to offer. In particular, creating climates focused on safety, especially in work environments that pose particular hazards. But what about less visible forms of damage to people at work? If injuries and visible workplace illness are the visible part of the iceberg, many Work Psychologists argue that stress and strain at work are the invisible damage that is done, invisibly beneath the surface.

STRESS AND STRAIN AT WORK

Although it is difficult to estimate the overall cost of work-related stress, many studies report that it has enormous impact in terms of both economic costs and human suffering. For example, survey research estimated that about half a million people in the UK believed they were suffering from work-related stress, depression or anxiety (Jones *et al.*, 2003) and that 14 million working days are lost in the UK due to workplace stress, depression and anxiety each year. The Health and Safety Executive estimates that the financial cost of work-related stress to employers was £531 million and to society nearly £4 billion per year. The total number of cases of stress in 2011/12 was 428 000 (40 per cent) out of a total of 1 073 000 for all work-related illnesses. There has been virtually no decline in either total or new cases of work-related stress in the UK over the past decade. The sectors with highest incidence are human health and social work, education and public administration, and defence. In particular nurses, teachers and welfare and housing professionals are most likely to suffer from work-related stress. The main causes of stress they report are work pressure, lack of managerial support and work-related violence and bullying.

The costs of stress stem not only from absenteeism and lost productivity, but also from compensation claims, health insurance and medical expenses. In the US, annual stress insurance claims in the California workers' compensation system have been estimated to be approximately $383 million (Beehr, 1995).

A study of employee health and well-being in the UK (Boorman, 2009) shows that, on average, National Health Service staff (of whom there are 1.4 million) lose 10.7 days through sickness absence each year (compared with 9.7 in the public sector as a whole and 6.4 in the private sector). Reducing sickness absence by one third (which is a realistic target given examples in other organizations) would save 3.4 million working days, equivalent to 14 900 additional full-time staff. The cost saving would be £555 million. Moreover, the report showed significant associations between staff health and well-being and other outcomes such as patient satisfaction and even infection rates in hospitals. Factors contributing to the high levels of stress in the NHS workforce included staff shortages and a lack of investment in skilled staff; inadequate resourcing; inconsistent and inadequate occupational health services; failure of top management to promote staff health and well-being ; failure to use information on the extent, and costs, of poor health and well-being in organizations; cultural barriers to investing money in services for staff; lack of consistent line management support to enable staff to benefit from health and well-being programmes.

What is work stress? When our ancestors were trying to survive in a hostile natural world 80 000 years ago, the challenges were probably enormous dangers from wild animals, or other humans, not to mention natural phenomena that were not fully understood (extreme weather or geological events), which must have made things a little tense. Today, sitting in an office, discussing the development of organizational strategy in the context of economic downturns does not have quite the same bite. Yet stress at work is a regular topic of conversation amongst those studying people at work. For some occupations it is easy to see why we might want to invoke this concept of 'stress'. The job of a soldier in Afghanistan is undoubtedly at times frightening, boring, dirty and lonely. Ambulance workers in inner cities face the threat of violence from people whose inhibitions have been lowered by alcohol. The call centre worker, with a large number of phone calls to deal with, some of which involve complaining customers crossing the line into personal abuse, might go home at the end of the day tense and angry. The social worker, who is anxious about a family she thinks may be abusing or neglecting a young child may lose sleep picturing herself in court over a failure to intervene. So is stress modern-day, self-indulgent angst or a serious issue that needs tackling if we are to create positive work environments?

What is Stress – Cause, Process or Outcome?

We can think of stress in a number of ways – as a cause of bad feelings (the abusive customer is a stressor); as a process – the means by which work pressures results in loss of sleep; or as an outcome – elevated blood pressure and absenteeism. The lack of consistency about how this term is used is one cause of controversy typical of this area of research (Briner, Harris and Daniels, 2004). A brief history of the concept will help us answer the questions we pose in this chapter.

The first model of stress was the 'Fight or Flight' model, proposed by Cannon (an animal physiologist) in 1929. He labelled as 'the fight or flight reaction' humans' physiological and psychological response to acute episodic stress. When our ancient ancestor was confronted by a predator, his body instantly reacted to prepare him to do battle or fly with all the speed his legs would give him. If you are crossing the street and a bus you had not noticed is suddenly upon you with the driver blasting his horn, you jump and run immediately to safety. You notice how fast your heart is beating and how quickly you are breathing. This is not simply a result of your leap to safety but a consequence of your bodily processes coordinating to prepare you for immediate and dynamic action – your heart rate speeds up to pump blood to your muscles immediately. Consider another modern-day situation where you become involved in an argument with a colleague in a meeting about a report you failed to produce on time. Once again, you feel your face flushing and your heart rate speeding up, though you are not preparing to run away at all speed or beat him senseless with a club. However, your body is giving you the capacity to do both these things. The problem with this reaction is that it takes the body some time to return to a resting baseline and the more frequently fight or flight reactions are produced the less time the body is at rest. In a worst case scenario, the failure to return to a state of relaxation leads to the basal level of arousal being permanently raised with associated negative consequences such as high blood pressure and coronary heart disease.

Hans Selye (1956), a Canadian endocrinologist, used the term 'stress' to describe a non-specific response of the body to any demand made on it. He distinguished between distress (harmful effects of demands) and 'eustress' (the enjoyment of challenging demands). Distress would be caused by conflicts with colleagues at work whereas eustress could occur in the process of running a very dynamic and exciting workshop with 20 senior managers developing ideas for new products for the future – demanding yes, but also exhilarating, exciting and offering a feeling of great accomplishment.

In developing his ideas, Selye went on to propose the 'General Adaptation Syndrome' (GAS) as a model for understanding how sustained stressors affect health. He described three stages: alarm, resistance and exhaustion.

In the first stage, the body produces an alarm reaction (for example in response to repeatedly dealing with angry callers on the telephone) and secretes stress hormones – adrenalin, noradrenalin, epinephrine and cortisol, that all serve to raise the level of arousal. The individual tries to adapt by coping with the stressors during the resistance stage and may well do so – there is sustained psycho-physiological arousal at a lower level of intensity than the alarm stage. However, resources are being used up and this impairs the ability to deal with other stressors. Managing angry customers is about within her abilities, but having to deal with demanding colleagues may be beyond her resources. Finally is the stage of exhaustion in response to sustained exposure to stressors. Over time, resistance generally decreases resulting in the person feeling burned out, becoming ill or, in the extreme, dying (for example from a heart attack). The GAS model describes longer-lasting chronic stress e.g. a sustained high level of workload, compared with the acute stress described in the fight or flight model.

In the last 20 years, models of stress at work have offered a more sophisticated representation of the phenomenon. For example Kahn and Byoserie (1992) presented a model of work stressors, moderators, perceptions and cognitions and the consequences or strains (see Figure 10.1) that reveal the processes by which work stressors affect individuals. It helpfully distinguishes between the causes (stressors) and the outcomes (strain) while identifying the processes that mediate or moderate the relationship between stressors and strain. The figure describes:

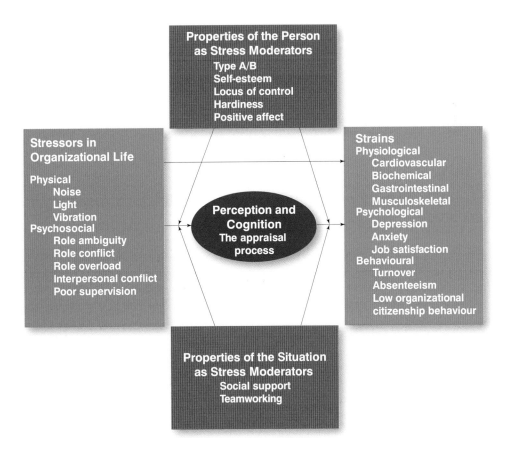

Figure 10.1   Theoretical framework for the study of stress in organizations

- Work stressors such as interpersonal conflict at work or poor supervision (over-controlling, bullying or neglecting). Work stressors subsume both task and role stressors. The task of an ambulance worker involves dealing with road accidents which are likely to be highly stressful. Roles may be ambiguous where it is not quite clear always what one is expected to do or how one's performance might be assessed as in the case of a social worker dealing with the needs of a family in poverty. Workload can be a role stressor. Air traffic controllers at a busy airport are often dealing with several planes and scheduling safe landings over a long period of time. A major study of stress in over 11 000 employees in 19 health care organizations in the UK National Health Service (NHS) (Wall *et al.*, 1997) suggested that high workload was the major cause of stress amongst these health-care workers. The research also revealed that 26.8 per cent of NHS workers had indications of minor psychiatric disorder (stress) compared with 17.8 per cent of people in the general population.

- Moderators. These are factors that can reduce or increase the effects of stressors upon outcomes. These moderators of the stress process could include teamworking (good teamworking will reduce the impact of stressors), social support (having supportive family, friends or colleagues buffers people from the effects of stressors), and recovery activities (participating in engaging activities such as sports, cooking and gardening as opposed to passive activities such as TV watching, helps people recover from stress and fatigue (Sonnentag *et al.*, 2010), and individual differences – warm, positive, optimistic people are less likely to be affected by stressors than anxious people (Seligman, 2002).

- Perception and Cognition. How we see, think about and interpret the world also affects the stressor – strain relationship. What to one person might seem a threat (giving a public talk) might be interpreted by another as an exciting challenge. How we appraise the world – our perceptions and cognitions, therefore, affect whether stressors translate into strain or not. The appraisal process is vital in determining whether stress is damaging to our functioning (Lazarus, 1991).

BOX 10.1

What is the frequency of high work stress? The Bristol Stress and Health at Work study

Smith *et al.* (2000a; 2000b) conducted the Bristol Stress and Health at Work study with three main aims: first, to determine the scale of perceived work stress in a random sample; second, to differentiate work stress and general life stress; and third, to determine whether objective measures of health and performance were related to reports of stress at work. A survey of 17 000 people, randomly sampled from the electoral register, was followed up 12 months later, along with a detailed investigation from a cohort of the original sample. The results suggested that approximately 20 per cent of the working population reported levels of work stress as 'very' or 'extremely stressful'; the effects of work stress were also largely independent from life stress and negative affectivity. This effect remained over time and was related to potentially stressful working conditions and to physical and mental health impairment. Generalizing these findings to the population of the UK, the implication is that five million workers may suffer from high levels of stress that could impair their health.

● Strain or the consequences of stressors. These include physiological consequences such as gastrointestinal and cardiovascular illness; the psychological consequences such as depression and anxiety; and behavioural consequences such as absenteeism, spillover of tensions into home life and lower levels of organizational citizenship behaviour.

Palmer and Cooper (2004) have developed a model of work stress in the UK which examines the impact at national level (Figure 10.2). Thus they show how hazards at work such as demands, role ambiguity and organizational change, affect employees which in turn leads to higher levels of individual and organizational ill health (absenteeism, turnover, reduced performance), which lead to negative outcomes for individuals (coronary heart disease, clinical depression) and organizations (reduced profit, more accidents) and huge national-level financial costs and losses (over £4 billion).

Another approach to understanding stress at work is the Conservation of Resources theory (COR) (Hobfoll and Shirom, 2000). This proposes that when people lose physical, emotional or cognitive resources they put energy into trying to limit the impact of the loss, which requires additional resources. Stress occurs when resources are threatened, when resources are lost or when resources are invested without the expected benefits. Thus, feeling you have too many tasks to complete at work

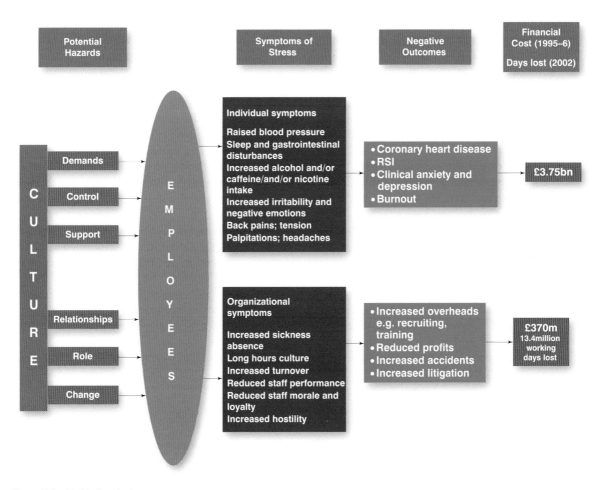

Figure 10.2   Model of work stress

and that you are losing the space you need to think, take breaks or relax might make you feel you have to work even harder to achieve those valued outcomes. But that in turn makes you feel even more stressed and therefore anxious. The theory further proposes that because humans are more focused on loss than gain, attention if focused on workplace factors that threaten resources such as negative feedback from one's boss or having to deal with a difficult conflict situation. Such resource threatening factors are much more salient than rewards. Particularly threatening is interpersonal conflict (Leiter and Maslach, 1988).

Moreover, there is evidence that the effects of loss of resources are chronic. Bakker *et al.* (2000) studied 2007 general practitioners over five years and found a correlation of 0.5 in stress levels, showing that levels of stress appeared to be enduring over this period of time. Schaufeli and Buunk (2003) studied five different samples over periods from three months to a year and found the correlation between stress levels at different points averaged 0.6. Stress is chronic so finding effective ways of managing stress is of huge importance. How do people cope with stressors and does their choice of strategies affects strain?

Stress Coping Strategies

There are three major types of stress coping strategies: problem focused, emotion focused and appraisal focused coping. The first strategy involves solving the problem by defining it, generating solutions, implementing solutions (Lazarus, 2000). For example, an office worker is unable to respond to all the customer requests in a timely fashion, causing them to become irate, because he is continually interrupted by colleagues who want his advice about issues to do with customer complaints. He defines the problem as interruptions to his core work. He generates solutions including the idea of producing a Frequently Asked Questions help sheet which he could give to all his colleagues along with a stipulation that they can only seek his advice between certain hours in the day. He implements this solution and finds that he is able to deal with almost all customers' complaints within one day of receiving them. Emotion focused coping involves trying to manage anxiety via denial or wishful thinking, or distancing oneself from the problem. Appraisal focused coping involves redefining the situation. For example, a junior manager might try to persuade herself that the presentation to the management team is not really important and it does not matter if she fails since the rest of her work is effective. Which approach is most successful? The research evidence suggests problem focused coping often helps to deal with a problem decisively and is most effective in preventing strain. What does not help is avoidance (for example in relation to continued conflicts with someone in another department of the organization) – pretending the problem does not exist or it will go away (Cartwright and Cooper, 1997).

Having recovery time to achieve psychological detachment is vital for coping with stress. *Psychological detachment* refers to disengaging mentally from work after the working day is over (Sonnentag and Fritz, 2007). Research evidence suggests that psychological detachment enables people to recover from job strain and is negatively related to health complaints, emotional exhaustion, depressive symptoms, negative mood, fatigue and sleep difficulties (Sonnentag, Mojza, Binnewies and Scholl, 2008) (see also Box 10.3).

What Causes Stress?

Stressors are factors in the environment that lead to strain. Below we list some of the most common stressors.

● Physical stressors – with advances in technology and its pervasiveness in working life, the physical office environment is increasingly stressful (McCoy and Evans, 2004). Temperature may also affect work (Gifford, 1997); some studies have shown that productivity is reduced when temperatures are high (McCormick, 1976) and that fine movement is impeded under very cold conditions (Fox, 1967).

Noise has been linked with increased risk of cardiovascular disease and increased mortality rates after long-term exposure (Zhao *et al.*, 1991; Ising *et al.*, 1999; Melamed *et al.*, 1999). Evans and Johnson (2000) found that a noisy office environment was associated with elevated stress hormones and poor task performance. Perceived control over the source of the noise is also thought to be a factor (Cohen, Evans, Stokols and Krantz, 1986; Wickens and Hollands, 2000). Glass, Singer and Friedman (1969) presented participants with an aversive noise stimulus and gave one group the option of pressing a button to stop the noise (but with encouragement not to do so), while the control group did not have this option. In the experiment, no one used the button, meaning all participants were exposed to the same noise stimulus. However, those with the option of stopping the noise were less affected on subsequent tasks and showed less post adaptive stress. Physical demands are also linked with stress. For example, continuous lifting and vibration has been shown to cause back and neck pain (e.g. Linton, 1990), as is poor ergonomic design such as poorly designed furniture (Goodrich, 1982; Wineman, 1986).

- Role stressors – role conflict, overload and role ambiguity, (Rizzo, House and Lirtzman, 1970). Role conflict describes a role where there are competing goals such as between quality of care and costs in health care or for control versus support of clients among probation workers. Role ambiguity is the degree to which a worker is unclear about the expectations of her own, or others' roles. Research has consistently shown links between these role factors and strain (Day and Livingstone, 2001; Jackson and Schuler, 1985; Netemeyer, Johnston and Burton, 1990).

- Workload. We described earlier how workload is a predictor of strain amongst health care workers. Some researchers have also distinguished between quantitative work load (the number of tasks, customers, products the role holder has to deal with) versus qualitative work load which relates to the intensity of the work such as the complexity of the task. This distinction has not proved very helpful in practice, however.

- Work pace – for example assembly line work where the worker has no control over the speed of the line; or time pressures, such as having to complete tasks within a specified period, for example, call centre workers may be told they have to complete all calls in an average of two minutes. Hurrell (1985) found, in a research study involving several thousand postal workers, machine paced workers suffered much more strain than those who controlled the pace of their work. Henning, Sauter and Krieg (1992) proposed that stress may result from a lack of synchrony between a worker's physiological internal rhythms and the rhythm set by a computer, for example in data input tasks. Moreover, tasks with high repetition and short time cycles are likely to result in repetitive strain and also create risks of musculoskeletal disorders if office ergonomics are neglected (McCoy and Evans, 2004).

- Work schedule – for example shift work is known to cause strain to varying degrees (Folkard and Monk, 1979). Typical shifts include the day shift (8am to 4pm), afternoon shift (4pm to midnight) and night shift (midnight to 8am). Rotating shift patterns typically require workers to rotate through the three shift patterns on a recurring basis (for example a week on days, then a week on afternoons, then a week on nights). Research indicates a high level of sleep disturbance amongst those on rotating shifts (Barton, 1994; Smith *et al.*, 1999). One problem is that such shift workers are unable to establish regular patterns of social activity since their leisure hours are constantly changing. Moreover, their leisure hours often do not coincide with those of their family and friends (Smith *et al.*, 1999). Control over shift patterns seems to make a difference. Workers who choose to work night shifts when compared with those assigned to rotating shifts report fewer sleep problems, health or domestic difficulties (Barton, 1994).

- Time rigidity. Flexitime, where employees have some choice over the time they go to work while fulfilling their contractual obligations in relation to total hours can be advantageous for child care (dropping off and picking up from school) and thus reduce strain (Lee, 1981). For example, Baltes et al. (1999) found that flexitime had little effect on productivity, absenteeism and performance, but that employees on flexitime showed less strain than others. Lee (1983) found that increasing flexitime allowed fathers to spend more time with their children thereby helping working mothers, while reducing the stress caused by work/family relationships. Lee (1981) suggested flexitime helped to alleviate stresses and strains directly related to childcare.

- Interpersonal conflict at work causes strain, especially where it is chronic (Reis and Gable, 2003). Passing conflicts do not appear to lead to problems. Conflict with co-workers, managers or clients all fall into the category of interpersonal conflict at work. De Dreu (2008) has reviewed research on conflict in teams and concludes that interpersonal conflict is damaging both to team effectiveness and to member well-being. Moreover, he argues that high task related conflict (what work to do and how to do it) is also damaging to the well-being of workers.

- Perceived control is now widely seen as a key factor in the stressor – strain relationship (Ganster and Murphy, 2000). A related concept in job design is autonomy (Hackman and Oldham, 1980 – see Chapter 4) – the amount of freedom the individual has to do the job in their own way. Control includes other factors, however, such as hours (flexitime), work pacing and decisions about the work environment (cleanliness, heat). Increasing control by increasing autonomy leads to reductions in stressors and therefore to strain. There is a widely held misperception that managers have more stressful jobs than others. While they do tend to have heavy workloads, deadlines, responsibility for complex decisions and many relationships to manage, stress-related diseases are much less common in managers than in blue-collar workers (Karasek and Theorell, 1990). One reason for this is that managers have greater control (autonomy) over their work. Karasek (1979) showed that the most damaging jobs have a combination of high demands (volume and pace of work) with low control.

- Emotional labour refers to the extent to which individuals at work have to manage their emotions in the course of their work. For example, cabin crew members in airlines have to smile and be helpful to passengers (not all of whom will be undemanding, pleasant or patient); police officers may have to deal with aggressive individuals on Saturday nights in city centres; ambulance workers have to manage the fear and pain of others while being confident and reassuring. Such emotional labour takes a toll and leads to strain. In short, the regulation of emotion to meet job or organizational demands produces strain over time. In particular, suppressing or showing false emotions is demanding and associated with job dissatisfaction, absenteeism, turnover and burnout (Brotheridge and Grandey, 2002). Grandey (2003) assessed 'surface acting' and 'deep acting' behaviour in employees in customer service type roles. Surface acting can be described as modifying facial expression (smiling) in order to present a positive image (when the employee is not feeling positive themselves), whereas deep acting is when the employee modifies her inner feelings in order to appear authentic to customers. In her research, Grandey found that those employees who exhibited more surface acting were more likely to experience emotional exhaustion. Conversely, there was no relationship between deep acting and emotional exhaustion. While this may seem counter-intuitive due to the effort required to modify inner feelings, it is possible that by doing so, emotional dissonance is reduced. This combined with the positive customer experience also associated with this behaviour may restore emotional resources of the employee while surface acting reduces the resources available (through emotional dissonance).

- Task content is itself a stressor and we describe some of the stressors in task content above in relation to the work of the police, ambulance workers and those in any organization dealing with customer complaints.

- Work–non-work life conflict (sometimes called work–family conflict). This refers to conflict between work roles and roles outside of work (mother, carer, etc.). Observation reveals this is a particular problem for women, given their relatively heavy burdens in the home and with child care. Such conflict can also damage relationships between partners. There are clear effects of work – non-work conflict on employee well-being (Grant-Vallone and Donaldson, 2001). Frone (2000) reported that those experiencing such conflict are 30 times more likely to suffer a mental health problem (depression or anxiety) than others. Hoonakker, Carayon and Schoepke (2004) found that employees with high work – family conflict experienced lower job satisfaction, high emotional exhaustion and increased turnover intention. Furthermore, they suggested that work – family conflict is negatively related to career opportunities and supervisory support, but that supervisors can help buffer their negative effects.

KEY THEME

Environment and Sustainability

Organizations play a key role in climate change through their production of carbon dioxide and the widespread use of pollutants. The planet we inhabit is a fragile and complex ecosystem. Understanding our place in it, our role as custodians and how we are affected by it are vital if we are to protect our vulnerable planet. Of particular interest in this chapter is how the natural environment affects human well-being and mental health. Research has clearly established that natural settings enhance our mental health with positive effects on cognitive, attentional, emotional and subjective well-being (Pryor, Townsend, Maller and Field, 2006). Moreover, exposure to nature has positive effects on the health and well-being of office workers, prisoners and hospital patients. For example, when hospital patients have views of natural settings such as parkland and trees, they experience less pain and stress, have better post-surgical outcomes and leave hospital sooner (Devlin and Arneill, 2003; Ulrich, 2006). The noise of cities and workplaces is inherently stressful and interferes with good cognitive functioning. Spending time in the relative silence of nature, hearing largely non-jarring sounds, has restorative effects on our attention and well-being (Berman *et al.*, 2008). Even children with attention deficit disorder function better after a walk in the park (Taylor and Kuo, 2009). Immersion in nature is good for us and both creating and protecting natural environments makes good moral, business, and people management sense for modern organizations. Surrounding work places with green spaces reduces stress and strain.

Consequences of Stressors – Strain

How then does strain manifest itself in people at work? Strain can sensibly be divided into three main categories: behavioural, psychological and physiological.

Behavioural

Information processing – strain leads to deterioration in memory, reaction time, accuracy and task performance. People make more errors on cognitive tasks and this has particular implications for health and safety. Strain is associated with medical errors amongst health care workers (Firth-Cozens, 1990). Hockey (1997) suggests that when perceived demands are unable to be met with normal work effort, either effort is increased with consequent negative psychological (e.g. irritability, fatigue) and physiological (e.g. increased secretion of cortisol) effects; or, that the task performance is reduced such as reduced levels of accuracy and speed. Lang, Thomas, Bliese and Adler (2007) studied effects of job demand and strain on performance on leadership tasks in army cadets. They reported that job demands had a negative effect on performance, which was mediated through strain. That is, demands increased the strain experienced by an individual, which then resulted in a decrease in performance. Collet, Averty and Dittmar (2009) found that physiological data from the autonomic nervous system and subjective reports of strain matched task demands in air traffic controllers. They conclude that 'Emotional factors are integrated in each step of information processing and are shown, through pathological manifestations (particularly a cortical lesion of orbito-frontal areas), to influence cognitive activity'. (p. 9).

Performance – strain has been suggested to have an 'inverted U' relationship with performance such that performance is best at moderate levels of strain or arousal and worst when strain or arousal are either very low or very high (Jex, 1998). However any stress seems to impair performance in complex tasks (Motowidlo, Packard and Manning, 1986). Motowidlo *et al.* (1986) found that stress was associated with less sensitivity, warmth and tolerance towards patients amongst a sample of nurses. The National Staff Survey for the NHS, conducted by Aston Business School, has repeatedly revealed associations between staff experience of stressful and unsupportive work environments and patient satisfaction, patient care and even patient mortality (Gov.UK, 2011).

Psychological

The most invoked concept to explain psychological consequences of sustained stress at work is that of 'burnout'. The metaphor is of an engine that has been run at such a high speed for so long, creating such a level of friction,that eventually the level of heat in the engine causes sustained and catastrophic damage, resulting in engine failure. Psychological burnout, first described by Maslach and Leiter (1997), refers to three sub-dimensions of strain – emotional exhaustion, depersonalization (the health care worker becomes hardened and starts to treat patients like objects), sense of ineffectiveness and lack of accomplishment (Maslach, Schaufeli and Leiter, 2001). This concept has been applied to and examined particularly amongst those in the caring professions. A measure to assess burnout (the Maslach Burnout Inventory – Maslach, Jackson and Leiter, 1996) has proved valuable in identifying at-risk samples of workers. Examples of items include:

- I feel I'm working too hard on my job.
- In my work, I deal with emotional problems very calmly.
- I worry that this job is hardening me emotionally.

Schaufeli and Bakker (2004) measured burnout and its opposite 'engagement' in employees from a number of organizations. They found that burnout was predicted mainly by job demands and to a lesser extent, job resources; that it is related to turnover intention and health problems; and that it mediates the relationship between job demands and health problems.

Physiological

Sustained stress leads to chronic activation of the sympathetic nervous system, which in turn leads to ill health because of excessive amounts of stress hormones circulating in the blood. Blood vessels also shrink and coronary arteries and the heart are damaged as a result of the thickening of plaque in the linings. Arteriolosclerosis (hardening and loss of elasticity in arterioles – often due to hypertension) is associated with increases in blood pressure and higher likelihood of heart attacks because the heart has to work so much harder. Because of the lack of oxygen associated with poorer cardiovascular function the body requires more oxygen and this therefore results in increased blood pressure. The evidence is clear that people in sustained stressful situations are at a higher risk of heart attacks (Krantz and McCeney, 2002).

There are also gastrointestinal (digestive) problems associated with stress. Levy, Cain, Jarrett and Heitkemper (2004) measured stress levels in women with and without irritable bowel syndrome (a dysfunction of the gastrointestinal system). They found that a positive relationship existed between daily symptoms and daily stress, and also that gastrointestinal patients reported higher stress levels than control groups.

Biochemical affects, such as the stress hormones, cortisol and catecholamine, increasing when the individual experiences strain. Long-lasting stress hormone increases contribute to decreased functioning of the immune system and to coronary heart disease (Cohen and Herbert, 1996; Krantz and McCeney, 2002).

There is clear evidence therefore that prolonged exposure to stressors can kill.

KEY FIGURE

Cary Cooper CBE

Cary Cooper CBE is Professor of Organizational Psychology and Health at Lancaster University Management School. He is a world-leading expert on stress and is often the first choice from the media to comment on workplace issues. He is the most influential Work Psychologist in Europe and his tireless work with the media has had a positive effect on the well-being of many thousands of workers across Europe. He has been extraordinarily effective in communicating understanding from research to the media and the general public. He has produced a huge volume of published work, including the 12 volumes of the *Blackwell Encyclopaedia of Management*. He also developed the Occupational Stress Indicator which has been translated into many languages and is used widely throughout the business and research world to diagnose and assess occupational stress. He has been an advisor to two United Nations agencies: the International Labour Office in 'Occupational Stress and Health', and the World Health Organization. He is a founding member of the British Academy of Management, founding editor of the *Journal of Organizational Behavior* and was appointed head of the Sunningdale Institute in 2005, which advises on issues facing UK public sector organizations. HR magazine ranked him 5th in the world of top HR thinkers in 2008.

UNDERSTANDING STRESS AT WORK

So far we have explored the basic ideas about stressors and strain at work and learned about the research evidence telling us what aspects of work experience lead to strain and how this strain can manifest. In order to go a little deeper and understand why these processes happen we next consider explanatory models. The most famous is the Demand–Control Model developed by Robert Karasek.

Demand–Control Model

Karasek (1979) argued that we could understand the effects of stressors upon strain by looking at the balance in work between demands and control (or decision latitude). He defined control as the degree of autonomy and discretion employees had for using different skills. Demands referred to the work-load and intellectual requirements of the job. He proposed that a combination of high demands and low control lead to health problems. Indeed, Karasek and Theorell found that those in such positions were two or three times more likely to become ill than others at work. We can understand these concepts better by looking at some practical examples of different combinations of demands and control.

- High demands and low control – waiter, assembly line worker, Post Office worker, computer help desk. In one postal sorting office I visited, I saw women typing the correct postcodes for letters that had the wrong or missing postcode. Each letter took less than five seconds to correct so the workers were completing more than 12 tasks a minute or 600 tasks an hour. They had a ten minute break after every 50 minutes and their speed of working was monitored by managers. They had very high demands and virtually no control.

- High demands and high control. Such a combination can be a real buzz or what Csikszentmihalyi calls 'flow' (Csikszentmihalyi, 2008). Such conditions can be exciting, stimulating and highly absorbing and those who experience them are likely to include lawyers, doctors and senior managers. Moreover, these conditions are likely to be health promoting.

- Low demands and high control, e.g. gardener. The job is not particularly demanding and you can choose how to do it. The ideal job if you want a peaceful life.

- Low demands and low control e.g. night watchman. The night watchman has little latitude about what there is to do on the job and what skills they can deploy. It is simply a case of 'keeping an eye on things' and getting through the night. Deeply boring and a great cure for insomnia!

Research evidence reveals the predictive validity of the model. For example, Ganster, Fox and Dwyer (2001) in a longitudinal study of 105 nurses found that those who perceived high demands and low control were ill more often and incurred the highest overall health care costs in the five years subsequent to perceptions of demands and control being assessed. Many studies have confirmed that a combination of high demands and low control is damaging to human health and this has been confirmed across cultures. For example, research in China confirmed the model's predictive power. In 1200 employees across five cities those people with the highest anxiety and depression were in jobs with high demand–low control characteristics, while the people who reported the highest job and life satisfaction performed jobs with high demand–high control characteristics (Xie, 1996).

Person Environment (PE) Fit Model

French, Caplan and Van Harrison (1982) proposed that to the extent that a person's skills and abilities match the job requirements and work environment within which they find themselves, the better will be their well-being and the lower their levels of strain. For example, a sociable, creative and well-travelled individual who seeks new projects continually is likely to make a good travel agent but not a software developer working on a long-term and detailed project. An anxious, attention-to-detail person who is highly risk avoidant and introverted will tend not to make a good leader. We can separate out 'PE fit' into two sub-components: person-job fit and person-organization fit. The person-job fit concept relates to the extent to which the skills, abilities and interests of the individual are compatible with job requirements. Person-organization fit refers to whether the values of the organization are consistent with the values of the individual. One of our MBA students had a senior role and very high salary in a major defence industry but felt that his values and the profit maximization values of the organization were in conflict. He had been suffering increasing illness and strain when he left to join an international aid agency on a much lower salary. After two years in the new job, he was happier and healthier than at any time in his career. Verquer, Beehr and Wagner (2003) performed a meta-analysis of PE fit and work attitudes confirming relationships with turnover intent, job satisfaction and organizational commitment. In an extension of this work, Hoffman and Woehr (2005) added behavioural criteria, finding relationships between PE fit, job performance and organizational citizenship behaviour.

Individual Differences in Response to Stress

While one person may find the prospect of working in a coal mine for six months rather scary, another person may see it as a great adventure. Taking responsibility for leading a team to introduce a culture of innovation in an organization might feel impossible to one person and exciting to another. Even with the same background of skills and experience, people differ considerably in how they respond to stress at work. The study of individual differences reveals that certain personality dimensions such as locus of control, hardiness and self esteem relate to people's reactions to stressors.

Locus of control describes the extent to which people believe that they are in control of events in their lives versus being at the mercy of factors and events outside their control. Rotter (1966) proposed that having an internal locus of control (believing generally that you control what happens to you in life) moderates the relationship between stressors and strain such that a strong internal locus is associated with less strain. Note how this theoretical approach parallels Karasek's ideas about perceptions of control.

Hardiness   refers to the extent to which people have orientations of commitment, control and challenge in their approach to their work lives: commitment to being involved in events and change rather than being isolated; a determination to try to control and influence events rather than feeling paralyzed or powerless; and an orientation to see change as a challenge rather than as a threat. Maddi and Kobasa (1984) studied employees of the Illinois Bell Telephone Company during a mass redundancy programme over a one year period, which involved cutting the 26 000 workforce by nearly half. Two thirds of employees suffered health and psychological problems during the change process but one third appeared to thrive, being healthier and more invigorated. Maddi and Kobasa (1984) found that the difference between the groups was accounted for by the commitment, control and challenge orientations described above. Similarly, Ghorbani et al. (2000) surveyed Iranian business managers, finding that the higher the hardiness level, the better their health and performance despite stressful situations. Bartone (1999) found that soldiers with a hardiness orientation were less likely than others to suffer from post traumatic stress disorder or depression, commonly experienced by soldiers in battlefield situations. Maddi's Hardiness Institute now offers training programmes to help people change their perceptions of stressful situations to view them as a challenge to be overcome.

Type A personality describes those who have a '… chronic struggle to obtain an unlimited number of poorly defined things from their environment in the shortest period of time and, if necessary, against the opposing effects of other things or persons in this same environment'. (Friedman, 1969, p. 84). Type A is also described as the coronary prone personality. Many years ago, I was working for a period in the idyllic setting of Bermuda and I met a recently retired senior executive who had suffered from a heart attack and recognized it was time to relax and change his life. He came to Bermuda, got into meditation and relaxation and worked to set up a holistic therapy institute. He channelled his considerable energies into this new venture and kept seeking help from me – so much so that he regularly called on Sunday mornings and indeed all hours of the day. He was a typical Type A, unable to stop his incessant striving, even while focused on relaxation and holistic living. Friedman and Rosenman in their 1974 book, *Type A Behavior and Your Heart*, describe the coronary prone personality as someone characterized by ambition, impatience, irritability and a sense of time urgency. They are engaged in a constant struggle to achieve more in even less time. Type B is described as relaxed, easy-going, patient and calm. It is noteworthy that Type A personalities achieve high work performance and career success. However, hostility is their main problem since they cannot help getting angry with others who fail to enable them to achieve their almost impossible aspirations (Krantz and McCeney, 2002). Research has suggested that there are two sub-components of Type A: Achievement striving and Impatience and irritability. Achievement striving is associated with success and good health (Bluen, Barling and Burns, 1990) and impatience and irritability with illness and strain (Barling and Boswell, 1995).

Our journey so far has helped us to understand the stressor – strain relationship and the factors that account for, mediate and moderate that relationship. Work and Organizational Psychologists are concerned with making a difference in the world of work. What can we therefore do to make a difference in this domain?

REDUCING AND MANAGING STRESS

Leading researchers in this area have settled on three broad methods of reducing and managing stress, grouped into three categories – primary, secondary and tertiary interventions (Quick *et al.*, 1997).

Primary Interventions

Primary interventions are stressor directed so they are aimed at modifying or eliminating stressors in the work environment. This might include ensuring the right levels of heat, light or noise; giving people more control over their jobs and work environments; redesigning the tasks they are required to do; or giving them more flexible work schedules (Cartwright and Cooper, 2005). Such interventions might also take a problem-focused approach by reducing noise, interruptions, time pressures, role ambiguity or number of hours worked. They might also involve changing appraisals of stressors via cognitive restructuring e.g. training employees to think 'this is not an overwhelming workload – it is a challenge to surf and be enjoyed; an exhilarating challenge'.

Secondary Interventions

Secondary interventions are more focused on people's response to stress. The focus is primarily on employees rather than changing aspects of the organization. So employees might be given relaxation exercises, stress management training and nutrition advice, or encouraged to undertake physical fitness training. Cary Cooper has called this the 'Band Aid approach' to stress management since it fails to deal with the underlying organizational causes, focusing instead on the symptoms (Cooper and Cartwright, 2001). Another example of secondary interventions is an encouraging emotion focused coping such as, telling staff to avoid, minimize or distance themselves emotionally from the stressors (e.g. the upset caused by unpleasant interactions, a co-worker). Other examples include training staff in negotiation and conflict resolution skills; stress management training, including cognitive behavioural therapy type training. Stress inoculation programmes also fall under the heading of secondary interventions, such as teaching people about stress (educational component) having them learn about time management, relaxation, problem solving methods (rehearsal) and then practising the skills in safe environments such as in workshops (application). Jones *et al.* (1988) found that using an organization wide programme in hospitals led to fewer medical errors and malpractice claims. Many organizations recommend secondary interventions in the form of relaxation exercises, meditation or biofeedback. There is some evidence that the regular practice of exercises such as meditation and mindfulness can significantly reduce arousal and anxiety (West, 1979a; 1979b; 1980; 1987).

Mindfulness practice involves learning (via practice) how to focus attention on our experience in the here and now without evaluation or intention, simply paying attention to our experience in the present moment. Research has demonstrated the beneficial effects of mindfulness practice in many domains including lower levels of emotional disturbance, depressive symptoms, anxiety and stress; higher well-being, positive affect and life satisfaction; greater awareness, understanding and acceptance of emotions; greater ability to correct or repair unpleasant mood states (demonstrated via use of functional medical resonance imaging); less reactivity to emotionally threatening stimuli; more adaptive immune responses; better relationship quality, reduced reactivity to conflict, increased sustained attention to social exchanges, higher levels of emotional intelligence; and greater compassion among medical students (Brown *et al.*, 2007). One study in the workplace found that mindfulness training was negatively associated with emotional exhaustion and positively associated with job satisfaction. (Hülsheger *et al.*, 2013).

Murphy reviewed research on the health effects of interventions at work designed to alleviate stress (1996). He looked at physiological and psychological outcomes, including blood pressure, headaches,

BOX 10.2
Open hearts build lives

Barbara Fredrickson argues that the experience of positive emotions enables people to explore new experiences and to build thereby their capacity to engage in life, thus coping more effectively with stressors and developing well-being. In a novel field experiment she trained half of a sample of 139 working adults in a meditation on loving kindness. The meditation group showed more positive emotions, social support, decreased illness and more of a sense of purpose in life. This in turn was associated with lower depression and greater life satisfaction.

BOX 10.3

The need for recovery from work

After a heavy day at work we all want to unwind – letting go of the tension of the day and refreshing our resources in order to be effective at work the next day. What is the best way of doing this? Feet up in front of the TV for a few hours with a beer? A game of tennis or cooking a meal. There is evidence that the recuperative quality of the time to unwind is affected by the nature of leisure or non-work activities during those times (typically in the evenings after work). Sonnentag, Binnewies and

Mojza (2008) found that challenging non-work activities such as sport, hobbies, creative activities (cooking, painting, playing music) predicted positive affect among their participants the next day whereas passive activities such as watching TV did not. After engaging in challenging activities during leisure time, participants in their research were more active, interested, excited, strong, inspired and alert than those who experienced more passive leisure time.

anxiety and job satisfaction; Muscle relaxation, biofeedback, meditation and cognitive behavioural training (CBT). His findings indicated that some interventions worked better for physiological outcomes (e.g. muscle-relaxation) and others for psychological ones (e.g. cognitive-behaviour skills). Meditation was the most effective intervention providing the most consistent results. It was only used in six of the sixty-four studies included in his review, however. Using a combination of techniques (CBT and relaxation or meditation) was found to produce the most positive outcomes rather than single techniques. He noted that none of the interventions were consistently effective in reducing job satisfaction or absenteeism.

Another secondary intervention involves increasing levels of social support for staff experiencing high levels of stressors at work. House (1981) distinguished between four types of social support: emotional, informational, instrumental and appraisal, and then went on to distinguish between verbal and enacted support. We consider each of these below and provide examples.

Emotional support is the kind of social support that we most readily identify. It is the notion of a shoulder to cry on, an encouraging word and sympathetic understanding of another's emotional pain.

Emotional support involves being an active, open listener. It does not involve giving advice or direction, rather it is simply providing the space within which people can express their emotions. It also involves a sense of compassion towards the person receiving the support.

Informational support is the second type of social support and involves providing helpful information that enables the person to cope such as explaining the steps to be taken when a customer becomes abusive.

Instrumental support refers to the practical, 'doing' support that team members offer to one another such as taking an additional shift in order to help a colleague with a sick child at home.

Appraisal support describes ways in which colleagues can help each other in the process of making sense of or interpreting a problem situation. This need not involve offering solutions, but would involve helping the individual examine a range of alternative appraisals of any given problem situations. Perhaps the individual has a challenging supervisor and reappraisal of the situation might involve suggesting that such a supervisor is offering rare and useful opportunities for growth and might also provide a reason for seeking beneficial additional training.

Within teams, the more that team members provide social support, the more cohesive the team becomes. This leads to better mental health of team members too since there is a strong and positive relationship between social support at work and job-related mental health (Ganster *et al.*, 1986; Manning *et al.*, 1996).

Buffer or moderator hypothesis The buffer hypothesis proposes that social support can buffer people from the effects of strain at work. Frese (1999), in a longitudinal study of 90 blue collar workers in the German metal industry, found that workers with more social support exhibited less anxiety, depression, irritation and strain. Allen, McManus and Russell (1999) found that first-year MBA students who worked in teams assigned to experienced second-year MBA students for peer-mentoring felt better supported in coping with stress than did those who simply received support from their year peers.

Tertiary Interventions

Tertiary interventions are symptom directed. They are focused on helping individuals cope with consequences of stressors. Again this means a focus on individuals rather than a focus on the organizations. One approach is to provide medical care in-house or outsourced for employees. Another is to use what are called employee assistance programmes or EAPs. EAPs have typically focused on employees' drug and alcohol problems, but have also been extended to dealing with employees' problems of stress at work. There is usually a significant counselling component to EAPs. Because they are usually 'in-house' programmes there is a great need for confidentiality and top management support since otherwise employees are unlikely to use the service. Cooper and Sadri (1994) found improvements in mental health and esteem amongst those participating in EAPs. Nevertheless, they represent a reactive approach since they are used for dealing with employees' problems after they arise rather than focused on creating positive work environments which minimize stressors.

In our studies of staff attitudes in the UK National Health Service, we have found that around one in seven of the 1.4 million NHS staff report being physically assaulted (usually by patients, their carers or relatives) each year. It is clear that the effects of those on the receiving end of such behaviours are very harmful. The research evidence suggests that bullying seriously affects the health of some victims at work and that the harasser is often a manager (Zapf and Gross, 2001). Greater awareness of these issues in the workplace has led many organizations to introduce bullying and harassment procedures designed to ensure the prevention and management of such problems at work.

BURNOUT AND ENGAGEMENT

A broad movement has developed within psychology, which focuses on how we can better understand human behaviour by paying at least equal attention to the strengths and potential in human behaviour rather than simply focusing on problems and weaknesses. A leading Dutch psychologist, Wilmar Schaufeli, has articulated this particularly in relation to the literature on stress, suggesting that there is an opposite of stress or burnout – job engagement. He suggests that instead of simply preventing and treating stress, we should be promoting positive work environments which encourage job engagement. He and colleagues define engagement as 'a positive work-related state of fulfilment that is characterized by vigour, dedication and absorption' (Schaufeli, Salanova, González-Romá and

Bakker, 2002, p. 74).Engagement affects both individual outcomes such as well-being and organizational outcomes (Saks, 2006; Schaufeli and Bakker, 2004).

Job and organizational characteristics proposed to predict job engagement include job characteristics that create psychological meaningfulness by providing challenging varied work (Saks, 2006), and psychological meaningfulness which results from a feeling of benefit to the self (such as self concept) as a result of role performance at work – think of the effect on the self concept of the ambulance team member successfully saving lives (Kahn, 1992); perceived fairness in how the organization manages employees will also encourage engagement. Harter *et al.* (2003), in a meta-analysis of engagement and organizational outcomes, found that businesses that experienced high levels of employee engagement averaged $80 000 to $120 000 higher revenue or sales per month than other businesses. Erickson (2005) suggests that engagement is more than merely job satisfaction or loyalty to the organization; it is also about passion, commitment and activation.

Schaufeli *et al.* (2002) propose that job engagement amongst employees is described by five core elements:

1 Urgency – the need to get this task done now.
2 Focus – on what is important now, not what might be most interesting.
3 Intensity – sense of significance and deep level of involvement in the work.
4 Adaptability – being proactive, not tied to job descriptions.
5 Personal initiative – thinking and working pro-actively and implementing new and improved ways of doing things.

Macey, Schneider, Barbera and Young (2009) suggest that job engagement is a consequence of four interacting elements:

1 Employees have *capacity to engage* – as a result of the motivation and autonomy they experience in their jobs. The organization gives them the information they need to do their job well; gives learning opportunities; provides feedback which builds confidence; and supports energy renewal through provision of flexi-time and work–non-work balance.
2 Employees have the *motivation to engage* – as a result of good job design. Jobs are intrinsically interesting (Hackman and Oldham, 1980) and the organization ensures people feel valued, respected and supported at work.
3 Employees have the *freedom to engage* – there is support and safety for them to innovate, and this is explicitly and implicitly provided by their manager and the wider organization. They are treated fairly and feel trust in their managers and the organization. People consequently feel safe to take action on their own initiative.
4 Employees focus their engagement on *the strategy and goals of the organization* – there is alignment between what employees do and the strategic goals of the organization. The organization has the right kind of culture for engagement which is communicated and enacted every day in every way throughout the organization. Staff know what the organizational priorities are and why, and when culture is aligned with these goals.

As a consequence, employees persist at tasks, even when it is tough; they respond pro-actively to emerging threats and challenges; they expand their roles at work because they are continually innovating and learning; and they adapt more readily to change.

Corporate Social Responsibility and Ethics

Creating cultures that engage staff and avoid harm

Increasingly those concerned with evaluating the worth of organizations are paying attention to how well employees are supported and managed. Why? Because there is good evidence that employee well-being predicts organizations performance. But more than that, there is recognition that it is part of corporations' social responsibility to contribute positively to their employees' health and well-being. It is unethical to create work places which cause psychological and physiological illness. Equally, it is part of an organization's ethical responsibility to create workplaces which enhance employee well-being and growth giving them opportunities for growth and development via engagement. What kind of culture creates a high level of job engagement? Macey *et al.* (2009) describe it as follows:

The central role of a culture of trust – trust in leaders, managers and the system including perceptions of fairness in relation to distributive justice, procedural justice and interactional justice (see Chapter 4).

What leaders pay attention to, monitor and measure is consistent with the organization's mission and they allocate resources on the basis of the core mission or values of the organization (e.g. quality of health care rather than cost in a health care organization).

The behaviours leaders model are consistent with the organization's stated values

The criteria for recruitment, selection, promotion and firing are aligned with the values and core purpose

Flat hierarchies, rituals and rites promote involvement, celebrations of accomplishment, encouragement of risk taking, and innovation. No good deed goes unrecognized

People are encouraged to talk about their work and how it affects them, how belonging to the organization is important to them and what they do to promote the organization and its staff

The focus of the organizations' systems and procedures is on the outcomes they value e.g. quality of service (not, for example, cost cutting above all else!) and employee health and well-being.

There is a dark side of engagement since it could lead to burnout. Schaufeli argues that there is a need for balance but that workaholism is associated with working unnecessarily and not in alignment with organizational goals and is associated with negative work experience. Engagement on the other hand derives from intrinsic and satisfying motivation to work so that work feels meaningful and important. Moreover, there is positive spillover into non-work life and this is the exact opposite of burnout and workaholism (Schaufeli, Taris and van Rhenen, 2008). Schaufeli *et al.* also show that workaholics work in less supportive social and psychologically fulfilling environments in contrast with those reporting high levels of work engagement.

One conclusion from this alternative perspective on stress and health at work is that '... organizations need to shift their emphasis from getting more out of people to investing more in them, so they are motivated – and able – to bring more of themselves to work every day'. Schwartz and McCarthy (2007, p. 64).

BOX 10.4
Staying well

In 2008, the New Economics Foundation was commissioned by the UK Government's Foresight Project to review the inter-disciplinary work of over 400 scientists from across the world. The aim was to identify a set of evidence-based actions to improve well-being, which individuals would be encouraged to build into their daily lives (**http://www.nhs.uk/Conditions/stress-anxiety-depression/Pages/**).

As an illustration of how government action can be explicitly directed towards improving well-being, the following briefly sets out the five evidence-based ways to well-being and the sorts of policy interventions which could help to enable them.

Connect

Social relationships are critical to our well-being. Survey research has found that well-being is increased by life goals associated with family, friends, social and political life and decreased by goals associated with career success and material gains. Governments can shape policies in ways that encourage citizens to spend more time with families and friends and less time in the workplace. For example, employment policies that actively promote flexible working and reduce the burdens of commuting, alongside policies aimed at strengthening local involvement, would enable people to spend more time at home and in their communities to build supportive and lasting relationships.

Be active

Exercise has been shown to increase mood and has been used successfully to lower rates of depression and anxiety. Being active also develops the motor skills of children and protects against cognitive decline in the elderly. Yet for the first time in history more of the world's population lives in urban rather than non-urban environments. Through urban design and transport policy, governments influence the way we navigate through our neighbourhoods and towns. To improve our well-being, policies could support more green space to encourage exercise play and prioritize cycling and walking over car use.

Take notice

Research has shown that practising awareness of sensations, thoughts and feelings can improve both the knowledge we have about ourselves and our well-being for several years (Brown et al., 2007). But the 21st century's never-ending flow of messages from companies advertising products and services leaves little opportunity to savour or reflect on our experiences. Policy that incorporates emotional awareness training, mindfulness and meditation practice, and media education into universal education provision may better equip individuals to navigate their way through the information superhighway with their well-being intact; regulation to create advertising-free spaces could further improve well-being outcomes.

Keep learning

Learning encourages social interaction and increases self-esteem and feelings of competency. Behaviour directed by personal goals to achieve something new has been shown to increase reported life satisfaction. While there is often a much greater policy emphasis on learning in the early years of life, psychological research suggests it is a critical aspect of day-to-day living for all age groups. Therefore, policies that encourage learning, even in the elderly, will enable individuals to develop new skills, strengthen social networks and feel more able to deal with life's challenges.

Give

Studies in neuroscience have shown that cooperative behaviour activates reward areas of the brain, suggesting we are hard wired to enjoy helping one another. Individuals actively engaged in their communities report higher well-being and their help and gestures have knock-on effects for others. But it is not simply about a one-way transaction of giving. Research by nef shows that building reciprocity and mutual exchange – through giving and receiving – is the simplest and most fundamental way of building trust between people and creating positive social relationships and resilient communities. Governments can choose to invest more in 'the core economy': the family, neighbourhood and community which, together, act as the operating system of society. Policies that provide accessible, enjoyable and rewarding ways of participation and exchange will enable more individuals to take part in social and political life.

The challenge for governments will be to create the conditions within society that enable individuals to incorporate these and other positive activities more consistently into their daily lives. By measuring the impact of their decisions on the components of personal and social well-being, government can provide a great boost to efforts to shape the policy cycle to one which explicitly promotes well-being.

AUTHOR EXPERIENCE

Team Climates for Safety in Coal Mines

When I left university, after seven years' educational training, I went to work as a coal miner in Wales for a year. The first two months, because it was such a dangerous environment, I was anxious about getting injured or worse. However, I soon realized that the best protection was the team I worked in. There was a strong culture of safety among the 1000 men working in the mine and they all took responsibility for their own and others' safety. But it was your immediate team which played the most powerful role, protecting you from harm, upbraiding you when you took risks and reinforcing safe working practices constantly. A culture of safety pervaded the organization and the team translated that culture into immediate work practices which ensured you minimized risk and danger. Creating a climate of safety requires not just policies and edicts from top management, but systems of training and reward that communicate to all employees the importance of safety and ensure that safe behaviours are practised throughout the organization.

BOX 10.5
The Black Reports

The UK government, partly in response to this and other research, began an initiative in 2005 focused on a strategy for the health and well-being of working age people. They commissioned a review of the links between health, work and wellbeing that underpinned emerging policy. In 2008, Dame Carol Black produced her report into the health of Britain's working age population – **Working for a healthier tomorrow** that led to further government responses. The focus then turned to mental health problems, because they have a greater impact on people's ability to work than any other group of disorders, with the production of a supplementary report on **mental health and work**. In 2011, Dame Carol Black and David Frost (Black and Frost 2011) **reviewed the sickness absence system** and made recommendations for improvement. The **government implemented some of the recommendations**, such as the introduction of an occupational health assessment and advice service to help people off sick for 4 weeks to return to work.

SUMMARY

This chapter emphasized the role of positive emotions and relationships for human health and well-being and stressed that creating workplaces characterized by such climates is an ethical responsibility on employers. Strains at work have a great impact on health and well-being and have concomitant effects on organizations' financial performance and effectiveness.

Levels of injuries and illness at work vary enormously depending on how well the workplace is managed to preserve the health and well-being of employees. Key indicators of problems in a work environment are high incidences of absenteeism and turnover.

Stress is the consequence when very high demands (or strains) are placed upon people at work, exceeding the physical, cognitive or emotional capacity they have to cope. Causes include physical role (such as nurses lifting patients in hospital), workload, work pace, relationships at work, perceived control, task content (the strain of some police work) and conflicts between work and home life.

The consequences of stress can be behavioural (inability to manage tasks such as memorizing material), poor performance on the job, burnout (emotional exhaustion, depersonalization and feeling ineffective) and ultimately physiological damage (e.g. heart disease). Stress coping strategies include problem focused, emotion focused and appraisal with problem focused appearing most effective.

Psychologists have provided a number of theoretical approaches, including the demands–control and Person–Environment (PE) Fit models. There are individual differences in how people respond to strain at work based on locus of control, hardiness Type A. Strategies for managing stress and strain at work include: Primary – dealing with the stressors directly such as reducing levels of noise; Secondary which involves training people to deal with stress via relaxation exercises or providing social support; and Tertiary which involves dealing with the symptoms of stress such as Employee Assistance Programmes (EAPs).

The chapter contrasts burnout with employee engagement, the latter characterized by workers' urgency, intensity, focus, adaptability and personal initiative. Prescriptions for employees to stay well are described, including the advice to connect, be active, take notice, keep learning and give in daily life. In particular, new understanding about techniques like mindfulness and the importance of opportunities for detachment and recovery from work are enhancing our ability to intervene to create workplaces that enhance rather than damage employee well-being.

DISCUSSION QUESTIONS

1 How can the competing perspectives of maximizing shareholder value and employee health and well-being be reconciled?

2 To what extent should governments legislate to force multinational companies to ensure employee health and well-being and should this be enforced internationally?

3 To what extent is stress just a 21st century Western nations, self indulgent, neurotic obsession?

4 What would you include in a comprehensive health and well-being programme in an organization?

5 What evidence is there that interventions to reduce stress and strain actually make a difference?

6 To what extent is stress at work an individual or an organizational phenomenon?

APPLY IT

1 Learn mindfulness and practise regularly for a month to discover what effects this has on your well-being.

2 Use mindfulness to become aware of the factors in your work that make you stressed.

3 Which of these factors is physical: role stressors, workload, work pace, work schedule, time rigidity, interpersonal, emotional labour stressors, low control, task content and work – non-work balance?

4 Then assess how you cope with each of these stressors. Do you use a problem

solving approach, emotion focused coping or appraisal focused coping?

5 How could you change your coping strategy in relation to each stressor to ensure you cope more effectively with it?

6 For each, what would be most effective – a primary, secondary or tertiary intervention and how would you design each of these to reduce your (and others') work stress?

7 How can you ensure you regularly engage in post-work activities that leave you refreshed, invigorated and renewed rather than depleted?

8 Look at the Five Ways to Well Being (Box 10.4) and determine how you can care for yourself more effectively by increasing connection, physical activity, learning, taking notice and giving to others.

WEB ACTIVITIES

Council Fined after School Janitor Loses Toe

Read this article at **www.press.hse.gov.uk** or by following the link in the digital resources online and discuss the questions below.

1 Which of the Zacharatos and Barling (2004) proposed HRM practices could have improved the Health and Safety outcome in this case?

2 What more could organizations do to prevent accidents such as these at work?

France: Stress and worker suicides mean the furure's not bright at Orange

Read this article by Angelique Chrisafilis published September 2009 at **www.gaurdian.co.uk** or by following the link in the digital resources online and discuss the questions below.

1 What issues for safety, health and stress at work are raised by the events at Orange?

2 What poor management practices are highlighted in the article that might give rise to the feelings and stress experienced by workers? How do these relate to models and theories in this chapter?

3 How would you approach this desperate situation at Orange in order to help and protect workers and to repair the harmful work culture?

FURTHER READING

Barling, J., Kelloway, E.K. and Frone, M.R. (eds.). *Handbook of Work Stress*. Thousand Oaks, CA: Sage.

Macey, W.H., Schneider, B., Barbera, K.M. and Young, S.A. (2009). *Employee Engagement: Tools for Analysis, Practice and Competitive Advantage.* Chichester: Wiley-Blackwell.

Quick, J.C. and Tetrick, L.E. (2003). *Handbook of occupational health psychology.* Washington DC, USA: American Psychological Association.

Schaufeli, W.B. and Buunk, B.P. (2003). Burnout: An overview of 25 years of research and theorizing. In M.J. Schabracq, J.A.M. Winnubst and C.L. Cooper

(eds.), *Handbook of Work and Health Psychology* (2nd edn., pp. 383–249). Chichester: John Wiley and Sons.

Seligman, M.E.P. (2002). *Authentic Happiness: Using the New Positive Psychology to Realize Your Potential for Lasting Fulfillment.* New York: Free Press/Simon and Schuster.

Shirom, A., Melamed, S., Toker, S., Berliner, S. and Shapira, I. (2005). Burnout and health review: Current knowledge and future directions. In G.P. Hodgkinson and J.K. Ford (eds.). *International Review of Industrial and Organizational Psychology* (pp. 269–308). Chichester: John Wiley and Sons.

REFERENCES

Allen, McManus and Russell (1999) Newcomer Socialization and Stress: Formal Peer Relationships as a Source of Support *** Tammy D. Allen, Stacy E. McManus, Joyce E.A. Russell Journal of Vocational Behavior Volume 54, Issue 3, June 1999, Pages 453–470

Bakker, A.B., Schaufeli, W.B., Sixma, H.J., Bosveld, W. and Van Dierendonck, D. (2000). Patient demands, lack of reciprocity and burnout: A five-year longitudinal study among general practitioners. *Journal of Organizational Behavior*, 21, 425–441.

Baltes, B.B., Briggs, T.E., Huff, J.W., Wright, J.A. and Neuman, G.A. (1999). Flexible and compressed workweek schedules: A meta-analysis of their effects on work-related criteria. *Journal of Applied Psychology, 84(4)*, 496–513.

Barling, J. and Boswell, R. (1995). Work performance and the achievement-strivings and impatience-irritability dimensions of Type A behaviour. *Applied Psychology: An International Review, 44(2)*, 143–53.

Barton, J. (1994). Choosing to work at night: A moderating influence on individual tolerance to shift work. *Journal of Applied Psychology*, 79, 449–454.

Bartone, P.T. (1999). Hardiness protects against war-related stress in Army reserves. *Consulting Psychology Journal: Practice and Research*, 51(2), 72–82.

Beehr, T.A. (1995). *Psychological Stress in the Workplace*. London: Routledge.

Benavides, F.G., Benach, J., Diez-Roux, A.V. and Roman, C. (2000). How do types of employment relate to health indicators? Findings from the Second European Survey on Working Conditions. *Journal of Epidemiology and Community Health, 54(7)*, 494–501.

Berman, M.G., Jonides, J., and Kaplan, S. (2008). The cognitive benefits of interacting with nature. *Psychological Science*, 19, 1207–1212.

Black, C. and Frost, D. (2011). Health at Work: An Independent Review of Sickness Absence, London: HMSO ISBN 9780101820523

Bluen, S.D., Barling, J. and Burns, W. (1990). Predicting sales performance, job satisfaction and depression using the achievement strivings and impatience-irritability dimensions of Type A behaviour. *Journal of Applied Psychology*, 75, 212–216.

Boorman, S. (2009). NHS health and well-being review: Interim report. Leeds, UK: Department of Health.

Briner, R.B., C.Harris. and Daniels. K. (2004). How do work stress and coping work? Toward a fundamental theoretical reappraisal. *British Journal of Guidance and Counselling, 32*, 223–234

Brotheridge, C. and Grandey, A. (2002). Emotional labour and burnout: Comparing two perspectives of 'people work.' *Journal of Vocational Behavior, 60*, 17–39.

Brown, K.W., Ryan, R.M. and Cresswell, J.D. (2007). Mindfulness: theoretical foundations and evidence for its salutary effects. *Psychological Inquiry, 18*, 211–237.

Bureau of Labour Statistics. (1997). *BLS Handbook of Methods*. Washington, DC: Author. Retrieved 29th July, 2009, from **http://www.bls.gov/opub/hom/homtoc.htm**

Bureau of Labour Statistics (2013) **http://www.bls.gov/iif/**

Cannon, W. (1929). *Bodily Changes in Pain, Hunger, Fear and Rage*. New York: Appleton.

Cartwright, S. and Cooper, C.L. (1997). *Managing Workplace Stress*. London: Sage.

Cartwright, S. and Cooper, C.L. (2005). Individually targeted interventions. In J. Barling, E.K. Kelloway and M.R. Frone (eds.), *Handbook of Work Stress*. Thousand Oaks, CA: Sage.

Cohen, S. and Herbert, T.B. (1996). Psychological factors and physical disease from the perspective of psychoneuroimmunology. *Annual Review of Psychology, 47*, 113–42.

Cohen, S., Evans, G.W., Stokols, D. and Krantz, D.S. (1986). *Behaviour, Health and Environmental Stress*. New York: Plenum Press.

Collet, C., Averty, P. and Dittmar, A. (2009). Autonomic nervous system and subjective ratings of strain in air traffic control. *Applied Ergonomics, 40(1)*, 23–32.

Colligan, M.J. and Cohen, A. (2004). The role of training in promoting workplace health and safety. In J. Barling and M.R. Frone (eds.), *The Psychology of Workplace Safety* (pp. 223–248). Washington, DC: American Psychological Association.

Collinson, D.L. (1999). 'Surviving the rigs': Safety and surveillance on North Sea oil installations. *Organization Studies, 20*, 579–600.

Cooper, C.L. and Cartwright, S. (2001). Organizational management of stress and destructive emotions at work. In R.L. Payne and C.L. Cooper (eds.), *Emotions at Work: Theory, Research and Applications for Management* (pp. 269–280). Chichester: John Wiley and Sons.

Cooper, C.L. and Sadri, G. (1994). The impact of stress counselling at work. In R. Crandall and P.L. Perrewe (eds.), *Occupational Stress: A Handbook* (pp. 271–282). Bristol, PA: Taylor and Francis.

Csikszentmihalyi, M. (2008). *Flow: The Psychology of Optimal Experience*. New York: HarperCollins Publishers.

Day, A.L. and Livingstone, H.A. (2001). Chronic and acute stressors among military personnel: Do coping styles buffer their negative impact on health? *Journal of Occupational Health Psychology, 6(4)*, 348–360.

De Dreu, C.K.W. (2008). The virtue and vice of workplace conflict: Food for (pessimistic) thought. *Journal of Organizational Behavior, 29(1)*, 5–18.

Devlin, A. and Arneill, A. (2003). Health care environments and patient outcomes: A review of the literature. *Environment and Behavior, 35*, 665–694.

Dunbar, E. (1993). The role of psychological stress and prior experience in the use of personal protective equipment. *Journal of Safety Research, 24*, 181–187.

Erickson, T.J. (2005). Testimony submitted before the US Senate Committee on Health, Education, Labour and Pensions, May 26.

Evans, G.W. and Johnson, D. (2000). Stress and open-office noise. *Journal of Applied Psychology, 85(5)*, 779–783.

Firth-Cozens, J. (1990). Source of stress in women junior house officers. *British Medical Journal, 301(6743)*, 89–91.

Folkard, S. and Monk, T.H. (1979). Shiftwork and performance. *Human Factors, 21*, 483–492.

Fox WF. Human performance in the cold. Human Factors. 1967;9(3):203–220.

Fox, D.K., Hopkins, B.L. and Anger, W.K. (1987). The long-term effects of a token economy on safety performance in open-pit mining. *Journal of Applied Behavior Analysis, 20*, 215–224.

Fredrickson, B.L. (2009). *Positivity: Groundbreaking Research Reveals How to Embrace the Hidden Strengths of Positive Emotions, Overcome Negativity and Thrive*. New York: Crown Publishers.

French, J.R.P., Caplan, R.D. and Van Harrison, R.V. (1982). *The Mechanisms of Job Stress and Strain*. Chichester: John Wiley and Sons.

Frese, M. (1999). Social support as a moderator of the relationship between work stressors and psychological dysfunctioning: A longitudinal study with objective measures. *Journal of Occupational Health Psychology, 4(3)*, 179–192.

Friedman, M. (1969). *Pathogenesis of Coronary Artery Disease*. New York: McGraw-Hill.

Friedman, M. and Rosenman, R.H. (1974). *Type A Behaviour and Your Heart*. New York: Knopf.

Frone, M.R. (1998). Predictors of work injuries among employed adolescents. *Journal of Applied Psychology, 83*, 565–576.

Frone, M.R. (2000). Work – family conflict and employee psychiatric disorders: The national comorbidity survey. *Journal of Applied Psychology*, *85(6)*, 888–895.

Ganster, D.C. and Murphy, L.R. (2000). Workplace interventions to prevent stress-related illness: Lessons from research and practice. In C.L. Cooper and E.A. Locke (eds.), *Industrial and Organizational Psychology* (pp. 34–51). Oxford: Blackwell.

Ganster, D.C., Fox, M.L. and Dwyer, D.J. (2001). Explaining employees' health care costs: A prospective examination of stressful job demands, personal control, and physiological reactivity. *Journal of Applied Psychology*. *86(5)*, 954–964.

Ganster, D.C., Fusilier, M.R. and Mayes, B.T. (1986). Role of social support in the experience of stress at work. *Journal of Applied Psychology*, *71(1)*, 102–110.

Ghorbani, N., Watson, P.J. and Morris, R.J. (2000). Personality, stress and mental health: evidence of relationships in a sample of Iranian managers. *Personality and Individual Differences*, *28*, 647–657.

Gifford, R. (1997). *Environmental Psychology: Principles and Practice* (2nd ed.). Boston: Allyn and Bacon.

Glass, Singer and Friedman (1969) Psychic cost of adaptation to an environmental stressor. Glass, David C.; Singer, Jerome E.; Friedman, Lucy N. Journal of Personality and Social Psychology, Vol *12(3)*, Jul 1969, 200–210

Goleman, D., Boyatzis, R. and McKee, A. (2002). *The New Leaders: Transforming the Art of Leadership into the Science of Results*. London: Little, Brown.

Goodrich, R. (1982). Seven office evaluations: A review. *Environment and Behavior*, *14*, 353–378.

Gov.uk (2011) NHS staff management and health service quality. https://www.gov.uk/government/news/nhs-staff-management-and-health-service-quality

Grandey, A.A. (2003). When 'the show must go on': Surface acting and deep acting as determinants of emotional exhaustion and peer-rated service delivery. *Academy of Management Journal*, *46(1)*, 86–96.

Grant-Vallone, E.J. and Donaldson, S.L. (2001). Consequences of work – family conflict on employee well-being over time. *Work and Stress*, *15(3)*, 214–226.

Hackman, J.R. and Oldham, G.R. (1980). *Work Redesign*. Reading, MA: Addison-Wesley.

Harter, J.K., Schmidt, F.L. and Keyes, C.L. (2003). Well-being in the Workplace and its Relationship to Business Outcomes: A Review of the Gallup Studies. In C.L.Keyes and J.Haidt (eds.), *Flourishing: The Positive Person and the Good Life* (pp. 205–224). Washington, DC: American Psychological Association.

Health and Safety Executive. (2013). *Annual Statistics Report for Great Britain*, http://www.hse.gov.uk/statistics/causinj/index.htm

Hobfoll, S.E. and Shirom, A. (2000). Conservation of resources theory: Applications to stress and management in the workplace. In R.T. Golembiewski (ed.), *Handbook of organizational behaviour* (2nd edn., pp. 57–81). New York: Marcel Dekker.

Hockey, G.J. (1997). Compensatory control in the regulation of human performance under stress and high workload: a cognitive–energetical framework. *Biological Psychology*, *45*, 73–93.

Hoffman, B.J. and Woehr, D.J. (2005). A quantitative review of the relationship between person-organization fit and behavioral outcomes. *Journal of Vocational Behavior*, *68*, 389–399.

Hofmann, D.A. and Stetzer, A. (1996). A cross-level investigation of factors influencing unsafe behaviours and accidents. *Personnel Psychology*, *49*, 307–339.

Hoonakker, P., Carayon, P. and Schoepke, J. (2004). Work-Family Conflict in the IT Work Force. *Journal of Organizational Behaviour*, *13*, 389–411.

House, J. (1981).*Work Stress and Social Support*. Reading, MA: Addison, Wesley.

Houston, D.M. and Allt, S.K. (1997). Psychological distress and error making among junior house officers. *British Journal of Health Psychology*, *2*, 141–151.

Hülsheger, U.R., Alberts, H.J.E.M., Feinholdt, A. and Lang, J.W.B (2013). Benefits of mindfulness at work: The role of mindfulness in emotion regulation, emotional exhaustion, and job satisfaction. *Journal of Applied Psychology*, *98(2)*, 310–325.

Hurrell, J. (1985). Machine-paced work and the Type A behaviour pattern. *Journal of Occupational Psychology*, *58*, 15–25.

Ising, H., Babisch, W. and Günther, T. (1999). Work noise as a risk factor in myocardial infarction. *Journal of Clinical and Basic Cardiology*, *2*, 64–68.

Jackson, S.E. and Schuler, R.S. (1985). A meta-analysis and conceptual critique of research on role ambiguity and role conflict in work settings. *Organizational Behaviour and Human Decision Processes*, *36(1)*, 16–78.

Jex, S.M. (1998). *Stress and Job Performance: Theory, Research, and Implications for Managerial Practice*. Thousand Oaks, CA: Sage.

Jones, J.R., Huxtable, C.S., Hodgson, J.T. and Price, M.J. (2003). *Self-Reported Work-Related Illness in 2001/02: Results from a Household Survey*. Sudbury: HSE Books.

Jones, J.W., Barge, B.N., Steffy, B.D., Fay, L.M., Kunz, L.K. and Wuebker, L.J. (1988). Stress and medical malpractice: Organizational risk assessment and intervention. *Journal of Applied Psychology, 73*, 727–735.

Kahn, W.A. (1992). To be fully there: Psychological presence at work. *Human Relations, 45(4)*, 321–49.

Karasek, R.A. (1979). Job demands, job decision latitude and mental strain: Implications for job redesign. *Administrative Science Quarterly, 24(2)*, 285–308

Karasek, R. and Theorell, T. (1990). *Healthy Work: Stress, Productivity, and the Reconstruction of Working Life*. New York: Basic Books.

Khan, R.L. and Byosiere, P. (1992). Theoretical framework for the study of stress in organizations. In M.D. Dunnette and L.M. Hough (eds.), *Handbook of Industrial and Organizational Psychology* (2nd ed.) (pp. 571–650). Palo Alto, CA: Consulting Psychologists Press.

Krantz, D.S. and McCeney, M.K. (2002). Effects of psychological and social factors on organic disease: A critical assessment of research on coronary heart disease. *Annual Review of Psychology, 53*, 341–369.

Lang, J., Thomas, J.L., Bliese, P.D. and Adler, A.B. (2007). Job Demands and Job Performance: The mediating effect of psychological and physical strain and the moderating effect of role clarity. *Journal of Occupational Health Psychology, 12(2)*, 116–124.

Layard, R. (2005). *Happiness: Lessons from a New Science*. London: Penguin Press.

Lazarus, R. (1991). *Emotion and Adaptation*. New York: Oxford University Press.

Lazarus, R. (2000). Evolution of a model of stress, coping, and discrete emotions. In V.H. Rice (ed.), *Handbook of Stress, Coping and Health: Implications for Nursing Research, Theory, and Practice* (pp. 195–222). Thousand Oaks, CA: Sage.

Lee, R.A. (1981). The effects of flexitime on family life – Some implications for managers. *Personnel Review, 10(3)*, 31–35.

Lee. R.A. (1983). Flexitime and Conjugal Roles. *Journal of Occupational Behaviour, 4(4)*, 297–315.

Leiter and Maslach (1988) The impact of interpersonal environment on burnout and organizational commitment. Michael P. Leiter and Christina Maslach Issue Journal of Organizational Behavior Journal of Organizational Behavior Volume 9, Issue 4, pages 297–308, October 1988.

Leiter, M.P. and Maslach, C. (2001). Burnout and health. In A. Baum, T.A. Revenson and J.E. Singer (eds.), *Handbook of Health Psychology* (pp. 415–422). Mahwah, NJ: Lawrence Erlbaum.

Levy, R.L., Cain, K.C., Jarrett, M. and Heitkemper, M.M. (1997). The relationship between daily life stress and gastrointestinal symptoms in women with irritable bowel syndrome. *Journal of Behavioral Medicine, 20*, 177–193.

Levy, Cain, Jarrett and Heitkemper (2004) Clinical Gastroenterology and Hepatology Volume 2, Issue 7, July 2004, Pages 585–596. Self-management for women with irritable bowel syndrome* Margaret M Heitkemper*, Monica E Jarrett*, Rona L Levy‡, Kevin C Cain§, Robert L Burr*, Andrew Feldll, Pam Barney*, Pam Weisman*.

Linton, S.J. (1990). Risk factors for neck and back pain in a working population in Sweden. *Work and Stress, 4(1)*, 41–49.

Loughlin, C. and Frone, M.R. (2004). Young workers' occupational safety. In J. Barling and M.R. Frone (eds.), *The Psychology of Workplace Safety* (pp. 107–125). Washington, DC: American Psychological Association.

Lyubomirsky, S., King, L. and Diener, E. (2005). The benefits of frequent positive affect: Does happiness lead to success? *Psychological Bulletin, 131*, 803–855.

Macey, W.H., Schneider, B., Barbera, K.M. and Young, S.A. (2009). *Employee Engagement: Tools for Analysis, Practice, and Competitive Advantage*. Chichester: Wiley-Blackwell.

Maddi, S.R. and Kobasa, S.C. (1984). *The Hardy Executive: Health Under Stress*. Homewood, IL: DowJones-Irwin.

Manning, M.R., Jackson, C.N. and Fusilier, M.R. (1996). Occupational Stress, Social Support, and the Costs of Health Care. *Academy of Management Journal, 39(3)*, 738–750.

Maslach, C. and Leiter, M.P. (1997). *The Truth About Burnout: How Organizations Cause Personal Stress and What to do About it*. San Francisco, CA: Jossey-Bass.

Maslach, Jackson and Leiter (1996) CA. Maslach, C., Jackson, SE, Leiter, MP, 1996. Maslach Burnout Inventory Manual, 3rd Edition. Consulting Psychologists Press, Inc., Palo Alto, CA.

Maslach, Schaufeli and Leiter (2001) JOB BURNOUT Annual Review of Psychology Vol. 52: 397–422 (Volume publication date February 2001) DOI: 10.1146/annurev.psych.52.1.397 Christina Maslach1, Wilmar B. Schaufeli2, and Michael P. Leiter3.

McCoy, J.M. and Evans, G.W. (2004). Physical work environment. In J. Barling, K.E. Kelloway and M.R.Frone (eds.), *Handbook of Work Stress* (pp. 219–266). London: Sage.

McCormick, E. (1976). *Human Factors in Engineering and Design*. New York: McGraw-Hill.

Melamed, S., Kristal-Boneh, E. and Froom, P. (1999). Industrial noise exposure and risk factors for cardiovascular disease: Findings from the CORDIS study. *Noise and Health, 4*, 49–56.

Milanovich, D.M., Driskell, J.E., Stout, R.J. and Salas, E. (1998). Status and cockpit dynamics: A review and empirical study. *Group Dynamics: Theory, Research and Practice*, 2, 155–167.

Motowidlo, S.J., Packard, J.S. and Manning, M.R. (1986). Occupational stress: Its causes and consequences for job performance. *Journal of Applied Psychology, 71(4)*, 618–629.

Murphy, L.R. (1996). Stress management in work settings: A critical review of the health effects. *American Journal of Health Promotion, 11(2)*, 112–135.

Neal, A. and Griffin, M.A. (2004). Safety climate and safety at work. In J. Barling and M.R. Frone (eds.), *The Psychology of Workplace Safety* (pp. 15–34). Washington, DC: American Psychological Association.

Netemeyer, R.G., Johnston, M.W. and Burton, S. (1990). Analysis of role conflict and role ambiguity in a structural equations framework. *Journal of Applied Psychology, 75(2)*, 148–157.

O'Dea, A. and Flin, R. (2000, *August*). *Safety Leadership in the Offshore Oil and Gas Industry*. Paper presented at the Academy of Management Annual Meeting, Toronto, Canada.

Palmer, S., Cooper, C. and Thomas, K. (2004). A model of work stress. *Counselling at Work (Winter)*: 2–5.

Parker, S.K., Axtell, C. and Turner, N. (2001). Designing a safer workplace: Importance of job autonomy, communication quality and supportive supervisors. *Journal of Occupational Health Psychology*, 6, 211–228.

Probst, T.M. and Brubaker, T.L. (2001). The effects of job insecurity on employee safety outcomes: Cross-sectional and longitudinal explorations. *Journal of Occupational Health Psychology*, 6, 139–159.

Pryor, A., Townsend, M., Maller, C. and Field, K. (2006). Health and well-being naturally: 'Contact with nature' in health promotion for targeted individuals, communities and populations. *Health Promotion Journal of Australia*, 17, 114–123.

Quick, J.C., Quick, J.D., Nelson, D.L. and Hurrell, J.J. (1997). *Preventive Stress Management in Organizations*. Washington, DC: American Psychological Association.

Quinlan, M. and Bohle, P. (2004). Contingent work and occupational safety. In J. Barling and M.R. Frone (eds.), *The Psychology of Workplace Safety* (pp. 81–105). Washington, DC: American Psychological Association.

Quinlan, M., Mayhew, C. and Bohle, P. (2001). The global expansion of precarious employment, work disorganization and consequences for occupational health: A review of recent research. *International Journal of Health Services*, 31(2), 225–414.

Reis, H.T. and Gable, S.L. (2003). Toward a positive psychology of relationships. In C.L.M. Keyes and J. Haidt (eds.), *Flourishing* (pp. 129–159). Baltimore, MD: United Books.

Rizzo, J.R., House, R.J. and Lirtzman, S.I. (1970). Role conflict and ambiguity in complex organizations. *Administrative Science Quarterly*, 15(2), 150–163.

Rotter, J.B. (1966). Generalized expectancies for internal versus external control of reinforcement. *Psychological Monographs: General and Applied*, 80(1), 1–28.

Saks, A.M. (2006). Antecedents and consequences of employee engagement. *Journal of Managerial Psychology, 21(7)*, 600–619.

Sauter and Krieg (1992) International Journal of Human-Computer Interaction Volume 4, Issue 3, 1992. Special Issue: Part II: Occupational Stress in Human-Computer Interaction. Work rhythm and physiological rhythms in repetitive computer work: Effects of synchronization on well-being Robert A. Henning Steven L. Sauter & Edward F. Krieg pages 233–243.

Schaufeli, W.B. and Bakker, A.B. (2004). Job demands, job resources and their relationship with burnout and engagement: A multi-sample study. *Journal of Organizational Behaviour, 25(3)*, 293–315.

Schaufeli, W.B. and Buunk, B.P. (2003). Burnout: An overview of 25 years of research and theorizing. In M.J. Schabracq, J.A.M. Winnubst and C.L. Cooper (eds.), *Work and Health Psychology* (2nd edn., pp. 383–249). Chichester: John Wiley and Sons.

Schaufeli, W.B., Salanova, M., González-Romá, V. and Bakker, A.B. (2002). The measurement of engagement and burnout: A two sample confirmatory factor analytic approach. *Journal of Happiness Studies*, 3, 71–92.

Schaufeli, W.B., Taris, T.W. and van Rhenen, W. (2008). Workaholism, burnout and work engagement: Three of a kind or three different kinds of employee well-being? *Applied Psychology*, 57, 173–203.

Schwartz, T. and McCarthy, C. (2007). Manage your energy, not your time. *Harvard Business Review*, 85, 63–66, 68, 70–73.

Seligman, M.E.P. (2002). *Authentic Happiness: Using the New Positive Psychology to Realize Your Potential for Lasting Fulfilment*. New York: Free Press/Simon and Schuster.

Seyle, H. (1956). *The Stress of Life*. New York: McGraw-Hill.

Smith, A., Brice, C., Collins, A., Matthews, V. and McNamara, R. (2000b). *The Scale of Perceived*

Stress at Work: A Further Analysis of the Impact of Demographic Factors and Type of Job. Contract Research Report/2000. Sudbury: HSE Books.

Smith, A., Johal S.S., Wadsworth E., Davey Smith. G. and Peters, T. (2000a). *The Scale of Perceived Stress at Work: The Bristol Stress and Health at Work Study. Contract Research Report 265/2000,* Sudbury: HSE Books.

Smith, C.S., Robie, C., Barton, J., Smith, L., Spelten, E., Totterdell, P. and Costa, G. (1999). A process model of shiftwork and health. *Journal of Occupational Health Psychology, 4,* 207–218.

Sonnentag and Fritz (2007) The Recovery Experience Questionnaire: Development and validation of a measure for assessing recuperation and unwinding from work. Sonnentag, Sabine; Fritz, Charlotte Journal of Occupational Health Psychology, *Vol 12(3),* Jul 2007, 204–221.

Sonnentag, S., Binnewies, C. and Mojza, E.J. (2008). 'Did you have a nice evening?' A day-level study on recovery experiences, sleep and affect. *Journal of Applied Psychology, 93(3),* 674–684.

Sonnentag, S., Mojza, E. J., Binnewies, C. and Scholl, A. (2008). Being engaged at work and detached at home: A week-level study on work engagement, psychological detachment, and affect. *Work and Stress, 22,* 257–276.

Sonnentag, S., Kuttler, I. and Fritz, C. (2010). Job stressors, emotional exhaustion, and need for recovery: A multi-source study on the benefits of psychological detachment. *Journal of Vocational Behavior, 76,* 355–365.

Takala J. (2002). Introductory report: *Decent Work – Safe Work.* Paper presented at the XVIth World Congress on Safety and Health at Work, Vienna: ILO.

Taylor, A.F. and Kuo, F.E. (2009). Children with attention deficits concentrate better after walk in the park. *Journal of Attention Disorders, 12,* 402–409.

Tjosvold, D. (1990). Flight crew collaboration to manage safety risks. *Group and Organization Studies, 15,* 177–191.

Turner, N. and Parker, S.K. (2004). The effect of teamwork on safety processes and outcomes. In J. Barling and M.R. Frone (eds.), *The Psychology of Workplace Safety* (pp. 35–63). Washington DC: American Psychological Association.

Ulrich, R. (2006). Evidence-based health care architecture. *The Lancet, 368,* S38–S39.

Verquer, M.L., Beehr, T.A. and Wagner, S.H. (2003). A meta-analysis of relations between person–organization fit and work attitudes. *Journal of Vocational Behavior, 63,* 473–489.

Wall, T.D., Bolden, R.I., Borrill, C.S., Carter A.J., Golya, D.A., Hardy, G.E., Haynes, C.E., Rick, J.E., Shapiro, D.A. and West, M.A. (1997). Minor psychiatric disorder in NHS Trust staff: Occupational and gender differences. *British Journal of Psychiatry, 171,* 519–523.

West, M.A. (1979a). Meditation: a review. *British Journal of Psychiatry, 135,* 457–467.

West, M.A. (1979b). Physiological effects of meditation: A longitudinal study. *British Journal of Social and Clinical Psychology, 18,* 219–226.

West, M.A. (1980). Meditation, personality and arousal. *Personality and Individual Differences, 1,* 135–142.

West, M.A. (ed.) (1987). *The psychology of meditation.* Oxford: Oxford University Press.

West, M.A. and Lyubovnikova, J. (2013). Illusions of teamworking in healthcare. *Journal of Health Organization and Management, 27,* 134–142.

Wickens, C.D. and Hollands, J. G. (2000). *Engineering psychology and human performance* (3rd ed.). Upper Saddle River, NJ: Prentice Hall.

Wineman, J.D. (1986). *Behavioural Issues in Office Design.* New York: Van Nostrand Reinhold.

Xie, J.L. (1996). Karasek's model in the People's Republic of China: Effects of job demands, control, and individual differences. *Academy of Management Journal, 39(6),* 1594–1618.

Zacharatos, A. and Barling, J. (2004). High-performance work systems and occupational safety. In J.Barling and M.R. Frone (eds.), *The Psychology of Workplace Safety* (pp. 203–222). Washington, DC: American Psychological Association.

Zapf, D. and Gross, C. (2001). Conflict escalation and coping with workplace bullying: A replication and extension. *European Journal of Work and Organizational Psychology, 10(4),* 497–522.

Zhao, Y., Zhang, S., Selvin and Spear, R.C. (1991). A dose response relation for noise induced hypertension. *British Journal of Industrial Medicine, 48,* 179–184.

Zohar, D. (1980). Safety climate in industrial organizations: Theoretical and applied implications. *Journal of Applied Psychology, 65,* 96–102.

Zohar, D. (2003). Safety climate: Conceptual and measurement issues. In J.C. Quick and L.E. Tetrick (eds.), *Handbook of Occupational Health Psychology* (pp. 123–142). Washington, DC: American Psychological Association.

CASE STUDIES FOR PART TWO: PROFESSIONAL PRACTICE OF WORK AND ORGANIZATIONAL PSYCHOLOGY

CASE STUDY 2.1

This case was prepared by Research Fellow Dr. Shaohui Chen at CEIBS. The case was prepared as the basis for class discussion rather than to illustrate either effective or ineffective handling of an administrative situation. Certain names and other identifying information may have been disguised to protect confidentiality. Used with permission.

Human Resource Management in B&Q China: Upgrading Action

Here is a case about performance measurement in B&Q in China, in which Executive Vice President of HRM and Training, Lily Chen, needs to think about how to design and implement a new performance assessment system.

In the winter of 2004, Lily Chen, an experienced HR and training specialist who had worked in several multinationals in China for more than ten years, decided to join B&Q China as Executive Vice President of HRM and Training. The multinational she quit had been operating in China for many years and had established a mature management system. Although this meant a stable job and income, she longed for a more challenging and innovative career platform. One of the prime motivators for her joining B&Q was David Wei, the President of B&Q China. Wei was the first Chinese to work as a president for a multinational's China business; all CEOs in Lily's previous company were foreign expatriates. However, undoubtedly, the most attractive part of this new role was the challenge associated with it. Wei had often emphasized the need to change the human resource management functions of B&Q China:

Human resource management needs some change. It should be capable of meeting the need for talent due to the expansion of B&Q China operations. The company can empower you to use your own discretion and innovative ability to propose and implement a human resource management framework which is suitable for the company's rapid development. The company hopes to have a strong human resource management team.

Lily knew that this was the opportunity she had been waiting for. From the first day of joining, Lily began to probe deeper to understand the significance of what David said.

The Speedy Development of B&Q China Business

B&Q is the number one DIY retailer in Europe and the third largest in the world. Since its establishment in Southampton, UK, in 1969, it has been developing its DIY business to become the first home improvement retailing brand in the UK. Currently B&Q employs over 35 000 people in over 370 stores across the UK. It also has a global presence with operations in more than ten countries. The parent company of B&Q is Kingfisher plc., which is listed among the Fortune 500 companies as one of the fastest developing companies in the world retailing industry.

With more than 30 years' expertise in franchise business management, B&Q started to expand its territory steadily in the global arena in the 1990s. In 1996, B&Q opened its first store outside the UK in Taiwan, China, marking its entry into the huge China market. In June 1999, based on in-depth market research and investigation in the Chinese market, especially Shanghai, the first B&Q store – Shanghai Hutai store – was opened to customers in mainland China.

In the following five years, B&Q opened chained warehouse stores in more than 20 big cities in China; B&Q stores are spread over central, south, north and east of China. It has now illustrated the real meaning of the economy of scale and positioned itself as a modern, reliable brand among the local Chinese customers. Since 2002, B&Q China is continually listed as the champion in the China Chain Store and Franchise Association (CCFA) in terms of the annual turnover and the average turnover of a single store in the home improvement materials retailing industry, making China the fastest growing market among all Kingfisher Group's global business. On November 2004, for the purpose of speeding up B&Q expansion in China, Kingfisher acquired five stores of Pricemart, a Chinese private-owned enterprise, and increased the number of B&Q China stores to 21. This acquisition strongly consolidated B&Q's position in the home improvement and decoration materials retailing business in China.

Lily realized that hiring new people would not be a problem as local labour is readily available in China. The real challenge would be the quality of labour – how to meet the HRM quality requirement raised by the B&Q mission of 'one-stop shopping and professionalized service' and the rapid business expansion and development.

Human Resource Management System in B&Q China

Lily Chen visited many functional departments and stores and communicated with managers. She found that the human resource management function was weak, both at the headquarters and the regional stores. In 2004, B&Q China had a workforce of more than 5000 employees and operated a decentralization model of human resource management system across B&Q headquarters, regional offices and stores. Lily said:

Firstly, I observed the structure. It seemed that the headquarter staff only took care of the headquarters' personnel matters and regional centres' staff took care of the regional staff. There was an HR director or manager in every

region who reported directly to the regional general manager, but did not report to the headquarters' HR department. In fact, the headquarters left a huge free space for HR management in regions and stores.

In short, this management practice shaped a pattern of 'the headquarter taking care of the headquarter matters and the regions taking care of the regional matters'. Every store manager and HR supervisor was responsible directly to the regional HR director or manager and the regional HR director or manager only reported to his regional general manager. He had no business with the HRM function and director at the headquarters. Therefore, the daily work of the HRM department in the headquarters focused on the personnel matters of 400–500 employees in the headquarters and exerted little influence on the HRM practices (planning, guiding, monitoring, training and development) of the regions and stores (see Exhibit 2.1.1). This resulted in lack of clarity and consistency regarding HRM policies and practices in the company. Lily commented:

In terms of HRM policies and initiatives, the regional HR management should follow the headquarters. But, in fact, every region drove their own initiative and our human resource management looked like different practices in different companies. We even had different training materials in our four regional centres, because every training manager developed his/her own material and thought they were the best. The headquarters did not pay heed to these kinds of practices.

Now Lily clearly understood what the company's CEO meant by building up a strong HR management department. She had not only to upgrade the whole HRM system, but also take care of the training and HR administrative functions. She clearly recognized:

Because the company is getting bigger and bigger, its HRM needs a higher degree of coordination and consistency, and should give consistent messages to company people.

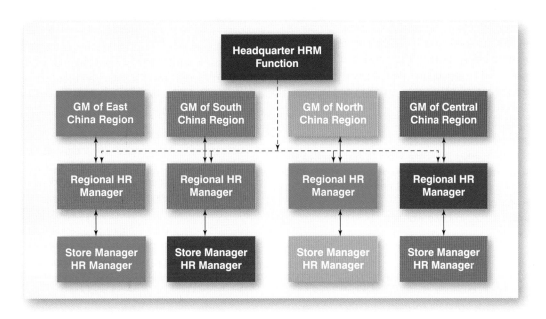

Exhibit 2.1.1   The reporting line of HRM function in B&Q China in 2004

Lily deemed that since the pace of opening new stores in every region was rapidly accelerating, and because the workload and complexity of staffing, training and motivation were constantly increasing, it would be very important to enhance the HRM capability of the headquarter. Referring to this aspect, she said:

Actually, this part (headquarter ability of managing regions and stores' human resource) was the most important. From the company perspective, the HR depart-ment in the headquarters should not only manage the staff there, but also support the HR management in other regions. And more importantly, it should also be capable of conveying and executing headquarters HRM policies and the best practices in regions and stores.

Undoubtedly, to utilize the capability of HRM more effectively, it was important to position the functional role of HRM in the company. In her words:

In fact, I personally think HRM is not only an administrative and supportive function, it should drive the business and should be a strategic

partner of company development. Any HRM policy the company initiates and implements should link to business development.

Main HRM Functions in B&Q

Basically, HRM in B&Q China included recruitment and staffing, compensation and benefits, training and development and employment relations. After monitoring these areas closely, Lily felt that some HRM practices needed to be changed from the root and that would be vital to exert the influence of HRM on business:

To speak concretely, we can take the exam-ple of staffing. Our company is developing faster, but the job descriptions (JD) are becoming irrelevant. The JDs of some posi-tions were being used for several years. They were not suitable and relevant to the current situation and needed some adjustments.

It seemed that a renewed job description system was imperative to guarantee the quality of HRM in the company. This would decide the basic content and evaluation criteria for recruitment and selection, performance management, compensation, training and employment relations. For assuring the competency of a large number of new recruits every year, it was essential to ensure that the training system was consistent across all regions, and measurable performance standards were set and attractive compensation and incentive schemes developed.

Moreover, during her discussions with managers and staff members (at different levels) about the performance appraisal system, she found that the current five-score method of performance evaluation did not provide valid performance data to the management or other members of the staff (Exhibit 2.1.2). In Lily's words:

I communicated with many managers and staff members about performance management in the company. Gradually, the issue was getting clearer during these conversations and the solution furthermore emerged from a discussion among the senior management. Most Chinese people like to use the word 'jiao-hao' (ok) to describe an average or below average performance. In 5-score performance evaluation, 1 stands for extreme unsatisfied performance, 2 stands for unsatisfied, 3 stands for average performance, 4 stands for good and 5 stands for excellent performance. Under this system, a majority of the staff would score 3 or 4, only a few would be marked at 5; however, none would be given a score of 1 or 2. Then we started to think that since none would score 1 or 2, why did we have these scores in the evaluation form?

Owing to the lack of a measurable performance evaluation system, the performance review unavoidably became a 'just-go-through movement' in the company, which did not have much of a bearing on employees' compensation and reward, and therefore, it failed to exert its influence on employees' performance as a motivator:

The store staff had no motive for excellent performance (the reward to them) as it depended on the performance of the whole company. For instance, if the company achieved the business target at the end of the year, all staff members would get 150 yuan as bonus (just a figure of speech, not the actual number of money); if the company exceeded the target, then everybody got 250 yuan as bonus. No matter how good or bad your performance was, all people ate the same rice from the big pot 'Da Guo Fan'. Similarly, at the year end, if a store performance was good, then everyone got a bonus, if the store's performance was not good, no one got bonus.

The management's decision was unanimous. Most managers believed that this performance management mechanism was not reasonable, because it could not identify and discipline the unsatisfied performer, but made good performers lose their inspiration and motivation. It did not emphasize on the fairness of rewards and punishment, and did not deliver a clear message about B&Q's result-oriented value to employees.

I. Performance Against Objectives

Objectives/Key Responsibilities	Measurable Performance Target	Rating 1–5
A.	–	–
B.	–	–
C.	–	–
D.	–	–

Rating: 1. Requires action 2. Partially meets job requirements 3. Fully meets job requirements 4. Exceeds job requirements 5. Excellent

Exhibit 2.1.2   B&Q China performance appraisal for office staff – 2005 (a part of performance review form)

In addition, Lily was aware that employment relations in the retailing industry is 'very sophisticated', and it is very important for the HRM function to properly conduct all HR-related work, such as recruitment and selection, contract continuity and termination. After a few years of operations in China, B&Q not only progressed in terms of business development, but also earned the reputation of being a 'very people-oriented company and employer'. However, there was a digression among B&Q staff regarding the understanding of what people-oriented management was:

B&Q gained the reputation of being a people-oriented company. However, some employees would misuse the concept of 'caring people'. According to their understanding, it seemed that because the company and management cared for the people, it should never fire people or terminate the employment contract. In fact, this was the thing of 'changing the concept stealthily'. It seemed that 'caring people' meant no punishment, no discipline and no rules. This understanding was, however, wrong.

Lily also felt that the company's management needed to have a better understanding about HRM functions and procedures. The differences between performance appraisal and performance management had to be clearly explained to managers and other members of the staff; a result-oriented performance management system had to be introduced and executed to actualize the company's strategic targets. More importantly, the company and management had to unmistakably convey this result orientation principle and should be capable of executing this principle in the day-to-day working of the management in headquarters, regions and stores.

However, since the company's HRM decentralization management model and the weak HRM foundation still needed improvement, Lily believed that the HRM department at the headquarters needed to take initiative:

The company's HRM department is very important. It should have an in-depth understanding of the company's values and senior management's intentions and the ability to carry them out. The HRM department must drive the change. If we do not drive, other departments will not do it.

According to the B&Q management procedure, David wanted Lily to propose an HRM improving and upgrading plan as soon as possible and submit it to the company's management committee for analysis and discussion. Once the upgrading plan was approved, the new set of HRM policies and procedures would be implemented in the company. Lily knew that to make the proposed upgrading plan effective, it would be essential to find a good starting point.

Questions

1 What advice and recommendations would you give to Lily about designing the new performance assessment system?

2 What steps should be taken to ensure that the system is consistent with the strategy at B&Q.

3 What other systems need to be considered to ensure that the assessments of performance are put to good use in improving performance?

4 What cultural factors should be taken into account in this context?

CASE STUDY 2.2

Managing the Management Consultant: Applying Professional Practice of Work and Organizational Psychology

This case is about the work of Management Consultants and is designed to help you integrate the material from Chapters in Part Two of the book. Read the following information about working as a Management Consultant and then complete the task that follows.

The Work of a Management Consultant

The work of management consultants focuses on improving efficiency and driving the growth of organizations through changes to organizational structure, strategy, management and operations. Management consultants can work with private and public sector clients over a wide variety of areas, from HR to supply-chain management. Management consultancy firms can be small, niche organizations specializing in specific services or industry sectors; or they can be made up of thousands of people all over the world delivering services regardless of location.

The typical work of a consultant involves preparing for and bidding on projects to work on, getting to know the client's organization, putting forward recommendations for change and implementing these solutions. Management consultants will often work as project managers, drawing together and maintaining the focus of teams with various specialisms, to implement bespoke solutions for clients. The work typically involves a lot of travel to client sites and to meet with project

teams. The nature of the work means there are targets to meet in short timeframes, so consultants typically work long hours to ensure work is ready.

Management consultants are responsible for ensuring the client understands and is satisfied with the project's progression and dealing with any concerns or resistance. Also, client requirements frequently change so consultants have to adapt quickly to deliver the best solution. Additionally, consultants will move from one project to the next straightaway, which means adapting to working with a different group of people and a new set of requirements rapidly. Exhibit 2.2.1 shows a set of competencies for management consultants.

Career Preparation and Trajectory

Many of the larger consultancy firms hire graduates straight from university, although mature candidates can move into the area with many years of work experience in a specific sector. Graduates can enter the profession from any degree background, from the Arts to Engineering, although often successful candidates have a Masters in a business-related subject or an MBA.

Graduate recruits typically begin their careers in an analyst role. Their time is spent conducting research, such as leading focus groups and conducting interviews with various employees and performing data analyses to build-up a picture of client organizations. They also help prepare project tenders and presentations to clients.

Progression is often fairly rapid, especially in the larger consultancies, where intense training and development will mean graduates are fulfilling the full consultancy role after about two years. Once they have reached this stage the work is more about identifying potential issues within organizations and providing possible solutions. At this level Consultants will often manage a specific

---

Competencies of a management consultant:

Communication

The extent to which an individual conveys oral and written information and responds to questions and challenges

Influencing others

The extent to which an individual persuades others to do something or adopt a point of view in order to produce desired results and takes action in which the dominant influence is one's own convictions rather than the influence of others' opinions

Organizing and planning

The extent to which an individual systematically arranges his/her own work and resources as well as that of others for efficient task accomplishment; and the extent to which an individual anticipates and prepares for the future

Problem solving

The extent to which an individual gathers information; understands relevant technical and professional information; effectively analyses data and information; generates viable options, ideas, and solutions; selects supportable courses of action for problems and situations; uses available resources in new ways; and generates and recognizes imaginative solutions

Teamwork and consideration of others

The extent to which an individual considers the needs of others, participates as a member of a group and is aware of the impact and implications of decisions relevant to others

Leadership

The extent to which an individual takes on the responsibility for providing focus to a team and develops members of that team

Drive

The extent which an individual originates and maintains a high activity level, sets high performance standards and persists in their achievement, and expresses the desire to advance

Tolerance for stress/uncertainty

The extent to which an individual maintains effectiveness in diverse situations under varying degrees of pressure, opposition and disappointment

---

Biggs, D.M. (2010) *Management Consultancy: A guide for students* Cengage Ltd London

Exhibit 2.2.1   Competencies of a Management Consultant

workstream within a project and be responsible for liaising with the relevant client stakeholders, presenting findings and implementing relevant recommendations.

After three years, graduates can expect to progress to Senior Consultant level and to project managing their own teams. After this point Consultants can go on to specialize in a specific sector, or progress to Director or Partner level. This means a more strategic role, regarding the growth of the firm, generating new business and maintaining relationships with clients. Alternatively, many

Consultants set up their own companies, using their contacts and experience.

Questions

Use the information provided in the case study to discuss the key areas of professional practice for Work Psychologists covered in Part Two, then prepare a plan to cover the following in relation to Management Consultants:

1   Appropriate recruitment and selection principles and processes.

2   Training and Development practices.

3   Performance Management.

4   Assurance of Safety and Health at work.

5   Career Development and Management.

PART THREE
ORGANIZATIONS

This final section of the book takes our perspective up a level to that of organizations as a whole. At this level, research and theorizing become more complex since account has to be taken of processes at individual and group level that influence and determine organizational processes. Account also has to be taken of the external environment within which organizations operate: their markets, countries, cultures, competitors and governments. Organizations vary considerably in size, purpose and processes. They are entities that can range from a small enterprise of perhaps 20 people working in a tool-making company, manufacturing parts for machinery used in car production, up to BP, one of the largest corporations in Europe, with 37 000 employees. Even that is tiny in comparison with the 1.4 million employees in the network of organizations that makes up the National Health Service in the UK. Organizations are created to align the activities of employees towards achieving organizational goals. This involves structuring activities and specifying goals and strategies; providing effective leadership which directs, motivates and enables employees to successfully achieve what is required; building effective teams and ensuring inter-team working; developing and reinforcing values and norms within the organization that sustain effective performance; and managing the change which is essential for organizations to adapt continually to their ever-changing environments. The next five chapters explore research and theorizing in these areas, providing a thorough grounding in understanding organizations, that we believe is essential for understanding Work and Organizational Psychology.

CHAPTER 11

ORGANIZATIONS: STRATEGY AND STRUCTURE

LEARNING OBJECTIVES

- To grasp the importance of strategy and structure as topics for study.

- To understand and be able to explain what is meant by organization strategy.

- To be able to compare and contrast the different perspectives on strategy adopted by theorists over the last 50 years, including management by objectives, bounded rationality, economic perspectives, resource-based view of the firm, emergent strategy and strategy as process.

- To be able to present the arguments for a value based perspective on strategy.

- To understand the structure of organizations and be able to explain how this can affect culture, behaviour and work attitudes in organizations.

- To have the ability to analyze the structure of any organization.

- To be able to explain how the environment of an organization affects its structure.

Psychologists are interested in human behaviour – individual, social and organizational (such as the study of culture and climate). In this chapter, we consider organizational strategies, structures and environments and the relationships between them. These are topics few organizational psychology texts address, so why do we think you should study them? More to the point, what difference will they make to your ability to understand and influence organizations for the benefit of those who work within them and are served by them?

> *Picture the following scenario: It is the credit crunch and economic recession of 2009 and you are working in a large company that makes a range of products for supplying the automotive industry. The industry is highly competitive and suppliers' prices are driven down by the large car manufacturers. The bottom has dropped out of the market and no one is buying cars. Not surprisingly, your company is suffering. The car companies have dramatically reduced their*

orders and they are bearing down hard on the prices your company charges for the products it supplies to them. They have smaller orders, they are in financial difficulties and they want your company to reduce costs and therefore prices too. The company has always been highly participative and consults its staff about major decisions – and you as a Work and Organizational Psychologist are always carefully listened to. The company is going to have to cut costs by at least 40 per cent or find new markets that will bring in an additional 40 per cent of revenue.

The company seems faced with a choice between two strategies. The first is to encourage innovation, to develop better products that differentiate it from competitors, and find innovative ways of reducing costs. This will involve everyone in the company coming up with new and improved ways of doing things. Ensuring a climate for innovation and ensuring that teams are focused on developing new and improved processes and products is vital. The alternative is to make a substantial proportion of the staff redundant to achieve the necessary cost savings to help the company stay in business. You are asked for your opinion as a Work Psychologist. Your advice is important because it could influence whether the company stays in business or goes bust. Your instincts as a psychologist are to keep people in work and to go for the innovation strategy – but is that a recipe for failure? It may very well be in the circumstances. 🔲🔲

And that is why those who study Work and Organizational Psychology should have an understanding of strategy, structure and environment – because it provides and indeed shapes the context for their work. If psychologists are to be leaders in organizations (and who better to lead them?), then they should understand structure of organizations and the nature of strategy.

In this chapter we explore organizations and their relationships with their environments via the topics of strategy and structure. To begin though, we must think carefully about what an organization is.

Huczynski and Buchannan (2007) define 'organization' as *a social arrangement for achieving controlled performance in pursuit of collective goals* (p. 6) and that generality makes it clear that organizations have been around for most of human history. We have had social arrangements for achieving controlled performance in pursuit of our collective goals for most of human history. It is notable that historically, few organizations, with the exception of the religious and the military, were ever bigger than about 30 people. Indeed, most people worked in small groups of three, four, five or six people. Organizations of 20 or more people tended to be unusual. All that changed with the Industrial Revolution, however, and for just the last 200 years, for the briefest eye blink of human history (probably about 0.2 per cent of out time here), large organizations have begun to proliferate. And with that proliferation has come an industry of management, consultancy, leadership and, yes, Work and Organizational Psychology. All have developed as we struggle to understand and manage these much larger social organizations that we have created to meet our economic needs. What practitioners, academics and management consultants are all concerned about is finding ways of ensuring that organizations survive, prosper and succeed in increasingly turbulent and competitive environments, so strategy is a word that dominates their conversations.

ORGANIZATIONAL STRATEGY

Much of our discourse about organizations is unquestioned since the words we use to discuss organizations proliferate in textbooks, newspapers and daily conversations about workplaces, so it is important to be aware that the concept of organizational strategy is relatively recent. The word strategy was always used to describe the tactics of generals in battle rather than the plans of organizational leaders. It is a concept embedded in the study of war. One of the earliest proponents of strategy as a concept taken out of the context of military manoeuvres was Niccolò Machiavelli. His writings in *The Prince* elucidated ideas about how Italian leaders in the 16th century could preserve their power and control their states, engage effectively with other states and prosper and succeed without the necessity of going to war. His name became a byword for manipulation and intrigue in common parlance, he was a master of power, politics and strategy. His writings on the subjects provide quotes for management scholars to this day. What he says about the challenges of innovation illustrate this by providing valuable insight into the psychology of the process of innovation:

> *... There is no more delicate matter to take in hand, nor more dangerous to conduct, nor more doubtful in its successes, than to set up as a leader in the introduction of changes. For he who innovates will have for his enemies all those who are well off under the existing order of things and only lukewarm supporters in those who might be better off under the new. This lukewarm temper arises partly from the fear of adversaries who have the laws on their side and partly from the incredulity of mankind who will never admit the merit of anything new, until they have seen it proved by the event.* Niccolò Machiavelli, Le Prince.

Although Machiavelli was therefore an early champion of the idea of strategy in organizations (albeit states), we have to wait until the latter half of the 20th century before the concept was being applied systematically to thinking about organization development

> *The end is still the same – to be victorious in the field of battle – it is merely the arena that has shifted. Competition is war by other means and, so the story goes, you need strategy to win it.* (Carter, Clegg and Kornhauser, 2008, p. 19.)

We will review its history from that point on, but first we must clarify what we mean by this word.

What is Strategy?

Strategy is variously defined as a concern of organizational leaders with the future and with the goals of the organization; as a metaphorical road map to guide the organization towards a desired destination; and as a means of achieving goals through the use of its resources. Because organizations are in competition with other organizations (other car parts suppliers in the example we used at the beginning), they need strategies to ensure they win (or at least do not lose – since losing can be fatal to the organization). The assumption in scholarly as well as popular writings is that strategy is the business of top managers. They are the people with the knowledge, skills and abilities to shape and implement strategy – it is what they are paid to do:

> *usually it is a top management privilege to spend time at expensive management retreats arguing with even more expensive consultants about 'what if ... scenarios'.* (Carter *et al.*, 2008, p. 10.)

According to most (though not all, as we will see) theorists, strategy is very much an organizational response to the environment and to changes in the environment. Just like an organism, an organization needs to adjust to changes in its environment in order to survive and prosper. Animals forage for food more widely when there is too little because of other predators; organizations seek new markets. Therefore, the strategy of the organization is a means of survival or defeating the opposition and provides a map for how to achieve these or other desired outcomes. Strategic decisions in turn leads to changes in the processes and operations of the organization. Indeed, theory suggests that strategy shapes the structure of the organization(in terms of hierarchies and divisions of operations) and influences its culture (values and practices).

If strategy shapes structures, determines policies and practices in organizations and influences values and behaviours, then self evidently, it should be of central concern to those studying Work and Organizational Psychology. It would be convenient therefore to offer a simple and coherent view of what scholars' take on strategy is but the ground has shifted a great deal over the last 60 years and is energetically contested. In order to help the reader understand this elusive concept of strategy, we will briefly review the history of theorizing over the last 50 years.

The Early History of Strategic Management

The development of strategic management as a discipline began in the 1950s when Philip Selznick (1957) introduced the idea that managers would need to 'fit' the organization to its external environment, 'strategy' being the set of decisions shaped by and responding to external factors. This led to the development of 'SWOT' analysis, in which managers carefully consider the Strengths and Weaknesses of their organizations, while also considering the Opportunities and Threats they face. Such an analysis, it was claimed, provided a basis for strategic planning.

The developing discipline of strategic management was given an intellectual coherence by the publication of Alfred Chandler's book *Strategy and Structure* in 1962. Until then, management had largely been seen as a series of separate activities – production, sales, marketing, R&D and finance. Chandler drew attention to the need for an integrated approach to management that took a long-term perspective and this approach was named 'strategy'. The structure of the organization, he argued, would then be consequent upon the strategic choices made by senior managers. The departments and hierarchies are structured in order to respond to the demands of the environment. Many theorists now argue that organizational structures (divisions, departments and hierarchies) are created to reduce uncertainty in the environment. There is a marketing department because it reduces uncertainty about customer needs and preferences; there is an R&D department because it reduces the uncertainty about how to create new products to meet shifting demands.

These models of strategy were based on a rational, neat and quasi-military approach to planning for the future. Environments were understood, decisions made and structures adapted in a rational, unambiguous and transparent way. The 'Rational Planning Model' had an early champion in Igor Ansoff (1965), an applied mathematician and business manager, who developed strategic management as a discipline by offering both dynamic models and a vocabulary that remains influential to this day. He distinguished between three broad activities in organizations:

- Administrative activities – direct production processes.
- Operational activities – maximization of efficiency of administrative processes.
- Strategic activities – directed to managing the organization's relationship with its environment and anticipating strategic turbulence or continual change.

Ansoff introduced the idea of 'gap analysis', a process of identifying the space between where the organization is today, where we would like it to be, and the necessary actions to reduce the gap. His Product Mission Matrix, which continues to influence thinking and practice today, integrates market and product analyses to produce the 2 by 2 matrix shown in Figure 11.1. Decisions about whether to focus on new or existing markets and to focus on existing or new products provide four broad strategies:

Market penetration involves selling more existing products/services into existing markets. The aim is to maintain or increase market share through having the most competitive prices, or effective advertising or using loyalty schemes so that customers always shop with you rather than your competitors because of the discounts they get. Dell computers has pursued this strategy very successfully, driving down prices and driving away competitors.

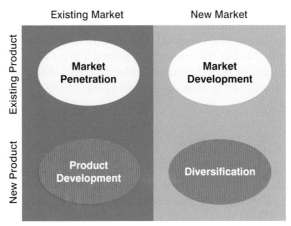

Figure 11.1   Ansoff's product market matrix

Market development involves selling existing products into new markets. Examples might be generating markets in new geographical areas. Japan uses barcode recognition on most of its mobile telephone devices. The companies that make these systems could adopt market development strategies by seeking to make them available in Europe and the US for example. Their widespread adoption would create huge new markets for these companies.

Product development is a strategy based on selling new products or services into current markets. For example, a vehicle breakdown service may begin offering car insurance to its customers followed by house and travel insurance.

DISCUSS WITH A COLLEAGUE

Identify four different organizations that use one of these strategies. Try to discover what it is about their products or markets that leads them to adopt this strategy. Do you think it is the right strategy for them? What strategy would you recommend, given their products and markets? Talk to managers in different organizations (they may be family or friends, colleagues on your course) and ask them which strategy is pursued by their organizations. Ask them if they are able to say why their organization pursues this strategy and whether one of the other three alternatives could work for them. Such conversations are likely to increase the sophistication of your understanding of strategy and enrich your appreciation of organizations more generally.

Diversification strategies involve selling new products or services into new markets. This means diversifying the products the organization seeks to sell and trying to sell them into markets the company has not operated in before. This might involve moving into the business of your suppliers – a car manufacturer deciding to make oil filters for its own cars and selling them to other car manufacturers; acquisition of other companies in order to diversify activities so the organization is not too dependent upon one market; or developing new product lines as a result of an accident (e.g. the weakly sticky Post-It note was the result of a failure to make a strong enough adhesive at 3M).

Having understood what we mean by strategy and explored briefly the beginnings of strategic management, we now explore major approaches to strategy in the last 60 years.

MAJOR PERSPECTIVES ON STRATEGY

Management By Objectives

One of the most influential management theorists of the 20th century, Austrian born Peter Drucker, asserted from a management perspective what Work and Organizational Psychologists see as axiomatic – the importance of clear objectives. Drucker emphasized clear objectives for the organization as a means of ensuring survival and success. His work led to the influential approach dubbed 'management by objectives' – ensuring the organization has clear objectives and that those of the departments, teams and individuals who make up the organization are derived from the organization's overall objectives. Managing by objectives is not just about setting objectives but also about monitoring progress towards them. He also gave credence to the notion of the *intellectual capital* of the organization – the fact that the knowledge that employees hold in their heads and that the organization retains in its 'memory' is a vital resource, as much as land, buildings and technology. Work and Organizational Psychologists should be interested in Drucker's work because it was grounded in theory and a strong commitment to intellectual understanding which shines through in the many influential books he authored. Moreover, unlike some of his predecessors and many economists, his interest was not in the behaviour of commodities, but the behaviour of people. Understanding behaviour of people within organizations was vital to both setting and managing strategy. For a good account of Drucker, his life and his extraordinary intellectual contribution to our understanding of organizations see Elizabeth Edersheim's book, *The Definitive Drucker* (2007).

Bounded Rationality Perspectives on Strategy

Academic thinking about strategy was profoundly influenced by the Nobel Prize winning economist Herbert Simon (1945). He argued, in contrast to assumptions of rational planning models, that, in real life, decision-making was far from perfect, not entirely rational and could only be understood as approximations to rationality. He coined the term 'satisficing' to describe what managers do when developing strategies and making decisions, a word which combines 'sufficing' and 'satisfying'. Simon's work suggests that managers should be focused on doing enough to get the job done rather than wasting time and energy seeking the very best decisions. Rationality is limited by lack of information, our cognitive limitations in processing a wide variety of complex and uncertain information, and simply the time available to manage complexity. What we see in organizational strategies and managerial decision-making is not rationality but 'bounded rationality': rationality bounded by these limitations. There are many other bounds to rationality, such as incorrect information, misinterpreted information, powerful interests dictating decisions and so on.

Cohen, March and Olsen (1972) took this thinking further with their startlingly named *garbage can model of decision-making*. Their analysis of strategy offered surprising insights into the randomness and complexity of strategic decision-making. They proposed that there are streams of events in organizations such as *problems* that can arise inside or outside the organization (loss of key personnel; economic downturn) and *solutions* (new product ideas; opportunities to sell into new markets; the serendipitous discovery of new products or processes). These solutions are not necessarily (or even usually) responses to problems and are often independent of them. Solutions are often discarded without being used (in the metaphorical garbage can) and managers then rummage around in the garbage can and find an appropriate solution when a problem occurs. The Post-It note adhesive was a failure and it was only the persistence of one choral singing employee, who saw the failed adhesive as a solution to marking the pages of his hymnal, that led to its identification as a potential new product. The failure became a solution, which produced a major new revenue stream for 3M.

There are also *choice opportunities* when organizations and their managers are expected to come up with a decision (even though there may be no rational need for a decision at that point). The Advisory Board is meeting and managers feel they should present a new strategy to them so, even though there is no problem, a choice opportunity exists and a garbage can solution can be selected. And then there are *participants*. Their involvement in particular problems, solutions or choice opportunities is also far from rational. People may have preferences for particular strategic solutions, problems or choice opportunities depending upon, for example, who is watching. If the CEO prefers certain strategic solutions, problems or choice opportunities, participants are likely to be vigilant for those and pluck them smartly from the garbage can.

DISCUSS WITH A COLLEAGUE

Pair up with a colleague also using this text. Think of a decision you have been involved in – perhaps in a sports club, social organization or with a group of friends. Thinking back to the process, can you see how the garbage can model might offer a better description of what actually happened than a rational planning model of decision-making? Better still if you can think of an example from a work organization. Both present your examples to each other and explain how the process was more garbage can than robotic decision-making. Then discuss what the implications are for organizations and how we might train managers to make strategic decisions (e.g., by seeking solutions regardless of problems, by seeking participants and creating choice).

These ideas have been extended to suggest that organizations are action generators. They generate problems for which they already have solutions. Total Quality Management is a solution – this involves continually improving the quality of every part and process of the organization. Business Process Re-engineering is another solution that focuses on finding ways of dramatically speeding up and making more efficient the processes in the business, whether it is making products or responding to customer complaints. These are ready-made solutions waiting for problems and each manager has their stock of them. Managers then generate problems (identifying situations as problems) to which these solutions are applied. The solutions are not driven by problems but strategies emerge (e.g., introducing culture change or leadership development programmes) because these strategic solutions are available and favoured by particular managers. Lean manufacturing is another example of a solution that generates problems. We may believe that lean manufacturing (optimizing production processes for example) is successful. We therefore come to see our secretarial processes as a problem to which we can apply 'lean', though no one has said the secretaries are not functioning well. Applying lean manufacturing principles to streamlining secretarial processes becomes a new strategy for improving the performance of the organization.

Michael Porter's Economic Perspectives On Strategy

This rapid transit through theoretical models of strategy takes us to the work of Michael Porter (1980, 1985), an industrial economist based at Harvard Business School. Porter argued that the potential of the organization and its strategy are dependent on the industry and the market within which it operates. The task of strategic decision-makers is to identify and exploit weaknesses and opportunities in these industries and markets. The airline industry is in trouble right now and there are very few opportunities, so cutting costs is a priority. The pharmaceutical industry, on the other hand, is in good shape and companies are investing in long-term research and development for new products. Strategy is therefore very much dependent on the industry within which the organization is embedded. Indeed, according to Porter, understanding the industry context is central to understanding organizational strategy. Competitive strategy must focus on product quality, manufacturing costs and product price, sales promotion and services and strength of sales channels – how effective the means of distributing products to retail outlets are. Note that we are using manufacturing terms here, but this equally applies to services such as insurance, selection and recruitment services and fund raising services.

Porter's analysis suggests three core strategies that organizations can pursue to secure competitive advantage in their markets:

- Product differentiation involves innovating to ensure your product is differentiated from those of competitors in a way that will be attractive to potential customers. This might involve adapting the product to include some new device or quality – as in the case of mobile phone manufacturers adding a camera facility, a music player or a barcode reader. It might also involve heavily advertising the product to give a sense that it has a unique and desirable quality. Coca-Cola is simply another highly sugared, fizzy vegetable drink, but massive global advertising presents it as 'the real thing'.

- Market segmentation involves analyzing the market and separating it out into discrete elements in order that you can target the different segments with appropriate products and advertising. This might be based on demography (people of different ages and genders will want different products and will be attracted by different advertising messages). It may also be done geographically (the climate in Greece is very different from that in Norway, so if you are advertising soft drinks, emphasizing qualities such as cool and refreshing may make sense in one place but not the other). Culture is another segment. Advertising in the US often relies on images of women. This will not appeal in some Muslim countries. Organizations can also segment markets on the basis of psychological factors. Those people who have developed an identity characterized by a strong commitment to the environment will find 'green' messages and 'organic' products and services more appealing.

- Price policy and cost leadership usually involves reducing costs and prices. Supermarkets adopt such an approach because they can benefit from the very large volumes they buy and sell. This means they can demand lower prices from their suppliers, reduce their own processing costs and pass low prices on to their customers. In some circumstances, pricing policy may mark the organization's products as high price but highly valued. A Luis Vuitton bag carries no more, no more safely and no more beautifully than the vast majority of other bags in the world. But the high price associated with it leads some people to value it highly and to buy one.

Porter's work also draws particular attention to the competitive environment, arguing that five forces determine bargaining power in negotiating prices with customers and suppliers. These five forces are listed below.

- *Rivalry among existing competitors* – this is the central competitive force. It is traditionally measured by the industry concentration, which is the percentage of the market taken by the top four firms: the greater the percentage, the less the competition.

- *Entrants* – ease of entry into a market determines the level of competition or rivalry. Governments may restrict entry by granting monopolies or quasi-monopolies to organizations; some postal services in Europe are examples, along with utilities such as water and energy. If a firm holds patents on a particular process or technology essential to the production of a product (e.g., pharmaceuticals with patents on a particular statin) this will restrict entry. Some products or services require highly specialized plants and technologies, which deters organizations from entering the industry such as Norway's sophistication in oil and gas exploration. Finally, there are economies of scale that result from a firm having built up capacity over the years and producing large quantities of a product at a low price, making it very difficult for new entrants to enter the market and compete.

● *Buyers* – the fewer buyers there are the more competitive the industry is. For example, governments buying military equipment for their armies from an arms production firm in the home country; or large auto manufacturers buying air filters for their cars from a small number of companies. The more dependent a company is on large buyers the greater the rivalry among competitors for that large contract, and the more competitively vulnerable the company is.

● *Substitutes* – the availability of substitutes also shapes the competitive environment. If it is easily possible to substitute one product for another then the environment is more competitive. Examples of substitutability are glass bottles and plastic bottles for aluminium drinks cans. Bus travel is a substitute for train travel and ferries offer an alternative to air travel for travellers from France wishing to visit the UK.

● *Suppliers* – are powerful if there is a significant cost to a company to switch suppliers. Part of Microsoft's strength as a supplier of operating systems is that it would cost PC manufacturers to redesign their computers to use other operating systems. Suppliers are also powerful if they are few and concentrated, such as the pharmaceutical industry in its relationships with health care systems. The greater the power of suppliers, the more competitive the environment.

Strategic management then requires the organization's decision-makers to understand the complexity of these forces and their interactions in such a way that they can produce a plan that will enable them to increase their profitability and ensure long-term survival, exploiting opportunities to reduce the power of their competitors and gain a greater industry concentration.

Porter's influential work did not stop there. His 1985 book, *Competitive Advantage: Creating and Sustaining Superior Performance*, focused on the concept of the value chain in production processes. The processes of production or delivery of services can be conceived of as a 'value chain' which transforms inputs (such as people's efforts, raw materials, knowledge and creativity) into final products or services. Porter proposed that the industry value chain depicted how different steps in the process add value (or do not) to services and products. Added value is the difference between the costs of production and revenue from sales. Thus we may assess the value added by the addition of attractive packaging to a particular product – customers pay more because packaging is glitzy. We may also assess the extent to which bureaucracy in an organization (requiring three signatures on a requisition for more materials) adds value. In effect, such an analysis leads us to question what specific parts of the organization add value, e.g., the work of Work and Organizational Psychologists, HR, R&D, sales team, etc. What does not add value? Does the ambience of a restaurant add to the final price that can be charged? Does the quality of raw materials make a difference? Does raising chickens organically and free range result in the ability to charge more? One of the consequences of such an analysis is that it reveals that some activities add less value than they would if the function was 'outsourced' (e.g., having a computing company provide email service and support rather than having this provided in-house).

Porter finally turned, at the request of US President Ronald Reagan, to consider the competitive advantage of nations in order to answer the question of what leads nations to success. It is important to be aware of this in understanding strategy since it identifies environmental factors that determine strategy, competitiveness and managerial decisions in organizations. As shown in Figure 11.2, Porter identified four key factors influencing competitive advantage and two secondary influencing factors.

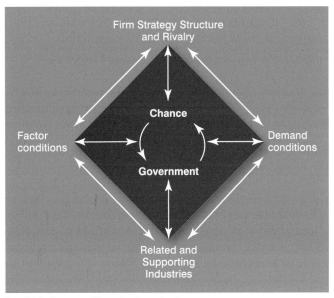

Figure 11.2   Porter's diamond model for the competitive advantage of nations

Factor Conditions   These include the availability of skilled labour, infrastructure (education health services, roads, airports, telecoms, etc.). Obviously, the more the better. Traditionally, natural resources have been seen as offering huge advantages but this is by no means a given. Take, for example, countries which have large quantities of oil or diamonds. Many of these countries are held back by corruption, conflict and lack of industry development. Because of these natural resources, governments do not need to encourage industry, entrepreneurialism and innovation and do not invest sufficiently in education, infrastructure, regulation and training. Countries with few natural resources such as Japan and the Netherlands have become outstandingly entrepreneurial, whereas those with many natural resources such as Nigeria and Chad are among the poorest in the world (Collier, 2007).

Demand Conditions   The more sophisticated customers there are in the home market, the more competitive the country will be, since customers will drive product and service innovation. Russia has traditionally not had a sophisticated domestic market because of the legacy of communism. Customers had to put up with what they were given by the state system. The legacy continues today with customers unlikely to be demanding in terms of services or product quality and therefore not forcing high levels of innovation and competitiveness on organizations. On the other hand, Japan's incredibly sophisticated customers for micro technology have meant that the country continues to lead the world in this sector.

Related and Supporting Industries   Where there are related and supporting industries, nations and industries will be more competitive. The most famous example is the concentration of computing firms in the Silicon Valley area of California. There is an abundance of suppliers, skilled labour with strong knowledge bases and also a great deal of knowledge diffusion.

Firm Strategy, Structure and Rivalry   The level of domestic competition will affect an industry and a nation's competitive advantage. Strong competition domestically ensures that companies become highly sophisticated and competitive, reducing thereby the likelihood of global competition. Domestic capital markets will also affect competitive advantage. For example, some countries emphasize a very short-term return on investments (e.g., the US and UK) and this leads to the development of industries that give a quick return (such as the automotive industry); other countries emphasize longer term returns, encouraging different types of industry (the chemical industry in Germany and the pharmaceutical industry in Switzerland are examples).

Secondary (and by implication less important) influencing factors are:

Government The state does or does not provide fiscal and economic stability; laws and systems that encourage enterprise – corruption discourages enterprise for example; and subsidies to firms (directly through grants or indirectly through creating roads to the places where the firms wish to locate).

Chance Of course chance also has a significant impact on competitive advantage. Carter *et al.* (2008) give the example of how American forces flooded Japan for strategic military reasons after the Second World War (because of the rise of the Soviet Union), but decided that bringing back empty ships made no sense. Those empty ships were instead filled with Japanese products, which were exported and sold in the US, providing the basis for the extraordinary economic development of Japan in the 20th century.

This analysis is not restricted to nations' competitive advantage, but also helps us understand industries. A sector will have its own diamond within a given region e.g., electronics in Eindhoven in the Netherlands. This will differ depending on sectors within a region. But the stronger a region's diamond within a sector, the more globally competitive the sector will be. In Sheffield, England, steel-making remains strong despite the huge drop in steel prices over the last 30 years because the factors in the diamond are strong and the region has innovative capacity.

Porter's influence on management thinking has been profound. His work continues to dominate in the field and to influence policy makers and senior leaders. It is important Work and Organizational (WO) Psychologists understand the thinking behind strategic decision-making in organizations so they can engage in debates at the table of top management, rather than being on the periphery, since their perspectives on organizations are vital to the flourishing of firms and those who work within them. But economists have also taken more nuanced approaches to understanding strategy closer to the perspectives of WO Psychology. One such approach is the resource-based view of firms.

Resource-Based View of Strategy

This perspective on strategy argues that it is the internal resources and unique capabilities of the firm that drive strategy. The 'Resource-Based View' (RBV) of the firm has been to suggest that resources determine the fit between the environment in which a firm operates and its capabilities or core competencies. This approach was articulated by Edith Penrose (1959), an American-born economist, who bravely defended colleagues against McCarthyism in the 1950s, before moving to the UK. Her ideas were revised by Wernefelt (1984), who proposed that resources were the key to profitability.

Unique resources such as knowledge, technology, skilled staff, brand names, efficient processes, organizational culture and innovation capacity ensure organizational advantage and survival. Such resources could come from training employees, takeovers of other companies, hiring employees with new skills or developing new technologies. Theorists have distinguished between *tangible resources* such as physical plant, capital and Intellectual Property Rights (IPR); and *intangible resources* such as reputation, brands, creativity and innovative capacity. Hamel and Prahalad (1996) extended these ideas by arguing, in contrast to Porter's industry emphasis, that the organization's resources are the key.

RBV theorists identify four types of resources:

- financial e.g., equity, capital and loans
- physical e.g., plant, equipment and land
- human e.g., the knowledge, skills and attitudes of employees
- organizational e.g., culture, climate and levels of trust within the organization.

Of course it is not just any old resources that firms must have. The RBV specifies *valuable resources*. To be valuable they must have four characteristics (referred to as the VRIN model):

- **V**aluable in enabling firm to exploit opportunities and gain advantage (for example a new technology which captures solar power effectively and cheaply).

- **R**are amongst competitor organizations.

- **I**mperfectly imitable – it is difficult to imitate this resource. Work and Organizational Psychologists can help develop a highly trained and motivated workforce through our knowledge. This is an imperfectly imitable resource since it is difficult to achieve without our specialist knowledge.

- **N**ot easily substitutable – having employees with a deep knowledge of the Alps working in the tourist industry in Switzerland is not easily substitutable, whereas the skills of call centre operatives are.

According to RBV, strategists should look inside their organizations for resources that have these VRIN characteristics and not keep scanning environment, if they are to develop brilliant strategies that will help them to win.

> *Sustainable competitive advantage can only be won by continuously developing existing resources incrementally while trying also to innovate products and services discontinuously in ways that play to the unique capabilities the organization has assembled, or can assemble, as it responds to changing market conditions.* (Carter, Clegg and Kornhauser, 2008, p. 58.)

Emergent Process of Strategy Making

You can see that strategic management has been dominated by the thinking of economists and those who adopt rational planning approaches. We have briefly considered the work of those who question such models (for example the bounded rationality perspective) and now go on to consider more radical alternatives, packaged as 'emergent strategy'. Among the theorists questioning rational planning were Cohen, March and Olsen (1972), Lindblom (1959) and Weick (1995), all of whose thinking originally derived from the work of Herbert A. Simon that we considered earlier. Their collective views can be summed up by saying that highly complex and dynamic environments require emergent strategy.

Strategizing (they argue) is a process of making sense of complexity and ambiguity and this sensemaking is an unfolding process. It is far more amorphous and fluid than is suggested by the models we have described thus far. Top down approaches to sculpting strategy may be fine in stable and simple environments, but in the real world of complex, dynamic situations it is a messy and experimental process that must be driven from bottom up, top down and sideways (Mintzberg, 1990). One view in the emergent school proposes that strategy is a process rather than a well worked out plan. For example, Pettigrew's comprehensive 1985 study of strategy in ICI, suggested that power and politics have often influenced strategic decisions as rational planning. Indeed, what masquerades as rationality is often shaped by -powerful influences within the organization. What the CEO and other leaders say is rational becomes rational. Alternative viewpoints from less powerful sources may be dismissed as uninformed or unintelligent.

Theorists in the emergent school question whether top management can ever know enough to come up with a sound strategic plan. They need information from all parts of the organization to have a sufficiently comprehensive understanding and they need information from the uncertain environment. To develop effective strategy requires employees to feed into the strategy or sense making process because their experience at the sharp end of the business, interacting with customers and suppliers, gives them important intelligence. However, they are often not motivated to engage because it is not a part of their jobs and they are not paid anything like as much as top management. Their concerns are with their psychological contract and their immediate work environment, not with abstract notions of strategy.

MINI CASE STUDY

W.L. Gore & Associates (UK) – Engaged employees

W.L. Gore (a US company) is famous for its high performance fabrics for outdoor activities, keeping clothes, boots and equipment protected from cold, wind and rain. Its 460 employees at the Livingstone plant in Scotland overwhelmingly believe they can make a valuable contribution to the success of the firm and are proud to work for the organization. The company has no job titles, no managers and no job descriptions. Employees are 'leaders' or 'associates' and they are paid according to their contribution, which is judged by their fellow associates. The most appropriate person (with the necessary skills) leads work groups at each stage of a project, and teamwork underpins the organization's activities. They manage their work time flexibly to deal with childcare or home deliveries, have a range of benefits available such as free dental care, health insurance, share options, childcare vouchers and sabbatical and career breaks. Moreover, employees say that they have fun at work and support their colleagues – team members care a lot about each other (adapted from **www.sundaytimes. co.uk** – best 100 companies)

Weick's (1995) work on the social psychology of organizing and on sense making through strategy is particularly relevant to psychological orientations towards organizational strategy. He explains how strategy provides a way of making sense of complexity in a way that gives the reassurance of direction. He uses the story of a group of soldiers lost in the Alps. One of them finds an old map in his pocket that offers hope. Carefully following the map at each turn and twist, the soldiers find their way back down from the mountains. On arriving back in civilization, they show the map to someone who points out that it is, in fact, a map of the Pyrenees. But it had done the job. Strategies are similarly simply a means of orientation – they give people confidence, provide directions and routes, and help to provide orientation. Strategy defines the terrain as the Alps for everyone and helps them find a way. It is a social construction of reality – constructing a reality it appears to mirror. Weick says strategy therefore has a number of functions:

- Gets people to work together to think about where they are and where they want to get to.
- Provides a way of thinking about the future – and just happens to use a language of visions, missions, and of Strengths, Weaknesses, Threats and Opportunities (SWOT).
- Motivates people and organizations.
- Represents the dreams of the organization (the community of employees).
- Manages the anxiety of potentially frightening futures such as organizational failure and large-scale redundancies.

It should not be surprising that emergent perspectives are less popular with managers than the clearly defined prescriptions of theorists such as Porter and those who offer the resource-based view. Popular management texts sell well and managers are hungry for guidance about how to develop strategy. There is a genre of best-selling books and a group of management gurus whose work has been particularly attractive over the last ten years. We consider their ideas that strategy should be revolutionary below.

Cognitive Perspectives

An important psychological perspective on strategy takes a cognitive orientation, arguing that strategy is often a consequence of the development of group mental models (Porac *et al.*, 1989). One study showed how managers from firms in the same sector in a geographic region developed a shared mental model of the nature of the competition in their sector in that region. Through their conversations and interactions they produced a model of the competitive domain which they came to believe, probably through a process of consensual validation. This led to the development of a rather narrow set of strategic alternatives – in effect, to a kind of 'groupthink' and to collective blind spots.

Another cognitive perspective is provided by models of phases of strategic decision-making. Schwenk (1984) suggested three phases: problem identification, generation of alternatives (strategies) and selection. Based on documentary evidence, he showed that, in the first phase, people seek information that confirms their initial beliefs. This also influences, of course, their consideration of alternatives along with a felt sense of personal responsibility as a strategic decision-maker. This sense of responsibility leads to group convergence, where decision-makers go along with group beliefs, as a way of reducing personal responsibility. If the majority adopt this approach, the individual is some-how less culpable when the strategy proves ill founded. In the final selection stage, leaders may rely on past experiences as a guide to their choices, despite major changes in the environment. The use of heuristics to guide decision-making can result in illusions of control and in misplaced certainty (Hodgkinson and Sparrow, 2002). Such cognitive perspectives enrich our understanding of strategic decision-making and demonstrate the value of psychological perspectives.

Those studying strategic decision-making and those making strategic decisions would benefit enormously in developing knowledge and awareness of the psychological processes such as emotional processes (e.g., the 'too much invested to quit' phenomenon) and social psychological processes (such as conformity and group polarization) that can affect hugely important decisions (Hodgkinson and Starbuck, 2012).

Strategy as Revolution

The approach adopted by some 'management gurus' proposes that strategy development should dramatically shake up the organization in order that its tendencies to inertia and unresponsiveness to a rapidly changing environment are counteracted. A leading proponent is Gary Hamel (1996), one of whose organizational exemplars was Enron, a company that failed spectacularly because of funda-mental flaws in strategy and values. He puts forward ten propositions for great strategy making:

1 Strategic planning should be about exploring the potential for revolution in the organization – for dramatic change.

2 It must be subversive – challenging accepted conventions within the organization and taken-for-granted assumptions.

3 The bottleneck is at the top of the bottle – the views of top managers are grounded in past experience. The need is for imagination and originality, not past experience.

4 Revolutionaries exist in every company so the task is to identify and engage them.

5 Change is not the problem, engagement is – engage revolutionaries and others in a discourse about the future, deliberately seeking challenging views.

6 Strategy making must be democratic.

7 Anyone can be a strategy activist within the organization.

8 Perspective is worth 50 IQ points – we can't make people smarter but we can give them new perspectives, which lead to shifts in thinking and practice.

9 Top down and bottom up are not the alternatives – both these and many more directions are needed.

10 You cannot see the end from the beginning – it is an open-ended process. It continually unfolds.

A more extreme version of these approaches to strategy development is offered by another 'management guru', Tom Peters (2003), whose messages include the recommendation to seek out the old and smash it. In a highly critical analysis of these ideas, Uchitelle (2006) points out in his book, *The Disposable American*, that these revolutionary ideas are associated with large-scale redundancy programmes and that the organizational revolutions these gurus advocate can lead to deep cost cutting, jobs lost and a cruel and dehumanizing culture.

> *At its core, the new cultural revolutionaries seek a totalizing creep into and envelopment of an increasing part of the organizational members' life world, in a manner that is difficult to see as other than corrosive or destructive.* (Carter, Clegg and Kornhauser, 2008, p. 96.)

MINI CASE STUDY
Napp Pharmaceutical Holdings

This Cambridge UK firm employs 838 staff to produce new drugs and its staff say they have strong leadership, good pay (39 per cent earn over £35k) and benefits and believe they are employed by a socially responsible company. A 'charter team' sets Napp's strategy by determining aims, direction and strategy. Half the team are senior managers and half are drawn from across the organization. The latter are people who will challenge conventional thinking and come up with radical innovations. Front-line staff who deal with customers and suppliers then decide on implementing the strategy, rather than this being a remote managerial decision. The company strives constantly to improve performance while maintaining a supportive culture. MD Antony Mattessich says 'Our culture is very different from that of the usual pharmaceutical company. We're a bit less hard edged: we really look for balance between the heart, head and body. You need to have all the standard attributes required in any pharmaceutical company, such as drive and intellect. However, that isn't enough. You need to be human: a nice person'. (www. http://napp.co.uk/).

KEY THEME

Environment and Sustainabilty
It's not just about turning off the lights

How can leaders integrate actions to reduce their environmental impact into their strategies? According to IBM, every dollar they save in energy spending drives an additional $6 to $8 in operational savings. Rich Lechner, Vice President of Environment and Energy (2009) argues that it's not only cash beneifts that arise from having an environmentally friendly strategy, there are brand and reputational benefits as well. He suggests organizations answer the following key questions as they seek to develop a strategy that incorporates environmental awareness.

- Are all aspects of the business, operations, IT and product lifecycle management, efficient and protective of our environment?
- Do we see environmental custodianship and energy consumption as key measures of our business success?
- Do we set challenging and public goals in our strategy related to environmental stewardship and energy consumption and make the data transparent?

- Are we acting as true leaders in these areas within our industry?
- Does our strategy involve reducing costs, complexity and inefficiency in all our activities so resources are saved?
- Are we simply reactive to regulation or do we take a proactive stance to energy and climate challenges, leading the way?
- Are energy conservation and environmental protection central to our business and brand strategies?

Lechner argues the environmental strategy must include people, information, product, IT, property and business operations and be core and integrated into the overall business strategy:

People: The strategy should identify ways of reducing (for example) commuting and business travel time and costs by using new technologies wherever possible.

Information: Companies must find efficient ways of collecting and storing data in order to minimize their data footprint. The by product is better information access and response.

Product: Companies must design products that have a lower environmental impact. Streamlining product development and manufacturing also results in less waste, fewer resources used and less energy usage.

Information technology: IT usage is costly in terms of power use and the need to keep machines cool. Businesses must focus their IT strategies to reduce energy costs and increase efficiency of IT systems in their contribution to the business goals.

Property: Companies need to ensure their buildings and transport systems are reducing constantly their environmental impact. When companies collaborate in transporting goods for example, there are far fewer empty and half empty trucks and containers travelling around the globe.

Business operations: Reducing energy or water consumption leads to reduced costs. Using good measures to compare existing use and conservation benchmarks is one starting point.

Addressing these key components of a business in combination, in relation to environmental impact, makes companies more competitive as well as socially responsible.

Strategy as Practice

Finally, the strategy as practice approach, perhaps similar to emergent strategy ideas, examines strategy as a process rather than an outcome. Researchers in this tradition are concerned to know where and how the work of strategizing and organizing is actually done. By researching the strategy process, it is suggested, we will better understand the nature of strategy. The approach seeks to answer questions such as who does it; what skills are needed; what are the common tools and methods; how is the work done, and how are the products of this work communicated and enacted? The focus is on strategy as a social practice; on the social interactions and negotiations of people throughout organizations as they engage in strategy formation (Jarzabkowski, 2005; Jarzabkowski and Spee, 2009). Studying strategy as practice, it is proposed, will help practitioners to develop reflexivity about their work by reflecting on what it is they are trying to achieve, how they are going about it and what they therefore need to change. It is an orientation that might especially appeal to Work and Organizational Psychologists since it is grounded in research, focused on social interactions and social psychological processes, and advocates a learning-in-action orientation to strategy formulation.

CONCLUSION

Reflecting on these different approaches to developing strategy, from Machiavelli through to Jarzabkowski, the reader might react with bewilderment and ask 'which approach is right?' 'What should guide me in my work?' The answers are that all these approaches and ideas enrich our understanding of how to shape the decisions and directions of organizations. Each adds value (to borrow from Drucker's notions). However, some stand out as more consistent with psychological and social psychological perspectives of organizations and probably provide a good fit with this work. These are the Resource-Based View of the firm, the strategy as practice view, and strategy as an emergent process. Psychologists can identify more easily with each of these rather more sophisticated approaches than perhaps they can with others such as the Product Market Matrix, the Rational Planning Model, Strategy as Revolution and Economic Models.

Finally, what is striking about the literature on strategy is how strategy appears to be discussed in a moral vacuum. Even war has its Geneva Convention, prescribing what is acceptable morally and what not. Yet little of the writing about organizational strategy discusses the fundamental moral issues that should be at the heart of strategy development. In recent years we have seen organizations fail on a massive scale because of a failure of values. These include dishonesty with the public; failure to learn from past mistakes; lack of wisdom amongst leaders more concerned with individual success than integrity; failure of regulation (the excesses and imprudence of banks); the damage done to our environment by organizations denying the reality of climate change; and the priority of organizational profit over contribution to the community. Integrating values with strategy development is essential. Two US psychologists, Peterson and Seligman (2004) have researched the fundamental human values in human communities cross culturally, surveying more than a million people, and have identified six core areas of values – Wisdom, Courage, Justice, Love, Temperance and Wonder. These are described with annotations on how they might apply to strategy development in organizations (see the Key Theme following).

This ends our exploration of strategy, but early in our exploration we noted how strategy determines structure and it is to an exploration of organizational structure that we now therefore turn.

KEY THEME

Corporate Social Responsibility and Ethics

Integrating values into strategy

Wisdom and knowledge – The acquisition and use of knowledge within organizations.

- **Creativity** [originality, ingenuity]: Thinking of novel and productive ways to conceptualize and do things within the organization.

- **Curiosity** [interest, novelty-seeking, openness to experience]: Taking an interest in ongoing experience for its own sake; finding subjects and topics fascinating; exploring and discovering.

- **Judgement and Open-mindedness** [critical thinking]: Thinking things through and examining them from all sides; not jumping to conclusions; being able to change one's mind in light of evidence; weighing all evidence fairly.

- **Love of learning:** Mastering new skills, topics, and bodies of knowledge within the organization.

- **Perspective** [wisdom]: Valuing wise counsel; having ways of looking at the world that make sense (e.g., focusing on climate change issues and corporate social responsibility).

Courage – Emotional strengths that involve the exercise of will to accomplish goals in the face of opposition, external or internal.

- **Bravery** [valour]: Not shrinking from threat, challenge, difficulty or pain; speaking up for what is right even if there is opposition; acting on convictions even if unpopular.
- **Perseverance** [persistence, industriousness]: Finishing what the organization starts; persisting in a course of action in spite of obstacles.
- **Honesty** [authenticity, integrity]: Speaking the truth, but more broadly, leaders presenting themselves and the organization in a genuine way and acting in a sincere way.
- **Zest** [vitality, enthusiasm, vigour, energy]: An organization characterized by excitement and energy; not doing things halfway or half-heartedly; work – life as an adventure; an organization that is alive and activated.

Humanity – An organizational strength that involves supporting and enabling all.

- **Caring:** Valuing close relations within the organization, in particular those in which sharing and caring are reciprocated; being close to people.
- **Kindness** [generosity, nurturance, care, compassion, 'niceness']: Doing favours and good deeds for others; helping them; taking care of them.
- **Social intelligence** [emotional intelligence, personal intelligence]: Being aware of the motives and feelings of those in the organization and those served by the organization.

Justice – Civic strengths that underlie healthy community life.

- **Teamwork** [citizenship, social responsibility, loyalty]: Working well as groups and teams; loyalty to the group.
- **Fairness:** Treating all people the same according to notions of fairness and justice; personal feelings not biasing decisions within the organization; everyone being given a fair chance.
- **Leadership:** Encouraging high performance and at the same time good relations within the organization.

Temperance – Strengths that protect against excess.

- **Forgiveness and mercy:** Forgiving those who have done wrong; accepting the shortcomings of others; giving people a second chance; not being vengeful.
- **Modesty and humility:** Letting accomplishments speak for themselves.
- **Prudence:** Being careful about organizational choices; not taking undue risks; not doing things that might later be regretted.
- **Organizational regulation** [control]: Regulating the organization; being disciplined; controlling organizational appetites and emotions.

Wonder and gratitude – Strengths that forge connections to the larger Universe and provide meaning.

- **Appreciation of beauty and excellence** [awe, wonder, elevation]: Noticing and appreciating beauty, excellence and/or skilled performance in various domains of life, from nature to art to mathematics to science to everyday experience.
- **Gratitude:** Being aware of and thankful for the good things that happen within the organization; taking time to express thanks.
- **Hope** [optimism, future-mindedness, future orientation]: Expecting the best in the future and working to achieve it; communicating that a good future is something that can be brought about.
- **Humour** [playfulness]: Laughter and fun within the organization; bringing smiles to the faces of people within the organization or served by it; the organization seeing the light side; organizational jokes.
- **Religiousness and spirituality** [faith, purpose]: Having coherent beliefs about the higher purpose and meaning of the universe and the contribution of the organization to this; knowing where the organization fits within the larger scheme; having beliefs about the meaning of life that shape the activities of the organization.

KEY FIGURE

Rosabeth Moss Kanter

Rosabeth Moss Kanter, one of the most famous management theorists of the last 50 years, believes that well-articulated values must guide the organizations of the future. She calls companies that are already moving in this direction 'the vanguard' and says that, in such companies, values, principles and attention to society have moved from the sidelines to the centre of business strategy. She gives the example of IBM, which in 2003, conducted a 'values jam' – a 72-hour web chat involving some 150 contributors focused on what IBM should stand for in the world. The CEO, Sam Palmesano, said 'Management is temporary, returns are cyclical. The values are the connective tissue that has longevity.' The jam produced three overarching values: dedication to every client's success; innovation that matters for the company and the world; and trust and personal responsibility in all relationships. Kanter gives other examples:

Procter and Gamble dedicate their strategy to improving the lives of the world's consumers for now and for generations to come. This led to breakthroughs in water purification via a not-for-profit company that saved many lives in the aftermath of the Asian tsunami.

Cemex is a huge building materials firm in one of the most polluting industries in the world, but its strategic commitment to improving working conditions and community development and its exploration of alternative fuels and environmental clean-up helped it win a World Environment Centre Gold Medal for International Corporate Achievement in Sustainable Development.

Omron, a Japanese electronics company, has as central to its strategy the motto 'at work for a better life, a better world for all' which drives innovations such as one of the world's first ATMs, a system to increase safety in laundries and a blood pressure monitor for women.

Banco Real's strategy (Brazil) makes social and environmental responsibility its top priority. Its commitment to the environment led the World Bank's International Finance Corporation to write the Equator Principles in 2003 (and revised in 2006). These are a set of environmental and social benchmarks for managing environmental and social issues in development project finance globally. The Equator Principles commit adopting banks and institutions to refrain from financing projects that fail to follow the processes defined by the Principles.

Kanter, R.M. *SuperCorp: How Vanguard Companies Create innovation, Profits, Growth, and Social Good* (Crown Business, 2009).

DISCUSS WITH A COLLEAGUE

Work with a group of fellow students (ideally in groups of six). Consider the strategies of six organizations in your home country (you can usually access these from websites or write to the company headquarters). Analyze the strategy statements in terms of the six values described in Key Theme Box: Corporate Social Responsibility and indicate on a scale of 1 to 7 the extent to which each of these values is present in the strategy document, with 7 indicating a dominant value in the document. Where possible provide examples of how you judge the value to be present. What values are missing entirely? Given that organizations are human communities and these six values represent the most important emphases in human communities across the world, what does it tell us about the nature of work organizations? What values (aside from the six listed) emerge as dominant in the strategy documents? What does this tell us about the nature of work organizations as human communities? Discuss in your groups of six and try to reach some conclusions. We would be keen to hear them – you can email the authors (m.a.west @lancaster.ac.uk and s.a.woods@aston.ac.uk).

ORGANIZATIONAL STRUCTURE

Organization Structure Defined

Organizational structure is the formal system of task design and management reporting relationships that controls, coordinates and motivates staff so that they work together effectively to achieve the organization's goals.

Contingencies such as the environment, technology and strategy of the organization will influence and determine the structure of the organization. The technology might be call centre technology, drug development technology or nuclear power plant technology. The nature of the technology will clearly influence structural design. In a nuclear power plant, control and safety will be vital so there will be tight control, clear hierarchy, role clarity, teamworking and a high level of recording and reporting. In a call centre, mass production and efficiency will be key so hierarchy, low levels of team working and clear job specification are the norm. In a pharmaceutical company, high-tech equipment and highly skilled technicians will be needed so there is more teamworking, less bureaucracy and a flatter and more cross-functional structure.

The environment includes some of the economic forces we have already discussed (such as the stage in the economic cycle – 2013 was characterized by a prevailing economic slump in Western Europe); competitors' strategies; government actions and decisions; the behaviour of suppliers and distributors; environmental forces (particularly climate change); and international forces (such as war between two countries). These environmental forces will influence the design of the organization and this, in turn, will affect the culture norms of organizations. Structure thus influences employees' experience (an innovative, entrepreneurial culture or a tight, control culture for examples).

A typical way of representing the structure is to depict it as a triangle – see Figure 11.3. The triangle is thin at the top where the CEO is located and broad at the bottom where the vast majority of employees are in such a typical hierarchical structure. In the figure there are seven levels in the organization, including the chief executive and the workers and, for most small and medium-sized enterprises, this represents a rather hierarchical organization. An organization of less than 1000 people could potentially manage within only three or four levels, thus improving communication and

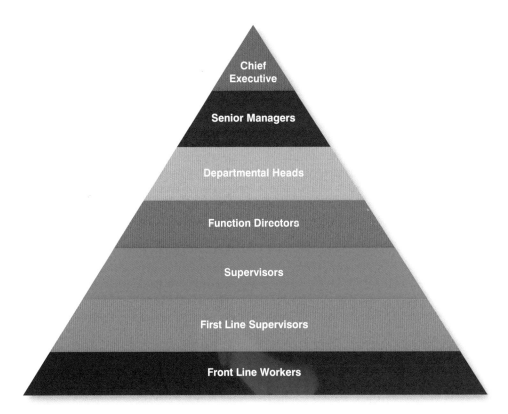

Figure 11.3   One view of organizational structure

speeding up decision-making (the example of W.L. Gore earlier depicted only two or at most three levels). But to understand structure in a more sophisticated way, it is necessary to revisit the seminal work of Max Weber and then to appreciate the body of research and theorizing spanning three decades that came to be known as the 'Aston Studies'.

Max Weber was trained in law in Germany and wrote at the beginning of the 20th century about his theory of bureaucracy and its role in the development of society and of organizations. He also proposed that the rise of Protestantism was responsible for the development of capitalism in Europe. The key element of organizations was hierarchy of authority that ensures members carry out the orders that underpin the organization. Organizational structure in his terms referred to the way authority was distributed. The rules of the organization are developed and implemented by a management group who also work to preserve their position of power. Weber viewed bureaucracy as a modern and superior organizational form that involved sets of jurisdictional areas ordered by rules. Duties, authority, qualifications, hierarchy of subordination, training, knowledge of rules, are all fundamental to an effective bureaucracy, according to Weber. He viewed modern organizations with their strong bureaucracies as an ideal form.

The largest body of research on modern organizations in the last half of the 20th century was conducted at Aston University in Birmingham and came to be known as the 'Aston Studies'. The first generation of researchers was led by Derek Pugh, and included Bob Hinings and David Hickson. Their focus was on organizational structure and links with environment, technology and organizational size. The second generation focused on the links between structure and climate and included Diana Pheysey, Kerr Inkson and Roy Payne. Google Scholar searches of these names reveal the extraordinary list of contributions they made to our understanding of organizations (see also Pugh, 1998 a, b, c). The final generation included Lex Donaldson, John Child and Charles McMillan who extended the research to examine international perspectives and relationships with organizational performance.

The Aston Studies took a systematic approach to understanding organizational structure by developing constructs and standardized measures:

- Specialization – the extent of specialized roles within organizations (as opposed to people being multi-skilled and 'jacks of all trades') and the number of specialized roles (think of roles on the railways to understand what this means – drivers, train dispatchers, revenue protection officers (ticket checkers to you and me!), etc.

- Standardization of work-flow activities – The degree to which there are standard rules and procedures in place to control wokr processes (think of call centres and you get the picture).

- Standardization of employment practices – processes for recruiting, promoting and disciplining employees.

- Formalization – the extent to which instructions and procedures are documented and saved (whether in electronic form or paper form). The civil service has been infamous for documenting everything and, prior to computerization, having everything in triplicate.

- Centralization – the degree to which decisions are made at the top of the hierarchy in the organization.

- Configuration – length of chain of command, span of control of managers and the percentage of specialized or support staff. Unlike the other measures this has multiple dimensions and is less useful.

The context of the organization was assessed in terms of:

- Origin and history, e.g. when and where it was set up and as what type of business (e.g., family owned originally).

- **Ownership** and control, e.g. public or private ownership and the degree of concentration of ownership (one shareholder versus thousands).

- Size, e.g. number of employees, financial turnover.

- **Technology**, e.g. degree of integration into the organization's work processes (the technology of trains is deeply integrated into the work processes of train companies for example).

- Location, e.g. single site, multiple sites, national or international.

- Dependence, e.g. the extent to which the organization is dependent on customers, suppliers, banks.

This approach offered a systematic way of analyzing the structure and processes in organizations for the first time and allowed comparisons between companies. The researchers carried out their first studies, using very carefully designed measures of the constructs, in the area around Birmingham in England. They revealed that specialization, standardization and formalization were highly positively correlated and were all correlated with organizational size. Larger size of organizations meant more of each. However, centralization was negatively related to each – the more centralization, the less the specialization, standardization and formalization. Larger size was also associated with less centralization. Replications of the original studies reinforced these findings, in particular the relationship between size and structure. The Aston Studies provided a wonderfully practical set of measures that researchers could use and this influenced the design of research for many years as we sought to understand the relationships between structure and processes in organizations (e.g., Patterson, West and Wall, 2004). You can use these measures to analyze any organization you encounter in your life to assess its structure and processes.

John Child (1984), one of the Aston Studies team members, offers a simpler way of describing or designing the structure of the organization. He identified five main questions:

1 Specialization. To what extent will jobs be specialized so that individuals complete rather narrow tasks but become very skilled in performing those tasks? The other extreme is to encourage workers to be 'jacks of all trades', able to do many jobs in the organization. The latter is typically necessary in much smaller organizations.

2 Hierarchy. How many levels will be needed to control and direct the organization? Will there be many layers of management to keep tight control? Alternatively, will the organization be 'flat' to encourage decision-making at the front line? If it is flat, the 'span of control' of each manager (the number of people who report to them) will be much greater. Decisions about hierarchy will influence employees' motivation and engagement (greater in flatter organizations), and communication effectiveness within the organization and costs.

3 Grouping. How are workers to be organized? Into functional groupings (production staff, R&D, HR, Sales and Marketing) or into cross-functional groups focused on particular products or services (all involved in commissioning and producing social science books working together and all those involved in commissioning and producing natural science books working together).

4 Integration. How are the different parts of the organization going to integrate their work together appropriately both vertically (workers influencing managers' ideas about strategy) and horizontally (HR working effectively with Finance)?

5 Control. What systems will be in place to ensure that quality is high across the organization, that costs are low and that managerial decisions are implemented? Will managers delegate authority to front line teams or maintain strict control? And should there be extensive formalization with lots of standard operating procedures and written rules and regulations? Who will have responsibility (an obligation to perform a task or function) and accountability (an obligation to report back on the discharge of their responsibilities).

Answers to these questions then determine the broad structure of the organization.

The structure is usually defined by an organization chart or organogram. Structures can be functional, product based or geography based. Figure 11.4a shows a functional structure (organized around the main functions of the organization). The disadvantages of such a structure are that it gets harder for the different functions to provide support for a wider and wider range of products as the business develops. Moreover, communication between the different functions may suffer as they operate like separate entities without excellent integration mechanisms.

Figure 11.4b shows a product-based structure with its advantages of specialization and disadvantages of replication of resource (for example HR) across the products and a lack of learning and development across boundaries. Good HR practice in Science Books may not be replicated in Arts Books.

Figure 11.4c shows a geographically based structure. This has the advantage of focusing on the needs of particular segments of the market (e.g., Far East) but the disadvantages of increasing operating costs (duplication across divisions), poor communication and likely competition for resources between divisions.

Figure 11.5 depicts a matrix structure in which the organization is structured around both products and functions. Thus there is a team working on developing, producing and selling garden tools; a team developing, producing and selling metal working tools and so on. Each team has members with R&D skills, with HR skills, manufacturing skills and sales and marketing skills. And each team member has two lines of reporting. Thus the R&D person on the garden tools team reports to the garden tools team leader and to the R&D team leader. Such a structure is likely to generate conflict between the competing needs of the different managers (R&D team leader and garden tools team leader). But, well managed and with excellent systems of communication, such structures can lead to high levels of innovation and responsiveness to the environment.

Figure 11.4a   A functional structure

Figure 11.4b   A product structure

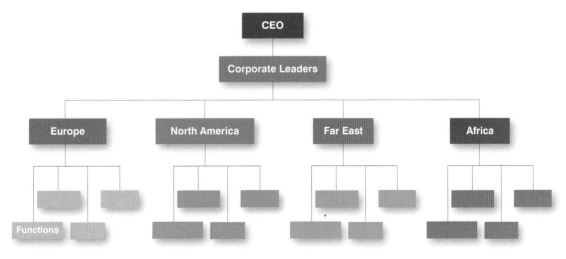

Figure 11.4c   A geographic structure

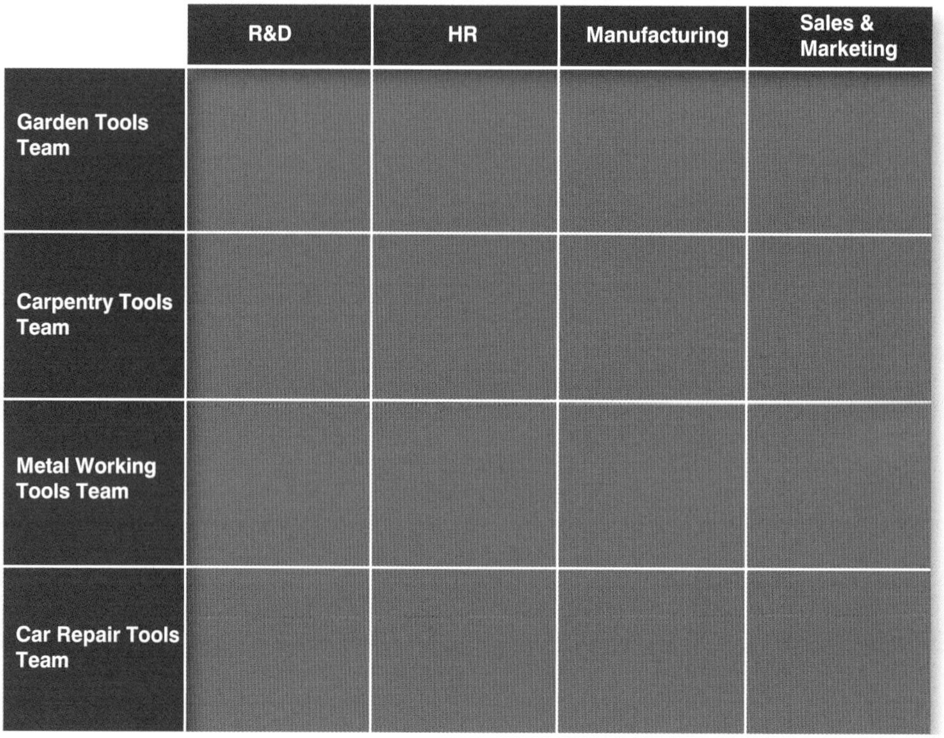

	R&D	HR	Manufacturing	Sales & Marketing
Garden Tools Team				
Carpentry Tools Team				
Metal Working Tools Team				
Car Repair Tools Team				

Figure 11.5   Matrix structure

Of course, there are many more advantages and disadvantages in all these forms of structure and they are presented far more simply than reality ever allows. There is no perfect structure because organization design is an approximate art, just like strategy development, and it is a continually unfolding process. The organization has to adjust continually to its environment and may do so successfully or unsuccessfully. The tendency to create hierarchical levels as a way of promoting people can be particularly dysfunctional. Organizational restructuring is dangerously attractive to senior managers since they can make such changes quickly and they appear to offer the chance of improving effectiveness. The English NHS is subject to repeated and sapping restructures by politicians with little effect. We know, however, that changing culture is much more difficult than changing structure, but is likely to have much more of an impact on organizational performance.

Another important distinction in thinking about organization structures is between *mechanistic* and *organic* organizations (Burns and Stalker, 1961). A mechanistic structure aims to ensure that the actions, decisions and processes in organizations are regulated, controlled and predictable. You can imagine that this would be necessary in a nuclear power plant, for example. Such organizations are characterized by a tall, centralized hierarchy of authority; top-down decision-making; detailed rules and standard operating procedures; and clearly specified tasks and roles. The major disadvantage of mechanistic organizations is that innovation and adaptability are inhibited. Given an unchanging environment and unchanging methods such a structure may be appropriate, although employees are increasingly seeking enriched jobs that give them opportunities for growth and development. In a buoyant market they are likely to seek employment in less rigid organizations.

Organic organizations seek to decentralize decision-making to the front line and to encourage high levels of communication, integration and innovation. In this way, the organization is able to respond quickly and effectively in an unpredictable environment or when faced with new tasks. W.L. Gore, the US company that makes waterproofing for outdoor wear, is continually innovating and is a highly organic organization, restricting the growth of any one plant (by creating new plants when they reach a certain size – more than 450) in order to maximize communication. Organic structures are characterized by a flat, decentralized hierarchy of authority; lateral communication and decision-making between people in different departments; great use of mutual adjustment in how the different parts of the operation work together; much face-to-face communication in task forces and teams; deliberately ill-defined tasks and roles; and a loose division of labour. They can be experienced as chaotic and uncontrolled, of course, and some find them too unregulated for comfort.

AUTHOR EXPERIENCE

The UK National Health Service (NHS)

Most of my work is now conducted in the UK NHS, which has a workforce of 1.4 million people – the largest organizational work force in Europe. It includes over 390 organizations responsible for providing primary health care, acute hospital care, mental health care and ambulance services. With health statistics for the UK generally good and a

spend of GDP on health considerably less than that of the US, it is an enviable system, providing free health care for all.

However, those charged with running these organizations are constantly in the public eye. With a million patient contacts every 36 hours, some go wrong, and the press and politicians are quick to criticize. It is also not surprising that senior management struggle to articulate strategies and design structures that will succeed when faced with the competing demands of patients, their relatives, staff, the media, national and local politicians, civil servants and pressure groups (such as Royal Colleges, unions and pharmaceutical companies).

Their approaches to strategy vary enormously. Understandably, some are very cautious while others 'build the bridge as they walk on it' (Quinn, 2004). Some are brave in developing new structures that devolve responsibility to front line teams delivering health care while others are defensively cautious, desperately trying to control procedures and set targets in almost every area of activity.

Our research has revealed the importance of how staff in these settings are managed, and has shown that this is strongly related to patient satisfaction and patient mortality (West et al., 2006). We also helped to run the NHS annual survey of staff experiences over a number of years, achieving a 55 to 60 per cent response rate each year (this is in the region of 180 000 to 200 000 responses a year – see **www.nhsstaffsurveys.com**).

Our research has led to many conversations with senior staff about how to run NHS organizations to achieve the best possible patient care. These conversations with policy makers, politicians and senior managers often come back to strategy and structure. Our ability to have these conversations and, at the same time, share perspectives from WO Psychology, has influenced policy in the NHS in directions most WO Psychologists would applaud. This had led directly to changes in HR policies and practices. Our ability to work and have influence with those charged with running the NHS at the most senior levels is a consequence of our knowledge of WO Psychology and its methods, and our ability to engage intelligently in conversations about strategy and structure. It is both a privilege and gratifying as a practitioner and as a researcher to feel that you have made a positive difference. That is also why these topics are so important in the training of WO Psychologists. For an overview of our recent work on strategy and culture in the NHS see Dixon-Woods *et al.* (2013).

Understanding organizational strategy, structure and environment enables WO Psychologists to understand other theoretical contexts for their work and to be able to influence senior managers more effectively in creating organizational environments that enable people to develop and thrive.

Another way of conceiving of organizational structure is the team-based organization. We will discuss this briefly in Chapter 12 in the context of the huge increase in the popularity of team working in organizations. Figure 11.6 depicts a team based organization structure in a health care organization with the focus on the patient pathway (the various functions and teams the patient encounters on his or her journey through the health care system). This structure makes

Figure 11.6   A team-based health care organization

the team the unit of analysis rather than the individual, and focuses on inter-team working rather than on hierarchical control (West and Markiewicz, 2003). It also identifies teams outside the organization (GPs) as included within the team-based organization since the patient experience is much affected by the interaction between the patient's general practitioner and the hospital. Such a structure emphasizes communication and collaboration in teams, focused on the needs of the customer (or in this case, the patient). Moreover, the traditional stem and leaf diagram of the organization chart is not appropriate for depicting team-based organizations. A more appropriate metaphor might be of a solar system with the management team representing the sun and other teams as planets or moons, affected by each other's gravitational pull (interacting and cooperating together) and particularly by the gravitational pull of the management team. Alternative perspectives on structure, such as this, are needed as organizations experiment with new and ever more varied ways of structuring their activities.

How does this description of organizational structures help our understanding of organizations? Just as in our consideration of strategy, it is important to recognize the powerful influence that structure has upon climate, culture and the experience of those working in organizations. It is important also to recognize that choices about structure should not be based on the preferences of senior managers but on the needs of the organization and on the fit between strategy, structure and environment. We turn now to consider the relationship between strategy and structure.

STRATEGY AND STRUCTURE

Thus far we have treated strategy and structure somewhat separately, occasionally pointing out the link between them. The most influential work on this relationship (Miles and Snow; 1986; Snow, Miles and Coleman, 1992) suggested that organizations could be understood as having one of four strategies in relation to the competitive environment and that their structures should complement that environment.

Prospector   The Prospector organization is the first to market with a product; they are innovators who make short-term products, moving on quickly to make new products as their competitors imitate them. Such organizations require a flexible structure with autonomous work groups responsible for local decision-making. At the same time, the organization is specialized and efficient. A good example would be Apple and its organization form – organic, with autonomous work teams.

Defender   Defender organizations have a limited but stable product line. They compete on the basis of cost and reduce their costs by constantly increasing efficiency. Such cost competitiveness is a good way of seeing off potential new entrants. They have mechanistic structures with centralized decision-making and a high degree of specialization. Call centres are typically of this type, always seeking to reduce costs, which helps to explain why they often give bad service by keeping you waiting and bizarrely assuming that tasteless piped music will mollify you.

Analyzer   The analyzer organization usually follows the Prospector, seeking to be second in the market. By copying the Prospector, but reducing costs and increasing quality, they can compete with them. Many Chinese companies have adopted the strategy of the Analyzer (it is a mix of both Prospector and Defender strategies). The Analyzer, according to Miles and Snow, should have a mix of functional and divisional structures to produce a matrix. Project and brand managers integrate project units and resource groups (such as Sales and Marketing). Some parts are flexible (such as R&D or parts of production to improve quality) while others are traditional and stable (such as other parts of production, reducing costs and increasing efficiency of production).

Reactor   Finally is the Reactor organization, which has no clear strategy. It simply responds ad hoc to whatever is going on in the environment at the time. The structure therefore is not stable and simply changes to fit the needs of the organization at that time.

This neat(ish) analysis provided by Miles and Snow is helpful in thinking about the relationship between strategy and structure. It should alert you to the fact that structure should follow strategy and reflect the environment within which the organization is operating. A dynamic, fast-changing, complex, unpredictable environment is no place for a hierarchical, tightly controlled organization. The point is to think carefully about the relationship between strategy, structure and environment in the organizations you encounter. Think about the extent to which their strategies and structures fit their environments and their cultures and what needs to change for the organization to be more effective.

DISCUSS WITH A COLLEAGUE

Choose a friend, relative or colleague on your course. First, discuss the organization they work within with a friend or relative, or a colleague on your course. Analyze with them the strategy they adopt in relation to their products or services and try to categorize them in terms of the four types described by Miles and Snow. What are the implications for the structure and processes of the organization of their adoption of this approach? How does it affect the work experience, motivation and work roles of those who work within the organization? Is the organization a pure type or a mix of the different types, or does it not conform to any of the four types described?

Second, given the demands of each type, what structures and methods of organizing work would you, as a Work and Organizational Psychologist, recommend for each?

An example will serve to illustrate the point. The authors of this book both work in business and management schools, which compete with 12 other business schools world-wide, many of which are outstanding and most of which are competing to attract the same students (and professors). Economic recessions, flu pandemics and reputation can all have dramatic effects on the profitability of our School. Our environment is dynamic, complex and challenging. We therefore need a strategy of innovation, quality and global appeal if we are to prosper. And protecting our reputation is vital. We encourage innovation via organic structures, but also retain control over quality by having standardized procedures for monitoring and controlling teaching and learning, research and administrative processes. Overall, we strive to be organic organizations but we also need some mechanistic elements to be successful.

New Forms of Organizing

While psychology may discover the enduring qualities of what it is to be human (such as the processes involved in short-term memory storage), organizations are swiftly evolving entities. What was true of organizations in the 1950s is not true today in many cases. Research suggests that new forms of organizing are developing and we need to monitor these new forms, learn from them and be vigilant about what organizational forms will enable people to give of their best, thrive, prosper and grow in organizations. Moreover, we need to recognize what forms of organizations are dehumanizing and do not take account of enduring human needs for connection, growth and development (call centres often sadly fit into this latter category).

Whittington *et al.* (1999), undertook research which charted the development of new forms of organizing. They studied, over four years, 450 European companies to discover what changes were associated with high performance and with reaping the benefits of organizational innovation. They found that companies had to make whole system or holistic changes and that the most successful companies over those four years were those which changed structures, processes and boundaries:

- Structures. Decentralization (but not of strategy development – this was retained within senior management); de-layering (reducing the number of hierarchical levels down from an average of 3.5 to 3.2); use of project teams; improving lateral communication; making better use of resources; and the introduction of sophisticated human resource management practices (including better systems of appraisal, induction, recruitment and selection).

- Processes. The most successful companies made major investments in their IT and intranet systems to enable and encourage better communication and share knowledge horizontally to encourage high levels of innovation. They spread accountability vertically making more people responsible for reporting on their fulfilment of responsibilities. Developing clear missions, investing in training and team building were increasingly emphasized in the best performing organizations.

- Boundaries. These companies focused on their core competencies rather than diversifying and spreading their resources too thinly. They outsourced the functions they were not expert in (catering, cleaning) and set up joint ventures and strategic alliances so that they could gain the benefits of access to other companies rather than competing and drawing strict boundaries around their own activities. In effect, they changed their boundaries in strategic ways.

The research suggested that high performance was the consequence when the companies changed all or nearly all of the following nine elements: decentralizing, de-layering, project forms of organizing, 'downscoping' (reducing size), outsourcing, developing strategic alliances, communicating horizontally and vertically, investing in IT, and introducing new HRM practices. Andrew Pettigrew, one of the project team leaders, warns against trying to achieve effective organizational development with simple and single changes (just changing structure) to achieve success. Change efforts needs to be wise, integrated, appropriate to the organization and to be introduced on multiple dimensions (compare this recommendation with systems approaches to change described in Chapter 14).

SUMMARY

In this chapter, we have proposed that strategy and structure are important topics since they are of fundamental concern to those charged with leading organizations. We have explained what we mean by organizational strategy. Strategy is defined as a metaphorical road map to guide the organization towards a desired destination and as a means of achieving goals through the use of its resources.

The chapter reviews the major perspectives on strategy thereby giving the reader a comprehensive and sophisticated understanding. These sought to achieve a fit between the organization and its environment. Market penetration, market development, product development and diversification are four approaches to strategy that have come to be known as the Product Market Matrix. Other major perspectives on strategy have included management by objectives (MBO) (Drucker); bounded rationality perspectives (Simon); and garbage can models (Cohen *et al.*). Economic perspectives on strategy have been dominated by the work of Michael Porter, which includes choices between market segmentation, product differentiation and price/cost leadership as strategies; industry perspectives such as the five forces model of industry competition and strategy, including the concept of the value chain; and national strategies for competitive advantage summarized in his diamond model.

The chapter also reviewed resource-based views of strategy, which argues that the unique resources of the firm should drive its strategy. Another perspective sees strategy as an emergent process of making sense of complexity and ambiguity and this sense making is an unfolding process. The strategy as revolution approach proposes that strategy development should dramatically shake up the organization in order that its tendencies to inertia and unresponsiveness to a rapidly changing environment are counteracted. Finally, the chapter described strategy as practice. Researchers in this tradition are concerned to know where and how the work of strategizing and organizing is actually done. The chapter particularly emphasized the importance of integrating values into the strategy development process and used a list of values recently developed by psychologists to show how values should be integrated into strategy development.

We have explored how and why organizations are structured the way they are. This reveals that structure plays an important part in influencing culture, behaviour and work attitudes. Organization structure is the formal system of task design and management reporting relationships. Contingencies such as the environment, technology and strategy of the organization will influence and determine the structure of the organization. The Aston Studies took a systematic approach to understanding organizational structure by developing constructs and standardized measures including specialization, standardization, formalization and centralization. Functional, product, divisional and matrix structures are described, and mechanistic structures are contrasted with organic structures. We also described the emerging form of team-based organizations. The chapter describes the relationship between strategy and structure and describes a typology of prospector, defender, analyzer and reactor strategies in fitting structure to strategy and environment.

Finally, we described new forms of organizing in recognition that the organizational landscape is constantly changing and forms that worked well 30 years ago are giving way to new forms dictated by dramatically different environments.

This chapter illustrates why simplistic recommendations for managing strategy, changing structures and managing the environments of companies are not helpful. If we wish to ensure the development of organizations that are effective and to ensure that those who work within them flourish, we must understand and shape the strategy and structure of organizations.

DISCUSSION QUESTIONS

1 Why are both strategy and structure important topics for you to study?

2 What is organization strategy and how would you advise a management team about how to develop a coherent and powerful strategy?

3 Compare three different perspectives on strategy adopted by theorists over the last 50 years, identifying the strengths and weaknesses of each.

4 Why should we adopt a value-based perspective on strategy and how do we decide within each organization what those values should be?

5 How do strategy and culture relate to each other?

6 How should we go about analyzing the structure of organizations?

7 To what extent is structure likely to influence culture, behaviour and work attitudes in organizations?

APPLY IT

Examine the strategy of your organization (or a selected organization) using an Appreciative Inquiry approach by asking:

1 What is good about the strategy?

2 What can we learn from this?

3 What is not so effective?

4 How can we take the learning from the good and apply it to the areas that need to be developed?

Consider the strategy from the following perspectives:

a. Management by objectives – from this perspective what is good about the strategy? What can we learn from this? What is not so effective? How can we take the learning from the good and apply it to the areas that need to be developed?

b. Bounded rationality – from this perspective what is good about the strategy? What can we learn from this? What is not so effective? How can we take the learning from the good and apply it to the areas that need to be developed?

c. Porter's economic perspective – from this perspective what is good about the strategy? What can we learn from this? What is not so effective? How can we take the learning from the good and apply it to the areas that need to be developed?

d. Resource based view – from this perspective what is good about the strategy? What can we learn from this? What is not so effective? How can we take the learning from the good and apply it to the areas that need to be developed?

e. Emergent strategy – from this perspective what is good about the strategy? What can we learn from this? What is not so effective? How can we take the learning from the good and apply it to the areas that need to be developed?

f. Corporate social responsibility and the environment – from this perspective what is good about the strategy? What can we learn from this? What is not so effective? How can we take the learning from the good and apply it to the areas that need to be developed?

g. Overall, based on this analysis, draw up proposals and associated rationale to reshape the organization's strategy.

WEB ACTIVITY

John Lewis' Business Model

Watch the video clip 'John Lewis Partnership Model Explained' on **www.youtube.com** or by following the link in the digital resources online and discuss the questions below.

1 The culture of the organization?

2 The work attitudes of employees?

3 The behaviour of employees?

Restructure at Microsoft

Read the article 'Microsoft restructure: Ballmer pins hopes on bringing devices together' by Stuart Dredge published in July 2013 at **www.guardian. co.uk** or by following the link in the digital resources online and discuss the questions below.

1 Discuss the restructure at Microsoft in terms of the models explored in this chapter.

2 What other systems might need to be changed in order to make this restructure work?

FURTHER READING

Edersheim, E. (2007). *The Definitive Drucker: Challenges for Tomorrow's Executives – Final Advice from the Father of Modern Management*. McGraw Hill.

Hodgkinson, G.P. and Starbuck, W.H. (eds.) (2012). *The Oxford Handbook of Organizational Decision Making*. Oxford: Oxford University Press.

Houlder, D. (2004). *Strategy: How to shape the future of business*. Norwich, UK: Format Publishing.

Weick, K. (1995). *Sensemaking in Organizations*. Thousand Oaks, CA: Sage.

West, M.A. and Markiewicz, L. (2003). *Effective teamwork: Practical lessons from organizational research*. Oxford: Blackwell.

Whittington, R., Pettigrew, A., Peck, S., Fenton, E. and Conyon, M. (1999). Change and complementarities in the new competitive landscape: A European panel study, 1992, 1996. *Organizational Science, 10(5)*, 583–600.

REFERENCES

Ansoff, I.H. (1965). *Corporate Strategy: An Analytic Approach to Business Policy for Growth and Expansion*. New York: McGraw-Hill.

Burns, T. and Stalker, G.M. (1961). *The Management of Innovation*. London: Tavistock Press.

Carter, C., Clegg, S.R. and Kornberger, M. (2008). *A Very Short, Fairly Interesting and Reasonably Cheap Book About Strategy*. Sage Ltd.

Chandler, A.D. (1962). *Strategy and Structure: Chapters in the history of American industrial enterprise*. Cambridge, MA: MIT Press.

Child, J. (1984). *Organization: A guide to problems and practice* (2nd edn). London: Harper and Row.

Cohen, M.D., March, J.G. and Olsen, J.P. (1972). Garbage can model of organizational choice. *Administrative Science Quarterly*.

Collier, P. (2007). *The Bottom Billion: Why the Poorest Countries are Failing and What can Be Done About it*. Oxford: Oxford University Press.

Dixon-Woods, M., Baker, R., Charles, K., Dawson, J., Jerzembek, G., Martin, G., McCarthy, I.,

McKee, L., Minion, J., Ozieranski, P., Willars, J., Wilkie, P. and West, M. (2013). Culture and behaviour in the English National Health Service: overview of lessons from a large multi-method study. *British Medical Journal: Quality and Safety*, published online and open access on 9 September 2013 as 10.1136/bmjqs-2013-001947.

Edersheim, E. (2007). *The Definitive Drucker: Challenges for Tomorrow's Executives – Final Advice from the Father of Modern Management*. McGraw-Hill.

Hamel, G. (1996) Strategy as revolution, Harvard Business Review, July-August, 69–82.

Hamel, G. and Prahalad, C.K. (1996). Competing in the new economy: Managing out of bounds. *Strategic Management Journal, 17(3)*.

Hodgkinson, G.P. and Sparrow, P.R. (2002). *The competent organization: A psychological analysis of the strategic management process*. Buckingham: Open University Press.

Hodgkinson, G.P. & and Starbuck W.H. (eds.) (2012) *The Oxford Handbook of Organizational Decision Making*. Oxford: Oxford University Press.

Huczynski, A. and Buchanan, D. (2005). Feature films in management education: Beyond illustration and entertainment. *Journal of Organizational Behaviour Education*.

Jarzabkowski, P. and A.P. Spee. (2009). 'Strategy as practice: A review and future directions for the field'. *International Journal of Management Reviews, 11(1)*, 69–95.

Huczynski and Buchannan (2007) Andrzej Huczynski, David A. Buchanan Organizational Behaviour: An Introductory Text London: *Financial Times Prentice Hall*, 2007.

Jarzabkowski, P. (2005). *Strategy as Practice: An Activity-Based Approach*. London: Sage.

Kanter, R.M. (2009). Bringing values back to the boardroom. *RSA Journal, Summer*, 30–33.

Lechner, R. (2009). The seven pillars of a 'green' corporate strategy. *Environmental Leader*, March 10.

Lindblom, C. (1959). The science of muddling through. *Public Administration Review, 34(4)*.

Machiavelli, N. (1988). *The Prince* (ed. Q Skinner and R. Price). Cambridge: Cambridge University Press.

Miles, R.E. and Snow, C.C. (1986). Organizations: New concepts for new forms. *California Management Review, 28(3)*.

Mintzberg, H. (1990). The design school: Reconsidering the basic premises of strategic management, *Strategic Management Journal, 11(3)*, 171–195.

Patterson, M., West, M.A. and Wall, T.D. (2004). Integrated manufacturing, empowerment and company performance. *Journal of Organizational Behavior, 25*, 641–665.

Penrose, E. (1959). *The Theory of the Growth of the Firm*. Oxford: Blackwell.

Peters, T. (2003). *Re-Imagine: Business Experience in a Disruptive Age*. London: Dorling Kindersley.

Peterson, C. and Seligman, M.E.P. (2004). *Character strengths and virtues: A handbook and classification*. Oxford: Oxford University Press.

Pettigrew, A.M. (1985). *The awakening giant: Continuity and change in ICI*. Oxford: Blackwell.

Porac, J. F., Thomas, H. and Bade-Fuller, C. (1989). Competitive groups as cognitive communities: The case of Scottish knitwear manufacturers. *Journal of Management Studies, 26*, 397–416.

Porter, M. (1980). *Competitive Strategy: Techniques for Analyzing Industries and Competitors*. New York: Free Press.

Porter, M. (1985). *Competitive Advantage: Creating and Sustaining Superior Performance*. New York: Free Press.

Pugh, D.S. (1998a). The Aston Studies, Volume 1. Aldershot, England: Ashgate.

Pugh, D.S. (1998b). The Aston Studies, Volume 2. Aldershot, England: Ashgate.

Pugh, D.S. (1998c). The Aston Studies, Volume 3. Aldershot, England: Ashgate.

Quinn, R.E. (2004). *Building the bridge as you walk on it: A guide for leading change*. San Francisco: John Wiley and Sons.

Schwenk, C.R. (1984). Cognitive simplification processes in strategic decision making. *Strateic Management Journal, 5*, 111–128.

Selznick, P. (1957). *Leadership in Administration*. New York: Harper and Row.

Simon, H.A. (1945). *Administrative Behaviour*, 2nd edn. New York: Free Press.

Snow, C.C., Miles, R.E. and Coleman, H.J. (1992). Managing 21st century network organizations. *Organizational Dynamic, 20(3)*, 5–21.

Uchitelle, L. (2006). *The Disposable American: Layoffs and Their Consequences*. New York: Knopf.

Weick, K (1995). *Sensemaking in Organizations*. Thousand Oaks, CA: Sage.

Wernefelt, B. (1984). A resource-based view of the firm, *Strategic Management Journal*. Volume 5, Issue 2, pages 171–180, April/June 198.

West, M.A. and Markiewicz, L. (2003). *Effective teamwork: Practical lessons from organizational research*. Oxford: Blackwell.

West, M.A., Guthrie, J.P., Dawson, J.F., Borrill, C.A. and Carter, M. (2006). Reducing patient mortality in hospitals: The role of human resource management. *Journal of Organizational Behaviour, 27*, 983–1002.

Whittington, R., Pettigrew, A., Peck, S., Fenton, E. and Conyon, M. (1999). Change and complementarities in the new competitive landscape: A European panel study, 1992, 1996. *Organizational Science, 10(5)*, 583–600.

CHAPTER 12

LEADERSHIP IN ORGANIZATIONS

LEARNING OBJECTIVES

- Understand the concepts of leadership and leadership effectiveness.

- Identify the main approaches to leadership research and the different levels of analysis.

- Know the key traits, motivations and competencies that predict leadership effectiveness.

- Describe the key elements, strengths and weaknesses of the trait, behavioural, contingency and leader member exchange approaches.

- Explain the transformational/transactional theory of leadership and the evidence for relationships with leadership outcomes.

- Understand the differences between cultures in leadership styles and expectations.

- Become a champion for fighting discrimination against women in leadership positions.

- Appreciate what is known about the effective leadership behaviours in organizations.

- Know the main forms of leadership development and the extent to which research evidence supports their effectiveness.

INTRODUCTION

Leadership is the most researched area of Work and Organizational Psychology; there are more research papers published in this area than any other. This is because leadership has an enormously important place in human society and in our thinking about our world. Whenever a group of people comes together to perform a task or make a decision, implicit and explicit leadership processes occur.

We rely on leaders to provide direction, to align efforts towards goals, to make decisions in a crisis and to inspire our commitmentus to achieve what we otherwise would not think was possible. Tales of leadership populate our literatures, our TV programmes, newpapers, mythologies and our films. We constantly focus on those who lead us politically, examining every nuance of their behaviour and speech, in order to gauge their trustworthiness, their intentions and their fitness to lead us. In work, we pay far more attention to the content of what our leaders and managers say than we do to the speech of others. Leadership is fundamental in human society.

DISCUSS WITH A COLLEAGUE

Think of three leaders that you admire (past or present). They could be people you worked with or people who you read about in the newspapers or see on television (such as Aung San Suu Kyi or Nelson Mandela) or they may be historical figures like Gandhi or Martin Luther King. Think about these three leaders and what it is about them as individuals or their behaviour as leaders that makes you admire their leadership. Try to come up with four or five examples of their behaviours and their traits that exemplify what you admire about their leadership. You are then in a position to attempt a definition of leadership. Try to write this out before you read on.

WHAT IS LEADERSHIP?

Offering a definition of leadership that would be accepted by most researchers and managers is a challenge since approaches to understanding this complex subject vary so greatly. A simple definition might be that leadership is directing the activities of a group towards a shared goal. However, such a definition ignores the many nuances of leadership that the following definitions illustrate:

- Leadership is … the influential increment over and above the mechanical compliance with the routine directives of the organization (Katz and Kahn, 1978, p. 528).
- Leadership is … the process of influencing the activities of the group toward goal achievement (Rauch and Behling, 1984, p. 46).
- Leadership is … the ability to step outside the culture. To start evolutionary change activities that are more adaptive (Schein, 1992, p. 2).
- Leadership is … about articulating visions, embodying values and creating an environment within which things can be accomplished (Richards and Engle, 1986, p. 206).
- Leadership is … to make decisions or take responsibility for the coordination or direction of other people (Nicholson, 2013, p. 12).

Leadership can be defined in terms of the traits or behaviours of the leader, as a set of influence processes, interaction patterns or role relationships. It may simply be defined also as the occupation of administrative positions (being the Chief Executive Officer) regardless of traits, behaviours or processes. Yukl (2013) says that most definitions of leadership see it as '… a process whereby intentional influence is exerted over other people to guide, structure and facilitate activities and relationships in a group or organization'. (p. 21). Leadership can therefore be seen as both a specialized role that an individual occupies and as a process of influence. We can distinguish between leaders and leadership. When we adopt a perspective of understanding leaders we are inevitably directed towards understanding who leaders and who followers are and why they occupy these roles. When we adopt the influence process perspective, we assume that anyone in a group or organization may exercise leadership at any point and that the complex interactions between people and situations will affect the emergence of leadership processes. Moreover, it is not either or – leadership is both a specialized role and an influence process. Yukl (2010) concludes therefore that:

> Leadership is the process of influencing others to understand and agree about what needs to be done and how to do it, and the process of facilitating individual and collective efforts to accomplish shared objectives. (p. 26.)

Leadership Effectiveness

Much of the academic and popular literatures focused on leadership centre on the need to know what factors predict effective leadership – understandably given the importance of leadership in human affairs. Implicitly, the question we want to answer is 'how can we identify those likely to be the most effective leaders?' This immediately leads to the question of 'what is effective leadership?'. Is it evidenced by the enthusiastic commitment of followers, by indifferent compliance or by reluctant obedience? The answer seems obvious.

When Nelson Mandela was released from prison after more than a quarter of a century, the African National Congress could finally unite behind their leader and overthrow the apartheid regime. The world waited with horrified foreboding anticipating ahead of a terrible civil war. Nelson Mandela went against the prevailing view of his followers and instead strained towards dialogue, reconciliation and negotiated transition rather than confrontation and violence. He achieved a reluctant obedience amongst his followers, which allowed a negotiated transfer of power without the bloodshed the world expected. So at times, reluctant obedience of followers may indicate highly effective leadership. Early resistance to a leader's behests might lead to later commitment when the wisdom of the approach is revealed.

Effectiveness may also depend on who is defining the term. Followers might focus on the achievement of task objectives whereas the leader might focus on the personal benefits he or she gains, such as promotion to a more senior position. This may seem a surprising way of thinking about leadership, but many leaders are in it to a greater or lesser extent for what they can get – more power, more influence or more money. From 2008 to 2009 the world's economy teetered on the edge of collapse as a result of the actions of some of the most powerful leaders in the financial world, working for their personal benefits. Many leaders are successful for their organizations and for themselves at the same time, achieving great things for their organizations and very large salaries and bonuses for themselves. Leadership has multiple motives therefore, and it is hard to disentangle selfish from altruistic motives, comfortable though it might be to see leadership effectiveness simply as selfless.

Another approach to leadership effectiveness is to see it as the product of intelligent, rational minds applied to complex problems solving. The effective leader analyzes the situation, develops effective strategies, allocates tasks, monitors performance and achieves goal outcomes. This was certainly a dominant perspective until the 1980s. In the last 25 years, we have seen much more emphasis on emotions and values, inspiration and motivation as hallmarks of effective leadership. Leaders are those who can inspire and motivate followers, and who can create positive, confident, optimistic work environments within which loyalty, commitment and engagement are dominant orientations.

Measures of effectiveness may therefore include the achievement of the group or organization's goals via improved performance, including measures such as productivity, share prices, return on investment, etc.; follower attitudes to and perceptions of the leader; the leader's contribution to enhancing group and organizational processes, including cohesion, culture, climate, cooperation and readiness for change and crisis; and the career of the leader – has she or he had a rapid advance up the hierarchy within or across organizations? It is difficult, therefore, to find a single measure of effectiveness since there are so many potential trade-offs. Increases in productivity might be associated with decreases in quality and decreases in staff commitment, for example. A bigger share dividend might be achieved at the expense of caring for the environment. Moreover, when should we judge the leader's effectiveness? Is it fair to judge the new CEO of a manufacturing company on the basis of productivity targets achieved after only four months? Most CEOs of UK hospitals are judged on targets that are hard to meet and require culture change in their organizations in order to meet them. Yet, the average tenure is less than two years – in which time they have had little chance to effect major change that impacts upon patient health outcomes. Leadership in organizations needs to be judged along multiple dimensions, depending on the context. This makes the job of researchers and leaders alike complicated.

RESEARCH INTO LEADERSHIP

Below we consider five major streams of research into leadership: the trait, behaviour, contingency, dyadic and charismatic/transformational theories. The trait approach suggests some people are natural leaders and many studies between 1930 and 1950 tried to identify what the traits of such people were. These were largely inconclusive but improved research designs over the last 50 years have yielded more convincing results and we will review these. In the 1950s and 1960s, the behavioural approach compared the behaviour of effective and ineffective leaders using survey research and examined correlations of questionnaire measures with measures of effectiveness. The approach has also been used to study how leaders and managers spend their time in order to probe the nature of managerial or leadership work, using direct observation, diary studies and job description questionnaires. The contingency approach examines leadership in the context of the characteristics of followers and of the task, context or organization. Dyadic approaches examine the varying nature of the relationships between the leader and his or her different followers and how favouritism can damage cohesion and leader effectiveness. Finally charismatic/transformational leadership theories place particular emphasis on the leader's ability to inspire and motivate followers by articulating an attractive vision, by intellectually stimulating followers, by encouraging them and by giving time and energy to their skill and career development.

Research approaches vary also in relation to the level of analysis of leadership and leadership processes. At the *intra-individual* level, researchers might use psychological theories of decision-making, cognition and motivation; they may focus on self management theory; or they may identify personal objectives and how leaders prioritize, manage time and monitor their own behaviour. The intra-individual approach has limited value because it neglects the social processes, which are at the core of leadership. The next level is *dyadic*, where the focus is on the relationship between two people. Leadership is a reciprocal influence process, usually with a focus on developing cooperative, trusting relationships in order to increase motivation and commitment. This approach too is limited, in this case by its failure to take account of the context within which dyadic relationships occur (for example in a team). Leadership can also be considered as a *group process*, where the team is taken into account, and research at this level would question how a leader contributes to group effectiveness and the role the leader plays in influencing the affective tone of the team. At the *organizational level*, leadership is conceived of as occurring in a larger open system in which groups or departments are subsystems characterized by intergroup relations and group-organizational relationships that the leader must manage. At this level, leadership research proposes might examine how effective leaders are at ensuring the organization adapt to its environment and acquire the resources needed to survive (see Chapter 14).

DISCUSS WITH A COLLEAGUE

If you now review your definition of leaders/ leadership you developed earlier, what assumptions did you make about the concepts of leader, effectiveness, approach and level of analysis. And how would you change your definition having explored the concept of leadership a little further?

Our initial introduction to the concept of leadership makes clear some of the complexities of the subject. The concept of leader itself is problematic as is the definition of effectiveness. We must also grapple with the decision about what approach we wish to take to understanding leadership and at what level of analysis. It should already be clear that this fascinating and complex area of research yields few easy answers.

TRAIT APPROACHES TO LEADERSHIP

We now go on to consider each of the major approaches to leadership, beginning first with the trait approach, then behavioural approaches, contingency approaches and then theories that examine the relationships between followers and leaders. We also consider situational variables affecting leaders' behaviour and followers' reactions. The approach is summarized schematically in Figure 12.1.

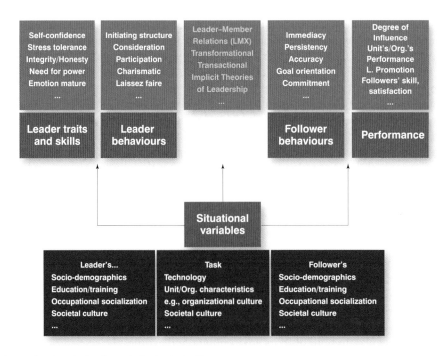

Figure 12.1   Approaches to understanding and effective leadership

Figure 12.2   Leadership traits, skills and motivations

First we consider theories that focus on the extent to which leadership emergence and effectiveness can be predicted from the personality traits (e.g., extraversion), motivations (e.g., need to achieve) and skills (e.g., specialist technical knowledge) of individuals (see Figure 12.2). This is the longest tradition in leadership research and represents a body of knowledge developed over the last 60 years. Those studies that use emergence as the outcome focus on who in a group becomes the eventual leader, whereas those that use effectiveness as the outcome are concerned with the extent to which leadership predicts outcome measures as diverse as productivity, innovation, group member satisfaction, group cohesion and peer evaluations.

Traits are relatively enduring patterns of behaviour and skills are abilities to perform a task effectively. Research has established that not only traits but also skills have a strong hereditary component (Arvey, Zhang, Avolio and Krueger, 2007), so if research establishes a strong relationship between traits, skills and leadership effectiveness it suggests that the notion of a born leader has some validity. Skills are usually divided into technical skills (knowledge about methods, processes and procedures), interpersonal skills and conceptual skills (knowledge and ability with ideas and concepts) and we consider these later. For now, we will focus on personality traits and their relationship with leadership effectiveness.

One of the largest meta-analyses of this question involved an examinations of 124 studies conducted between 1904 and 1948 (Stogdill, 1948), and a follow-up of studies from 1949 to 1970 (Stogdill, 1974), confirmed and extended the original findings. Together they revealed that effective leaders were: adaptable to situations, alert to the social environment, ambitious, achievement oriented, creative, assertive, co-operative, decisive, dependable, dominant, energetic, persistent, self-confident, tolerant of stress and willing to assume responsibility. Key skills included clever, conceptually skilled, diplomatic and tactful, fluent, knowledgeable about the work, good administrative ability, persuasive and socially skilled. However, such a list of leadership requirements would rule virtually all humanity out of contention for leadership and Stogdill pointed out that this was not a definitive list and none of the traits emerged as an absolute must for leadership. Moreover, the situation that leaders operated in appeared to exert a significant and profound influence on what was effective at any moment in time.

Chapter 3 described the use over the last 20 years of the Big Five dimensions for understanding personality. Not surprisingly, considerable research effort has gone into identifying which of the Big

Five dimensions are associated with leadership effectiveness. Notwithstanding the fact that effectiveness has continued to be operationalized in research in differing ways, three of the five dimensions appear to be associated with leadership effectiveness. Openness to Experience, and Extraversion are positively correlated and Neuroticism is negatively correlated (e.g., Judge, Bono, Ilies and Gerhardt, 2002). The desire to learn and explore new opportunities is clearly important for leaders in modern organizations, as is the commitment to seeing things through effectively, being dependable and having integrity. Moreover, being warm, positive, energetic and confident, as we have already seen, is important for effective leadership. However, being anxious, relatively pessimistic and emotionally unpredictable is problematic in a leader, not least because of the impact on followers. Agreeableness does not correlate with leadership effectiveness, consistent with the suggestion that need for affiliation is not a high priority for a leader. However, there are correlations between four of the five dimensions and leadership emergence (who emerges as a leader in a group situation). Again extraversion, emotional stability (the polar opposite of neuroticism) and openness are positively correlated, but with conscientiousness also proving to be quite strongly related (see Figure 12.3).

Managerial Motivation

McClelland and colleagues undertook a major programme of research to understand how achievement motivation of leaders was related to performance (McClelland, 1985). The research was conducted using the Thematic Apperception Test, which involves research participants telling a story based on ambiguous pictures of people. McClelland and colleagues discerned three motivational themes underlying the stories their leaders told: need for achievement; need for affiliation; and need for power. Need for power had two sub-dimensions: socialized power orientation and personalized power orientation. The latter refers to a motivation orientation to acquire power in order to advance the organization's aims, make a contribution or enable followers to develop their skills and careers. Such leaders tended to have strong self-control. Another type of power orientation was 'personalized power orientation', characterized by a desire for power to advance the leader's own interests by dominating others in order to fulfil their own desires. The research suggested that effective leaders or managers in large organizations have a moderately high need for achievement, a relatively low need for affiliation and a highly socialized rather than personalized power orientation (McClelland and Boyatzis, 1982).

Leadership	Emergence	Effectiveness
	β / R	β / R
Neuroticism	−.09	−.10 *
Extraversion	.30 *	.18 *
Openness	.21 *	.19 *
Agreeableness	−.14 *	.10
Conscientiousness	.36 *	.12
Multiple R	.53 *	.39 *

Based on 222 correlations from 73 samples with total N ~ 43.000 (Judge, et al., 2002)

Figure 12.3   Big Five and leadership emergence and effectiveness

Another approach to understanding the motivations of effective leaders (Miner, 1977; Berman and Miner, 1985) used a qualitative measure called the Sentence Completion Test. Again, content was investigated qualitatively to identify motivational themes in leaders'/managers' responses to the incomplete sentences. Miner used this approach to examine the motivations associated with advancement in large organizations He identified six motivation themes and found that three were related to managers' advancement in their organizations' hierarchies. Those that correlated most consistently were: desire to exercise power; desire to compete with peers; and a positive attitude towards authority figures. Those that did not correlate consistently with advancement were: desire to stand out from the group; desire to perform routine administrative functions; and desire to be actively assertive. The results were not so clear for leaders in smaller organizations, indicating the importance of context in research into managerial and leader effectiveness; what may lead to career advancement in a large organization of 1000 people may be irrelevant in small enterprises of say ten to fifteen employees.

Competencies

A body of research that has influenced both practitioners and researchers (Boyatzis, 1982) focused on the competencies related to managerial effectiveness. The competencies explored by Boyatzis include personality traits, motives, skills, knowledge, self-image and some specific behaviours. The main research method employed was the 'behavioural event interview'. This asked managers to identify critical incidents in their work and the ways in which they dealt with them. These were analyzed in depth to reveal underlying competencies. The sample included 253 managers who were rated as low or high in effectiveness.

Effective managers proved to have a strong efficiency orientation; high achievement motivation; high work standards; and a focus on task objectives. Confirming McClelland's earlier work, they had a strong socialized power orientation; had a high desire for power; liked having power symbols such as grand titles and large offices; were assertive in their behaviour; had a strong tendency to attempt to influence others; were concerned about the reputation of the organization; had high self-confidence and were decisive rather than hesitant; made proposals in a firm manner, with appropriate poise, bearing and gestures; had high self-efficacy and a high internal locus of control; initiated action rather than waited for things to happen; took steps to circumvent obstacles; sought information from a variety of sources, and accepted responsibility for success or failure. The research also suggested that effective managers (unsurprisingly) had good interpersonal skills; good oral presentation skills, including the ability to use symbolic, verbal and non-verbal communication devices to make clear and convincing presentations. They were good at building team spirit and encouraging a sense of group identity and loyalty. Finally, effective managers had strong conceptual skills, including the ability to identify patterns or relationships in information and events (what the researchers called 'inductive reasoning') and the ability to communicate this effectively to the people they led.

This influential research has been taken up by many organizations, which have sought to build their leadership capacity by testing for, and developing, these competencies in managers. The major problem with this approach is the lack of parsimony. The list of competencies is so long that it suggests few people would have or could develop all these competencies effectively. What works for whom in what context is unclear.

Assessment Centres

The advent of assessment centres in the last 40 years offered another means for determining which traits predicted advancement in an organization. The most outstanding research using this approach was conducted in the US AT&T company (a major telecommunications organization). The research focused on data gathered in assessment centres (Howard and Bray, 1990) and monitored each candidate's progress into middle management. Assessment centres scores were related to advancement eight years and twenty years later. Such a long-term research study is unusual and the design offers fascinating insights into the personal attributes that predicted advancement. The traits that best predicted advancement were (not surprisingly) desire for advancement, along with dominance, interpersonal skills, cognitive skills (creativity and critical thinking) and administrative skills. Other important predictors included need for achievement, self confidence, energy levels and low need for security. Particularly interesting is that the individual's first job was an important moderator of the relationship between traits and ultimate advancement. The more opportunities for learning and development in the first role, the greater the job challenge (within limits), and the better the person's boss as a role model of success and achievement orientation, the quicker the individual advanced in their career.

Derailing

Another way of gleaning understanding about what predicts effective leadership is to focus on what predicts failure. The Center for Creative Leadership (CCL) is one of the most enlightened work and organizational psychology consultancy organizations in the world. One example of their commitment to research is the study of what predicts the success or, unusually, the failure of top executives (Lombardo and McCauley, 1988). Failure is termed 'derailing'. Derailed managers are those who are dismissed, transfer, retire early or just fail to continue to advance. In the CCL study, there are many similarities between both those who succeeded and those who failed but certain traits seemed to be particularly important for predicting failure.

Emotional stability and composure Managers who derailed were less able to handle pressure. They were moody, had angry outbursts and displayed inconsistent behaviour.

Defensiveness Managers who derailed were more likely to be defensive about failure. They attempted to cover mistakes and blame other people.

Integrity Successful managers were more focused on the immediate task and on the needs of subordinates than on competing with rivals or impressing superiors.

Interpersonal skills Managers who derailed were likely to have less developed interpersonal skills and were often abrasive or intimidating towards others.

Technical and cognitive skills Those who derailed were often outstanding in terms of technical knowledge when they were at lower levels in the organization. As they moved up, this technical competence led to arrogance and over-confidence about their opinions and decisions. So the strength became a weakness.

Summary

Over the last 70 to 80 years a considerable amount of research has sought to determine the traits predicting leadership effectiveness and, though some commentators argue that this has been a blind alley, it is possible to identify some core personality traits associated with leadership effectiveness. Yukl (2010) identifies the following:

1 *High energy level and stress tolerance* Effective leaders are people who have high levels of stamina and can work effectively over long periods. They maintain relatively high levels of energy throughout the day. They are also less likely to be affected adversely by conflicts, crisis events and pressure, maintaining an equilibrium that is relatively unusual. In particular, they are able to think calmly in crisis situations and to communicate calmness and confidence to others.

2 *Self-confidence* They are self confident, believing that they can be effective in difficult situations and giving those they lead a sense of confidence and efficacy. They tend to be optimistic and confident in the face of difficulties and this optimism is often a self-fulfilling prophecy. As a consequence they are more likely to deal with difficult situations rather than deny or avoid them. However, excessive self-confidence or self-esteem can make leaders prone to making highly risky or downright wrong decisions.

3 *Internal locus of control* Effective leaders believe that what happens around them is more under their control than the control of external forces and so are motivated to take action to influence and control events. This is associated with a tendency to be pro-active rather than passive. They also believe that they can therefore influence, persuade and motivate others as well as win their allegiance to courses of action.

4 *Emotional maturity* They have higher levels of emotional maturity which includes emotional intelligence. They are less prone to moodiness, irritability and angry outbursts. Indeed, they are more likely to be positive and optimistic, communicating their positivity to others. Emotionally mature people have awareness of their own strengths, weaknesses and typical reactions to situations. They have a high level of moral integrity. Emotional maturity is associated with a socialized rather than a personalized power orientation.

5 *Personal integrity* Consistency between espoused values and behaviour is characteristic of those with high levels of personal integrity, along with honesty, transparency and trustworthiness. Such leaders also keep promises to staff and other stakeholder groups and tend not to use their leadership primarily out of self interest.

6 *Socialized power motivation* Effective leaders seek power, but primarily in order to achieve organizational objectives and to support the growth, development and advancement of those they lead.

7 *Moderately high achievement orientation* Not surprisingly, high achievement orientation is associated with leadership effectiveness. However, this is not a linear relationship. Those managers with very high achievement orientation can become insensitive to the effects of their desires on those around them who feel too driven by their leader's ambition.

8 *Low need for affiliation* Need for affiliation refers to the need to be liked and accepted by those around us. Effective leaders do not have high needs for affiliation. Those who did would be likely to put their need to be liked ahead of making good decisions in difficult situations or ahead of having to manage poor performance among their followers. Neither do they have extremely low affiliation needs, uncaring for the opinions or liking of others. That would suggest imperviousness to social relationships and the need for belonging, which is central in healthy human growth and development.

Turning to skills and competencies, the research to date suggests the following are important for leaders:

1 *Technical competence* is important because it wins the respect of followers. It includes knowledge about the organization, its strategy, structure and processes; knowledge about products and services and production methods and technologies; and knowledge about the organization's environment.

2 *Conceptual skills* are important because having an understanding of the complex environments of organizations (both internal and external) enables sense-making and reduces anxiety that the situation is too complex to be comprehended and therefore managed. The ability to analyze, organize, plan and make decisions is central to organizational functioning, so leaders who have conceptual skill will increase confidence of followers within the organization.

3 Finally, *interpersonal skills* are vital to effective management and leadership. Understanding the needs and feelings of followers, monitoring the effects of one's own behaviours on followers and being aware of one's own emotional reactions are central to effective leadership.

Caveats that need to be born in mind in considering these conclusions are:

- Only a few studies have rigorously tested the assumption that personality traits have a causal impact on leader effectiveness or the emergence as a leader.
- For at least some personality traits, it is not clear which comes first, being in a leadership position or possessing the trait in question.
- Implicit theories of leadership held by followers can facilitate leadership emergence (e.g. leaders should be 'extraverted') rather than leader traits predicting emergence.
- The trait approach provides little guidance concerning what advice or training to give current or aspiring soon-to-be leaders.

BEHAVIOURAL THEORIES

The discussion so far has concentrated on the personality and competencies of leaders. We now turn to using a different approach to understanding leadership, which involves studying the behaviour of leaders. Below, we consider two streams of research. The first looks at the nature of leadership and managerial work and the second at two important research programmes that adopted a behavioural approach conducted respectively at the universities of Ohio and Michigan during the 1950s and 1960s.

The Nature of Leadership and Managerial Work

We have discussed leaders and leadership, but inevitably the words 'managers' and 'management' have also peppered the text. In this section we begin by asking who are the leaders and who are the managers? The reality is that leadership roles require a great deal of management and managers are also required to be leaders. Different researchers have offered pithy differentiating statements: 'Managers are those who do things right, leaders are those who do the right things'; 'managers seek stability, leaders seek innovation'. However, the reality is that leading and managing are distinct processes, not different types of people (Bass, 1980). We have already defined leadership and much of management can be understood as the day-to-day processes of ensuring that leadership goals are achieved via supporting, monitoring, directing and motivating performance.

What is it like to lead and manage in modern organizations? Yukl (2013) suggests that the research evidence shows the pace is unrelenting. Managers tend to work long hours and to deal constantly with requests for information, requirements for decisions to be made and requests for assistance or direction. The content of the work is varied and fragmented, each component necessarily of brief duration. Half of the tasks managers undertake take less than nine minutes and only one tenth take an hour. One of the biggest challenges for managers and leaders therefore is finding the time to undertake tasks, which take much longer. Consequently, interruptions are frequent, multi-tasking is essential and important activities are interspersed with relatively unimportant tasks. Indeed, Sumantra Ghoshal (described by *The Economist* – a news magazine – as a 'EuroGuru') once observed that the challenge of leadership is to learn to focus on the difficult, tough, major tasks which really will make a difference to organizational performance, and not to manage the inevitable (see Birkinshaw and Piramal, 2006 for an appreciation of Ghoshal's work).

Because of the large number of tasks and requests, managers have to react to some and ignore or give minimal attention to others. There are always more challenges and problems than can be handled so the need to make wise choices about which must be attended to and with how much attention and effort is a constant. Human beings are effort minimizers (as are all animal species) so there is a tendency to deal with easy problems, with problems for which solutions already exist, with problems for which solutions have been found in the past, or with problems where the people are amenable rather than difficult. Of course, problems that bosses raise tend to get dealt with first, though clearly customers' problems should also take precedence. These high levels of demands mean that managers may have little time for reflection and may avoid tasks that take time such as team-building, writing, developing strategy and reflecting on what the organization is trying to achieve, its processes and its success. Instead, fire fighting, responding to immediate demands and doing emails tend to take front and centre stage. Good leadership and management involve making wise choices about how scarce and valuable leadership time is used. And how managers make decisions is not so much linear as a disorderly process with strong political elements. Decisions are made as a consequence of many conversations, new information, unfolding events often evolve haphazardly rather than as a result of a careful, rational process.

One response is to suggest that leaders will benefit from learning mindfulness practices that help them relate to the present moment of their leadership, by becoming more able to give attention to the totality of their present experience in an accepting and non-judgemental way. As a result they are more likely to be able to offer effective leadership (see for example, Glomb *et al.*, 2012) by developing response flexibility, affect regulation, empathy, persistence, better communication, improved memory, increased self-determination, coping more effectively with stress and developing less biased decision-making. That said, managers usually take the time to engage in much consultation about important decisions since such decisions tend to go through prolonged and highly political processes.

So far we have considered the skills, traits and motivations of leaders and how they relate to leadership effectiveness. During the 1950s and 1960s, research in this area focused more on what leadership behaviours were related to effectiveness (Figure 12.4). The research was concentrated in two centres: Ohio State University and the University of Michigan. The two centres produced similar though not entirely overlapping conclusions about effective leadership behaviours.

Ohio State Leadership Studies

Researchers from this group identified 150 items of good examples of leadership behaviours and developed a series of questionnaires to measure these behaviours. The questionnaires included the Leader Behaviour Description Questionnaire (LBDQ), the Supervisory Behaviour Description

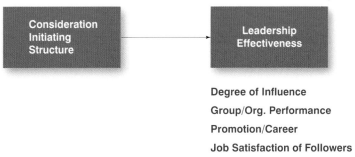

Figure 12.4 Behavioural theories of leadership

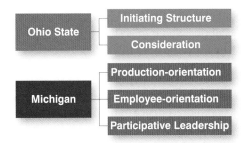

Figure 12.5   Ohio and Michigan behavioural studies

Questionnaire (SBDQ) and the Leader Opinion Questionnaire (LOQ). Factor analysis revealed two broad categories of leader behaviours: *consideration* and *initiating structure* (see Figure 12.5).

- *Consideration:* Behaviour indicating that a leader trusts, respects and values good relationships with their followers.
- *Initiating Structure:* Behaviour that a leader engages in to make sure that work gets done and that subordinates perform their jobs acceptably.

Consideration describes leader behaviours focused on the employee, such as listening to and valuing employees, helping them solve problems, supporting them, giving positive feedback and being friendly, supportive and respectful in interactions with them. Initiating structure behaviours are focused on the task and include clarifying employees' roles and objectives, setting performance standards, monitoring task performance and correcting poor performance. The two factors proved to be relatively independent of one another suggesting that leaders could have high levels of both, low levels of both or high levels of just one.

The key question is which of these behavioural styles predicted performance. It is not a surprise that consideration predicts employee satisfaction but neither had strong (only weak) positive relationships with effectiveness measured in terms of task performance (Judge, Piccolo and Illies, 2004).

Michigan Leadership Studies

During the same period, virtually identical research was being undertaken at the University of Michigan where interviews were used to gather data on leader behaviours and objective measures of group productivity were developed (Likert, 1967). The researchers found that effective leaders displayed three patterns of behaviour: *production orientation, employee relations orientation* and *participative leadership* (see Figure 12.5). Production or Task Orientation included setting objectives, finding necessary resources (equipment, supplies) and planning and scheduling. This was similar to, but rather broader than the initiating structure pattern identified in Ohio. Relations-oriented behaviours included supporting employees, listening to their problems, supporting their skill and career development and showing appreciation for their contributions. Again, this was a broader category of behaviours than the consideration constellation identified at Ohio. The third category identified group level behaviours such as working with a team rather than just individuals, setting up and facilitating meetings, ensuring participation in group decision-making and promoting cooperative group working.

Limitations of Behavioural Approach

The approach taken by these two centres (which were highly influential in their day) has been criticized on several grounds. First, it is difficult to determine causality in the studies – were the leaders displaying these behaviours because their teams had been successful or were the teams successful because their leaders behaved this way? Many studies used only self-report questionnaires for both leader behaviour measures and outcome measures, so it is difficult to know whether relationships are the result of the measurement process rather than reflecting real relationships. Moreover, the questionnaires themselves have been criticized for the ambiguity of many items and the response bias they inadvertently create. Overall, the research suggests that increases in relations-oriented behaviours result in higher levels of staff satisfaction and that changes to task-oriented behaviours produce inconclusive results.

Blake and Mouton's Managerial Grid

It may have already occurred to you that it would be interesting to compare the effectiveness of leaders who display high levels of both consideration and task orientation or task structure with leaders low on both or just one dimension. Blake and Mouton (1964) (Figure 12.6) proposed such a model with four extreme categories:

- High consideration, high structure.
- High consideration, low structure.
- Low consideration, high structure.
- Low consideration, low structure.

Those low on both dimensions were termed laissez faire in their behavioural style, since they were likely to leave employees to largely manage themselves. The two high-low configurations were termed either people-oriented or task-oriented. The researchers were particularly interested in what came to be called the 'high high' leader, predicting that this configuration of behaviours would be highly effective. Research has generally been inconclusive, which is not surprising given that the model assumes a simplicity that is at odds with reality. A leader's behaviour in any situation may have a complex mix of both consideration and task structuring so it is not easy to categorize behaviour.

Amabile, Schatzel, Moneata and Kramer (2004) used diary data from 26 project teams over several weeks. They found that effective leaders used more relations-oriented behaviours such as giving psychological support, consulting with team members and recognizing their contributions. They also used task behaviours, such as clarifying roles and objectives, monitoring progress and dealing with problems. But the timing of these behaviours proved at least as important as the level of the

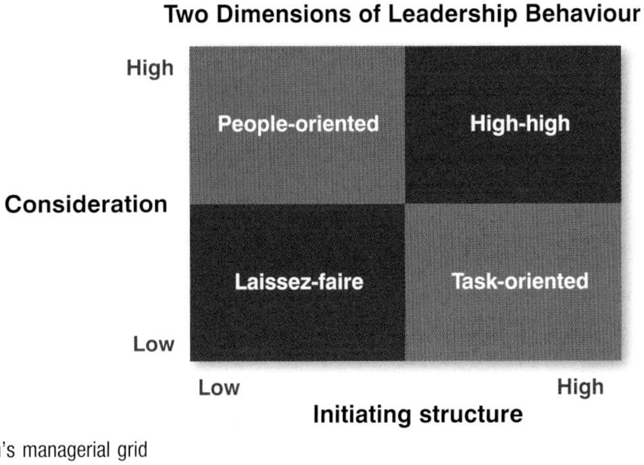

Figure 12.6   Blake and Mouton's managerial grid

Leadership Behaviour	Consideration/People Orientation	Initiating Structure/ Task Orientation
	r/p	r/p
Leader effectiveness	.39 *	.28*
Followers' motlivation	.40*	.26*
Satisfaction with leader	.68 *	.27 *
Job satisfaction	.40*	.19
Group/Org. performance	.23 *	.23
Overall average	.49 *	.29 *

Based on 400 correlations from 200 studies with 300 samples (Judge et al., 2004, Journal of Applied Psychology)

Figure 12.7   Effects of leadership behaviours

behaviours. Negative behaviours by leaders such as making mistakes, inappropriately chastising team members or failing to take appropriate action created negative spirals.

Figure 12.7 shows the results of a meta-analysis of research on the relationships between the dimensions in the Ohio and Michigan studies and a variety of potential leadership effectiveness measures (Judge *et al.*, 2004). What is clear is that the relationships between the consideration/employee relations measures and the outcomes are stronger than those between the structuring/task orientation measures and the outcomes.

Overall, the behavioural approach tends to ignore the context or situation within which leader behaviours occur. In some situations (crises for examples), task-oriented behaviour will be vital, whereas at other times, relations-oriented behaviour will build loyalty and commitment. It appears that Initiating Structure is more susceptible to situational differences than is Consideration because in some situations task orientation is positively associated with satisfaction whereas in others it has negative effects.

The approach has also been criticized for its narrow focus on two broad behavioural areas (consideration and initiating structure). Leadership involves more than two dimensions of behaviours. It includes scanning the external environment, developing visions and strategies, managing conflicts, establishing coalitions with other parts of the organization or other organizations, influencing external stakeholders and so on. The list is almost endless, but the management of change is a particularly important category.

In reviewing the extensive research in this area, Yukl (2010) argues for an integrative framework of leader behaviours subsuming three broad categories: task-oriented behaviours, relations-oriented behaviours and change-oriented behaviours. Change-oriented behaviours include:

- Monitoring the external environment.
- Interpreting events to explain the urgent need for change.
- Studying competitors' ideas for innovation.
- Envisioning exciting new possibilities for the organization.
- Encouraging people to view problems and opportunities in new ways.
- Encouraging innovation.
- Encouraging and celebrating progress in implementing change.

The most serious criticism of this approach is that it fails to address the question of which leadership behaviours are appropriate in which situations? In a crisis, when a customer is complaining because the meal is late in a restaurant, using consideration as a style in the kitchen may not be at all helpful. After the dinner has been successfully served, it may be. We therefore need a much greater understanding of the situations in which different leader behaviours are most and least helpful. The major problem therefore with both trait and behavioural approaches is that they offer very simple answers to very complex questions.

CONTINGENCY APPROACH

The study of the trait and behavioural approaches leads to the conclusion that the effectiveness of leadership is determined not just by leaders' traits or behaviours alone but is dependent on situational factors – leadership effectiveness is contingent upon factors such as the task, followers and other aspects of the environment. This has led to the development of 'contingency' theories of leadership (Figure 12.8) within which and below we consider two examples: *situational leadership* and the *path-goal theory* of leadership.

Situational Leadership Theory

Hersey and Blanchard (1977) proposed that effective leadership was contingent on the maturity of followers. They distinguished between job maturity – how skilled the followers were at their jobs; and psychological maturity – how confident the followers were. The less mature the subordinates, the more task orientation or structuring the leader needed to provide. At intermediate levels of maturity, leaders (it was proposed) should use more consideration and less structuring. When followers were mature, leaders could withdraw and provide minimal structuring and support since followers were self-directed. Although there is little empirical support for the theory, it does draw attention to the fact that leadership behaviours do have to be adjusted depending on the characteristics of followers and that a participative approach is not appropriate in every situation (Figure 12.9).

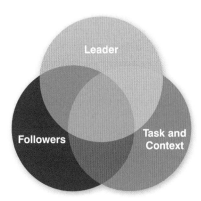

Figure 12.8   Contingency approaches to leadership. Leader effectiveness is determined by both the personal characteristics of leaders and by various characteristics of the situation in which leadership takes place.

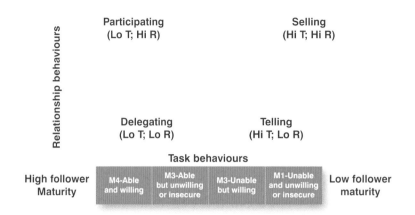

Figure 12.9   Situational leadership (T = task orientation; R = relations orientation)

Participative Leadership

Participation in decision-making by followers seems like an obvious strategy for leaders to promote. Leaders who encourage those they lead to contribute to decisions gain a number of advantages from this style of leadership. Those who influence a decision tend to see it as more their own decision and support it. Their motivation to implement it is increased. As a result of being involved in the process and thinking through the decision, they have a better understanding of the nature of the decision and their anxieties are likely to be reduced. Moreover, they can resist the decision if it appears likely to threaten their interests. Finally, simply by expressing their anxieties in the course of participating in the decision, their resistance to the decision is likely to be reduced. And of course, having the views, experience and knowledge of a variety of colleagues is likely to lead to a more sophisticated and comprehensive analysis of the decision-making issue, producing better-quality decisions.

However, there are disadvantages to participation. For example, participation takes time and, in a crisis, time may not be available. Staff may not be in full possession of the facts or may make self-interested decisions. If the leader does not take account of their views, they may become resentful and distrustful. Participation is not always a cost-free process. And those who are not included in the decision-making process may feel left out. It is difficult to know where to draw the line. Participation can be a recipe for avoiding making decisions leading to organizational inertia.

Think through your own approach to leadership and times when you have been called upon to lead. When did you use one or more of the styles below? What was it about the situation or about you at that time that led you to use each of these styles? What conclusions do you draw about the relationship between leadership styles and situational factors affecting behaviour?

- *Autocratic decision*: the leader makes the decision, not taking into account the opinions or suggestions of staff. They therefore have no direct influence on the decision. This style involves no participation.
- *Consultation*: the leader invites staff to contribute their opinions and ideas. However, he or she still makes the decision alone after taking into account the views of staff.
- *Joint decision*: the leader invites the views of staff in a meeting. Everyone's comments are contributed and the group collectively arrives at a decision. The leader does not make the final decision; this is made on the basis of consensus in the group.
- *Delegation*: the leader asks staff to take responsibility for making the decision. The staff members given this responsibility may have to seek the leader's approval for the final decision. Delegation is greater to the extent that the individual staff member does not have to seek final approval.

Figure 12.10 Path-goal theory. 'Clarifying path to better goal attainment and removing barriers'

Path-Goal Theory

Robert House offered a more sophisticated version of contingency theory in the form of *path-goal theory*. House suggests that the leader should make desired rewards available (goal) and clarify for the subordinate the kinds of behaviour that will lead to the reward (path). The theory proposes four types of leader behaviour and two situational variables (Figure 12.10). The four types of leadership behaviours are:

- Directive – sets goals and gives guidance.
- Supportive – shows concern for followers' needs.
- Participative – consults before decision-making.
- Achievement-oriented – sets challenging goals and expects followers to perform at highest level.

Each of these strategies is enacted by taking into account the nature of subordinates and their tasks. Path-goal theory proposes two classes of situational or contingency variables that moderate the relationship between leadership behaviour and outcome:

- *Environment:* Task structure, formal authority system, work group autonomy.
- *Subordinate:* Locus of control, experience, perceived ability.

When the leader compensates for things lacking in either the work setting or the employee, performance and employee satisfaction are likely to be high. If there is low task structure then the leader will need to be directive. Where there is high work-group autonomy, the leader can be consultative. When subordinates have a low internal locus of control, leaders will need to be directive. If employees have high perceived ability and experience, then an achievement-orientated style makes sense. When the task is stressful, tedious or dangerous, supportive leadership is more appropriate as a style. Overall, this approach has produced more support than the other contingency approaches in terms of predicting effective leadership (Podsakoff, MacKenzie, Ahearne and Bomer, 1995), but the results are not conclusive.

Contingency theories therefore take us a little further than trait or behavioural theories in representing more accurately the complexity of leadership in real organizations. They have been criticized for being too simplistic, despite their attempts to take account of situational factors. The criticism centres on the suggestion that real life situations are too complex to be reduced to single variables (follower maturity, task structure). In practice, leadership situations are multi-faceted, dynamic and subject to only limited control. Moreover, given the fast pace of their work, leaders and managers do not have the luxury of analyzing the situation using what may seem contrived or unrealistic models. Their value lies in reminding leaders of the need to monitor the changing situation.

A final criticism of contingency approaches is that followers are treated as an homogenous group, assumed to share characteristics – all relatively mature, able and experienced; or all with a low internal locus of control. We now turn to examine a theory which presents a quite different approach by focusing on leader – follower relationships.

DYADIC THEORIES OF LEADERSHIP: LEADER–MEMBER EXCHANGE THEORY

This theory describes the different kinds of relationships that may develop between a leader and a follower and what the leader and the follower give to and receive back from the relationship. The model proposes that leaders have different reactions to different followers (Graen and Cashman, 1975). When the leader has subordinates with whom they get on well or who are similar to them (personal compatibility) or subordinates who they perceive to be competent, they both trust and spend more time with them than they do with other subordinates. The reverse applies to those who are perceived as less compatible or competent (Figure 12.11). Not only do leaders spend less time with them, they also have more formal relationships with them. The theory also suggests that subordinates know very well which group they are in – the 'in-group' or the 'out-group'. The attributions of leaders to members of these different groups are systematically different. The successes of in-group members are attributed to their ability or hard work while their failures are attributed to situational or environmental factors. The reverse is true for out-group members. In-group members are trusted with the more interesting assignments and desirable tasks, are given more information and are taken into the leader's confidence much more.

A widely used seven-item measure is available to test the nature of relationships – the LMX7. Subordinate ratings of their leaders are influenced by whether they see the leader as fair, whereas the ratings provided by leaders are influenced by whether they see their subordinates as competent. Research using this and other LMX measures generally supports the model (Martinko, Harvey and Douglas, 2007). Given its predictive validity and the obvious implications for practice, the model has been used to develop a set of prescriptions about how to correct performance deficiencies apparent amongst followers in ways other than adopting favourites (summarized by Yukl, 2010, pp. 243–246):

- Gather information about performance problems rather than jumping to conclusions about employees' motivation or competence.
- Try to avoid attributional biases that assume the problem lies with the person rather than the situation.

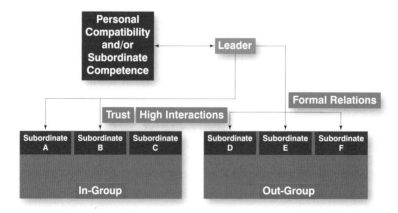

Figure 12.11   Leader–member exchange model

- Provide corrective feedback as soon as possible after the performance problem becomes apparent.
- Describe the problem briefly to the person.
- Explain the consequences (for the team, customer, organization) of the performance problem.
- Be calm and professional rather than angry, resentful or embarrassed.
- Work together with the employee to try to identify the reasons for the problems in performance.
- Invite suggestions for ways of correcting the performance problem.
- Express confidence in and support for the employee.
- Show a sincere commitment to helping the person.
- Agree on the steps forward to correct problems.
- Summarize and agree the content of the discussion.

CHARISMATIC AND TRANSFORMATIONAL LEADERSHIP

The most influential recent approaches to leadership focus on *charismatic* and *transformational leadership*. Charismatic leadership describes a self-confident, enthusiastic leader able to win followers' respect and support for their vision of how good things could be. Followers identify with such leaders because of their desire to please an individual who seems extraordinary because of their strategic insights, unconventional (even radical) views, strong convictions, high energy levels and self confidence.

This attractive description should not blind us to the dangers of charismatic leadership. Both Winston Churchill (typically seen as a benevolent leader) and Adolf Hitler (a tyrant) have fitted the charismatic leader profile. Theorists and researchers propose that negative charismatics have a personalized power orientation and intentionally seek devotion from followers rather than support and loyalty. They use ideology when it suits them, changing the rules for personal benefit, and they tend to dominate and weaken followers, increasing their dependence. Their concern is with self-glorification and increasing power rather than with the well-being of followers (Howell and Shamir, 2005).

On the other hand, in two studies, Erez and Johnson (2008) found that leader charisma was positively associated with followers' positive affect and negatively associated with followers' negative affect. The authors hypothesized that leaders' positive affect, positive expression and aroused behaviour would mediate the relationships between charisma and affect. Their research showed that firefighters under the command of a charismatic officer were happier than those under the command of a non-charismatic officer and that these relationships were mediated by the leader's positive affect and expressed positivity.

A closely related concept is *transformational leadership*, which is defined as leadership that inspires followers to trust the leader, to perform at a high level, and to contribute to the achievement of organizational goals. Bass (1985) describes transformational leadership as having four key components:

- *Idealized influence:* leaders behave in admirable ways so that followers tend to identify with them (e.g. they display conviction; they portray role modelling behaviours consistent with a vision; they appeal to the commitment and loyalty of followers on an emotional level as well as rational level).
- *Inspirational motivation:* leaders articulate a vision which is appealing and inspiring to followers (e.g. this provides meaning for the work task; they set high standards and communicate optimism about the achievability of the vision).
- *Intellectual stimulation:* leaders stimulate and encourage creativity in their followers (e.g. challenge assumptions, take risks, ask followers for their ideas and for suggestions on how to develop them into practice).

- *Individualized consideration:* leaders attend to each follower individually (e.g. by acting as a mentor or coach, and by listening to their concerns and paying attention to their needs, including their skill and career development needs).

The theory contrasts two styles of behaviour called *transformational* and *transactional leadership*. Transactional leadership motivates followers by exchanging rewards for high performance and noticing and reprimanding subordinates for mistakes and substandard performance. Transactional leadership consists of three dimensions underlying leaders' behaviour:

- *Contingent reward:* leaders set up constructive transactions or exchanges with followers, e.g. clarifying expectations, establishing rewards in order to motivate and shape their performance. Other examples include exchanging rewards for appropriate levels of effort, or responding to followers' self-interests as long as they are getting the job done.
- *Active management by exception:* leaders monitor follower behaviour, anticipate problems and take corrective action before serious difficulties occur.
- *Passive management by exception:* leaders wait until the followers' behaviour has created problems before taking action.

These leader behaviours are therefore very much task-focused and behavioural rather than emotional. Theorists such as Bass (1985) suggest that transformational and transactional behaviours are not mutually exclusive but that effective leaders use both styles. However, it is proposed the most effective leaders use the transformational approach more since it increases follower motivation and performance more. Figure 12.12 reveals what research suggests about the two styles. Transformational leadership does appear more effective than management by exception (passive management by exception appears to be negatively related to effectiveness). Both contingent reward and transformational leadership are positively and relatively strongly related to leadership effectiveness.

The final category, *laissez-faire leadership*, represents the absence of leadership. It differs from passive management by exception, where at least some influence is exerted. In effect, this involves leaving staff to manage themselves and make their own decisions regardless of their competence or of the need to structure the task. The meta-analysis in Figure 12.12 reveals that this approach is strongly negatively related to effectiveness. Why would anyone use either passive management by exception or laissez faire styles? Observation suggests the answer is 'out of necessity'. Where leaders must oversee very

	Outcome*
	r/p
Transformational leadership	.44*
Transactional leadership	
Contingent reward	.39*
Active management by exception	.15
Passive management by exception	−.15
Laissez-faire leadership	−.37*

[a]A combined outcome measure of follower job satisfaction satisfaction wilth leader, motivation, leader performance, effectiveness and group/organization performance.
Based on 626 correlations from 87 studies with a total N > 38.000 (Judge, et al., 2004).

Figure 12.12   Relationships between transformational and transactional leadership outcomes

large groups of staff or where the task is simple, predictable and structured, leaders may be inclined to adopt these approaches. However, the research evidence suggests that such styles are nevertheless counter-productive.

Overall, the research evidence suggests that transformational leadership is effective and that a combination of transformational leadership and contingent reward is powerful in producing desirable outcomes such as effectiveness (productivity, profitability), innovation, employee commitment and engagement and employee well-being. Recent studies also suggest its value in encouraging employee creativity and corporate entrepreneurship. Gong, Huang and Farh (2009) examined the relationship between transformational leadership, employee creativity and job performance. Transformational leadership predicted employee creativity, which in turn predicted employee sales and supervisor-rated employee job performance. Another showed the effects on top management teams (TMTs) of CEO transformational leadership. Ling *et al.* (2008) proposed that transformational CEOs influence TMTs' behavioural integration, risk propensity, decentralization of responsibilities and long-term compensation and that these TMT characteristics impact corporate entrepreneurship. Data from 152 firms supported most of these hypothesized links, underscoring how the CEO-TMT interface helps explain transformational CEOs' role in promoting corporate entrepreneurship. Transformational leadership also predicts commitment to organizational change among followers (Herold *et al.*, 2008).

KEY THEME

Cross Cultural Issues

Global Leadership and Organizational Behaviour Effectiveness (GLOBE)

Do leadership styles and follower preferences for leadership styles vary across countries? These questions led to the creation of the GLOBE programme in 1993, involving 170 researchers from 63 countries. The focus of the research was on the relationship between societal culture, organizational culture, leadership prototypes (what people implicitly expect of their leaders) and organizational effectiveness. Data was gathered from 17 000 middle managers in 900 organizations concentrated in three industry sectors (finance, telecommnications and food).

The GLOBE programme investigated leader behaviours and attributes reported to be effective or ineffective in each societal culture. The methodology relied primarily on the development of a questionnaire instrument, translated, back-translated and tested in each of the 63 countries, covering all major cultural regions in the world (Brodbeck *et al.*, 2000; Den Hartog *et al.*, 1999; House *et al.*, 1999).

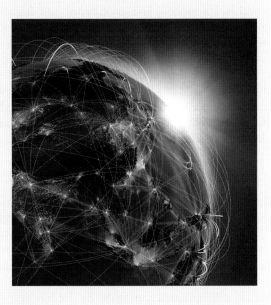

We now move on to examine three important questions in leadership research: are there cross-cultural differences in leadership styles? Do men and women differ in their leadership styles? And can leadership be developed via training programmes and other interventions? We begin with a key theme, focusing on cross-cultural differences in leadership.

LEADERSHIP ACROSS CULTURES

Leadership is recognized by the fit between what the individual implicitly believes leadership constitutes and the behaviours observed in someone in a leadership role (Lord and Maher, 1991). The implicit model carried in the individual's mind is called their 'leadership prototype'. The better the match between the individual's leadership prototype and their leader's behaviour, the more they are influenced by the leader. For example, research on transformational leadership suggests that charismatic/transformational leadership styles are closer to followers' perceptions of 'ideal' leadership than other styles (e.g. transactional leadership). This research also suggests that when employees see a leader as close to ideal, the leader can influence them in ways which go well beyond the influence deriving from the formal authority position.

GLOBE tested the hypothesis that differences in leadership prototypes exhibit predictable within-country consistency and between-country differences and that the differing prototypes mirror cultural norms, values and assumptions deeply ingrained in societal culture. In other words, people develop leadership prototypes that mirror their societal cultures. Leadership prototypes will therefore be widely shared within particular cultures and there will be predictable cross-cultural differences in these prototypes. In our increasingly connected world, characterized by more interaction, global travel, global business and international working, understanding these variations becomes important. A style of leadership that works well in the United States may not go down so well in the Middle East or in Turkey. The leadership prototype in Germany may be discordant with the leadership prototype in Sweden. Understanding what works where and why is important for understanding which leadership styles work well in which countries and for training leaders to be more protean – changing their styles to suit the situation they find themselves in. It is also important because most research on leadership over the last 100 years has been conducted in the US. Our knowledge is therefore biased towards US models and prototypes and highly ethnocentric. For the fast-growing economies of countries such as India, China and Brazil (for example), this research may have limited applicability or may be misleading.

The GLOBE research identified 21 leadership prototypicality dimensions grouped into six broad categories (see Figure 12.13) which reliably differentiated leadership prototypes across cultures. The dimensions include some that vary across cultures ('culturally contingent leadership') and some that are valued across all cultures ('universal leadership concepts'). The latter include charismatic/value-based; team-oriented; humane-oriented; autonomous; self-protective and participative. The sub-elements making up these six dimensions from among the 21 are depicted in Figure 12.13.

Culturally contingent leadership concepts

Those dimensions which varied across cultures included: ambitious, cautious, compassionate, domineering, formal, humble (self-effacing), independent, risk-taking and self-sacrificing.

Taking the European sub-sample which involved more than 6000 middle managers from 22 European countries, the results clustered into five broad groups of countries: Anglo, Nordic, Germanic, Latin and Near East countries. The results showed that leadership prototypes were similar within and different between the five culture clusters. Further analysis revealed three higher order dimensions which differentiated countries by leader prototypes: 1) *Interpersonal Directness and Proximity*

1. Charismatic/Value-based

Charismatic 1: Visionary

Charismatic 2: Inspirational

Charismatic 3: Inspirational

Integrity

Decisive

Performance-oriented

2. Team-oriented

Team 1: Colloborative team orientation

Team 2: Team Integrator

Diplomatic

Malevolent (reverse scored)

Administravely competent

3. Self-protective

Self-centered

Status conscious

Conflict Inducer

Face saver

Procedural

4. Participative

Autocratic (reverse scored)

Non-participative (reverse scored)

5. Humane-oriented

Modesty

Humane-oriented

6. Autonomous

Autonomous

Figure 12.13   The GLOBE leadership dimensions

(i. e. low face-saving, low self-centred, low administrative; high inspirational and integrity), 2) *Autonomy* (i.e. individualistic, independent, autonomous, unique), and 3) *Modesty* (i.e. modest, self effacing, patient). For example, the 'Interpersonal Directness and Proximity' dimension separates the South/East from the North/West European countries (the exceptions are former East Germany and Portugal). In the Germanic, Anglo and Nordic countries, people expect leaders to have high inter-personal directness and proximity, whereas this is not the case in South/East European countries. The Germanic cluster, Georgia and most prominently the Czech Republic expect and prefer leaders with high levels of autonomy (individualistic, independent, unique), and much more so than is the case in the Anglo, Nordic, Central, Latin and Near East European countries.

Universal leadership concepts

In at least 95 per cent of the 62 countries studied in GLOBE, three dimensions were always associated with effective leadership. These are Integrity, Inspirational and Team Integrator. Two were always found to be negatively related to effective leadership – Malevolent and Face Saver (Den Hartog *et al.*, 1999). House *et al.* (1999) originally proposed that charismatic/transformational leadership (Integrity, Visionary, Inspirational, Self-sacrificing, Decisive and Performance-oriented) is a universally endorsed leadership constellation but and, though this hypothesis received some support, only two elements out of the five (Inspiration, Integrity) were completely universally endorsed. Across all countries the following items indicated leadership effectiveness: motive arouser, foresight, encouraging, communicative, trustworthy, dynamic, positive and confidence builder (Den Hartog *et al.*, 1999). Figure 12.14 shows those clusters around the world in which particular prototypes are rated as high, medium or low.

Societal Cluster	Charismatic/ Value Based	Team-Oriented	Participative	Humane-Oriented	Autonomous	Self-protective
Eastern Europe	M	M	L	M	H	H
Latin America	H	H	M	M	L	M
Latin Europe	M	M	M	L	L	M
Confucian Asia	M	M	L	M	M	H
Nordic Europe	H	M	H	L	M	L
Anglo	H	M	H	H	M	L
Sub-Saharan Africa	M	M	M	H	L	M
Southern Asia	H	M	L	H	M	H
Germanic Europe	H	M	H	M	H	L
Middle East	L	L	L	M	M	H

Key: H a high score on this dimension; M a medium score on this dimension; L a low score on this dimension.

H, L indicate the highest or lowest score on this dimension in comparison with the other societal clusters
e.g., Eastern Europe had the highest score of all the culture clusters for 'Autonomous' and Latin America had the lowest.

Figure 12.14   Summary of societal rankings for GLOBE dimensions of leadership (adapted from Chhokar, Brodeck and House, 2007)

Where a particular dimension is seen as prototypical across cultures, we should recognize that this does not mean that these characteristics are necessarily expressed in the same way. As we shall see in Chapter 14, there are major differences across cultures that influence values and behaviours. Inspirational or charismatic leadership may be valued across all societies, but may be seen in rather different ways. In some places, such leadership is seen as potentially dangerous because of the risk that the leader may exploit followers. The risk-taking associated with inspiration may be viewed ambivalently in cultures that are avoidant of uncertainty. Consequently, the expression of transformational leadership or charismatic leadership is likely to be moderated and expressed in different ways across cultures that nevertheless value that leadership prototype.

The GLOBE project will have a considerable influence on our understanding of leadership across cultural boundaries for a long time to come thanks to the scale, ambition and methodological sophistication of the work. In particular, it serves to show how important cross-cultural issues are in our understanding of behaviour at work, and the extent to which reliance on findings largely from one or two cultures may blind us to understanding of leadership specifically and work behaviour in general across cultures (Chhokar, Brodbeck and House, 2007; House, Hanges, Dorfman and Gupta, 2004).

People and Teams are the Key to Successful Leadership

I was the formally designated leader of a large business school in the United Kingdom. The School had some 190 staff, including 105 academics and 85 support and administrative staff. The School had an annual turnover of about £37 million and provides education for over 3000 students, the majority of whom come from outside the European Union. It competed with about 12 000 other business schools worldwide and its biggest challenge is to be towards the front of that enormous race. That required a very high degree of fitness. What is it like to lead such an institution? There are multiple challenges constantly and most of them are strategically important. It is vital that the School can align around an inspiring and exciting vision of what it can become (**http://www1.aston.ac.uk/aston-business-school/**) and that all staff in the School are engaged by that vision. They must have the confidence that the School can achieve its aims so that has to be reinforced continuously. At the same time, there is the day-to-day reality of ensuring that this business is run effectively and that means paying lots of attention to income, spending and investment for the future where possible. The School must have a strategy for its future and the objectives of the Management Team, every programme and department, every professor and every lecturer, are all clear and aligned around the strategy. Progress must be measured and monitored via key performance indicators. A close watch must be kept on the world around us: the economy, government legislation on higher education or foreign visitors' (students') visa requirements, on the new courses other business schools are putting on and on global trends and events such as climate change, international tensions, etc. As a leader I also had to build good partnerships between the Business School and the other Schools in Aston University, as well as ensuring effective relationships with the Central Services departments such as Finance, HR, Estates, Library and Information Systems. A lot of my time was spent meeting with people from other organizations and countries: other business school deans with whom we were building partnerships; potential collaborators in China, the Middle East, Africa, India, Sweden, France and Mexico; leaders of City Councils; politicians; business leaders and philanthropists; and, of course, members of the press who often had questions to ask about current affairs.

The core of the job though was working with the people who make up the business school – ensuring teams are effective, ensuring staff have good relationships at work and enjoy their jobs, and ensuring everyone feels valued, respected and supported in relation to what they do in the organization. I spent a lot of time working to ensure that there was a positive culture and that people were rewarded and appreciated and are very clear about what they are required to do in their jobs. Leading a business school was a great privilege and it was a hugely demanding but also enormously rewarding role. What made it possible to do this at all successfully in my experience was the nature of the top team that works with you. Having bright, skilled, committed, professional and supportive colleagues makes a challenging job eminently do-able.

GENDER AND LEADERSHIP

It is clear that in almost every country in the world there is widespread discrimination against women at senior levels of leadership in organizations. Good progress is being made however, In the UK, women account for 17.3 per cent of FTSE 100 and 13.2 per cent of FTSE 250 board directors (2013), up from 12.5 per cent and 7.8 per cent in 2011. However, there are only three female CEOs of the top 100 companies: Carolyn McCall at easyJet, Angela Ahrendts at Burberry and Alison Cooper at Imperial Tobacco. Across Europe there was an increase in the number of women on boards from 13.7 per cent in 2012 to 15.8 per cent in January 2013. This represents an average of 17 per cent of non-executive board members and 10 per cent of executive board members. Least discriminatory is Norway following the country's decision to introduce a legal quota of 40 per cent female representation on the board of public companies. France and Spain have also introduced such quotas. In the US, taking the Fortune 500 companies, in 2012, women held 16.6 per cent of board seats; less than one-fifth of companies had 25 per cent or more women directors, while one-tenth had no women on their boards. Only 4 per cent of CEOs were women. .According to CNN Money, in 2006, there were only ten women running US Fortune 500 companies, and only 20 in the top 1000. Women make up 8.5 per cent of European corporate boards (385 of the 4535 positions available) according to research by the European Professional Women's Network. Least discriminatory is Norway with 28.8 per cent of board members being women. Sweden is not far behind with 22.8 per cent, followed by Finland (20 per cent) and Denmark (17.9 per cent). Eighty-six per cent of UK boards have at least one female member, but the overall percentage of women directors is still only 11.4 per cent.

Despite decades of debate, discussion and awareness-raising, it remains the case that women are dramatically under-represented as CEOs and on the boards of corporations, as well as in political life. In effect, the leadership potential of many women is not fulfilled and their contribution to businesses, corporations and organizations is lost. There is a desperate need for leaders at senior levels of most organizations, yet the potential contributions of women are wasted. The effects on women aspiring to leadership positions are also deeply damaging. To quote the Business Editor of *The Observer*, Ruth Sunderland: 'Women are the single biggest – and least acknowledged – force for economic growth on the planet. This is not a claim made by rampant feminists, but by *The Economist*, which suggests that over the past few decades women have contributed more to the expansion of the world economy than either new technology or the emerging markets of China and India. But surprise, surprise: technology and emerging markets have gleaned acres of coverage in the business press; the potential of women, seen as a "soft" issue, has not'.

What are some of the reasons for this discrimination, sometimes called the 'glass ceiling'? Lyless and Heilman (2006) suggest that women need more skills than men to advance to executive positions. Others offer the following explanations. Women are denied access to roles and positions which provide important experience or visibility that will enable promotion. Women are excluded from networks that provide connections and supports for promotion to senior positions. Women are less likely to focus on promotion and exert effort in that direction than men. Senior industry figures are less likely to provide mentoring for women than men because they do not see them as future leaders. Competing family demands, such as child-care duties, make career progress more difficult for women. Senior managers do not take decisive action to encourage equality of opportunity in their organizations. Senior managers are biased and tend to promote people with similar characteristics to themselves, including gender. Some men intentionally try to preserve the top echelons for men (see Yukl, 2010 for more discussion of these explanations). There is some evidence that all of these factors are at play within organizations and create the circumstances that prevent women from assuming leadership positions.

Research has examined the extent to which there are differences between men and women in terms of leadership style and leadership effectiveness, since this might be one explanation for some of the differences. Eagly, Johannsen-Schmidt and Van Engen (2003) undertook a meta-analysis to investigate leadership styles and concluded that women used transformational leadership styles a little more than men. They were also more likely to use contingent reward as a transactional style, whereas men used passive management by exception rather more. Their transformational style involved more use of individualized consideration – supportive behaviour towards those they lead and a focus on developing subordinates' skills and confidence. Such findings, given our earlier analysis, suggest women should be more likely than men to be offered leadership positions, given this configuration of leadership style.

There is little difference in leadership effectiveness (Eagly *et al.*, 1995). Women are more likely to be effective when the role requires strong interpersonal skills and men are more likely to be effective in roles which require strong task skills. However, the differences in leadership style and role performance are small; so small in fact that is safer to assume that there is no difference in leadership effectiveness between men and women.

The key is to ensure that organizations make best use of the talents that are available to them. Currently, the majority of organizations in Europe fail to do this because of their long-standing discrimination, favouring the promotion of men over women to senior positions.

LEADERSHIP DEVELOPMENT

A question asked of those who study leadership by many business people is 'Are leaders born or is it possible to train people to be leaders?' That question reflects a lack of understanding about the nature of leadership. Certainly some traits with a strong genetic component are important for leadership such as extraversion (positively) and neuroticism (negatively), but it is equally true that everybody is called upon at points in their lives to provide leadership. Moreover, leadership is highly dependent upon the situation in which people find themselves as we have seen above.

Nevertheless, the question of whether leadership competence can be enhanced by training is an important issue. In Chapter 7, we saw that the effectiveness of training programmes depends on how well they are designed. They range in quality from the frankly hopeless to good. Simply analyzing leadership interventions to see whether they work is not a useful exercise. More important is examining the design elements and fortunately we do know something about quality of design (Baldwin and Ford, 1988; Lord and Hall, 2005; Salas and Cannon-Bowers, 2000; Tannenbaum and Yukl, 1992). Based on the existing research, Yukl (2010) identifies eight factors that determine the success of leader training:

1 Clear learning objectives – the training programme must specify a limited number of very clear objectives in order that it is appropriately focused.

2 Clear meaningful content – the content must be clear to the trainees in order that it can guide their thinking and behaviour and it must be meaningful in its relation to the objectives of the training and the development of effective leadership. Periodic summaries of content help to ensure understanding. Models should be simple enough for people to understand and memorable enough for them to be able to access and apply them in the workplace.

3 Appropriate sequencing of content – models should be presented before people are asked to acquire techniques derived from them. Material should progress from the simple to the more complex. And having intervals in training so that people can practice techniques and digest the learning between training sessions is valuable.

4 Appropriate mix of training methods – there should be a mix of training sessions rather than a diet of only one method. Formal lectures, practice sessions, role plays, coaching and experiential exercises can all be used, but should be appropriate both to the capacities of learners and the particular skills being taught.

5 Opportunity for active practice – trainees should be asked to restate the principles they have been taught, try them out in a safe way (e.g., through role plays) and then put them into practice back in their workplaces, with an opportunity to review effectiveness.

6 Relevant, timely feedback – feedback is fundamental to all animal learning, and no less to humans. Therefore information about the success or otherwise of leadership behaviours during the training process is vital for effective training.

7 Promoting the self-confidence of trainees – by reassuring and praising trainees, their confidence is likely to be developed and their leadership skills to improve. By beginning with relatively simple tasks, trainees can experience success before moving on to more complex and challenging tasks.

8 Follow-up activities – in order to sustain learning it is helpful to have review sessions or to have trainees carry out specific leadership tasks back in their organizations and then to review their success and problems in order that learning can be sustained.

Leadership development is a huge industry in most countries, soaking up enormous amounts of money spent by organizations on training. Below we briefly review evidence on the effectiveness of different types of interventions to promote leadership effectiveness.

Multi-source Feedback Via Questionnaire

This method of promoting leadership effectiveness involves the individual and several others with whom they work completing a questionnaire assessing the leader's behaviours and effectiveness. This is sometimes called 360-degree assessment because subordinates, peers and bosses are all asked to assess the individual. The leader is then encouraged to reflect on the differences between self-ratings and those of the others; to reflect on the ratings of those they work with or report to; and to reflect on how the ratings compare with those of other leaders in organizations, using the norm data available for that particular instrument. There are many variations of such instruments available with widely varying psychometric properties. Some are very widely used personality questionnaires, which have limited validity data (such as Myers Briggs) while others are based on considerable research in psychology, such as some 'Big Five' measures. Feedback to the individual can be in the form of a written report (the least useful), a one-to-one discussion with someone expert in understanding the results or a workshop with a group of leaders sharing and discussing their results together.

How effective is multi-source feedback? A number of studies have produced mixed results (Seifert, Yukl and MacDonald, 2003), some suggesting positive effects and others no effects. In a review that took in some 131 studies (not confined to leadership), Kluger and DeNisi (1996) found only a weak positive effect of multi-source feedback on performance. Indeed, in one third of studies the relationship was negative. It may be that, used in conjunction with training or other interventions, this approach is useful, but there is no clear evidence for this. More research is needed to determine the effectiveness of this approach. Meanwhile, it is a highly profitable industry for consultancies and soaks up a considerable amount of managers' time in organizations.

Developmental Assessment Centres

Assessment centres were described in detail in Chapters 6 and 7. Here we consider their effectiveness in promoting leader development. Such assessment centres, usually spread over two to three days, involve multi-source feedback, in-basket exercises, aptitude tests, interviews, group exercises, writing assignments and intensive reflection processes. There is evidence that such processes do have positive effects on subsequent leader performance (Engelbracht and Fischer, 1995). The problem is that with such a mix of interventions, it is very difficult to know what elements are potent in enabling leadership development and what are redundant. The design of such programmes is therefore a pick and mix in the dark process for those charged with encouraging effective leadership development. More sophisticated questions, such as which elements are most effective for which leaders, cannot be addressed by the existing corpus of research.

Developmental Assignments

The best way to learn to lead, many argue, is through experience rather than through formal training, so giving potential leaders challenging assignments can be helpful (McCall, et al., 1988). These could include specific challenging projects on a 'task and finish' group, managing a new project, leading a 'blue sky' team proposing new products or services, working on secondment in another part of the organization, having an assignment in another country or chairing a special task force.

The research at AT&T (Bray et al., 1974) suggested that experiencing diverse and challenging work enhanced subsequent career development and research at the Center for Creative Leadership (CCL) (McCauley, Eastman and Ohlott, 1995) reinforced that. In the CCL research, managers reported that they learned new and valuable skills, but this was dependent upon the project they were involved in. Moreover, the data were both retrospective and self-report and therefore weak. The research evidence and anecdotal reports indicate that much depends on the quality of the assignments and the size of the assignment challenge. Having a challenging assignment is best, but this should not be to the point where the individual feels they are sinking or where they fail. The greater the variety of tasks, in general, the better the learning people derive. Moreover, the better and more timely the feedback, the more effective the learning from assignments is.

Job Rotation

Job rotation is a system of encouraging leadership development by assigning people to multiple jobs within the organization in a short space of time. Managers are usually encouraged to work in up to five or six different jobs over periods usually up to two years. The purpose is for them to experience a range of aspects of the business, to interact with different customers, to get to know different technologies, to experience different country cultures in a multinational organization and to increase their network of contacts within the country. Participants report the value of such experiences, although the constant change and learning can be stressful and overwhelming. Campion, Cheraskin and Stevens (1994) found that participants reported increased technical, managerial and business knowledge. However, there was also evidence of lower productivity because of the frequent requirements for new learning and there were negative effects on subordinates who reported lower satisfaction when exposed to constant changes of manager. Because job rotation is often employed to rapidly increase the skills and careers of outstanding individuals (called 'fast tracking'), this can generate resentment among others at their exclusion from the programme. Overall, there is little research evidence to support the value of this method of encouraging leader development – simply because there have been too few studies to provide a clear picture.

Action Learning

Action learning groups are formed of individuals who meet regularly together while working on a specific project in their work areas or organizations. They meet under the guidance of a facilitator to set objectives, review progress, problem solve and share experiences. By working in such a group, motivation is increased and there is a strong sense of mutual support. There is some evidence that this works best when a whole team works together. The logic of action learning groups is reasonable and participants report valuable outcomes. For example, knowing that they will have to report on progress at the next Action Learning Group meeting, spurs them to make progress on the project. Moreover, having the support and guidance of the group gives confidence. Very few published studies have evaluated outcomes, however. Prideaux and Ford (1988) report positive outcomes, but these are based only on retrospective self-reported benefits. This is another area of leadership development research where considerably more effort is needed to advance our understanding.

Mentoring

Mentoring refers to situations where an experienced manager works with a less experienced individual to support their leadership development. The role has two functions or advantages. The more senior person can advise, support and counsel the person based on their greater experience and knowledge. And they can help to advance the career of the mentee by promoting and protecting them and winning good assignments for them. Indeed, there is some evidence that mentees do have greater career success as a result of this patronage (Whitely and Coetsier, 1993). It is noteworthy, however, that women seem to have more difficulty finding a mentor within organizations (Ragins and Cotton, 1993). Mentees generally report better career advancement, higher levels of satisfaction, higher organizational commitment and lower turnover. The evidence suggests that mentoring is useful, but there is little to suggest it leads to higher levels of leadership effectiveness.

Executive Coaching

It is mainly high-level leaders and managers in organizations whose development needs are provided by executive coaches. The coach is usually a high-level (often retired) manager or specialist (such as a Work Psychologist). Coaches can be internal or external personnel and coaching has become such a large industry that there are many executive coaching companies offering their services internationally. The purpose of coaching is to help the individual leader learn new skills, handle difficult problems, manage conflicts or learn to work effectively across cultural boundaries. The relationship should be characterized (rather like a therapeutic relationship) by strict confidentiality, rules for ethical conduct and a sense of psychological safety and trust between the two parties. However, the ethics of executive coaching has not kept pace with the financial growth of the industry. Executive coaching is usually contracted over a limited period and includes regular meetings between the coach and the leader.

The advantage of this approach to development is that there is a strong, clear focus on specific issues faced by the leader, in contrast to training programmes, which may be generic, abstract and not sufficiently relevant to participants' day-to-day work problems. The disadvantages are the cost and variable coach competency.

There has been only limited research so far examining the effectiveness of coaching, but what there is has been favourable. Hall, Otazo and Hollenbeck (1999) reported on a study of 75 people from six companies for whom executive coaching was helpful. However, this study was based on self reports and was retrospective, limiting the confidence we can place in the findings. Olivero, Bane and Kopelman (1997) assessed outcomes associated with a three-day training workshop, augmented by eight weeks of executive coaching focused on individual action projects. The results suggested the managers were more productive as a result of the training and these effects were augmented by the coaching; indeed coaching had the stronger effects of the two interventions. A study by Bowles, Cunningham, De La Rosa and Picano (2007) produced similarly positive results. However, all these studies are deeply flawed methodologically and do not employ adequate controls so, although the results are encouraging, they offer little by way of solid support.

Outdoor Pursuits Programmes

This approach to leadership development involves groups of participants engaging in challenging activities, usually in wild and wonderful places. Rock climbing, white-water rafting, building bridges, hiking and other challenging pursuits form the core of the experience. The aim is to make links between these activities and organizational leadership. There is usually an experienced facilitator whose role is to assist in this process. The experience is supposed to encourage personal growth, build self-confidence, build self-control, encourage trust between participants and enable risk-taking in a controlled environment.

Very few studies have examined the efficacy of such interventions. In the area of team building, the results are not encouraging (Tannenbaum *et al.*, 1996). Marsh, Richards and Barnes report long-term improvements in leaders' self confidence but Wagner, Baldwin and Roland (1991) find only weak effects three months after the interventions. Perceptions of team work did improve where intact teams participated in programmes. There is little evidence that these programmes are effective (other than self report evidence and it is clear from this that many participants do enjoy the experience). The conclusion has to be that such interventions are lots of fun for those who participate in them and make lots of money for those who run them. A few headline cases have resulted in serious injury to physical or mental health when the programmes are run by people without adequate training.

Reflections on Leadership Development

Overall, there is little evidence for the effectiveness of leadership development programmes. Undoubtedly some programmes work for some people some of the time, but evaluating their effectiveness empirically is very challenging. The interventions are so diverse, the participants have quite different challenges very often and those providing the programmes have hugely varying experience, knowledge and sensitivity. What is needed is research, which asks the simple questions of what interventions work for what leadership development objectives with which individuals in which work contexts? We are very far from being able to answer such questions. Vast sums of money are spent on leadership development in organizations; if only 1 per cent was spent on research into effective interventions, there is no doubt we could save a great deal of wasted money and produce a great many more effective leaders. What is clear is that experience in the job of leadership is hugely valuable in enabling leaders to develop their skills, but without guidance and support much of that experience can be wasted (Day, 2000; Day and Harrison, 2007).

KEY THEME

Ethics and Corporate Social Responsibility

Ethical Leadership

Interest in ethical leadership in Work and Organizational Psychology has grown rapidly in the last 20 years. A key characteristic is the leader's focus on influencing the ethical behaviour of others in ther organizations. The following values are emphasized in theories of ethical leadership (Yukl, 2013):

- Integrity: demonstrates consistency between espoused values and lived values; shows openness and honesty; admits mistakes; keeps promises; does not manipulate and deceive people.

- Altruism: focuses on helping others without expectation of personal gain; makes personal sacrifices to help others.

- Humility: acknowledges others' efforts in success rather than claiming responsibility; is modest about accomplishments and capabilities; is respectful of others; does not seek to differentiate on the basis of status symbols; admits limitations and errors.

- Empathy and healing: is aware of the challenges others face; is focused on taking intelligent action to help others; encourages forgiveness in the workplace.

- Personal growth: focuses on others' growth and development; offers opportunities for growth and advancement; provides mentoring and coaching for others; sees mistakes by others as a learning opportunity for all.

- Fairness and justice: treats others equally; stands up for those who are relatively powerless; speaks out against injustice and manipulation; speaks truth to power.

- Empowerment: encourages others to voice opinions and influence change; provides a high degree of autonomy and employee 'voice'; shares sensitive information to enable others to have organizational insight; encourages others to express dissent or minority views.

Current conceptualizations of ethical leaders paint a relatively clear picture of the behaviours that describe ethical leadership. Ethical leaders serve followers and the organizations and place their needs behind those of others. They balance and integrate the competing views and needs of stakeholders. They develop a vision based on the values, input and needs of those they lead. They act in a way that is consistent with the values they express. They are willing to make personal sacrifices and take personal risks to achieve the vision of the team or organization. They are open and transparent in communicating information in a timely fashion. They encourage criticism and diverging contributions from followers, valuing challenge to their own opinions. They make extensive use of coaching, mentoring and training to develop followers. Listening to others is their primary orientation.

Above all, ethical leaders set clear standards for ethical conduct; model ethical behaviour; help people to find fair ways of resolving conflicts and dealing with problems; oppose ethical practices in their organizations; and implement programmes to support ethical behaviour within their organizations.

KEY FIGURE

Robert House

Robert House has been the Joseph Frank Bernstein Professor of Organizational Studies at Wharton since 1988. He received his Bachelors degree from the University of Detroit in 1955 and an MBA from the University of Detroit in 1958. He received his PhD from Ohio State University in 1960 and was profoundly influenced by the work going on there at the time on behavioural theories of leadership. He has had a glittering academic career. He received the Irwin Career Award for Scholarly Contributions to Management from the Academy of Management in 1991. Other positions include Senior Management Training Specialist, North American Aviation, Inc., 1958–59; Personnel Analyst, Chrysler Corporation, 1955–58; Management Development Research Analyst, Corporation, 1956–58. He is Co-founder (1989) and Executive Editor of the journal *Leadership Quarterly*.

His theoretical contributions have been wide-ranging. He developed the path-goal theory of leadership described in this chapter in 1971. He argued that 'The motivational function of the leader consists of increasing personal payoffs to subordinates for work-goal attainment and making the path to these pay-offs easier to travel by clarifying it, reducing roadblocks and pitfalls and increasing the opportunities for personal satisfaction en route'. (House 1971, p. 324). The initial

version of path-goal leadership had two leadership behaviours (supportive and directive leadership – similar to the Ohio studies). Later House and Mitchell (1974) added two others – participative and achievement-oriented leadership. In 1996, House extended the theory to include behaviours derived from charismatic and transformational leadership studies.

House helped to develop charismatic theory with reference to traits and skills of such individuals and explored in depth the conditions in which charismatic leaders are likely to emerge. He argued that follower behaviour indicates a person's values and self concepts as well as their goals; their self concept is based on a hierarchy of values and social identities; people seek to enhance their self esteem; and people are motivated to have a consistent and integrated self concept. Charismatic leaders enable followers to build positive self concepts and identities which enhance their self esteem. House contributed to our thinking by also describing how negative charismatics can be recognized by their personalized power orientation – they seek power for their own ends rather than for the benefit of others.

Houses' second main contribution has been through the GLOBE studies, described in this chapter. In 1991, he first conceived the idea for the research and he wrote the first proposal a year later while visiting leadership scholars in various countries. He won funding in 1993 from the Eisenhower Leadership Education Program in the US. By 1994 he had identified and won the collaboration of around 170 Country Co-Investigators (CCIs) from 65 countries. In 1994, the GLOBE Coordination Team was established, with 11 members from six countries covering five continents, and data collection began in earnest. Three years later, in 1994, the initial round of data collection from 62 countries was complete. In 1999, the first academic journal articles began to appear in the top leadership journals. In 2004, the first comprehensive GLOBE book was published. Three years later, in 2007, the second comprehensive GLOBE book was published to great acclaim and won the 2009 Ursula Gielen Book Award for International Psychology, at the American Psychological Association Division 52 meeting.

Given what you have learned about leadership in
this chapter, design a training programme that you
think would help leaders to become more effective
in their work. Remember also to draw on the information contained in Chapter 7 to enable you to offer
something more effective than that offered by most
leadership development providers.

CONCLUSION

From the preceding discussion of our knowledge of leadership, it may feel difficult to identify what is
known about the key elements of leadership. Gary Yukl, a leading theorist and researcher in the
leadership area over many years summarizes understanding of effective leadership behaviours in a
helpful way. In reviewing the extensive research, Yukl (2013) argues for an integrative hierarchical
framework of leader behaviours subsuming three broad categories: task-oriented behaviours,
relations-oriented behaviours, change-oriented behaviours, and External behaviours:

Task-oriented	Clarifying
	Planning
	Monitoring operations
	Problem solving
Relations-oriented	Supporting
	Developing
	Recognizing
	Empowering
Change-oriented	Advocating change
	Envisioning change
	Encouraging innovation
	Facilitating collective learning
External	Networking
	External monitoring
	Representing

SUMMARY

This chapter began by making clear the importance of leadership in human society and therefore the importance of understanding what constitutes effective leadership. Huge advances in understanding have been made in the last 100 years, but very large areas of ignorance remain. This is partly because defining leaders and leadership is complex and challenging. It was proposed that:

> Leadership is the process of influencing others to understand and agree about what needs to be done and how to do it, and the process of facilitating individual and collective efforts to accomplish shared objectives.

Leadership effectiveness is similarly complex and depends on which stakeholder group is defining it. Effectiveness can subsume productivity, innovation, personal benefits, employee attitudes, long-term outcomes or short-term outcomes, cohesion, culture, group identity and successful management of change. Effectiveness may also be defined in terms of the career of the leader – has she or he had a rapid advance up the hierarchy within or across organizations?

The chapter described trait theories that assess the extent to which personality predicts leader emergence and effectiveness. The Big Five personality dimensions correlate with leader effectiveness, with extraversion and openness correlating positively and neuroticism correlating negatively. Four of the five dimensions correlate with leader emergence (extraversion, conscientiousness, openness and – negatively – neuroticism. Overall, leader effectiveness and emergence are predicted by traits such as high energy level and stress tolerance; self-confidence; internal locus of control; emotional maturity; personal integrity; socialized power motivation; moderately high achievement orientation; low need for affiliation; and by technical competence; conceptual skills; and interpersonal skills.

The behavioural approach has focused on the nature of leadership and management and illustrates the complexity of these roles – high demand and high variation. The Ohio State and Michigan University studies examined the extent to which leaders focus on managing relationships with followers or getting the job done. The former approach (relations orientation) appears more effective, with a task approach having a weak association with outcomes. The behavioural approach ignores the complexity and variety of situations that leaders face and assumes that certain leader behaviours will be effective across all situations. Moreover, they neglect the importance of leadership focused on changing organizations.

Contingency approaches seek to take account of the situation and explore both task and follower characteristics. Situational leadership examines the maturity (confidence and ability) of followers and proposes that, with greater maturity, less task structuring is required. House's path-goal theory proposes that the leader clarifies rewards for followers (goal) and the desired behaviours to achieve this (path). Two contingencies determine the appropriate leader style (directive, supportive, participative, achievement-oriented): environment and followers. When the leader compensates for factors lacking in followers or in the environment, he or she will be most effective. There is some limited support for the contingency approach.

Dyadic theory focuses on the leader member exchange process. Where followers are perceived by the leader to be similar to them or technically competent they are treated as favourites and damaging 'in-groups' and 'out-groups' are created. The best leadership is apparent when there are few differences in relationships between leaders and followers in terms of preferences and when followers view their leaders as fair.

The chapter described the more recent focus on charismatic and transformational leadership, pointing out that charismatic leaders are attractive but can be dangerous. The transformational leader uses idealized influence, inspirational motivation, intellectual stimulation and individualized consideration to promote follower motivation and loyalty. This is contrasted with transactional leadership, which consists of three dimensions underlying leaders' behaviour: contingent reward, active management by exception and passive management by exception. The most effective styles appear to be transformational and contingent reward.

The chapter explored leadership across cultures, using the results from the GLOBE study. This describes six core dimensions of leadership behaviour: charismatic/value-based; team-oriented; humane-oriented; autonomous; self-protective and participative. Some descriptions of leadership are valued differently across cultures such as ambitious, domineering and self-effacing. Some are valued in all cultures, including integrity, inspirational and team integrator. This research reminds us that leadership is culturally specific and that leaders must learn how to lead in different cultural settings. Moreover, reliance on research from only one culture will blind us to very real differences across cultures.

Women are appallingly underrepresented in leadership in companies around the world. There are a variety of explanations for this, but differences in leadership style or effectiveness is not one of them. Although women tend to have a slightly more transformational and participative style, these differences are so small as to be immaterial (and anyway should confer advantage). There is a desperate need for the widespread discrimination against women in the world of work to be ended.

Overall, there is little evidence for the effectiveness of leadership development programmes. Undoubtedly some programmes work for some people some of the time, but evaluating their effectiveness empirically is very challenging. Much research remains to be done in this and other areas of leadership research.

DISCUSSION QUESTIONS

1   What is leadership and what is leadership effectiveness?

2   To what extent are leaders born rather than made?

3   What are the most effective leadership behaviours?

4   How can leaders have different relationships with subordinates and still be fair? How can leaders learn to be charismatic and transformational?

5   How would you design a study to determine what aspects of leadership training are most effective?

6   How do you explain the fact that some leadership attributes are universally valued while others are culturally dependent? What is it about the former group of attributes or values that makes them so important?

APPLY IT

Yukl (2013) has distilled from the theory and research on leadership a statement of the essence of effective leadership (see below).

1   Consider your own strengths and areas of development as a leader (or those of your current leader) in relation to each of these behaviours.

2   In relation to which qualities are you strong? What can you learn from this?

3   How can learning help you to develop those areas where you are less effective?

- Helping to interpret the meaning of events. Effective leaders help their followers make sense of change, catastrophes, successes and the future. They provide a narrative which both makes sense to people and inspires them to give of their best and make a positive difference. Martin Luther King's 'dream' speech is a fine example.

- Creating alignment around strategies and objectives. Effective leaders clarify direction, strategy and the priorities for people's efforts. They help to create shared understanding and agreement about direction. They define the key priorities (few in number) and make clear what we are not going to do rather than overwhelming people with inspirational priorities. They help to define clear, challenging, measureable objectives for all.

- Nurture commitment and optimism: they encourage belief in the team or organization about likely efficacy and a sense of the value of the work. They encourage positive attitudes and experiences rather than cynicism or defeatism and they do so with humour, belief and a sense of purpose which inspired others to be committed.

- Encourage trust and cooperation: they emphasize the importance of people supporting each other, backing each other up and valuing each other's contributions to build trust and cohesion. They work to continually develop mutual respect, trust and cooperation among followers. They help to resolve conflicts quickly and fairly. They continuously build a strong sense of community and supportiveness that ensures people act cooperatively and supportively with colleagues.

- Create a sense of collective identity: they encourage a strong and positive vision of the value of the team's/organization's work and a sense of pride in the efficacy of the group. They encourage a sense of identity for the group or organization such that people derive value from being part of that collective. They enable the group/organization to see how their work makes a positive difference and nurture a sense of the group's character, uniqueness and identity through rituals, celebrations, humour and narrative.

● Organize and coordinate work efforts: they ensure that people are clear about their roles and contributions and help them work together in a coordinated way towards success. They are practical and timely in dealing with systems difficulties and coordination problems so that the group/organization can be successful.

● Enable collective learning: they ensure that followers engage in collective learning about errors, successes and means of ensuring continually improving quality. They ensure the group regularly takes time out to review objectives, strategies and processes so that they collectively learn and improve.

● Ensure necessary resources are available: they ensure that the group or organization has the resources (money, staff, IT support, time) necessary for them to get the job done and work actively and tirelessly to ensure

these resources are in place. This may involve political acumen and risks in dealing with the wider organization, customers and other stakeholders but they are consistent in working tirelessly to ensure the group/organization can get necessary resources to be effective.

● Develop and empower people: they focus on ensuring the continued growth and development of their followers; they provide high levels of autonomy and development opportunities to empower those they work with and ensure they continue to develop efficacy and confidence. They encourage followers to believe in their ability to respond successfully to greater challenges and responsibility while providing the necessary supports and resources to achieve this.

● Promote social justice and morality: they emphasize fairness and honesty in their dealings with all, challenging unethical practices or social injustices on behalf of all, not only their followers. They set an outstanding example of ethical/moral behaviour, especially when it requires them to sacrifice their personal interests.

WEB ACTIVITY

Leadership: the Richard Branson Viewpoint

Read the article 'Sir Richard Branson talks to HR magazine about leadership' by Peter Crush published in July 2010, which can be accessed at **www.hrmagazine.co.uk** or by following the link in the digital resources online and discuss the questions below.

1 How would you describe Richard Branson's style of leadership?

2 In what ways could leaders be socially responsible in their activity? How does this relate to the content of this chapter?

3 What are the issues to consider for leaders in managing people in large businesses?

Women in Leadership at Wal-mart

Read the article 'Women Accuse Wal-Mart of Bias' by Jami Crush, which can be accessed at **www.abcnews.go.com** or by following the link in the digital resources online and discuss the questions below.

1 What are the issues of leadership and gender raised by this story?

2 What are the barriers that women face to becoming senior leaders in organizations?

3 What could companies like Wal-mart do to create a culture in which women and men have equal progression opportunity?

FURTHER READING

Bass, B.M. and RIggio, R.E. (2006). *Transformational leadership* (2nd edition). Mahwah, NJ: Lawrence Erlbaum.

Chhokar, J.S., Brodbeck, F.C. and House, R.J. (2007). *Culture and Leadership around the World: The GLOBE Book of In-depth Studies of 25 Societies*. Mahwah, NJ: Lawrence Erlbaum.

Eagly, A.H., Johannesen-Schmidt, M.C. and van Engen, M.L. (2003). Transformational, transactional and laissez-faire leadership styles: A meta-analysis comparing women and men. *Psychological Bulletin*, *129*, 569–591.

Nicholson, N. (2013). *The 'I' of Leadership: Strategies for Seeing Being and Doing*. Chichester, UK: JOssey Bass.

Nohria, N. and Khurana, R. (eds.). 2010. *Handbook of Leadership Theory and Practice: A Harvard Business School Centennial Colloquium*. Harvard: Harvard Business School. Yukl, G. (2010). Leadership in Organization, 87th ed. New Jersey: Pearson Prentice Hall.

REFERENCES

Amabile, T.M., Schatzel, E.A., Moneta, G.B. and Kramer, S.J. (2004). 'Leader Behaviours and the Work Environment for Creativity: Perceived Leader Support.' *Leadership Quarterly, 15(1)*, 5–32.

Arvey, R.D., Zhang, Z., Avolio, B.J. and Krueger, R. F. (2007). Developmental and genetic determinants of leadership role occupancy among women. *Journal of Applied Psychology*, 92, 693–706.

Baldwin, T.T. and Ford, J.K. (1988). Transfer of training: A review and directions for future research. *Personnel Psychology*, 41, 63–105.

Baldwin, Wagner and Roland (1991) Wagner, R.J., Baldwin, T.T. and Roland, C., "Outdoor Training: Revolution or Fad?", Training & Development Journal, Vol. 45 No. 3, 1991, pp. 50–7.

Bass, B.M. (1985). *Leadership and Performance beyond Expectation*, New York: Free Press.

Berman, F.E. and Miner, J.B. (1985). Motivation to change at the top executive level: A test of the hierarchic role-motivation theory. *Personnel Psychology, 38*, 377–379.

Birkinshaw, J. and Piramal, G. (2006). Sumantra Ghoshal on management: A force for good. London: Financial Times Press.

Blake, R. and Mouton, J. (1964). *The Managerial Grid: The Key to Leadership Excellence*. Houston: Gulf Publishing Co.

Bowles, S., Cunningham, C.J.L., De La Rosa, G., Picano, J. and Meekins, R. (2007). Coaching leaders in middle and executive management: Goals, performance, buy-in. *Leadership and Organization Development, 28(5)*, 388–408.

Boyatzis, R.E. (1982). *The Competent Manager*, NY: John Wiley.

Bray, D.W., Campbell, R.J. and Grant, D.L. (1974). *Formative years in business: A long-term At&T study of managerial lives*. New York: John Wiley.

Brodbeck, F.C., *et al.* (2000). Cultural variation of leadership prototypes across 22 European countries. *Journal of Occupational and Organizational Psychology*, 73, 1–29.

Campion, M.A., Cheraskin, L. and Stevens, M.J. (1994). Career-related antecedents and outcomes of job rotation. *Academy of Management Journal*, 37, 1518–1542.

Chhokar, J.S., Brodbeck, F.C. and House, R.J. (2007). *Culture and Leadership around the World: The GLOBE Book of In-depth Studies of 25 Societies*. Mahwah, NJ: Lawrence Erlbaum.

Day (2000) The Leadership Quarterly Volume 11, Issue 4, 2000, Pages 581–613 Leadership development: A review in context David V. Day.

Day and Harrison (2007) Human Resource Management Review Volume 17, Issue 4, 2007, Pages 360–373 David V. Day Michelle M. Harrisonb A multilevel, identity-based approach to leadership development

Den Hartog, D.N., House, R.J., Hanges, P.J., Ruiz-Quintanilla, S.A., Dorfman, P.W. and Associates (1999). Culture specific and cross-culturally generalizable implicit leadership theories: Are the attributes of charismatic/transformational leadership universally endorsed? *Leadership Quarterly, 10*, 219–256.

Eagly et al. (1995) Gender and the effectiveness of leaders: A meta-analysis. Eagly, Alice H.; Karau, Steven J.; Makhijani, Mona G. Psychological Bulletin, Vol 117(1), Jan 1995, 125–145.

Eagly, A.H., Johannesen-Schmidt, M.C. and van Engen, M.L. (2003). Transformational, transactional and laissez-faire leadership styles: A meta-analysis comparing women and men. *Psychological Bulletin, 129,* 569–591.

Engelbracht, A.S. and Fischer, A.H. (1995). The managerial performance implications of a developmental assessment centre process. *Human Relations, 48,* 1–18.

Erez, A., Johnson, D.E., Misangyi, Vilmos F.; LePine, Marcie A.; Halverson, Kent C. (2008). 'Stirring the Hearts of Followers: Charismatic Leadership as the Transferal of Affect.' *Journal of Applied Psychology, 93,* 602–616.

Glomb, T.M., Duffy, M.K., Bono, J.E. and Yang, T. (2011). Mindfulness at work. *Research in Personnel and Human Resources Management, 30,* 115–157.

Graen, S.G. and Cashman, J.F. (1975). A role-making model of leadership in formal organizations: A development approach. *Organization and Administrative Sciences, 6,* 143–165.

Gong, Y., Huang, J.-C., Jiing-Lih Farh (2009). Employee learning orientation, transformational leadership and employee creativity: The mediating role of employee creative self-efficacy. *Academy of Management Journal, 52,* 765–778.

Graen, S.G. and Cashman, J.F. (1975). A role-making model of leadership in formal organizations: A development approach. *Organization and Administrative Sciences, 6,* 143–165.

Hall, D.T., Otazo, K.L. and Hollenbeck, G.P. (1999). Behind closed doors: What really happens in executive coaching. *Organizational Dynamics, 29* (Winter), 39–53.

Herold, D.M., Fedor, D.B., Caldwell, S. and Yi, L. (2008). 'The Effects of Transformational and Change Leadership on Employees' Commitment to a Change: A Multilevel Study.' *Journal of Applied Psychology 93,* 346–357.

Hersey, P. and Blanchard, K.H. (1977). *The management of organizational behaviour,* 3rd ed. Englewood Cliffs, NJ: Prentice Hall.

House (1971). Administrative Science Quarterly Vol. 16, No. 3, Sep., 1971. A PathGoal Theory of Leader Effectiveness.

House and Mitchell (1974). RJ House, TR Mitchell; Path-goal theory of leadership. Journal of Contemporary Business, 3 (1974), pp. 81–97.

House, R.J., Hanges, P.J., Ruiz-Quintanilla, S.A., Dorfman, P.W., Javidan, M., Dickson, M.W. and Gupta, *et al.* (1999). *Cultural influences on leadership and organizations: Project GLOBE.* In W.H. Mobley, M.J. Gessner and V. Arnold. (eds.).

Advances in Global Leadership. (pp.171–233). Stamford, CN: JAI.

Howard, A. and Bray, D.W. (1990). 'Predictors of managerial success over long periods of time.' In Clark, H. and Clark, M. (eds.). *Measures of Leadership,* Leadership Library of America, West Orange, NJ, pp. 113–30.

Howell and Shamir (2005). The Role of Followers in the Charismatic Leadership Process: Relationships and Their Consequences Jane M. Howell and Boas Shamir ACADemy of MANAGEMENT REVIEW, 2005 vol. 30, 96–112.

Judge, T.A., Bono, J.E., Ilies, R. and Gerhardt, M.W. (2002). Personality and leadership: A qualitative and quantitative review. *Journal of Applied Psychology, 87(4),* 765–780.

Judge, T.A., Piccolo, R.F. and Illies, R. (2004). 'The forgotten ones? The validity of consideration and initiating structure in leadership research.' *Journal of Applied Psychology, 89,* pp. 36–51.

Katz, D. and Kahn, R.L. (1978). *The social psychology of organizations,* 2nd ed. New York, NY: John Wiley and Sons.

Kluger, A.N. and DeNisi, A.S. (1996). The effects of feedback interventions on performance: Historical review, meta-analysis, a preliminary feedback intervention theory. *Psychological Bulletin, 119,* 254–284.

Likert, R. (1967). *The human organization: Its management and value,* New York: McGraw-Hill.

Ling, Y.A.N., Simsek, Z. Michael H. Lubatkin, John F. Veiga (2008). Transformational leadership's role in promoting corporate entrepreneurship: Examining the CEO-TMT interface. *Academy of Management Journal, 51,* 557–576.

Lombardo, M.M. and McCauley, C.D. (1988). *The dynamics of management derailment.* Technical Report No. 34. Greensboro, NC: Center for Creative Leadership.

Lord, R.G. and Maher, K.J. (1991). *Leadership and information processing. Linking perceptions and performance.* Boston: Unwin-Hyman.

Lord, R.G. and Hall, R.J. (2005). 'Identity, deep structure and the development of leadership skill.' *Leadership Quarterly, 16,* 591–615.

K.S. and Heilman, M.E. (2006). When fit is fundamental: Performance evaluations and promotions of upper-level female and male managers. *Journal of Applied Psychology, 91,* 777–785.

McCall, M.W. Jr., Lombardo, M.M. and Morrison, A. (1988). *The lessons of experience.* Lexington, MA: Lexington Books.

McCauley, C.D., Eastman, L.J. and Ohlott, P.J. (1995). Linking management selection and development through stretch assignments. *Human Resource Management*, *34(1)*, 93–115.

McClelland, D.C. and Boyatzis, R.E. (1982). 'The leadership motive pattern and long-term success in management.' *Journal of Applied Psychology*, *67(6)*, 737–743.

McClelland, D.C. (1985). *Human Motivation*, Glenview, IL: Scott, Foresman.

Martinko, Harvey and Douglas (2007). The role, function, and contribution of attribution theory to leadership: A review Mark J. Martinko, Paul Harvey, Scott C. Douglas The Leadership Quarterly Volume 18, Issue 6, Pages 561–585.

Miner, J.B. (1977). *Motivation to manage: A ten-year update on the 'studies in management education' research*. Atlanta: Organizational Measurement Systems Press.

Nicholson, N. (2013). The 'I' of Leadership: Strategies for seeing, being and doing. Chichester, England: John Wiley.

Olivero, G., Bane, D.K. and Kopelman, R.E. (1997). Executive coaching as a transfer of training tool: Effects on productivity in a public agency. *Public Personnel Management*, 26, 461–469.

Podsakoff, P.M., MacKenzie, S.B., Ahearne, M. and Bommer, W.H. (1995). Searching for a needle in a haystack: Trying to identify the illusive moderators of leadership behaviours. *Journal of Management*, *21*, 423–470.

Prideaux, G. and Ford, J.E. (1988). Management development: Competencies, teams, learning contracts and work experience-based learning. *Journal of Management Development*, 7, 13–21.

Ragins, B.R. and Cotton, J.L. (1993). Gender and willingness to mentor in organizations. *Journal of Management*, 19, 97–111.

Rauch, C.F. and Behling, O. (1984). Functionalism: Basis for an alternate approach to the study of leadership. In J.G. Hunt, D.M. Hosking, C.A. Schriesheim and R. Stewart (eds.), *Leaders and managers: International perspectives on managerial behaviour and leadership*. New York: Pergamon Press, pp. 45–62.

Richards, D. and Engle, S. (1986). After the vision: Suggestions to corporate visionaries and vision champions. In J.D. Adams (ed.), *Transforming Leadership*. Alexandria, VA: Miles River Press, pp. 199–214.

Salas, E. and Cannon-Bowers, J.A. (2000). The anatomy of team training. In L. Tobias and D. Fletcher (eds.), *Handbook on Research in Training*. New York: Macmillan.

Schein, Edgar. H. (1992). *Organizational Culture and Leadership*, 2nd ed. San Francisco: Jossey-Bass.

Seifert, C., Yukl, G. and McDonald, R. (2003). Effects of multi-source feedback and a feedback facilitator on the influence of behaviour of managers toward subordinates. *Journal of Applied Psychology*, *88(3)*, 561–569.

Stogdill, R.M. (1948). Personal factors associated with leadership: A survey of the literature. *Journal of Psychology*, *25*, 35–71.

Stogdill, R.M. (1974). *Handbook of leadership: A survey of the literature*. New York: Free Press.

Tannenbaum, S.I. and Yukl, G. (1992). 'Training and development in work organizations.' In *Annual Review of Psychology*. eds. P.R. Rozenzwig and L.W. Porter. Palo Alto, CA: Annual Reviews, Inc. pp. 399–441.

Tannenbaum, S.I., Salas, E. and Cannon-Bowers, J.A. (1996). Promoting team effectiveness. In M.A. West (ed.), *Handbook of Work Group Psychology* (pp. 503–529). Chichester: Wiley

Whitely, W.T. and Coetsier, P. (1993). The relationship of career mentoring to early career outcomes. *Organization Studies*, *14(3)*, 419–441.

Yukl, G. (2013). Effective leadership behavior: What we know and what questions need more attention. *Academy of Management Perspectives*, *26*, 66–85.

Yukl, G. (2013). *Leadership in Organization, 8th* ed. New Jersey: Pearson Prentice Hall.

CHAPTER 13

TEAMS AND TEAMWORK

Think of a group of humans working together, some examples are:

● Early humans on the savannah 80 000 years ago, working together to catch an antelope so they could survive.
● A lifeboat crew working to rescue a couple from a floundering yacht in a storm.
● A top management group, trying to ensure their company increases productivity and profitability so they can stay in business through a recession.
● Breast cancer care professionals working together to correctly diagnose and determine the best possible treatment for a mother who shows symptoms.
● A group of academics located in five different countries who are conducting a cross-national study of the effectiveness of virtual teamworking.
● A production cell, manufacturing the fascia of car dashboards for three different automotive companies and involving 20 different designs.
● A Champions' League football team, working to claw back a 2–0 deficit from the first round.

What they have in common is that they are trying to achieve shared objectives by working interdependently, communicating about their work together, playing specific roles in the process and, though they have one or more leaders, sharing some responsibility for the outcome of their work together. They are teams.

WHAT IS A TEAM?

Having described several teams, it is useful to clarify what we mean by a 'team'. It might be argued that the fans at the football game are a team; so are the rest of the people in the hospital or all of those working in the manufacturing company. As in many areas of social science, psychologists love to argue about definitions (see Delarue, Van Hootegem, Procter and Burridge, 2008; Hackman, 1987; Rasmussen and Jeppesen, 2006; West and Lyubovnikova, 2012; West, Tjosvold and Smith, 2006, for debates on definitions of teams).

One definition is:

> *A team is a relatively small group of people working on a clearly defined, challenging task that is most efficiently completed by a group working together rather than individuals working alone or in parallel; who have clear, shared, challenging, team-level objectives derived directly from the task; who have to work closely and interdependently to achieve these objectives; whose members work in distinct roles within the team (though some roles may be duplicated); and who have the necessary authority, autonomy and resources to enable them to meet the team's objectives.*

Unpacking this definition, we can see that members of the team have shared objectives in relation to their work – rescuing yachters, catching meat, winning games, successfully diagnosing and treating breast cancer. Second, they have sufficient autonomy and control so that they can make the necessary team decisions about how to achieve their objectives without having to seek permission from senior management – in effect senior managers would just be telling people what to do; there would not be teamwork. Third, they have both responsibility and accountability – they have to decide the tactics and put them into operation so it is down to them if it doesn't work out. Fourth, they are dependent upon and must interact with each other in order to achieve their shared objectives. They have to discuss strategy, tactics and roles and adapt their individual work depending on what others in the team do. Fifth, they have an organizational identity as a work group with a defined organizational function (e.g. the HR team responsible for all aspects of personnel management). Finally, they are not so large that they would be defined more appropriately as an organization, which has an internal structure of vertical and horizontal relationships characterized by sub-groupings. In practice, this is likely to mean that a team is smaller than ten to fifteen members and larger than two people. Research evidence generally suggests teams should be as small as possible to achieve their objectives efficiently and ideally should be no bigger than six to eight members (Hackman, 2002).

Kozlowski and Bell (2003, p. 334) weighed many definitions of 'teams' and selected out what they believed to be the key elements:

> *Work teams and groups are composed of two or more individuals who exist to perform organizationally relevant tasks, share one or more common goals, interact socially, exhibit task interdependencies, maintain and manage boundaries and are embedded in an organizational context that sets boundaries, constrains the team, and influences exchanges with other units in the broader entity.*

Both definitions refer to shared objectives and task interdependence. However, the first definition focuses more on group level features, such as autonomy, identity, teams' roles and cooperation, whereas Kozlowski and Bell's (2003) definition, takes an organizational level perspective, looking at how the team interacts with, and is influenced by, the wider organization, a theme we will return to later. Both definitions offer useful and complementary perspectives in understanding teams.

Salas *et al.* (2009) suggest that there are five core components of teamwork. The first is leadership which incorporates the search for and structuring of information to help the team perform its task; the use of information to solve problems; the management of team members; and the management of resources (e.g. IT). Leadership may also be shared when the leadership function is transferred between members for particular tasks, depending on who has the knowledge, skills and abilities to enable the team to perform a particular task. Second is adaptability, which is the team's ability to adapt its performance processes in response to changes or cues in the environment. Third is mutual performance monitoring between team members to ensure teamwork is on track. Fourth is 'backup behaviour' – team members supporting each other when they have a workload problem. Fifth is team orientation, which refers to the team's robustness in maintaining effective teamwork even under pressure or stress. These components are facilitated by three coordination mechanisms: shared mental models, which are knowledge structures or representations of the team's work, processes or environment that are shared or distributed (to a greater or lesser extent) throughout the team and enable them to work in a compatible way. The second coordination mechanism is closed loop communications, whereby a message is sent by team members, received by other team members and followed up by the sender to ensure the message was appropriately received and interpreted. Finally is mutual trust, which exists when team members can rely on each other to do what they say they will do and when they support each other in their shared endeavour.

Because many people report working in very large teams or in teams that do not have clear objectives, or whose members do not meet regularly, researchers have argued that what are often called 'teams' in organizations are in reality only 'pseudo teams' (Dawson *et al.*, 2008; West and Lyubovnikova, 2012). And such pseudo teams may lead to ineffectiveness rather than effectiveness in organizations.

'Real' versus 'Pseudo' Teams

A typical example of a pseudo team is where employees report that they are part of a team but observation reveals that they merely work in close proximity to each other and have the same supervisor. Hackman (2002) argues that, in such cases these are not real teams, as their task does not require them to work together collectively, nor are all members accountable for the task's completion. A team is a 'real' team when team members work closely and interdependently towards clear, shared objectives. Real teams also have regular and effective communication, usually in the form of team meetings, in which they reflect upon their performance and how it could be improved. Hackman (1993) proposed that in organizations, where the potential for error is inevitable, effective teams can act as 'self-correcting performance units', whereby team members anticipate and respond to each other's actions, and coordinate tasks as a seamless and collaborative whole.

In contrast, a pseudo-team is a team without clear goals, or one in which team members do not communicate, or who do not work interdependently to achieve common goals. In these groups, members are less likely to be satisfied, committed and effective and there are likely to be high error rates and low effectiveness. And indeed, in health care settings, research suggests that the more people who work in pseudo teams, the higher the levels of errors that could harm patients or staff, the higher the levels of violence by patients or their carers towards staff and the poorer the quality of patient care (Dawson *et al.*, 2008; West and Lyubovnikova, 2013). Having clarified the distinction between real teams and pseudo teams, it is helpful to consider the different types of (real) teams we find in organizations.

Types of Teams in Organizations

There are multiple types of teams in organizations, which can be grouped into categories such as these:

- Strategy and policy teams, e.g. management decision-making teams; university committees setting standards on teaching quality; politicians at cabinet level deciding on how to reduce carbon emissions in the nation's cars.

- Production teams, e.g. manufacturing assembly teams in a mobile phone-producing company; production process teams in an aluminium smelting company; bottling teams in a brewery; teams in a garden nursery that grow plants and display them ready for sale.

- Service teams, e.g. teams that service photocopiers in client organizations; radiography teams in hospitals; advice centre teams for a computer sales organization; health care teams in primary care.

- Project and development teams, e.g. research teams; new product development teams; software development teams; problem-solving teams trying to determine the cause of defects in a carbon fibre coating system.

- Action and performing teams, e.g. surgical teams; negotiation teams; cockpit crews in commercial airliners; ambulance teams; firefighting teams; lifeboat crews; football teams; string quartets and rock bands.

Key dimensions on which they differ include:

- Degree of permanence – project teams have a defined life time that can vary from weeks to years; cockpit 'teams' are together for only hours.

- Emphasis on skill/competence development – breast cancer care teams must continually develop their skills over time to a high level, whereas decision-making committees usually have little emphasis on skill development.

- Genuine autonomy and influence – manufacturing assembly teams may have little autonomy and influence whereas top management teams have considerable discretion and are powerful.

- Level of task from routine through to strategic – short-haul airline flights involve crews in routine tasks, whereas a government cabinet may be determining penal strategy for a ten-year period.

A very different approach to understanding the structure of teams is offered by an organizing framework (Hollenbeck, Beersma and Shouten, 2012) which identifies three underlying dimensions that can be used to describe work teams: *skill differentiation, temporal stability*, and *authority differentiation*. First, skill differentiation describes the extent to which members of a team have specialist knowledge, expertise or functional capabilities, which would make it difficult to interchange team member roles or substitute team members. Some may be described as unidisciplinary, such as a group of pediatric nurses working together in a hospital ward. Interdisciplinary (also referred to as multiprofessional/cross-disciplinary) teams are composed of members from a range of different occupational groups and disciplines with high levels of knowledge and skill differentiation. The second dimension is temporal stability, which refers to the extent to which a team has a history and is likely to remain intact in the future. Membership stability is argued to facilitate the development of shared mental models regarding both task and teamwork processes. The third team descriptor is authority differentiation, referring to the degree to which decision-making power lies with the team as a whole or individual members/subgroups who occupy leadership roles. Research has shown that a hierarchical authority structure, in combination with a culture deeply rooted in individual professional autonomy and poor communication can create barriers to establishing a safe culture in health care teams.

Implicit in this exploration of types of teams and team is that there are certain tasks that are best performed by teams and others that are best performed by individuals or groups of individuals working serially or in parallel. The second learning objective of this chapter is to understand what tasks are best performed by teams.

WHAT DO TEAMS DO?

The point of having a team is to get a job done, a task completed, a set of objectives met, whether it is catching an antelope for meat, rescuing people at sea or developing a business strategy for financial survival. When teams are created to perform a task, the tasks they perform should be tasks that are best performed by a team. Building a house does not necessarily require the bricklayers to work interdependently and in close communication over decisions. Each of those laying bricks simply needs to know which is his or her section of the wall. On the other hand, a team of chefs preparing a dinner for 80 people will have to work very closely together with a high degree of communication and coordination to ensure the diners have a delightful dinner. Similarly, sports teams are called teams since they have to work interdependently, to communicate constantly, to understand each other's roles and to collectively implement a strategy in order to achieve their goal of winning.

What tasks are best performed by teams rather than individuals? The following dimensions can be used to analyze the appropriateness of tasks in organizations for teamwork:

- Completeness, i.e. whole tasks – not simply putting the studs on the car wheels but assembling the whole transmission system plus wheels. Just doing a small and routine element of a task is not motivating or enjoyable.
- Varied demands – the task requires a range of skills that are held or best developed by a number of different individuals, such as a hotel conference centre team, requiring audio-visual technical skills, planning skills, sales and marketing skills and people management skills.
- Requirements for interdependence – the task requires people to work together in interdependent ways, communicating, sharing information and debating decisions about the best way to do the job (as in the case of the breast cancer care team described earlier).
- Task significance – the importance of the task in contributing to the achievement of organizational goals or to the benefit of the wider society. Examples are a top management team in a £25 million turnover company or a crisis management team set up following a natural disaster, that is working to provide shelter, food and safety for hundreds of people.
- Opportunities for learning – providing team members with chances to develop and stretch their skills and knowledge because the task demands and offers that. We see that in sports teams constantly of course, but it is no less true in other teams in organizations. Running a business requires marketing, R&D, production, strategy, people management, financial management, innovation and sales skills. The top management team of a company that is not constantly learning is leading a company towards failure.
- Developmental possibilities for the task – the task can be developed to offer more challenges to the team members, requiring them to take on more responsibility and learn new skills over time. The shop floor manufacturing team might be asked to take responsibility for continuously developing adaptations of existing products or developing new products.
- Autonomy – the amount of freedom teams have over how to do their work, ranging from when and how often to have review days (during which they stop work to reflect, plan and take action) through to offering new products and services they have developed and to hiring new staff.

The first objective of this chapter was to define teams and distinguish them from other organizational groups. From the discussion so far, it should be clear what is and is not a team. Working in the same office area does not make a group of people a team. Neither does working in the same department. So, it should be clear that working in teams is not just about having coffee and cakes together at 11am on Wednesdays! It is challenging, takes hard, extra work, careful thought and may involve interpersonal conflict. Why would organizations therefore invest resources in teamworking if it is so difficult? This brings us to the third learning objective: to understand how teamworking affects organizational performance.

WHY WORK IN TEAMS?

Why do modern organizations use teams as a means of structuring work and what evidence is there for their value? Teams have been used to accomplish large complex tasks that individuals working alone cannot take on. Moreover, they offer the potential for innovation in responding to the requirements of customers and the demands of fast-changing environments. According to Cohen and Bailey (1997), in their influential review of teamwork, there are several important reasons for implementing team-based working, including the following:

- *Teams* are the best way to enact organizational strategy. Authority for decisions can be devolved to teams, rather than being taken by senior managers and teams can respond quickly and effectively in the fast-changing environments most organizations encounter.
- *Teams* enable organizations to *speedily develop and deliver products and services* cost effectively. Teams can work faster and more effectively with members working in parallel and interdependently whereas individuals working serially and separately are much slower.
- Teams *enable organizations to learn* (and retain learning) more effectively. When one team member leaves, the learning of the team is not lost. Team members also learn from each other during the course of teamworking.
- Cross functional teams promote *improved quality management*. By combining team members' diverse perspectives, decision-making is better because team members can question ideas and decisions about how best to provide products and services to clients.
- Cross-functional design teams can undertake *radical change*. The breadth of perspective offered by cross-functional teams produces the questioning and integration of diverse perspectives that enables teams to challenge basic assumptions and make radical changes to improve their products, services and ways of working.
- *Creativity and innovation* are promoted within team-based organizations through the cross-fertilization of ideas (West, Tjosvold and Smith, 2003).

West and Markiewicz (2004) argue that well-managed, team-based working in organizations offers a number of benefits: efficient processes; flexible response to change; improved effectiveness; reduced costs; increased innovation; effective partnering with other organizations (teams from two separate organizations or parts of one organization can combine their expertise to achieve solutions to problems); customer involvement (teams can give more attention to and engage with customers in a way individuals working alone would be less able to do); employee commitment and well-being; and more comprehensive utilization of the skills of employees. What is the evidence for these wide-ranging claims? Does teamworking really produce the goods?

Delarue *et al.* (2008), reviewed the research evidence on links between team-based working and various outcomes (operational, financial, structural and worker). They concluded that there were significant positive associations. Levine and D'Andrea-Tyson (1990) found that employee participation leads to sustained increases in productivity and that teams effectively enable such participation. Cohen, Ledford and Spreitzer (1996) reported associations between teamworking and both efficiency and quality when a work organization developed teams whose members were given a voice in decision-making. In a review of 12 large-scale surveys and 185 case studies of managerial practices, Applebaum and Batt (1994) concluded that team-based working led to improvements in organizational performance. A number of other surveys have also reported links between team-based working and improvements in both labour productivity and quality (e.g., Banker, Field, Schroeder and Sinha, 1996; Batt, 1999; 2001; Benders and Van Hootegem, 1999; Elmuti, 1997; Mathieu, Gilson and Ruddy, 2006; Paul and Anantharaman, 2003; Procter and Burridge, 2004; Stewart and Barrick, 2000; Tata and Prasad, 2004; West, Brodbeck and Richter, 2004). Positive effects of teamwork on productivity have been recorded in settings as diverse as US steel mills (Boning, Ichniowski and Shaw, 2001), the US apparel industry (Dunlop and Weil, 1996) and the Australian economy (Glassop, 2002). Overall, research suggests that well managed teamwork is likely to have a positive impact on performance (Delarue *et al.* 2008).

There are similarly positive relationships between teamwork and financial outcomes. In a meta-analysis of 131 field studies on organizational change, Macy and Izumi (1993) found that interventions with the largest effects upon financial measures of organizational performance were team development interventions. Zwick's (2004) study of German organizations showed that economic value increased after the introduction of teamwork. Another meta-analysis of 61 independent samples found that working had a significant though small positive relationship with both performance outcomes and staff attitudes (Richter, Dawson and West, 2011). The analyses showed that team working had a stronger relationship with performance outcomes if accompanied by complementary HR measures.

A core purpose of team-based working is to decentralize decision-making to lower levels in the organization (Bacon and Blyton, 2000). Organizations that use self-managing work groups have been shown to be less hierarchical in structure and have a broader span of control (Glassop, 2002). This enables them to be more adaptive and agile in response to changes in their environments, since there are fewer levels in decision-making to be negotiated when changes are proposed.

Do those working in teams feel more satisfied at work? In a survey of Canadian employees, Godard (2001) found that team-based working was associated with job satisfaction, empowerment, commitment, citizenship, task involvement and belongingness. Why should this be so? The activity of a group of people working cooperatively to achieve shared goals via differentiation of roles and using elaborate systems of communication is basic to our species. We have worked this way throughout most of our evolutionary history. Human beings work and live in groups because groups originally enabled survival and reproduction (Ainsworth, 1989; Buss, 1991). By living and working in groups, early humans could share food, easily find mates and care for infants. They could hunt more effectively and defend themselves against their enemies. Individuals who did not readily join groups would be disadvantaged in comparison with group members as a consequence (West, 2001). 'Over the course of evolution, the small group became the survival strategy developed by the human species' (Barchas, 1986, p. 212). The benefits of teamworking are therefore not only improved task performance (West, 1996), but also emotional benefits for team members (Carter and West, 1999; Patterson and West, 1999). It follows that organizations which make extensive use of teamworking have lower levels of employee turnover (Glassop, 2002), and reduced absenteeism (Delarue, Van Hootegem, Huys and Gryp, 2004)

Overall, therefore, the evidence suggests that teamworking contributes to organizational performance in positive ways. But as the comments earlier in this chapter suggested, this is likely to be dependent on

BOX 13.1
Teamwork in hospitals and other health care organizations

As governments have struggled to cope with the increasing health care demands of ageing populations, higher expectations and increased health care costs, they have identified teamworking as one way to provide better health care in hospitals and primary health care teams. Does teamworking in health care organizations lead to better patient outcomes?

- Poor teamworking can jeopardize patient safety (NCEPOD, 2002). Conversely, successful teamwork is associated with effective health care delivery (West et al., 1998).

- Innovative, high-quality care is most likely to be provided by teams whose members have clear, shared work objectives, emphasize quality, communicate well and hold good quality meetings.

- Teamwork is associated with lowered hospitalization rates and reduced physician visits while maintaining function for elderly patients with chronic illness and functional deficits.

- Teamworking also contributes to performance in health care organizations by reducing errors and improving the quality of patient care.

- Poor teamwork is associated with early retirement and increased sickness absence in doctors.

- The higher the percentage of staff working in teams in hospitals, the lower the patient mortality.

- Team functioning predicts innovations in health care in community mental health, primary health care and breast cancer care teams (West et al., 2003).

- There is evidence that team-based working leads to lower stress amongst doctors (itself a predictor of medical errors).

- Members of effective health care teams report high job satisfaction, role clarity and well-being (Mickan and Rodger, 2005).

For a review, see West and Spendlove, 2005; Borrill et al., 2000.

(or mediated by) how well the teamworks together. Establishing clear objectives, good communication and regular reviews have been mentioned a number of times as important elements in creating effective teams. These are all examples of team processes and this brings us to our fifth learning objective – to understand the factors influencing the performance of teams. Critical to influencing the performance of teams are 'inputs' and 'team processes'. We will now turn to consider these.

WHAT MAKES AN EFFECTIVE TEAM?

What models might help us understand the functioning of teams from lifeboat crews to top management teams to football teams? The model of choice over the last 30 years is the input-process-output (IPO) model (see Figure 13.1). More sophisticated representations can be used to guide research and practice (see Mathieu et al., 2008 for this and for a valuable review of research on team effectiveness), but the value of the IPO model is that it shows the relationships between team inputs and outputs. It also proposes that team processes mediate input-output relationships – team inputs (such as team member skills) affect team processes (such as communication) and thereby have an effect on outputs.

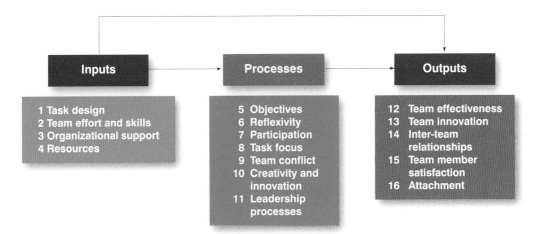

Figure 13.1   An input-output model of team performance

For example, having team members with diverse knowledge and experience leads to more informed and better decision-making and therefore to higher levels of team effectiveness. Moreover, inputs also directly affect outputs – having sufficient resources such as phones on each team member's desk enables the team to respond quickly to customer orders, making the team more effective.

Figure 13.1 describes the broad categories of factors that influence team effectiveness and team-based working – the inputs, processes and outputs. In addition the figure shows the four core dimensions of inputs, the seven dimensions of processes and the five key dimensions of the outputs. Each of these 16 components is an important element of what influences team effectiveness and the effectiveness of team-based working across an organization. The elements of the IPO model are described in more detail below.

Before describing the IPO model in detail, it is useful to have in mind the key criticisms of this approach. There are two. First, IPO models have been criticized for simplifying too far the complex processes of teamwork. Teams have multiple concurrent performance episodes that overlap so there are often quite different processes occurring at the same time. Critics suggest that the IPO model should be used to understand each of these separately, not simply sum them all to present a rather crude picture of the team. Moreover, the model does not incorporate a feedback loop from outputs to inputs and processes, but clearly learning and change are consequences of performance and other outcomes. Second, the model is criticized because it takes too broad a time slice and offers a static picture that ignores the long-term development of the team. Teams learn, develop and mature over time and this is neglected in IPO models (Salas *et al.*, 2009).

Team Inputs

Team task

Inputs include the most important aspect of any model of teams – the task a team is required to perform. Is it a task best done by teams or would it be better accomplished by individuals working alone? And is the task complete, challenging, relevant? Does it, in short, reflect well the dimensions of team tasks we described above? Where it does not, then the team will not perform effectively. The task determines team members' roles, collective goals, task-related interactions and team coordination and workflow processes (Kozlowski and Ilgen, 2006) see Table 13.1. First and most important is the task; second is the people who make up the team. We reviewed key dimensions of team tasks above.

Table 13.1 Team inputs	
Dimension	**Components**

Task design	Complete task
	  Autonomy
	  Task relevance
	  Feedback
	  Interdependence

Team effort and skills	Team member motivation and effort
	  Appropriateness of team members' skill to the task in hand
	  Team potency-team members' belief in likelihood of the team's ability to succeed

Organizational support	Information and communication
	  Training for teamworking
	  Climate in support of teamworking

Resources	Material and human resources, e.g. IT support, administrative support

Key dimensions of teamwork include degree of permanence; emphasis on skill/competence development; genuine autonomy and influence; level of task from routine through to strategic. Tasks best performed by teams have high levels of the following characteristics: completeness, varied demands, requirements for interdependence, task significance, opportunities for learning, developmental possibilities for the task and autonomy.

TEAM COMPOSITION

How do we go about selecting the people for the team? We address this question by first asking whether diversity of team composition is an advantage or disadvantage. Then we consider personalities of team members, their social skills and their teamwork knowledge, skills and abilities. However, the overriding principle is the skills required to perform the task. If a hospital manager wishes to create a team that will provide breast cancer care services, he or she needs to ensure access to the skills to investigate biopsies and offer a diagnosis (a medical oncologist), operative skills for conducting biopsies and remove cancerous growths (a breast surgeon), the skills to undertake nursing care pre- and post-operatively (breast cancer care nurse) and the skills to provide ongoing support to someone recovering at home (such as a medical social worker). Teams are there to do a job and the first and overriding principle is ensuring that all the skills needed for accomplishing the team task are either held by one or more team members or can quickly be developed by them.

KEY THEME

Cross Cultural Issues

Team diversity

A key issue to understand in composing teams is whether heterogeneity (or diversity) is advantageous or disadvantageous to teams and their members. Is it better to put together a team whose members are very different from each other? This may be in relation to observable characteristics such as age, gender, ethnicity or status in the organization; or on underlying dimensions such as skills, attitudes, experience; or even personality. Or is team functioning disadvantaged by such diversity?

Van Knippenberg and Schippers (2007) have reviewed the effects of team diversity on team performance. They define diversity as the degree to which there are objective or subjective differences between people within the team and conclude that we can view diversity from two theoretical perspectives.

The first is an Information/Decision-making Perspective. This suggests:

- Diversity is an informational resource since it creates a bigger pool of information for a team to draw from in its decision-making.
- Consequently this offers the prospect of better problem-solving, decision quality, creativity and innovation.
- Diversity is therefore good for performance.

The second, and competing, perspective is a Social Categorization Perspective that suggests:

- Diversity is a source of intergroup bias – we distinguish between those who are like us and not like us in our team and biases develop between 'us' and 'them'.
- This intergroup bias produces less liking for, trust in and cooperation with dissimilar others in our team and leads to poor communication, interpersonal challenges, misunderstandings and incivility.
- This creates conflict, suspicion and lack of trust and disrupts performance.

For the most part, the evidence suggests that diversity, when well managed through good team processes (such as clarifying objectives, clear roles, good communication and regular reviews of team effectiveness), leads to performance gains rather than losses in the long term (van Knippenberg et al., 2010). However, initial performance in heterogeneous teams is likely to be affected by process difficulties more than in homogeneous teams and teams may never recover from this.

Research by Van Knippenberg and his colleagues reveals that when team members believe in the value of diversity, diversity is more likely to have positive effects on team performance. The leader, in particular, plays a vital role in encouraging the development of positive beliefs about diversity in the team. Edmondson and Roloff (2009) argue that psychological safety and learning are key factors to effective collaboration in diverse teams.

Size Does Matter

The evidence suggests that teams should comprise the least number of members required to enable the team to accomplish its task. This is because having more team members than necessary leads to perceptions among team members that there is unequal distribution of workload and perceptions that some individuals are putting in more effort than others, creating feelings of resentment and reducing motivation (Hackman 2002). And having more members than are needed is simply inefficient. Once the team gets above eight to ten members, coordination and communication become more difficult, and more formalized rules for working together have to be developed to ensure the team remains effective (West, 2012).

Personality and Ability

How do people with different personalities work together in teams? This question has led to a variety of enormously popular models of team personality which suggest what mix of personalities is best for effective teams. The best known is Belbin's Team Roles Model, which proposes that a mix of team roles (dominant leader, facilitating leader, creative person, warm supporter, task completer, external networker) predicts team performance. This idea has intuitive appeal to managers, but researchers have found little or no supportive evidence. Moreover, the instruments developed to measure the team role types (Belbin, 1981; 1993) do not appear to have good psychometric properties (Anderson and Sleap, 2004; Furnham, Steele and Pendleton, 1993).

Do more rigorous approaches suggest that a mix of personalities in teams predicts better team performance or is it best for all team members to be agreeable people, primarily focused on getting on with other team members? The 'Big Five' model of personality (Goldberg, 1990; see Chapter 3) offers a robust personality model that we can use to analyze the mix of personalities in teams and the effects on team performance. The model describes five dimensions of personality:

- Extraversion – positive emotions, gregariousness and warmth.
- Agreeableness – trust, straightforwardness and tender-mindedness.
- Conscientiousness – competence, order and self-discipline.
- Emotional Stability versus Neuroticism – calmness and stability versus anxiety, self-consciousness and vulnerability.
- Openness to experience – fantasy, actions and ideas.

Research evidence suggests that the particular personality dimensions that predict team effectiveness depend on the type of task. In interdependent teams where individual contributions to team success are easily recognized and rewarded, hardworking and dependable team members are most successful (Mount, Barrick and Stewart, 1998; Barrick *et al.*, 1998). High levels of conscientiousness accompanied by low variability of this trait between team members is associated with team effectiveness. Other team members see these conscientious individuals as valued team members because they can be relied upon to perform their part of the work. Conscientiousness is particularly important in team settings because hierarchical control is reduced, so there is a need for self-discipline.

Having high levels of agreeableness per se in teams does not appear to be related to team performance, but having any very disagreeable individual in a team undermines effectiveness. One aggressive or manipulative member or someone who is low in conscientiousness (and so does not pull their weight) can dramatically undermine team performance (De Dreu and Weingart, 2003). Task conflict is managed better in teams with high levels of emotional stability and openness (Bradley *et al.*, 2012). Teams with high levels of extraversion are good at decision-making (for example management teams), probably because their warmth and optimism helps them in persuading others to accept their decisions. For teams requiring creative decisions or innovation, openness rather than conscientiousness or extraversion is likely to be important. In general, however, the research evidence suggests that *teams composed of conscientious people with high levels of extraversion are likely to be most effective.*

Teamwork Skills

When we create teams we need to consider the technical skills required to perform the task, such as a chemist, marketer and production specialist for an R&D team making cosmetics. However, we also need to consider other skills which we might label 'generic teamworking skills'. In our experience these are rarely considered in organizations when managers are putting together teams. This includes people's preferences for working in teams; whether they have an individualist or collectivist approach to working with others; their basic social skills such as listening, speaking and cooperating; and their teamworking skills such as collaboration, concern for the team and interpersonal awareness. Do they express appreciation, build optimism, contribute to cohesion and enhance a sense of team potency?

Generic teamwork skills include social skills such as:

- Active listening skills – being able to listen to others and engage effectively in understanding their views and experiences.
- Communication skills – understanding how to communicate effectively, taking into account the receiver, the message and the appropriate medium – for example email for routine communications, telephone conversation for more complex discussions and face-to-face for communications involving conflicts.
- Social perceptiveness – being aware of others' reactions and understanding why they react the way they do (this is often referred to as one dimension of 'emotional intelligence' – see Chapter 3).
- Self monitoring – being sensitive to the effects of our behaviour on others (so called because it involves monitoring the effects of the self on others).
- Altruism – working to help colleagues without necessarily expecting reciprocity.
- Warmth and cooperation – smiles, appreciation, humour, support and small talk, oil the wheels of teamwork.
- Patience and tolerance – accepting criticism and dealing patiently with frustrations (Peterson *et al.*, 2001).

The application of such skills builds a sense of trust, safety and mutual respect in teams. Selecting team members for these skills or coaching them to develop these skills creates better conditions for team effectiveness.

Another way of thinking about generic skills for working in teams is in relation to the knowledge, skills and abilities (KSAs) for teamwork. In teamwork settings, employees need the abilities to perform the job as individuals as well as the abilities to work effectively in a team because both are important for team performance. Stevens and Campion (1993; 1999) propose that effective team functioning depends on teamwork abilities, focusing on team members' knowledge of how to perform in teams that extend beyond the requirements for individual job performance. Based on the literature on team functioning, they identified two broad skill areas (interpersonal KSAs and self-management KSAs), consisting of a total of 14 specific KSA requirements for effective teamwork (see Table 13.2).

Stevens and Campion (1999) also developed a 35-item multiple-choice test in which respondents are presented with scenarios they may face in the workplace and asked to identify the strategy they would most likely follow. Examples are shown in Box 13.2.

Table 13.2 Steven's and Campion's knowledge, skills and abilities for teamworking	

1 Interpersonal Team Member KSAs

A conflict resolution	1	Fostering useful debate, while eliminating dysfunction conflict
	2	Matching the conflict management strategy to the cause and nature of the conflict
	3	Using integrative (win – win) strategies rather than distribution (win – lose) strategies
B Collaborative problem solving	4	Using an appropriate level of participation for any given problem
	5	Avoiding obstacles to team problem solving (e.g. domination by some team members) by structuring how team members interact
C Communication	6	Employing communication that maximizes an open flow
	7	Using an open and supportive style of communication
	8	Using active listing techniques
	9	Paying attention to non-verbal messages
	10	Warm greeting to other term members, engaging in appropriate small talk, etc.

2 Self-management Team KSAs

D Goal setting and performance management	11	Selling specific, challenging and acceptable team goals
	12	Monitoring evaluating and providing feedback on performance
E Planning and task coordination	13	Coordinating and synchronizing tasks, activities and information
	14	Establishing fair and balanced roles and workloads among team members

The researchers found that team members' scores on this test were significantly related to team performance in several studies (McDaniel *et al.*, 2001). Regardless of their task specialism or their preferred team role, there are certain attributes that all team members need to demonstrate if the team is to achieve its goal according to this model, and that is teamwork KSAs. (The correct answers by the way are B, A and C).

So far, in our consideration of team inputs, we have focused on the team's task, the mix of team members, including the team size, the task related skills of members, their personalities, social skills and teamworking KSAs. Now we move on to consider the organizational context within which teams function. If teams are seeds, the organization is the seed bed within which teams grow. If the bed is rocky and infertile, teams will fail. If the bed is correctly prepared and maintained, teams will thrive and flourish.

BOX 13.2
Example items from a measure for selection into teams

Suppose you find yourself in an argument with several co-workers about who should do a very disagreeable, but routine task. Which of the following would likely be the most effective way to resolve this situation?

A Have your supervisor decide because this would avoid any personal bias.

B Arrange for a rotating schedule so everyone shares the chore.

C Let the workers who show up earliest choose on a first-come, first-served basis.

D Randomly assign a person to do the task and don't change it.

Your team wants to improve the quality and flow of conversations among its members. Your team should:

A Use comments that build upon and connect to what others have already said.

B Set up a specific order for everyone to speak and then follow it.

C Let team members with more say determine the direction and topic of conversation.

D Do all of the above.

Suppose you are presented with the following types of goals. You are asked to pick one for your team to work on. Which would you choose?

A An easy goal to ensure the team reaches it, thus creating a feeling of success.

B A goal of average difficulty so the team will be somewhat challenged, but successful without too much effort.

C A difficult and challenging goal that will stretch the team to perform at a high level, but attainable so that effort will not be seen as futile.

D A very difficult or even impossible goal so that even if the team falls short, it will at least have a very high target to aim for.

Organizational Supports

Developing teamwork in organizations requires that the organization provide the right context for teamworking. For example, encouraging the development of teamworking in an organization that has a high level of bureaucracy and many rules and regulations is unlikely to be successful. Teams, because of their diverse perspectives, are innovative. If that innovation is stifled by excessive bureaucracy, teamwork will be stifled too. Below are some of the key characteristics that are required to sustain teamworking in organizations.

Organization structure: vertical and horizontal linkages

In considering the structure of the organization, including the layout of the organization chart, it is important to consider the number of hierarchical levels within the organization. The simplest way of doing this is to count the number of levels from the most senior manager to the person who is lowest in the organization hierarchy, including both in the count. Where there are more than three levels in a small to medium-sized organization (between 20 and 250 employees), there may well be a case for considering reducing the number of layers to increase the effectiveness of teamworking.

Another important element of the structure of the organization is the degree of integration between departments and functions. To what extent do different departments and functions interact together, share information and have influence over each other's decision-making? Organizations are sometimes described as constructed in separate silos where finance, production and marketing (for examples) do not cooperate or interact. There are tensions and conflicts between departments. In other organizations there are cross-functional teams which ensure effective pooling of knowledge and expertise and good communication to provide a seamless service to customers.

One reason for the introduction of team-based working is to improve the degree of integration between departments, functions and especially between teams. A high degree of integration within the organization supports effective team-based working since innovations (which almost always require cooperation across team boundaries) can be facilitated rather than blocked. Mechanisms to ensure teams and departments communicate, cooperate, share best practice and innovate across boundaries will enable effective team-based working, since teamworking is as much about bridging across teams as it is about bonding within teams. A simple way is requiring every team to have as one of its five or six objectives: *improving the effectiveness and supportiveness with which we work with other teams in the organization.*

Organization culture

Organizations can be described in terms of their cultures – the shared meanings, values, attitudes and beliefs of members (Schein, 1992; see Chapter 14). Surface manifestations of culture include: the number of levels in the hierarchy; pay levels (how big the gaps are between the highest and lowest paid for example); how rigid or inspirational the job descriptions are; informal practices and norms such as 'dress down Friday' when everyone comes in to work dressed more informally; espoused values and rituals, stories, jokes and jargon and the physical environment. The introduction of team-based working in the organization requires that a number of key elements of culture are in place or are developed in parallel. These key elements are likely to include:

- Trust.
- Communication.
- Involvement and participation.
- Support for training.
- Support for teamworking.

DISCUSS WITH A COLLEAGUE

Work with a colleague and discuss and decide why it is suggested that these five elements of culture are important for effective teamworking in organizations. Explain why you think each cultural element is important for effective teamworking and try to develop practical examples to illustrate your arguments:

- communication
- involvement and participation
- trust
- support for training
- support for team working.

AUTHOR EXPERIENCE

Two Top Teams with Two Very Different Leaders

I worked with a team of professionals brought together from several different countries in a multi-national pharmaceutical company. Their task was to develop a range of new products to bring in a huge new revenue stream. They were from diverse functional as well as cultural backgrounds, had a huge budget, custom-designed office space and the freedom to think as differently as they liked. They were a creative team charged with developing and implementing breakthrough ideas. And their leader was senior, influential and committed to success. My job was to help facilitate the team towards its goal. They failed and so did I. The reason was that the leader was dominant in a way that was threatening, controlling and dama-ging to team members. He had clear ideas about the way forward and everyone's ideas were wel-come as long as they were consistent with his. He got angry easily, banged his fist on the table and expressed frustration constantly about the team not moving fast enough. The team was eventually disbanded and the leader moved out of the com-pany, the whole venture having failed because of a failure of leadership.

The second team was the top management team of one of the largest UK hospitals. We were studying levels of innovation in top management teams of hospitals to discover the factors that pre-dicted their success. Faced with a huge rebuilding programme, a major change in their status and massive national change in health services function-ing, the members of this particular team were under enormous pressures. The eight team members were led by an intelligent, inclusive and thoughtful team leader. During their busy meetings, he would listen carefully to other team members' ideas before taking time to summarize the content of discussions regularly. He would also pull the team members back when they had skipped over someone's con-tribution with an interjection such as 'Hang on, let's just go back to the point that Marion started to make that seemed like it might help us. Marion, can you elaborate a little on what you were saying?' The unhurried inclusiveness, reflexivity and capacity to summarize progress and issues in team meetings predicted this team's performance as the most inno-vative, radical and effective of the 26 top manage-ment teams we studied (West and Anderson, 1996).

For an excellent discussion of team leadership, see Zaccaro, Heinen and Shuffler (2009).

Climate for team-based working

This requires a commitment within the organization to this way of working and an organizational climate which promotes team-based working. Supportive and challenging environments are likely to sustain high levels of team performance, especially those which encourage risk taking and idea generation. Also important are egalitarianism and valuing innovation. Where climates are character-ized by distrust, poor communication, personal antipathies, limited individual autonomy and unclear goals, the implementation of these ideas is inhibited. HRM systems should be geared to support team working. This includes recruiting for team working, socializing people for effective team and inter-team working and appraisal and reward systems focused on teams.

Appraisal and performance review systems

In a team-based organization attention should be focused on the development of performance criteria against which teams can be measured. These include:

- *Team outcomes* – the team's performance, be it producing parts, treating patients, or providing customer service is likely to be best defined and evaluated by the 'customers' of the teams.
- Team *member growth and well-being* – the learning, development and satisfaction of team members. In well-functioning teams, members learn from each other constantly.
- *Team innovation* – the introduction of new and improved ways of doing things by the team. Teams, almost by definition, should be fountains of creativity and innovation since they bring together individuals with diverse knowledge, orientations, skills, attitudes and experiences in a collective enterprise, thus creating the ideal conditions for creativity (West, 2002).
- *Inter-team relations* – cooperation with other teams and departments within the organization. Teams must not only be cohesive, they must also cooperate and work effectively with other teams and departments (West and Markiewicz, 2004).
- *Team goal setting* – perhaps the most powerful component of appraisal is goal setting and this applies no less to teams. The overall direction of a team's work – its purpose – should be clearly articulated by the team leader or the senior management team. This purpose should link tightly to the overall purpose of the organization. Team goals should be operationalized as six or seven clear, challenging and measureable objectives that team members have been involved in setting. Where clear goals and objectives are not set for teams in organizations, conflict and ineffectiveness are likely consequences.

Reward systems

To encourage a focus on effective teamworking, rewards should be based on team performance to some extent. Where such rewards are related to the achievement of predetermined team goals, rewards may then be distributed equally to each member of the team or they may be apportioned by senior management, by the team leader or in a manner determined by the team itself. It is worth noting, however, that where team rewards are used, team members who do not pull their weight are seen even more so than usual as 'free riders' and their failures lead to resentment and demotivation amongst other team members.

Using systems of team rewards to complement individual and organization based rewards focuses staff on the importance of teamwork. But the reward system has to be seen as transparent and fair and as not inappropriately rewarding those who do not pull their weight. Of course, team rewards may not always involve money. The organization may provide team level rewards in other forms, such as an away day in a luxury spa, dinner for the team or new office furniture or equipment.

These then are the inputs into teamworking – the elements that make up the construction of the boat. Now we turn to explore team processes or the sailing of the boat out on the seas. The key elements of team processes are shown in Table 13.3.

Table 13.3 Team process	
Dimension	**Components**
Objectives	Clarity of objectives
	Team members' commitment to the objectives
	Agreement within the team about the appropriateness of the objectives
Participation	Decision-making
	Communication
	Regular meetings
	Trust, safety and support
Task focus	Customer/client focus
	Concern with quality of work or commitment to excellence
	Constructive debates about task performance
	Error management
Team conflict	Task-related conflict
	Interpersonal conflict
Creativity and Innovation	Practical support for new and improve products and services
	Climate for creativity and innovation
Reflexivity	Reflection on performance

Team Processes

We create teams in order to utilize the skills, knowledge and abilities of people who make up the team in ways that ensure their collective efforts enable them to accomplish tasks they could not manage alone. To be in a team means to interact, to share information and ideas, to debate fully and intelligently the best way of accomplishing the task, and to develop the products or provide the services that the organization or the customers or clients need and want. What are the key team processes that influence the effectiveness of teams?

Team objectives

There is no more important process of working in teams than clarifying the objectives of the team and ensuring that team members are both committed to these objectives and agree with them. Their objectives will be dependent upon the nature of the task they are required to perform – making car parts, delivering computer support, providing Accident and Emergency services or providing cabin service in an airliner. Clarifying the objectives requires that the team state clearly six or seven measureable aims. There should be a limited number since this helps the team to both focus and prioritize and, given the limitations of human short-term memory, six or seven is a suitable maximum. These objectives should be stated in a way that enables their achievement to be measureable, and they should be challenging or stretching. As indicated in Chapter 4, goals are most motivating when they are clear and challenging. There is a consistent positive relationship between how challenging goals are and performance, whether at individual or team level (Locke and Latham, 2013). However, team members should also be committed to these goals since commitment is associated with higher levels of motivation (hardly surprising) and that commitment is more likely to be evident when team members have worked together to define their objectives (and this is certainly unusual in organizations). Finally, it is important that team members show agreement with these goals – they understand them, are committed to them and agree that they are the objectives they should be seeking to fulfil. And, as indicated earlier, all teams embedded in organizations should have one goal focused on improving their inter-team cooperation and effectiveness.

A useful test of the clarity of team objectives is to ask all team members to write down their team objectives, without consultation with each other, and check how well they agree. In many teams there is a very low level of agreement (beyond vague aspirations such as 'to be really effective as a team' or 'to deliver great customer service') and this leads to ineffectiveness, mistakes and team member dissatisfaction.

Participation

Being part of a team involves participation, the essence of teamwork, which can be described by the three I's: Interacting, Information sharing, Influencing decision-making.

Interaction In order for a group of individuals who share a common goal to be called a team they must have some degree of interaction through meetings, teleconferences, email interchange etc., and particularly through face-to-face meetings on a regular basis, otherwise their efforts are essentially uncoordinated and un-aggregated. Interaction provides opportunities for exchanging information, communicating, building trust, giving each other feedback and just generally 'touching base', which enables the team to coordinate individual member efforts to achieve their shared goals. By meeting, communicating and interacting, they learn to dance the dance of teamwork better. Imagine how successful a sports team would be that only met to play together once or twice a year, never discussed or compared tactics or gave each other feedback on performance or planned playing strategies. Compare this with a team of equally skilled players that played together and discussed their performance every week. Virtual teams in particular are faced with many challenges of not interacting regularly other than via electronic media (Hertel *et al.*, 2005).

Information sharing Information in a team context is data which alter the understanding of the team as a whole and/or of individual team members. Within teams, the ideal way of giving information is in face-to-face meetings, except for giving routine messages which can be done via email or in other written form. Of course, there is a temptation to avoid such direct communication since this takes time. In general, teams err on the side of electronic mail messages and communicate too little face-to-face. Yet the whole basis of teamwork is communication, coordination, cooperation and transfer of information in the richest possible form.

Influencing decision-making A principle assumption behind the structuring of organizational functioning into work teams is that teams will make better decisions about performing their task than individual team members working alone. However, there is much research to show that teams are subject to social processes which undermine their decision-making effectiveness:

1 One is the tendency for team members to focus on and discuss information all team members share before the discussion starts and to ignore new information that only one or two team members know about. Even when those one or two members introduce this information into the discussion, team members are likely to ignore it since it is not information they all already share. This is referred to as the hidden profile phenomenon and teams can avoid it by ensuring that members have clearly defined roles so that each is seen as a source of potentially unique and important information; that members listen carefully to colleagues' contributions in

decision-making; and that leaders work to alert the team to information that is uniquely held by only one or two members and to ensure that each team member's voice is heard (Stasser, Vaughan and Stewart, 2000). Poor medical decision-making often occurs when the unique information about the patient's symptoms offered by one member of the team is ignored by the others.

2   Team members tend to go along with the majority opinion and are thus susceptible to social conformity effects causing them to withhold opinions and information contrary to the majority view (Brown, 2000).

3   The team may be dominated by loud, confident or aggressive individuals who take up disproportionate 'air time' (how long you speak for in team meetings) or argue so vigorously with the opinion of others that they always win. And winning often means making many poor decisions. 'Air time' and expertise are positively correlated in high-performing teams and uncorrelated in teams that perform poorly. In other words, time speaking on a topic in high performing teams is apportioned most to those who have most expertise on the particular topic.

4   Status and hierarchy effects can cause problems because some members' contributions can be valued and attended to disproportionately. Leaders' views will always tend to have an undue influence on the outcome. Good team leaders hold their views in abeyance until all other team members' views have been heard.

5   'Group polarization' refers to the tendency of work teams to make more extreme decisions than the average of individual members' opinions or decision. Team decisions tend to be either more risky or more conservative than the average of individuals members' opinions or decisions (Semin and Glendon, 1973; Walker and Main, 1973).

6   In his study of failures in policy decisions, social psychologist Irving Janis, identified the phenomenon of 'groupthink', whereby tightly-knit groups may err in their decision-making because they are more concerned with achieving agreement than with the quality of the decisions made. This can be especially threatening to organizational functioning where different departments see themselves as competing with one another, promoting 'in-group' favouritism and groupthink. The crash of the space shuttle *Columbia* has been attributed directly to problems of 'groupthink'. It is also likely to occur when the leader of the team is especially dominating. Margaret Thatcher and George W. Bush have both been identified as political leaders who tended to reject disagreement or views conflicting with their own, leading to flawed decision-making and foreign policy failures (see for example Nicholson, 2013).

7   The social loafing effect is the tendency of individuals in teams to work less hard than they do when individual contributions can be identified and evaluated. In organizations, individuals may put less effort into contributing to high-quality decisions in meetings, if they perceive that their contribution is hidden in overall team performance (Karau and Williams, 1993). When each person in the team has a clear role, social loafing is much less likely to occur. Well designed team working will undermine the effects of social loafing and reduce the tendency of team members to lose motivation as a result of perceiving others as making less effort than themselves.

8   The study of idea generation in groups (sometimes called 'brainstorming groups') shows that quantity and often creativity of ideas produced by individuals working separately, are consistently superior to those produced by a group working together. Individuals working alone generate about 50 per cent more ideas than those working in a group for an equivalent period of time. They also produce ideas of at least equivalent and usually superior creativity. This is due to a 'production-blocking' effect. Individuals are inhibited from both thinking of new ideas and

offering them aloud to the group by the competing verbalizations of others (Diehl and Stroebe, 1987). Yet almost everyone in organizations goes straight into the process of idea generation in groups resulting in poor performance. By simply giving all team members five minutes to quietly develop their own ideas before all share their ideas in the group, idea generation in groups ('brainstorming') would be much more effective.

Underpinning all team processes should be a sense of mutual trust, safety and support. Otherwise, teamworking is like swimming against the current. Where team members feel they may be attacked by colleagues (verbally or physically), teamwork will fail. Each team member has a responsibility to promote safety. This involves encouraging others to offer their views and then supportively exploring those ideas. Trust in teams is vital to team members' preparedness to cooperate (Korsgaard *et al.*, 2003). Safety, trust and support are also essential for the team to manage disagreements and enable helpful debates about the best way to achieve the team's objectives (Edmondson, 1999). A focus on task excellence rather than cohesion and agreement is essential for this. Teams that are more concerned with agreeing than with doing a great job are ineffective and potentially dangerous. Task focus rather than cohesion focus is therefore vital.

Task focus

Task focus is the team's practice of examining their team performance critically. Dean Tjosvold, in a career of research into cooperation and competition in teams, has coined the term 'constructive controversy' to describe the conditions necessary for effective questioning within a team (Tjosvold, 1998). His work shows that when teams explore opposing opinions carefully and discuss them in a co-operative context, quality of decision-making and team effectiveness are dramatically increased (see also West, Tjosvold and Smith, 2003).

> *Controversy when discussed in a cooperative context promotes elaboration of views, the search for new information and ideas and the integration of apparently opposing positions.* (Tjosvold, 1991)

Tjosvold believes that a lack of constructive controversy can lead to poor team decisions and tragedies such as the *Challenger* space shuttle disaster. In the latter case, engineers suppressed controversy over the appropriateness of launching the shuttle in cold weather, with tragic consequences. Constructive controversy has three elements: elaborating positions; searching for understanding; and integrating perspectives.

1 Elaborating positions: team members carefully describe their positions on the issue under discussion, explaining how they have come to their conclusions. They also indicate to what extent they are confident or uncertain about the positions they have adopted.

2 Searching for understanding: people with opposing viewpoints seek out more information about each other's positions and attempt to restate them as clearly as possible. There are attempts to explore areas of common ground in opposing positions along with an emphasis on personal regard for individuals whose positions oppose their own. This process leads to creativity and more productive outcomes.

3 Integrating perspectives: team members work together to influence the team in an effort to reach a solution based on shared, rational understanding rather than attempted dominance. Finally, members strive for consensus by combining team ideas wherever possible rather than using techniques to reduce controversy, such as majority voting. Strategies such as voting may merely postpone controversy. Box 13.3 shows the conditions within which team constructive controversy can exist.

KEY THEME

Ethics and Corporate Social Responsibility

Aston Organization Development (**www.astonod. com**) was created to apply the results of research in Work and Organizational Psychology on teams within organizations (mostly health service organizations) in 2003. The company has pioneered the concept of Team Based Working, helping organizations to create structures and cultures which improve performance through high levels of staff engagement. The company helps organizations to assess and develop team effectiveness using diagnostic tools. The Management Team is assiduous about ensuring that feedback following the use of diagnostic tools is managed in a supportive way that ensures that no harm is done to individuals or organizations, in line with ethical guidelines. The key aim of this organization has always been to ensure that practice is informed by evidence in a way that improves both performance and employee well-being. The Management team believe that this approach will develop long lasting relationships with clients which bring mutual rewards. They have never pursued a policy of maximizing profit as a goal in itself.

The company also uses a variety of team development tools and exercises to help teams and organizations bring about change and improvement. This includes designing and implementing effective strategies for improving organizational performance. These are generally evidence based and their impact is continually evaluated to ensure the tools do no harm and also add value. Demonstrating improved performance, employee well-being and recipient satisfaction is a core part of the company's work.

The company selects only highly experienced consultants who have a clear understanding of the research and theory underpinning the interventions. They also must have supported many organizations to create sustainable change and have a deep understanding of the process of implementation of Team Based Working. It is a requirement also that consultants can work with people at all levels in the organization, including directors and senior leaders in order to enable change strategies to become operational reality. Many organizational interventions fail because they do not gain practical as well as espoused commitment from senior leaders.

The company is committed to enabling its clients to become self-sufficient rather than consultant dependent. It does so by helping organizations develop in-house capacity by providing skills training for team coaches, team leaders and team facilitators. The aim is to create sufficient expertise to develop the structures, processes and behaviours which will maintain high performing teams at all levels across organizations.

Error management

How teams manage errors is a good barometer of their ability to achieve a high level of task focus in the interests of their customers, clients or patients. Team members and leaders can respond to an error by seeking who to blame or by asking 'what can we learn from this?'. A good example of this principle is a study on safety in teams. Edmondson (1996) studied newly formed intensive care nursing teams and their management of medication errors (giving too much or too little of a drug, or administering the wrong drug). In some groups, members openly acknowledged and discussed their medication errors and ways to avoid their occurrence. In others, members kept information about errors to themselves. Learning about the causes of these errors, as a team, and devising innovations to prevent future errors was only possible in groups of the former type. Edmondson (1996; 1999) argues that learning and innovation only take place where group members trust other members' intentions. Where this is the case, team members believe that well-intentioned action will not lead to punishment or rejection by the team. Edmondson argues that safety … 'is meant to suggest a realistic, learning-oriented attitude about effort, error and change – not to imply a careless sense of permissiveness, nor an unrelentingly positive affect. Safety is not the same as comfort; in contrast, it is predicted to facilitate risk.' (Edmondson, 1999, p. 14).

Culture too can affect error management in multicultural teams. Gelfland *et al.* (2011) and colleagues have proposed that uncertainty avoidance, humane orientation, tightness-looseness of control, fatalism, power-distance and individualism-collectivism will have significant effects on such teams' approaches to error management (see for more on these aspects of culture).

Team conflicts

Constructive conflict is desirable in teams (Deutsch, 1973). Constructive team conflict can be a source of excellence, quality and creativity. However, high levels of conflict in teams makes team members uncomfortable, anxious and angry. Team performance is then undermined (De Dreu and van de Vliert, 1997). Carsten De Dreu, from the University of Amsterdam, has conducted extensive research on the associations between relationship conflict, task conflict, team performance and team member satisfaction (see De Dreu and Weingart, 2003). His research shows strong and negative correlations between relationship conflict and team performance, and team member satisfaction. It also shows strong and negative correlations between task conflict and team performance, and task conflict and team member satisfaction. How do we square this with the idea of constructive controversy?

BOX 13.3
Encouraging constructive controversy in teams

- Teams can encourage constructive controversy by coaching team members to explore all team members' views in an open-minded way, so that creative ideas emerge.

- Independent thinking is encouraged by having the team consider all team members' views and suggestions.

- Team members should consider all team members' views based on whether their proposals would improve the team's service to its clients. They base judgements then on quality, not (for example) on the status of the person proposing the idea.

- Team members should have vigorous and supportive discussions of alternatives since such comprehensive decision-making encourages all team members to develop their critical thinking and to learn from each other in the course of teamwork.

- Team leaders can encourage team members not to focus on winning in the process of making decisions. They should be primarily concerned with making excellent decisions that lead to the best products or services for their clients.

- Constructive controversy does not exist when there are competitive team climates.

- If team members publicly question their colleagues' competence, destructive arguments about team decisions erupt and quality of decision-making suffers.

- Team members should build co-operative team climates, characterized by trust, supportiveness, safety and a professional approach to work.

- Leaders should also encourage team members to communicate their respect for each other's competence and commitment. In this way, they will feel that disagreements do not represent attacks on each other's ability and this will be clear to all.

Constructive controversy is different from task conflict in its effects. Conflict is emotionally uncomfortable whereas constructive controversy is not personalized. Individuals feel supported rather than attacked. In productive and creative teams, constructive task conflict is not only endemic but desirable (Tjosvold, 1998). Team diversity and differences of opinion about how best to meet customers' needs should be a source of excellence, quality and creativity. *But too much conflict (whether it is about the task or not) or conflict experienced as threatening and unpleasant by team members can destroy relationships and the effectiveness of the team.* What may be a comfortable level of debate for you, can be intensely uncomfortable for your colleagues who may feel threatened, attacked or put down. When that happens people withdraw and stop engaging open-heartedly and enthusiastically in the team.

How do we resolve conflicts in teams? We can *avoid* the conflict by pretending it does not exist, probably just postponing the conflict if the issue is likely to recur. We can give in and *accommodate* the other person. They get what they want and I don't. I feel resentful and they expect me to accommodate them every time. We can *compete* to win against them and, if we do, their needs are not met and they may carry resentment into the next conflict we have and be determined to win whatever. *Compromise* sounds like a sensible way to manage conflict, but actually it means that neither of us get our needs fully met. Or, we can *collaborate* to find an integrative, creative solution that meets (or even exceeds!) both our needs. This is a 'win – win' solution. It is the ideal since both parties are happy and their relationship is stronger because of the successful conflict negotiation. Here is an opportunity for team members to exercise their creativity and develop innovative solutions that promote the long-term effectiveness of the team.

Imagine two people in a top management team who are in a conflict. One wants innovative action taken quickly to achieve the aims of providing brilliant products and services to customers rather than being blocked and frustrated by bureaucracy. The other, who controls the budget, is anxious that there should be careful processes of review, probity and decision-making in place to control the situation. They keep finding themselves in conflict. Avoidance, compromise, competition and accommodation are not working. An integrative solution might be for them to meet weekly to discuss new ideas together, ahead of full team meetings, so that they can deal quickly with new ideas together. This is based on the principle of both of them committing to the principles of probity and innovation. They bring their integrative solutions in each case to the wider team for discussion and approval rather than using up time in team meetings in repeated conflicts.

Of course team members will not necessarily be best friends. After all, we are thrown together by chance with people at work who are often very different from us. But if we are clear about, and committed to, a shared team vision and clear team objectives, we are less likely to allow our small differences to interfere with team success. We don't need to vote for the same political party in order to work together successfully to ensure we correctly diagnose breast cancer and offer the patient we are serving the best possible care and support.

Creativity and innovation

Creativity is the development of ideas; innovation implementation is making them happen in practice. Innovation includes both creativity and implementation therefore (West, 2002). Team innovation is the introduction of new and improved processes, products or services by a team (See Box 13.4). Levels of team innovation are high when team members expect, approve and practically support attempts to introduce new and improved ways of doing things. Team members may reject or ignore ideas or they may offer both verbal and practical support. High levels of both verbal and practical support will lead to more attempts to introduce innovations in teams. Verbal support is most helpful when team members initially propose ideas. Practical support can take the form of cooperation in the development of ideas, as well as the provision of time and resources by team members to apply them (West, 2002).

BOX 13.4
Team creativity and innovation

How can teams promote their levels of creativity and innovation? Problem solving has a number of distinct and important stages. Each requires different kinds of skills and activities. These are: problem exploration, developing alternative ideas, selecting an option and implementing the preferred option.

Exploration – Probably the most important stage of team problem solving is clarifying and exploring the problem. Team members usually begin to try to develop solutions to problems before clarifying and exploring and, if necessary, re-defining the problem itself. But the more time spent in exploring and clarifying a problem before attempting to seek solutions, the better the quality of the ultimate solution.

Ideation – Having suspended attempts at solution development during Stage 1, the next step is to develop a range of alternative solutions to the problem. When making decisions, teams generally seek for 'one way out'. One idea is proposed and the team goes with that idea, making appropriate modifications as are perceived necessary. Research on team problem solving suggests that it is most effective to begin by generating a range of possible solutions. It should be a stage which is both playful and challenging, when all ideas are welcomed and encouraged.

Selection – In this stage, the aim is to encourage constructive controversy about appropriate ways forward; to be critical and judgemental, but in a way that is constructive and personally supportive. If Stage 2 has generated many solutions, it may be necessary to select the three or four solutions that appear most promising, but it is important to avoid selecting only those which fit the current way of doing things. At least one potential solution should be 'blue sky' – a completely new way of dealing with the issue. Teams should not select a solution simply because it is a solution rather than because it is the *best* solution. In an eagerness to achieve 'closure' and avoid further uncertainty or ambiguity, teams are sometimes too prepared to overlook problems inherent in solutions they have adopted.

Implementation – Teams that conduct the first three stages carefully, will find that implementation is the least difficult and most rewarding stage of the problem-solving process.

These then are four distinct stages of problem solving. If you would like to explore techniques which teams can use at each of these stages of creative problem solving see Van Gundy (1988) and West (2004).

Reflexivity

Team reflexivity is the extent to which team members collectively reflect upon the team's objectives, strategies and processes, as well as their wider organizations and environments, and adapt accordingly. After the open-heart surgery, the team comes together and reviews their performance – what went well, what was problematic, what can we learn from this and what do we need to change for next time? There is increasing interest in this concept because it is seen as a means for developing teamwork generally (Schippers *et al.*, 2008; Schippers, Dawson and West, 2012; West, 2000; Widmer, Schippers and West, 2009; www.reflexivity.com).

Team reflexivity is conceptualized as a process involving three stages or components: *reflection, planning* and *action or adaptation*. The first stage, *team reflection*, refers to a team's joint exploration of work-related issues and includes behaviours such as questioning, planning, exploratory learning, analysis and reviewing past events. This is what a good sports team does at half time and at the end of the game. Effective teams will ask questions that help them reflect on their performance such as:

'Do people think we communicate information about patients well within this team?' 'Let's think about some alternatives in terms of how we could best improve our product design processes?'. 'So we agree that our communication about patients is hampered by professional divisions within the team?'.

The second stage, *planning*, refers to the activities that enable reflections to change into action or adaptation. *Planning* involves four dimensions: *detail* – the extent to which a plan is worked out in detail before as opposed to being worked out only during action; *inclusiveness of potential problems* – the extent to which a team develops alternative plans in case of inadvertent circumstances; *ordering of plans* – the extent to which plans are broken up into sub-plans before actions are commenced; and *time scale* – the extent to which both short and long time frame plans are drawn. Effective teams will reflect but will not spend their time navel-gazing. They translate their insights about their own team's functioning into plans for change and action (West, 2000).

The third stage is *action or adaptation*. The action component of reflexivity can be assessed on four dimensions: magnitude – the scale of an action or change initiated by the team; novelty – how new or different the action or change is for the team, organization or other stakeholders; radicalness – the change to the status quo the action or change represents; and effectiveness – the extent to which the action or change achieves the goals the team members intended.

Non-reflexive teams show little awareness of team objectives, strategies and the environment in which they operate. Non-reflexive teams tend to rely on the use of habitual routines. In other words, they tend to repeatedly exhibit a similar pattern of behaviour when problems arise without explicitly discussing it or selecting it over other possible ways of action. This lack of exploration of alternative hypotheses ultimately leads to stagnation, lack of innovation and inability to adapt to a changing environment.

DISCUSS WITH A COLLEAGUE

You are invited to help solve a problem in a team that provides training for other teams in a service-oriented organization that offers help for people with disabilities. Alarmingly, you are told that team members have become so hostile recently that it resulted in physical violence. How would you go about using the information you have acquired so far to help you understand what factors may have led to the breakdown in relationships and what you can do about it. Note that this was a situation your author faced. If you would like to check your answers, please email m.a.west@aston.ac.uk in order that you can be given feedback on the wisdom of your strategy.

Research in both experimental and field settings has found positive effects of team reflexivity on team performance. These effects were observed in samples comprising management, production and teams, coming from a variety of sectors, including banking, government, health care, chemical industry and R&D. In these studies, the impact of team reflexivity is particularly powerful in teams charged with complex endeavours which require non-routine activities. Reflexivity is particularly relevant when the environment is uncertain (see publications listed on the reflexivity network – **www.reflexivity.com**).

Team Outputs

If team inputs and team processes are well managed, team outputs should follow, according to the IPO model. Table 13.4 shows the main dimensions of team outputs.

Table 13.4 Outputs	
Dimension	*Components*
Team effectiveness	Goal achievement
	Productivity
	Managerial praise
Innovation	Development of new process, services, ways of working
Inter-team relationships	Cooperation with other teams
	Effectiveness in working with other teams
	Absence of destructive conflict with other teams
Team member satisfaction	With recognition for condition
	With responsibility
	With team member support
	With influence over decisions
	With team openness
	With how conflicts are resolved
Attachment	Attachment to the team and its members
	Sense of belonging in the team

The first is team effectiveness – is the team achieving what it is required to, whether rescuing people at sea, providing great customer services, building cars or enabling university students to learn about Work Psychology (for an excellent analysis of team outcomes, see Brodbeck, 1996). Second is innovation. In complex teamworking settings, innovation is likely to be one of the best barometers of team functioning. Bringing together a group of people with diverse skills and backgrounds to address a challenging task should lead to creativity and innovation, if team processes are effective. If not, something is wrong with those processes (West, 2002).

Key to team effectiveness is inter-team relationships. There is a danger that the development of a number of individually successful teams within an organization will lead to levels of inter-team competition which could in the long term be detrimental to organization performance (Richter *et al.*, 2006). Organizations must encourage the development of individual team identity whilst ensuring that communication and feedback flows between teams. This allows teams to avoid duplication of effort, to learn from each other's experiences and to coordinate efforts to achieve the broader goals of the organization. A key dimension of effective teamworking is therefore the extent to which teams work cooperatively and effectively with other teams within the organization. Teams must work together for the organization to be effective (sales teams and production teams for example), constantly devising ways of promoting their shared effectiveness (West and Markiewicz, 2004).

Finally are the 'softer' elements of team effectiveness, but nonetheless important for that. These are the satisfaction and attachment of team members to their teams. Do they feel satisfied with how the team functions and do they have a sense of frequent interaction, continuity of the team, absence of conflict and presence of strong mutual support that are the hallmarks of belonging (Baumeister and Leary, 1995)? Given the importance of positivity in human relationships and human experience, we should recognize that optimism, cohesion and a collective sense of efficacy/potency are key outcomes of inputs and processes. Effective inputs and team processes will enable all these dimensions of team effectiveness to be achieved.

KEY FIGURE

George Elton Mayo (1880–1949)

George Elton Mayo (1880–1949), an Australian organization theorist, lectured at the University of Queensland before moving to the US where he spent most of his academic career at Harvard Business School. He is known as the founder of the Human Relations Movement, arguing that performance at work is largely a consequence of motivation, relationships and group processes rather than mechanistic management techniques.

His conclusions arose from a series of studies in the Western Electric Hawthorne Works in Chicago between 1924 and 1932, and suggested how group processes and teamworking could influence performance. He began by studying how fatigue, monotony, rest breaks, work pacing and even illumination could affect the performance of a group of people at work. But careful investigation revealed that:

1 Belonging, recognition and security matter much more to people at work than physical conditions.

2 Work is a group rather than individual activity.

3 Much of adult social life is a consequence of workplace interactions.

4 Work groups exercise powerful influences on the behaviour and attitudes of people at work.

5 Giving a team attention, support and involving them in decision-making will increase their motivation and improve their performance.

Mayo was surprised by his findings and it changed his views about performance at work. It led to the notion of the Hawthorne Effect. If you offer any intervention such as team building in the workplace, people's motivation will increase and their performance will improve. It is sometimes called 'Somebody upstairs cares' – management is showing an interest in the workers.

Knowledge of the Hawthorne Effect requires that when we wish to conduct intervention studies (designed to test whether performance is improved by a training intervention) we must control for the Hawthorne effect to ensure that benefits are due to the specific aspects of the intervention rather than to the effects of increased attention to the team. The only way to do this is to compare two 'treatments' that are equally credible and offer an equal amount of time and attention to those involved. Few studies that employ such controls are used in psychology outside of psychotherapy research, whereas the use of such placebo controls is common (and far easier) in medical research.

However, the data from the illumination experiments have recently been reanalyzed by Steven Levitt and John List, two economists at the University of Chicago. They found no systematic evidence that levels of productivity in the factory rose with changes in lighting. They suggest that in fact lighting was always changed on a Sunday, when the plant was closed. On Mondays output rose compared with Saturdays, the last working day and continued to rise for subsequent days. Levitt and List compared this with weeks when there was no experimentation and found that output always went up on Mondays. Workers tended to work hard for the first few days of the week and then slacken off, regardless of what the experimenters were up to.

Levitt and List (2009) 'Was there Really a Hawthorne Effect at the Hawthorne Plant? An Analysis of the Original Illumination Experiments'. NBER Working Paper #15016, http://www.nber .org/papers/w15016.pdf

Mayo, E. (1993) *The Human Problems of an Industrialized Civilization*

Trahair, R.C.S. (1984) *The Humanist Temper. The Life and Work of Elton Mayo*. Transaction Publishers

SUMMARY

In response to increasing complexity and change, many organizations have made the team the functional unit of the organization. Instead of individuals being responsible for separate pieces of work, groups of individuals come together to combine their efforts, knowledge and skills to achieve shared goals. Teamworking is one solution adopted by modern organizations for responding to the challenging environments in which they find themselves.

In this chapter we explored theory, research and application to understand how to create effective teamwork within organizations. We defined a work team in terms of its task, working relationships between team members and the embedding of teams within organizations. The chapter distinguished between the rhetoric of teamwork in organizations and the reality by characterizing the difference between real teams and pseudo teams. The former have clear objectives, members work interdependently, and the team meets regularly to review performance and how it can be improved.

Several broad categories of teams are strategy and policy teams; production teams; service teams; project and development teams; and action and performing teams. Key dimensions of teamwork include degree of permanence; emphasis on skill/competence development; genuine autonomy and influence; level of task from routine through to strategic. Tasks best performed by teams have high levels of the following characteristics: completeness, varied demands, requirements for interdependence, task significance, opportunities for learning; developmental possibilities for the task and autonomy.

Teamwork is associated with organizational effectiveness, team member well-being and high levels of organizational responsiveness, adaptability, innovation and creativity. The chapter also presented evidence on the value of teamworking in health care settings for patient benefits and staff well-being, including relationships with patient mortality.

What factors contribute to team effectiveness was considered, using the input-process-output framework. Inputs included task design, team member effort and skills, organizational support and resources. Team member characteristics included size, diversity (which we considered from two theoretical perspectives), personality and ability, teamwork skills, and team member knowledge skills and abilities. In terms of organizational supports we reviewed organizational structure, organizational culture and climate, and appraisal and reward systems.

Team processes include objectives (clarity, challenge, specificity); participation (information sharing, influence over decision-making and interaction frequency); task focus (constructive controversy, error management); team conflicts (task related and interpersonal); support for creativity and innovation (espoused and enacted); and reflexivity (reflection, planning and action). Finally, we considered the dimensions of team effectiveness including task performance, team innovation, inter-team relationships, team member satisfaction and team attachment.

The chapter has shown how, with effective management of team inputs and processes within organizations, teams can be outstandingly effective not just in achieving organizational aims but in meeting the human needs for growth, belonging and a sense of effectiveness, for those people who make up the team.

DISCUSSION QUESTIONS

1   In practice, how would you know whether a team in an organization was a real team or just given that name for convenience sake?

2   How can diversity in teams be best used as a source of creativity and effectiveness?

3   What team inputs should organizations pay most attention to when designing work teams?

4   What three or four team processes are most important in determining the performance of teams?

5   To what extent would the knowledge accumulated through research into teams be of use in developing, leading and coaching a sports team to success?

6   Given the detailed examination of inputs and processes in this chapter, how would you go about forming and leading a team?

7   How would you measure team performance?

APPLY IT

How well does your team function and how can you ensure it is effective in achieving its aims and creating a positive climate for success? Consider each of the following questions and for each, reflect on the strengths of the team in this area. What can you learn from that about improving your team's working in areas where it is less effective?

1   The team has a strong **team identity** – we agree about what the team is there to achieve; we know who is in the team and feel a sense of affinity with other team members; we have a sense of distinctiveness as a team; we all feel positive or proud about being a part of this team.

2   All team members are clear about and committed to our **team objectives** and these are challenging, clear, measured and centrally relevant to our work. We have no more than seven team objectives and all of them focus on improving our performance and functioning.

3   All of us understand our own **roles** and how they fit with others within the team. We also understand each other's roles clearly and how we can help each other be successful. And we do help and support each other by backing each other up in the performance of our individual roles.

4   All team members are actively involved in **decision-making** about the work of the team and how it is carried out. Everyone contributes their views and there is supportive discussion of everyone's inputs. Everyone's view is valued equally and we are good at listening carefully to each other.

5   The team has **constructive debates** about how best to do our work and about how to improve our outcomes but this is almost always respectful and not acrimonious. Team members come away from these debates saying the discussions were stimulating and useful rather than feeling angry or hurt.

6   Team members meet regularly to review the performance of the team and to learn together. There is **effective communication** between all team members during and between these meetings. Team members generally look forward to these meetings because these are seen as useful and constructive.

7   The team is cooperative and supportive in working with **other teams** within the

organization and within partner organizations. We recognize that internal service determines the quality of service to customers so we work hard to support other teams within the organization (and in partner organizations) and resolve conflicts quickly and fairly. We have a strong interest in meeting the needs of these other teams.

8 We are a supportive, optimistic and cohesive team with a high level of **team positivity**. There are good levels of humour, lots of appreciation and a strong ethic of professionalism. We generally have fun as a team, strongly believe in our ability to achieve our objectives and we are committed to continuously improving our performance.

WEB ACTIVITY

High-performance Teams

Read the article 'Teaming with bright ideas', published by *The Economist* July 2006, available at the link below or in the digital resources online and discuss the questions below.
http://www.economist.com/node/5380422

1 What should organizations do to ensure they create effective teams and teamworking practices?

2 In addition to selecting the right people, how could consultancies ensure that teams they assemble will work together well?

3 The article talks about distributed groups of people in businesses. Are they real teams?

The Tour de France Winning Team

Read the article 'Wiggins tour win shows team unity' by Geraint Roberts, July 2012 on **www.bbc.co.uk/ blogs** or in the digital resources online and discuss the questions below.

1 What can organizations learn from sports teams such as the Sky cycling team?

2 Use theory and models from the chapter to evaluate the team described in the article.

FURTHER READING

Flood, P., MacCurtain, S. and West, M.A. (2001). *Effective top management teams*. Dublin, Ireland: Blackhall Press.

Mohrman, S., Cohen, S. and Mohrman, L. (1995). *Designing team-based organizations*. London: Jossey Bass.

Sala, E., Goodwin, G.F. and Burke, C.S. (2009). *Team effectiveness in complex organizations: Cross-disciplinary perspectives and approaches*. London: Routledge.

Tjosvold, D. (1991). *Team organization: An enduring competitive advantage*. Chichester: John Wiley and Sons.

West, M.A. and Markiewicz, L. (2012). *Effective teamwork: Practical lessons from organizational research*. (3rd edition). Oxford: Blackwell.

West, M.A., Tjosvold, D. and Smith, K.G. (eds.), (2003). *The international handbook of organizational teamwork and cooperation*. Chichester: John Wiley and Sons.

REFERENCES

Ainsworth, M. (1989). Attachments beyond infancy. *American Psychologist*, 44, 709–716.

Anderson, N. and Sleap, S. (2004). An evaluation of gender differences on the Belbin Team Role Self-Perception Inventory. *Journal of Occupational and Organizational Psychology*, 77, 429–437.

Applebaum, E. and Batt, R. (1994). *The New American Workplace*. Ithaca, NY: ILR Press.

Bacon, N. and Blyton, P. (2000). High road and low road teamworking: Perceptions of management rationales and organizational and human resource outcomes. *Human Relations*, 53, 1425–1458.

Banker, R.D., Field, J.M., Schroeder, R.G. and Sinha, K.K. (1996). Impact of work teams on manufacturing performance: A longitudinal field study. *Academy of Management Journal*, 3, 867–890.

Barchas, P. (1986). A sociophysiological orientation to small groups. In E. Lawler (ed.), *Advances in group processes*: Vol. 3. (pp. 209–46). Greenwich, CT: JAI Press.

Barrick, M.R., Stewart, G.L., Neubert, M.J. and Mount, M.K. (1998). Relating member ability and personality to work-team processes and team effectiveness. *Journal of Applied Psychology*, 83, 377–91.

Batt, R. (1999). Work organization, technology and performance in customer service and sales. *Industrial and Labour Relations Review*, 52, 539–564.

Baumeister, R.F. and Leary, M.R. (1995). The need to belong: Desire for interpersonal attachments as a fundamental human motivation. *Psychological Bulletin*, 117, 497–529.

Belbin, R.M., (1981). Management Teams: Why they succeed or fail. London Butterworth-Heinemann.

Belbin, R.M. (1993). *Team roles at work: A strategy for human resource management*. Oxford: Butterworth, Heinemann.

Benders, J. and Van Hootegem, G. (1999). Teams and their context: Moving the team discussion beyond existing dichotomies. *Journal of Management Studies*, 26, 609–628.

Boning, B., Ichniowski, C. and Shaw, K. (2001). *Opportunity Counts: Teams and the Effectiveness of Production Incentives*. NBER Working Paper No. 8306. Cambridge, MA: National Bureau of Economic Research.

Borrill, C., West, M., Shapiro, D. and Rees, A. (2000). Teamworking and effectiveness in the NHS. *British Journal of Health Care Management*, 6, 364–371.

Bradley, B.H., Klotz, A.C., Postlethwaite, B.E. and Brown, K.G. (2013). Ready to rumble: how team personality and task conflict interact to improve performance. *Journal of Applied Psychology*, 98, 385–392.

Brodbeck, F.C. (1996). Criteria for the study of work group functioning. In M.A. West (ed.). *Handbook of work group psychology*. (pp. 285–316). Chichester John Wiley and Sons.

Brown, R. (2000). Group processes (2nd edn.) Oxford, UK: Blackwell.

Buss, D.M. (1991). Evolutionary personality psychology. *Annual Review of Psychology*, 42, 459–491.

Carter, A.J. and West, M.A. (1999). Sharing the burden – teamwork in health-care settings. In J. Firth-Cozens and R. Payne (eds.). *Stress in health professionals* (pp. 191–202). Chichester: John Wiley and Sons.

Cohen, S.G. and Bailey, D.E. (1997). What makes Teams Work: Group effectiveness research from the shop floor to the executive suite. *Journal of Management*, 23, 239–290.

Cohen, S.G., Ledford, G.E. and Spreitzer, G.M. (1996). A predictive model of self-managing work team effectiveness. *Human Relations*, 49, 643–676.

Dawson, J.F., West, M.A. and Yan, X. (2008). Positive and negative effects of teamworking in healthcare: 'Real' and 'Pseudo' teams and their impact on health-care safety. Paper submitted for publication.

De Dreu, C.K.W. and Weingart, L.R. (2003). Task versus relationship conflict, team performance and team member satisfaction: A meta-analysis. *Journal of Applied Psychology*, 88, 741–749.

De Dreu, C.K.W. and Van de Vliert, E. (1997). Using conflict in organizations. London: Sage.

Delarue, A., Van Hootegem, G., Huys, R. and Gryp, S. (2004). *Dossier: Werkt teamwork? De PASO-resultaten rond arbeidsorganisatie doorgelicht.* Leuven: Hoger Instituut voor de Arbeid, Departement TEW, Departement Sociologie (KU Leuven).

Delarue, A., Van Hootegem, G., Procter, S. and Burridge, M. (2008). Teamworking and organizational performance: A review of survey-based research. *International Journal of Management Reviews*, 10, 127–148.

Deutsch, M. (1973). *The resolution of conflict: Constructive and destructive processes*. New Haven, CT: Yale University Press.

Diehl, M. and Stroebe, W. (1987). Productivity loss in brainstorming groups: Towards the solution of a riddle. *Journal of Personality and Social Psychology*, 53, 497–509.

Dunlop, J.T. and Weil, D. (1996). Diffusion and performance of modular production in the US apparel industry. *Industrial Relations*, 35, 334–355.

Edmondson, A.C. (1996). Learning from mistakes is easier said than done: Group and organizational influences on the detection and correction of human error. *Journal of Applied Behavioural Science*, 32, 5–28.

Edmondson, A.C. (1999). Psychological safety and learning behaviour in work teams. *Administrative Science Quarterly*, 44, 350–383.

Edmondson, A.C. and Roloff, K.S. (2009). Overcoming barriers to collaboration: Psychological safety in diverse teams. In E. Salas, G.F. Goodwin and C.S. Burke (eds.) (2009). *Team effectiveness in complex organizations: Cross-disciplinary perspectives and approaches* (pp. 183–208). London: Routledge.

Elmuti, D. (1997). The perceived impact of team-based management systems on organizational effectiveness. *Team Performance Management*, *3*, 179–192.

Furnham, A. Steele, H. and Pendleton, D. (1993). A psychometric assessment of the Belbin Team Role Self-Perception Inventory. *Journal of Occupational and Organizational Psychology*, *66*, 245–261.

Gelfland, M.J., Frese, M., and Salmon, E. (2011). Cultural influences on errors: prevention, detection, and management. In D. A. Hofman and M. Frese (eds.). *Errors in Organizations* (pp. 273–316). London, UK: Lawrence Erlbaum Associated, Taylor and Francis.

Glassop, L.I. (2002). The organizational benefits of teams. *Human Relations*, *55*, 225–249.

Godard, J. (2001). High performance and the transformation of work? The implications of alternative work practices for the experience and outcomes of work. *Industrial and Labour Relations Review*, *54*, 776–805.

Goldberg (1990). An alternative "description of personality": The Big-Five factor structure. Goldberg, Lewis R. Journal of Personality and Social Psychology, vol *59(6)*, Dcc 1990, 1216–1229. doi: 10.1037/0022-3514.59.6.1216.

Hackman, J.R. (2002). *Leading Teams: Setting the Stage for Great Performances*. Harvard, USA: Harvard Business School Press.

Hackman, J.R. (1987). 'The design of work teams.' In Lorsch, J. (ed.), *Handbook of Organizational Behaviour*, (pp. 315–42). Englewood Cliffs, NJ: Prentice-Hall.

Hackman, J.R. (1993). Teams, leaders and organizations: New directions for crew-orientated flight training. In E.L.Wiener, B.G. Kanki and R.L. Helmreich (eds.). *Cockpit Resource Management* (pp. 47–69). CA: Academic Press.

Hertel, G., Geister, S. and Konradt, U. (2005). Managing virtual teams: A review of the current empirical research. *Human Resource Management Review*, *15*, 69–95.

Hollenbeck, J.R., Beersma, B. and Shouten, M.E. (2012). Beyond team types and taxonomies: A dimensional scaling conceptualization for team description. *Academy of Management Review*, *37*, 82–106.

Karau, S.J. and Williams, K.D. (1993). Social loafing: A meta-analytic review and theoretical integration. *Journal of Personality and Social Psychology*, *65*, 681–706.

Korsgaard, M.A., Brodt, S.E. and Sapienza, H.J. (2003). Trust, identity and attachment: Promoting individuals' cooperation in groups. In M.A. West, (ed.). *Handbook of Work Group Psychology*. Chichester: John Wiley and Sons.

Kozlowski, S.W.J. and Bell, B.S. (2003). Work groups and teams in organizations. In W.C. Borman and D.R. Ilgen and R.Klimoski (eds.) *Industrial/ Organizational Psychology*, Vol. XII: John Wiley and Sons.

Kozlowski, S.W.J. and Ilgen, D.R. (2006). Enhancing the Effectiveness of Work Groups and Teams. *Psychological Science in the Public Interest*, *7*, 77–124.

Levine, J.M. and D'Andrea-Tyson, L. (1990). Participation, productivity and the firm's environment. In A.S. Blinder (ed). *Paying for Productivity* (pp. 183–237). Washington, DC: Brokkings Institution.

Locke, E.A. and Latham, G.P. (2013) (eds.). *New Developments in Goal Setting and Performance*. London: Routledge.

Macy, B.A. and Izumi, H. (1993). Organizational change, design and work innovation: A meta-analysis of 131 North American field studies-1961–1991. *Research in Organizational Change and Design* (Vol. 7). Greenwich, CT: JAI Press.

Mathieu, J., Maynard, T.M., Rapp, T. and Gilson, L. (2008). Team Effectiveness 1997–2007: A Review of Recent Advancements and a Glimpse Into the Future. *Journal of Management, 34*, 410–476.

Mathieu, J.E., Gilson, L.L. and Ruddy, T.M. (2006). Empowerment and team effectiveness: An empirical test of an integrated model. *Journal of Applied Psychology*, *91*, 97–108.

McDaniel, M.A., Morgeson, F.P., Finnegan, E.B., Campion, M.A. and Braverman, E.P. (2001). Use of situational judgement tests to predict job performance: A clarification of the literature. *Journal of Applied Psychology 86*, 730–40.

Mickan, M.S. and Rodger, S.A. (2005). Effective Health Care Teams: A model of six characteristics developed from shared perceptions. *Journal of Interprofessional Care*, *19*, 358–370.

Mount, M.K., Barrick, M.R. and Stewart, G.L. (1998). Five-factor model of personality and performance in jobs involving interpersonal interactions. *Human Performance*, *11*, 145–65.

(NCEPOD, 2002). Working as a team. The 2002 Report of the National Confidential Enquiry into Perioperative Deaths. London: NCEPOD.

Nicholson, N. (2013). *The 'I' of Leadership*. Chichester, England: Jossey Bass.

Patterson, M.G. and West, M.A. (1999). Employee attitudes as predictors of organizational performance. Manuscript submitted for publication.

Patterson, M., Warr, P. & West, M.A. (2004). Organizational climate and company productivity: The role of employee affect and employee level. Journal of Occupational and Organizational Psychology, 77, 193–216.

Paul, A.K. and Anantharaman, R.N. (2003). Impact of people management practices on organizational performance: Analysis of a causal model. *International Journal of Human Resource Management*, 14, 1246–1266.

Peterson, N.G., Mumford, M.D., Borman, W.C., and Jeanneret, P.J. (2001). Understanding work using the occupational information network (ONET): Implications for practice and research. *Personnel Psychology*, 54, 451–92.

Procter, S. and Burridge, M. (2004). Extent, intensity and context: Teamworking and performance in the 1998 UK Workplace Employee Relations Survey (WERS 98). *IIRA HRM Study Group Working Papers in Human Resource Management*, No. 12.

Rasmussen, T.H. and Jeppesen, H.J. (2006). Teamwork and associated psychological factors: A review. *Work and Stress*, 20, 105–128.

Richter, A.W., Dawson, J.F. and West, M.A. (2011): The effectiveness of teams in organizations: a meta-analysis, *The International Journal of Human Resource Management*, 22(13), 2749–2769.

Richter, A.W., West, M.A., van Dick, R. and Dawson, J.F. (2006). Boundary spanners' identification, intergroup contact and effective intergroup relations. *Academy of Management Journal*, 49, 1252–1269.

Salas, E., Rosen, M.A., Burke, C.S. and Goodwin, G.F. (2009). The wisdom of collectives in organizations: An update of competencies. In E. Salas, G.F. Goodwin and C.S. Burke (eds.) (2009). *Team effectiveness in complex organizations: Cross-disciplinary perspectives and approaches*. (pp. 39–79). London: Routledge.

Schein, E. H. (1992). Organizational Culture and Leadership. New York: John Wiley.

Schippers, M.C., West, M.A. and Dawson, J.F. (2012). Team reflexivity and innovation: The moderating role of team context. *Journal of Management*. published online 17 April 2012. DOI: 10.1177/0149206312441210

Schippers, M.C., Den Hartog, D.N., Koopman, P.L. and Van Knippenberg, D. (2008) The role of transformational leadership in enhancing team reflexivity. *Human Relations*, 61, 1593–1616.

Semin, G. and Glendon, A.I. (1973). Polarization and the established group. *British Journal of Social and Clinical Psychology*, 12, 113–21.

Stasser, G., Vaughan, S.I. and Stewart, D.D. (2000). Pooling unshared information: The benefits of knowing how to access information is distributed among group members. *Organizational Behaviour and Human Decision Processes*, 82, 102–116.

Stevens, M. J., & Campion, M. A. (1994). The knowledge, skill, and ability requirements for teamwork: Implications for human resource management. Journal of Management, 20, 503–530.

Stevens, M.J. and Campion, M.A. (1999). Staffing work teams: Development and validation of a selection test for teamwork settings. *Journal of Management*, 25, 207–28.

Stewart, G.L. and Barrick, M.R. (2000). Team structure and performance: Assessing the mediating role of intra-team process and the moderating role of task type. *Academy of Management Journal*, 43, 135–148.

Tata, J. and Prasad, S. (2004). Team self-management, organizational structure and judgements of team effectiveness. *Journal of Managerial Issues*, 16, 248–265.

Tjosvold, D. (1991). Team organisation: An enduring competitive advantage. Chichester: John Wiley and Sons.

Tjosvold, D. (1998). Cooperative and competitive goal approaches to conflict: Accomplishments and challenges. *Applied Psychology: An International Review*, 47, 285–342.

Van Gundy, Jr, A.B. (1988). *Techniques of structured problem solving*. New York: Van Nostrand Reinhold.

van Knippenberg, D., Dawson, J.F., West, M.A. and Homans, A. (2011). Diversity faultlines, shared objectives, and top management team performance, *Human Relations*, 64(3), 307–331.

Van Knippenberg, D. and Schippers, M.C. (2007). Work group diversity. *Annual Review of Psychology*, 58, 515–41

Walker, T.G. and Main, E.C. (1973). Choice shifts in political decision-making: Federal judges and civil liberties cases. *Journal of Applied Social Psychology*, 3, 39–48.

West, M.A. (2000). Reflexivity, revolution and innovation in work teams. In M. Beyerlein (ed.), *Product development teams: Advances in interdisciplinary studies of work teams* (pp. 1–30). Greenwich, CT: JAI.

West, M.A. (2002). Sparkling fountains or stagnant ponds: An integrative model of creativity and innovation implementation in work groups. *Applied Psychology: An International Review, 51*, 355–87.

West, M.A. (ed.) (1996). *Handbook of Work Group Psychology*. Chichester: John Wiley and Sons.

West, M.A. (2001). The human team. In N. Anderson, D.S. Ones, H. Sinangil and C. Viswesvaran (eds.), *Handbook of Industrial, Work and Organizational Psychology, Volume 2, Organizational psychology* (pp. 270–288). London: Sage.

West, M.A. (2004). The Secrets of Successful Team Management. How to lead a team to innovation, creativity and success. London: Duncan Baird Publishers.

West, M.A. (2012). *Effective Teamwork: Practical lessons from organizational research*. (3rd edition). Oxford: Blackwell.

West, M.A. and Anderson, N. (1996). Innovation in top management teams. *Journal of Applied Psychology, 81*, 680–693.

West, M.A., Borrill, C.S. and Unsworth, K.L. (1998). Team effectiveness in organizations. In C.L. Cooper and I.T. Robertson (eds.), *International Review of Industrial and Organizational Psychology, 13*, (pp. 1–48) Chichester: John Wiley and Sons.

West, M.A., Brodbeck, F.C. and Richter, A.W. (2004). Does the 'romance of teams' exist? The effectiveness of teams in experimental and field settings. *Journal of Occupational and Organizational Psychology, 77*, 467–473.

West, M.A. and Lyubovnikova, J.R. (2012). Real teams or pseudo teams? The changing landscape needs a better map. *Industrial and Organizational Psychology, 5(1)*, 25–28.

West, M.A. and Lyubovnikova, J.R. (2013). Illusions of team working in health care. *Journal of Health Organization and Management, 27(1)*, 134–142.

West, M.A. and Markiewicz, L. (2004). *Building team-based working: A practical guide to organizational transformation*. Oxford: Blackwell Publishing Inc.

West, M.A. and Spendlove, M. (2005). The impact of culture and climate in health-care organizations. In J. Cox, J. King, A. Hutchinson and P. McAvoy (eds.) *Understanding doctors' performance*. Radcliffe Publishing: Oxford, pp. 91–105.

West, M.A., Tjosvold, D. and Smith, K.G. (eds.) (2005). *The essentials of teamworking: International perspectives*. Chichester: John Wiley and Sons.

West, M.A., Tjosvold, D. and Smith, K.G. (eds.) (2003). *The international handbook of organizational teamwork and cooperative working*. Chichester: John Wiley and Sons.

Widmer, P S., Schippers, M C. and West, M A. (2009). Recent developments in reflexivity research: A review. *Psychology of Everyday Activity, 2(2)*.

Zaccaro, S.J., Heinen, B. and Shuffler, M. (2009). Team leadership and team effectiveness. In E. Salas, G.F. Goodwin and C.S. Burke (eds.) (2009). *Team effectiveness in complex organizations: Cross-disciplinary perspectives and approaches* (pp. 83–111). London: Routledge.

Zwick, Thomas (2004). "Employee participation and productivity," Labour Economics, Elsevier, vol. *11(6)*, pages 715–740.

CHAPTER 14

ORGANIZATIONAL CULTURE, CLIMATE AND CHANGE

LEARNING OBJECTIVES

- Understand the concept of organizational culture.

- Understand ways of assessing and studying organizational culture.

- Compare and contrast different models of culture.

- Understand the concept of organizational climate and how climate relates to organizational outcomes.

- Understand the concept of corporate social responsibility as an element of culture.

- Understand what forces cause organizations to change.

- Understand key strategies that Work Psychologists can use to achieve or shape organizational change.

In this chapter, we explore what makes organizations different from each other and the differing experience of employees who work within them. These are encapsulated in the concepts of organizational culture and climate. We explore the concepts of culture and climate and differentiate between them, showing how they can be uncovered in organizations and how they can be studied. We also explore how culture and climate predict outcomes such as organizational performance and employee satisfaction. We also focus on the forces that cause organizations to change and the factors that influence employees' reactions to cause employees to sometimes resist the changes leaders wish to introduce. The chapter describes methods of reducing resistance to change and techniques for successfully introducing change and seeing it through. The overall aim of the chapter is to help the reader become adept at comprehending the different cultures in organizations, understand how to measure climate and to successfully manage change in organizations.

ORGANIZATIONAL CULTURE

You can be an expert very quickly in understanding organizational culture, just by paying attention. Like an explorer visiting a country for the first time, you need to pay close attention, watch, listen and learn to discover. By paying conscious attention you can discover the culture and climates of the organizations you encounter every day. Whenever you engage with any organization, whether you walk in to a government employment agency, visit your primary health care team or enter the headquarters of a voluntary organization, or are interviewed for a job in a manufacturing company, you can be a student of culture and climate. But you have to pay attention to discover what is often hidden from those who work within the organization. The goldfish may never know there is water in the bowl whereas the outsider is likely to see it by paying attention. For an illustration of a more systematic study of culture and an example of a large and multi-method study of cultures across the National Health Service in England see Dixon-Woods *et al.* (2013).

For a ten-year period I led a research programme designed to discover what managerial practices made a difference to company performance (Patterson *et al.*, 2004). This involved the team in visiting over 100 manufacturing organizations across the UK every other year for several years, interviewing senior managers, surveying the staff, touring the shop floor and examining the production systems. From the very first phone call our engagement with the organization was a source of information about the culture and climate. How were we dealt with on the phone? Put on hold, peremptorily dealt with, welcomed, informed or listened to? When we arrived for our first interviews at 8am in the morning, what was the reception area like? Clean and bright? Were the plants in reception healthy? Were we offered coffee, kept waiting, smiled at, ignored? Was the mission of the organization on the wall in a smart frame or was there a faded painting, partially hidden by dirty glass? Were quality accreditations visible and was the documentation on the tables up to date?. Were visitors welcomed or treated as a nuisance?

When we entered deeper into the territory of the organization, what did we discover? Did all the staff eat together at lunchtime or were there separate canteens for managers and shop floor staff? How clean, safe and tidy were the shop floor areas? Did the Chief Executive claim all the glory or was he or she full of appreciation for everyone else? How did they talk about customers and suppliers – as partners or as enemies? Were the toilets clean? Was the manufacturing equipment modern or ancient? What stories were we told about the organization and its history and what did they imply about what was valued in the organization? What jokes were told and what did these tell us about the culture? To what extent did managers engage with staff on the shop floor and the staff with us as visitors? How did it feel overall – warm and welcoming, professional and businesslike, creative and exciting, sloppy and drab? We could go on, but the point is that every experience, sight, sound and conversation potentially tells you about the culture and climate of the organization. It is all data! And you can gather this data in your daily interactions with every organization you come across.

Organizations can be described much as we might describe to our friends the experience we had in visiting a foreign country. We might talk about the dress, laws, physical environment, buildings, nightlife, recreational activities, language, humour, food, values and rituals. Similarly, organizations can be described in terms of their cultures – meanings, values, attitudes and beliefs. And they can be described in terms of their climates – what it feels like to work there or to visit the organization.

DISCUSS WITH A COLLEAGUE

Try describing to a fellow student two organizations you have worked in or encountered as if you were describing the experience of visiting a foreign country and ask him or her to reciprocate. Your conversations will quickly reveal key differences and similarities and also the fundamental dimensions you both use to describe organizations. Then you begin to get a sense of what is meant by organizational culture.

Try giving your descriptions of the same two organizations to each other again, but using just the dimensions described in Table 14.1. This time the descriptions will probably be more disciplined and you will probably discover you need more information to produce a comprehensive description.

Of course, in one sense you are just offering your idiosyncratic descriptions and those will depend on the lenses through which you view organizations because of your past experience. What Organizational Psychology can offer is a richer perspective based on theory and research. For example, one model describes culture along the dimensions shown in Table 14.1.

Table 14.1 Surface manifestations of culture	
Hierarchy	Such as how many levels from the head of the organization to the lowest level employee. The greater the number of levels relative to the number of employees, the more bureaucratic and the less innovative the organization will generally be.
Pay levels	High or low, whether there is performance-related pay, and what the differentials are between people at different grades. Pay matters to people and how it is managed has a big effect on culture.
Job descriptions	How detailed or restrictive they are and what aspects they emphasize, such as safety or productivity, cost saving or quality. How rigid or flexible they seem to be and whether they are regularly reviewed.
Informal practices such as norms	Management and non-management employees sit at separate tables in the dining area; dress is strictly formal, or there are uniforms, or dress is casual and varied. People turn up late to meetings frequently or everyone is always there on time. Customers are spoken about warmly as partners or treated as a target group.
Espoused values and rituals	An emphasis on cooperation and support versus cut-and-thrust competition between teams; cards, gifts and parties for those leaving the organization or such events are not observed. There are always festivities at key points in the calendar (summer barbeque and religious celebrations such as Christmas) and people behave wildly versus social events are dignified and restrained.
Stories, jokes and jargon	Commonly told stories about a particular success or the failings of the chief executive; sarcasm about the HR department for example; and jargon or acronyms (most hospitals have a lexicon of acronyms and jargon and the language is often beyond patients).
Physical environment	Office space, eating areas, rest rooms; are all spaces clean, tidy and comfortable, or is it only the areas on public display? Are there decorations such as plants and paintings and good facilities such as water fountains? Is the place overrun with paper or cables? Does it feel pleasant, urgent, uncomfortable, overwhelming or exciting to be in?

Organizational Culture Defined

So what do we mean by organizational culture? Culture has been described as the shared meanings, values, attitudes and beliefs that are created and communicated within an organization (for a thorough treatment of this topic, see Ashkanasy, Wilderom and Peterson, 2000; Schneider, Ehrhart, and Macey, 2013). Schein (1992), a pioneer of research into culture, offered this definition:

> *Organizational culture is the set of shared, taken-for-granted implicit assumptions that members of an organization hold and that determines how they perceive, think about and react to their various environments.*

Models of culture

Schein's model distinguishes between different levels of culture. *Espoused values* are those that are captured in mission statements, visions and company brochures. They are the values the organization wishes to be known for. Then there are enacted values that are expressed in artefacts and in basic underlying assumptions. *Artefacts* include the number of levels in the hierarchy, pay levels, documents, meeting practices (set agendas for example), ritual celebrations (leaving, long-lasting service awards and performance excellence awards) and so on. Indeed almost any sustained visible aspect of the organization and its functioning. Then there are *basic hidden assumptions* that tell a great deal about the organization's true values. Like the goldfish's water, these are often invisible to members because they are taken for granted. An example might be that arriving up to ten minutes late for meetings is normal, acceptable and expected. You can imagine that an outsider coming from an organization where punctuality was the norm, would notice and be irritated by this laxity about time. Others, maybe you, never disagree with the Chief Executive; whatever you ask for will always take much longer than is promised; or people will always drop everything to help a customer who has a problem. A revealing exercise is to ask people you know who work in an organization to write down one unwritten rule in their organization. This is one way of encouraging the discovery of basic hidden assumptions in organizational culture. In effect, Schein suggests that culture is rather like an iceberg with visible artefacts and espoused values above the waterline, but hugely influential and often unconscious values and behaviours hidden below the water line. Our task as psychologists is to understand all.

Leaders clearly have a strong influence in determining culture, but it is ultimately a product of the values (what is important) of all those who make up the organization. In one organization we visited there was a strong emphasis on productivity amongst managers, but when we talked to shop floor workers who resented the lack of reward for improved performance, there was a collective effort to avoid increasing speed of workflow. Their value (resisting management pressure) was an important part of the culture.

Goffee and Jones: Sociability Versus Solidarity

Is there a simpler way of thinking about culture? Goffee and Jones (1998) believe that culture can be represented by two fundamental dimensions. The extent to which the organization emphasizes sociability and the strength of commitment to solidarity. They define sociability as sincere friendliness or the emotional non-instrumental relations among individuals who regard one another as friends (an emphasis on social relations). Solidarity refers to the emphasis on common tasks and shared goals (an emphasis on task performance). Putting these dimensions together into a two-by-two matrix gives four possible configurations (see Figure 14.1).

The 'Networked Organization' is characterized by high sociability and low solidarity. Task performance is less highly valued but what is emphasized is warmth, positive feelings and good social relations. High sociability encourages informal sharing of knowledge, innovative thinking and strong, positive morale.

On the other hand it discourages a full exploration of criticisms and disagreements (for fear of upsetting friends). Consequently, poor performance may be tolerated. Family-owned firms may be more likely to develop such networked cultures where social relationships are more important than firm performance.

The 'Mercenary Organization' is characterized by low sociability and high solidarity. There is much emphasis on productivity and performance with little concern with the quality of social relations. It is performance that matters, not how well people get on or even whether they know each other. The point is to get the work done. This sense of shared purpose, regardless of social relationships, pervades the mercenary organization. Professional service firms, such as law firms, are often characterized by such a mercenary culture. The downside of such an orientation can be a tournament culture where members question the personal value of decisions and policies and where battles for power and status take up energy and attention.

The 'Fragmented Organization' is characterized by low sociability and low solidarity. There is little emphasis on either performance or quality of social relations. Examples might include a university department where researchers are focused on their own research and writing and are not concerned with the performance of their department or university overall. Moreover, social relationships are not well developed since the researchers come in to the department only once or twice a week to give their lectures to students and pick up their post, the rest of the time working at home.

Finally, the 'Communal Organization' is characterized by both high sociability and high solidarity. There is a strong emphasis on both performance and quality of social relations. Examples might include an aid agency such as OXFAM operating in an area struck by a disaster. Staff provide each other with strong support since they are all facing huge challenges, but they are also united in their solidarity of a focus upon relieving suffering and providing fresh water for those affected by the disaster. And in case you think this is the 'best' form, Goffee and Jones say the communal culture may be inappropriate in some contexts. During periods of change, growth or acquisition, the communal elements of culture may interfere with the need for a hard focus on driving change through and ensuring success. Moreover, there may be an underlying tension between these two cultural elements, which can only be managed by a dynamic, charismatic and powerful leader.

Which of these four orientations is most appropriate will depend on the environment the organization faces, the tasks it is required to perform and the success of the organization. Where recruitment and retention of staff are vital and there is a shortage of skilled labour, the organization might want to increase sociability. Goffee and Jones say this can be achieved by promoting sharing of ideas and emotions within the organization and by recruiting compatible people – people who are agreeable and will get on with each other. Sociability can also be increased by reducing formality (first names terms rather than titles) and limiting hierarchical differences. Leaders can also act like a friend rather than like a boss. Increased solidarity can be achieved by raising employees' awareness of competitors through briefings, newsletters, videos, emails, memos ('we have to focus and work hard to survive given the strength and hunger of our competitors'). By creating a sense of urgency, stimulating the will to win and encouraging commitment to shared corporate goals, the organization will become more mercenary (in the absence of a strong emphasis on sociability).

DISCUSS WITH A COLLEAGUE

Again take your examples and plot descriptions of the same two organizations, but using just the two dimensions described in the Goffee and Jones model. This time the descriptions will probably be very simple and you will probably discover you can do this relatively easily.

Competing Values Model

A more complex and influential two-by-two model of organizational culture is offered by the Competing Values Model (Cameron and Quinn, 1997; Quinn and Rohrbaugh, 1981). This model incorporates two fundamental dimensions of organizational effectiveness into a single model – emphases upon flexibility versus control and internal versus external orientation. The framework's four quadrants (see Figure 14.1) present a set of valued outcomes and a managerial ideology about the means through which they may be achieved. It calls attention to how *opposing* values exist in organizations and how 'individual organizations are likely to embrace different mixtures of values that are reflected in their desired ends and in the means to attain them, such as their structural designs and mechanisms of coordination and control' (Zammuto and O'Connor, 1992, p. 711). Quinn argues that organizations will emphasize all four quadrants but to a greater or lesser extent so that rather than being located in one of the quadrants, they will have value emphases in all four but the degree of emphasis or strength in each will vary between organizations and within organizations arguments over time. Thus, instead of a single point, each organization will be represented by a 'blob' on Figure 14.1 but the shape of the blob will vary depending on the particular emphasis of the organization.

DISCUSS WITH A COLLEAGUE

Again take your examples and plot descriptions of the same two organizations, but using just the Competing Values Model. Each time you do this work, your understanding of the cultures of the two organizations becomes richer, more valuable and should provide you with a more sophisticated representation than most working in those organizations would be able to achieve. You are already becoming an expert on organizational culture.

A major strength of this model is its derivation from four orientations to the study of organizational effectiveness, reflecting long traditions in Work and Organizational Psychology. Thus the rational goal approach (external focus but with tight control within the organization) reflects a rational economic model of organizational functioning in which the emphasis is upon productivity and goal achievement (Hall, 1980; Clinebell, 1984). The open systems approach (external focus and flexible relationships with the environment) emphasizes the interaction and adaptation of the organization in its environment, with managers seeking resources and innovating in response to environmental (or market) demands (Shipper and White, 1983). The internal process approach reflects a Tayloristic concern with formalization and internal control of the system in order that resources are efficiently used. Finally the human relations approach reflects the tradition derived from sociotechnical (Emery and Trist, 1965) and human relations schools (e.g. McGregor, 1960), emphasizing the well-being, growth and commitment of the community of workers within the organization. Quinn (1988) argued that a balance of competing organizational values is required for organizational effectiveness.

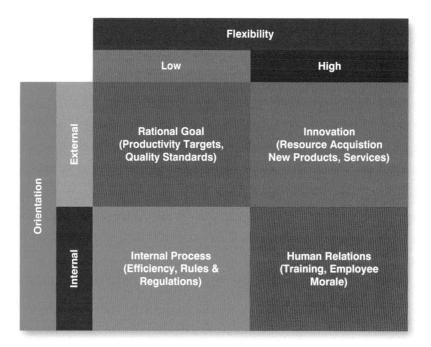

Figure 14.1   The competing values model of team performance

Intergration, Differentiation and Fragmentation Model

Martin (1992) suggested three broad and quite different perspectives on culture – integration, differentiation and fragmentation. By adopting all three perspectives we can increase our ability to understand culture quite profoundly.

1   The integration perspective. Those who adopt this view believe that a 'strong culture' will lead to more effective organizational performance. A strong culture is one that is shared by those throughout the organization – there is organization-wide consensus and clarity. Senior management set the values and develop a mission statement. When this is effectively communicated and implemented via managerial practices, organization-wide consensus is shaped. So employees know what they are supposed to do and agree on the value of doing it.

Macdonald (1991) described such a culture in the Los Angeles Olympics (1984) Organizing Committee. The employees wore attractive uniforms, developed elaborate rituals, introduced brightly coloured stadium decorations, adopted an intense working pace and told many stories about their charismatic leader, which all reinforced an organization-wide commitment around a shared set of values. However, organizational psychologists now believe that culture is more complicated than the integration perspective alone implies.

2   The differentiation perspective. This view recognizes that employees or members have differing interests, task responsibilities, backgrounds, experiences and expertise, which means that work attitudes and values, as well as pay and working conditions, will vary throughout the organization. Add the differing social identities due to gender, class and ethnic background, and,

according to this perspective, the concept of a unifying culture simply overlays an average of widely differing sub-cultures (rather like saying that China – or Russia or the UK – is one culture when in fact there are huge regional and sub-cultural differences within them). Instead, it is proposed that within the organization there are overlapping and nested sub-cultures, which coexist in relationships of harmony, conflict or indifference.

Van Maanen (1991) found just this differentiation even in the 'strong culture' of Disney-land. Food vendors and street cleaners were at the bottom of the status rankings whereas, among ride operators, those responsible for 'yellow submarines' and 'jungle boats' had high status. Some tension was noted between operators, supervisors and even customers as the different groups interacted. At the same time, supervisors were engaged in an endless struggle to catch operators breaking the rules. According to Van Maanen, the conflict or differentia-tion perspective offers a more realistic account of organizational culture than the integration perspective.

3 The fragmentation perspective. Ambiguity is a defining feature of many organizations. According to the fragmentation perspective, this ambiguity occurs because there simply is no consensus about meanings, attitudes and values of the organization.

Meyerson (1991) demonstrated this approach in a study of a social work organization. Where goals were unclear, there was no consensus about appropriate ways to achieve them, and success was hard to define and to assess. In this organization, ambiguity was the salient feature of working life. As one social worker reported: 'It just seems to me like social workers are always a little bit on the fringe; they're part of the institution, but they're not. You know they have to be part of the institution in order to really get what they need for their clients, but basically they're usually at odds with the institution' (p. 140). Clearly this is not a description of every organization, but it is probably accurate for parts of most organizations, particularly with moves to 'out-sourcing' of key functions and to the blurring of boundaries (many health-care organizations employ agency staff and locums who may not feel integrated into the organization).

How Do Cultures Develop?

Leaders in organizations are not simply observers of cultures, they play a powerful role in shaping culture. Indeed, the founder and early leaders of organizations determine the culture and its development over a long period of time. What leaders say, and more equally importantly, do, communicates what the organization values. By paying large bonuses to financial traders who take big risks to make and win huge profits, employers encourage risk taking with the public's pension funds and savings. That is why banking and finance sector leaders are rightly blamed for the banking collapse in the US and many European countries of 2008–2009. Their values decision-making determined the culture of risk taking that destroyed the pension hopes of millions of workers. Culture is also affected by the selection practices of organizations – what sorts of people are recruited and selected,; with what competencies and characteristics; and are they generally sociable and supportive team workers or hard-driving, successful innovators who are committed to success above all? You can see how selection processes might contribute to increasing sociability or solidarity, using the Goffee and Jones model of culture. Socialization processes will also affect the culture – what employees are told about the organization and its expectations of them will affect what they understand to be the organization's values. US marines are stripped of their prior values and expectation (and even of their hair) and told that their success is based on them obeying orders unquestioningly. A strong set of values is deeply ingrained in them from their very first day until there is no questioning. Then they can be sent into battle in confidence that they will simply do what they are ordered to do. Allen and Meyer (1990) review the literature on organizational socialization and describe a study demonstrating how organizations can foster commitment and different levels of innovation among newcomers to organizations.

There is considerable debate about the types of cultures that are associated with organizational effectiveness, but some researchers have gathered data from the employees of successful companies on which characteristics they associate with their companies' success. These include emphases on customer service, quality of goods and services, involvement of employees in decision-making, training for employees, teamwork and employee satisfaction. Increasingly it is argued by pundits and policy makers in government, however, that a key cultural value for success is corporate social responsibility.

KEY THEME

Corporate Social Responsibility

Corporate social responsibility is a cultural value that emphasizes the importance of organizations promoting business activities that bring simultaneous economic, social and environmental benefits and, by extension, not undertaking activities that have the opposite effects. This involves the organization working in partnership with:

- Other organizations – for example, having open, mutually supportive and transparent relationships with suppliers to avoid their exploitation. Large supermarket chains are often accused of doing the opposite.

- Community bodies – for example promoting the arts by sponsoring ballet or providing free marketing advice for a homeless charity.

- Unions – by working collectively with unions to create better quality of work life for employees in the belief that this approach will benefit all along with and certainly the productivity of the organization.

- Consumers – by adopting an ethical approach to claims made about products and services,

giving a realistic picture of what is on offer and not hiding bad news in the small print.

An organization with a strong commitment to CSR would ensure a high level of performance in areas such as health and safety, the environment and equal opportunities. Intrinsic to this approach is the notion of responsible behaviour in business, encouraging increased awareness of ethical issues, open, constructive dialogue and trust with key stakeholders (employees, consumers, suppliers, governments, the public). Much emphasis is now placed also on environmental responsibility within business, reducing carbon output by avoiding unnecessary energy use and reducing waste. Increasingly businesses are choosing their suppliers, based on whether they have environmental quality accreditation in place (such as ISO 12001).

CSR at a society level is about social progress, effective protection of the environment, prudent use of natural resources and high and stable levels of economic growth and employment to ensure a better quality of life for everyone, both in the present and for future generations. There is evidence that proponents of CSR argue that it is good for long-term business success as well as good for wider society, but the evidence for this is not clear at present, largely because it is still a new area of research and understanding of what CSR actually means in practice (enacted versus espoused values) is still unclear.

Some suggest that CSR is just glossy claims by public relations specialists with little commitment in practice to changes in values and behaviours in organizations. For example, some large mulrinationals will make very public commitments (relatively small amounts) of money to supporting cancer charities, but spend many times more on paying accountants and lawyers to help them find ways of legitimately avoiding tax payments. The reputations of Google, Starbucks and Amazon have been built on their corporate social responsibility but they are adept at avoiding taxes, while staying within the law on a grand scale in many countries where they operate, denying governments revenue that could make a major difference to human and social well-being. Others see CSR as a source of business opportunity and improved competitiveness (consumers will buy products that do less harm to the environment such as recycled paper). And some leaders see CSR as sound business practice focused on reducing waste and increasing the commitment of employees. Many organizations see CSR as an irrelevance to the single goal of maximizing shareholder returns. After the collapse of the banking industry in the West in 2008 and 2009 and the increasing effects of global warming, more people see CSR as a business obligation and the topic should now be one of central concern to business leaders.

KEY THEME

Globalization and Culture

Organizational cultures occur in the context of national cultures and a major challenge for very large organizations that span many countries is how to ensure their values are appropriate for and implemented across international boundaries with varied national value emphases. The most influential analysis of national cultures was articulated by Geert Hofstede (1980; 1983), a Swedish researcher, who undertook a detailed study of variations in the cultures of outlets of IBM across the world, He concluded that there were four underlying dimensions of national culture:

Individualism-Collectivism

This refers to the extent to which people define themselves in relation to individual characteristics (football player, jokey person, someone who reads a particular broadsheet newspaper) versus identity being based on belonging to particular groups (family, profession, political party, social club, work organization). Eastern cultures tend to be high in collectivism, whereas countries such as the UK and US are high in individualism.

Power Distance

This refers to the extent to which people in a particular culture obey authority figures and are respectful of those in authority. Turkey and many Middle Eastern countries are high in power distance while Western European countries (for the most part) tend to be low.

Uncertainty Avoidance

High uncertainty avoidant cultures plan carefully ahead, require clarity about tasks, roles, goals and responsibilities and find ambiguity threatening and uncomfortable. It is sometimes referred to as tolerance of ambiguity.

Masculinity-Femininity

This dimension contrasts an emphasis on achievement, winning and recognition with an emphasis on interpersonal relations and support. Countries such as Norway and Sweden tend to have high femininity and it is interesting to note that there is a strong correlation between this dimension at national level and representation of women on boards of companies and in government.

Some years after his initial research, Hofstede agreed that a fifth dimension was useful – *Long Term Perspective* typical, for example, of Chinese culture. Subsequent studies have tended to provide broad support for Hofstede's analysis though controversy persists about the precise number and content of dimensions. The individualism-collectivism dimension has emerged as a highly robust description, however.

These cultural variations have a profound influence on organizational culture since it is difficult for work organizations to develop values that are at variance with the dominant national values of the countries within which they are located.

ORGANIZATIONAL CLIMATE

So far we have explored in depth the concept of organizational culture, but there is a related concept in Work Psychology – organizational climate. If culture is what makes the organization distinctive, climate is 'what it feels like to work here'. It is based on employees' perceptions of the work environment (Rousseau, 1988). Climate can designate descriptions and perceptions at the individual, group or organizational level of analysis, i.e. what it feels like to me, how the group or team feels, how the whole organization feels. Individual perceptions of the work environment are usually termed psychological climate, and when shared to a level sufficient for aggregation to the group or organizational level, are labelled group or organizational climate. Schneider *et al.* (1990; 2013) suggests that organizational climate perceptions focus on the behaviours which are rewarded and supported in an organization. Most also agree that individuals also interpret processes, practices and behaviours in the organizational environment in relation to their own sense of well-being (James, James and Ashe, 1990) and this contributes to the experience of climate. Where supervisors are authoritarian and demanding, employees' well-being will be negatively affected and thus the organizational climate will be poor.

Individuals can describe the organizational environment both in an overall global sense, as well as in a more specific, targeted manner. The latter are sometimes called domain-specific climates and might be focused on the climate for safety (is there a high emphasis on safety in the organization?), climate for service (a strong emphasis on meeting customers' needs) or a climate for innovation (lots of encouragement for employees to come up with and implement ideas for new and improved ways of doing things). In relation to the global organizational climate, James and his colleagues (James and

James, 1989) describe four dimensions of global organizational climate, which have been identified across a number of different work contexts:

a　Role stress and lack of harmony (including role ambiguity, conflict and overload, subunit conflict, low organizational identification and low management concern and awareness).

b　Job challenge and autonomy (as well as job importance).

c　Leadership facilitation and support (including leader trust, support, goal facilitation and interaction facilitation and psychological and hierarchical influence).

d　Work group cooperation, friendliness, and warmth (as well as responsibility for effectiveness; (James and McIntyre, 1996).

Patterson *et al.* (2005) have developed a measure of overall climate based partly on the Competing Values Model and partly on dimensions identified in previous research – called the Organizational Climate Measure. This assesses climate in relation to 17 dimensions is shown in Figure 14.2.

Climate Versus Culture

Are you clear about what the difference is between culture and climate so far? No? Well neither are most scholars. They tend to agree that culture is about the shared values and meanings of those within an organization and use an anthropological metaphor to communicate this (imagine being a traveller in a foreign land trying to understand its culture). Climate refers more to how it feels to work in the organization – the experience of it. Climate is a meteorological metaphor so it's about the weather – is it cold, hot, stormy, changeable or mild. For organizational climate read is it friendly, competitive,

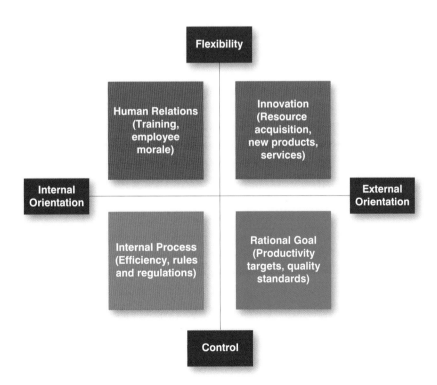

Figure 14.2　The organizational climate measure: dimensions mapped against competing values quadrants

busy, laid-back or authoritarian? There are many attempts to differentiate and contrast the two concepts since they are both used to provide a summative description of the organization. One key difference that writers refer to is the measurement methods associated with each. Some researchers argue that climate is accessible through quantitative survey measures while culture is only accessible using qualitative methods (observation, interview, document analysis, etc.). These are artificial dichotomies, however. It is rather like comparing apples and cars. The key to understanding the two concepts is the metaphorical basis of them. Culture is about traditions, ways of doing things, values, hidden assumptions – the metaphor of understanding national cultures. Climate is a more generalized notion and is derived from the concept of typical weather patterns in an area (cold, wet, stormy, warm, changeable, dark, etc.). Climate is very much infused with the affective reactions of employees to their work environment. Climate is often described as members' surface experiences and perceptions, while culture shapes (almost unseen) taken-for-granted and even unconscious assumptions about how to behave in the organization and the meaning of events.

Climates for Success

Climate perceptions provide the context for understanding employee attitudes and behaviour (Schneider *et al.*, 2000). Research has suggested that climate perceptions are associated with a variety of important outcomes at the individual, group and organizational levels. These include leader behaviour (Rousseau, 1988; Rentsch, 1990), turnover intentions (Rousseau, 1988; Rentsch, 1990), job satisfaction (Mathieu, Hoffmann and Farr, 1993; James and Tetrick, 1986; James and Jones, 1980), individual job performance (Brown and Leigh, 1996; Pritchard and Karasick, 1973), and organizational performance (Lawler, Hall and Oldham, 1974; Patterson, Warr and West, 2004). The domains of climate and culture that some researchers (Wiley and Brooks, 2000) believe are the key to organizational success are:

- Customer service:
  - Strong emphasis on customer service.
  - Company provides quality service.
  - Customer problems corrected quickly.
  - Delivers products/services in a timely fashion.

- Quality:
  - Senior management committed to quality service and demonstrates quality is a priority.
  - Supervisors provide guidance for service and set good examples in relation to quality.
  - Quality of work is rated.
  - Clear service standards are met.
  - Quality is a priority vs meeting deadlines.
  - Quality is a priority vs cost containment.
  - Continuous improvement.

- Involvement:
  - Front-line staff have the authority to meet customer's needs.
  - Encouragement to be innovative and participate in decisions.
  - Sufficient effort is made to get opinions of staff.
  - Management use employees' good ideas.

- Training:
  - Plans for training and development.
  - Opportunities for staff to attend training and to improve skills.
  - Staff have the right training for them to improve.
  - Staff are satisfied with training opportunities.
  - New employees get necessary training.

- Information/knowledge:
  - Management gives clear vision/direction.
  - Staff understand goals clearly.
  - Staff are informed about issues.
  - Departments keep each other informed.
  - Enough warning about changes.
  - Satisfaction with organizational information.

- Teamwork/organization:
  - Cooperation to get the job done.
  - Management encourages teamwork.
  - Workload fairly divided.
  - Enough people to do the work.
  - Problems in teams corrected quickly.

- Overall satisfaction:
  - High job satisfaction.
  - Jobs use skills and abilities.
  - Work gives a feeling of accomplishment.
  - Satisfaction with organization.
  - Rate the organization as a place to work.
  - Proud to work for the organization.
  - Would recommend working for the organization.
  - High job security.
  - Not seriously considering leaving the organization.

Others argue that there can be no universals and that success will be dependent on the differing contingent relationships between task, environment and cultures that each organization faces. Still others argue that we must look at more specific aspects of climate and culture and relate these to specific outcomes (domain-specific approaches).

Domain-specific climate has been linked with several important work outcomes. Using their model of service climate, Schneider and colleagues demonstrated that service climate is related to customer perceptions of service quality (Schneider, 1980; Schneider, Parkington and Buxton, 1980; Schneider, White and Paul, 1998; Salvaggio *et al.*, 2007; Schneider *et al.*, 2009). Safety climate has also been linked with safety behaviours and accidents (Hofmann and Stetzer, 1996), and safety compliance in the health sector (Murphy, Gershon and DeJoy, 1996). Research in the area of innovation also suggests that group climate factors influence levels of innovative behaviour in health care and top management teams (West and Wallace, 1991; West and Anderson, 1996).

From the exploration of culture and climate so far it is clear that they are dynamic concepts. Culture and climate change as a consequence of many different forces. Indeed change in organizations is a central concept in Work Psychology. Below we explore why change occurs, types of change, why employees sometimes resist and sometimes welcome change and the strategies managers can use to achieve change. We also describe different methods of managing the change process.

AUTHOR EXPERIENCE

The Energy of Innovative Organizations

As part of a major research project on corporate performance, I visited a wire and cable company and spent the day interviewing senior managers and touring the manufacturing plant learning about its operations (Patterson *et al.*, 2004). This company operates in a highly competitive market, but its market share is growing. At the end of nine hours of interviewing, I left exhausted and somewhat anxious that I had gathered too little information. The next day I visited another company which manufactures UPVC windows. Again I interviewed senior managers and spent some time watching the production process. This company also has a market share which is growing, despite the fact that it is in a highly competitive environment. After four hours of relatively relaxed discussions with senior management and a tour of the shop floor, I left feeling I had gathered all of the information I needed. I also felt that the second company – the window manufacturers – was much less likely to be in business in ten years' time than the first company. The reason for this is that the wire and cable company is innovating in almost every area of its operations while the window manufacturer only makes changes when competitors develop a new fitting or design which threatens their market position.

The reason why the difference in length of interview time was so great between these two companies was because the wire and cable company was busy developing new ways of doing things. Employers and employees were so enthusiastic and eager to talk about these that there was an enormous amount of information to absorb. In contrast, in the UPVC window company, shop floor employees had been deskilled; each worked on a strict job cycle time of two and a half minutes, and the company had little or no strategy for training, human resource management, quality control, communication or teamwork. Consequently, only the senior managers had much information to offer about the company. Nevertheless, the company is efficient and doing well financially. However, their problem is that their highly efficient operation is readily imitated by others in the industry. Indeed, their own strategy of innovating only in response to competitors' new ideas demonstrates this neatly.

Climate and culture concepts enable us to understand and articulate the differences between organizations and to begin to understand how we can go about helping them to change for the better. As psychologists we are not only concerned with understanding and describing organizations, but also with making them more nourishing and developmental environments within which people can flourish.

ORGANIZATIONAL CHANGE

Organizations are like organisms. They must adapt to their environmental circumstances in order to survive. In 2008, we saw the world plunged into a major financial crisis as banks lost billions of dollars and some collapsed altogether. Credit, which businesses need in order to fund innovation and expansion, was no longer available. Moreover, with changes in bank lending, some existing loans became more expensive. As the confidence felt by consumers fell ('the economy is in bad shape, I might lose my job, so I must spend less') demand worldwide dropped. Moreover, in some countries (the US, Japan, the UK, Germany) the property market collapsed and house prices fell by over 20 per cent after years of rapid growth. This led house owners to become even more worried about the drop in the value of their assets. The loss of confidence became a vicious cycle. The effects on employment levels, business bankruptcies and business growth are sudden, dramatic and global.

Faced with these changed circumstances, some businesses dug the trenches within which to weather out the storm, stopped spending, and worked even harder at what had worked well in the past. Others began to look for new markets, or made redundancies to reduce costs. Others decided to spend more on R&D to develop new products and to cut spending in areas such as staff training or travel. Some companies tried to be smart about the decisions to cut R&D spending. They did this by identifying the best bets for new products, cutting out 60 per cent of investment in product development (saving 60 per cent) and increasing by 20 per cent the spend on those they thought were the best bets, thereby saving 40 per cent overall. However, they actually increased the spending on the areas they felt were most important. All these changes occurred because the organizations were trying to survive or even prosper. Economic factors, therefore, cause change. But a wide variety of other factors lead to organizational change, such as:

- Actions of competitors. When i-Phone produced the new touch phone, their competitors were left behind and the i-Phone sold out in days. Immediately there was a rush to develop and market new touch phones (Nokia was one of the quickest to change and produce a competitor product). If the local supermarket cuts prices on its products, the next supermarket down the road is likely to follow suit.

- Government legislation. When a government requires organizations to pay for the cost of transport in major cities (such as a traffic 'congestion charges'), businesses may decide to relocate in order to reduce costs, moving to a more rural area or another city where such charges do not apply. If a government introduces better maternity benefits (longer paid leave for mothers), some businesses may relocate their activities to other countries with less enlightened policies in order to reduce their wage bills.

- Environmental factors. Climate change requires businesses to have ever 'greener' policies and practices since many businesses will only do business with companies that have environmentally sound approaches. Reducing energy costs by changing the way products are made may be a response to higher oil prices.

- Demographic factors. As the European population ages, businesses are finding it tougher to recruit young skilled workers. They are persuading some employees to stay at work later in their lives, seeking skilled workers from other countries or relocating their operations to countries where the supply of skilled labour is greater (such as India) and the costs of such labour are lower.

- Ethics. Recognizing the discrimination against women in salary levels which exists internationally, some organizations take action to ensure equality. Concerns with corporate social responsibility may lead some organizations to recognize that exploring every possible loophole in the tax regulations to reduce the amount they pay (including investing assets as much as possible outside the country in 'tax havens') might be considered unethical. They may then reduce the number of accountants and tax lawyers they employ and commit to paying higher tax bills. This is sadly unusual in practice.

- Leaders. One insightful Dilbert cartoon describes 'Bungee Bosses' who fly in on a bungee rope, announcing 'I'm your new boss, let's change everything before I am reassigned, whoops, too late – bye' – before he or she disappears on the retracting elastic rope. New leaders are very likely to want to demonstrate impact through their interventions and usually initiate change. Barack Obama's first actions as President were to sign an order closing the infamous Guantanamo Bay prison and to set a date for the withdrawal of US troops from Iraq. He also swiftly announced a huge federal budget to stimulate the ailing economy.

Anything can change in organizations (except perhaps the fact that change is continuous), but the main domains of change are usually:

- organizational goals and strategies
- organizing arrangements: organizational structure, policies and procedures, reward systems, physical setting
- social factors: management style
- individual attributes: knowledge, skills and abilities (KSAs), motivation, behaviour
- work methods: technology, job design, information technology, work-flow design.

Change in one area is likely to have an impact in other domains also, so changing reward systems will affect motivation while changes in technology will require changes in KSAs amongst employees.

Models of Change

Episodic and continuous change

Weick and Quinn (1999) believe there are two types of change – episodic and continuous, sometimes respectively referred to as planned and emergent change. Episodic is planned and potentially revolutionary. Its aim is to make a fundamental and lasting change in some aspect of the organization's functioning. Such change tends to be big, noisy and involve lots of major resources in the form of time or money. Making large-scale redundancies, restructuring the organization to reduce the number of layers in the hierarchy, acquiring another organization, opening up a new operation in Malaysia or closing down an existing factory in Ireland – they all involve high profile, planned and revolutionary change. Weick and Quinn argue that such change is less likely to be successful than continuous change because it is an either – or gamble.

The second type is continuous change. Organizations with a climate of continuous change seek to ensure that there is continuous improvement and adaptation, encouraging continuous reflection and learning. This can be achieved by encouraging all within the organization to take responsibility for learning and change. It is their responsibility to decide how to improve task performance, whether it is maintaining the manufacturing equipment or winning new customers. Such a strategy is more likely to be effective where bureaucracy is minimized and there are relatively few hierarchical levels so that employees do not feel they generally have to seek permission to implement new ideas, secure in the knowledge that innovation will generally be supported by managers.

Systems perspective on change

The systems perspective on organizational change views the organization as a dynamic system of interrelated components. The perspective gives rise to systems thinking, Senge's (1990) so-called Fifth Discipline. The basic tenet of the systems perspective is that organizations are composed of a multitude of subsystems that vary in their size and scope, and that change into one system will effect change in other related systems. Theories in this perspective don't necessarily agree on the best ways to conceptualize the core subsystems of organizations.

Miller (1967) identified four subsystems: organizational goals and values, technical subsystems, psychosocial subsystems and managerial subsystems. Nadler and Tushman (1997) also identified different four systems:

- **The work.** The day-to-day activities carried out by employees. Process design, pressures on the individual and rewards are part of this element.
- **The people.** The knowledge, skills, attitudes, experiences and characteristics of those who work in the organization.
- **The formal organization.** The structure, systems and policies in place.
- **The informal organization.** This consists of all the processes that emerge over time, such as power, influence, values and norms.

The model suggests that in considering change, all four components must be considered as interrelated elements. If you change one element, the others three will need to be attended to. If we change the type of work done, we must also consider how this aligns with individual skills (people), how this fits with the current organization of work in departments and teams (formal organization) and what activities, influences and power relationships will be affected by the change (informal organization). If this alignment is not managed the organization will not change, but homeostasis will be maintained. Change will fizzle out.

Systems theories generally extend their perspective to define organizations as 'open' systems. This means that they consider the impact of external or environmental stimuli on organizational systems – organizations are essentially reactive to external change.

The systems perspective on organizational change is a good illustration of how change can morph and develop over time. From this perspective, organizations comprise interconnected subsystems and the links between these subsystems means that change in one will lead to changes in others. Planned change in one system might lead to unforeseen consequences in others and so this may call for a development of the change strategy. The constant iterations of the change strategy mean that it is, in itself, constantly evolving. To help understand how systems and their reciprocal effects upon one another, Work, Psychologists and organizational theorists have constructed guiding models. Two are presented below.

The McKinsey 7S model The 7S model, designed by McKinsey (a major management consultancy firm) is a framework identifying seven interdependent systems in organizations (Figure 14.3). The model is probably overly simplistic, but is a useful way to analyze internal issues in an organization. A key omission, however, is the external environment. The model is shown in Figure 14.3, indicating the seven systems. Practitioners use the model as a framework for analysis of organizations, and in the analysis of change, potential barriers and facilitators of change can be identified:

- strategy: the organization's long-term mission and strategy
- structure: the way that the organization is structured, including reporting lines
- systems: the systems and procedures that govern how people in the organization work
- shared values: core values of the company evident in organizational culture and group norms
- style: the style of leadership adopted by senior leaders
- staff: the human resources of the organization, their motivation and satisfaction
- skills: the skills and competencies of the employees.

The Burke-Litwin model This model (Burke and Litwin, 1992) is a comprehensive, and arguably one of the most useful models of organizational performance and change. The model identifies a number of key factors and their relationships with one another. The model is designed to show the progression from environmental demands, through macro-level changes to factors like leadership and strategy, and subsequently through to individual and organizational performance. The model is shown in Figure 8.1 in Chapter 8. The key features of the model and approach are:

- The distinction between transformational factors (mission and strategy, leadership, organizational culture) and transactional or operational factors (structure, systems, management, practices and climate). If transformational factors are changed, they have an effect across the whole organization. If transactional factors are changed, they are less likely to have an organization-wide impact.
- The external environment is the most powerful driver of organizational change.
- Changes in the external environment affect transformational factors. These in turn lead to changes in the transactional factors.

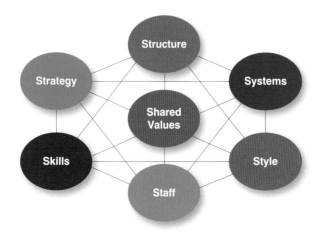

Figure 14.3   The McKinsey 7S model

- Together, these changes in transformational and transactional factors affect motivation, which in turn affects individual and organizational performance.
- The 12 components of the model interact in particular ways – changes in one will likely lead to specific changes in the others.
- The key factors for major change are the transformational factors.
- Transactional factors are more relevant for optimizing or fine-tuning the organization.

The Learning Organization

Another perspective on change proposes that we need to have a pro-active approach to change and create cultures within which learning happens continually at all levels to ensure that organizations are shaping as much as being shaped by change. This has led to the development of the notions of action learning and the learning organization. Action learning proposes that organizations should continuously review their functioning, diagnosing gaps between current and desired performance, identifying objectives for change, implementing change, evaluating the outcomes and institutionalizing the whole approach. These steps in action learning are depicted in (Figure 14.4).

The *learning organization* works to create, acquire and transfer knowledge in order that the organization adapts itself continually on the basis of new knowledge and insight, as well as to the myriad of powerful external forces that influence its survival. Those who advocate a culture of learning (e.g. Senge, 1990) believe that the rate at which individuals and organizations learn may be the only sustainable competitive advantage in a world characterized by rapid change, highly integrated economies and an increasingly interconnected information world. To produce the conditions for organizational learning and continuous change, managers must put in place mechanisms that encourage employees to take responsibility for learning and for sharing insights with others (Van der Krogt, 1998). These mechanisms include:

- A training and development plan linked to the business strategy (for an organization intent on developing more international market, training for staff in cross-cultural working might be part of the training and development plan).
- Line managers developing employees, e.g. through coaching them to improve their skills.
- The use of personal development and performance reviews to enable employees to develop objectives to improve their work performance and develop their knowledge, skills and abilities.
- Enabling employees to learn about ways of working outside their immediate job role, such as through secondments, visiting external suppliers/customers, work shadowing, job rotations (employees fulfilling a variety of roles on a regular basis rather than staying in one job permanently) (Shipton *et al.*, 2002).

Figure 14.4   The steps in action learning

How do Employees React to Change?

Managers are often those who drive change in organizations and they do so (hopefully almost always) because they foresee benefits for the organization, its customers or its employees from the change. Some change is welcomed by employees, such as schemes to reduce wasteful uses of energy or to improve the speed of information given to customers so that the latter are happier with the service they receive. And some change is not welcomed or is resisted by employees, especially those that employees believe will make it more difficult for them to do their jobs well.

Managing change involves understanding the reasons why people resist change in organizations and recognizing that resistance to change is not necessarily good or bad. In some instances it is a normal and natural reaction to change. In other instances it is a reasonable reaction to an inappropriate attempt to change the status quo. Not all innovation and change is for the best, nor is it always well thought out. Resistance to change can be an important force for ensuring that change is introduced wisely or it can be an instinctive and unhelpful reaction to the uncertainty change heralds.

Why do people sometimes resist change? One reason is the feelings of *uncertainty and insecurity* that reduce people's acceptance of change. When changes to methods of production are proposed with the development of teamworking, employees may feel anxious that their fellow teamworkers will not be up to the job or that they may not get on with them. Another is *selective perception and retention* – when people hear about the change they listen more to and remember better the potentially threatening aspects: 'Team working will mean I won't get credit for the work I do, it will be invisible in the team's efforts. Therefore I won't get my bonus.' A related cause of resistance to change is *misunderstanding* about the nature of the change and its consequences. This often occurs when there is inadequate consultation and information sharing about the changes to be introduced. Consequently, suspicions and misunderstandings grow and people inevitably resist or even sabotage the change. Managing change effectively means informing very fully all those affected by, or who perceive they may be affected by, the change. Then of course there is *habit* – 'we have always done it this way and it will just be hard work to change things.' Change is often perceived as posing *threats to status, security, pay, job role or the social environment*. People resist change if they see it threatening their job security, power, status, pay differentials or the variety of their jobs. Working in teams may be seen as being forced not to work with the people I have always got on with and working with people I don't know so well who I may not get on with. And, as we have already suggested, employees are good judges and may see that *the change is unwise*. Sometimes we simply *KNOW* that it is not going to help us do our jobs better.

But it is not just individuals that resist change. Sometimes organizations as a whole have powerful means for resisting change – even change that is necessary for the organization to survive and prosper. Argyris (1993) termed these processes by which organizations accomplish this as 'defensive routines'.

As a consequence of their scale and complexity, organizations can be compared with organisms that have a personality and life of their own. Analogous to living organisms, they develop immune systems to fight against attacks that threaten them. These immune systems in one sense are found in the norms and unwritten rules of the organization and can be very difficult to detect. Where they are detrimental to the organization's long-term effectiveness, these organizational defences are referred to as 'defensive routines'. As routines they are set into motion automatically and often without deliberate intent on the part of any one individual. Defensive routines are often designed to reduce difficulty and embarrassment within organizations and so can inhibit learning. Because they are designed to maintain the status quo, they often prevent the organization from dealing with the root causes of problems. They are one of the most important causes of failures in the implementation of changes, because anything, which threatens to change the status quo, is likely to be dealt with as a virus. According to Argyris, who conceived the notion, defensive routines are so closely entwined with organizations' norms that they are undiscussable and their undiscussability is also undiscussable! Defensive routines make the unreasonable seem reasonable and are often disguised as virtues.

An example is where people in an organization continually blame market conditions, political changes and economic circumstances for problems the organization is experiencing. Regardless of what goes on within the organization, problems are always explained in terms of what is occurring outside. Consequently, a kind of cohesion is maintained between people within the organization who collude together in not addressing their own performance problems and the need to change.

Another example is denial of the existence of a problem in the first place. The organization might have before it the evidence of a market downturn in sales and orders, but senior managers keep dismissing this simply as a 'blip' in the market, although the blip is clearly, to any outside observer, a major precipice. Another example of this 'faking good' is an immediate reaction of crushing any suggestions for new and improved ways of doing things on the basis that it has been tried and failed elsewhere, or that it will cost too much or that the initiator does not really understand the complexities of the situation. In some organizations, large numbers of people have survived by 'faking good' and marking time in their work. Innovation represents a threat to the cosy system they have created and is habitually resisted. Therefore, the reaction of those within such organizations is always to reject new ideas, but their reaction is undiscussable. Indeed, in such organizations innovation is often promoted verbally, but in practice any attempt to introduce innovation is sharply thwarted. Suggestions for new ideas are tolerated and the innovator is placated by luke-warm words of support, but without the practical follow-through of resources, time and real commitment.

Exposing defensive routines is all the more difficult because they are so very hard to detect. People become immensely frustrated at the struggle involved in implementing a clearly sensible innovation, particularly when they are unable to understand why it is proving so difficult and why it arouses so much hostility. Below are some strategies for confronting defensive routines:

- Have arguments well thought out; reasons should be compelling, vigorous and publicly testable.
- Do not promise more than can be delivered; unrealistic promises can be seized upon to reject what is essentially a good idea.
- Be prepared to admit mistakes and then use them as a means of learning (for yourself and the organization).
- Always try to look beneath the surface. Continually ask 'why?' of those who resist the change.
- Surface and bring into the open subjects which seem to be undiscussable, despite the hostility this may generate.
- Learn to be aware of when you are involved in or colluding with defensive routines.
- Try to see through the issues of efficiency (doing things right) to the more important questions of effectiveness (doing the right things).

Forcefield analysis of change

Kurt Lewin, a leading social psychologist of the early 20th century (1890–1947) argued that change occurs when the forces favouring change strengthen, resistance to change lessens or both occur simultaneously. Otherwise organizations remain in equilibrium. This statement (which will probably strike you as self evident) contains within it a useful means for thinking through how to manage change. Lewin described all situations in which we find ourselves as in a 'temporary equilibrium held in place by two sets of forces: driving forces which push change along and restraining forces which pull back against change' (Lewin, 1997). Understanding those forces will help the innovator towards successful implementation. Lewin also suggested that we will often be more successful in implementing change when we reduce the forces against change. The temptation of managers is often just to focus on the forces in favour of change (such as the number of employees who agree with the idea) and they typically do this by trying to increase, via persuasion about the value of the change, the numbers of employees who agree. But forces resisting change are often more powerful (for example, because we resist losses /rises more than we seek potential gains -- Kahneman, 2011) and when these are reduced, forces FOR change automatically become more important.

Figure 14.5 describes a strategy for reducing resistance to change based on a combination of stakeholder and forcefield analysis. This exercise enables the development of an overview of how much resistance to change is likely to be present and where major problems may arise within an organization. It enables strategy planning for managing resistance to change and participation processes within an organization

DISCUSS WITH A COLLEAGUE

Using the forcefield and stakeholder analysis, first identify a change you would like to make in your university or another organization and then develop a plan to bring the change about. Put this plan together, consulting carefully with colleagues and decide the steps you would need to take to achieve success. Present the plan to your tutor and ask them to provide feedback on what you may have missed in your analysis and get their guidance on whether they feel it is appropriate for you to pursue the idea. Then decide whether you would like to go ahead and try to make the change. Carefully consider the ethical implications of any change you propose to make in any organization.

DESIGNING AND IMPLEMENTING CHANGE AND INNOVATION

Richard Daft (1992) has made major theoretical contributions to the understanding of change and innovation in organizations. He proposes an integrative strategy for implementing change based on seven stages or elements.

1 Diagnose a true need for change. Correctly identifying the nature of the problem is fundamental to effective change or innovation. It is therefore important to spend sufficient time diagnosing the true need for change and correctly identifying the nature of the problem.

2 Find an idea that fits the need. This means making sure that the correct match is found between the nature of the problem and the idea for change.

3 Get top management support. Innovation and change attempts are (much!) more successful to the extent that people with power support them.

4 Design the change for incremental implementation. Daft argues that the prospects for success for innovations are improved dramatically if each part of the process can be designed and implemented sequentially. Then so-called 'teething problems' can be managed one by one as they appear, rather than trying to deal with a whole jaw full of problems at the same time.

5 Develop plans to overcome resistance to change. Align plans for change with the needs and goals of users. Here it is important to ensure that the innovation meets a real need. If people within the organization do not believe that the change has value, or if top management does not support it, the organization will resist the change. Ways of overcoming resistance include:

Step 1 Define the change you wish to implement. The outcome of the change will be the equilibrium which you are hoping to achieve in the future. It is therefore important that this outcome is clearly defined.

Step 2 Now identify all those individuals and groups which could have an influence on your ability to introduce the change in your organization. For each of these 'stakeholders' identify major advantages and disadvantages which may accrue to them with the introduction of the change.

Stakeholder	Advantages	Disadvantages
_____	_____	_____
_____	_____	_____
_____	_____	_____

Step 3 The forcefield. Draw a 'forcefield' with an arrow to represent each stakeholder. For each arrow in the forcefield you will need to decide:

(a) the direction of the arrow, for or against – although it is sometime difficult to know exactly how others are thinking, for the purposes of this exercise you must make a decision based on your current knowledge of the situation. If the arrow represents a group within which there are mixed opinions, you must still decide which side, on balance, the group as a whole will be. You may, however, indicate the situation within the arrow – for example by patchy shading.

(b) the size of the arrow – this will represent the relative power of the individual group or factor to influence the introduction of the change. You may wish to use colour and shading to make the arrows as representative of your view of the situation as possible. The greater their influence, the bigger the arrow and the more you therefore need to concentrate on them.

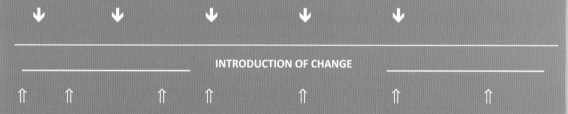

Step 4 Action planning. After contemplating the forcefield that you have drawn, you may have some new insights into the situation. Does the environment for the introduction of the change look more positive than you had thought? Alternatively, are the arrows more heavily weighted on the restraining side of the change line? A review of the forcefield will enable you to decide where you need to exert energy in order to:

(a) decrease the power and influence of the restraining forces

(b) increase the power and influence of the driving forces

Based on the analysis, what actions could you take to reduce the influence of the restraining forces and increase the power of the supporting forces? Your action plan should be helpful in determining strategies for moving forward. Try to identify ways in which the balance of the forces can be weighted more strongly in your favour. This may be by finding new helping forces, or by trying to eliminate or lessen the effect of some of the hindering forces. People often find that it tends to be easier to do the latter. To use the car analogy, it is as if one's foot is already down on the floor and there is no way to increase the driving force. The easiest solution may well be to take off the handbrake!

Figure 14.5   Analyzing and managing resistance to change

- Communication and education. Clear and persistent communication about the nature of the need, the value of the change and the process of implementation is likely to reduce resistance to change. Daft rightly argues that far more communication and education than managers think is necessary should be undertaken, since typically the amount required is underestimated.
- Participation and involvement. Extensive and early involvement of those affected by the change is required in order to reduce resistance to change. Participation in the design of the change is the single most potent way of reducing resistance.

6 Create change teams. Organizational changes are implemented more successfully if teams are created which carry responsibility for their successful implementation.

7 Foster change champions. Champions are volunteers who are deeply committed to a particular innovation or change. They have the responsibility of ensuring that all necessary resources and technical supports are available and they persuade people about the value of the implementation.

Even following these prescriptions, many changes are not implemented successfully in organizations. John Kotter (1995) has identified eight core reasons for the failure of organizational changes. They are the failures to:

- Establish a sense of urgency about need for change.
- Form a powerful guiding coalition to drive the change forward.
- Create a vision of the benefits and value of the change.
- Communicate the vision to all affected by the change.
- Empower others to act on the vision, giving employees the opportunity to help make the change happen.
- Plan for and create short-term wins so that people are quickly convinced of the value of the change.
- Consolidate improvements and produce still more change.
- Institutionalize new approaches so that the change is embedded and stable.

Organizational change is constant. The challenge for psychologists and other leaders in organizations is to understand and manage change so that it is shaped to support the fundamental purposes of the organization and to enable the effectiveness and flourishing of those who work within and are served by organizations. That is our challenge and existing theory and research has taken us some way towards this. One of the biggest challenges is educating leaders in how to manage change effectively in practice.

DISCUSS WITH A COLLEAGUE

What would you identify as the four or five most important principles in managing change, based on the material you have read in this chapter?

Bejamin Schneider

Benjamin Schneider is senior research fellow, CEB Valtera, and professor emeritus of Psychology at the University of Maryland. Ben moved to CEB Valtera in 2003 after retiring from full-time academic work. For many years, he was the head of the Industrial and Organizational Psychology programme at the Univeristy of Maryland. Schneider has wide-ranging interests in service quality, organizational climate and culture, staffing issues, and the role of manager personality in organizational life. Ben was awarded the Year 2000 Distinguished Scientific Contributions Award by the Society for Industrial and Organizational Psychology; the 2006 Career Contributions to the Service Discipline Award from the Services Marketing Special Interest Group (SERVSIG) of the American Marketing Association; the 2009 Michael R. Losey Award from the Society for

Human Resource Management (SHRM) for career contributions to HR; the 2009 Herbert J. Heneman Jr. Career Contributions Award from the HR Division of the Academy of Management; and the 2013 Lifetime Achievement Award from the Organizational Behavior Division of the Academy of Management. He was awarded the Year 2000 Distinguished Scientific Contributions Award by the Society for Industrial and Organizational Psychology. For the purposes of this chapter, one of his most famous contributions is the Attraction-Selection-Attrition (ASA) model of organizational behaviour. The central argument of the ASA model is that people matter much more than structures, environments and tasks and that climates and cultures are ultimately a reflection of the unique collection of people who make up organizations. Organizations seek to attract people who share the organization's values (the latter influenced disproportionately by the values of the leader). Organizations then select people whose values mirror their own. And employees who do not share the values of the majority of others in the organization will leave or are pushed out (i.e. attrition). Such a process is likely to produce an integrated and cohesive organization. However, diversity of perspective is needed to promote innovation. So a lack of diversity could also lead to a failure to change and innovate in response to environmental changes. Being aware of the ASA theory could help leaders avoid the problems of creating too homogeneous an organization. Schneider's theory has played a major role in affecting how we think about the development of culture and climate in Work Psychology. His contribution was reflected in the publication in 2008 by his peers of a book to celebrate his work – *The People Make the Place.* And he is a very nice guy!

SUMMARY

This chapter describes how to study organizational culture by maintaining awareness of all your experiences within organizations. Key dimensions for describing culture include hierarchy, pay differentials, job descriptions, norms (dress formality for example), espoused values and rituals (award ceremonies, mission statements), stories, jokes and jargon and the physical environment. Organizational culture is defined as the set of assumptions held by organization members about the organization. Schein's levels of culture are described – artefacts, espoused values and hidden assumptions. Other models of culture are also presented, including Goffee and Jones Sociability versus Solidarity Model; Quinn and Cameron's Competing Values Model and Martin's Integration, Differentiation and Fragmentation approach. The development of culture is described and the key roles of leaders and socialization tactics are illustrated.

The importance of corporate social responsibility in determining cultural values is shown as a key theme in modern organizations. An alternative approach to culture, using the concepts of values from positive psychology, presents a challenging perspective on corporate social responsibility also. Cross-cultural variations in values are described, including masculinity-femininity, power distance, uncertainty avoidance, individualism versus collectivism and long term versus short term time perspective.

Organizational climate is defined as what it feels like to work here and is contrasted with the concept of culture. Dimensions of climate include role stress and lack of harmony, job challenge and autonomy, leadership facilitation and support and work group cooperation, friendliness and warmth. An instrument for measuring climate (Organizational Climate Indicator) is described. Climates for success include emphases on customer service, involvement, quality, training, information, teamwork and cooperation, and overall satisfaction.

The chapter identifies the forces leading organizations to change, including economic forces, actions of competitors, government legislation, environmental factors, demographic factors and leaders. Two types of change are described – episodic and continuous. The chapter describes models of change, including Weick and Quinn's episodic and continuous change; and systems models that see change as encompassing multiple elements in the organization. These include Nadler and Tushman's model of interrelated systems, the MacKinsey 7S model and the Burke-Litwin model.

Learning organizations seek to create continuous positive change and use mechanisms such as action learning to promote continuous improvement, learning and development plans for employees, job rotations and secondments to ensure employees continually improve their knowledge skills and abilities.

Employees' reactions to change include selective perception and retention, uncertainty and insecurity, misunderstanding, habitual ways of responding and resistance. Organizational responses to change can include defensive routines designed to protect the organization from change. Strategies for overcoming defensive routines and resistance are described, including the use of forcefield and stakeholder analysis.

The chapter also describes how to diagnose and implement change by diagnosing a true need for change; finding an idea that fits the need; getting top management support; designing the change for incremental implementation; developing plans to overcome resistance to change; creating change teams; and fostering innovation champions. You have been introduced to the complex and exciting topic of organizational change, in order – as Kanter (1983) puts it – that you may become masters rather than victims of change.

DISCUSSION QUESTIONS

1   What is the difference between organizational climate and organizational culture? What is the value of each approach and in what circumstances, as a psychologist, would you focus on one or the other?

2   How is national culture likely to affect organizational culture and climate?

3   How helpful to managers and leaders are notions of culture and climate and how can they use them?

4   Can we change organizational culture and, if so, how?

5   Can you describe an organizational change that you have experienced? Was it successful and, if so, what factors made it successful or unsuccessful? What implications does that have for our understanding of organizational change?

6   Compare the value of the different models of change in describing an organizational change you have experienced.

APPLY IT

1   Review the 'Discuss with a colleague' exercises focused on organizational culture early in this chapter and select one of the organizations you used for the exercise. Ideally, this is an organization you are currently working in (it could be your university) or an organization with which you are very familiar.

2   Based on your analysis, what aspect of the culture would you particularly recommend be changed? It could be that people don't cooperate sufficiently across different departments or that employees do not give high quality service to customers. Or it could be that the organization is not sufficiently environmentally aware.

3   Clearly state the change you would recommend making. Then, use the 'forcefield and stakeholder analysis' described in Figure 14.5, to explore and plot the forces that will enable the change and those that will produce resistance to the change. Identify the relative strength of the driving and restraining forces by using different thickness of arrows.

4   Plan the design of a change process that will reduce resistant forces and increase driving forces.

5   Think through steps 3 and 4, taking account of all four components identified in Miller's systems perspective (the work, the people, the formal organization, the informal organization) and the seven elements identified in the McKinsey 7S model (strategy, structure, work systems, shared values, style, staff, skills). Not all will necessarily be relevant to the change you are proposing but make sure you consider each element of both the Miller and McKinsey models.

6   Repeat the forcefield and stakeholder analysis but this time considering all the elements in the Burke-Litwin model of organizational performance and change. Again, not all will necessarily be relevant but take the time to methodically think through each element of the model.

7   Having completed steps 3 to 6, design a change strategy and process to ensure successful change, based on your analysis. Structure the change process around the seven stages or elements identified by

Daft – identify a true need for change; find an idea that fits the need; get top management support; design the change for incremental implementation; develop plans to overcome resistance to change through communication, education, participation and involvement; create change teams; and foster change strategies.

8　Now further elaborate your plan by trying to incorporate the guidance offered by Kotter – establish a sense of urgency; form a powerful coalition; create a vision of the benefits; communicate the vision; empower others to act; create short-term wins;

consolidate improvements; and institutionalize the changes (not all will be relevant but make sure you consider each prescription).

9　Practise this type of analysis/change planning during your career and you will be a master of change in a world where such mastery is in desperately short supply.

10　Reflect on each of the models you have used (e.g., Burke-Litwin, Kotter, Miller, Daft) and consider which is most useful in practice and in the context of the particular organization and change you were considering.

WEB ACTIVITIES

Culture Change in the NHS

Read the article 'Creating a culture of compassion in the NHS after the Francis report' by Lubna Haq, March 2013 at **www.guardian.co.uk** or in the digital resources online and discuss the questions below.

1　How could you frame the issues in this article around models of organizational culture and climate?

2　What would be the practical steps of creating a culture of compassion? What models would help?

Changing Failing Businesses

Read the article 'How to turn around a failing company' by James Hurley, August 2013 at **www. telegraph.co.uk** or in the digital resources online and discuss the questions below.

1　The article focuses on core business issues (business finance, profitability, etc). What management barriers might exist in organizations to turning around performance?

2　How would you advise a failing business to manage people through a change process to ensure the change was effective?

FURTHER READING

Dixon-Woods, M., Baker, R., Charles, K., Dawson, J., Jerzembek, G., Martin, G., McCarthy, I., McKee, L., Minion, J., Ozieranski, P., Willars, J., Wilkie, P. and West, M. (2013). Culture and behaviour in the English National Health Service: overview of lessons from a large multimethod study. *British Medical Journal: Quality and Safety*, published online and open access on 9 September 2013 as 10.1136/bmjqs-2013-001947.

Iles, V. and Sutherland, K.I. (2002). *Organisational change: A review for health care managers*. London: NCCSDO.

Quinn, R.E. (2004). *Building the bridge as you walk on it: A guide for leading change*. San Francisco: John Wiley.

Schein, E. (2004). *Organizational culture and leadership* (3rd ed.). San Francisco: Jossey-Bass.

Schneider, B., Ehrhart, M.G. and Macey, W.H. (2013). Organizational climate and culture. *Annual Reviews of Psychology, 64*, 361–388.

Schneider, B. and Barbera, K. M. (Eds.) (2014). *Oxford handbook of organizational climate and culture*. New York: Oxford University Press.

REFERENCES

Allen, N.J. and Meyer, J.P. (1990). Organizational socialization tactics: A longitudinal analysis of links to newcomers' commitment and role orientation. *Academy of Management Journal, 33*, 847–858.

Argyris, C. (1993). *Knowledge for Action. A Guide to Overcoming Barriers to Organizational Change*. San Francisco: Jossey Bass.

Ashkanasy, N.M., Wilderom, C.P.M. and Peterson, M.F. (2000). *Handbook of Organizational Culture and Climate*. London: Sage Publications.

Brown, S. and Leigh, T.W. (1996). A new look at psychological climate and its relationship to job involvement, effort and performance. *Journal of Applied Psychology, 81*, 358–368.

Burke, W.W. and Litwin, G.H. (1992). A causal model of organizational performance and change. *Journal of Management, 18*, 523–545.

Cameron, K.S. and Quinn, R.E. (1997). *Diagnosing and Changing Organizational Culture*. San Francisco: Jossey-Bass.

Clinebell, S. (1984). Organizational effectiveness: An examination of recent empirical studies and the development of a contingency view. In W.D. Terpening and K.R. Thompson (eds.), *Proceedings of the 27th Annual Conference Midwest Academy of Management* (pp. 92–102). Department of Management, University of Notre Dame.

Daft, R.L. (1992). *Organizational Theory and Design*, (4th ed.). New York: West Publishing Company.

Dixon-Woods, M., Baker, R., Charles, K., Dawson, J., Jerzembek, G., Martin, G., McCarthy, I., McKee, L., Minion, J., Ozieranski, P., Willars, J., Wilkie, P. and West, M. (2013). Culture and behaviour in the English National Health Service: overview of lessons from a large multimethod study. *British Medical Journal: Quality and Safety*, published online and open access on 9 September 2013 as 10.1136/bmjqs–2013–001947.

Emery, F.E. and Trist, E.L. (1965). The causal texture of organizational environments. *Human Relations, 18*, 21–32.

Goffee, R. and Jones, G. (1998). *The Character of a Corporation: How your Company's Culture Can Make or Break your Business*. London: HarperBusiness.

Hall, R.H. (1980). Effectiveness theory and organizational effectiveness. *Journal of Applied Behavioural Science, 16*, 536–545.

Hofmann, D.A. and Stetzer, A. (1996). A cross-level investigation of factors influencing unsafe behaviours and accidents. *Personnel Psychology, 49*, 307–339.

Hofstede, G. (1980). *Culture's consequences: International differences in work-related values*. Beverly Hills, CA: Sage.

Hofstede, G. (1983). The cultural relativity of organizational practices and theories. *Journal of International Business Studies, 14*, 31–46.

James, L.A. and James, L.R. (1989). Integrating work environment perceptions: Explorations into the measurement of meaning. *Journal of Applied Psychology, 74*, 739–751.

James, L.R., James, L.A. and Ashe, D.K. (1990). The meaning of organizations: The role of cognition and values. In B. Schneider (ed.), *Organizational Climate and Culture* (pp. 40–129). San Francisco: Jossey-Bass.

James, L.R. and Jones, A.P. (1980). Perceived job characteristics and job satisfaction: An examination of reciprocal causation. *Personnel Psychology, 33*, 97–135.

James, L.R. and McIntyre, M.D. (1996). Perceptions of organizational climate. In Kevin R. Murphy (ed.), *Individual Differences and Behaviour in Organizations*. San Francisco: Jossey-Bass.

James, L.R. and Tetrick, L.E. (1986). Confirmatory analytic tests of three causal models relating job perceptions to job satisfaction. *Journal of Applied Psychology, 71*, 77–82.

Kahneman, D. (2011). *Thinking Fast and Slow*. New York: Farrar, Straus and Giroux.

Kanter, R.M. (1983). *The Change Masters: Corporate Entrepreneurs at Work*. London: Allen and Unwin.

Kotter, J. (1995). Leading change: Why transformation efforts fail. *Harvard Business Review, 73*, 59–67.

Lawler, E.E., Hall, D.T. and Oldham, G.R. (1974). Organizational climate: Relationship to organizational structure, process and performance. *Organizational Behaviour and Performance, 11,* 139–155.

Lewin, K. (1997). *Resolving Social Conflicts; and Field Theory in Social Science.* New York: Harper and Row. (Reprinted from *Field theory in social science,* 1951)

Martin, J. (1992). *Cultures in Organizations: Three Perspectives.* Oxford University Press, London.

Mathieu, J.E., Hoffman, D.A. and Farr, J.L. (1993). Job perception-job satisfaction relations: An empirical comparison of three competing theories. *Organizational Behaviour and Human Decision Processes, 56,* 370 387.

McDonald, P. (1991). The Los Angeles Olympic Organizing Committee: Developing organizational culture in the short run. In P.J. Frost, L. Moore, M. Louis, C. Lundberg and J. Martin (eds.), *Reframing Organizational Culture* (pp. 26–38). Beverly Hills, CA: Sage Publications.

McGregor, D. (1960). *The Human Side of Enterprise.* New York: McGraw-Hill.

Meyerson, D. (1991). Normal ambiguity? A glimpse of an occupational culture. In P.J. Frost, L. Moore, M. Louis, C. Lundberg and J. Martin (eds.), *Reframing Organizational Culture* (pp. 131–144). Beverly Hills, CA: Sage Publications.

Miller, E. (1967). *Systems of organization.* London: Tavistock.

Murphy, L.R., Gershon, R.M. and DeJoy, D. (1996). Stress and occupational exposure to HIV/AIDS. In C.L. Cooper (ed.), *Handbook of Stress, Medicine and Health.* Boca Raton, FFL: CRC Press.

Nadler, D.A. and Tushman, M. (1997). *Competing by design: The power of organizational architecture.* Oxford: Oxford University Press.

Patterson, M.G., Warr, P.B. and West, M.A. (2004). Organizational climate and company performance: The role of employee affect and employee level. *Journal of Occupational and Organizational Psychology, 77,* 193–216.

Patterson, M.G., West, M.A., Shackleton, V.J., Dawson, J.F., Lawthom, R., Maitlis, S. and Robinson, D.L. (2005). Validating the organizational climate measure: Links to managerial practices, productivity and innovation. *Journal of Organizational Behaviour, 26,* 379–408.

Patterson, M., West, M.A. and Wall, T.D. (2004). Integrated manufacturing, empowerment, and company performance. *Journal of Organizational Behaviour, 25,* 641–665.

Pritchard, R.D. and Karasick, B.W. (1973). The effects of organizational climate on managerial job performance and satisfaction. *Organizational Behaviour and Human Performance, 9,* 126–146.

Quinn, R.E. (1988). *Beyond rational management: Mastering the paradoxes and competing demands of high performance.* San Francisco, CA: Jossey-Bass.

Quinn, R.E. and Rohrbaugh, J. (1981). A Competing Values approach to organizational effectiveness. *Public Productivity Review, 5,* 122–140.

Rentsch, J. (1990). Climate and culture: Interaction and qualitative differences in organizational meanings. *Journal of Applied Psychology, 75,* 668–681.

Rousseau, D.M. (1988). The construction of climate in organizational research. In C.L. Cooper and I.T. Robertson (eds.), *International review of industrial and organizational psychology* (Vol.3) (pp. 139–159). Chichester: John Wiley and Sons.

Salvaggio, A.N., Schneider, B., Nishii, L.H., Mayer, D.M., Ramesh, A. and Lyon, J.S. (2007). Manager personality, manager service quality orientation and service climate: Test of a model. *Journal of Applied Psychology, 92,* 1741–1750.

Schein, E. (1992). *Organizational Culture and Leadership.* San Francisco: Jossey-Bass.

Schneider, B. (1980). The service organization: Climate is crucial. *Organizational Dynamics, 9,* 52–65.

Schneider, B. (1990). The climate for service: An application of the climate construct. In B. Schneider (ed.), *Organizational climate and culture* (pp. 383–412). San Francisco: Jossey-Bass.

Schneider, B., Ehrhart, M.G. and Macey, W.H. (2013). Organizational climate and culture. *Annual Reviews of Psychology, 64,* 361–388.

Schneider, B., Parkington, J.J. and Buxton, V.M. (1980). Employee and customer perceptions of service in banks. *Administrative Science Quarterly, 25,* 252–267.

Schneider, B., White, S.S. and Paul, M.C. (1998). Linking service climate and customer perceptions of service quality: Tests of a causal model. *Journal of Applied Psychology, 83,* 150–163.

Schneider, S., Bowen, D.E., Erhart, M.G. and Holcombe, K.M. (2000). The climate for service: evolution of a construct. In N. M. Ashkanasy, C.P.M. Wilderom and M.F. Peterson (eds). *Handbook of Organizational Culture and Climate.* London: Sage Publications, 21–36.

Schneider et al. (2009). Organizational Service Climate Drivers of the American Customer Satisfaction Index (ACSI) and Financial and Market Performance Benjamin Schneider1, William H. Macey2, Wayne C. Lee3 and Scott A. Young4. Journal of Service Research August 2009 vol. 12 no. 13–14.

Senge, P. (1990). *The Fifth Discipline*. London: Century Business.

Shipper, F. and White, C.S. (1983). Linking organizational effectiveness and environmental change. *Long Range Planning, 16(3)*, 99–106.

Shipton, H, Dawson, J., West, M.A. and Patterson, M. (2002). Learning in manufacturing organizations: What factors predict effectiveness? *Human Resource Development International, 5(1)*, 55–72.

Van der Krogt, F. (1998). Learning network theory: The tension between learning systems and work systems in organizations. Human Resource Quarterly, *Summer*.

Van Maanen, J. (1991). The smile factory: Work at Disneyland. In P.J. Frost, L. Moore, M. Louis, C. Lundberg and J. Martin (eds.), *Reframing Organizational Culture* (pp. 58–76). Beverly Hills, CA: Sage Publications.

Weick, K.E. and Quinn, R.E. (1999). Organizational change and development. *Annual Review of Psychology, 50*, 361–388.

West, M.A. and Anderson, N. (1996). Innovation in top management teams. *Journal of Applied Psychology, 81*, 680–693.

West, M.A. and Wallace, M. (1991). Innovation in health-care teams. *European Journal of Social Psychology, 21*, 303–15.

Wiley, J.W. and Brooks, S.M. (2000). The high-performance organizational climate: How workers describe top-performing units. In N.M. Ashkanasy, C.P.M. Wilderom and M.F. Peterson (eds.), *Handbook of Organizational Culture and Climate* (pp.177–192). Thousand Oaks, CA: Sage.

Zammuto, R.F. and O'Connor, E.J. (1992). Gaining advanced manufacturing technologies' benefits: The roles of organizational design and culture. *Academy of Management Review, 17*, 701–729.

CASE STUDIES FOR PART THREE: ORGANIZATIONS

CASE STUDY 3.1

Leadership Development at Petronas

PETRONAS is the national oil company of Malaysia. Incorporated in 1974, the organization was established in order to commercialise the huge natural oil resource of Malaysia for the benefit of the nation. It is a multinational oil and gas business in the fullest sense, now ranked in the FORTUNE Global 500 largest corporations. On their website, PETRONAS give a clear sense of their vision, mission and values (Exhibit 3.2.1).

The oil and gas sector, and energy sector more broadly, are amongst the most scrutinized in the world. Concern about the use of natural carbon resources to meet global energy needs, and their impact on the world's climate present important economic and operating challenges to oil and gas organizations, and more specifically to their leaders.

PETRONAS clearly identified in the early years of their business, the importance of leadership in achieving their strategic mission. In 1979, an internal training function was established to focus on the development of leaders at the company. That training group grew to become the PETRONAS Leadership Centre (PLC). PLC is now a major provider of leadership development in the oil and gas sector more broadly in Malaysia, and beyond. Their objectives are to unleash the potential of programme registrants so that they are able to develop, grow, and lead effectively in their teams.

Programme developers at PLC reflect the dynamic challenges that leaders face at different stages of their careers in a variety of programmes. There are development tracks for new or early career leaders, people making the step to general management, and to senior management.

One of their "signature programmes" is the Leadership Excellence at PETRONAS (LEAP) programme. The LEAP programme is a 10-day course, spread across five modules that, over a 3-month period, aim to build the leadership competencies and capabilities of trainees. The programme focused on development to General Management level comprises modules on:

- Introduction to Leadership at General Management level
- Leading Self
- Leading Others

The programme is augmented by applied learning modules in which trainees participate in coached applied practice in their teams, to transfer and put their new skills to work. At the end of

Vision Statement

To be a Leading Oil and Gas Multinational of Choice

Mission Statement

- We are a business entity
- Petroleum is our core business
- Our primary responsibility is to develop and add value to this national resource
- Our objective is to contribute to the well-being of the people and the nation

Shared Values

Our values are embedded in our culture as the backbone of our business conduct, reflecting our sense of duty and responsibility in upholding our commitment towards contributing to the well-being of peoples and nations wherever we operate.

Loyalty: Loyal to nation and corporation

Integrity: Honest and upright

Professionalism: Committed, innovative and proactive and always striving for excellence

Cohesiveness: United in purpose and fellowship

Exhibit 3.2.1   PETRONAS Vision, Mission, and Shared Values

the programme, a reflective performance review module, enables the trainees to reflect on their progress and identify their next learning challenges (see Exhibit 3.2.2).

Leadership development clearly remains a central concern and interest at PETRONAS as it continues to grow, and work towards realizing its strategic vision and mission.

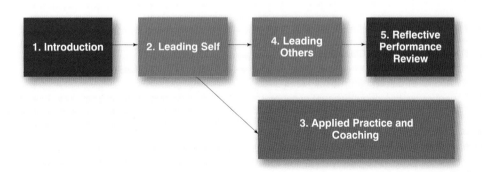

Exhibit 3.2.2   Programme Structure of the PLC Leadership Excellence at PETRONAS programme.

Further Reading

http://www.petronas.com.my/
http://www.petronasleadershipcentre.com.my

Questions

1 What will be the challenges of new leaders at PETRONAS, given the economic, social and environmental context that the oil and gas sector operates in currently?

2 How could research and theory on leadership and other areas of Work and Organizational Psychology be applied in the LEAP programme?

3 What will be the success factors in ensuring that the LEAP programme enables leaders to contribute effectively to the PETRONAS Vision, Mission, and Shared Values?

4 How could research on teams and team effectiveness help leaders undertaking the LEAP programme to manage their teams?

5 Do you have any ideas that could enhance leadership development at PETRONAS further? How and in what ways would these ideas contribute?

CASE STUDY 3.2

European Companies and Their Organizational Structures and Strategies

This case is about the organizational structures and strategies of some European companies.

Organizational structures

An organizational structure is a mostly hierarchical concept of subordination of entities that collaborate and contribute to serve one common aim. There are various types of organizational structures, some of which include:

Functional structure: a company organized with a functional structure groups people together into functional departments such as purchasing, accounts, production, sales, marketing. These departments would normally have functional heads that may be called managers or directors depending on whether the function is represented at board level.

Divisional structure refers to a hierarchical organization wherein each division (focusing on specific products or specific markets) is responsible for all or most of its functional activities.

Geographical structure refers to an organizational design that focuses on the geographic location of operations. Geographical structures include units that may be responsible for both functional and divisional operations within a geographic region.

In recent times, most companies adopt mixed structures depending on the size of the company and the company strategy. Examples of such companies include:

Bayer AG of Germany

Bayer AG is one of the largest and oldest chemical and health-care products companies in the world. Because of massive sales gains and increased activity overseas in the early 1980s, Bayer announced a re-organization in 1984. Bayer had been successful with a conventional organizational structure that was departmentalized by function. However, in response to new conditions the company wanted to create a structure that would allow it to achieve three primary goals: (1) shift management control from the then West German parent company to its foreign divisions and subsidiaries; (2) restructure its business divisions to more clearly define their duties; and (3) flatten the organization, or empower lower level managers to assume more responsibility, so that top executives would have more time to plan strategy.

Bayer selected a relatively diverse matrix management format to pursue its goals. It delineated all of its business activities into six groups under an umbrella company called Bayer World. Within each of the six groups were several subgroups made up of product categories such as dyestuffs, fibres or chemicals. Likewise, each of its administrative and service functions were regrouped under Bayer World into one of several functions, such as human resources, marketing, plant administration or finance. Furthermore, top managers who had formally headed functional groups were given authority over separate geographic regions, which, like the product groups, were supported by and entwined with the functional groups. The net effect of the reorganization was that the original nine functional departments were broken down into 19 multidisciplinary, interconnected business groups. After only one year of operation, Bayer management lauded the new matrix structure as a resounding success. Not only did matrix management allow the company to move towards its primary goals, but it had the added benefits of increasing its responsiveness to change and emerging opportunities, and of helping Bayer to streamline plant administration and service division activities.

DuPont of France

Founded in 1802 in France, DuPont puts science to work by creating sustainable solutions essential to a better, safer, healthier life for people everywhere. Operating in more than 70 countries, DuPont offers a wide range of innovative products and services for markets, including agriculture, nutrition, electronics, communications, safety and protection, home and construction, transportation and apparel.

From 1919 to 1921 DuPont operated a 'functional structure'. This is where a 'President' was responsible for departments with functions of sales, purchasing, treasury, development, production and engineering.

However, as a result of product diversification (strategy) and company expansion, DuPont had to decentralize into separate divisions for each product, hence adopting a product divisional structure. This is where a chairman and CEO were responsible for divisions based on products, e.g. speciality fibres, performance coatings, agriculture and nutrition, polyester, pigments and chemicals etc. DuPont was the first company in the world to hit upon the structural solution to the problem of diversity.

ABB of Switzerland

ABB is a leader in power and automation technologies that enable utility and industry customers to improve performance while lowering environmental impact. The ABB Group of companies operates in around 100 countries and employs about 120 000 people. ABB was formed in 1988 from the merger of the Swedish ASEA group and the Brown Boveri company of Switzerland. The then CEO, Percy Barnevik, imposed a matrix structure on the company comprising two key dimensions – business segments and geography segments. By the late 1990s, ABB was experiencing considerable frustration with its structure. When a new chief executive took over from Barnevik, one of his first actions was to abolish the regions and restructure the business segments into seven more focused product divisions, apparently taking the company back to a product divisional structure, however, within the structural framework of a network multidivisional. This multidivisional structure comprised various geographical divisions, each operating individual product divisions with regional functional divisions. This type of structure separates operational responsibility for the individual diversified businesses from strategic responsibly from the make-up and performance of the overall corporate portfolio.

Questions

Consult the websites of the companies concerned to help you deepen your analysis.

1 Compare the choices made by these companies in structuring their activities. What are likely to be the consequences for, and strengths and weaknesses of the organizations?

2 Which approach, given the nature of each of the businesses, is likely to be most successful?

Organizational strategies

Unilever of Netherlands (*Unilever's diversification strategy – 'Path to Growth' strategy*)

Unilever is one of the largest packaged consumer goods companies specializing in hundreds of different brands. Unilever is based in Holland and the UK and is jointly owned by Unilever N.V and Unilever. Miles and Snow stated that there are four types of organizational strategies pursued by companies; Defenders, Prospectors, Analyzers and Reactors. Unilever is a company that uses the 'Prospectors' organization type. Prospectors are organizations which almost continually search for market opportunities, and they regularly experiment with potential responses to emerging environmental trends.

Unilever was founded on soap and margarine – both products essentially sharing the same raw materials – with diversification into other business areas starting in the mid-fifties. In the mid-1950s, rapid growth in the Western world resulted in increased competition and lower margins in the company's traditional categories. Unilever's strategy was an active diversification programme through acquisition. The vigour with which this was pursued, while successfully introducing the company into valuable new categories, also brought in a lot of peripheral activities.

Unilever's 13 core business sectors are: ice cream, tea-based beverages, culinary products, hair care, skin care and deodorants (all with superior growth potential); spreads, oral care, laundry care and household care (steady growth); and frozen foods, fragrances and professional cleaning (selective growth).

More recently, Unilever launched its 'Path to Growth Strategy' in 1999, in order to increase competitive advantage and revive the company. A major strength of the company's global environment is the geographic diversification of its major product markets. In 2003, Unilever had sales and marketing efforts in 88 different countries. The key is that it gave decision-making power to its managers in different countries so that they could tailor their products to the market's specific preferences and consumers' local tastes.

Nestlé of Switzerland (*market/product development strategy and horizontal integration strategy*)

Nestlé with headquarters in Vevey, Switzerland, was founded in 1866 by Henri Nestlé and is today the world's leading nutrition, health and wellness company. Sales for 2008 were CHF 109.9bn, with a net profit of CHF 18.0bn. They employ around 283 000 people and have factories or operations in almost every country in the world. Nestlé adopts a variety of strategies depending on geographical location.

The company's strategy is guided by several fundamental principles. Nestlé's existing products grow through innovation and renovation, while maintaining a balance in geographic activities and product lines. Long-term potential is never sacrificed for short-term performance. The company's priority is to bring the best and most relevant products to people, wherever they are, whatever their needs, throughout their lives.

Another strategy that has been successful for Nestlé involves striking strategic partnerships with other large companies. In the early 1990s, Nestlé entered into an alliance with Coca-Cola in ready-to-drink teas and coffees in order to benefit from Coca-Cola's worldwide bottling system and expertise in prepared beverages.

In Asia, Nestlé's strategy has been to acquire local companies in order to form a group of autonomous regional managers who know more about the culture of the local markets than Americans or Europeans. Nestlé's strong cash flow and comfortable debt-equity ratio leave it with ample muscle for takeovers. Recently, Nestlé acquired Indofood, Indonesia's largest noodle producer. Their focus will be primarily on expanding sales in the Indonesian market, and in time will look to export Indonesian food products to other countries.

StatoilHydro of Norway (*diversification strategy*)

StatoilHydro is an integrated, technology-based international energy company primarily focused on upstream oil and gas operations. Headquartered in Norway, it has more than 30 years' experience from the Norwegian Continental Shelf, pioneering complex offshore projects under the toughest conditions. The culture is founded on strong values and a high ethical standard.

They aim to deliver long-term growth and continue to develop technologies and manage projects that will meet the world's energy and climate challenges in a sustainable way. StatoilHydro is listed on NYSE and Oslo Stock Exchange.

Following 30 years of growth that gave Norway's national oil company a solid upstream portfolio, Statoil ASA (NYSE: STO) is now pursuing a diversification (growth) strategy that will take it beyond crude oil production on the Norwegian Continental Shelf. This type of diversification strategy is called horizontal diversification, where the company acquires other companies in line with its growth strategy. For example, in 2005, Statoil acquired EnCana's entire Deepwater US Gulf of Mexico portfolio

Questions

Consult the websites of the companies concerned to help you deepen your analysis.

1 Compare the choices made by these companies in their strategies. What are likely to be the consequences for the organizations in terms of success, culture and management processes?

2 What challenges are they most likely to face and how might the knowledge of Work and Organizational Psychology be of value as they go forward?

Company websites:

Bayer AG of Germany – **http://www.bayer.com/en/homepage.aspx**
DuPont of France – **http://www2.dupont.com/DuPont_Home/en_US/index.html**
ABB of Switzerland – **http://www.abb.com/**
Unilever of Netherlands – **http://www.unilever.com/**
Nestlé of Switzerland – **http://www.nestle.com/**
Statoil of Norway – **http://www.statoil.com/en/Pages/default.aspx**

CHAPTER 15

THE PSYCHOLOGY OF WORK AND ORGANIZATIONS

Take out the list of questions that you wrote down at the very start of the book and look over each one. What did you learn about your questions? Did you get answers to them? Do you think you asked the right questions? Are there any you didn't get answers to? Remember, if there are unanswered questions on your list, email them to us. We will be genuinely interested to know about areas of people management in organizations as yet unaddressed by Work and Organizational Psychology.

If our proposition was correct though, and you did in fact get answers to most, if not all of your questions, then we would like to pose two of our own questions:

1 Why is Work and Organizational Psychology not a core topic on all Bachelor programmes in business and management, and in psychology?

2 Why don't all businesses and organizations have a Work and Organizational Psychologist (or indeed a small team of them) amongst their staff?

If we could answer these questions, then we might understand the single most important barrier that limits the impact of research and theory in Work and Organizational Psychology: the failure to adequately penetrate businesses and organizations and to make the insights of Work and Organizational Psychology invaluable to those working in them.

This is the focus of this final chapter, in which we identify some of the major emergent issues in the three parts of this book, and consider ways in which they could be put to work more effectively in organizations. We also return to the contemporary themes that were highlighted in Chapter 1 and think about how they might feature in the future of Work and Organizational Psychology.

INSIGHTS FROM WORK AND ORGANIZATIONAL PSYCHOLOGY

In the first section of this chapter, we will consider the main insights and implications for organizations that stem from the three parts of this book. Our purpose is to briefly recap on some of the major contributions of Work and Organizational Psychology to business and organizations.

Part One: Understanding the Foundations of Work and Organizational Psychology

In Part One of the book, we examined some of the core foundations of Work and Organizational Psychology, many of which are drawn from theories and research in psychology more generally. The key implications of these chapters come from understanding people and their behaviour at work.

Scientific foundations

A defining feature of Work and Organizational Psychology is its scientific approach to dealing with problems of business, organizations and management. This has been emphasized at various and numerous junctures in the book. One of the defining propositions of a psychological approach to understanding people and their behaviour at work is that principles and techniques from scientific research methods offer the most effective means of building knowledge and understanding. Evidence-based problem solving techniques are employed in both practice and research in Work Psychology, and represent models that can easily be adopted by people working in organizations.

Perhaps the most important principle of the scientific emphasis of Work and Organizational Psychology is that decisions about management in organizations, including those around problem solutions, should be based on sound investigation and evidence. That evidence should be reliable and obtained systematically, not simply based on hearsay and anecdotal accounts. The plain truth is that far too much practice in business is based on opinion, ideology, or very weak evidence and evaluation. Such practices occur because organizations seldom have employees readily at their disposal with the necessary skills and knowledge to kick outlandish claims of 'proof or evidence of effectiveness' into touch. A first key implication for people in organizations is therefore to know when to ask questions about the scientific evidence underpinning practices and interventions, to know what questions to ask, or if nobody in the organization knows, to know where to find someone who does.

The differences that define people, and that matter

Research on individual differences is long-standing in psychology and in Work and Organizational Psychology. Theory and research into intelligence and personality traits have evolved alongside societal trends and attitudes and have waxed and waned in popularity through the course of the past 100 years. Currently, the field of differential psychology is strong and the personality trait paradigm particularly has witnessed a resurgence, backed up by findings from numerous meta-analyses that show that personality traits of the Big Five model of personality predict important life outcomes, including those at work, most significantly job performance. Theory in this area is also rich and constantly developing. Likewise, there is strong evidence for the importance of cognitive ability in job performance and success, and longitudinal cohort studies will no doubt continue to underscore the long-term life advantages of high cognitive ability and certain combinations of personality traits and emotional styles. The major insight for organizations comprises improved understanding for determining why some people perform certain jobs better than others, or more specifically, why different people tend to behave or perform differently in similar situations, or during similar work activities. There are also important implications for development.

The practice of psychometric assessment in organizations has taken on a tradition and agenda of its own in recent years and this is a potential area for concern. The evidence of the validity of individual difference assessment has catalyzed the emergence of a whole host of specialist companies, and a multitude of different assessment tools (tests and diagnostic questionnaires). The quality of these varies considerably, and the extent to which assessments of individual differences have any impact in organizations depends strongly on the quality of the tools that are used. Compounding this problem is the widening gap between research in individual differences and the practice of assessment. There have been precious few innovations in assessment practice in the past quarter century, whereas new findings in personality and ability research are published routinely. For people in organizations, the challenge is to cut through consultant sales spin to ensure that the products used with employees are robust and defensible for personnel decision-making.

Making sense of attitudes and behaviour at work

The complexity of behaviour at work means that making sense of it is challenging. People at work rely too often on implicit ideas about the roots of behaviour, and we know from attribution theory that people are biased towards ascribing dispositional causes to behaviour rather than social or situational ones. The study of behaviour in organizations attempts to address these issues by blending insights from social psychology with those from differential psychology and research and theory on topics such as attitudes, emotions and cognitive processes like perception.

Powerful research findings in this area identify the processes that facilitate, control or modify people's behaviour. Studies of reinforcement, for example, show how behaviour can be managed in organizations, although the notion of manipulation inherent in behaviour modification makes it unpalatable to some. Perhaps the most informative findings from the field are from the study of attitudes at work. To have answered the happy-productive worker question (by showing that people who are satisfied at work, also tend to perform well) is a major step in management research. However, the challenge now is to understand the nature of the relationship – why do satisfied workers tend to be productive, and under what circumstances are they not productive? Alongside these concerns sits research that reveals some of the things that promote satisfaction, engagement and commitment at work, attitudes that are positive for employees as well as organizations.

An idea that has not had the impact it should have done in organizations is also related to attitudes and behaviour: the theory of planned behaviour. This theory has stood up to empirical tests and could help to explain many of the barriers that people in organizations face when attempting to change attitudes and behaviour. It is an example of how social forces (in this case judgement of social norms) influence behaviour at work. There are many other social influences, which among other things, help us to understand how issues of diversity at work might be managed.

Motivating people

Theories and models of motivation at work tell us about how people's effort and behaviour at work is initiated, directed and maintained over time. There are multiple perspectives on motivation and each offers a slightly different insight. Some theories and models of motivation have received strong empirical support and are, moreover, practical with some of the clearest implications for people management practice in organizations.

Goal setting is a good example. Setting people goals that are specific, challenging, attainable, measurable and time-bound is a very reliable way of improving motivation performance, and in virtually all scenarios, works better than telling people to do their best. Research has uncovered some of the mechanisms that facilitate the link between goal setting and performance.

Perceptions of justice and fairness at work are also immensely important for motivation. Work in this area has shown that when people are fairly rewarded for their efforts, and when systems and procedures for recognizing and rewarding performance are fair, they feel better and work harder. An emergent concept in research is interactional justice, or the extent to which people feel that they are treated with respect and dignity, and kept informed about decisions. These will be key areas for research in the future. More widely, the study of motivation through job design has knocked down once and for all the notion that motivation comes solely from within people. Designing jobs so that they are meaningful and give people freedom and responsibility all contribute significantly to commitment, job-involvement, satisfaction and motivation.

Part Two: Practicing Professional Applications of Work and Organizational Psychology

The second part of this book outlined major professional practice areas of Work and Organizational Psychology. These represent the areas in which Work and Organizational Psychologists have had the most significant impact on practice in organizations. If you have encountered a Work Psychologist in the past year, then they are most likely to have been involved in one of these activities. If you are planning to be a Work Psychologist, then these activities represent the staple areas that you are likely to work in. As with Part One, we present some summary thoughts on the major implications for organizations.

Recruiting and selecting

No other area of Work and Organizational Psychology has produced an equivalent volume of research, clarity of findings or impact on practice than recruitment and selection. The major theme in much of the contribution of Work and Organizational Psychology to the practice of recruitment and selection has been the reduction of bias and sources of unreliability in selection assessment. For practitioners, there are critical findings such as the value of psychometric assessment, the importance of structured forms of interviewing and the effective use of work sampling and assessment centre methodology. In very simple terms, the introduction or incremental improvement of systematic techniques of assessment in any organization is one of the most straightforward and dependable ways of improving selection decisions and raising productivity.

One of the reasons for the impact of theory and research on recruitment and selection practice is undoubtedly that psychologists, particularly in the UK and Europe, have disseminated knowledge effectively, training practitioners to use assessment techniques and therefore effectively delegating their implementation to others. This has proven a successful strategy, and the in-roads made into HR processes such as managerial and graduate selection are in no small way down to the fact that HR managers can apply the techniques themselves. There are issues raised by this strategy, for example, once outside the training environment, psychologists release control of the quality management of assessment. There are plenty of horror stories about how techniques are employed by some practitioners, but equally one encounters good practice too. The model is a sound one though, and could prove useful if Work and Organizational Psychology is to make a similar impact in other areas.

Despite successes, some organizations continue to persist in the use of unstructured and unsystematic techniques, and more needs to be done to understand why this is so. One promising line to explore is the notion of fit. Managers and practitioners believe in the value of fit much more than psychologists do, and sometimes make decisions about the suitability of job candidates on that and almost nothing else. By failing to acknowledge and operationalize organization fit adequately in selection practices, there is a very real risk of alienating a proportion of managers and others in organizations. Moreover, there is need to examine recruitment and selection research from an organizational strategic point of view and to understand how different techniques can be deployed in different kinds of organization and for different recruitment needs.

Developing and training

The past decade or so has witnessed considerable advances in the training and learning literature in Work and Organizational Psychology. The traditional functions captured by the training cycle (training needs assessment, training design and training evaluation) have been elaborated and explored, offering a wealth of guidance to practitioners about how to most effectively implement learning and training activities in their organizations. The major implications for practice are again concerned with the structure of approach and evidence base used for making decisions about whether to invest in learning and, once interventions have been made, the extent to which they have produced the desired results.

Outside of this traditional focus, some of the most exciting developments have come from the literature on individual differences in learning processes and preferences. These include an emergent body of research on goal orientation and the differences between performance and learning goal orientation. There is plenty of work to do in this area, including the clear establishment of the role of goal orientation on performance and the ways in which goal orientation can be developed or modified.

The other major emergent insight into employee learning is from work on active learning. The experience of many people in organizations is that they often shape their own learning and development, selecting self-directed or directed learning activities themselves. The process of doing so implies a self-appraisal of development needs and this falls outside of traditional procedures for training needs analysis. There is a strong probability that more and more organizations will go down this route, delegating responsibility for development decisions to people themselves, particularly those in complex, technical or autonomous jobs. More, therefore, needs to be known about how people self-appraise, and the extent to which active learning produces effective outcomes.

Managing performance

At the start of Chapter 8, we discussed the observation that performance measurement and management is often a weak point in HR strategy in organizations. Some companies use ad-hoc or unstructured systems, others employ very elaborate mechanisms for capturing performance data that managers find difficult and laborious to apply. Some do get the process right though, and the insights that come from Work and Organizational Psychology can help practitioners to improve performance management systems in two areas: performance measurement and performance improvement. In the field of performance measurement, academics have been concerned with modelling the performance domain. Work conducted in this area is highly technical, so much so, that very recent articles are beyond most psychologists, let alone most people working in organizations. This is one area where the drive for ever more elaborate statistical models has seriously limited the impact of the work in practice. It is as though researchers in the field have willingly ignored the real concerns of people working in organizations. Without clarity of guidance, managers are left to develop their own approaches, so it is little wonder that performance measures fall short on occasions.

Practically minded researchers and psychologists have, among other things, considered the role of competencies in performance assessment. Competencies have received a mixed response in academic research, although there are important recent advances, but have certainly made a big impact in organizations because of their practical utility. Competencies are easy to understand, and to apply. The challenge for Work and Organizational Psychology is now to work further to understand whether competencies work, and how they work most effectively.

In the field of performance improvement, important insights for managers and practitioners are around the implementation of goal setting interventions and provision of feedback. If delivered in the right ways, goal setting and feedback have proved themselves to be robust processes for facilitating performance improvement. Research in Work and Organizational Psychology has resulted in models explaining the pathways from goal setting and feedback to performance improvement, and the factors that influence these pathways.

Guiding and managing careers

The stories of our working lives are played out as careers, and vocational psychology examines the development of those stories across the lifespan, the decisions that people make within them and the factors that determine outcomes and endings. New research looking at the impact of our work and our careers on our personality and identity underline the centrality of work to people's lives and development.

The staple areas for the study of careers have traditionally been career development and career choice. Theories and models of career development aimed to map out the various stages of people's careers and to determine common experiences of individuals as working life progressed. The theories relied on stable, predictable work expectations and environments, but as society has changed, so these have changed too. Theories of development have been superseded by more flexible models and perspectives, including concepts such as boundaryless careers and employability, reflecting the changing realities of organizations, and the internationalization of the working world. From a developmental perspective, there is also increasing interest on the place of work in people's lives more generally, for example how work influences development of personality across the lifespan. There are lessons for managers and practitioners concerning the expectations of employees about their relationships with organizations, and about their development and progression.

One of the most useful models to have emerged from Work and Organizational Psychology is Holland's RIASEC model of career preferences and environments. There is still work to be done on establishing whether all of the predictions of Holland's theory are supported, but, nevertheless, the theory provides an elegant framework for people to begin exploring the kinds of careers that match their individual interests. Career counsellors are typically aware of the model and use it where appropriate, but what about practitioners in organizations who coach staff, providing informal career guidance? The benefits of Holland's model can still be realized in these situations. A simple implication is the importance of helping people to find work activities and roles that match their individual differences. More specifically, assessments of RIASEC interests are simple to use and understand, and could be built into development discussions.

Creating healthy workplaces

We are discovering a great deal about the importance positive emotions and relationships play at work and the value for business and employees of creating climates with these characteristics. We also know a great deal about how to prevent work-related illnesses and injuries as a result of research. A safety climate is key and there are well understood steps for creating such a climate. In particular, it requires managerial commitment and control. Given how well-developed our knowledge is in this area, there is little excuse for organizations to have poor records of health and safety at work.

Similarly, in relation to stress and strain at work, research has advanced understanding dramatically. We know the causes, processes and consequences of stress at work, from psychological through to biochemical processes. And we know that sustained stress causes heart disease, gastrointestinal disorders, increases in stress hormones and, ultimately, death. Unfortunately too much effort in organizations is put into managing the symptoms of or responses to stress – encouraging employees to cut down their drinking or to take up relaxation classes. Instead, organizations should be focusing on what are now the clearly identified causes of stress, such as role factors, workload, work – life balance, low control, work pace and emotional labour.

Recent work has contrasted burnout with engagement – a positive work-related state of fulfilment characterized by dedication, vigour and absorption. Organizations should be encouraged to adopt enlightened approaches to management which focus on increasing levels of engagement, control and individual growth and development by investing in rather than neglecting, or worse, exploiting those who work within organizations. The level of knowledge about stress and health at work is now so well developed that an agenda of creating healthy workplaces should dominate this area of work with a sustained effort at designing and evaluating interventions designed to create outstanding work environments for staff.

Part Three: Creating Effective Organizations

In one sense, Part Three of the book represents a culmination of the understanding communicated in the first two parts, with the added perspective that comes from considering whole organizations. We covered a number of key topics that provide the real world context for most of the topics covered in the book.

Building organizations and determining direction

We have bewailed the fact that the evidence from Work and Organizational Psychology is not sufficiently influential in the way organizations are developed and led. One reason is because researchers in the field have paid insufficient attention to organizational structure and strategy. Leaders and managers in organizations are obsessed with both, and if experts do not understand strategy and structure development their expertise will be doubted. It is important that those researching or practicing in this area understand the choices available to leaders in how they structure their organizations. It is also important that we understand that structure should be related both to the environment of the organization and to its strategy. Organizational structures are, in one sense, created to reduce uncertainty – marketing departments exist to gather information on customer preferences. And strategies also shape structure. If we want to encourage innovation in a company operating in a highly competitive market, then hierarchy is a barrier.

We need to understand how strategy is developed in organizations and encourage the use of evidence from research in Work and Organizational Psychology in that development process. Strategy is an emergent process of making sense of complexity and ambiguity, and this sense-making is an unfolding process. The addition of evidence-based approaches from the field will significantly improve the strategy development process. Strategy development should not be a value-free process. The strategies of some of the largest financial corporations worldwide have brought the world economy to the brink of collapse in recent years and all have a responsibility to remind leaders that values should be core rather than peripheral to the strategy development process. Strategy is ultimately about people.

Leading organizations

There is more discussion, debate, misunderstanding and simplistic thinking about leadership in organizations than any other topic in Work and Organizational Psychology. That is because leadership is archetypal in human affairs and there is a strong need in society to find, appraise and follow leaders. There is also a hard-wired tendency to test the trustworthiness of leaders, particularly their integrity to determine if investing our trust, energies and resources in them is worthwhile. Many people aspire to become leaders, some with a need to use leadership for their own ends and others with a strong desire to do good for others. This explains the dominance of books on leadership in railway station and airport bookshops.

What research and theorizing has revealed, however, is that understanding leadership and leadership effectiveness is challenging since it is so complex and we should be especially wary of the snake oil merchants who offer quick and simple prescriptions for effective leadership. So much is written about leadership and the challenge for the student is to separate out what is robust and useful from what is conjecture or devoid of applicable value. We know that personality is an important predictor of effective leadership – particularly elements of the Big Five. And we know that high energy level; stress tolerance; self-confidence; emotional maturity; and particularly personal integrity are key to leadership effectiveness. People will follow those they trust. Humility too is emerging as a hitherto neglected characteristic of effective leadership. Positivity and interpersonal skills are also important. Some of these qualities can be learned and some are influenced genetically. All of us are called upon at times to be leaders and having a vision of the difference we want to make; being positive, confident, optimistic; building positive relationships; working across boundaries; taking time to reflect on strategy and processes; having the courage to make the right decision and acting in a kind way, are all skills that can be learned. Critically, so is acting with integrity, humility and honesty.

We have seen the widespread discrimination against more than half of the world's population in terms of the conferment of leadership positions both in business and politics. It is extraordinary how we waste the leadership potential of so many when good leadership is such a scarce commodity. Those seeking to create more effective organizations and just societies should vigorously focus on this issue to ensure we advance human society by drawing on the resources offered by both men and women. Much more research is needed to determine the circumstances that enable this aspiration most effectively.

Much more research is also needed to determine which interventions are most effective in developing leaders. We saw that there is little evidence to support any of the training and development methods for leaders in organizations, yet vast, truly vast, sums are spent annually throughout the world on interventions that either make no difference or whose efficacy has yet to be demonstrated. This is an important and challenging agenda for the future in leadership research.

Working together in teams

There has been a big increase in the use of teams in modern organization, although this is probably the unit of production that humans have developed most in our evolutionary history. As with other areas at work, interest has spawned quick-fix models that evidence suggests are not effective. Team roles theory and team building gimmicks are two examples of this.

We have seen how many organizations incorporate rhetoric about teamwork but the reality is loose groupings of people who happen to work in the same department or physical area. The rhetoric of teamwork creates conditions where errors, dissatisfaction and conflict are more likely to occur when it is not matched by good practice. Good practice means ensuring teams are working on a task suitable for teamwork; that they have a limited number of clear, challenging objectives; that they meet regularly to review performance and how it can be improved; and that team members are clear about their roles in the team. There is a considerable amount of change needed in many or most organizations to ensure these simple guidelines for effective teamwork are in place and therefore plenty of scope for us to make a positive difference.

Teamworking in organizations is also about working effectively with other teams, and this has been neglected by both researchers and practitioners. Ensuring that one of the core objectives of any team is improving how it works with the other teams in the organization to provide products and services, is a simple way we can improve organizational functioning generally. We also need to ensure that organizations that rely on teamwork, have processes, climates and practices that are consistent with a team-based working culture (such as team level appraisals).

The very stuff of organizations – cultures, climates and changes

Studying organizations that we encounter every day is fascinating and fun. Rather than going in and out of them asleep we can be alert to their characteristics, foibles and unique qualities. This involves truly becoming a student of organizations. Through maintaining awareness of organizational culture we can become experts at analyzing the nature of organizations, especially when we use the models described in the literature. Building such a capacity has an important value for society more generally because the more we understand the culture of organizations, the more we can discern those that are enacting for real the principles of corporate social responsibility, rather than acting the part. Organizations are part of the societies and communities within which they are located and have a responsibility to contribute to rather than detract from those communities, to protect the environment and to treat people equally and with dignity and respect. Work and Organizational Psychology is not and should never be a value-based discipline if we want to make a positive difference in the world. Encouraging cultures of social responsibility and 'outing' cultures of exploitation is part of the legitimate work of change agents in society.

Work and Organizational Psychology should therefore be about improving cultures and climates in organizations. Many people work in organizations where they feel moderately unhappy rather than experiencing a sense of growth, development and flourishing. The discipline has amassed enough evidence of how to create the conditions for climates and cultures for promoting the well-being and development of employees. Organizations now need to focus on using models of change to bring this about. That will be difficult since we have too little evidence of what change interventions are most effective. This is therefore an agenda for future research and practice: determining which change interventions are most effective in creating climates and cultures within which employees and the organization thrive and flourish.

THE POTENTIAL CONTRIBUTIONS OF WORK AND ORGANIZATIONAL PSYCHOLOGISTS

The preceding discussion of the main insights from Work and Organizational Psychology highlights some important practical contributions that Work and Organizational Psychologists could potentially make in organizations:

1 Evaluate practice and proposed problems solutions to determine the evidence base to support their efficacy.

2 Evaluate and manage the use of assessment tools to help make decisions based on individual differences.

3 Use theories of organizational behaviour to facilitate engagement and change in organizations, and to foster positive attitudes and emotions, and interpersonal and intergroup relationships among diverse groups at work.

4 Devise evidence-based strategies for improving motivation by, among other things, improving goal setting and reward systems, creating fairness and equity and designing jobs.

5 Improve recruitment and selection systems by enhancing procedures to ensure more people with the potential to perform are selected, and are done so fairly and ethically.

6 Develop systems for appraisal and analysis of learning needs, learning and development intervention, and evaluation, including calculation of return on investment of learning and development.

7 Evaluate and improve performance assessment systems and develop guidance on procedures and programmes for performance improvement.

8 Develop strategies for employee career development, breaking down career barriers, and helping employees to find activities or roles that appeal to their individual difference and interests.

9 Design organizations, jobs and work in ways that minimize stress, illness and injury and maximize engagement and positive relationships.

10 Integrate evidence-based knowledge from Work and Organizational Psychology into the strategy development process in organizations to ensure it plays a central role.

11 Promote leadership based on integrity, transformational and reward contingent styles and discourage leadership characterized by favouritism, laissez-faire and management by exception. Design evidence-based training programmes that reinforce positive styles of leadership.

12 Ensure organizations are populated by real teams with clear objectives, clear team member roles, regular reviewing of performance and good inter-team working.

13 Create cultures and climates that are positive, supportive, task-focused, support the growth and development of employees, and that are characterized by strong corporate social responsibility, care of the environment and contributions to the community.

We believe that there are two ways to view these contributions. First, they represent core areas of expertise for Work and Organizational Psychologists. Placing a psychologist in an HR team would instantly provide all of these contributions. Second, they represent areas of study in Work Psychology, and with the right guidance, people without specialist knowledge of psychology could study specific areas in depth to grasp the theoretical foundations and practical implications. In short, managers and other practitioners could develop sufficient knowledge and skills in specific areas to apply the insights of Work and Organizational Psychology. This brings us to the question of why neither of these things happens particularly often, and we feel that it is because of three barriers that exist in the field. We commented on two of these barriers in the first edition of this book, and feel that they are equally relevant now in the second edition. However, we also now identify a third barrier that is equally important.

Barrier One: the Scientist–Practitioner Divide

Much has been written about the scientist–practitioner divide in Work and Organizational Psychology. We discussed it in detail in Chapter 2. The essence of the division is that practitioners frequently feel that the implications of research for practice are unclear or are not stated in research articles. Worse, the concerns of academic researchers often do not tally with the concerns of people working in organizations. Some academics get frustrated at the unwillingness of practitioners to see their perspective, and point out that one of the responsibilities of science is to create new knowledge that is not driven by the needs of one interest group or organization. A parsimonious solution is the notion of pragmatic science; a preference for research that is scientifically sound, but that addresses real problems faced by people in organizations, presenting the results and implications in ways that they understand.

More scientific research needs to be pragmatic science, but this requires a change in the way that research is evaluated in the field. One of the criticisms implicit in the practitioner perspective is that scientists intentionally ignore practical implications and exercise a form of intellectual arrogance. The truth is that the way that articles are published in the field still exerts a bias towards research that is technically and theoretically advanced rather than that which is practical. We definitely do not advocate poor science, but we would rather that applied journals view the practical implications of research with as much importance. There is some evidence that perspectives on this problem are changing, but more needs to be done by those in powerful positions in the field, namely funding bodies, journal editors and editorial board members who determine the way that knowledge is established in the field. Scientists themselves could ask stretching questions about their work, including: How does my research help people to be more effective or satisfied at work, and how does it enhance the way we understand people at work, or change for the better the way people do things in organizations?

Barrier Two: Work Psychology and Business

The scientist–practitioner divide is influential in limiting the impact of some areas of research, but it is an inwardly focused debate. If you are a Work Psychologist, or training to be a Work Psychologist, then the previous two paragraphs will have probably interested you. If you are in neither of these groups, then you probably care nothing for the internal wrangling of Work and Organizational Psychologists. And there, in part, lies the second, silent barrier that limits the impact of Work and Organizational Psychology. Psychologists have spent so long convincing themselves that the problem of impact is with each other, that they have missed the more important gap, and that is the one between Work Psychology and businesses. It is a systemic problem in the field, propagated by the ways that the insights of Work and Organizational Psychology are shared, disseminated and applied.

The feature of the field that gives rise to the barrier between Work Psychology and business is exclusivity. Work and Organizational Psychologists train as specialists, and to be qualified, you typically need to go through university education for at least four years, with further training needed depending on where you practice. Much education is conducted in Schools of Psychology, not Business Schools, and the values and perspectives in modern psychology schools are very different from the concerns of people in business. Compounding the problem is that many people move from basic high-school education (ages 11–18) through to university education and a specialism in Work Psychology, without working in anything more than part-time employment. The exclusivity of the field lies in the facts that psychologists do not allow non-specialists to gain the knowledge of the field, and frequently fail to encourage students to learn and experience business.

As a consequence, Work and Organizational Psychologists have failed to be open, to share ideas and expertise with those in business, and to allow new ideas in. For example, why have Work and Organizational Psychologists typically seen it as acceptable to ignore issues of strategy, structure and environment? How can we hope to be credible if we ignore these huge management issues? To see the benefits of opening up practice, one need look no further than recruitment and selection. The successes and impact of recruitment and selection theory and practice have undoubtedly come from the systems by which managers, HR professionals and other practitioners have been able to get access to not only the knowledge of selection from Work and Organizational Psychology, but also the tools and methods. People can be trained to use psychometrics effectively, to interview more systematically, and to observe and rate behaviour more objectively. The result is improvements to selection practice in organizations, and as a knock-on effect, more business and work for psychologists. The next challenge for the field is understanding how the insights from other areas of the field could be disseminated and operationalized in the same way.

Barrier Three: Higher Education

The field of Work and Organizational Psychology, as we have discussed, has insights to offer that are relevant to all people working in organizations. Moreover, a background in psychology, whilst acting as a solid foundation, is not a requisite for understanding many of these insights. Given the accessibility and relevance of the field, it is extraordinary that it is not included more often in the curricula of business schools and in psychology schools. In the UK for example, very few business schools offer a Bachelors module on Work and Organizational Psychology (with some content rather included in modules on Organizational Behaviour or HRM), and we are unaware of any school of psychology that includes a core module on the area, despite the numbers of practicing Occupational Psychologists in the UK.

This is a fundamental barrier to the field having influence in the leaders and managers of tomorrow. A sound understanding of Work and Organizational Psychology would have huge benefits to people leading, managing, and working in organizations. Furthermore of course, those that have learned about the field are more likely to stay engaged and to apply theory and research in their practice, and to work with psychologists on relevant business problems.

Overcoming the Barriers

Of these two barriers, it is the latter two which present the biggest limitations on the impact of Work Psychology. The scientist–practitioner divide could be addressed in the ways highlighted above, but it is an internal matter. The barrier between Work Psychology and business, and the absence of the field from higher education programmes requires more practical intervention, and we feel that there are three things that organizations and Work Psychologists could do to work together to bring knowledge from the field into practice for mutual benefit:

1 Systems for training and education in Work and Organizational Psychology need to do more to make Work Psychologists valuable in organizations. Work and Organizational Psychologists should enter practice with enough practical skills to slot into a business as managers or HR specialists and instantly be able to make a valuable contribution. The knowledge base is available, it just needs to be provided to trainees in an enabling format.

2 People in organizations need only be open to the ideas from Work and Organizational Psychology. We have tried to communicate them in an accessible way in this book, and if you are an HR manager, and you have seen value in these ideas, then consider recruiting a Work Psychologist to your team. There is sometimes confusion about what they could offer beyond an HR graduate, but the list of contributions above, combined with the technical knowledge held by psychologists illustrates the potential benefits. The 'need' is for managers in organizations to look beyond HR, and to see Work and Organizational Psychologists as key complementary workers who can enhance the HR function in important ways. Instead of buying in psychologists as consultants, consider taking them on as staff – the value for money is much better for one benefit.

3 Ideas from Work and Organizational Psychology need to be shared more effectively. That means presenting knowledge from the field widely to business in an accessible, inspiring and effective way. Practitioners in the field are sometimes precious about holding onto specialist knowledge, but real impact comes when people in organizations think differently about problems at work. So whatever field you are working in, and for whatever reason you decided to read this book, use the ideas to think about business, work, organizations and the people in them and apply the ideas in solving work-related challenges and problems. That is exactly the outcome and impact that we hoped for and intended for this book.

4 Psychologists need to work with business schools and psychology schools to ensure that the subject is included on curricula for higher degrees. This means engaging with and communicating with leaders of academic institutions and schools. You can help with this as a reader of this book. If you liked learning about the field, then tell your friends and colleagues, ask them to request it from their academic school. If you are working in or leading such a school, and want to offer it to students, then find a Work and Organizational Psychologist to help (and if you cannot, then email us, we can recommend some).

CONTEMPORARY THEMES AND CHALLENGES

Throughout the book, we have highlighted three important contemporary themes and challenges in organizations and management:

1 Ethics and Corporate Social Responsibility.
2 Globalization and Cross-Cultural Working.
3 Sustainability.

Ideas from Work and Organizational Psychology have implications in these areas, and at various junctures in the book, we have picked out specific points at which areas in the field interact with the three themes. Collectively, they represent potential contemporary emphases for the style and application of Work Psychology in organizations. Here we briefly recap on the main implications.

Ethics and Corporate Social Responsibility

The major issues to emerge around ethical and socially responsible working are concerned with providing a framework and perspective for management practice. One of the key implications of Work and Organizational Psychology for management practice is the focus on not only productivity and effectiveness, but also the well-being and satisfaction of people who work in, or who are served by organizations. In fact, much of the evidence we have reviewed shows that productivity and well-being have the potential to reciprocally enhance each other. This dual focus represents an integration between both economic and social outcomes in business and organizations. The challenge for practitioners is to ensure that both outcomes remain central to the application of psychology at work, since they are symbiotic rather than exclusive.

More practically, work represents an important means of social and societal development. Employment gives rise to social status, and the benefits of work, including pay, enable people to improve their lives, and the lives of their families and children. Employment is an important means of increasing opportunity and raising aspirations. Through closer examination of processes and systems in organizations (such as recruitment and selection, and performance management), barriers to social mobility and social development can be identified, weakened or stripped out completely. With this theme in mind, one emphasis in the application of ideas and techniques from Work and Organizational Psychology is how they can be applied to enhance ethical and socially responsible management practice. Organizations both benefit from and contribute to society. They derive their success from society and they should contribute success to society. Corporate social responsibility (CSR) is not a luxurious afterthought. It should be part of the culture of every organization. Profit maximization alone is a dangerous orientation as so much experience in recent years attests. As practitioners and researchers we should be unashamed of praising and criticizing organizations for their commitment to CSR.

Globalization and Cross-Cultural Working

We have already suggested in this book that there is a strong probability, much stronger than in years previously, that you will spend time working in another culture or working with people from other cultures. The integration of the diverse values and interests of employees in a global environment is a key contemporary challenge for organizations. There are some important areas of research and theory in the field that help practitioners and managers to think about cross-cultural working. Many are based around differences in cultural values. The work of Hofstede on cultural values and the GLOBE project on cross-cultural leadership are good examples, as is research on diversity in teams and in organizations more broadly. The literatures on expatriate workers and the role of cultural adjustment also reveal how research can contribute to a better understanding of success and failure in cross-cultural working.

There are many areas, however, in which the role of culture is not well understood. Theory and research conducted in typically Western cultures is unlikely to apply in exactly the same way to different cultures. In many areas of Work and Organizational Psychology, theory and research is at the point where people have ideas about when, how and why culture might be important, but no clear evidence to support those ideas. Literature and research will emerge though, and over the next 10–15 years, we predict that people will be in a much better position to describe and identify the influences of culture on the major areas of the field.

Sustainability

Of our three themes, it is this one that has, so far, had the least impact in Work and Organizational Psychology. Many of the ideas discussed in this book have clear benefits for the economic health and sustainability of businesses, but little attention has been given to sustainability of other kinds. Environmental sustainability is set to be *the* global challenge of the 21st century. In order to address the challenge, it is critical that all industries, and indeed all people in organizations, ask themselves how they could contribute to working in ways that are more environmentally sustainable. Work and Organizational Psychology can contribute in two specific ways to begin with.

First, areas of practice could be examined, and potential carbon costs of those activities reduced. We provided examples relating to e-learning in Chapter 7, but other good examples of using technology are evident in delivery of psychometric assessment for example. Alongside development in technology should be research that aims to establish that the effectiveness of techniques is maintained when delivered using new technology. Second, ideas and insights from Work and Organizational Psychology have a critical contribution to make as organizations and governments work to change attitudes and perceptions about sustainable working. There is no shortage of practical guidance from social psychology and organizational behaviour about techniques that promote attitudinal and behavioural change. Moreover, research on change in organizations should now be focused on the factors that predict success of companies in achieving new levels of environmental sustainability (such as ISO 14001, the environmental management standard), given the fundamental importance of this area to all our futures.

SUMMARY AND CONCLUSION

Work and Organizational Psychology is the study of people and their behaviour at work, and of the organizations in which people work. Work Psychologists develop psychological theory and apply the rigour and methods of psychology to issues that are important to businesses and organizations. The intent is to promote and advance understanding of individual, group and organizational effectiveness at work, and the well-being and satisfaction of people working in or served by organizations.

Throughout this book, we have illustrated the major areas of Work and Organizational Psychology, considering the main theories and key research findings in the field, as well as their practical implications for organizations and management. Along the way, we have also considered some contemporary themes, and the ways in which Work and Organizational Psychology can help organizations and businesses to address the challenges that arise from them.

In this final chapter we have argued that the impact of the psychology of work and organizations could be so much more than it is already, and that the major barriers to achieving this are between Work Psychology and business, and in the preparation of the leaders of tomorrow in higher education. In order to help overcome these barriers, we propose that Work and Organizational Psychology seek to be less exclusive and more inclusive as a discipline, and that business schools and psychology schools be encouraged to include the subject much more widely in higher education programmes. These steps would enable leaders, managers, practitioners and others in organizations feel more confident and at liberty to apply and use the ideas and insights from the field.

At the start of the book, we presented a written task in which you listed seven questions about people and their behaviour in organizations. Now, at the end of it we have another, which we hope will start breaking down the barriers between Work Psychology and business. Take the piece of paper with your questions on, and turn it over (re-using it is better for the environment). Write down seven ways in which your learning from this book will change the way that you think at work, or better still, seven ways in which your learning will change what you do at work. Therein lies the purpose and value of the Psychology of Work and Organizations.

CREDIT PAGES

All figures and boxes *not* listed on this credit page are the authors' own work and so do not require any credit lines, permissions acknowledgements or referencing citations.

Photo Credits

The following photographs have all been reproduced with permission of the copyright holders, and the credit lines are listed below:

Authors' image – © Steve Woods and Mike West; Part 1 opener – © iStock; page 25 – © iStock; page 32 – Courtesy of UCL Library Services, Special Collections, Pearson Papers; page 37 – © iStock; page 45 – © Bettman/Corbis; page 57 – © iStockphoto.com/joan Vicent Cantó; page 66 – © iStock; page 87 – © iStock; page 103 – Courtesy of Timothy A. Judge; page 112 – © iStock; page 133 – Courtesy of Edwin A. Locke, Dean's Professor of Motivation and Leadership (Emeritus), University of Maryland; and Gary Latham, Secretary of State Professor of Organizational Effectiveness, Rottman School of Management; page 137 – © Shutterstock; page 138 – © iStock; page 157 – © Shutterstock; page 170 – © Shutterstock; page 183 – Courtesy of Prof. Filip Lievens, Ghent University; page 191 – © Shutterstock; page 204 – Courtesy of Irwin Goldstein, Senior Vice Chancellor for Academic Affairs at the University System of Maryland; page 208 – © Shutterstock; page 210 – © Shutterstock; page 258 – © iStock; page 261 – © iStock; page 278 – Courtesy of John L. Holland Papers, Western Historical Manuscript Collection – Columbia, MO; page 282 – © Shutterstock; page 290 – © iStock; page 295 – © iStock; page 306 – © Shutterstock; page 317 – Courtesy of Prof. Cary L. Cooper, CBE from Lancaster University; page 325 – © Shutterstock; page 327 – © Shutterstock; page 345 Part 3 opener – © Shutterstock; page 362 © iStock; page 364 – Courtesy of Prof. Rosabeth Kanter; page 371 – © Shutterstock; page 401 – © Shutterstock; page 405 – Davies, J. and Thomas, H. (2009). What do Business School Deans do? Insights from a UK Study. Management Decision, 47, 1396–1419. and Courtesy of Aston Business School; page 413 – Courtesy of Dr. Robert House; page 432 – © Shutterstock; page 438 – © Shutterstock; page 450 – Courtesy of the University of Adelaide Archives (Series 1151); page 467 – © Shutterstock; page 468 – © iStock; page 472 – © iStock; page 483 – Courtesey of Dr. Benjamin Schneider; page 490 Case Study 3.1 image – © Shutterstock

Figures, Tables and Boxes Credits

The following third party figures, tables and boxes have been reproduced from the originals, with the kind permission from the copyright holders and the credit lines are reproduced below:

Figure 4.2 – Ajzen, I. and Fishbein, M. (1977). Attitude–behaviour relations: A theoretical analysis and review of empirical research. *Psychological Bulletin, 84,* 888–918

Figure 7.6 – Gully, S. and Chen, G. (2009). Individual differences, attribute-treatment interactions, and training outcomes. In S.W.J. Kozlowski and E. Salas (eds.) *Learning, Training, and Development in Organizations*. New York: Routledge

Figure 8.4 – Locke, E.A. and Latham, G.P. (2002). Building a practically useful theory of goal setting and task motivation: A 35 year old odyssey. *American Psychologist, 57 (9)*, 705–717

Figure 9.2 – Holland, J.L. (1973). Holland, J.L. (1994). *Self-Directed Search: Assessment booklet, a guide to educational and career planning*. Odessa, FL: Psychological Assessment Resources

Figure 9.4 – Woods, S.A. and Hampson, S.E. (2010). Predicting adult occupational environments from gender and childhood personality traits. *Journal of applied psychology*, 95(6), 1045.

Figure 10.1 – Khan, R.L. and Byosiere, P. (1992). Theoretical framework for the study of stress in organizations. In M.D. Dunnette and L.M. Hough (eds), *Handbook of Industrial and Organizational Psychology* (2nd ed.) 571–650. Paolo Alto, CA: Consulting Psychologists Press

Figure 10.2 – Falmer, S., Cooper, C. and Thomas, K. (2004). A model of work stress. *Counselling at work (Winter)*: 2–5

Figure 12.3 – Judge, T.A., Bono, J.E., Ilies, R. and Gerhardt, M.W. (2002). Personality and leadership: a qualitative and quantitative review. *Journal of Applied Psychology*, 87 (4), 765–780

Figure 12.13 – Dorfman, P., Hanges, P.J. and Brodbeck, F.C. (2004). Leadership and Cultural Variation: the identification of culturally endorsed leadership profiles. In R.J. House, P.J. Hanges, M. Javidan, P. Dorfman, and V. Gupta (eds) Leadership, Culture, and Organizations: The Globe study of 62 societies 669–719. Thousand Oaks, CA: Sage Publications, Inc

Figure 12.14 – Chhokar, J.S., Brodbeck, F.C. and House, R.J. (2007). *Culture and Leadership around the World: The GLOBE Book of In-depth Studies of 25 Societies*. Mahwah, NJ: Lawrence Erlbaum

Figure 14.2 – Aston Organization Development, 2003

Figure 14.3 – www.Mckinseyquarterly.com/enduring_ideas_2170

Table 13.1 – West, M.A., Markiewicz, L. and Dawson, J.F. (2006). Aston Team Performance Inventory: Management set. London: ASE

Table 13.3 – West, M.A., Markiewicz, L. and Dawson, J.F. (2006). Aston Team Performance Inventory: Management set. London: ASE

Table 13.4 – West, M.A., Markiewicz, L. and Dawson, J.F. (2006). Aston Team Performance Inventory: Management set. London: ASE

Discuss with a Colleague page 60 – Woods, S.A. and Hampson, W.E. (2005). Measuring the big five with single items using a bipolar response scale. European Journal of Personality, 19 (5), 373–390

Box 8.1 Coleman, V.I. and Borman, W.C. (2000). Investigating the underlying structure of the citizenship performance domain. *Human Resource Management Review*, 10, 25–44. Elsevier Ltd

Box 8.3 Campion, M.A., Fink, A.A., Ruggeberg, B.J., Carr, L., Phillips, G.M. and Odman, R.B. (2011). Doing competencies well: Best practices in competency modeling. Personnel Psychology, 64(1), 225-262

Box 9.1 – Arnold, J. (1997). Managing Careers into the 21st Century. London: Sage

Exhibit 2.2.1 Biggs, D.M. (2010). Management Consultancy: A guide for students. Cengage Ltd London

The following Figures and Tables have all been adapted and changed from the original sources but below are citation references to the research, for referencing purposes:

Figure 2.3 – Hodgkinson, G.P., Herriot, P. and Anderson, N. (2001). Re-aligning the Stakeholders in Management Research: Lessons from Industrial, Work and Organizational Psychology. *British Journal of Management*, 12 (S1), S41-S48

Figure 3.1 – Ackerman, P.L. and Heggestad, E.D. (1997). Intelligence, personality, and interests: evidence for overlapping traits. *Psychological Bulletin*, 121 (2), 219–245

Figure 4.1 – Robbins, S.P. and Judge, T.A. (2009). *Organizational Behavior (Pearson International Edition)*. London

Figure 4.4 – Meyer, J.P. and Allen, N.J. (1991). A three-component conceptualization of organizational commitment. *Human Resource Management Review*, 1, 61–89

Figure 4.5 – Ashkanasy, N.M. and Daus, C.S. (2002). Emotion in the workplace: The new challenge for managers. *Academy of Management Executive, 16,* 76–86

Figure 4.6 – Guillaume, Y.R., Dawson, J.F., Priola, V., Sacramento, C.A., Woods, S.A., Higson, H.E., Budhwar, P. S. and West, M.A. (2013). Managing diversity in organizations: An Integrative Model and Agenda for Future Research. *European Journal of Work and Organizational Psychology*, (Ahead-of-print), 1-20

Figure 5.3 – Humphrey, S.E., Nahrgang, J.D. and Morgeson, F.P. (2007). Integrating Motivational, Social, and Contextual Work Design Features: a meta-analytic summary and theoretical extension of the work design literature. *Journal of Applied Psychology*, 92 (5), 1332–1356

Figure 7.4 – Anderson, J.R. (1996). ACT: A simple theory of complex cognition. *American Psychologist*, 51, 355–365

Figure 8.1 – Burke, W.W. and Litwin, G.H. (1992). A Causal Model of Organizational Performance and Change. *Journal of Management*, 18 (3), 523–545

Figure 8.3 – Murphy, K.R. and Denisi, A.S. (2008). A Model of the Appraisal process. In P.S. Budhwar and A.S. Denisi (eds), Performance Management Systems: A Global Perspective (pp. 81–96). London: Routledge

Figure 9.1 – Nicholson, N. (1990). *On the move: the psychology of change and transition*. Chichester: John Wiley and Son Ltd

Figure 9.3 – Holland, J.L. (1973). Making Vocational Choices: A Theory of Vocational Personalities and Environments. Ddessa, FL: Psychological Assessment Resources. or Holland, J.L. (1994). Self-Directed Search: Assessment booklet, a guide to educational and career planning. Odessa, FL: Psychological Assessment Resources

Figure 11.1 – Ansoff, I.H. (1965). *Corporate Strategy: An Analytic Approach to Business Policy for Growth and Expansion.* New York: Mcgraw-Hill

Figure 11.2 – Porter, Michael E. (1990). *The Competitive Advantage of nations*, The Harvard business review (offprint) free press

Figure 12.6 – Judge, T.A., Piccolo, R.F. and Illies, R. (2004). 'The forgotten ones? The validity of consideration and initiating structure in leadership research', *Journal of Applied Psychology*, vol. 89, pp. 36–51

Figure 12.12 – Judge, T.A., Piccolo, R.F. and Illies, R. (2004). 'The forgotten ones? The validity of consideration and initiating structure in leadership research', *Journal of Applied Psychology*, vol. 89, pp. 36–51

Figure 14.1 – Cameron, K.S. and Quinn, R.E. (1997). *Diagnosing and Changing Organizational Culture.* San Francisco: Jossey Bass

Table 6.2 – Hough, L.M., Oswald, F.L. and Ployhart, R.E. (2001). Determinants, Detection and Amelioration of Adverse impact in Personnel Selection Procedures: Issues, Evidence and Lessons learned. *International Journal of Selection and Assessment*, 9, 152–194

Table 9.1 – Levinson, D.J. (1978). *The season's of a man's life.* New York: Knopf

Table 9.2 – Super, D.E. and Hall, D.T. (1978). Career development: Exploration and planning. *Annual Review of Psychology*, 29, 333–372

Table 9.3 – Super, D.E. and Hall, D.T. (1978). Career development: Exploration and planning. *Annual Review of Psychology*, 29, 333–372

Table 9.4 – Holland, J.L. (1994). *Self-Directed Search: Assessment booklet, a guide to educational and career planning.* Odessa, FL: Psychological Assessment Resources

Table 13.12 – Stevens, M.J. and Campion, M.A. (1999). Staffing work teams: Development and validation of a selection test for teamwork settings. *Journal of Management*, 25, 207–28

INDEX